PULITZER

Also by Denis Brian

*Murderers and Other Friendly People: The Public
and Private Worlds of Interviewers*

The Enchanted Voyage: The Life of J. B. Rhine

*The True Gen: An Intimate Portrait of Ernest Hemingway
by Those Who Knew Him*

Fair Game: What Biographers Don't Tell You

*Genius Talk: Conversations with Nobel Scientists
and Other Luminaries*

Einstein: A Life

PULITZER

A Life

Denis Brian

John Wiley & Sons, Inc.

New York • Chichester • Weinheim • Brisbane • Singapore • Toronto

Published by John Wiley & Sons, Inc.
Published simultaneously in Canada

This publication is designed to provide accurate and authoritative information in regard to the subject matter covered. It is sold with the understanding that the publisher is not engaged in rendering professional services. If professional advice or other expert assistance is required, the services of a competent professional person should be sought.

Library of Congress Cataloging-in-Publication Data:

Brian, Denis
    Pulitzer : a life / Denis Brian.
      p. cm.
    Includes bibliographical references and index.
    ISBN 0-471-33200-3 (cloth : alk. paper)
    1. Pulitzer, Joseph, 1847–1911. 2. Journalists—United States—Biography.
I. Title.
PN4874.P8 B75 2001
070′.92—dc21
[B]

                                             2001026916

Printed in the United States of America

10 9 8 7 6 5 4 3 2 1

Acknowledgments

The following invaluable sources left their firsthand impressions of Joseph Pulitzer: John Heaton, Don Carlos Seitz, Dr. George Hosmer, James Barnes, Alleyne Ireland, George Cary Eggleston, Norman Thwaites, Walt McDougall, Nellie Bly, James Creelman, George St. Johns, Harold Pollard, and Charles E. Chapin. Chapin, a former *Evening World* city editor, who idolized Pulitzer, composed his memoir in a Sing Sing prison cell, where he was serving a life sentence for killing his wife in a failed double suicide attempt.

Also of great help were William Robinson Reynolds's Ph.D. thesis on Pulitzer; Allen Churchill's *Park Row*; W. A. Swanberg's *Pulitzer* and his *Citizen Hearst*; James Wyman Barrett's *Joseph Pulitzer and His* World; George Juergens's *Joseph Pulitzer and the* New York World; Daniel W. Pfaff's *Joseph Pulitzer II and the* Post-Dispatch: *A Newspaperman's Life*; Brooke Kroeger's *Nellie Bly, Daredevil, Reporter, Feminist*; Joyce Milton's *The Yellow Kids*; John Winkler's *William Randolph Hearst*; David Nasaw's *The Chief: The Life of William Randolph Hearst*; the *St. Louis Post-Dispatch*; the *New York World*; the *New York Journal*; the *New York Sun*; the *New York Times*; James V. Maloney, corporate secretary for Pulitzer, Inc.; and the extensive Pulitzer archives at Columbia University and the Library of Congress.

Many thanks to John Gable, Executive Director, Theodore Roosevelt Association; Sylvia Jukes Morris; Ann Morris, Director, Western Historical Manuscript Collection, University of Missouri; Dorothy Dyer, Curator, Bar Harbor Historical Society; Ross MacTaggart, Motor Yacht Historian; Jill Radel, Museum of Yachting, Newport, R.I.

My wife, Martine, worked with me enthusiastically on every aspect of the book, and her advice, critical acumen, and penchant for *le mot juste* enhanced the finished product enormously.

My editor, Hane Lane, gave wise and welcome suggestions, persuaded me that less is more, and was patient and encouraging.

Contents

Joseph Pulitzer and His "Indegoddampendent" *World*

Every issue of the paper presents an opportunity and a duty to say something courageous and true; to rise above the mediocre and conventional; to say something that will command the respect of the intelligent, the educated, the independent part of the community; to rise above fear of partisanship and fear of popular prejudice.

—Joseph Pulitzer

Always fight for progress and reform; never tolerate injustice or corruption; always fight demagogues of all parties; never belong to any party; always oppose privileged classes and public plunder; never lack sympathy for the poor; always remain devoted to the public welfare; never be satisfied with merely printing the news; always be drastically independent; never be afraid to attack wrong, whether by predatory plutocracy or predatory poverty.

—Joseph Pulitzer

At eighteen, Joseph Pulitzer, a penniless, gangling Hungarian emigrant recruited in Europe to fight in the Civil War, threw himself from the ship bringing him to the United States and swam ashore to collect the bounty he thought should come to him and not to his recruiter. He fought in the Union Army and after the war, while working at various menial jobs, taught himself enough English to become a lawyer, a U.S. congressman, a superb journalist, and eventually the multimillionaire owner of two great American newspapers, the *St. Louis Post-Dispatch* and the *New York World*. At its peak in the late 1890s the *World* had a million daily readers.

Always a hands-on owner, Pulitzer focused on his high-minded, informed, and intelligent editorials.

One of his early editors, John Cockerill, who often handled the news pages, defined news as "any hitherto unprinted occurrence which involves the violation of any one of the Ten Commandments and, if it involves a fracture of the Vth, VIth, VIIth, VIIIth, or IX Commandments and by those people whose names people have heard and in whose doings they are specifically interested by knowledge of their official and social position, then it is great news."

Perhaps this explains why the *World* had a mass audience.

Pulitzer, however, insisted that "Sensationalism as generally understood is to be avoided. Cheap crimes are not to be seized upon to play up. A sensational story that is worth featuring is to be pushed to the limit. But no faking."

He told *World* reporter James Creelman, "I want to attack anything that is wrong in public service, the police department or elsewhere. I believe in the paper being a moral teacher of what is right and what is wrong. It must take part. I should turn in my grave if the paper sat on a fence. The paper should not run the government or make tariffs but it should lead public opinion."

And lead it did. Pulitzer's influence became so great that he elected a president—Cleveland—prevented a war between the United States and Britain, exposed and cleaned up corrupt insurance companies, surpassed Theodore Roosevelt in trust-busting, and outsmarted banker J. P. Morgan for the financial good of the country. Without Pulitzer there would be no Statue of Liberty. He successfully fought slumlords, crooked police, and shady politicians. Even his most ferocious rival, William Randolph Hearst, acknowledged that Pulitzer was "a mighty democratic force in the life of the nation" and "a towering figure in national and international journalism."

One of Pulitzer's less known achievements was to create a new way of swearing that caught on, such as his assertion that his *World* was "indegoddampendent." That he invented it was confirmed by American language expert H. L. Mencken, and is "absobloodylutely" part of today's talk and known as an "infix."

A contemporary called him the most interesting man on the planet, and the *Texas Newspaper Union,* "the greatest journalist on earth." To his friend Henry Watterson, editor of the *Louisville Courier-Journal,* Pulitzer's life read "like a story out of the books of giants, goblins and fairies." Theodore Roosevelt once praised the *World* as "magnificent and strong" and called its editorial page "the finest in the country"—until Pulitzer called Roosevelt a liar in his effort to cover up the bribery and corruption involved in buying the land for the Panama Canal. Then Roosevelt sued him for criminal libel and tried to send him to prison—an episode the ex-president failed to mention in his memoirs.

But there was a time when Pulitzer betrayed his high principles. For several months before and during the Spanish American War he engaged in a frantic attempt to outsell William Randolph Hearst's *New York Journal,* which earned both men disrepute as purveyors of the sensational "yellow press." As a visiting English newspaperman saw it, theirs seemed like "a contest of madmen for the primacy of the sewer."

After the war, Pulitzer bitterly regretted the exaggerations, rumors, and out-right lies his paper had printed, and redirected the World to regain its former glowing reputation as a great newspaper—which it did.

He was a blind invalid for the last twenty-two years of his life—and so sensitive to noise that he traveled in a soundproofed yacht—but he remained in active control of the World, relying on a group of secretaries to keep him informed and to write out his ideas, complaints, orders, reminiscences—even his personal letters to his wife and children. Most if not all of these records are in the archives of Columbia University and the Library of Congress, and provide rich sources for a Pulitzer biographer.

He died in 1911, at age sixty-four. His World survived him by nineteen years. His Post-Dispatch still exists and flourishes. Among his other legacies are the annual Pulitzer Prizes, the Columbia University School of Journalism—and the fountain in front of Manhattan's Plaza Hotel.

Pulitzer's son Joseph Jr. said that "a flame of integrity was extinguished at the death of my father but its light will always radiate to newspapermen of conscience everywhere."

More recently, Arthur Krock of the New York Times wrote: "Joseph Pulitzer had a shining personal character, humility in possession of power, and compassion for the unfortunate. He hated cant, sham, injustice and corruption and was incapable of any of these. He was one of the few gifted with both humor and a sense of consecration."

His plea at a political convention in 1875 is still strikingly apposite over 125 years later: "The growth of money power in this country has been fabulous and its connections with and interest in the Government [are] alarming . . . Let us never have a Government in Washington owing its retention to the power of the millionaires rather than to the will of the millions."

The evidence suggests that the restless, pain-racked, nerve-racked, disease-ridden—and perhaps manic-depressive—genius was the Einstein, Shakespeare, Churchill of journalists, and is still the greatest newspaper editor of all time, at least in the English-speaking world.

CHAPTER 1

The Fighting Immigrant

1864–1869

—

17 to 22 years old

S eventeen-year-old Joseph Pulitzer couldn't take it anymore. He adored his
mother, but got into so many fierce arguments with his stepfather that he
was desperate to leave home. A military career seemed a way of escape. He was
prepared, as it turned out, to fight for almost any country that would accept him.

Joseph was born in Mako, Hungary, on April 10, 1847, the eldest son of
Hungarian Jews. His father, Philip, a prosperous grain merchant, retired in
1853 and moved with his family to Budapest, where Joseph and his younger
brother, Albert, were educated in private schools and by a tutor who taught
them French and German. When Joseph was eleven his father died of heart
disease, and a few years later his beloved mother, Louise, married Max Blau, a
businessman—the man Joseph had grown to hate.

The scrawny, almost six-foot-three-inch tall, high-strung teenager looked as
martial as a beanpole. Yet he hoped to follow in the footsteps of two of his
maternal uncles, officers in the Austrian Army. But when the Austrian Army
rejected him for his weak eyesight and emaciated appearance, he was undeterred. He traveled to Paris to join the French Foreign Legion for service in
Mexico. When the French declined his offer, he crossed the Channel to England, where he volunteered to serve with the British forces in India. Again, failure. Bitterly disappointed, he reluctantly headed for home, stopping en route
in Hamburg, Germany. And there he met his destiny.

Shortly before, in America in the summer of 1863, U.S. President Abraham Lincoln, his country torn by civil war, his army depleted by casualties, disease, and desertions, had planned to turn stalemate into checkmate by a mass
attack against the Confederacy. Lincoln intended to bolster his weakened army
by drafting three hundred thousand men from New York City alone. But many

5

of the eligible males there were recent Irish and German immigrants who lived in squalor and didn't give a damn who won the war.

In resisting the draft, they looted and torched draft-office buildings and prevented firemen from dousing the flames. Motley groups of policemen and convalescing soldiers were sent to quell the riot. They had orders to take no prisoners and kill every man who had a club. But they were overwhelmed by the mob: beaten, stabbed, kicked to death, or shot with their own muskets. Survivors retreated in panic from a barrage of bricks, stones, and dead animals.

Responding to anguished cries to save the city, the army hurried thousands of battle-scarred Union troops with field guns and howitzers to take back control of Manhattan's streets. For men who refused to join the army, the rioters proved fierce fighters: some two thousand died, and about ten thousand were wounded. After this tragic fiasco, Union Army agents looked for urgently needed recruits in less dangerous territory, especially Europe, under the guise of encouraging emigration.

Languishing in Hamburg after his failed missions to join any of three armies, Pulitzer met one of the Union recruiting agents. Assured that he could ride a horse and fire a gun, the agent put the unlikely recruit aboard a Boston-bound ship.

The gangling, nearsighted youngster soon showed his spirit and audacity by jumping ship in Boston Harbor, swimming ashore through almost freezing water, and taking a train to New York. There he collected the three-hundred-dollar bounty for enlisting—which otherwise would have gone to the agent he'd outsmarted. But when Pulitzer arrived at Remount Camp, Pleasant Valley, Maryland, on November 12, 1864, the captain in charge took one jaundiced glance at him and, according to biographer Don Carlos Seitz, who presumably got it from Pulitzer himself, yelled, "Take that . . . little . . . away from here! I don't want him in my company!"

He stayed, despite the frigid reception, and spent the rest of the war in L Company of the First New York Lincoln Cavalry. Taking their cue from the captain, fellow soldiers ridiculed his appearance, inadequate English, and guttural accent, although many of them were of German origin. Some took his name (pronounced Pull-it-sir) as an invitation to grab his large nose. When a sergeant tried it, Pulitzer struck him hard—the only injury he inflicted in the war.

Saved from a court-martial for striking a superior by an officer who admired his prowess at chess, he took part in minor skirmishes on horseback against the enemy at Antioch, Liberty Mills, Waynesborough, and Beaverdam Flat, ending the war in the comparatively peaceful Shenandoah Valley as a Major Richard Hinton's orderly.

After Confederate general Robert E. Lee's surrender, Pulitzer rode with his regiment for the victory parade in Washington on May 23, 1865, his view of General William Tecumseh Sherman and Secretary of War Edwin Stanton taking the salute completely blocked by the men riding their horses so close beside him that they bruised his knees.

What now? Certainly not a military career.

Competition for jobs among Civil War veterans was desperate. In Manhattan, a city of astonishing contrasts, about fifteen thousand panhandlers worked the streets, some hiring deformed babies to raise their take. A district known as Five Points on the Lower East Side, crammed with desperately poor immigrants, depraved criminals, and prostitutes, scared even the police away. Nearby was another world, a booming, war-fueled Wall Street, mansions, flourishing businesses, and affluent individuals window-shopping on Broadway. Realizing he stood less chance of emulating them than of joining the Hell's Kitchen crowd, which welcomed army veterans, Pulitzer, a good sailor, followed a tip and traveled to New Bedford, Massachusetts, to apply for a deckhand's job on a whaler. But the whaling industry had not recovered from its destruction by Confederate cruisers, and the only ship's captain seeking a crew turned him down.

Despite the odds against him, he returned to New York City, where Irish immigrants had a lock on jobs for waiters, laborers, longshoremen, and other employment requiring some English. Though—thanks to his successful grain-merchant father, Philip—Pulitzer had been well educated by tutors and was fluent in German, French, and Hungarian, his English was all but incoherent. Unable to pay to rent a room, he was reduced to sleeping in the streets in his frayed army uniform and scuffed shoes, some nights on a bench in City Hall Park.

With his last few cents he walked into the luxurious French's Hotel for a morale-raising shoeshine. But a porter thought he might offend the snooty clientele and told him to beat it. (Pulitzer's life often resembled a fable. Twenty-three years later he bought that same French's Hotel, had it demolished, and replaced it with the tallest building in the city—a two-million-dollar golden-domed skyscraper to house his newspaper offices.)

Having his topcoat stolen was the last straw: he decided to check out and head for St. Louis, Missouri. Some joker had advised him that unlike Manhattan, crowded with German immigrants after the same nonexistent jobs, there weren't any Germans in St. Louis. Pulitzer also liked the idea that in a German-free environment he would have to learn English fast—or starve.

Unaware that he'd been fooled—St. Louis had a huge German population—he sold his only capital, a silk handkerchief, for seventy-five cents to buy food for the long journey. Then he took a train west, as a stowaway, arriving on the night of October 10, 1865, at East St. Louis, across the river from St. Louis. (The railroad bridge to reach St. Louis was not completed until 1874.)

He got off the train, broke, tired, and shivering with cold. A downpour of sleety rain soaked him to the skin. But he hardly noticed it. For him the shimmering lights in the distance, barely visible through the curtain of rain across the Mississippi River, were not just the lights of a city but of a promised land. Attracted by the voices of deckhands on a ferryboat and puzzled to hear them speaking German, Pulitzer walked to the riverbank and asked how to get across without paying. He was lucky. Their fireman had just quit. Could the young man fire a boiler?

"In my condition I was willing to say anything and do anything," he recalled. One deckhand "put a shovel in my hand and told me to throw some coal on the fire. I opened the fire box door and a blast of fiery hot air struck me in the face. At the same time a blast of cold driven rain struck me in the back. I was roasting in front and freezing in the back. But I stuck to the job and shoveled coal as hard as I could."

The captain resented his limited and awkward English, bullied him, and worked him to exhaustion. After a few days the harsh talk escalated into a violent quarrel, and Pulitzer walked off the boat for good—into St. Louis. He later told his biographer Seitz, "I still have a painful recollection of firing that ferryboat with its blasts of hot air on my face, and the rain and snow beating down on my back."

After renting a room, he headed for the nearest library, where he read in the want ads of a local German-language newspaper, *Westliche Post*, that an army barracks needed a caretaker for sixteen mules, pay to include free meals. Ex-cavalryman were preferred.

The weather turned unexpectedly hot as he walked the four miles to the barracks, discovered he'd left his discharge papers behind, ran to get them from his room, then ran back, panting and sweating. He was hired, but not for long. The food was inedible and the mules impossible. He stood it for two days, then quit.

Then he took almost anything he could get: as a deckhand, laborer, stevedore, hack driver—all poorly paid, dead-end jobs. The "promised land" was becoming a mirage. However, he did learn enough English to work as a waiter at Tony Faust's restaurant, where at least he had bright surroundings, but all too briefly. Apparently he couldn't balance his tray and was fired for dropping a juicy steak onto a good customer.

When, on his next job as a laborer, the foreman who paid his wages failed to turn up with the cash, Pulitzer, now nineteen, struggled with a moral dilemma: How could he face his landlady without the room rent? He knew no one well enough to borrow the money, and had just ten cents in his pocket. He solved the problem by sleeping under the stars after eating a dime's worth of apples. The next day the foreman had recovered from a brief illness and appeared with Pulitzer's wages. That evening, when he handed over the rent a day late and explained his "disappearance" from bed and board, his landlady teased him for being too sensitive. But he made sure there was no repeat performance by saving money for rent from moonlighting.

Working sixteen-hour days at two jobs, he was still so anxious to master English quickly that he also spent four hours in the local library—leaving fewer

Pulitzer *(right)* with his friend librarian Udo Brachvogel.

than four hours for sleep. Between temporary jobs he almost lived in the library. Each morning he waited impatiently on the library steps for librarian Udo Bachvogel to open up, kept reading all through lunchtime while munching apples, and only left in the evening just as the doors were being locked. Udo helped him with English conversation, and they became friends for life.

But a chance encounter with a scam artist—not his hard labor—put him on the road to his remarkable career. With some forty others he paid five dollars to this smooth talker, who promised good jobs on a Louisiana sugar plantation, shipped them by steamboat to a desolate spot forty miles south of St. Louis, and dumped them. Realizing they had been taken, they began to trudge back to the city, resolved to murder the man. "Whether or not this reckless program would have been carried out it is impossible to say," according to biographer Alleyne Ireland, "for when, three days later, the ragged army arrived in the city, worn out with fatigue and half dead from hunger, the agent had decamped."

By chance a reporter, who had heard something of the story, met Pulitzer and persuaded him to write an account of the scam. It was published in the *Westliche Post*, the German-language paper through which he had landed his first civilian job.

Pulitzer's energy, intelligence, and way with words appealed to its part owner and coeditor, Dr. Emil Preetorius, who started to give him writing assignments. Eventually other tenants in the *Post* building sensed something worth cultivating in the intense, driven young man, especially attorneys William Patrick and Charles Johnson, and physician Joseph McDowell.

Dr. McDowell asked him to help in the summer of 1866 when a cholera epidemic terrorized St. Louis, killing 1,686 residents in two weeks. More than a quarter of the population of 260,000 fled the city. Victims of the disease were to be buried on dreaded Arsenal Island, and Dr. McDowell was appointed health officer for the area. Piles of corpses awaited burial because officials in charge of the job had panicked and left for the mainland. Though McDowell had known Pulitzer for only a few months, he recommended him to be in charge on Arsenal Island. Pulitzer found the place almost deserted, even by the convicted murderers from prisons on the mainland who had been promised their freedom if they helped to bury the dead. Some had taken advantage of the offer, only to escape to unknown parts. Pulitzer stayed, helped to bury many of the cholera victims, and also kept the records. When the epidemic was over in October, having killed 3,527 in St. Louis, he was again in need of a job.

The two attorneys in the newspaper building pointed him toward work in wild Ozark country for a railroad company in the early stages of incorporation. He rode there with a black aide. Both men were swept from their horses while trying to cross the flooded Gasconade River. The aide and his horse sadly drowned, but Pulitzer, a strong swimmer, and his horse survived.

He dragged himself up the bank, drenched to the skin and worried by the prospect of having to catch his mount, which had started off on a cross-country gallop. Then he saw an elderly farmer sitting on a tree stump, watching him with intense interest.

"The first thing he did," said Pulitzer, "was to take me to the farmhouse and hand me a tumbler three parts full of whisky. When I refused this he looked at me as though he thought I was mad. 'Yer mean to tell me yer don't drink?' he said. When I told him no, I didn't, he said nothing, but brought me food. After I had eaten he pulled out a plug of tobacco, bit off a large piece, and offered the plug to me. I thanked him but declined. It took him some time to get over that, but at last he said: 'Yer mean to tell me yer don't chew?' I said no, I didn't. He dropped the subject, and for an hour or so we talked about the war and the crops and the proposed railroad. That man was a gentleman. He didn't take another drink or another chew of tobacco all the time. Finally, before he went to bed, he produced a pipe, filled it, and handed the tobacco to me; but I failed him again, and he put his own pipe back in his pocket, firmly but sorrowfully.

"Well, my God! It was nearly half an hour before he spoke again, and I was beginning to think that I had really wounded his feelings by declining his hospitable offers, when he came over and stood in front of me with an expression of profound pity. 'Young feller,' he said, 'you seem to be right smart and able for a furriner, but let me tell you, you'll never make a successful American until yer learn to drink, and chew, and smoke.'"

Next morning, having dried his clothes and caught his horse, Pulitzer started to work for what would become the Atlantic and Pacific Railroad. It required him to master complicated articles of incorporation involving twelve counties, which he later recorded from memory. This feat so amazed the lawyers who had steered him to the job that they encouraged him to become a lawyer, letting him study at a desk in their office and giving him a free run of their law library.

He took time off on March 6, 1867, to visit St. Louis's Court of Criminal Correction, where he renounced his allegiance to the emperor of Austria and became an American citizen.

Shortly after, his sixteen-year-old brother, Albert, left Hungary to join him in St. Louis. Having already taught himself English, Albert soon got work teaching German to local high school students.

Joseph was a remarkably quick study. The following year, in 1868, he was admitted to the bar and became a notary public. But handicapped by his youth—he was now twenty-one—odd appearance, scruffy clothes, and still imperfect English, he attracted few clients and none of consequence. One, a ferryboat captain who wanted some documents sealed, immediately recognized him as the youngster he had hired to stoke the boiler on his boat. "He stopped short," Pulitzer recalled, "as if he had seen a ghost and said, 'Say, ain't you the damned cuss that I fired off my boat?' I told him yes, I was. He was the most surprised man I ever saw, but after he had sworn himself hoarse he faced the facts and gave me his business.'"

Despite his apparent failure as a lawyer, Pulitzer caught the attention of Carl Schurz, the high-principled other coeditor and co-owner of the influential and prosperous *Westliche Post*. As a youth in Germany, Schurz had been inspired to become a revolutionary by Gottfried Kinkel, his art history professor at the University of Bonn. In 1848 Kinkel founded the newspaper *Democratic Union*, which Schurz helped him to edit, and a year later they both joined an uprising against the oppressive Prussian government.

Prussian troops captured Kinkel, who was sentenced to life in Spandau Prison. Schurz escaped arrest by hiding in a sewer. Then he risked his life to free Kinkel by traveling on a false passport to Berlin, where he persuaded a sympathetic prison guard to lower Kinkel by rope to the ground. Waiting nearby with a horse and carriage, Schurz eventually helped Kinkel reach Scotland. After escaping from Germany himself, Schurz landed in England, where he married. He and his wife immigrated to the United States in 1856.

As a political activist, Schurz had enthusiastically campaigned for Lincoln, who, in 1861, had appointed him minister to Spain. Schurz had hardly arrived in Madrid when he turned back to fight in the Civil War as a Union major general. He led his mostly German American troops at Bull Run, Chancellorsville,

Carl Schurz had been Lincoln's minister to Spain.

Gettysburg, and Chattanooga, and fought alongside Sherman in North Carolina. Idolized by his men, Schurz in turn idolized Lincoln.

After the war, although Schurz devoted more time to politics than to the *Westliche Post,* he did discuss the paper's need for a new reporter with his partner, Preetorius, and the city editor, Louis Willich. They eventually agreed on a short list: either Pulitzer, inexperienced but promising, or a veteran reporter named Ahrenberg. Willich had his own agenda. Afraid that the experienced man might covet his job and unseat him, he put in a strong plug for hiring the "harmless" Pulitzer—and prevailed.

"I could not believe it," Pulitzer recalled years later. "I, the unknown, the luckless, almost a boy of the streets, selected for such responsibility—it all seemed like a dream."

But it was a nightmare for Willich. He had chosen the wrong man. Pulitzer willingly worked nonstop all day and night and into the next morning, turned in reams of good copy, covered breaking news and politics, showing such a mastery of the job and tenacity in getting a story that he was promoted over Willich to virtual partnership with the paper's owners. He was also a threat to rival St. Louis reporters, who tried to put down this newcomer who was scooping them. They scoffed at his enthusiasm, shaky English, large nose, small chin, and tall, gaunt figure. But "it was not long before the editors of the English sheets were advising their young gentlemen to cease guying 'Joey' and endeavor to imitate him if they expected to hold their jobs, as it was a little monotonous to be compelled to secure the best stuff by translating from the columns of the *Westliche Post*."

Among those "threatened" reporters were Henry Morton Stanley, later famous for tracking down Livingstone in Africa, and William Fayel—who gave this account of Pulitzer in action: "One sultry day nearly all of the reporters of St. Louis were drawn to an alley behind the Old Post Office, at Second and Olive Streets, by some incident. Suddenly there appeared among us the new reporter, of whom we had all heard but whom we had not yet seen. He had dashed out of the office without stopping to put on his coat or collar. In one hand he had a pad of paper, and in the other a pencil. He announced that he was the reporter for the *Westliche Post*, and began to ask questions of everybody in sight. I remarked to my companions that for a beginner he was exasperatingly inquisitive. The manner in which he went to work to dig out the facts, however, showed that he was a born reporter." In Fayel's opinion, Pulitzer was such a go-getter that "he became a positive annoyance to others who felt less inclined to work, and as it was considered quite fitting and proper in those days to guy the reporters of the German papers, the English reporters did not hesitate to try to curb his eagerness for news. On more than one occasion he was sent out from the Coroner's office on a wild-goose chase. But it was soon observed that, while taking this banter in good part, he never relaxed his efforts."

His publishers were so dazzled by this talented workaholic and his knowledge of the law that they sent Pulitzer to cover the state legislature in Missouri's capital, Jefferson City. There he continued to work sixteen-hour days, impressing one colleague with his "unquenchable thirst for news," and another by what appeared to be his "chief ambition—to root out public abuses and expose evildoers. In work of this kind he was particularly indefatigable and absolutely fearless." He was also full of surprises: a sort of intellectual Superman who disarmed the opposition. When, for example, a secret Democratic caucus was held in Jefferson City, only reporters for Democratic papers were invited, and the doors were locked. But early in the session, Pulitzer broke open the doors, sending the doorkeepers sprawling on the floor, and calmly walked to the reporters' table, took a seat, and opened his notebook, while the members watched in silent astonishment. No one objected or even questioned his presence. The next day his was the only Republican paper in the state with a report of the meeting.

The cynical deal-making politicians and corrupt lobbyists he despised and tried to expose ridiculed his efforts and appearance, mimicking his guttural speech by calling him "Choe Bulitzer," "Joey the German," and "Joey the Jew." But he had equally influential admirers, especially Lieutenant Governor Henry Brockmeyer, a philosopher and nephew of the German statesman Bismarck. "They think," said Brockmeyer, "because he trundles about with himself a big cobnose and bullfrog eyes that he has no sense; but I tell you he possesses greater dialectical ability than all of them put together. Mark me, he is now engaged in the making of a greater man than Editor Preetorius, or even Schurz."

In 1869, although he'd only recently moved to the state, Carl Schurz was elected U.S. senator for Missouri, the first German-born American to enter the Senate. It encouraged Pulitzer to dream of a political career for himself.

CHAPTER 2

Upright, Spirited, and Dangerous

1869–1872

21 to 25 years old

U nexpectedly, Pulitzer's political dreams became a reality, of sorts, when he attended a Republican Party meeting on December 14, 1869, as a reporter, and left—the most surprised man in the place—as their candidate for Missouri state senator. Attorney Chester Krum, first choice to fight for the seat, declined to run. Everyone else who was proposed chickened out. And who could blame them? The Democrats had the election in the bag. When Pulitzer, simply there to report the event, left the room for a moment, someone light-heartedly proposed him. His nomination was greeted with a storm of applause, a mixture of derision, delight, and desperation. What had they to lose? He returned to renewed applause, tried to take it as the joke it was meant to be, but couldn't resist the unanimous ovation. He called their bluff and accepted, say-ing that he had not sought the honor but would campaign in earnest. He was, of course, supported by his own paper, which characterized him as a thor-oughly upright young man with spirit, education, and talent.

His confident Democratic opponent, Samuel Grantham, a local tobac-conist, was always the front-runner; his only disadvantage, pointed out by the *Westliche Post*, was that he had fought in the Confederate Army—though this was hardly an obstacle in Missouri.

Pulitzer kept his word to run a lively race. From morning to night he exhorted his constituency to support him and went from door to door to can-vass the voters, arousing an unusual interest in the campaign. The *Missouri Democrat*, a Republican publication despite its name, hung back, waiting until

15

voting day, December 21, then gave him a halfhearted endorsement. "Mr. Pulitzer," it read, "is neither an old resident, a great man, nor a rich man. He has lived here only since his return from service in the army. But he is a young man of thorough honesty, [who understands] the workings of our City Government, and he has a fine education and natural ability." A snowstorm kept the old and infirm indoors, which seemed another strike against him. But those who braved the weather beat the odds. They gave Pulitzer an upset victory of 209 to 147. He was four years too young to be a state senator, so when the proud twenty-one-year-old took his seat in the legislature on January 5, he was breaking the law. If anyone caught on, they kept quiet. And he soon "aged" himself with a reddish beard and mustache. Depending on his mood, it gave him a benign or a ferocious appearance.

Afraid of losing their hot property to politics, the owners of the *Westliche Post* persuaded him to stay—and handle both jobs.

In the state senate he held his fire briefly, voting in 1870 with the majority to support the Fifteenth Amendment, which gave blacks and other minority males the right to vote. But almost everywhere he looked, he found crooked deals: among the judges, lawyers, and many fellow Republicans, who were ruthless in their efforts to sustain the system. As Seitz explained, during the Reconstruction period the halls of the legislature were crowded "with adventurers and the lobby with agents of corruption." These Pulitzer attacked in his paper and on the state Senate floor "with all the zeal of his fiery soul. He was soon in a very unhappy position. The old hands in the lobby tormented him incessantly, while his high sense of duty and lofty ideas put him much out of place among his careless and often corrupt colleagues. He fought for honesty, against the sale of law, and engendered much hostility. To be in a position to follow up his crusades on the floor with the power of a newspaper of such strength as the *Westliche Post* then enjoyed was held unfair in the eyes of his fellow members, with the result that he soon became a storm center."

To their alarm, Pulitzer dared to introduce a bill to abolish their power base—the five-member County Court. This judicial den of thieves used their position to fleece the public, appointed all county officials, and fattened their own wallets with kickbacks from lobbyists and contractors.

One of these judges, heading a committee to oversee the building of a county poorhouse, supplied the building material himself, submitted an inflated bill, approved it, and then cashed it from the public treasury. Until Pulitzer arrived, such shady business would have remained unreported. The placid local press was no threat to the judges, lobbyists, and contractors, who despised its reporters as *schnorrers* (spongers).

To make his point, Pulitzer focused on Edward Augustine, a lobbyist and contractor who profited from the crooked system and had been assured that he would get the contract for several hundred thousand dollars to build a new insane asylum at Allenton. Fearing that Pulitzer's reform bill would lose him

Joseph Keppler cartoon of Joseph Pulitzer *(standing left)* at a church festival in St. Louis.

this plum, Augustine and several other lobbyists arrived in Jefferson City to urge its defeat.

In his dual role of reporter-politician, Pulitzer had questioned Augustine's motives and asked who was financing him. Claiming his honor had been impugned, Augustine threatened to "insult the young jackanapes to his face." They confronted each other at Schmidt's Hotel, where political delegates from St. Louis gathered for a meeting on the evening of January 27. When Augustine, a bully with a prizefighter's physique, arrived, he shook a meaty finger at the tall, skinny Pulitzer and yelled, "You're a damned liar!"

Everyone expected Pulitzer to respond in kind. Instead, he merely told him not to use such language. Even when taunted by his friend *St. Louis Dispatch* reporter Wallace Gruelle, "Why didn't you knock that man down when he called you a damned liar? You must keep up the esprit de corps, man!" Pulitzer muttered incoherently and walked away. In fact, to the fierce but frail Pulitzer, his only hope of saving face was with a bat or a bullet.

There were conflicting reports of what happened next. Not in dispute is that Pulitzer went to his nearby room and told his roommate Anthony Ittner that Augustine had insulted him and he intended to "return the compliment with interest." He then took a four-barreled Sharp's pistol from his suitcase unobserved by Ittner and returned to the hotel. En route he met Gruelle heading for the telegraph office and advised him, "If you'll wait a little while, you'll have an item."

Pulitzer was about to see more action than during the Civil War. He found Augustine still in the hotel and insulted him with a few well-chosen adjectives, echoes of his military days. Augustine held his ground and kept his cool, saying: "I want to tell you in clear and simple English that you are a damned liar and puppy!" Then he rushed him. As he did, Pulitzer raised his gun. They fell to the floor locked together in a frenzied tussle, during which Pulitzer fired twice. One bullet hit Augustine below the knee; the other made a hole in the floor. Pulitzer had a head wound. The place was in an uproar as politicians and reporters tried to separate the contestants. Someone grabbed Pulitzer's gun, and someone else called for a doctor.

Accounts of what happened next differ.

According to Pulitzer, he knew that Augustine always carried a revolver and brass knuckles, so when Augustine came at him holding "a yellow, gleaming instrument in his raised hand," and smashed him over the head, he fired his own gun in self-defense. Other witnesses claimed that Augustine did not have a gun and that Pulitzer got the head wound when he hit the floor during the struggle.

Pulitzer's roommate Ittner, in a bowling alley when he heard of the shooting, hurried to Schmidt's Hotel, surprised to see Pulitzer looking quite cheerful and washing blood from a cut on his head. "Hello, Tony," Pulitzer greeted him with a big grin.

Strangely, Augustine was still in the same room, sitting in an armchair and smoking a cigar. He seemed to be feeling little pain and was surrounded by an excited group of friends. One of them suggested that they punish Pulitzer "as the officers of the law in Jefferson City were not in his opinion very eager to protect citizens from assault." But no one took him up on it and Pulitzer returned to his room with Ittner, unmolested.

Press reports of the fight also differed. One, pro-Pulitzer, written by Gruelle, stated that Augustine did have a gun: "Tonight [January 27], about half past 7 o'clock, Mr. Pulitzer shot at and wounded Mr. Augustine in the office of the Schmidt Hotel. It appears that Mr. Pulitzer—and, by the way, I am on Pulitzer's side, not because he is a newspaper man, but he is a clever, affable gentleman. Only two shots were fired, one of which took effect in Augustine's leg. Augustine struck Pulitzer on a head with a Derringer, [here Gruelle supports Pulitzer's account] or some other kind of pistol, cutting his scalp and ending the battle."

The *Missouri Democrat's* anti-Pulitzer version, implying that he shot an unarmed man, reads: "Augustine called him a puppy, when Pulitzer called him a liar. Augustine started toward him, when Pulitzer drew his pistol, aiming at his breast, but Augustine seized his arm and directed the shot downward, which took effect in the right leg below the knee. A second shot struck the floor, when Augustine pressed him into a corner and knocked him down, cutting his head severely. The act is generally declared one of shameless and murderous intent [and] a disgrace to St. Louis."

Gruelle again came to Pulitzer's defense in a letter to the "Editors of *Dispatch*": I know the correspondent of the *Democrat* to be a perfect gentleman yet, misled doubtless by rumor, he has done Mr. Pulitzer injustice. I am no upholder of assassination, but because a man unfortunately gets himself into a scrape, I do not see the necessity of hounding him down. Politically Mr. Pulitzer and I are enemies. Personally we are friends. I have stood by him and I will stand by him. I may not justify the step he took, but then I want justice done this man."

Gruelle wrote for his own paper, the following day, a lighthearted piece apparently meant to ease the situation and showing no sympathy for the wounded Augustine: "Pulitzer is blamed more than he ought to be. As I told him last night, after he reached his room, I had a great notion to shoot him for aiming at Augustine's breast and hitting him only in the leg. Bad marksmanship is to be deprecated on all occasions, and when a member of the press— and a legislator, to boot—essays to burn gunpowder I want him to go the whole hog. [I am going to] put Pulitzer under a severe course of training and I will bet, at the end of that time, he can snuff a candle at ten steps. If he can't, I now and here pledge you my word of honor that I will shoot him myself."

A policeman arrested Pulitzer and took him and Ittner to a magistrate. Ittner posted bond and they were both free to spend the night at home. In court next morning, the magistrate gave Pulitzer a small fine for disturbing the peace. But there was more to come. Although Augustine had only sustained a flesh wound in his leg, Pulitzer was also charged with assault with intent to kill, his trial to take place in the late fall.

The next day in the state legislature a fellow senator proposed appointing a committee to investigate the fight, intending at least to embarrass Pulitzer and at most to cripple his political career. Others heatedly opposed the idea, afraid apparently that it might boomerang and expose them to investigation for minor peccadilloes such as fraud and fornication. The proposal lost by a vote of 58 to 42.

Waiting to come to trial through the summer and fall, Pulitzer continued to work as both politician and reporter. Part of his job was to scan other foreign and domestic newspapers for story leads, especially the lively *New York Sun*, which specialized in human-interest stories and what Pulitzer agreed was the brightest and sprightliest news. He sent a fan letter to its editor and part-owner, Charles A. Dana, calling it "the most piquant, entertaining, and without exception, the best newspaper in the world," which Dana published in the *Sun* on August 24, 1871.

Three months later, on November 20, 1871, Pulitzer stood trial in Jefferson City, accused of shooting Augustine with murder in mind. Defended by

Charles Johnson, his friend and mentor from St. Louis who had volunteered for the job, he was found guilty. But he got away with a slap on the wrist and a $405 fine.

He had nowhere near that amount, but friends rallied around, including Daniel Taylor, a former mayor of St. Louis, and the lieutenant governor, E. O. Stanard, and paid the fine. Years later, Pulitzer repaid them all.

Even though these were violent times, it was odd that a man found guilty of a such a crime did not spend a day in prison. It eventually came out that "a professional lobbyist who knew that Augustine had intentionally incited Pulitzer into attacking him, coldly told Augustine's supporters that unless they ceased their prosecution of the youngster he would reveal all of their rascalities and wreck a number of reputations. 'If that boy goes to prison, he will not go alone,' was his ultimatum. This 'argument' won out. 'It was the first hit [success] I ever made,' observed Mr. Pulitzer [in an unintentional double-entendre] thirty years afterwards."

Surprisingly, the affair did not diminish his political influence: Pulitzer's reform bill passed—both depriving Augustine of his potential ill-gotten gains and ridding the County Court of its corrupt judges.

CHAPTER 3

Survives Fire and Marries

1872–1878
—
25 to 31 years old

D espite or perhaps because of his criminal record, soon after his gunfight with Augustine, Pulitzer was appointed to a part-time job as one of Missouri's three police commissioners. He took it seriously and bolstered his reputation as a straight shooter by gunning for corrupt officials and going easy on the small fry. It was a busy life of politics, running the *Post* six days a week, and fighting crime. Having completed his term as state senator, he joined Carl Schurz's Liberal Republican movement to reform the Republican Party. Under President Grant it had become the party of northern big business, tolerating judges for sale to the highest bidder and crooked stock-market manipulators.

As a convention secretary at the reform movement's national convention in Cincinnati in May 1872, Pulitzer supported Horace Greeley as the man to topple Grant. Greeley was the most admired journalist of his time, but his critics ridiculed him as a crackpot who had hired Karl Marx as a foreign correspondent and claimed to speak with the spirits of the dead. Still, many Democrats were so eager to dump Grant that they, too, supported him, even though he had dismissed them as traitors, horse thieves, and idiots.

At the convention Pulitzer met three men who would play significant roles in his life: Henry Watterson, the one-eyed, outspoken editor of the *Louisville Courier-Journal*; Whitelaw Reid, Greeley's editorial assistant; and John Cockerill, managing editor of the *Cincinnati Enquirer*.

Greeley was no shoo-in at the convention. It took six ballots before Liberal Republicans chose him as their presidential candidate. But Pulitzer was enthusiastic and set out to make some sixty stirring speeches promoting Greeley throughout Missouri and Indiana. He lost to Grant in the presidential election, but even had he won, he would never have reached the White House.

Cartoonist Joseph Keppler's view of Pulitzer as a leader in Carl Schurz's Liberal Republican Party.

Unknown to Pulitzer and almost everyone else, Greeley had been on the verge of madness during the campaign and died that winter in a mental hospital.

Greeley's defeat was Pulitzer's opportunity. Preetorius longed to retire, and Schurz believed that the *Westliche Post's* influence had been crippled by supporting the losing contender. Fearing it would be further damaged if Pulitzer left, they offered the twenty-five-year-old—who worked sixteen-hour days—controlling interest in the paper at a bargain price and deferred terms.

As co-owner and managing editor of the *Post*, he moved to the Lindell Hotel, favored by bachelors with active social lives, one of whom remembered him as "a good story teller, full of fun and much inclined to practical joking." He also relaxed from his demanding work by horseback riding. But his days at the *Post* were numbered. Afraid apparently that this take-charge dynamo would soon gain complete control, Schurz and Preetorius bought him out for thirty thousand dollars, leaving him with only a small financial interest in the paper.

That winter of 1872, with cash to spare, Pulitzer took off for Europe. In Budapest he had an emotional reunion with his beloved mother, Louise, whose

Horace Greeley, the
most admired journalist
of his time.

portrait he always carried with him. His good news was that both her emigrant
sons had made it; his younger brother Albert, having quit teaching in St. Louis,
had moved to Manhattan to work as a reporter on the popular *New York Sun*—
the paper Pulitzer most admired.

Back home in St. Louis, Pulitzer made a comfortable living by practicing
law. But his driving interest was newspapers, both to express his views and as
potential moneymakers. In January 1874 he learned that the bankrupt *St. Louis
Staats-Zeitung* still had a valuable asset: a franchise to publish news from the
Associated Press. He put in the winning bid of a few thousand dollars at the
auction. Then he quickly sold the franchise to the *St. Louis Globe* for twenty
thousand dollars, and the printing press to another paper for a healthy profit.
Now a man of means, he moved to the city's affluent South Side near his former friend and colleague Senator Carl Schurz and next door to composer
Charles Balmer. A frequent guest at musical evenings when Balmer's three
daughters sang, Pulitzer briefly showed a romantic interest in one singer, as
well as in Schurz's daughter, but not enough to commit himself.

Pulitzer's mother, Louise, a portrait he always carried with him.

As a Shakespeare buff, he saw arresting performances of *King Lear* and *Hamlet* by Irish American John McCullough and went backstage to congratulate him. The actor had been hiding in Canada since Lincoln's murder, fearing that simply as an intimate of the assassin, John Wilkes Booth, his own life was in danger. Now that the heat was off he dared to return to America, to which, like Pulitzer, he had immigrated as a youngster. The two became close.

Most mornings Pulitzer went riding with attorney friends. Some evenings he spent with his best friend and roommate Thomas Davidson, a freethinking Scottish philosopher who knew William James and spoke five languages. Together they studied Plato and Aristotle in the original Greek at meetings of the Aristotle Society. Plato's disillusionment with politics echoed Pulitzer's own feelings, especially about President Grant, whom he despised as an incompetent drunk surrounded by crooks and relatives on the take. Because Grant had no worthy Democratic opponent, Pulitzer helped to create the People's Party as a new political force to fight the president at the next election. But when the People's Party convention in Jefferson City nominated farmer William Gentry to be Missouri's next governor, Pulitzer wanted out. He disavowed a published interview in the *St. Louis Globe* on September 7, 1874, quoting him as calling Gentry an ass nominated by asses, but conceded that he considered People's Party candidates inferior to the Democrats.

"Not that I fail to recognize in the movement some excellent men and good intentions," he continued, in a letter to the Democratic *Missouri Repub-*

lican. "But without referring to that particularly warm place said to be paved with good intentions, the result of the convention reminds me very much of that leg of mutton on which old Dr. Johnson dined on the way to Oxford, and which he declared to be: 'Ill-fed, ill-kept, ill-killed, and ill-dressed.' Platform and ticket are ill-born, ill-reared, ill-principled and ill-led. To men of thought and principle both platform and ticket are deaf and dumb." His most damning complaint was the failure "to protest against the real causes of the prostrate condition of the country—the corruption, the lawlessness, the usurpation and the profligacy of Grant's national administration."

Though he had helped to create the third party, he told the Democratic *Republican* that he was bolting the platform and the ticket to become a Democrat—and a Democrat with a strong independent streak he remained for life. Almost immediately, in October 1874, he began stumping the state for the Democrats, including Charles M. Hardin, their candidate for governor of Missouri. Hardin won, as did all thirteen of Missouri's Democratic congressmen up for election, giving them a whopping majority in Congress. Politics to Pulitzer was not the art of compromise, but rather the determination to stick to one's well-aimed guns. He emphasized this, as Seitz reported, in responding to a fellow Democratic delegate at the Missouri Constitutional Convention on December 20, 1875:

"I am not here, sir, as a trader or trafficker; we are not selling and bargaining. Principles, convictions and motives are neither sold nor bargained for!"

At the convention Pulitzer found strong opposition to his belief that the state had a moral responsibility to prevent crime by giving the poor a good public education. Yet he said, "I heartily despise demagogical appeals against the rich, or any particular class, but this question is so grave that it must be treated without gloves. The growth of money power in this country has been fabulous, and its connections with and interest in the Government [are] alarming. We all want prosperity, but not at the expense of liberty. Poverty is not as great a danger to liberty as is wealth, with its corrupting, demoralizing influences. Let us never have a Government at Washington owing its retention to the power of the millionaires rather than to the will of millions."

After the convention Pulitzer made a failed attempt to buy a German-language newspaper in New York, then left for an extended vacation in Europe.

On his return in the fall of 1876 he was incensed to learn that his good friend and mentor Carl Schurz had gone over to the enemy. Schurz had switched back from the reform Liberal Republicans to the regular Republican Party—"the party of corruption"—and was stumping the Midwest for its presidential candidate, Ohio governor Rutherford B. Hayes. Pulitzer reacted fast and furiously, making a clean break from Schurz and trying to destroy his influence. After selling his small remaining interest in the *Post* he stalked Schurz on his speaking tour of Indianapolis, Detroit, and Buffalo and eloquently refuted his pro-Hayes speeches.

Though a lively and witty speaker, Schurz turned down Pulitzer's challenge to a debate, which spurred the Democratic *St. Louis Times* to comment on September 4, 1876: "Mr. Schurz will not consent to a discussion of the issues of the campaign with Mr. Pulitzer, because he would be the last man to acknowledge the intellectual equality of his former lieutenant and associate, but there is nothing that would be more satisfying to the Democracy and we fancy nothing more gratifying to Mr. Pulitzer. With all the strength and analytical resources of Mr. Schurz, he is immeasurably the inferior of the other in nimbleness of intellect, in practical knowledge."

Pulitzer lashed out at Schurz before a Detroit Opera House crowd, saying it was "ludicrous" that "Carl Schurz, distinguished in the past and extinguished in the future, advocates the election of Hayes on a reform platform." He burst a blood vessel in his fiery attack, and when he followed Schurz to Manhattan, was coughing blood. Nevertheless, he addressed a standing-room-only audience at Cooper Union, advocating New York governor Samuel Jones Tilden, a Democrat, as the true reform candidate for the presidency and stressing reconciliation with Southerners because "whoever endeavors to array one section against another is a traitor to his country."

While in Manhattan, Pulitzer had briefly met Tilden, like himself a bachelor and attorney, and with an apparently flawless record as governor. A member of the antislavery faction and an effective reformer, he had helped to destroy the notorious "Tweed Ring"—even though its members were fellow Democrats—by exposing corrupt judges who made the ring possible.* However, there were persistent rumors but no credible evidence that Tilden was a syphilitic drunk, and some questioned the source of his $6 million fortune. He had, after all, been a friend of Boss Tweed before he helped to bring him down.

Pulitzer was soon in the thick of things, reporting the action from Washington, D.C., for Charles A. Dana, editor of his favorite newspaper, the *New York Sun*. Dana had hired him as a special correspondent to cover the election—perhaps as a consolation for turning down Pulitzer's proposal to produce a German-language edition of the *Sun*. Both men made no secret of their support for Tilden, despite his apparent and obvious defects. This charisma-deprived presidential candidate invariably looked as if he had a foul smell under his nose—an appropriate expression during the election, because the stench of dirty politics was palpable. He clearly won the presidency with 4,300,590 popular votes and 196 electoral votes to Hayes's 4,036,298 and 173. Yet Hayes became president!

Pulitzer discovered how it happened: through Republican bribery, forgery, and perjury, especially in Louisiana and Florida, where crooked Republican

---

* Tweed and Tammany Hall cohorts stole some $200 million from New York City. They forced all contractors doing business with the city to pad their bills enormously and hand over the loot. Consequently it cost almost $2 million to plaster one city building, and forty chairs and tables cost $170,729.60.

election boards threw out thousands of "illegal" Democratic votes. When Tilden's supporters learned of the trickery they resorted to similar sleazy tactics, as well as violence and intimidation, but it was too little, too late.

Congress tried to calm the country by appointing a bipartisan commission of seven Republicans, seven Democrats, and one independent. But, at the last moment, the independent, Supreme Court Justice David Davis, retired and was replaced by Supreme Court Justice Joseph P. Bradley, a Republican. The commission's seven Democrats and eight Republicans voted strictly on party lines. Bradley and his fellow Republicans switched the electoral votes to give Hayes a razor-thin majority of one—185 to 184—putting Hayes in the White House despite Tilden's popular-vote plurality of 264,292. Although Tilden did nothing to challenge the stolen election, Pulitzer joined his friend Henry Watterson at a protest meeting in, of all places, the Ford's Theater, the scene of Lincoln's assassination.

From the stage where Booth, the assassin, had broken his leg, Watterson called for a hundred thousand Democrats to storm Congress. An impassioned Pulitzer followed him, urging the excited crowd to "come fully armed and ready for business!"—as if advocating another civil war, which seemed a frightening possibility.

The *Albany Argus* predicted the "prospect of war in every street and on every highway of the land" if Tilden was cheated out of the presidency. Several battalion commanders of state militias offered to place their men at Tilden's command. A friend warned Hayes that the Democrats were secretly organizing an army to fight for Tilden. President Grant even prepared for battle. He ordered troops with light artillery to assemble near Washington and had the commander of the Army's Eastern Department, believed to be a Democrat, transferred far afield.

Despite Pulitzer's rabble-rousing speech, no armed mob responded, nor did he himself appear at the Capitol with a drawn gun. But he did attack, in print, the man whose partisan vote made Hayes president: Joseph P. Bradley. Putting the judge on trial, in the *Sun*, Pulitzer's verdict appeared on February 15, 1877: Bradley's "face is dark as if the shadow of his soul hangs over it and on his forehead could plainly be read, 'Guilty.'" Bradley *was* guilty according to most prominent historians of then and now, who agree that Republicans stole the 1876 presidential election. Even Grant privately admitted that Tilden should have been president.[†]

[†] Though, in 2000, there was no threat of an armed insurrection during the controversial presidential election campaign between Vice President Al Gore and Governor George W. Bush, it was in many respects a remarkable repetition of 1876, with the Democrat, Gore, winning the popular vote and shenanigans reported in Florida depriving him of a possible victory. The 2000 election was also decided by a theoretically impartial body—the U.S. Supreme Court—which voted along party lines for the Republican!

Disgusted with national politics after his temporary reporting assignment for the *Sun*, Pulitzer returned to St. Louis. He moved into a suite in the fashionable Southern Hotel, where he made several new friends, including the German consul, Dr. Gerlact, and resumed his law practice.

After celebrating his thirtieth birthday with friends on April 10, 1877, he returned to his hotel late that night. Two hours later, the place was ablaze. The fire was so devastating that an account of it appeared three days running on the front page of the *New York Times*. Fatalities first estimated at fifty were finally established as seventeen. Because the hotel's fire alarm wasn't working, Pulitzer and other residents were warned only by the smoke and flames, the general noise and kicking in of doors by firemen and hotel employees. But by the time the residents were aroused, "almost every avenue of escape had been cut off by the suffocating smoke," reported the *Times*. "Few of them were able to descend the stairways, and were driven back to their rooms, thus making escape from the windows the only means available. Then began a scene of the most agonizing and horrible nature. Men, women, and children appeared at the windows and eagerly bending down, wildly called for help."

The Fire Department had arrived too late to save the building but rescued many terrified, screaming residents by ropes and ladders, watched by a crowd estimated at five thousand, some shouting for those at the windows to "Jump! Jump!," others imploring them to wait until ladders reached them. "The excitement was intense," said the *Times*. "Men and women were running around frantically calling for missing friends; many fainted from the excitement, while others stood appalled at the terror of the spectacle." Several among the seventeen who died leaped from the fourth, fifth, or sixth stories, among them a woman who, "mounting the window-sill, threw her arms in the air and made the fearful leap, turning over twice in her downward flight," to land on her feet "but with fatal effect."

Pulitzer's friend George Frank Gouley, grand secretary of the Masonic Fraternity of the state, died in the fire, leaving a young widow. Another friend, Dr. Gerlact, the German consul, broke his leg jumping to safety from a window, but his wife was uninjured. As for Pulitzer, he feared he'd choke to death from the smoke, but eventually escaped otherwise unhurt. All his personal belongings were destroyed in the fire, except for the pants he had hurriedly put on.

Soon after, he moved to Washington, D.C., where he considered practicing law. There he renewed his acquaintance with twenty-three-year-old Kate Davis, an intelligent, affectionate, and down-to-earth young woman with a teasing sense of humor. They had first met when he was reporting the presidential election, and he had become infatuated with this strikingly attractive brunette daughter of a Georgetown judge, and a distant cousin of Jefferson Davis, former president of the Confederacy.

Pulitzer lived in Washington's Willard Hotel, a favorite meeting place for lawyer-lobbyists who were so powerful in their ability to control the fate of a bill that they were known as Congress's "third house." Pulitzer despised most of them as men who sold their souls to the highest bidder. And knowing it was virtually certain that to be a successful lawyer in Washington he'd also have to become a lobbyist, he decided to look for another occupation.

Not sure that Kate Davis returned his affection, he took his time about proposing to her. When he did nervously pop the question, she agreed to marry him. But his joy was tempered by the fear that, because of his uncertain future, she'd eventually come to her senses and dump him.

After a lovers' quarrel, he left for a business trip to St. Louis. From there he sent her what he called his "first love letter," saying he had been miserable away from her despite the friends, flattery, and business pressures awaiting him in his hometown, and adding: "I have an ideal of home and love and work— the yearning growing greater in proportion to the glimpse of its approaching realization. I am almost tired of this life—aimless, homeless, loveless, I would have said, but for you. I am impatient to turn over a new leaf and start a new life—one of which home must be the foundation, affection, ambition and occupation the corner stones, and you my dear, my inseparable companion. Would I were not so stupid always to be serious and speculative! Would I had your absolute faith and confidence instead of my philosophy! I could not help thinking how utterly selfish men are in love compared with women, when I read your letter and feel its warmth. I am too cold and selfish, I know. Still, I am not without honor, and that alone would compel me to strive to become worthy of you, worthy of your faith and love, worthy of a better and finer future. Don't of course, show my letters to anybody. I can't bear that thought. Confidential correspondence, much more even than conversation, depends upon strict privacy. Men would certainly not make certain declarations in the hearing of others." He asked her to write to him every day and signed off, "Goodbye till Wednesday, J.P."

Although they agreed to a honeymoon in Europe, he was unable to name a day for their wedding. The best he could say was sometime in the summer. Exactly when depended on his ongoing negotiations to invest in various newspapers. When these fell through, he told Kate to set the date, and returned to join her in Washington. There, by chance, he met his Shakespearean actor friend John McCullough, passing through the city. The actor was also off to Europe that summer, and they arranged to travel together on the same transatlantic liner. Kate, it seems, did not object to having a stranger along on their honeymoon trip.

They married at Washington's Episcopal Church of the Epiphany on June 19, 1878, following in the footsteps of Kate's parents thirty years before who, according to biographer W. A. Swanberg, had been greatly shocked by Kate's choice of a guttural-speaking "foreigner" as a husband. Doubtless, as devout Anglo-Saxon Protestants, they would have been devastated had they known he was the son of Hungarian Jews, which explains why he didn't tell them. Even

Pulitzer's wife, Kate, a
distant cousin of Jefferson
Davis.

Kate mistakenly believed that his mother was a Catholic. Pulitzer may even
have thought so, too, though he himself was an agnostic with no religious affil-
iations or prejudices.

However, during the wedding ceremony the thirty-one-year-old bride-
groom was not preoccupied with religious matters but with the impression he
was making. The shoeshine porter had scrawled the number of his hotel room
on the soles of his shoes. And as he knelt at the altar, Pulitzer worried that the
congregation would mistake the figure 17 for the size of his feet.

CHAPTER 4

Buys *St. Louis Post-Dispatch*

1878–1879
—
31 to 32 years old

When the dying *St. Louis Dispatch* was up for auction on December 9, 1878, someone said "It's not worth a damn," another suggested forty thousand dollars. "Not worth a damn" seemed the consensus at the auction. There were few bids, and Pulitzer topped them at twenty-five hundred dollars.

He turned up at the dingy newspaper office at ten the next morning and supervised the production of the paper. The building and equipment were on their last legs. Ropes were missing to the elevator on which forms containing type were usually lowered from the composing room to the press room, so the staff improvised, carefully sliding them down the stairs. It was touch and go, but eventually some one thousand copies of the paper came off the worn and battered flatbed press. Pulitzer had budgeted twenty-seven hundred dollars to revitalize the paper. When that was exhausted, if it hadn't turned a profit, he and the *Dispatch* would be kaput.

That same day, John Alvarez Dillon paid a visit. The Irish American, Harvard-educated owner of the rival *Evening Post* suggested combining their papers and sharing expenses and profits. Pulitzer had the advantage of a Western Associated Press franchise. He, Dillon, had the advantage of experience. Rather than destroy each other in a battle for only so many readers, why not work together? Dillon asked. Pulitzer liked the thirty-five-year-old publisher immediately and shared his progressive views and intellectual interests. He agreed to the merger on condition that in editorial policy he had the last word.

Then he moved fast. Having a poor opinion of the *Dispatch* staff with one exception, Pulitzer fired the rest. He offered a job to the exception, who declined.

On December 12, 1878, a reporter in the *Post's* office at 321 Pine Street looked up from his desk and saw "a tall, distinguished looking young man (enter and look) appraisingly about, I knew without being told that it was Joseph Pulitzer. He was more than six feet tall and wore rimless glasses, a soft hat and a blue chinchilla overcoat, obviously tailored in New York."

That afternoon, the new publishing partners turned out forty-two hundred copies of their joint venture, the *Post and Dispatch.* To regular readers of the *Post* nothing seemed changed except the name of the paper. As usual, there was something for everyone. On page one: the crimes of local crooks as revealed in that day's Four Courts trials, under the alliterative heading VAGARIES OF VICE; for farmers concerned with the weather, an update on a flood in the East titled TRAIL OF THE TIDE; and for foreign-news junkies, an account of Russian troops occupying parts of the Balkans.

But those who read the editorials on page two of the four-page paper had to notice the change. Pulitzer had taken over. His succinct, muscular style announcing the new proactive editorial policy had replaced Dillon's elegant, polished prose and laissez-faire attitude:

"The POST *and* DISPATCH will serve no party but the people; will be no organ of 'Republicanism,' but the organ of truth; will follow no caucuses but its own convictions; will not support the 'Administration,' but criticize it; will oppose all frauds and shams wherever and whatever they are; will advocate principles and ideas rather than prejudices and partisanship. These ideas and principles are precisely the same as those upon which our Government was originally founded, and to which we owe our country's marvelous growth and development."

Pulitzer put words to work in the paper's December 30 issue when he declared George Vest, a lawyer who had served in the Confederate Congress, his candidate for the U.S. Senate, against fellow Democrats Samuel Glover and railroad magnate Thomas Allen, whom he portrayed as fronting for big-money interest, adding: "If it is a crime to sympathize with the struggle of a poor but pure and brilliant man like Vest against the combined power of money, offices, patronage, newspaper influence and slander, we plead guilty."

When the Democratic *Missouri Republican,* with its twenty-thousand circulation several times that of the *Post and Dispatch,* called the "pure" Vest "corrupt," Pulitzer shot back that it was "an unmitigated lie." When the *Republican* hinted that Vest was a boozer, Pulitzer called it "a gross slander" used to defame "nearly every prominent man in the history of the state."

Pulitzer's editorial of January 10, 1879, stated "The Great Issue" of the campaign: "Democracy means opposition to all special privileges. Republicanism means favoritism to corporations. The tremendous power and influence of nearly all corporations and favored classes are notoriously on the Republican side. Money is the great power today. Men sell their souls for it. Women sell their bodies for it. Others worship it. The money power has grown so great that the issue of all issues is whether the corporations shall rule this country or the country shall again rule the corporations. [Corporate influence] reaches the Supreme Court, and the White House itself! Yet it is seriously proposed by purchased papers and political prostitutes to send the most conspicuous creature of 'capital and privilege' in this State [railroad magnate Tom Allen] to the Senate of the United States as a representative of the Missouri Democracy."

As if to underscore the power of Pulitzer's little paper, Vest won the election—and kept his seat for twenty-four years.

Fresh from that triumph, Pulitzer launched a daring in-your-face campaign to make the affluent residents of St. Louis pay their fair share of state property taxes. He opened with a striking front-page headline "TAX-DODGING," referring to the richest man in town, J. C. B. Lucas.

Under the daring subhead "Wholesale Perjury as a Fine Art" was a copy of Lucas's state tax return for 1878, in which he had listed his property as:

Two horses, mares and geldings;	$100.00
One cow	25.00
Two clocks	20.00
Two watches, chains appendages	50.00
One sewing machine	15.00
Gold and silver plate	500.00
Jewelry, all kinds	250.00
Household, kitchen furniture	1500.00
One library	75.00
Two carriages	200.00

According to this declaration, the paper pointed out, Lucas had not one cent on hand, not one dollar in a bank or safe, no stocks, bonds, or other assets. And in his editorial on the next page, Pulitzer called for a grand jury to investigate tax dodgers because "Millions and millions of property in this city escapes all taxation. When persons like Charles P. Chouteau, the Lucases, or Gerald B. Allen, swear that they do not have one cent in cash, or in bank, don't own one cent's worth of bonds and stocks or notes or other securities, they commit a falsehood, both ridiculous and monstrous. And a much stronger term could be used without danger of libel suits. Tax dodging has become so universal, thanks to the indifference of the press and the officials, that change is imperatively demanded."

The exposure was a sensation. Bitter complaints poured in from the city's "best citizens." Droves of advertisers withdrew their advertising in a concerted effort to bankrupt the paper. Still, Pulitzer kept the heat on by publishing more questionable state tax returns day after day.

To protests that he had gone too far, Pulitzer replied that he'd not gone far enough. To cries of "Invasion of privacy!" he stated: "The tax returns are not private secrets; they are public documents. We would not willingly injure an honest man, but we do not care how many dishonest men are injured by the publication of their own sworn statements."

Pulitzer estimated that because these fat cats refused to declare their $70 million in personal wealth, the middle and working classes, even the poor, had to make up for it. He dramatized his point by publishing "the returns of poor men, of mechanics, printers, plasterers, and widows, showing that the scanty and hard-earned savings of the poor are made to contribute their full share of the taxation."

After weeks of unrelenting attack a grand jury was convened. However, Henry Laughlin, the judge in charge, said he had made a careful study of the subject of tax-dodging but that the tax law was so full of defects it was impossible to enforce. Then he dismissed the grand jury. Pulitzer protested that the statute was crystal clear and that the grand jury could have indicted the worst offenders for perjury. But the judge's ruling stood, and after a few more weeks of the campaign, Pulitzer threw in the towel. Nevertheless, he pursued his crusade to clean up the city, exposing the "respectable" owners of brothels, "who rent and lease homes to the frail sisterhood for immoral purposes," by printing their names and addresses. His exclusive story wowed the journalistic community nationwide.

On January 11, 1879, the British launched a preemptive strike against the Zulus in South Africa. The previous year, the British in the neighboring colony of Natal had threatened to invade Zululand unless its militant king, Cetshwayo, apologized and atoned for the abduction and subsequent killing of two Zulu women who had sought safety in Natal. When the king ignored the thirty-day ultimatum, British forces crossed the border. The Zulus launched a massive, overwhelming counterattack. The result, wrote historian Brian Roberts, "was one of the most devastating massacres in the annals of British colonial warfare."

When the news reached Pulitzer in February 1879, he compared it with the conflict between Americans and the native Indians. His one-sided sympathies were obvious: "The most painful features of our Indian warfare are reproduced with startling accuracy in the accounts of the bloody battle between the Zulus and the English. In each case the opposing forces are civilization and barbarism, and in each case civilization, relying on its superiority in tactics and armament, is lulled into a false and fatal security. Of the final result of the struggle there can be no doubt in either case, but the difference between the value of the life of an American or English army officer on the one hand and a painted savage on the other, makes the victory cost all it is worth."

He was right about the eventual winners, both at home and abroad. After a series of battles, the British finally beat the Zulu army decisively on July 4, 1879, and King Cetshwayo was exiled—but only for a while. He was eventually to be Queen Victoria's guest in England, and allowed to return to Zululand to rule a much smaller area.

The big news in St. Louis was a secret state senate investigation of two men suspected of connections with an illegal gambling ring, who had been appointed to a police board by Missouri's governor. Hearings to decide if the rumors were true were being held in St. Louis's Lindell Hotel. The press was banned, so Pulitzer and Dillon had their own secret meeting with their English-born city editor, Henry Moore. How could they report the hearings they believed the public had a right to know about? Moore, an audacious man, had the answer. He knew a physician whose office adjoined the hotel room in which the secret hearings were taking place. A door between the two had been sealed. Moore persuaded the physician to allow a *Post and Dispatch* reporter to hide in his waiting room, out of sight of the patients. There, for two days, he pressed his ear against the sealed door, listening to the hearings.

Though too cramped to take notes, he had a phenomenal memory and, as he knew the senators and witnesses involved, could identify them by their voices. At dawn he gave his city editor an almost verbatim account of the "secret" hearings to date, which filled eight columns of the February 18, 1879, issue, melodramatically headed THE VEIL IS RENT.

As newsboys yelled "Secret Committee Hearings! Exposure of the Gambling Ring!" the hearings were continuing through the evening. Warned that the secret was out, the committee chairman left the room to buy a paper and, to his astonishment, found the entire story "more complete than his own secretary had recorded it."

Even rival papers acknowledged it as the greatest journalistic coup in years. "It stamps the *Post and Dispatch* as one of the most enterprising papers in the country," applauded Morrison Mumford, a Kansas City editor. Accolades also came from St. Louis papers, which picked up the story and credited it to the *Post and Dispatch*. But when Pulitzer made a front-page splash of a young army man's suicide headlined "Lost Through Love," and printed the suicide note explaining the motive as unrequited love, the *Globe-Democrat* panned him for "unscrupulous sensationalism." To this, Pulitzer replied: "The press may be licentious, but it is the most magnificently representative moral agent in the world today. More crime, immorality and rascality is prevented by the fear of exposure in the newspapers than by all the laws, moral and statute, ever devised."

Sharing *Sun* editor Dana's creed, "Whatever the Divine Providence permitted to occur I was not too proud to report," Pulitzer published stories headlined, "A Well Known Citizen Stricken Down in the Arms of His Mistress," with details in the report from the grieving mistress, and "A St. Louis Heiress Chooses A Husband Against Her Father's Will—And the Wrathful Parent Disinherits His Spirited Daughter."

In the spring, Pulitzer named members of an illegal gambling ring headed by a prominent citizen, Alanson Wakefield, who was indicted for perjury on April 24, found guilty, and sent to prison for two years. Fifty of his employees paid heavy fines. Two years later, Missouri made gambling a felony.

Pulitzer was quick to skewer his rivals for their mistakes. In fact, he was so irritated by the *St. Louis Star,* which frequently stole his news stories, that Pulitzer set a trap, publishing a "cabled" report of a revolt against the British in

Afghanistan. Next day, the *Star* printed it. When Pulitzer revealed that it was a fake story meant to catch the *Star* in the act, the public humiliation ended the practice and accelerated the paper's rapid demise.

By May, when the *Star* gave up the ghost, Pulitzer bought and buried the remains—for $790—and hired the best of the survivors to work for him. Now his was the only evening paper in St. Louis.

Soon after Kate became pregnant in the fall of 1878, the Pulitzers moved to larger quarters, at 2929 Washington Avenue, an affluent area of town. From his new home Pulitzer was taken to his office every day in a horse-drawn brougham driven by Eugene Stewart, a black man, who kept the job for life.

En route to and from his office, little escaped Pulitzer's notice. Firsthand painful experience of the potholes in muddy streets and the lack of open space spurred him to pressure the city into cleaning and repairing the roadway and providing more parks.

Pulitzer worked at a desk in the editorial office in an alcove "masked by a curtain, from behind which he would leap out from time to time with some new thought or criticism for his associates." His energy and enthusiasm were infectious and exhausting. He did every job on the paper, recalled one of his staff: "One day he rushed into the editorial rooms, just as excited as a cub reporter, with an account of a runaway which he had written himself. The runaway horse had only damaged a cheap buggy," but, wrote biographer Swanberg, Pulitzer's "account obscured this fact" until the last line.

After a hurried lunch of beer and a sandwich with friends, he eagerly returned to work. At times Kate accompanied him to the office and joined him in the evenings for dinner. He was back at his desk after dinner and worked by a single gas light on editorials and ideas for the next day's edition, sometimes till the early morning hours. Or, as he put it, "I worked on that carcass like a slave." Although this meant he spent less time with Kate, their marriage seemed ideal to their friends.

On March 10, 1879, Pulitzer moved the paper to a three-story building at 111 North Street. To celebrate its new home and name, the *St. Louis Post-Dispatch*, twenty-thousand copies of a special eight-page edition were to be printed on a new four-cylinder Hoe press, said to be capable of producing that number in one hour. Well-wishers packed the building to give the new press a send-off. It sprang to life at 2:30 P.M. and rolled along smoothly for several minutes as Pulitzer and Dillon proudly watched the product of their joint effort. Then, suddenly, disaster: the blank paper tore, and onlookers were splattered with ink and threatened by waves of ruined newsprint.

Only the pressmen could save the day. They quickly stopped the press, cleaned up the mess, and, crossing their fingers, restarted the machine. That evening every subscriber got a copy, though a little later than usual.

The new move and equipment had made inroads into what was left of Pulitzer's twenty-seven-hundred-dollar investment in the paper. Now, immediately on arrival at the office, he held urgent, whispered conferences with the cashier. As he recalled: "Harris had so nearly exhausted my personal account that I drew out of it three hundred dollars and put it in a trunk at home, against the coming expenses of the birth of my first child."

Pulitzer's crusades increased both circulation and threats against him, so he began to carry a gun for protection. One evening his wife, Kate, subject to the unexpected appetites of a pregnant woman, sent him a message to bring home a bag of tomatoes. He was carrying them and almost home when a thug he recognized approached him. Pulitzer anticipated trouble but didn't draw his gun, perhaps recalling the Augustine episode. Instead he threw the bag of tomatoes at the man and rushed into his house.

After their first son, Ralph, was born on June 11, 1879, Pulitzer surprised his staff by staying home on Sundays, normally a working day, to spend the time with his wife and baby. Kate was a "remarkable beauty," recalled newsman O. O. Sealey, and she "called at his office with her firstborn nearly every evening. Although having done the work of seven men, he would freshen up at seeing his wife and child [and] be joyous as if they had just returned from a trip to Europe. He would have as many compliments for Mrs. Pulitzer as would a young lover. In such an atmosphere those were happy days for everyone." The couple's idyllic existence was shadowed only by Kate's fear that someone her husband had exposed in his paper would make her a widow. He tried to reassure her by continuing to pack a gun.

That summer Pulitzer encouraged a reporter to try to outsmart the city's bungling detectives who had failed to find a well-known hoodlum suspected of killing a local policeman. The reporter soon announced that he was following hot leads that would probably lead to the arrest of the notorious murderer. Almost daily for a week the paper reported, in deathless prose, the progress of the exciting manhunt. Then—nothing. In fact, not one lead developed by the reporter panned out. At the time the killer was hiding in Canada, and was arrested in Chicago four years later.

Even though the reporter had failed, Pulitzer judged the enterprise worthwhile—it had been the talk of the town, increased circulation, and enthralled regular readers.

Anyone who thought Pulitzer's attempts to bring in a cop-killer meant he had gone over to the establishment was quickly disabused when, that same summer, he condemned the police for brutality, citing their shooting of an apparently innocent black man for resisting arrest, and the callous treatment that caused the death of an eleven-year-old boy in a Four Courts jail.

In the fall, Pulitzer investigated six failed insurance companies. Revealing that they had collected twenty-three million dollars in premiums and handed out a mere eight dollars in benefits before going belly up, he asked, "Where has the money gone?," adding, "Fifteen million dollars systematically stolen. Even the James boys [notorious bank and train robbers] seem perfect heroes compared with the pious frauds and hollow hypocrites who under the very cover of respectability could perpetrate such robbery. What mockery upon all society that not one of them is in the Penitentiary!

"Who can wonder at the growing discontent of the poor? Who can fail to see that Socialism, or Communism, is bred, not from below, but [from] above . . . where these 'respectable' wreckers of insurance companies, banks and watered railroads steal their millions, to move, not into prison, but into 'best' society."

James Priest was among the implicated directors named by Pulitzer. A Missouri member of the Democratic National Committee, Priest had previously been promoted in the *Post-Dispatch* for political office. Discovery of Priest's insurance fraud ended Pulitzer's support. The exposure had some effect: a court made Priest repay seventy-five hundred dollars, and in 1880 the state legislature toughened laws regulating insurance companies.

By year's end, with circulation grown by two thousand to about five thousand, and with advertisers flocking back to the paper, Pulitzer and Dillon had made a profit of some eighty thousand dollars. But Dillon wanted out. Pulitzer's dynamic and driven personality was too much for him. Dillon also had been embarrassed by Pulitzer's exposure of tax dodgers. Political enemies had publicized Dillon's tax return, which was not correct to the penny. They had hoped to discredit Pulitzer on the same ground but failed—he was clean as a whistle. They parted friends, after Pulitzer paid Dillon forty thousand dollars for his share of the paper. Now the Hungarian-born dynamo was in total control of every aspect of the paper.

His first move was to respond to a libel suit that singer Carlotta Patti had brought against the *Post-Dispatch* for describing her as drunk during a performance in Leavenworth, Kansas. Her attorney, Hermann, claimed that the report was false and had damaged her reputation. Convinced that the story was true and apparently having some dirt on Hermann, Pulitzer counterattacked on December 5, 1879. In the piece he both ridiculed and tried to intimidate the lawyer: "Mr. Hermann is not so well provided with character himself that he can afford to be dancing in front of the newspaper offices in war paint and feathers, and we may take a notion one of these days to set up where the public can admire his beautiful moral proportions. " Hermann was not intimidated, but when he brought the case to court, the judge threw it out.

In its brief lifetime the paper had taken on powerful forces, attacked bankers and insurance executives, tax dodgers, the police, brothel owners, a gambling ring, a whiskey ring, rival newspapers, labor union agitators, the gas company's monopoly, and the horse car street railway monopoly. In sensational terms and blaring headlines it had exposed the private foibles and failings of individuals, and mocked the pretensions of the middle class in St. Louis who made "guys of themselves bedecked in the regalia of the British Indian cavalry" in staging a medieval tournament with jousting knights and fair damsels.

But nothing he had written was as provocative as his attack on the corrupt municipal government. "We are ruled," he declared, "by the alliance of whisky and gambling; and the corruption bred by these noxious influences permeates our whole local government and our local politics. . . . The pollution of bribery has silenced a servile press, has corrupted an obsequious police, has defiled the very judgment seat of justice itself. The congenial alliance between the gambling hall and brothel, the convenient service of the pander and the capper [a decoy], the coercion of the spy and the blackmailer—these have been the influences which have ruled St. Louis." On behalf of decent citizens he promised that his paper would continue to speak the truth about these "corrupt and malignant influences" in an attempt to destroy them.

He lived up to his promise. And, as a result, he was repeatedly sued for libel, but he won every case. Is it any wonder he carried a gun? Nothing, it seemed, but a bullet would stop him.

CHAPTER 5

President Garfield
Assassinated

1879–1881

—

32 to 34 years old

P ulitzer chose thirty-four-year-old John Cockerill as his managing editor for
the *St. Louis Post-Dispatch* and to take charge when he was out of town or
otherwise engaged. They first met and clicked seven years earlier, at the
Cincinnati political convention. During the Civil War Cockerill had been a
drummer boy in his father's Union regiment, the Seventieth Ohio. As one of
America's first foreign correspondents, he had reported the Russo-Turkish War
in 1877–1878. "A hard taskmaster," according to a colleague, Lafcadio Hearn,
"a tremendous worker, and a born journalist. Not a literary man, nor a wellread
man, nor a scholar—but he had immense common sense, and a large experience of life, besides being, in a Mark Twainish way, much of a humorist." Typical was his response to a clergyman who objected to an irreligious cartoon:
"My Dear Sir: Will you kindly go to hell?"

Depending on his mood and the situation he "could be highly agreeable
or effectively repulsive and had the faculty of acquiring the affection of his
men." Cockerill was also, like Pulitzer, fearless in his promotion of unpopular
crusades. But no one on the staff showed more energy than Pulitzer himself,
"who was everywhere in the office—appearing most unexpectedly and at odd
times, now arguing with a reporter in the city room on some story—anon dashing into the composing room," according to historian Julian S. Rammelkamp.
James Creelman, who worked as a reporter for Pulitzer, noted that: "Nothing
escaped his keen, gray-blue eyes. He wrote editorials, edited the news and
contrived striking headlines. What he wrote himself he altered and polished
and condensed, and sometimes the press had to wait while he worked on the

John Cockerill shot and killed an angry reader.

proofs with such eagerness to improve on himself that his corrections amounted practically to a rewriting of the article. No such worker had ever been seen in a St. Louis newspaper office before." This prompted Cockerill to say, "Mr. Pulitzer was the damndest best man in the world to have in a newspaper office for one hour in the morning. For the remainder of the day he was a damned nuisance."

On January 23, 1880, a fire destroyed much of the composing and printing equipment. Joe McCullagh came to the rescue and let Pulitzer use the presses of his morning *Globe-Democrat*. Two weeks later the *Post-Dispatch* was back in action in its own repaired premises.

One of Pulitzer's motives for hiring Cockerill was to have more freedom to pursue his political goals. As he confided to a friend, "I can never be president because I am a foreigner, but some day I am going to elect a president." Not if William Hyde could stop him. Hyde was the short-tempered editor of what had been one of Missouri's most powerful Democratic papers, misleadingly named the *Missouri Republican*. Its rigid proestablishment line had become too obvious, and the paper was already losing influence when Pulitzer arrived on the scene as a rival and challenged Hyde's choice of Tilden as their best hope in the next presidential election.

Pulitzer was getting the better of Hyde in the battle of words, which explains why Hyde launched a preemptive strike. On March 2, 1880, the two men passed each other walking along Olive Street without a word. Then Hyde suddenly turned and landed a haymaker on Pulitzer. In that evening's *Post-Dispatch* Pulitzer described Hyde's sneak attack, which had knocked him flat onto the sidewalk and sent his glasses flying. Hyde, too, lost his glasses when he struck the blow. Both nearsighted editors scrambled to recover them before resuming the fight, during which Pulitzer tried to pull a revolver from his pants pocket, made difficult because he wore a heavy overcoat. But when he managed to get it out, someone wrestled the gun from him, and other onlookers separated the two men. Pulitzer biographer W. A. Swanberg suspected "that he was hardly as trigger-itchy as he made out—that this public advertisement of his hip-pocket pistol was calculated to discourage further attacks on him." Perhaps.

In May, with Cockerill firmly in control of the paper, Pulitzer left town for the Democratic state convention in Moberly, where he urged all candidates opposed to Tilden to join forces against pro-Tilden candidates led by Hyde. Tilden's people had packed the convention galleries with St. Louis toughs to howl Pulitzer down, but he stayed on the platform for almost an hour until they had exhausted themselves, and then he began his speech. It did the trick and confounded the opposition. He was elected for the upcoming national convention at Cincinnati as one of the delegates of an anti-Tilden delegation.

Then fate took a hand: the sixty-six-year-old Tilden withdrew from the race. So did Pulitzer's candidate, Horatio Seymour. Finally the Democrats nominated General Winfield Scott Hancock, and the Republicans, James A. Garfield, with Chester A. Arthur as his running mate.

In a blatant about-face, Pulitzer first strongly opposed Hancock, then, when nominated, just as vigorously recommended him. Before the convention he thought a general in the White House would be "a stupendous mistake" and that "the teaching of American history, the example of every Republic that has yet existed and perished, the admonition of Washington, the instinct of the common sense and the general intelligence of the country, all agree in pointing [out] the danger of a soldier in the place of the chief magistrate." But on June 24, the day after Hancock's nomination, Pulitzer saw him in an almost dazzling light: "Although a soldier all his life, he has ever been on the side of civil supremacy, habeas corpus and a strict construction of the Constitution. He was a gallant and faithful officer during the war, and his nomination puts the quietus to the attempt of Garfield and his followers to make the war and military service the paramount issue in this campaign."

In June, Pulitzer also attended the Republican national convention in Chicago, along with his political reporter, John Reavis, an intellectual and energetic go-getter, and John McEnnis, a witty Irishman with a keen eye for human-interest stories. Though a committed Democrat, Pulitzer tried to live up to his editorial promise to be evenhanded. So the tall, handsome Garfield was all but eulogized as "a man of genius, oratorical talents, scholarly attainments and intellectual force who will unite the entire Republican party." The cocksure Democrats had better watch out, Pulitzer warned, because Garfield would be a tough nut to crack. Then came the sting in the tail: Garfield had a shady past. As chairman of the House Committee on Appropriations he had been involved in several scandals. He'd even taken a $329 payoff from Crédit Mobilier of America, which owned the Union Pacific Railroad, though he claimed it was a stock dividend. As for running mate Chester Arthur, he had a weak record as customs collector for the Port of New York, from which he had been fired by President Hayes for refusing to reform the place. Other Republican candidates were a corrupt bunch, said Pulitzer, whose crimes he would reveal during the campaign. Hardly evenhanded—it was reporting with a hell of a twist!

Pulitzer failed to mention, for example, that as a lawyer in New York in 1854 and 1845, Arthur had successfully pleaded two remarkable cases upholding the civil rights of blacks, both slave and free. The first established that slaves brought into New York while traveling between two other states were free; the other, that blacks were entitled to the same accommodations as whites on New York City's streetcars.

After returning to St. Louis from the conventions, Pulitzer began to campaign for Thomas T. Crittenden to be governor of Missouri. Crittenden won the nomination and the election. Then Pulitzer sought political office for himself, as a U.S. congressman for St. Louis's Second District, a safe Democratic seat. The thought of Pulitzer in political power stirred archenemy William Hyde into taking another swipe at him by promoting railway magnate Thomas Allen to oppose him. Pulitzer's response seems to have been written with gritted teeth. Restating his policy to be fair and candid, he called Hyde and his colleagues "sordid, malevolent, and domineering" for trying to impose Allen on the Democratic Party, which is "the hereditary enemy of the kings of every character and the jealous watcher over the Railway Kings who purchase legislation, corrupt official life and encroach upon the rights of the poor and defenseless. Does anyone suppose for an instant that Mr. Allen, if sent to Congress, would sacrifice his personal interests to public good?"

Pulitzer's loss was astonishing: 709 votes to Allen's 4,254. But he wasn't surprised. And the next day, September 24, he explained exactly how Allen had stolen the election from him:

"The Missouri Pacific Railroad ordered their men to quit work at three o'clock and provided them with carriages to take them to the polls, compelling them to vote for the Allen ticket. The same was the case with the Market and Olive street railroad lines. All the employees were forced to vote for Allen. The Transfer Company, the Bridge Company, the Elevator Company and the Gas Company did likewise. Every corporation and monopoly in the city was most active for Mr. Allen. With the railroads; with the corporations; with the monopolies; with nearly the entire press under the direct money obligations to Mr. Allen passionately proclaiming innumerable dirty lies against his competitor, no wonder such an extraordinary vote was cast."

Even more amazing was the vote in the Ed Butler–controlled First Ward. Like Pulitzer, this muscular, illiterate Irish blacksmith had arrived in St. Louis penniless and built a flourishing business. He shoed all the horses and mules used to pull city transport and had built a political machine in the working-class district able to deliver votes to either party. Butler got favors for himself and his pals by payoffs to city officials and made sure they were reelected. He intended to vote for Pulitzer until political leaders and business big shots warned him to change sides or lose his horseshoeing monopoly. Butler caved. The night before the primary, he and his cronies hurried through the Second District with new orders. At two the next morning Butler arrived at the Republican office with the news that he had "every damned one of 'em switched." Almost. In Ed Butler's ward the vote was 641 to 1 for Allen.

Humiliated by the massive defeat masterminded by William Hyde, Pulitzer decided to abandon public life for good, which may have pleased the pregnant Mrs. Pulitzer, who, a week later, on September 30, 1880, gave birth to their second child, Lucille Irma. Their first child, fifteen-month-old Ralph, had developed asthma, and to give him relief the Pulitzers wintered in Aiken, South Carolina, an area recommended for those suffering with respiratory problems, because of its balmy, pine-forest-scented breezes. Back home in their three-story house, though they often entertained, Pulitzer's thoughts were almost always on work and invariably involved politics.

Knowing how he'd been cheated in his own bid for office, he resolved to clean up the local Democratic Party, first by getting rid of the mayor, Henry Overstoltz, who was up for reelection in cahoots with Ed Butler.

Late in December 1880 Pulitzer helped to organize a protest meeting at Armory Hall. It was packed with reform-minded Democrats who applauded loudly when he declared: "I will not lend any support to any ticket which has not a pure record." In his zeal to topple the Democratic mayor and clean up the party, Pulitzer supported a Republican mayoral candidate, William Ewing, who was hardly a pure politician—if there is such an animal. Pulitzer's campaign was extremely effective. In April 1881 Ewing won with some twenty-four thousand votes to eleven thousand for Overstoltz.

Encouraged by the success of the campaign, Pulitzer concentrated on exposing corruption wherever he found it. Circulation soared as he developed the paper into an enticing mix of important national and international news and moral crusades, with sensational accounts of vice, crime and corruption, gossip, humor, sports, and entertainment. It was as if he wanted the reader to gasp, groan, and laugh at the realities of their wicked and wonderful world and eagerly await the next day's account.

Pulitzer rarely found English-born Henry Moore, his tough but respected city editor, wanting. At Christmas, Moore assigned reporter John McEnnis to investigate the influence of the criminal underworld in spawning illegal gambling throughout the city. McEnnis came up with a gambling den catering to young men from "the best families." The story, which ran on December 28, 1880, and headed A HELL FOR BOYS, propelled Pulitzer into a mass attack. He took all six local reporters off their current assignments to discover as many illegal operations as they could throughout the city. Their report, which made the front page on January 3, 1881, seven columns of inside information headed IN FULL BLAST, revealed that some four hundred gamblers patronized seventeen illegal establishments. Because the police had made no attempt to close them, Pulitzer wrote in an accompanying editorial, "the gamblers themselves are beginning to think that they are conducting a legitimate business. We do not say that gamblers pay for immunity here, but it will be interesting to note the policy that will be pursued by the authorities now. What will the police do about it?"

The following Sunday, he had his commandos "raid" the Variety theaters near the city's red-light district. They came back with Monday's page-one story headlined THE ROAD TO RUIN, which told how "nearly a thousands boys" crowded the balconies of the "man-traps baited with harlots and rotgut whisky," gazing at "professional women" displaying "the female form divine." Pulitzer explained "that in making war on the gambling dens and Variety Halls we are not actuated by a desire to create a journalistic sensation. We fight these shams and frauds because we believe it to be right. There is nothing Puritanical or illiberal about the POST-DISPATCH, but there are certain fixed principles of morality which it is the duty of every public journal to maintain. We believe that the prosperity and moral health of St. Louis could be advanced by the suppression of gambling and the regulation of Variety Show."

Cynics may compare this stance to that of clergymen who take a suspiciously obsessive interest in reforming "fallen" women by associating with them, and of the "crusading" newspaper that deplores but reproduces the "shocking photos" printed by other publications and then announces, "more shocking photos inside." However, there is no evidence that Pulitzer was anything but a decent man in public and private life. Where he does appear to be either something of a hypocrite or deluded is in denying that he wanted to create a journalistic sensation. Of course he did, and he often said so, but his main motive, he claimed, was to attract more readers to the serious columns in which he expressed his heartfelt views on life and politics.

He miscalculated, however, when he urged ministers and their congregations to join the fight against Satan. They wanted to go even farther and close down all Sunday entertainment, including operas, and the publisher was forced to do a moral U-turn in which he suggested that "the dear [church] ladies" were distorting his mission.

After attacking gambling dens and sleazy theaters, he unleashed his team of reporters on lottery runners, fortune-tellers fronting for abortionists, opium dens, and prostitutes working out of houses owned by "eminently respectable" individuals "who profit by the wages of sin." A grand jury investigated the houses of prostitution but declined to release names of the property owners.

Once more Pulitzer dared to bring things out in the open: "The reporters of the POST-DISPATCH have found little trouble in securing the matter which the grand jury thought ought to be published, but were unwilling to. Below is given a list of the keepers of houses of ill-repute, with the names of owners.

The territory from Chouteau to Case avenue, and from the river to Fourteenth street, embracing the heart of the city, is dotted thickly with plague spots." He was certainly on to something. In January 1881 he had sold ninety-three hundred copies. Two months later, when he published the names, twelve thousand.

Libel suits soared, too. He won them all with one exception, which was settled out of court. Meanwhile, the police bowed to Pulitzer's pressure and arrested 145 gamblers, but only 4 from dens controlled by gambling syndicate boss Robert Pate. However, when the *Post-Dispatch* charged that police had been bribed to go easy on Pate's operations, 4 policemen were arrested and indicted. Because Pate had powerful political contacts he soon resumed operations, backed by businessmen who saw gambling as a "necessary evil" to attract visitors to the city with money to spend. In his editorial column, Pulitzer agreed that "the gambling instinct is very strongly implanted in man. So is the whisky appetite, the inclination to steal and a hundred other passions [but] professional gamblers are a dangerous class in any large community. If they are prosperous they are certain to elevate to power men who are decidedly lax in morals and inclined to look leniently on vice—and if they are not prosperous they are likely to stimulate all sorts of small crimes in an effort to be so." It would take another year before Pate was indicted for conducting a gambling den—a felony for which he faced a steep fine and prison.

Almost every issue of the paper produced targets of his crusades determined to silence him. Pulitzer was returning to work from lunch the day after he broke the police-corruption story, when a tough-looking character confronted him with obvious intent. Ready for trouble—this wasn't the first time—Pulitzer slammed the man against a store window, rushed to his office, and wrote an account of the encounter headed WHO HIRED HIM?

In another incident soon after the street attack, Jake Usher, irate owner of a brothel, stormed in to give Pulitzer a piece of his mind. A reporter nearby reckoned that "Usher's indignation was a summer breeze competing with a Kansas cyclone. Mr. Pulitzer had the loudest voice on the Mississippi, and the flow of words came like Niagara. After describing the disgrace Usher was to St. Louis, he started for Usher who lost no time in getting away. " Aware that Usher might be the first of many, and that others might be more dangerous, managing editor Cockerill kept a loaded revolver in his desk drawer.

Although murder was rampant in St. Louis, that year's biggest murder story came out of Washington, D.C., when President Garfield was gunned down in a railroad station. The assassin was Charles J. Guiteau, a demented and disgruntled Chicago lawyer. On one of his visits to the White House to apply for the job of U.S. consul in France, Guiteau had the gall to steal the president's stationery. When he was turned down for the job, he set out to assassinate Garfield. He got within range one evening in late June, but panicked and walked away—only to stalk the president again, on July 2.

En route with two of his sons for a reunion at his alma mater, Williams College, in Williamstown, Massachusetts, Garfield was waiting for their train in the Baltimore and Potomac railroad station when the assassin approached him from behind, fired his .44-caliber Bulldog revolver twice, and yelled triumphantly, "I am a Stalwart and now Arthur is president!"

Stalwarts were Republicans who wanted to retain the corrupt spoils system, as did Vice President Chester Arthur. Garfield had infuriated the Stalwarts by backing the investigation of a post office scandal spawned by the spoils system.

One bullet grazed Garfield's arm; the other lodged in his back, near his pancreas. Guiteau was arrested, and the wounded president was taken to the White House.

Pulitzer ordered the largest type in stock for the front headline that day—GARFIELD'S LIFE—and worked far into the night on what was virtually the president's obituary. He printed a record thirty-one thousand copies, which sold out.

For weeks Garfield lay in his bed in great pain while at least fifteen doctors poked and prodded in futile attempts to locate the bullet, spreading infection through his body with their unwashed fingers. A primitive air-conditioning system in his bedroom gave him some relief, and inventor Alexander Graham Bell also tried and failed to locate the bullet with an electrical device he'd invented to detect metal. No one seemed to realize that the steel springs in the mattress were causing a field of interference. In fact, nature was trying to save Garfield. A protective cyst had grown around the bullet, making it harmless. Had the doctors left him alone, he might have recovered.

In subsequent reports, Pulitzer dared to dispute the daily "rose-colored" bulletins from the White House doctors. He pointed out that Garfield's temperature of 104 degrees indicated a burning fever, and suggested that because the president read his doctors' bulletins they might be telling white lies to protect a mortally wounded man.

On August 11, 1881, the *Post-Dispatch* came out with the headline HE IS DYING, a startling contradiction of the doctors' upbeat bulletins. The next day, to find out the facts for himself, Pulitzer was off to Long Branch, New Jersey, near the ocean home to which Garfield had been taken to escape the stifling heat.

Strangely, while Pulitzer was away, Cockerill wrote positive editorials about the doctors. Yet Pulitzer, the man on the spot, gave them hell. He stated with astonishing confidence that far from recuperating, as the doctors claimed, Garfield had chronic blood poisoning, which, unless cured, would be fatal: "The physicians and bulletins and [other] reporters have lied for days and weeks and months denying this fact. The official bulletins are entirely untrustworthy, Dr. Bliss's particularly. Everybody here knows he is a reckless liar. The best that the most hopeful of physicians and attendants say is that he is holding his own, but that means little when it is remembered that he was dying—when

abandoned even by Dr. Bliss a fortnight ago, and death was arrested by stimu-
lants, artificial means and something like a miracle."

Pulitzer obviously had first-class inside information and so was able to give
precise details: "His blood is poisoned from the original wound he has in his
back. The glandular swelling has gone, but only to leave a terrible wound or
large sore covering part of his face and head, affecting the ear, jaw, head and
leaving a hole in the cavity of his mouth. Sores all over his body and on his rec-
tum make every motion and even quietude painful. Boils here and there indicate pus and bad blood, but what probably is the worst sign of all is the frequent
coughing. The President is slowly dying. He may possibly linger for some time,
but at present there seems to be no reason for the expectation of his recovery. I
give the facts as I find them, not as they ought to be or are wished to be."

He had it right. Four days later the *Post-Dispatch* page one headline read:

THE LUNGS AFFECTED.

———

Notwithstanding the Official Bul-
letins the President is in a
Critical Condition.
The Predictions of the Post-
Dispatch Specials Com-
pletely Verified.

———

Even Dr. Bliss Now Admits the
Fact.

———

The Chances of Recovery Strongly
Against the Patient—The Truth
Told in Our Special
Telegrams.

Pulitzer exposed the official bulletins as shams because they failed to "contain the faintest allusion to the lung complication. . . . Why should Dr. Bliss be
so magnificent a liar? Every day last week, for instance, I telegraphed that a
new trouble with the lungs was approaching. Every day last week and even yesterday until a late hour of the night Dr. Bliss repeatedly and emphatically
asserted that there was no trouble whatever with the lungs. Now he suddenly
admits that the right lung is not only affected, but that it is a very serious thing.
Everybody in the inner circle knew that for nearly two weeks, still Dr. Bliss
insisted that the lungs were perfectly sound. Is such lying pardonable?"

On September 15, 1881, Pulitzer reported: "The best sign of this morning
is the absence of Dr. Bliss, who has gone to New York. But unfortunately he
will be back soon. He has probably gone for some instruments, as another operation is to be performed. The pus on the lung is to be removed by means of a
hollow needle, which will cause the poor, patient President great suffering.

The official bulletins are entirely untrustworthy, Dr. Bliss, particularly. Everybody here knows he is a reckless liar."

The blood poisoning was not cured, and four days later, on September 19, Garfield died from an infection and internal bleeding. Guiteau, in prison, now faced a murder trial.

Critics complained that in Pulitzer's sensational reports he had prematurely killed off the president. He replied that on the contrary he had hoped and prayed for Garfield to survive but that he had not been fooled by the doctors' bulletins and had tried, as always, simply to tell the truth—backed presumably by expert advice and inside information. Dr. Bliss, the "reckless liar," did not sue him for libel.

Pulitzer, who had shown himself to be a superb reporter, left the awful heat of New Jersey to report breaking stories from New York, including a post office scandal, before returning to St. Louis.

There he kept up his driving pace, taking on the fire department and the law courts.

After calling the fire chief incompetent, the fire department undermanned and underfunded, and the firemen demoralized, Pulitzer promised to build "a small fire of our own" under the fire department. The mayor, responsible for the situation, took the heat without flinching—until a two-block factory on Clark Avenue went up in smoke. Then he felt obliged to hold hearings, but they fizzled out in finger-pointing. Nothing happened until St. Louis underwriters announced a 20 percent hike in fire insurance rates. Then the city government acknowledged that Pulitzer had a point by increasing firefighting funds and ordering the mayor to reorganize the fire department.

In his campaign to clean up the city, Pulitzer complained that while murder rates in St. Louis rivaled Chicago's, no one had been hanged for murder in the past six years. Instead, a killer could expect to spend a year or two in jail, then be freed to prey on society. "A brutal murder was committed yesterday," Pulitzer wrote. "The lawyers of the desperado are already at work on his defense, while the Circuit Attorney is away summering in the mountains. In other words, the State is idle while the criminal is at work. We kill mad-dogs for the protection of the community and we must kill human mad-dogs for the same reason." He got quick results, though the timing was unfortunate. A month later, in the season of goodwill, he reported: "Good news for Christmas! There will be five hangings within the next three weeks."

Good news for newsboys who hawked his paper on the streets was that Pulitzer was giving them a Christmas dinner. They thanked him for it with three cheers, and it became an annual affair. Everyone agreed that he was a generous and concerned employer (except, no doubt, those he fired) who paid his male and female staff well, and rewarded reporters for exceptional work: a gold watch for one and an extra week's wages for another.

The day after Christmas, Pulitzer was again on the warpath—this time against the police department as totally inadequate, with "three policemen to the square mile and two hoodlums to the square yard." The previous summer Pulitzer had regretted nudging Governor Crittenden into firing Police Chief James McDonough, a decent man but too old and easygoing for the job. Now, he thought even less of his replacement, Ferdinand Kennett, calling his conduct reprehensible for protecting illegal gambling, and virtually challenged him to sue for libel. Kennett took up the challenge but lost the suit.

On December 31, 1881, the *Post-Dispatch* moved into 515–517 Market Street, a four-story building with the editorial offices on top and, in the basement, two of the latest Hoe presses, capable of printing twenty thousand newspapers an hour.

Hopes were high. Pulitzer was out of debt and making a profit. Sales were increasing almost daily. In their euphoria, no one on the staff could have anticipated what would happen within a year—although, considering the nature of his crusades, the virulence of the attacks, and the characters of his enemies, the tragedy that occurred now seems all but inevitable.

CHAPTER 6

Jesse James
"Shot Like a Dog"

1882
—
34 to 35 years old

E arly in 1882 Pulitzer visited New York, where brother Albert was making his name writing for the *New York Herald*, and then went north to Boston, on the lookout for talent and bright ideas. There he met Charles Taylor, editor of the *Boston Globe*, and discussed with him how to bring a paper to vibrant life. They agreed on the same *modus operandi*: cater to the masses and earn their trust.

Back on home ground, he decided to expand sporting news—not baseball, in which interest seemed to have died, but boxing matches and cockfights, even though both were banned in Missouri. Conceding that prizefighting, as it was called, was "coarse, demoralizing, and vulgar," he promised to provide coverage for those who wanted it.

To reassure his more sophisticated readers that he was also catering to their interests, Pulitzer told them he was providing a daily diet of some four thousand words of foreign and domestic news from a New York wire service as well as from Associated Press reports.

He even scooped the British press in reporting a seventh and last assassination attempt on the British monarch, Queen Victoria—a sure circulation-booster. Roderick MacLean, a twenty-seven-year-old grocer's assistant, fired a gun as she drove from Windsor railroad station on March 2, 1882, missing her but denting the carriage. The police seem to have been otherwise engaged, because it took two Eton schoolboys to prevent a second shot by beating the would-be assassin into submission with their umbrellas. Three days later the Queen invited nine hundred Eton schoolboys to Windsor Castle, where she

thanked the young heroes. Britain's Liberal prime minister, William Gladstone, probably thinking of both the Fenians fighting for Irish home rule, and
the recent murder of President Garfield, remarked that foreign assassins always
had political motives, but English assassins were always insane. It was certainly
true in the case of MacLean, who said he shot at the queen because he was
hungry. Had he been sane, someone suggested, he would have shot his local
grocer. In fact, he had recently been released from a lunatic asylum.

Pulitzer's scornful attacks on royalty were always blunted when it came to
Victoria. He saw her as a lonely, decent, and dignified woman who, although
not brilliant "in any respect," was far superior to her Hanoverian forbears, one
of whom Pulitzer mocked for his "ugly and hungry mistresses," another for losing America through ignorance and obstinacy, and a third for contributing
nothing "to history and humanity except Mrs. Jordan and half a dozen illegitimate children." He forgave Victoria for being an ultraconservative because she
rarely allowed it to show "in an objectionable manner, and never to interfere
with the clearly expressed will of the people. Had she fallen victim to the assassin, her death would have been lamented the world over, and none more sincerely than in the land her grandfather lost."

After the attempt to kill Queen Victoria, Pulitzer didn't have long to wait
for another front-page sensation: Governor Crittenden's offer of a ten-thousand-
dollar reward for the capture, dead or alive, of legendary outlaws Frank and
Jesse James had found a taker willing to squeeze the trigger.

The James brothers, sons of a Baptist missionary turned Missouri farmer,
had been fierce fighters for the Confederate cause. During the Civil War Frank
James had joined Colonel Quantrill's guerrilla force in a merciless raid on
Lawrence, Kansas, an antislavery stronghold, during which they slaughtered
150 men and destroyed the town. This earned Quantrill his reputation, at least
among Northerners, as the bloodiest man in American history. Frank's brother
Jesse fought under another ruthless leader, "Bloody Bill" Anderson, a Quantrill
lieutenant, and took part in the massacre of 25 unarmed Union soldiers on fur-
lough at Centralia, Illinois. Soon after, they killed more than 100 Union militia and mutilated many of the corpses.

At war's end Jesse, then eighteen, was severely wounded by federal soldiers
but escaped capture. When he recovered, he persuaded his brother Frank and
some friends to resume their wild wartime guerrilla attacks—where the money
was. Jesse led his gang in raids on trains and stagecoaches with the reins in his
teeth and both guns blazing. Over the years they also robbed individuals,
killing all who resisted. They boasted of never robbing a friend, a preacher, a
Southerner, or a widow. But they were great widowmakers. To many in the
community of farmers on the Missouri-Kansas border, Jesse James was a Robin
Hood–style hero who shared with them a fierce, undying loyalty to the Southern cause. They bought his claim to have been driven to crime by the Yankee
authorities who persecuted him because of his devotion to a lost cause. Pro-

tected by this community, the outlaw brothers escaped capture for seventeen years. But after Governor Crittenden's reward offer, Jesse James, now thirty-four, had only months to live. Fellow gang member Robert Ford had contacted the governor to offer to hand over Jesse for the reward money and amnesty for himself and his brother Charley. Crittenden agreed. Then Robert decided to kill rather than capture Jesse. Pulitzer's headline and subheads told the story in surprisingly sympathetic terms:

A DASTARD'S DEED.

Cold-Blooded Treachery
at Last Conquers
Jesse James.

The Noted Border Bandit
Shot Like a Dog
From Behind.

By a Man Who Was Eating
His Bread and Was
His Friend.

By a Coward Traitor's Hand Missouri Vanquishes Jesse
James.

Historians have confirmed the *Post-Dispatch* account as generally accurate. Dated April 4, 1882, it read: "Jesse James was shot and killed in his house . . . by Robert Ford, at 10 o'clock yesterday morning. The murderer, in company with his brother Charles, had been living with Jesse James for some time and both were completely in his confidence. A plan had been on foot between the two brothers for some months past to murder James, yesterday morning presenting the first favorable opportunity.

"Immediately after breakfast Charley Ford and Jesse James went out into the stable, in the rear of the house, for the purpose of currying their horses, to be used that night, as Ford says, in an attempt to rob the bank in Platte City. Upon returning to the house Jesse James divested himself of his coat and vest and his belt, in which were his pistols, and threw them on the bed. As James turned his back to adjust a picture on the wall, Robert Ford,

QUICK AS A FLASH, DREW A REVOLVER

and fired, the ball striking the outlaw in the back of the head, penetrating the brain and coming out through the eye. The ball was fired from a .45-caliber

Colt improved, and death was instantaneous. Mrs. James, hearing the shot, rushed into the room, and, lifting Jesse's head in her lap, tried to revive him, but without effect.

JESSE NEVER SPOKE A WORD

after the ball entered his head.

"The murderer then ran out of the house, but came back at the request of Mrs. James. He was then accused of the murder, which he strenuously denied, claiming that the pistol had been discharged by accident."

Frank James escaped a similar fate when he surrendered to Governor Crittenden on October 5, 1882.

In a rare tribute to the bandit, Pulitzer published two editorials about him on the same page. The first began: "However much we may feel inclined to rejoice over the removal of the desperado JESSE JAMES from the warm precincts of eternal day, every sentiment of manhood and humanity must revolt against the manner of his taking off. He was an outlaw, an enemy of society, and the blood of innocent men fairly reeked on his hands, and yet there is no evidence that he ever took a human life through methods that were cowardly or treacherous. [Wasn't it cowardly to shoot unarmed men?] There must be a feeling of sympathy in the inner heart of every thorough man for this hunted outlaw shot down like a dog, unarmed, in the midst of his own family, by two boys . . . regarded by him as friends." The second, only slightly less sympathetic editorial, read: "Mr. JAMES leaves behind him a record dark with cruelty and wanton murder. He disgraced the State of Missouri in the eyes of the civilized world, retarded immigration and menaced the peace of some of our best people. His removal is a cause for general rejoicing . . . but it is to be regretted that the measure of poetic justice was not filled. After such a life of turmoil and bloodshed Mr. JAMES should have perished with his boots on. The messenger overtook him in a moment of *dolce far niente*, so to speak, when his pedal extremities were covered only with socks."

Pulitzer attacked Missouri governor Crittenden as the villain of the piece, accusing him of taking "advantage of his power, like Henry II of England, to make one man a murderer in order to get rid of another man who incommoded the State."

Crittenden dismissed Pulitzer's charge as an attempt to create a sensation. Whether it was or not, it worked. The controversy raised the circulation that month from 20,000 to 26,600 copies daily. And the story refused to die.

Pulitzer had made the mistake of all but eulogizing a ruthless bandit. Bitterly disappointed in Governor Crittenden for protecting gamblers, he was damned if he would congratulate him, even for ridding the country of a killer, and he defended his position: "It must not be thought that we have a particle of kindly sentiment for the late Mr. JAMES. He was a murdering, thieving bandit and a shame and injury to the State. We have no patience with the weakminded people who regard him as a hero or sympathize with his family on account of his fate. We simply claim that, as a criminal, he was entitled to be adjudged and dealt with under the laws."

The *Kansas City Times* didn't buy it, charging that "Frank James might find a safe asylum in the *Post-Dispatch* office at St. Louis which mourned the loss of his brother Jesse as it had never mourned the loss of any of Missouri's great men." Judging by the *Post-Dispatch*'s headlines first reporting his death, they had a point.

Pulitzer disagreed. "A villainous and utterly indefensible lie," he replied. "We have never failed to express satisfaction with his death, and to congratulate the State now that he is no longer alive." He did concede "that we have severely criticized our asinine Governor for the lawless and uncivilized way in which he compassed the bandit's murder."

When Major John Edwards, editor of the *Sedalia Democrat*, urged the James gang to kill Ford in revenge, Pulitzer protested: "If this advice is followed the western end of the State will soon be covered with an inch of human gore [and] the Democratic party will be held responsible for the Sedalia Democrat's wild utterances. It will be claimed that Maj. Edwards has voiced the true sentiment of the Confederate Democracy of our 'robber-ridden' State, and [then] it will be easy for the Republican party to demonstrate that JESSE JAMES was a representative Democrat and the openly expressed sympathy for him shows Missouri to be a State in which the pistol is held to be above the law and an instrument more sacred than the Constitution." Pulitzer also revealed that Edwards had been a friend of the James brothers during the Civil War and their apologist ever since, helping, as their enthusiastic historian, to make heroes of them.

He soon had another reason for attacking Crittenden. At long last, thanks to Pulitzer's efforts, gambling boss Pate was sentenced to six months in jail. But the governor immediately pardoned him. Pulitzer then roused the public to force a second trial, in which Pate was again sentenced to jail—and again pardoned by the governor! However, Pate was so shaken by the subsequent outcry that he indefinitely delayed reopening his gambling dens.

Pulitzer's aim to tell the truth at all costs partly explains his brutal obituary that spring of Cornelius Vanderbilt, who killed himself in a New York hotel. To Pulitzer it merely added "another scandal to the record of this family, so strangely compounded of greed, vice and wealth. Cornelius was a reckless, dissipated youth. At one time he was known as a card-sharper and the associate of questionable men. His father virtually discarded him. . . . It was claimed that he was subject to epilepsy. He was not out of funds when he shot himself—he had simply grown tired of his own disgusting companionship. After he shot himself, his austere brother William, who felt for him the affection that Cain experienced for Abel, drove up in his carriage, looked at the corpse and drove away. Money is a great and worshipful thing in modern society, but there are scores of thousands of families in this country struggling along today on $2,000 a year that would hardly exchange their peace, content and loving pride for a share of the Vanderbilt name and treasure."

Ironically, one of Pulitzer's sons would marry a Vanderbilt!

Pulitzer's skepticism about Vanderbilt's epilepsy was unjustified. He did in fact suffer from it so badly that his father had him confined in various lunatic asylums because in those days it was thought to be a mental disease. Pulitzer might at least have quoted Henry Clews, a friend of Vanderbilt who attended that last birthday party. He said: "Let us throw the mantle of charity over that tragic scene in the Glenham Hotel, and hope that his soul may have found the rest which, in its poor afflicted body, it vainly sought for here."

Spurred perhaps by Vanderbilt's wasted life, Pulitzer decided to dramatize the extremes of rich and poor nearer home. He printed a list of St. Louis millionaires (he was not yet one of them) and featured the lifestyle of a wealthy dermatologist who had made his bundle quickly and retired, in contrast to tenement life in Clabber Alleys, the city's toughest neighborhood. There, the paper reported, "upon a filth begrimed floor, reclined in beastly drunkenness several negro men and women and three white women, the latter in a half-nude condition. One of the white women, whose face was partially destroyed by a disease, with the utmost sang-froid requested a 'chaw of tobacco.' Stretched in one corner of the room, upon a bed of straw saturated with filth, lay a white child whom the above-mentioned woman claimed as her own. Emaciated with disease and probably hunger, the little thing moaned feebly, its pitiful wails failing, however, to reach the stony heart of the mother," a "vile creature" with "an imbecile grin."

Outside, the reporter found hogs and children wallowing in deep mud, and a black woman and a white woman fighting over who was going to rob the white man they'd lured into the alley.

The *Post-Dispatch* headlined the piece "What Can Be Seen in a Big Christian City."

When such true dramatic vignettes were in short supply, the paper inflated trivial events into shocking scandals, announced invariably by an alliterative headline. One such was: ROCK AND RYE, subheaded, "Rev. Lofton Goes Up Upon a Saintly Spree . . . He Is said to Have Been Intoxicated and Grossly Insulted a Lady . . . A Terrible Clerical Scandal Involving the Pastor of the Third Baptist Church . . . Gen. Sherman Views the Reverend Gentleman's Escapade—A Shocking Story of a Divine."

The report was something of a letdown: Having been ill, a clergyman had taken an alcoholic stimulant on his doctor's advice. When he sat next to a woman on a streetcar, she was offended by his alcoholic breath and simply moved to another seat.

Pulitzer was an equal-opportunity publisher when it came to embarrassing clerics. He encouraged reporter Frank Bigney to break the story of a Catholic priest suspected of fathering a child by a beautiful young woman. That issue sold a thousand extra copies. And as a result of the unsubstantiated rumor, the bishop of St. Louis suspended the priest. Far from condemning Pulitzer for giving credence to a rumor, the journalistic community praised him for his enterprise.

Crime stories were part of the mix, and the paper always tried to be first with the most. Readers had been intrigued by the news that Zoe Watkins, a visitor to St. Louis, had disappeared on her way to mail a letter. A few days later, at seven-thirty in the evening, city editor Moore got a tip that her body had been discovered in the river. Moore immediately sent a reporter for the details and had the story written, edited, headed, and printed as an extra edition — and on the street by ten that night, fast work that increased that day's sales by five thousand copies.

In June 1882, Pulitzer covered the hanging of President Garfield's assassin, Guiteau, in obsessive detail: how, as a prisoner, he had survived two attempts on his life; how he slept, cried, and prayed; what he ate just before his execution; and medical opinions on his mental and physical condition. Pulitzer even persuaded clergymen to discuss whether Guiteau would "wing his way to heaven or hell," and what he would do in the next life. *Post-Dispatch* reporters interviewed other murderers in the prison to discuss Guiteau's crime, sanity, their opinion of hanging — they were against it — and whether they anticipated a future life after their executions.

Pulitzer had no doubt that Guiteau got his just deserts.

The hanging issue of the paper, with an artist's impression of Guiteau in his deathwatch cell and three men inspecting the scaffold, sold a record 45,720 copies. On that same day the Pulitzers' third child, Katherine Ethel, was born.

After enjoying the euphoria of record sales and a new addition to his family, Pulitzer was discouraged. Readers had lapped up the attempt to kill Queen Victoria, the betrayal of Jesse James, and Guiteau's hanging, but showed little interest over the paper's first big war story in July, which began when the British navy bombarded the port of Alexandria. Ostensibly the quarrel was with a rebellious Egyptian army chief, Urabi Pasha, whose followers went berserk on June 11, slaughtering some fifty Europeans and severely wounding the British consul. This, explained British prime minister William Gladstone, had created "a situation of *force* . . . which could only be met by force." But the naval attack had another motive: to establish a protectorate in Egypt to ensure the safety of the Suez Canal — Britain's vital passage to India for military and commercial purposes.

Pulitzer printed a map of the area and made it easy for busy readers to follow the fighting by headlines alone, from the first SHOT AND SHELL on July 11 to MASSACRE OF EUROPEANS BY THE ALEXANDRIANS and BRITISH SAILORS AND MARINES LANDED FROM FLEET to the final defeat of the Egyptian army. Urabi was deported to Ceylon.

Pulitzer expressed his disappointment that the war news had neither aroused nor increased his readers in an editorial in which he also revealed his rare pro-British bias:

"The Battle of Tel-e-Kebir was the most important to us of any that had occurred since the Franco-Prussian war, for it involved a nation to which we are allied by blood, language and commerce. The fate of 25,000 troops depended on the turn of this struggle and yet it created less sensation in St. Louis than an ordinary item of local news."

Nevertheless, business was good, and he shared his success with his staff. Cockerill got a twenty-five-hundred-dollar bonus. Senior reporters at thirty-five dollars a week were now the highest-paid in the city. Women compositors received the same wages as men, and everyone got a two-week vacation with pay, unheard of on almost all other newspapers. As well as an annual Christmas dinner, the newsboys were rewarded for good work with gold watches, pocket knives, and new suits.

As for himself, now wealthy enough to take extended vacations and confident that Cockerill could hold the fort, Pulitzer took his family to their favorite spot at Aiken, intending to spend much of the winter there with occasional forays to New York. He could hardly have anticipated that soon after he left for South Carolina, Cockerill would almost destroy the paper.

With Pulitzer's general approval, Cockerill lit the fuse with an explosive campaign against James Broadhead, a Democratic candidate for Congress, calling him an unprincipled thief, and backing the accusation by citing his record: As a lawyer with a ten-thousand-dollar retainer from the city to negotiate disputed prices with the local gas company, Broadhead had agreed to its outrageously high rates. Then, when the city tried to cancel the gas company's franchise, Broadhead switched sides and represented the gouging gas company. Accepting fees from both parties in the gas dispute, Cockerill concluded, was "about as honorable as breaking into a man's house and appropriating his valuables." Throughout the fall, Cockerill's unremitting, vitriolic editorials exposed Broadhead to contempt and ridicule: He was a puppet controlled by corrupt power broker Ed Butler. His conflict-of-interest work for the gas company had cost St. Louis taxpayers three million dollars. He had "the cowardice rather than the courage of his convictions" and was "a political and legal weathercock" who sold the city's interests to a gas monopoly. "His political record is one of vacillation, duplicity, deceit and indecision."

When, despite this onslaught, Broadhead won the primary against the other Democratic candidate, John Glover, it provoked Cockerill into aping his opponent and becoming a "political weathercock" himself. He promised that the *Post-Dispatch* would switch its party allegiance and enthusiastically support any Republican candidate of good character who entered the race against Broadhead. Broadhead's friend and law partner Colonel Alonzo Slayback thought the insults reflected on him, too, and, at a Democratic Party meeting, excoriated the *Post-Dispatch* and its staff.

Cockerill decided the time was ripe to respond and the risk acceptable. He counterattacked next day with an open letter, describing Slayback's outburst, when "without personal provocation he proceeded to apply a string of vile and virulent epithets to the Post-Dispatch and its conductors, making charges which he knew to be false." Among others, he wrote, Slayback had charged that the paper resorted to blackmail. The sting was in the tail when Cockerill quoted John Glover, the recently defeated candidate, who had called Slayback a coward.

Slayback and a friend read Cockerill's letter in an early copy of the paper and hurried to the newspaper building and up the narrow stairs to confront Cockerill in his office. He was at his desk chatting with business manager John McGuffin and composing-room foreman Victor Cole when the two visitors burst in.

Almost incoherent with rage, Slayback intended to slap the editor's face and demand that he retract the insult.

McGuffin later recalled that Cockerill's gun was lying on a table when Slayback rushed in and asked, "'Is that for me?'" and Cockerill replied, "'No, sir, only for self-defense.'"

Slayback then pulled a self-cocking gun from his pocket and pointed it at Cockerill. But before he could squeeze the trigger, McGuffin jumped forward "and grabbed the pistol just as the hammer fell, catching the hammer between the thumb and forefinger preventing the pistol from going off. At the same time Cockerill [rose,] grabbed his [own] pistol and fired. The ball struck Slayback in the left breast, killing him almost instantly."

The gunshot brought startled reporters and several people from the street crowding into the room to see Cockerill wiping blood from his face, and Slayback sprawled on the floor, a bullet wound in his chest, blood gushing from his mouth.

Cockerill asked City Editor Henry Moore to send for a doctor, and one arrived in a few minutes. But Slayback was already dead. Spattered with blood, Cockerill made his way through the group without a word and took a carriage to the nearby Lindell Hotel to change his clothes.

Word of the killing quickly spread through the city, and a crowd gathered outside the newspaper building, threatening to torch it.

That evening Cockerill surrendered to the police at the Four Courts and was put in a cell. Several friends arrived to give him moral support.

A nationwide battle of words began between those who despised Pulitzer's newspaper, and its champions. A longtime rival, editor William Hyde of the *Missouri Republican,* called the tragedy the "fruits of aggressive and sensational journalism of the 'Post-Dispatch' school." Deliberately intending to fuel the fire, he charged that Slayback had been "singled out by the 'Post-Dispatch' as a victim of its venom," and when he went to the paper "to vindicate his manhood," he found "the editor with a revolver ready at hand."

Harper's Weekly agreed that Slayback's killing was "a direct result of personal journalism. There is a desire in men to hear ill of their neighbors, and it is this 'long-felt want' that personal journalism undertakes to supply. . . . A newspaper skillfully conducted for the purpose of skillfully goading private persons or public officers to fury will not lack an audience. . . . There is a risk that the worm may turn, that the bull may gore. . . . Slayback turned, and if he had shot Cockerill there would have been a poetic justice in the transaction."

A slap on the wrist and a hearty pat on the back came from the *St. Louis Criterion*: "We admire the progressive and fearless spirit of the Post-Dispatch [but] feel that it has been too aggressive and bitter in some respects, but that it has accomplished much for morality in this city is not to be denied and this is a virtue of sufficient magnitude to counterbalance many of its faults."

William Rockhill Nelson, founder and editor of the *Kansas City Star*, emphatically disputed denigrators of Pulitzer's work as "a frightening example of journalistic depravity." What they decry as "personal journalism," he wrote, "is the hope and protection of the country. Every bribe-taking official, every public plunderer, every greedy monopolist, every rascal in the land deprecates 'personal journalism.' The Post-Dispatch has antagonized all the evil elements in the city, and has not hesitated to attack wrong, however securely entrenched in power. There isn't a rogue in St. Louis who does not hate [the paper] and all the rascally elements would have been delighted to have seen its building razed to the ground and its editor lynched after the recent tragedy. But this was not to be. A powerful public journal cannot be wiped out in this manner by a howling mob, even when it is led by so-called 'prominent citizens.'"

That, however, didn't stop them from trying.

Pulitzer was in New York when the bomb dropped. A reporter found him in the Fifth Avenue Hotel, with several doctors who were treating three-year-old Ralph after a serious asthma attack. The news shocked and amazed Pulitzer. He was deeply sorry for Slayback and his family but was convinced that Cockerill had acted in self-defense. Pulitzer quickly returned to St. Louis. Always loyal to his staff, he visited Cockerill in jail and assured him of his complete support.

He took responsibility for all that had happened during his absence and added: "The charge of blackmail is the worst that can be proffered against any honest paper or editor. If Mr. Cockerill had remained silent under it, he would, by his silence have confessed its truth. [His response] under the circumstances was purely in self-defense, made inevitable by Col. Slayback's own provocation. If Mr. Cockerill had allowed the public stigma and brand of blackmailing to go unresented he would have been unfit for his position and would have ceased to be managing editor of the paper."

It was a tough time for Pulitzer. Slayback, a staunch Democrat, had been a friend of his, and was a popular man around town, a kindhearted, public-spirited, and talented attorney. Hundreds attended a benefit for his family.

At the inquest, which the *Post-Dispatch* reported in full without comment, McGuffin and Cole testified that Cockerill grabbed a gun from his desk and fired it in self-defense after Slayback had rushed into the office and aimed a gun at him. But William Clopton, who had accompanied Slayback to the office, swore that his friend was unarmed and removing his coat for a fistfight when Cockerill shot him.

Even the cautious *New York Times* called it "a sensation" when six weeks later pawnbroker Morris Michael testified before a grand jury that the gun McGuffin said he had taken from "Slayback in the *Post-Dispatch* office really belonged to Slayback." According to the *Times* report, Michael had sold it to Slayback and it retained Michael's private trademark. "This overthrows that part of Mr. Clopton's testimony which stated that Col. Slayback was not armed."

Although Cockerill was exonerated and freed, his enemies continued to hound him, claiming that someone from the *Post-Dispatch* must have planted the gun on Slayback. Important *Post-Dispatch* advertisers canceled, and within a few weeks circulation had fallen by thirteen hundred and continued falling. Clearly, Pulitzer's enemies were winning.

Broadhead was elected in November—a sure sign that the paper was losing prestige as well as supporters.

Hyde's hostile *Missouri Republican* kept after Cockerill with what to him seemed "almost inhuman malignancy." It denounced the inquest verdict, pressured the local bar association into condemning the *Post-Dispatch* for its "wanton employment of intemperate, licentious, and defamatory language," persuaded Slayback's widow to sue Cockerill in civil court, and organized public protest meetings throughout the city, which continued to fuel the fire.

To save the paper from extinction and restore staff morale, Pulitzer was forced to replace Cockerill. But time would show that Pulitzer had not deserted him when he eventually reemployed Cockerill. Fortunately, Pulitzer's previous partner, John Dillon, was willing to edit the paper in this emergency. As a St. Louis native and member of a leading family, with a lighter touch than Pulitzer's and Cockerill's, he was more acceptable to readers and advertisers—though he still carried on the fight against corruption.

Though by no means emasculated, after the Slayback killing *Post-Dispatch* editorials became less inflammatory, focusing on subjects that, surprisingly, are still hot topics today. Election finance reform was one: "We are far behind England in his matter and the popular indifference to the ordinary corruptions of election times does not speak highly of our political morality or our political sense. Nothing is publicly known, and apparently no information is desired about the amounts of money raised for campaign purposes, nor about the way in which the money is spent."

And on education: "A reporter for the New York Mail and Express has been going the rounds of the public schools of that city and publishing a variety of evidence and opinion about the discipline, sanitary conditions and general management of those institutions. One principal said: 'The course of study is almost useless. The boys are hurried on from grade to grade, so that when they reach the third grade they cannot read well or spell well, or write a good letter, or compute a sum in interest and all this botany and physiology and vocal music and mineralogy and French and German are a mere waste of time. The idea of having to teach the three R's to the highest grade boys of fourteen or eighteen years old who have presumably spent from eight to twelve years in the Public Schools!'"

Pulitzer's precarious health worsened after Slayback's tragic death and its aftermath. He and Kate no longer enjoyed living in a city where they had once been happy and were now socially ostracized. He considered making a fresh start elsewhere, maybe in New York City, where brother Albert—a fleshier, less fastidious version of himself—was flourishing. On November 16, 1882, Albert had launched his own daily newspaper, The *New York Journal*, on capital of twenty-five thousand dollars. Joseph had contributed a small amount.

Unlike Joseph, Albert had no desire to change the world. His purpose was to make money to satisfy his earthy appetites—and the paper reflected his interests. Known as "the chambermaids' delight," it provided a daily diet of gossip, spicy scandals, society romances—and was an immediate success, especially at one cent a copy. Joseph's *Post-Dispatch* cost five.

But Joseph was in no shape to attempt to emulate his younger brother with a new enterprise. It was all he could do to keep his own paper afloat. In fact, he had never considered starting a new newspaper in New York City, though he knew that the major Manhattan newspapers were overwhelmingly Republican and there was a need for an influential paper to support the Democratic presidential candidate in 1884. At least twice he had planned to buy one already in operation, but negotiations had fallen through.

Never robust, he now had a constant cough that prevented him from sleeping. He was losing weight and suffered from excruciatingly painful headaches. And he worried over the health of his asthmatic three-year-old son, Ralph. One way or another, it looked as if his enemies would soon be rid of both him and his paper.

CHAPTER 7

Pulitzer Takes Over
the *World*

1883

—

35 to 36 years old

T he enraged St. Louis community was still hellbent on destroying the paper
and Pulitzer. Kate was fearful of thugs waiting to beat him up or to kill
him. His doctor saw that he was heading for a breakdown and advised leaving
the city immediately for a long, restful vacation. Pulitzer was wounded but not
a man to retreat from a fight. He stayed, working behind the scenes, where he
kept pulling the strings until April 1883, when Dillon reported that the worst
was over—readers and advertisers were slowly returning to the paper. It would
survive. Only then did Pulitzer set off for a trip to the Mediterranean.

Soon after, Pulitzer arrived in Manhattan with his family and checked into
the plush Fifth Avenue Hotel. They meant to stay there for a few days of shopping and sight-seeing before sailing for Europe. Then he heard that a New York
newspaper, the *World*, was for sale—and could think of nothing else. Its owner,
the notorious "robber baron" Jay Gould, had acquired it as part of a stock deal
four years previously. But it was a losing proposition, robbing *him*, for a change,
of a steady forty thousand dollars a year. He was naturally anxious to unload it
and looking for a sucker to meet his inflated price.

Pulitzer's irresistible appetite to take over a New York newspaper—having
tried unsuccessfully several times before—made him a likely candidate. Yet he
was well aware of Gould's sordid reputation. It would be almost like bargaining
with the devil himself, a man who, according to one biographer, was "furtive as
a deadly spider, fed on the betrayal of friends, fattened on the ruin of stockholders, lied and bribed his way to a power that raised him above the law." The

New York Herald named him "the skunk of Wall Street," and a fellow trader called him "the worst man on earth since the beginning of the Christian era. He is treacherous, false, cowardly and a despicable worm incapable of a generous nature."

Gould's stranglehold on railroad companies had even reached St. Louis, and Pulitzer had once lambasted him in the *Post-Dispatch* as "one of the most sinister figures that ever flitted bat-like across the vision of American people."

Broadhead and until recently Slayback had represented Gould's legal interests in St. Louis. Pulitzer's mouthpiece Cockerill had called one a thief and killed the other. Surely Gould would refuse to do business with a man who appeared to be his implacable enemy? Dealing with Gould would, at the very least, be a tricky situation. Kate could see that just the thought of running a New York paper had worked wonders: suddenly her husband was much less a physical and nervous wreck than when they had arrived. Knowing how much it meant to him—almost his life's blood—she encouraged him to go ahead. They could take the Mediterranean cruise some other time. A new paper was all he needed. He took a carriage ride to Gould's Broadway office in lower Manhattan to meet the monster. Instead he found a frail, well-mannered, soft-spoken, almost effeminate man who went straight to the point. Gould asked for more than five hundred thousand dollars for the equipment, an Associated Press franchise, and the paper's good name. He meant to keep the three-story building for himself.

Pulitzer was surprised if not amused. Who was he kidding? Half a million bucks for a financial basket case! But he remained equally polite, said he'd think it over, and called on his brother Albert, now himself a newspaper tycoon, for advice. Albert almost had a fit. Was Joseph crazy? The city couldn't take two Pulitzers! The competition was already brutal. And his own paper, the *Morning Journal*, was barely one year old. They'd be fighting for the same readers and both go kaput. Forget it, he told his brother, the place was already swamped with newspapers. As for the *World* itself, everyone knew it was "the largest white elephant in captivity." Albert told Joseph that if he bought it, he would lose his shirt and what was left of his precarious health. St. Louis had almost killed him, and New York would finish him off. He was insane even to think of it.

Joseph argued that no New York paper represented the Democratic views of its working-class population and that Albert's paper had no political mission. Their papers would be radically different—reflecting their very different tastes and attitudes.

You're an idiot and you'll be sorry, Albert warned him.

Returning to his hotel, Joseph got cold feet. Maybe Albert was right. After what he'd endured in St. Louis, he didn't have it in him to revive the dying and discredited *World*, let alone deal with Gould. He tried to persuade a Chicago newspaper publisher, Melville Stone, to become his partner. Stone declined. He offered his old friend Henry Watterson the job of managing editor, and to write his own paycheck. Watterson said no: he was happy at the *Courier-Journal.*

Joseph feared he'd made a big mistake. It was foolhardy in his shaky state to consider taking on another paper. There was too much competition in Manhattan. Albert was right. Let's forget it, he told Kate, and take the next boat to Europe. But she tried to talk him out of his fears. She was sure he'd succeed. If that's what he really wanted, he should take a shot at it. After a sleepless night, he made his decision.

Buoyed by Kate's optimism and encouragement, he returned to Gould on May 10, 1883, and offered him $346,000, to be paid in installments. Gould accepted, but, about to sign the agreement, he suddenly remembered giving a small block of the newspaper stock to his son. He assumed Pulitzer wouldn't object to the boy "keeping this little holding."

Not, replied Pulitzer, if you don't "object to seeing it stated each morning that the Gould family has no control or influence in the property."

Gould didn't press the matter, and they shook hands on the deal.

The World was Pulitzer's—except for the bricks and mortar.

It was located at 32 Park Row in lower Manhattan, on the same street as formidable competitors: the *New York Tribune, Sun, Herald, Journal, Times, Star, Mail & Express, Daily News,* and *Commercial Advertiser,* several edited by men of national reputation, and all of the Republican persuasion.

The day he was to take charge of the paper, Pulitzer rose at dawn to work out the changes he planned. And when this almost elemental force, taking the stairs three at a time, burst into the second-floor newsroom, the somewhat staid and stuffy staff responded like deer caught in headlights.

"I hardly knew the place," one told a friend. "A cyclone had struck, men were hurrying around with excited faces. Messenger boys coming and going in droves. J. P. seemed to be everywhere, now arguing with a reporter, now dashing to the composing room, now suddenly descending on the market editor. He loves argument." An argument, he said, enabled him to judge a person's moral courage—without which no one worked for him for long.

He warned the staff: "You have all been living in the parlor and taking baths every day. Now you are all walking down the Bowery."

Taking this to mean a pay cut, several resigned on the spot. But he meant, as he wrote in the first issue, that the *World* would no longer cater to the interests of the affluent. It was "dedicated to the cause of the people rather than the purse of potentates [and] will expose all fraud and sham, fight all public evils and abuses [and] serve and battle for the people with earnest sincerity. Performance is better than promise. Exuberant assurances are cheap. I make none. I simply refer the public to the *World* itself. There is room in this great and growing city for a journal that is not only cheap but bright, not only bright but large, not only large but truly democratic—In that cause and for that end solely the new *World* is hereby enlisted and committed to the attention of the intelligent public. Joseph Pulitzer."

The first edition under Pulitzer's control hit the streets on May 11. It cost two cents, with eight pages of six columns each, and sold 22,761 copies. Under Gould it had sold at most 11,000 on weekdays and 15,000 on Sundays. It still looked as dull as any other paper on the market, with small headlines and masses of uninterrupted print. The difference between the old and the new *World* was its gee whiz! contents. Instead of a politically correct paper for "gentlemen," about as exciting, someone said with a sneer, as Thomas Gray's "Elegy Written in a Country Churchyard," Pulitzer provided murder, mayhem, and mystery.

To entice people to support his crusades, he first had to get them to read his paper. So the front page featured the following: two executions, one at Sing Sing, where the murderer refused to see a priest, shouting, "I'm not a Catholic! I'm a Democrat!" and the other at Pittsburgh, where the condemned man yelled at his executioners, "Good-bye, all ye murderers! Yer hangin' an innocent man!" An account of a thunderstorm's terrible toll in New Jersey was headed THE DEADLY LIGHTNING! and subheaded "Six Lives and One Million Dollars Lost." Catering to curiosity about the ups and downs of the high and mighty, Pulitzer reported the bankruptcy of a Californian millionaire, James Keene, who was unloading a painting of cattle for eight thousand dollars—and taking a four-thousand-dollar loss. The buyer, of all people, was Jay Gould! And finally the mystery: who started the recent bloody revolt in Haiti, and was dynamite used to massacre some four hundred victims? So page one had something for almost every taste.

Pulitzer sent a reporter to witness the execution of Angelo Cornetti at Sing Sing, an account of which was headlined:

SCREAMING FOR MERCY.
HOW THE CRAVEN CORNETTI
MOUNTED THE SCAFFOLD.
Gagged and pinioned by the Guards and
Dragged Resisting to a Prayer-
less Doom.

The failure to mention *why* Cornetti had been hanged was remedied in the next day's paper: he had slashed a fellow inmate's throat while in prison for beating his wife to death during a drunken brawl. Graphic descriptions of executions were not part of a crusade to end capital punishment. Pulitzer believed that murderers and rapists should be executed. The gory and gruesome details he published reflected the cruelty of the times: the Civil War had made people less sensitive to human suffering.

Pulitzer was off to a good start. His friendly rival in St. Louis, the *Globe-Democrat*, wished him well, and his biggest booster, William Nash of the *Kansas City Star*, suggested that "There is scarcely a man, west of the Allegheny mountains who does not wish Mr. Pulitzer success [and no one] doubts that he will carry the 'Western method' into the *World* office. His paper will no longer be the organ of dudes and dudines of Fifth and Madison avenues. It will cease to devote its space to the coaching trips of DeLancey Kane and the postings of the Oscar Wildes. It will devote itself to the news."

Archenemy Hyde of the *Missouri Republican* kept silent.

Pulitzer even persuaded publicity-shy Jay Gould to critique the paper's new look. "First-rate," Gould replied. "All that I'm afraid of is that it will be a little too bright and pitch into me. It is wonderfully improved, but its new editorial tone is not to my liking. I am afraid it might become dangerous."

He could be sure of that. Pulitzer essentially confirmed his fears that same day by bringing Cockerill from St. Louis to join him as managing editor and within a week printing the paper's support of a tax on all that Gould held dear: luxuries, inheritances, large incomes, monopolies, and privileged corporations.

Using the paper's Sunday editions as laboratories to discover which "human interest" features had the biggest appeal, Pulitzer found, like today's tabloid editors, that the wilder the better, so there were features on cannibalism at sea; the practice of human sacrifice in the United States by fanatical religious sects; and unusual murder weapons—including a nail, a coffin lid, a red-hot horseshoe, an umbrella, a matchbox, and a teakettle.

Later he even ran a report in the Sunday *World* headed, "French Scientist and Explorer Discovers a Race of Savages with Well-Developed Tails." An accompanying illustration showed a male of the species, called a "man-monkey," up a tree. In a reassuring touch, apart from his tail the artist made him look not unlike the man next door who'd forgotten to shave. Obviously Pulitzer failed to follow the reporting precept "When in doubt, leave it out."

How did he reconcile printing such tripe with his emphatic demand for accuracy? Perhaps the sources swore the stories were true, and there were no DNA tests, telephones, telephotos, tape recorders, or other witnesses to disprove them. Maybe, in striving for excitement, Pulitzer was susceptible to being duped. Even today, for various reasons, the most respected and sophisticated publications sometimes get caught and print phony news stories. Or, perhaps, rather than trying to verify iffy but enticing stories, Pulitzer's energy was engaged in attracting more readers from the hundreds of thousands of immigrants and working-class people in the city.

A false rumor that Jay Gould was secretly his partner threatened to undermine his proclaimed support of the underdog. Pulitzer quickly killed the rumor with editorials disparaging the selfish rich, and mocking their pretensions and conspicuous consumption. What also disgusted him was "the sordid aristocracy of the ambitious matchmakers, who are ready to sell their daughters for barren titles to worthless foreign paupers, and to sacrifice a young girl's self-respect and happiness to the gratification of owning a lordly son-in-law," dooming the young woman to "a cold, calculating life, full of frivolity and abuse. Such an aristocracy ought to have no place in the republic."

This editorial comment was sparked by the arrival of a delegation of aristocratic Koreans who had no handles "to their Korean names, such as Earl,

French Scientist and Explorer Discovers a Race of Savages with Well-Developed Tails.

NEW YORK, SUNDAY, DECEMBER 15, 1895.—COPYRIGHTED BY THE PRESS PUBLISHING CO., 1895.

The Missing Link.

THE HUMAN MAN-MONKEY WITH A TAIL, DISCOVERED BY A FRENCH EXPLORER.

The *World* went wild on Sundays.

Marquis, Viscount or even Sir. Fortunately," wrote Pulitzer, tongue-in-cheek, "this will check any matchmaking attempts by title-hunting mothers because they would be unable to boast of 'My daughter, the Countess of Ik,' or 'My darling child, the Viscountess of Sik.'" Pulitzer believed that the honest workingman who had earned his family's love was the true American aristocrat. "And it is to such men as Abraham Lincoln, and Jefferson and Jackson and Franklin, all most lowly born, that we owe most of our greatness as a nation. Out of poverty and ignorance [they] carved honor and renown. This is the proudest fact in our history. We make men, we do not inherit them." Yet women especially were agog for tidbits about the so-called aristocrats he despised. He satisfied that appetite, without betraying his principles, with illustrated features about their fabulous homes, fancies, foibles, and fortunes—glorifying none, and exposing some to ridicule or contempt. In this respect he led the way in stripping society butterflies and moneyed moguls of their glamour and mystery.

On such occasions he went on the attack in a fine frenzy. When dictating an editorial on "Collis Huntington's extremely ill-gotten wealth, Jay Gould's railroad-wrecking or Cyrus Field's income," cartoonist Walt McDougall recalled,

Pulitzer's "speech was so interlarded with sulphurous and searing phrases that the whole staff shuddered." When the customary curses didn't always fit his fury, he created his own. Pulitzer was the first man McDougall "ever heard who split a word to insert an oath. His favorite was 'indegoddampendent'!" Pulitzer doubtless responded with a similar oath to surprising news that his *World* was the talk of St. Louis and the comments "are complimentary to you—a great change in the last six months towards you. The misfortune of last fall [Slayback's death] is never mentioned and seems to be altogether forgotten." The latter is hard to believe. The only concern of the writer, his friend Charles Gibson, was that "with your tender feelings & well grounded affections your family may absorb much of the time & brain power, which your national position—for that is what it is—demands." This was the first acknowledgment that Pulitzer was a power to be reckoned with on the national scene. As for putting his family before his work, that was unlikely, except on isolated occasions. He was such a committed and driven workaholic that if the paper ever fell below his exacting standards, he returned home feeling physically ill.

Editorial writer William Merrill had reason to recall Pulitzer's dedicated modus operandi:

The scene: the *World* newsroom. Time: evening. Merrill is at his desk, writing about a bill U.S. senators will vote on that night. He glances at his watch, stands, and walks toward the door. Pulitzer emerges from his office and inquires where he's off to. Home to dinner, Merrill replies. "I'll come back to finish the report."

Pulitzer's raised eyebrows indicate astonishment. "Why go all the way uptown and back?" he asks, as if Merrill is off his rocker. "Why not stay here till the Senate acts and eat dinner later?"

"Because," says Merrill, "in twenty-five years I've never missed dinner at seven."

"My God!" Pulitzer is incredulous.

Merrill continues: "I rise at seven, breakfast at seven-thirty, read the papers until eight-thirty, ride my horse in Central Park until nine, and then take the El downtown. By ten, I am at my desk. I lunch at one; finish my work and go home for dinner. At ten-thirty I am in bed."

"What boredom!" Pulitzer says with a gasp. "I breakfast when I get up, lunch when I get the chance. If I never get it, I forget it. Sometimes I dine at seven, sometimes at midnight; sometimes not at all; and I never get to bed until four or five in the morning. Everything depends on the news; the hours make no difference to me."

"Perhaps not. But sooner or later this will break down your health," Merrill warns. "No constitution could stand it."

As Merrill leaves for dinner, Pulitzer, now bemused rather than belligerent, pats him on the back affectionately, saying, "my dear Old Man!"

Even if he did miss dinner, Pulitzer wouldn't miss supper. A street vendor invariably appeared at midnight with sandwiches, which Pulitzer and his staff chewed as they chatted or kept working, washed down by ice water or a slug of whiskey. Kate adapted to his uncertain hours and led an active social life, pleased when she could persuade him to join her. He had found a permanent place for them to live nearer his office at 17 Gramercy Park, a fashionable spot on the Lower East Side, with room for his coachman and several other servants. The ailing Samuel Tilden, failed presidential candidate, lived next door, and Pulitzer paid at least one visit, when he admired Tilden's superb wine cellar.

At about that time, a mixed message came from Pulitzer's rival Charles A. Dana, the *Sun*'s editor. He was surprised "that journals of this city have not paid much attention to Mr. Joseph Pulitzer. There is a natural disposition against gratuitous advertising, but this need not prevent our welcoming a clever man, especially when he was once a correspondent for the *Sun*, which shines for all. Mr. Pulitzer possesses a quick and fluent mind with a good share of originality and brightness; but he has always seemed to us rather deficient in judgment and in staying power. Anyway, we tender him all sorts of friendly wishes."

Pulitzer replied: "We are delighted to receive a cordial welcome from the successful and shining *Sun*. Our delight is somewhat dulled by the melancholy statement that the editor of the *World* is deficient in judgment and staying power. He has always stayed where he pleased to plant himself until ready to move, and he has never made any moves which were not clearly for the better. We can say the same thing for the gifted editor of the *Sun*, who was long ago accepted as our model, guide and preceptor in journalism. It may have been bad judgment on the part of Mr. Dana to employ the present editor of the *World* as a correspondent for his paper; but if the editor of the *World* has shown deficiency of judgment in journalism heretofore, it has been because he tried not only to imitate but even to excel the *Sun* in its truthfulness, fearlessness, independence and vigor."

In May, Pulitzer seized the chance to excel in covering the opening of the Brooklyn Bridge. Its construction had been a great human drama of triumph and tragedy. His reporters had been compiling a dramatic history of the sixteen-year effort to create this engineering marvel, the first bridge to wed Manhattan to Brooklyn across the East River, and he had prepared his own innovation to match the occasion—an engraving of the bridge to splash across four columns of page one—the first time the *World* had illustrated a news story.

And what a tale there was to tell. The brilliant designer of the bridge, John Augustus Roebling, had died in an accident in the first year of its construction. His son, Colonel Washington Roebling, then took over as chief engineer. But in 1872, surfacing from a dive in the murky water, he suffered an attack of the bends that left him permanently crippled and confined him to a wheelchair. It didn't deter him, however. He had already shown ingenuity in overcoming an explosion, a fire that lasted for weeks, a vital cable snapping, and fraud by a steel-wire contractor that forced Roebling to replace tons of cable. For the next eleven years, sitting in his Columbia Heights, Brooklyn, apartment, he had looked through field glasses to supervise the project from afar. And his wife, Emily, relayed his instructions to the men at the site.

Pulitzer and Cockerill returned from the bridge-opening ceremony eager to put out a special edition about it to hit the street the next morning. But they discovered that the printers had gone on strike to protest business manager McGuffin's economy drive, which deprived them of customary free soap, and of ice for their drinking water. Pulitzer and Cockerill quickly huddled with the union representative in Keenan's Café next door and agreed to restore the soap and the ice. The strike was over.

McGuffin normally ordered fresh ice every day. Now he refused to concede complete defeat by not ordering ice the following Sunday, hoping there'd be enough left over from Saturday's quota. He was out of luck. It was a very hot day. And Pulitzer's lively word-splitting lingua franca made it clear that he did not enjoy drinking warm water. After that they never lacked ice.

On Memorial Day the Brooklyn Bridge was again front-page news. As holidaymakers were crossing the East River on the bridge's pedestrian walkway, someone started a rumor that the structure was collapsing. In a wild stampede to get off, twelve were crushed to death, and others were badly injured. Pulitzer and Cockerill dropped everything to lead a team of reporters to the site a stone's throw from their office, to interview witnesses. Circulation soared for the next day's paper, with its front page devoted to dramatic firsthand accounts of the tragedy headlined BAPTISED IN BLOOD.

A poignant story made page one for May 28. A young woman, abandoned by her husband and denied charity assistance, had tried to drown herself and her children in the East River. Headlining her pathetic words "LET ME DIE! LET ME DIE!" as she was dragged from the river, Pulitzer went to town in an editorial, comparing her plight with the good life of Fifth Avenue's perfumed pets. A few days later he discovered the woman was an alcoholic, desperate—not to get food for her kids, but booze for herself. He made a front-page apology to readers for misleading them.

Pulitzer found time to make a lightning one-day visit to the *Post-Dispatch*, and after assuring himself that all was well, instructed department heads to send him weekly reports.

Each morning in his *World* office he chaired an 11:00 A.M. editorial meeting with Cockerill, city editor Dave Sutton, and editorial writers William Merrill and Douglas Levine, to discuss the contents and treatment of the upcoming issue. All men with the courage of their convictions, they often vigorously defended their views—overheard free entertainment for the rest of the news staff because Pulitzer's office was separated from them by only a thin partition.

"As the voices of JP and his advisers rose higher and louder," wrote Pulitzer biographer William Barrett, "Duneka and Shipman at the city desk furnished the gestures, combining the thunder of Demosthenes with the acrobatics of Billy Sunday." (Sunday, an evangelist and former professional baseball player, accompanied his sermons with exaggerated baseball-playing gestures.)

Despite what had happened in St. Louis, Pulitzer took no action to protect himself or his staff from irate or crazy visitors—though he probably still carried a gun. There was no bodyguard, doorman, or reception room. Anyone could come off the street, climb the narrow stairs to the second floor, and walk into the newsroom.

One day, a Tammany Hall politician burst in, and pounding on city editor David Sutton's desk, yelled at him, "What the hell do you mean by printing all this stuff about me? By God, I'll have the law on you! What's more, for two cents I'd —"

Roused by the noise, Douglas Levine, a tubby, white-haired little seventy-year-old, emerged from Pulitzer's office where he had been working, grabbed the politician by the neck and pants, rushed him across the room and booted him down the stairs. "Damn fool was making so much noise I couldn't write my editorial," Levine explained. As a youngster he had been a wrestler and circus strongman known as "Little Hercules." He was a good man to have on your side. Perhaps Pulitzer had a bodyguard after all.

By August his circulation had risen from 22,761 to 39,000 and climbing. He celebrated by joining Kate at the opera and one day managed to tear himself away from work to lunch aboard Jay Gould's 250-foot yacht *Atalanta*, its floors covered with Oriental rugs, the crew dressed in Gould's colors, white and blue. Dana of the *Sun* was also a guest. Not immune to the lure of luxury, Pulitzer began to fancy a yacht for himself.

Prompted by this visit, he confided to his readers that it was understandable why rich newspaper owners such as Bennett and Dana had capitalistic prejudices: they were protecting their luxurious lives. "They cannot help it. It is only human nature. Man is greatly controlled by his environment. A newspaper conductor with an income of a quarter or half a million a year or more, with yachts, town houses and country houses to keep up, with an intimate circle of millionaire friends to entertain and be entertained by—above all, with a surplus income which must be invested and which naturally goes into bonds and stocks and other securities of corporations and monopolies—which side would he be apt to drift into? Is he likely to be eager and zealous and earnest in resisting the encroachments of monopoly and the money power, in defending the rights of the common people? [But] there is one newspaper not controlled nor in any way swayed or influenced by this side of capital. That is the *World*."

It was no empty boast. He remained true to his principles. His support of the poor against the rich—although, of course, he was now one of them—eventually lost him wealthy friends, which he sometimes bitterly regretted.

His championing of the poor—deploring "the un-republican spectacle of excessive riches and excessive poverty, of enormous fortunes gathered in the hands of the few, of abject poverty the lot of only too many"—brought more and more readers who sympathized with his message.

Pulitzer became the first publisher of a New York daily to create a separate sports department, with H. G. Crickmore, a horse racing expert, in charge, which explains why St. Blaise winning the English Derby in 1883 made page one of August 20. But boxing and baseball were the sports that transformed casual readers into fervent fans.

Irish American John L. Sullivan, the world's heavyweight boxing champion, attracted fiercely loyal supporters, especially among New York's large Irish American population. He was frequently featured in the paper, often as an example of how the manly art had been reduced to a demonstration of brute strength, patronized by thugs and thieves. It enraged some readers by reporting that Sullivan had turned up for one fight drunk. Obviously not a fan, Pulitzer called boxing barbaric, and remarked that "every blow is given with the object of disabling and with a good prospect of killing the person at whom it is aimed. It is a matter of wonder that these fights have not before now resulted in manslaughter." While Pulitzer deplored the sport in his page four editorials, his boxing expert wrote enthusiastic page one accounts, with positive headlines such as VAST ASSEMBLAGE ALMOST FRENZIED WITH EXCITEMENT and, when American Jack Dempsey beat Englishman Tom Henry, DEMPSEY WORSTS HENRY . . . AFTER SIX TERRIFIC ROUNDS.

At times, despite his reservations, Pulitzer conceded that such occasions were great spectacles. Writing about the fight in which John L. Sullivan knocked out Herbert Slade in the third round, Pulitzer admitted, "it was a great exhibition and it showed the natural brutality of human nature. A fierce joy thrilled in every breast and burned in every eye as the magnificent ruffian Sullivan delivered his powerful blows and knocked his helpless antagonist about the ring at his pleasure. It looked as if a yell of delight would have burst forth if he had given the poor wretch a death blow. When the unequal battle was over shouts went up as for a great victory and the vanquished dragged himself away unnoticed and left a bloody track as he went. After all, the world is not very different now from what it was when gladiators fought to the death in the presence of 'gallant knights and ladyes faire.'"

An "expert's" prediction that "slugger" Sullivan had neither the intelligence nor the endurance to lick an English boxer, Charles Mitchell, brought an avalanche of Irish rebuttals. Typical was "Shorty" McCaull's: "I will bet $100 to a cent that your expert is an Englishman." Another correspondent, who signed himself D.H.D., blamed the police for breaking up Sullivan's bare-fist fights before he could obliterate his opponents. D.H.D's hero was "as brave a man as ever split a cheek or stove a jaw. I have known John L. Sullivan for ten years and a braver man doesn't live. But he never has a show. Just as he gets warmed up the police or somebody else stops him. What's the use of having bravery if a man can't be left to show it? Is this fair? Is this just? Is this treating a brave man right? But that's the way it is with an Irishman."

Although baseball was called the national sport, its wide acceptance was still a year away. Football, too, was a minority interest. Even when Yale beat Harvard for the national championship before a wildly excited crowd of eight thousand, it rated only a small spot on page five of November 30.

While sports fans were exercised over the cops tying Sullivan's hands, Pulitzer was on another social crusade—turning the spotlight on developers who produced jerry-built houses that were slums even before the foundations had settled.

More and more readers were informed of such scams: by the fall his sales had soared to more than fifty thousand copies a day, five times what the old *World* had sold less than a year before.

That fall Pulitzer catered to readers who fancied themselves amateur detectives by inaugurating a new way to cover murder cases: he provided detailed accounts of the killings and keyed sketches of the crime scenes. For example, on the September 19 front page, the *World* reported how a New York clergyman named Kemlo had slashed his wife to death, then cut his own throat and jumped from a fourth-floor window. With the story Pulitzer printed a bird's-eye-view sketch of the apartment where the tragedy occurred, with the following keys:

A—Door stained with blood, B—Window stained with blood from which Kemlo leaped, C—Bed covered with blood, D—Table set and covered with blood, E—Chair in which Mrs. Kemlo sat, F—Sink in which knife was found, G—Pool of blood. He used the same X-marks-the-spot treatment for a Long Island double murder, and a New Jersey rape-murder. The idea caught on. Soon other papers copied him.

In November Pulitzer started an advice and gossip column mainly targeting women, but from the flood of incoming letters, obviously many men were also interested. The advice columnist floated the daring idea that instead of being stuck with the same dancing partner all night, a gentleman might escort her back to her seat—and then presumably play the field. And it was deemed highly improper for a gentleman when writing to a lady to enclose a stamped and self-addressed envelope. If she "cares enough about a gentleman to answer his notes she will be only too happy to provide her own postage stamps." The female who asked if it was acceptable to flirt with a male acquaintance was given the go-ahead, the columnist calling the idea that one should only flirt with strangers "preposterous." Readers who wanted to lose weight were advised to eat less.

Pulitzer took women's issues seriously, and although a man of his time, believing a woman's place was in the home and voting and jury duty should be left to men, he also thought that a woman doing the same job as a man should get the same pay.

He thought Oscar Wilde's place was in the home, too, or back in his home country, judging by his response to a complaint by the playwright's mother that the American press had maligned him during his lecture tour in the States: "Inasmuch as the divine sunflower apostle took several thousand dollars out of this country and left nothing but the memory of a very ugly young man with a profusion of hair, a wealth of cheek and an insane pair of legs, it would seem that he ought to feel like congratulating himself and that his ma ought to be happy."

Had Pulitzer known Wilde was not English but an Irishman, he might have gone easier on him.

Pulitzer's contempt for those who enriched themselves by exploiting the weak, or who squandered or hoarded inherited wealth, was unrelenting. With rare exceptions, he never met a millionaire he liked. Even when John D. Rockefeller gave forty thousand dollars to the Chicago Baptist Theological Seminary, Pulitzer scoffed: "It was about time for Rockefeller to do something religious."

The catalyst for a year-long attack on William Henry Vanderbilt had been the snarling response by the railroad tycoon's son William Kissam Vanderbilt to a question about the public's comfort: "The public be damned!!"

Pulitzer then lit into the father with "What respect is due to a man who counts his wealth by the hundred millions and spends it wholly for the gratification of his own whims and pleasures? Who in the coarse and vulgar language of a horse jockey* extols his son, not for his culture, not for his patriotism or public spirit, but for his sharpness in Wall Street gambling and because 'he never squeals.'"

By "squeal" he was referring to a painful and pathetic practice of stableboys. To test the quality of a hunting dog, a boy would grab its ear or tail between his teeth, then lift the dog off the ground. Dogs who squealed were considered mongrels, nonsquealers—thoroughbreds. No doubt Pulitzer would have liked to grip both Vanderbilts between his teeth until they squealed. Publicly, through his paper, in June alone, he called Vanderbilt a fraud, plunderer, and blackmailer, and referred to his railroad as malignant, a cancer, and monumentally mismanaged.

Toward the end of the year, perhaps out of angry epithets, Pulitzer took a different tack: he calculated that Vanderbilt's $200 million fortune represented 350 tons of gold, which would need 7,000 strong men to lift, 25 freight cars to haul, 1,400 horses to pull, and 70 elephants to carry. He left it for the public to decide if it was fair for one man to possess so much loot while a few hundred feet from his mansion, children were starving.

A couple of weeks later Pulitzer pounced on snobbish socialites who regarded the visit of Britain's prince of Wales as the most exciting event in the city's social life, rivaled only by the American Jennie Jerome's marriage to Lord Randolph Churchill (eventually Winston Churchill's parents). These "rabid victims of the Anglomania disease," as he called them, had the gall to sing "God Save the Queen" at a dinner at Delmonico's to celebrate the centenary of

---

*Pulitzer was on shaky ground here. A master of creative cursing, he himself swore like a trooper with a temper tantrum and then some.

the British withdrawal from New York City. He reminded readers that "New York under Cornwallis, Tryon and Clinton [British generals during the Revolutionary War] was not half as mad about the British as it is under the Union Club, the Murray Hill regime and the worship of British lords and the Prince of Wales. [Then] the natives did not drop their h's and the American ladies did not try to ride to hounds or marry English titles. English ways were unpopular, English poodles [sic] were not the fashion, and English actors scarce."

Strangely, Pulitzer himself seemed to have contracted Anglomania. Only a few weeks before, he had supported Queen Victoria's son Prince Edward when he was snubbed by an American actress. The actress, Mary Anderson, a favorite of theatergoers for her portrayals of "pure" women, aware of Edward's well-earned reputation as a philanderer, had declined an invitation to meet him. Pulitzer's first response was to suggest that the international incident was a publicity stunt by the actress's press agent, who sent her photo to the prince to spark his interest. Pulitzer suggested that Americans might admire her spirit yet reprove her for being unnecessarily rude to the future monarch. Addressing his "sensitive" women readers, he asked, "Why should virtue have anything to fear from the courtesies due to men in exalted positions; or why should an actress imagine that an introduction to a Prince could sully her reputation independent of her own conduct? Do not some of the best and purest women in England [meet] His Royal Highness occasionally without fear or moral ruin?" On page one a month later Pulitzer updated the story, headed MARY ANDERSON'S TRIUMPH, in which he noted how, despite the actresses's snubbing of the prince, his wife, the princess of Wales, had attended one of her performances. As a result, "society circles profess themselves to be profoundly astonished at the lack of spirit shown by the Princess of Wales in honoring Miss Anderson with her presence."

Pulitzer sympathized with the prince, who, because of his "exalted" position, should have expected deference, criticized the princess for disloyalty to her husband, and both praised the actress for her spirit and scolded her for her bad manners. One would have expected him to insist that an American woman had every right to refuse to meet anyone in the world, however exalted his position. But, he was sometimes inconsistent. One glaring example was his attitude toward William Kissam Vanderbilt, whom he ridiculed for trying to buy his way into high society by building a three-million-dollar gray limestone château on the corner of Fifth Avenue and Fifty-second Street and filling it with expensive antiques, tapestries, and suits of armor. Amazingly, in December, despite his pulverizing by Pulitzer, Vanderbilt invited the *World* to cover a grand ball there. And Pulitzer accepted.

Equally unexpected was his treatment of the affair. Instead of heading it VULGARIANS VULGAR DISPLAY or GLITTERING GATHERING OF GLUTTONS, he chose MAGNIFICENCE UNSURPASSED and SCENES OF DAZZLING SPLENDOR AT THE GREAT MANSION. He even rated it "the most brilliant private ball which has ever been given in this city, and probably in the United States."

Only a few months before, he had tried to explain his apparent ambivalence: "We have been accused of being bitterly opposed to the wealthy. That is generally untrue. We respect wealth when it is made the instrument of good. We despise wealth when it accumulates in the hands of money lords who seek to establish an aristocracy of dollars [or] when it is prostituted to shoddy display and to the gratification of coarse and vulgar tastes." Presumably he thought Vanderbilt's ball was in a good cause or in good taste, or good copy for the Christmas season.

As George Juergens suggests in his superb record and critique of Pulitzer's early years at the *World*, "[His] criticism of the wealthy families in New York City, finding fault with how they made their money and what they did with it, stemmed from [his] liberal political bias. Reform meant changing the conditions of life and labor which men like Vanderbilt [and] Gould had created, and which they did most to perpetuate. For Pulitzer and his staff, criticizing their values was but another way of attacking them as political foes. [Pulitzer] hoped, by showing that the emperor wore no clothes, to dissuade tens of thousands of New Yorkers from slavishly conceding the superiority of one class over another. [He] hoped to prevent the rise in the New World of a peasant mentality inherited from the Old . . . hoped to forestall, if not class consciousness, at least class war. They were important aims at a time when unchecked immigration and wracking poverty made one-half of the city strangers to the other."

He also knew that women especially enhanced their drab lives through vicariously "sharing" those of their "betters," eager to know the smallest detail about them. He catered to this curiosity with accounts of their liaisons, descriptions and illustrations of their lavish homes, and by naming the estimated four hundred millionaires living in New York City and the widows in the city who had inherited millions.

Juergens explains this journalistic schizophrenia: "The World attacked the titans of Wall Street as buccaneers, and their style of living as unsocial and vulgar [yet] glorified them as living symbols of the American dream of success. If the paper contradicted itself with almost every issue it delivered to the newsstand, the contradiction was part of its appeal. It did no more than reflect the idealism and crassness of the community that produced it, which is another way of saying that it was a paper of and for the people." This also explains why Pulitzer persisted in reporting events some high-minded individuals considered too shocking to print. Despite the criticism he endured for going to town on such sensational stories, Pulitzer was proud of his work. He showed this when he asked a staff reporter how he had developed his muscular arms. "By exercising to keep fit, which is vital in this business," replied the young man. "In your profession," Pulitzer corrected him. "Don't think I'm criticizing you, my dear boy, but journalism is a profession—*the* profession."

According to Pulitzer's credo, "A newspaper should be scrupulously accurate, avoid everything salacious or suggestive that could offend the good taste or lower the moral tone of its readers; but within these limits it is the duty of a newspaper to print the news. I do not mean the good taste which is offended by every reference to the unpleasant things of life or the kind of morality which refuses to recognize the existence of immorality. I mean the kind of good taste which demands that frankness should be linked with decency, the kind of moral tone which is braced and not relaxed when it is brought face to face with vice."

What wouldn't Pulitzer print? For one, the account of two young boys sexually molesting a six-year-old girl, which Horace Greeley's successor, Whitelaw Reid, put on the front page of the antisensationalist *New York Tribune*. Pulitzer pitched the same story into a wastebasket, as he reported in an editorial—and so gave publicity to a story he thought shouldn't have it!

CHAPTER 8

Puts a Democrat in the White House

1884
—
36 to 37 years old

From the start and for years to come, Pulitzer beat the competition by transforming the news they missed, or muffed, into provocative human-interest stories, such as his exclusive account, published in late January, of a recently married couple in Virginia's Shenandoah Valley. For thirty-eight years one of them, described as a "man-woman," had "masqueraded" as a female, until a real woman persuaded him to have "a simple and painless operation," change his name from Elizabeth to John, and marry her. The *World* interviewed a clergyman who had anticipated a visit from Elizabeth—unaware of her sex and name change—but being short of guest rooms had invited "her" to share his wife's bed. The offer had been accepted. Now, learning that he had invited a man to sleep with his wife, the preacher was mad as hell until, apparently, the reporter persuaded him to turn the other cheek. Such reports spurred some readers to damn Pulitzer for lowering the tone of the press to sell newspapers; one even asked him to omit all sensational news, especially about crimes, murders, and executions. He replied, "The attempt of a few narrow purists to charge upon the daily press some share of the responsibility for this lamentable condition of things is a futile one. The daily press publishes vice, no doubt, but it does not idealize or palliate it. It publishes also the inevitable consequences of vice."

A month later, he elaborated: "The complaint of the 'low moral tone of the press' is common but very unjust. A newspaper relates the events of the day. It does not manufacture its record of corruptions and crimes, but tells of them as they occur. If it failed to do so it would be an unfaithful chronicler. The daily journal is like the mirror—it reflects that which is before it. Let those who are startled by it blame the people who are before the mirror, and not the mirror, which only reflects their features and actions."

A Presbyterian minister preaching against the evil of Sunday newspapers provoked Pulitzer into claiming to be the more effective moralist of the two: "Sinners do not shrink from vice, but they are awfully afraid of exposure in the newspapers. No pulpit orator can reach the evil-doer like a Sunday newspaper with a quarter of a million readers."

No question, Pulitzer believed "that a sensational newspaper could serve high social goals."

He wasn't alone in this. People expected newspapers to expose a system that let killers get away with murder. And they went berserk when that happened in Cincinnati, Ohio, in March. Alerted by their local paper that murderer William Berner had been given a reduced sentence, an enraged mob of ten thousand attacked the prison, to lynch him. But he had been removed for his safety to another prison. The frustrated rioters dynamited and set fire to the courthouse and terrorized the city for three days and nights, before the police and members of the Ohio National Guard took control. But it came at a terrible cost: 39 killed and 122 injured.

Pulitzer covered his front page with the story for four days, suggesting that "the destruction of property, the sacrifice of innocent life could not be charged only to the escape of one boy who deserved hanging. Robespierre, Marat and Danton were not accidents. They were the natural product of long-continued abuses and outrages. Does Fifth Avenue forget that it is flanked by the tenements of Eleventh Avenue and Avenue B, and outnumbered 1,000 to 1 in point of mere numbers? Our bankers and brokers cannot too speedily recognize the peril of teaching the people to despise all law." Hinting at the danger of another American revolution not unlike the French Revolution, he warned: "We cannot ride roughshod over the liberties of the people by purchasing elections with money of favored corporations and monopolies. The terrible reaction is sure to come, no matter how patient the people are. And the reaction is apt to be more terrible than the evil itself."

In the following weeks, Pulitzer was preoccupied with his two sick children: his infant daughter stricken with pneumonia, his son suffering from recurring asthma attacks. With them on his mind, he was naturally sensitive to the evidence that dealers adulterated milk to enhance profits, rationalizing the practice by saying it satisfied the demand for cheap milk. It hit the poor hardest, by depriving their children of vitamins, and many became sick or died from vitamin deficiencies. Although the law forbade adding water or other foreign substances to milk, a doctor said he had a collection of toads and small snakes that New York inspectors had found in milk, proving the dealers had stopped at roadside pools or streams to top up their cans. The most alarming report, by the State Charities Aid Association, estimated that "the deaths of 45% of children under five and 35% under one, could largely be attributed to impure milk."

True to his watchwords "Never drop a thing until you have gone to the bottom of it" and sensing that someone at the top was also skimming profits, Pulitzer told his reporters to find and name the culprits. They fingered the railroad companies. By charging sixteen times more for transporting milk than for other products, they all but forced dealers to dilute it to keep the cost down. Pulitzer concluded that "but for the greed of the railroad corporations," New York dealers could sell milk at about half its present price and still make a fair profit. "[Now] a good portion of the sum is unjustly extorted by the railroad companies."

As for the adulteration, he revealed in a story headed MAGGOTY MILK SUPPLY that "milk from along the Harlem line road is, with few exceptions, so much rank poison for babes and little children to drink. [It] passes the lacometer test and therefore sells freely in New York. Its richness, however, is due to the presence of diseased particles which, imbibed by the child, produce cholera, diarrhoeal complaints and oft-times death."

Pulitzer continued to agitate for tighter regulations to ensure the purity of milk—twenty years before the birth of the Food and Drug Administration—at a price the poor could afford.

Another big problem was police reluctance to enforce laws already on the books. As in St. Louis, many of the New York police were hard to distinguish from the crooks. Pulitzer frequently exposed police as corrupt, brutal, and inefficient: he told of detectives who earned about the same wage as poorly paid reporters, but made fortunes through blackmail and extortion; of police on the beat who smashed the skulls of the guilty and innocent alike; and he ridiculed the police department for letting the nation's most notorious fence, Fredericka "Marm" Mandelbaum, escape to Canada while out on bail.

At 5 feet, 1 inch and 250 pounds, this mother of three presumably couldn't outrun the police, but she could certainly pay them off from her twelve-million-dollar haul. She threw fabulous balls for her crooked suppliers and buyers, taught a class for female pickpockets on the third floor of her brownstone home on Clinton Street, and during her twenty-two-year career outwitted and outfitted the police. She reached Canada with an estimated ten million dollars of her ill-gotten gains—diamonds, pearls, rubies, lockets, pins, and brooches. The *World* printed an artist's sketch of Mandelbaum with which the Canadian police identified her. She was curious to know who had tipped off the police.

Pulitzer claimed the credit with a succinct front-page headline:

MARM MANDELBAUM ARRESTED.

Taken in Canada Through "The World's" Portrait of Her. With Ten Pounds of Jewels.

"When THE WORLD published portraits of the 'Missing Mother of Thieves' and her 'Darling Boy' the first link was forged in the chain of their capture. The pictures were cut out by a reporter for the *Evening Times* here and shown to the Chief of [Hamilton, Ontario] Police. The Chief asked for another inspection and they were given to him. Mrs. Mandelbaum's picture was shown to the keeper of a cheap hotel near one of the railway stations and he said: 'Why that woman's upstairs!' The Chief and Detective Castell found mother and son and took them in charge. She and Julius [her son] asked the Chief to see them alone in the room, as they wanted to speak to him. Speaking to him meant bribing him to release them. They had 'spoken' to many New York officers, they said, and were astonished to find that this easy way of escaping the law did not prevail here."

Two days later Pulitzer answered his critics: "While some of our esteemed, aesthetic contemporaries assume to censure the frequent illustrations in the *World* as sensational, we have the satisfaction of knowing that our perfect portrait of Eno [Manhattan stockbroker John Eno, wanted for fraud] led to his recognition and arrest in Montreal. *The World's* beautiful picture of 'Marm' Mandelbaum brought about her arrest in Hamilton, Ontario. Thus, while we are contributing our share toward the advancement of American art and are educating as well as amusing our numerous readers we are subserving the cause of public justice."

That wasn't the case with "Marm" Mandelbaum. It only led to a temporary inconvenience. At her December 12 trial in Hamilton, for bringing stolen jewelry into the country, the police chief said he had no instructions from the New York authorities, and no evidence to offer. As there were no witnesses against her from the United States, she was acquitted. Laughing all the way to her hoard, there being no extradition treaty for receiving stolen goods, she lived out the rest of her life north of the border, in luxury, dying five years later, in 1889, at age seventy-one.

Pulitzer's *bête noire* Leander Richardson, editor of the *Journalist*, a trade journal, mocked the publisher for his "champion nerve" and "exhibition of childish vanity" in boasting "that the arrest of John C. Eno, Julius, and Mother Mandelbaum were effected through the likenesses of these distinguished personages which had appeared in the *World*. Mandelbaum has been known by sight to every well-ordered detective in America for twenty years. As for Eno, he was arrested through the descriptions furnished for the Canadian police."

He was wrong. A Detective Farey of Montreal acknowledged that he had taken Eno into custody when he recognized him from his picture in the *World*. Richardson was a prejudiced commentator who previously had been hired and fired by Pulitzer.

Murder, milk, and Mandelbaum were not Pulitzer's sole preoccupations. In a prudish age when people put skirts on table legs and separated male and female authors on their bookshelves, Pulitzer followed the fashion, objecting, for example, to the plunging necklines of female operagoers. He also complimented himself and other papers for refusing to spell out the "odious remark" a man had made about a woman, which had him expelled from a private club, though Pulitzer claimed to have the juicy details and name of the woman, which the public was panting to know.

But restraint was hardly the watchword of Pulitzer's reporters. If Horace Greeley started the modern style of question-and-answer interviewing by giving Brigham Young the third degree in 1859, Pulitzer increased the pressure, urging his reporters to use a no-one-is-sacrosanct and no-question-is-out-of-bounds approach.

When a competing editor took exception to an in-your-face *World* interview with plutocrat Jay Gould, Pulitzer pretended he couldn't control his gung-ho reporters: "The insolence and impertinence of the reporters for the World, when approaching such men as Jay Gould, fill the refined and esteemed heart of the delicate editor of the Commercial Advertiser with a sorrow that is almost as mellow as a paw-paw poultice. We have observed at times a disposition on the part of our reporters to be obtrusive and unrelenting in their efforts to acquire information, but the majority of them are young and inexperienced, and we cannot muster the nerve to reprove them. Besides, this is a rushing, busy world, and we do not always have the time to look after the deportment of our reporters. We are thinking seriously, however, of having dress suits made for all of them." Two months later, Pulitzer's man in Washington, Theron Crawford, got an exclusive interview with General Grant, putting "The World ahead of the pack on a major news story." As Pulitzer noted, Grant, though usually reluctant to talk to the press, chose the *World* in which to endorse John Logan for the Republican presidential nomination.

The biggest foreign news came from Pulitzer's man in England, who had interviewed Sir Henry Gordon. He was sure that his brother, General Gordon, was alive and well. The British general was then in Khartoum to evacuate forces threatened by Sudanese rebels. Alive at the time of the interview, Gordon was stabbed to death by rebels on January 27, 1885. The *World* got the news late but made the most of it on February 6 (beating the *Times* by five days) and eulogizing Gordon as a hero.

Despite his chronic Anglophobia, Pulitzer was delighted and said so when he read a report that during a U.S. lecture by English poet and intellectual Matthew Arnold, he was shown a copy of the *World*, which he thought hilarious. Arnold passed muster because he liked the racy and sensational *World*, but few other foreigners—except for the Irish, Germans, and Hungarians—escaped Pulitzer's xenophobic contempt.

Hearing of a fatal duel in Mexico, he resorted to black humor: "Duelling is looking up. Two Mexicans have actually succeeded in mutually slaughtering each other on the field of honor. This sort of thing should be encouraged—in Mexico." Learning that Mexican officials in Tampico had boarded an American ship and lowered its flag for alleged port violations, he urged: "If any Mexican greaser pulls down the American flag, beat him over the head with the flag-staff!"

An equal-opportunity bigot, Pulitzer believed that "the modern Greek is a treacherous, drunken creature. To call a man a 'Greek' is equivalent to branding him a liar and a cheater. For 400 years Greece was under the heel of the cruel Moslem. Some of the worst national traits may be the result of the long years of oppression and degradation to which they were subjected by their haughty conquerors."

He was anxious to distinguish immigrants working as scabs in Pennsylvania coal mines from his own distinguished background: "These foreigners, who, it is said, 'work for fifty cents a day and live like hogs,' are not Hungarians. They are Sclavs [sic]. They simply come from Hungary, but they are hated as intensely by the true Magyars as they are by the Pennsylvania miners. [Pulitzer's father was of Magyar-Jewish descent.] They are Asiatic invaders." He dismissed the Chinese as "barbarians" and the Italians as living happily "and contentedly in the midst of filth and foul odors."

As for the French, they were incorrigible idiots to admire Voltaire, Rousseau, and Hugo. And he never expected them to see the light, because you can "expect to extract sunshine from a cucumber before you hope to dislodge this gross ignorance from the French cranium." Such blatant bigotry seems surprising in a man of Pulitzer's intelligence, experience, and general outlook. He was, however, a man of his time, when the Irish looked down on the Germans; the Germans looked down on the Italians; the Italians looked down on the Jews; and presumably the Jews looked down on all of them. The *World* even looked down on members of the House of Lords, "the rulers of Great Britain," as "spendthrifts, libertines, wife-beaters, and drunkards." Nothing equaled the paper's savaging of royalty: Spain's King Alphonso was "a pitiful little specimen, a nonentity—brainless, characterless and worthless. Still he is a King, and, considering his origin and bad breeding, is 'as good as could be expected.' He might have been a tramp."

The *World* again ripped into royalty in a feature headed A PRECIOUS LOT OF GOOD-FOR-NOTHING PRINCES AND DUKES, where the duke of Edinburgh is "cold, selfish and miserly." His wife was proud, arrogant, and domineering. And the duke of Cambridge, commander in chief of the British army, "is utterly unfit for the position as has been painfully demonstrated [during the Crimean War, 1854–1856] when he showed the white feather [a symbol for cowardice] in a way that would have ruined another man."

Pulitzer was hardly exaggerating. Queen Victoria had been horrified when the duke applied for sick leave to avoid fighting, and wrote to him: "I hope you will be back in the Crimea by this time. Forgive my telling you frankly that I hope you will not let your low spirits and despondent feelings be known to others; you cannot think how ill natured people are here, and I can assure you that the Clubs have not been slow in circulating the most shameful lies about you."

Even Pulitzer's sympathy for the poor evaporated when it came to the English. Given "a fairly habitable apartment," he wrote, poor Londoners "would stuff the broken windows with rags, lie on dirty straw and wallow in filth, gin and degradation." This, of course, could be said of some of the poor in every city in the western world—including New York. Perhaps Pulitzer was simply pandering to the Anglophobic Irish, who outnumbered the combined English, Scottish, and Welsh population of New York by more than five to one.

Pulitzer-hater Leander Richardson thought so, pointing out that "There was nothing that could be done by the British government in connection with Ireland that did not meet with the most violent demonstrations of disapproval on the part of the *World*. The paper thirsted for British gore with a thirst that passed all understanding. It even went so far as to secure the services of a celebrated Fenian leader [James Stephens] as its Paris correspondent." (Fenians, members of a secret revolutionary society, fought for Irish freedom from British rule. Its American members invaded British Canada in 1866, 1870, and 1871, but were driven back by Canadian volunteers.)

Although Pulitzer was a fervent supporter of Irish independence, he deplored "the use of dynamite by the Celtic enemies of England as a destructive, cruel, senseless crime, for it accomplishes nothing but the slaughter and maiming of innocent persons. The employment of this dreadful agent is going to hurt the cause of Ireland more than anything else." For those who didn't get the written message, he published a cartoon showing named Irish terrorists as devils burning in hell while dead and injured children lay near the Tower of London, the site of a recent explosion.

From the start, Pulitzer had supported justice and equal rights for all—with no exceptions—but especially for the Irish, Germans, Scandinavians, and Jews. When a reader complained that a news report included the sentence "The Jew is accused of assaulting him," Pulitzer apologized: "It is the standing order in the *World* office—as in all intelligently conducted newspaper establishments—that no distinctions of race or creed are to be made in presenting the news. Occasionally, through oversight, something of the kind complained [about] slips into the *World*, but it is rare indeed. We assume that the nationality and the religious beliefs of persons who fall into the newspaper can be of no particular interest to the public."

Apparently no one asked him how he reconciled this attitude with hisslurs on the Slavs, Greeks, French, English, Chinese, and Italians. Yet Pulitzer was curiously inconsistent because, for example, he crusaded on behalf of badly treated Italian laborers. As for the Chinese, he was prepared to sympathize with them "so long as they remain at home. We do not want them here, but that is no reason why we should uphold the French in shooting them down. We never endorse injustice of any kind, even though barbarians are the victims."

Because of its pro-Irish stance the *World* looked like an Irish newspaper, especially in the spring. Then, for eight days running it gave front-page accounts of a 610-mile walking race dominated by Irishmen, and eventually with two Irishmen, Rowell and Fitzgerald, in the lead. HURRAH FOR FITZGERALD! was the headline tribute to the winner on May 4, and New York's Irish celebrated as if they'd won a war.

Sports news on page one gave way to the Wall Street crash that month, which panicked the moneymen. Gould lost more than forty-one million dollars,

Cartoonist Walter McDougall saw wealthy victims of the Wall Street crash as rats in a cage. William H. Vanderbilt is shown wearing a crown.

and Vanderbilt and associates, almost fifty million dollars. When the brokerage firm of Grant & Ward went belly up, owing customers sixteen million dollars, Ferdinand Ward, ex-president Grant's partner, got ten years in prison for swindling customers. Grant was exonerated. Pulitzer despised these men he regarded as money-mad and published a Walt McDougall cartoon of Vanderbilt and his crowd as caged rats.

While the moguls were grieving over their bank balances, Pulitzer and his wife were grieving over the heartbreaking death through pneumonia of their daughter Katherine Ethel on May 9, six weeks short of her second birthday.

Pulitzer handled it by losing himself in his work, especially in the imminent battle for the White House. He would play a vital role in the filthiest, most fiercely fought presidential campaign yet, with both contenders accused of having impregnated women to whom they were neither married nor engaged at the time.

At a mass meeting of maniacs, as the *Nation* called delegates at the June Republican convention, James G. Blaine was nominated the presidential candidate. His supporters almost worshiped this spellbinding speaker of Irish-Scots ancestry, whose spectacular career had taken him from teaching school and editing a country newspaper, to Speaker of the House, U.S. senator from Maine, and President Garfield's secretary of state. Blaine had been with Garfield when he was assassinated.

The pride and hope of the Republican Party had one major flaw: he was on the take, and had amassed a fortune of at least a million dollars on a salary never exceeding five thousand dollars a year. Consequently, according to writer Gil Troy, "Republicans went insane over him in pairs, one for, one against." Those for Blaine seemed to have had more cash, according to the *Nation*, which concluded that Blaine had been nominated because "Wall Street was in the saddle and Blaine was Jay Gould's man."

Pulitzer gave all-out support to the Democrats' choice, Grover Cleveland, a stocky, bull-necked, 260-pound bachelor known to his nephews as "Uncle Jumbo." As a lawyer during the Civil War, with two brothers in the Union army, and a mother and two sisters to support, he had paid $150 for a substitute to take his place in the firing line. After the war, as sheriff of Erie County, New York, he had hanged two murderers himself rather than have his deputies do it. This was a striking example, some thought, not of sadism or concern for the sensibilities of others, but of an inability to delegate authority. Later, as mayor of Buffalo, he was known as the "veto mayor" because he consistently squashed the self-serving bills of political grafters.

Pulitzer rated him honest, sincere, and "more of a Reformer than a Democrat" who worked "like the devil" and enjoyed it—not unlike himself, in fact. Certainly Cleveland lacked Blaine's brilliance and charisma, said Pulitzer, but he'd make a damn good president because he came from common people, with no aristocratic ancestors; had succeeded by his own efforts and strong character; was not a Wall Street speculator; and had no connection with railroads or Blaine. Most of all, he was "repulsive to the rascals who are preying on the government and who must be driven out of Washington."

Because of a petty personal grudge against Cleveland, Charles Dana gave him only halfhearted support, leaving Pulitzer's *World* as Cleveland's greatest newspaper champion.

Reform-minded Republicans led by Carl Schurz, who had deserted Blaine because of his questionable record, were ridiculed by an aggressive Republican New York state assemblyman, Theodore Roosevelt. He shared the reformers' low opinion of Blaine but chose to hold his nose and vote for him to ensure a Republican in the White House at almost any cost.

But Pulitzer was determined to elect a Democratic president. Launching what became a lifelong campaign to discredit Roosevelt's support of Blaine, Pulitzer ridiculed him for opposing a bill to limit the workday of horsecar drivers to twelve hours as a "communistic" idea and damned him as "a reform fraud and Jack-in-the-box politician. What an exhibition he makes of his reform professions when he signifies his intention to elect a President of the

United States a man he admits to be venal and corrupt, and for whom he blushes to speak."

Pulitzer gave voters four reasons for supporting Cleveland:

> He is an honest man.
> He is an honest man.
> He is an honest man.
> He is an honest man.

It was an inspiring rallying cry to a jaded public who thought of "politician on the take" as almost a law of nature. Then a Buffalo newspaper dropped a bombshell that made Blaine's victory all but inevitable.

"Honest" Grover Cleveland, said the paper, had a shocking secret. He had led a dissolute life as a young man ten years before in Buffalo, carousing with a winsome and willing widow, Maria Halpin. As a result, he had sired her son, named Oscar Folsom Cleveland, now in an orphan asylum, and driven her, the victim of his lust, into an insane asylum.

Republicans were ecstatic. They had already challenged Pulitzer's claim that Cleveland was a man of integrity by referring to him vaguely as an immoral drunk, and now here was specific dirt they could use to destroy him— the knockout blow. So-called respectable papers made the charge against Cleveland seem disgusting beyond description, typically by referring to "revolting details," but being too high-minded to cite them.

While Cleveland's supporters were reeling from the scandal, the *Indianapolis Sentinel* counterattacked. It released a skeleton from Blaine's cupboard, accusing him, while a teacher in Kentucky, of getting his future wife pregnant and then refusing to marry her. Found hiding out in Pittsburgh, said the paper, he was forced to marry the woman—three months before their son was born. The boy had died as an infant.

Pulitzer played straight man, cautiously linking the amorous activity of the two contenders. "The opponents of Cleveland at Chicago," he wrote, "are telling stories about the Governor's early days in Buffalo which reflect upon his chastity. They are probably the same kind of fellows who talk about Blaine and his schoolteaching days in Kentucky, which were marked by an excess of animal vitality."

The mention of Blaine's animal vitality infuriated the *Journalist's* Leander Richardson into anti-Semitism: "I should like to point out to Jewseph [sic] Pulitzer that the man who casts nameless slurs at another is a thousand times dirtier a coward than he who boldly makes public his charges and places himself in a position to be punished under the law, if what he tells is shown to be false."

Blaine struck back at his accusers by suing the *Indianapolis Sentinel* for libel, giving the story new life as a court case open to the press and public.

On the other side, Democratic Party leaders asked Cleveland for his response to the dirt on him, desperate for a denial. Instead he advised them to do what they considered political suicide, to tell the truth, implying that the rumors were essentially true.

Pulitzer couldn't believe it and called the charges contemptible and "baseless rumor, transparently false and libelous," to which only dolts would give credence, and dismissed them as a political trick. A week later he upped the ante: "A villainous libel was fastened upon Cleveland by a vicious, dirty journal in Buffalo, and all the respectable Republican journals have indirectly given it their endorsement."

Dana's *Sun* not only endorsed it, but also suggested a nightmare scenario in which, if Cleveland won, "the coarse debauchee might bring his harlots to Washington and hire lodgings for them close to the White House." And, allying himself with "indignant, deluded and outraged" Democrats, Dana declared that he could no longer support the "coarse" candidate, Cleveland.

Clergymen grouped to rescue Cleveland, headed by a Boston Unitarian minister, Dr. James Clarke Freeman, who questioned the embattled candidate and reported: He "cheerfully admits the indiscretion, but denies that he railroaded Maria Halpin into an insane asylum or that he led a 'dissolute life.'" Rev. Kingsley Twining, editor of a religious weekly, the *Independent*, also investigated Cleveland, and Pulitzer printed his conclusion that there was "a culpable irregularity of life, living as he was, as a bachelor, for which it is proper he should suffer but there was no seduction, no adultery, no breach of promise, no obligation of marriage." Twining was willing to forgive Cleveland, according to biographer James Barrett, but was outvoted by religious colleagues who couldn't stomach his "personal impurity," and agreed that "the attempt to force such a candidate upon the people would disgrace the party and the whole nation, if he should be elected."

Now Pulitzer knew the score, and instead of conceding defeat, he attacked. First he went after the *Sun*, a paper he had once rated the country's best, for its filthy record. Next he took on everyone who had smeared Cleveland, whom he glorified as a humane and generous man.

Under the headlines:

CLEVELAND'S VINDICATION.

THE SCANDALS ABOUT HIS PRIVATE
LIFE ALL EASILY DISPROVED.

Investigation Shows that Instead of Being a
Villain He Saved the Honor of Two Families
by Taking on Himself the Sins of Other Men.

the *World* explained that "after the child was born the woman made a habit of visiting every man with whom she had been intimate and demanded money under a threat of exposure. Three of her four admirers—for she was an attractive woman—were married, and the man who in reality was the father of the infant had an interesting daughter whom he idolized. He was in constant dread that his offense should reach his wife and child, and Cleveland, being the only unmarried man, relieved him of the embarrassment by shouldering all the responsibility. The man is dead and the child is his perfect image in manner and looks."

Cleveland suspected that his married law partner, Oscar Folsom, was the child's father.

In a masterly example of political spin, Pulitzer switched the subject from Cleveland's fornication to his self-sacrifice and to his having done the decent thing: "Cleveland acted a heroic part, suffering the obloquy that his friends might not bring unpleasantness to their hearthsides. He did everything in his power for them, and he provided for them until the woman became a confirmed victim to alcoholism and made it impossible by her condition for him to have anything to do with her. He accepted responsibilities that not one man in a thousand has shouldered." It was later confirmed that when the widow, a hopeless alcoholic, had suffered a mental breakdown, Cleveland had had her institutionalized, and the boy adopted by a childless couple. He never saw either of them again. Maria later recovered, remarried, and lived in New Rochelle, New York. The boy eventually became a prominent doctor.

Emboldened by his own rhetoric, Pulitzer dared to ask: What if he did once have "a sporadic association with a middle-aged female, was such an offense unpardonable? How many unmarried men are there in the world who are in a position to safely and conscientiously cast the first stone at the offender?" And he suggested that "If Grover Cleveland had a whole family of illegitimate children, as he has not, he would be more worthy of the Presidential office than Blaine, the beggar at the feet of railroad jobbers [crooked public officials], the prostitute in the Speaker's chair [Blaine was Speaker of the House in 1868], the representative and agent of corruptionists, monopolists and enemies of the Republic."

That summer of 1884 a pitiful and horrifying story took readers' minds off the presidential race. American explorers stranded in the Arctic had survived by eating their dead companions. The *New York Times* broke the story, and the *World* followed with its own reports on August 15 and 16. A few days later, Pulitzer admonished other papers for continuing to drag out the story and its gruesome details: "The casket containing the remains of Whistler, one of the Greely party, has been opened and the evidences of cannibalism obtained. What good does all this do? The whole country is convinced that the poor wretches constituting the Greely party were compelled to eat each other in order to subsist, and there is no further need of breaking open tombs. It is not proposed to prosecute the survivors, and no sensible people condemn the cannibalism under the circumstances. We have had enough of these sickening revelations to make Arctic exploration rather unpopular for some years. So let the matter drop."

The *New York Times* didn't drop the subject entirely, reporting the result of an investigation into the failure of the expedition, which blamed General William B. Hazen, the "incompetent Chief of the Signal Service," for the deaths of nineteen of the twenty-five Arctic explorers—without mentioning cannibalism.

The story of Blaine's shotgun wedding soon reclaimed the public's interest when he brought a libel case against the paper that had exposed him. A stupid move, thought Pulitzer: "If he had left the scandal unnoticed, it would have died in its birth." Pulitzer had it both ways, expressing in editorials his high-minded decision not to give the trial publicity, while printing the juicy details on the front pages.

Unleashed to find more dirt about Blaine, *World* reporters unearthed someone who knew his older brother as the black sheep of the Blaine family. According to this source, Blaine's brother had jumped bail in St. Louis to avoid a trial for forgery, been imprisoned in Georgia, and was "always up to some meanness or other. I suppose he has gone to the dogs in his own way."

Pulitzer himself was up to some meanness in late September when he implied, without convincing evidence, that Blaine had tampered with his dead son's gravestone to obscure the child's birth date, and also published the view of a "prominent" pro-Cleveland physician that Blaine was a very sick man with Bright's disease, and if elected, would probably die in office. In fact, Blaine lived for nine more years and in 1889 became President Benjamin Harrison's secretary of state.

In the midst of the dirty campaign Pulitzer was persuaded to run for Congress, but only when assured that the Ninth District in New York City was such a safe seat he wouldn't have to campaign. He won by almost two to one. An admiring St. Louis friend, Charles Gibson, predicted that Pulitzer would become a leader in the House, but wondered how he expected to run two great newspapers and play his part on the national stage.

Gibson's question must have occurred to Pulitzer. He was already running himself ragged producing two daily newspapers in two cities. In St. Louis, Dillon was only nominally the editor of the *Post-Dispatch*; Pulitzer still made all editorial decisions, even minor ones. Dillon confirmed this when he complained of his role as Pulitzer's puppet:

"You have a right to ask why I have sat here like a dummy, and blindly followed your orders," he wrote to his boss in September. "In all cases in which my judgment has dissented from yours you have been so invariably right and I so invariably wrong that you have relieved me of the necessity of thinking for myself. I can say with truth that I have done for you what I have never done for anyone else in my life, in surrendering my judgment to yours without question."

Despite his self-imposed workload, Pulitzer had an overpowering urge to do more for his country, which he saw as heading for disaster. Apparently he thought he could be more effective as a legislator than as a crusading publisher. Though neither socialist nor Communist, he was obsessed by the abject poverty of the many and the enormous fortunes of the few in America. He continued to give readers vivid glimpses into the tragic lives of the poor and obscene extravagance of the superrich. The situation drove him, in private, to passionate polysyllabic invective, and in public to a series of editorials proposing a national income tax on all with incomes above ten thousand dollars. Under the scare headline AN AMERICAN REVOLUTION, Pulitzer quoted a German socialist's warning of an imminent crisis in America between the workers and the wealthy. Pulitzer agreed that if nothing was done, violent revolution was all but inevitable, and almost alone among New York's publishers he persistently pointed out the inequities in American society.

When Dana in the *Sun* denied that there were distinct classes in the country, Pulitzer responded: "Everywhere we hear of reduced wages and discharged hands, and the tenement-houses in New York are filled with unemployed but willing workmen whose families are pinched by want. But turn the kaleidoscope of beneficent Republican policy, and what do we see? Vanderbilt, the king of a grand Republican monopoly, driving his fast horses or picking his teeth on the hotel balcony at Saratoga. Gould, the beneficiary of Republican legislation, sailing sweetly in his magnificent steam yacht. Yet, despite these kaleidoscope views, the *Sun* tell us there are no 'classes' in the country. No 'classes' in this country, forsooth! Would to God there were none! But twenty-four years of Republican rule have succcessfully built up classes and each year the Republican power lasts the distinction between the 'classes' will be more sharply defined."

To celebrate the record-breaking Sunday sale of his *World*, topping 100,000 for the first time, and reaching 103,670 on September 28, 1884, Pulitzer gave a silk top hat to all male employees, money bonuses to the women, and persuaded the authorities to fire a hundred-cannon salute in City Hall Park facing the *World* building. He believed that the paper's soaring popularity "demonstrated that the Eastern public appreciates a style of journalism that is just a bit breezy while being honest, earnest, and sincere."

And at Thanksgiving, everyone got a turkey.

But the euphoria was short-lived. Late in October Pulitzer feared he would fail in his drive to put a Democrat in the White House, expecting thousands of normally Democratic Irish Americans, shocked by Cleveland's sex life, to defect to Blaine. But just when his election seemed in the bag, Blaine blundered.

At his meeting with hundreds of Protestant clergymen on October 29, one of them assured Blaine: "Notwithstanding all the calumnies that have been urged in the papers against you, we stand by your side [shouts of 'Amen!']. We are Republicans and don't propose to leave our party and identify ourselves with the party whose antecedents have been Rum, Romanism and Rebellion. We are loyal to our flag. We are loyal to you."

It had been a grueling campaign. Exhausted or preoccupied, Blaine did not respond. His Irish Catholic supporters could laugh off the rum and rebellion allusion, but not the implication of disloyalty through their allegiance to

World cartoon by Walt McDougall ridicules Republican presidential candidate James G. Blaine.

Romanism (a disparaging term for Roman Catholicism). In fact, Blaine was not anti-Catholic: his mother was Catholic and his sister the mother superior of a convent. But his silence implied otherwise, and even convinced some that the Republican Party had an anti-Catholic bias.

That same evening Blaine made a fatal mistake by attending a fund-raising banquet at Delmonico's Hotel. Pulitzer had already called Blaine a political prostitute. But the most devastating blow to his chances was the *World's* front-page spread of October 30—a Walt McDougall cartoon across all seven columns headed THE ROYAL FEAST OF BELSHAZZAR BLAINE AND THE MONEY KINGS. It showed Blaine at the banquet with his backers, among them Jay Gould, Andrew Carnegie, John Jacob Astor, William H. Vanderbilt (wearing a crown), and Chauncey Depew.* They were about to guzzle Gould Pie, Lobby Pudding, and Monopoly Soup while ignoring a starving couple and their child begging for a share. (According to Old Testament prophet Daniel, Belshazzar was a Babylonian ruler at whose feast the writing on the wall signaled the city's destruction.)

---

* In fact, Vanderbilt wasn't at the banquet. McDougall had drawn the cartoon in advance of the event—a common practice—assuming Vanderbilt would attend because he was on the guest list.

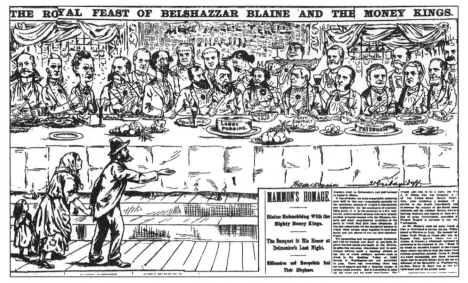

World cartoon that helped to destroy Blaine's presidential aspirations and elect Cleveland.

The accompanying news report, headed MAMMON'S HOMAGE, read: "From Rum, Romanism, and Rebellion, Mr. Blaine proceeded to a merry banquet of millionaires. The mask is off and Blaineism stands revealed in its true colors. Up to the present time we have heard from Blaine nothing but expressions of affection for the workingman of the country and eulogies from the Republican Party as their 'protector.' Read the list of Blaine's banqueters who are to fill his pockets with money to corrupt the ballot-box, to raise a corruption fund of $500,000 to defeat the will of the people. Are they friends of the workingman? What humbug! Are they in sympathy with labor? Fraud! Are they not mostly railroad kings, Wall Street millionaires, greedy monopolists, lobbyists, speculators?"

That day's *World*, naming the men Blaine was fronting for, delighted members of the Democratic National Committee, who made thousands of copies of the cartoon to be used on placards. Cleveland supporters carried them in parades in various cities, chanting:

Blaine! Blaine! James G. Blaine!
The Continental Liar from the State of Maine!

His supporters countered by reviving the Cleveland scandal, marching through the same cities, and calling out the taunting phrase in unison:

Ma! Ma! Where's My Pa?

To which crowds of Democrats would gleefully yell back:

Gone to the White House! Ha! Ha! Ha!

On November 2 tens of thousands of men marched up Broadway and Fifth Avenue to salute Cleveland, the Democratic contender, as he stood on a flag-draped reviewing stand at Madison Square. Many were former Republicans. And the *World* rejoiced:

A REVOLUTION
SUSPENDING BUSINESS TO
GREET CLEVELAND
50,000 SOLID MEN MARCH-
ING UP BROADWAY
A SPLENDID ARRAY OF BUSINESS
MEN'S CLUBS.
BANNERS, CHEERS, SONGS AND MARCHING.
CRIES FOR REFORM.
A PROCESSION OF VOTERS FIVE
MILES IN LENGTH.
EVERY MOTTO AND EVERY VOTE A
PROTEST AGAINST BLAINISM.

The next day's headlines reported even dirtier and deadlier Republican tactics than during the Tilden-Hayes race:

DOING MURDER IN ARMOR.
LOUISIANA REPUBLICANS ARMED FOR A
FIGHT AND GUARDED BY CORSELETS.
Attempted Intimidation of Democratic
Colored Voters Leads to the Bloody
New Iberia Riot—Eighteen Bodies
Collected to Date—One at Least
Dead of Fright—Kellogg Ruffians in
Louisiana Fire Upon Democrats.

On election night an excited Pulitzer rushed wildly about the *World* offices, convinced Cleveland would win and carry New York by 60,000. Equally optimistic Democrats gathered at polling places, singing:

Hurrah for Maria!
Hurrah for the Kid!
We Voted for Grover!
And We're Damn Glad We Did!

Exhilarated, Pulitzer watched five editions go to press—148,000 copies—and saw the final edition off at eight in the morning, its front page confidently headlined:

VICTORY!

He was nearly wrong. Cleveland carried New York by only 1,100 votes. However, this gave him 36 vital electoral votes toward his total of 219. Without New York he would have lost. Blaine got 182 electoral votes. Out of 9,759,351 popular votes, the Democrat beat the Republican by a mere 62,683.

Years later, Cleveland acknowledged Pulitzer's major role in his narrow victory: "I can never lose the vividness of my recollections of the conditions and incidents attending the Presidential campaign of 1884. How brilliantly and sturdily the World then fought for Democracy. It was here, there and everywhere in the field, showering deadly blows upon the enemy and it was won against such odds and by so slight a margin as to reasonably lead to the belief that no contributing aid could have been safely spared. The contest was so close that if it had lacked the forceful and potent advocacy of Democratic principles at that time by the New York World the result might have been reversed."

After the victory Pulitzer blamed the dirty campaign on Republican journals "that dragged the sewers to find filth to fling at Grover Cleveland. They have . . . thrust into the very faces of females and spread before the young of both sexes filth that they knew to be false as it was feculent. They have done more in the short campaign to debauch and defile the country than all the disseminators of obscene literature have been able to accomplish in the past half century."

The next day his vindictive critic Leander Richardson hit back with snide anti-Semitic vigor: "The vileness of the World's conduct throughout has been simply shocking. As a business manager of a clothing establishment somewhere in the direct vicinity of Chatham Street, Jewseph [sic] Pulitzer would be an honor to his race and a glory to his surrounding."

None of the contenders' hands were clean, but Pulitzer's were cleaner than most, and he was almost justified in claiming: "Despite great provocation, we refused to cast filth for filth. If we suppressed truth in any instance it was to the advantage of the Republican candidate and in the interest of decency."

The one exception was the cheap shot in a World feature headlined WAS BLAINE HIMSELF THE INFAMOUS PERPETRATOR OF THE DEED?, suggesting that Blaine had been the vandal who chiseled out the last figure on the birth date on his dead son's gravestone (implying that Blaine had done it to scotch the rumor that his wife had been pregnant when they married).

The big loser in the newspaper world was Pulitzer's rival Dana. By supporting Blaine, the Sun's circulation had plummeted from 137,000 to 85,000. The usually Republican New York Times having reluctantly joined the Mugwumps (independents) and promoted Cleveland, saw a mass desertion by loyal Republican readers, and its profits fell from $188,000 in 1883 to $56,000 in 1884.

On several fronts, Pulitzer's success was phenomenal. In fewer than two years he had raised the World's daily sales to 125,000, ten times what they had been under Gould. Pulitzer had played a crucial, decisive role in putting a Democrat in the White House—against the odds. But it wasn't enough. By next year he meant to double circulation *and* be a congressman who made a difference.

CHAPTER 9

Saves Statue of Liberty

1885

—

37 to 38 years old

"**O**ur splendid society is threatened by socialism, communism and anarchism," Chauncey Depew warned an anxious YMCA audience early in 1885. Told of the lecture, Pulitzer had his editorial for the day. He knew that as a Republican politician, railroad tycoon, and friend of the Vanderbilts, Depew was indeed a member of "a splendid society": Fat cats incorporated. Foreign ideologies are only dangerous, Pulitzer responded, when the bosses mistreat the workers: "Labor must be starved, overtaxed with work, abused in every way before it rises in rebellion. Mr Depew [should have] pointed out to the greedy corporations and monopolies of which he is so brilliant a representative that there is no Communism in this country and can be none except through the insane folly of corrupt wealth. It is a painful and poisonous plant of foreign growth. If law prevails and is made to reach the rich as well as the poor, if capital uses its power justly and makes no attempt to oppress and outrage Labor, all the Communism in the United States will be confined to a few beer cellars and Sunday meetings. But if corporations encroach on the people's rights our soil may eventually be prepared for the seed of Communism and prove as congenial as the soil of Europe."

The spring brought a chance to dramatize his point when Missouri Pacific Railroad workers, provoked by their mistreatment, went on strike. Pulitzer was one of the few publishers to support the strikers, whose wages had recently been cut twice to pay higher dividends to the owners of the company. Prominent among the owners was a man frequently in Pulitzer's sights, Jay Gould. And what a vulnerable target Gould made during the strike as he cruised on his yacht *Atalanta*, his daily expenses equal to the wages of two hundred of his railroad workers, the cost of one bottle of his wine enough to support a worker and his family for two weeks.

Pulitzer stated the case succinctly: "Dividends paid on watered [artificially overpriced] stock have gone to add to the hoards of millionaires who are sailing in their floating palaces. Wages cut down to a miserable pittance of $1 or $1.18 a day, out of which the workingman must feed and clothe a family." The *World's* vigorous campaign on behalf of workingmen helped to sustain and strengthen trade unions in their efforts to obtain a living wage for their members. Without the support of those unions, wrote social worker Jacob Riis, "in a population of a million and half, very nearly half a million persons [had been] driven, or chose, to beg for food, or to accept charity. There is no mistake about those figures. They are drawn from the records of the Charity Organization Society."

On the domestic front the Pulitzers were expecting their fourth child in late March, which curtailed Kate's social life, but Joseph was busier than ever. Though he wouldn't take his seat in Congress for several months, he had been bombarded by friends and strangers asking him to use his influence with Cleveland to get them one of the hundred thousand available jobs in the new administration. Out of those he chose to recommend Charles Gibson, a good friend from St. Louis and a loyal Democrat, as minister to Berlin, and Dr. Montrose Pallen, an intelligent New York physician, to be consul-general in London.

Cleveland took an upper-floor suite in Manhattan's Victoria Hotel to interview such office seekers or their patrons. The lobby was already crowded when Pulitzer arrived to promote his friends. He handed his card to one of a squad of bellboys shuttling between the lobby and Cleveland's suite, then mingled with senators and congressman, all waiting to be called to see the man who handed out the jobs. Pulitzer stayed until he realized he wasn't going to be called. Knowing how much he had helped to elect Cleveland, he left in a fury. Afterward, Cleveland apologized and explained that Pulitzer's card had been mislaid in the general commotion, and when it was found the jobs had been filled.

But when Pulitzer attended the presidential inauguration on March 4, 1885, his mood had completely changed, as reflected in the next day's high-spirited *World* headlines:

AT HOME
In the old Democratic
White House Again.
After Twenty-Four Years Wander-
ing in the Wilderness
President Cleveland, by the
grace of God
And the Supreme Will of the
American People

Cynics predicted that Pulitzer was now in Cleveland's pocket and would be the voice of the administration. He replied that he'd "gladly and zealously support all that is good in President Cleveland's administration," but would oppose whatever was "clearly wrong or mistaken. We regard the editorship of The *World* as a great public trust, as Mr. Cleveland regards the Presidency."

Pulitzer's prominence in national affairs had embittered Charles Dana, the man he had once admired as a liberal editor of the country's greatest paper. But Dana, having become a conservative and a staunch supporter of laissez-faire capitalism, had lost tens of thousands of *Sun* readers to the *World*. He now saw Pulitzer as a dangerous threat who jeopardized the very existence of the *Sun*, and his previously good-natured rivalry turned to an unscrupulous effort to destroy him.

To discredit Pulitzer, Dana gave credence to the rumor that he was a vulgar and unsophisticated hick who had once been coach driver for a St. Louis engineer, James B. Eads, and had pressured people into nominating him for his congressional seat.

In retaliation, Pulitzer called Dana "the able and aged [sixty-six] bully and blackguard of the *Sun*," denied that he had ever worked for Eads, and asserted that his nomination for Congress was "totally unsought, unexpected and undesired." After that accurate rebuttal, he counterattacked with: "We would a thousand times rather be an honest coachman enjoying the esteem of honest people than the present editor of the *Sun*."

James Eads, who had been in Manhattan on January 19, read Pulitzer's response and offered to testify that when they first met, Pulitzer was co-owner of the *Westliche Post*. Pulitzer didn't take him up on the offer, but threw fuel on the smoldering fire when he again expressed his selective xenophobia: "To what race of human beings does Charles Anderson Dana belong? . . . The Danas although a New England family of considerable Puritan and literary pretensions, have unquestionably a Greek derivation. The modern Greek is a treacherous, drunken creature. Mr. Charles Ananias Dana may be descended from a Greek corsair. If so, his career of treachery, hypocrisy, deceit and lying could be easily accounted for."

On the same editorial page Pulitzer claimed that Dana had once been on a sinking ship, and although a strong swimmer and wearing two life preservers, when a terrified young woman pleaded with him either to save her or to hand over one of his life preservers, he had refused. Instead, said Pulitzer, he replied "with grammatical precision, 'At a time like this the motto is *sauve qui peut*' [everyone for himself], and then slid into the water and swam easily ashore." Pulitzer did not name the woman, mention if she survived, nor who was the source of this devastating charge.

That was only the first in a salvo of Pulitzer's attacks. Dana's insults had so infuriated him that one can imagine the glee and accompanying expletives with which, three days later, he composed his exposure of Dana as a hypocrite for demeaning "office-beggars" while having been one himself. Pulitzer had the evidence—a seventeen-year-old letter Dana had sent to President Andrew Johnson begging for a federal appointment:

"This letter [from Dana to the president] is not modest, but it is self-reliant, bold and beseeching. It is couched in beautiful language. We doubt whether the Anglo-Saxon tongue was ever more adroitly employed in the art of office-begging. The fact that this letter produced no results—that it was a case to the winds, as it were—should not discourage ambitious gentlemen who long to serve the public. The style and diction are what we commend. With an honest, decent man's name at the bottom this style of letter ought to 'fetch' a small post-office . . . every time."

Other critics joined Dana in ganging up on Pulitzer for running questionable ads in the World. Leander Richardson led the pack, decoding ads in the World's personal columns as lightly disguised come-ons from pimps and prostitutes. And he panned Pulitzer for turning his paper into a "sewer for the stream of vice and filth which courses through the great city under the surface of decent life, the channel of communication between massage harlots and their victims, and the assignation house keepers and their licentious customers."

Hoping to bait Pulitzer into an admission of guilt, ignorance, or carelessness, Richardson reprinted the evidence: A REFINED YOUNG LADY OF HIGHEST RESPECTABILITY, stranger in the city, temporarily distressed in finances, desires the ACQUAINTANCE OF A WEALTHY, HONORABLE GENTLEMAN, WHO WOULD PROVE A FRIEND. Address Helena P. Hamilton, Brooklyn Post-Office. "Was not this," Richardson asked, "a plain enough request for bids upon the kind of merchandise in which this particular young woman deals?"

Richardson also accused Pulitzer of disgusting taste in running an ad "for various kinds of loathsome diseases [including gonorrhea] with a picture, the filthy suggestiveness of which is seldom equalled in the cesspool pages of the Police Gazette." Even an unscrupulous newspaper owner, he suggested, would refuse to print such an ad unless tempted by big bucks, yet, he claimed, the World got a mere $300 "for publishing this nauseating news."

Sometimes Pulitzer's critics hit the mark. In subsequent issues the World published an ad by Duffy's Barley Malt Whiskey, touting the drink as a sure cure for consumption, dyspepsia, and all wasting diseases, with a fake testimonial from President Cleveland commending the whiskey.

The exposure of the phony Cleveland ad spurred Pulitzer to explain that he could not "vouch for the honesty of the thousands of advertisers. Advertisements which appear fair and honorable upon their face are accepted. If swindlers occasionally get access to our columns, we have only to be informed of the fact to apply the remedy." But by the time he replied, Richardson had been replaced as the Journalist's editor by the more benign W. G. MacLaughlin.

Richardson's main charge against Pulitzer had been that he printed filth. Strangely, Pulitzer lodged the same complaint against Émile Zola's realistic novels describing contemporary French slum life. Instead of welcoming the zealous reformer, a man after his own heart, Pulitzer the prude complained:

"Zola is very fond of narrating how near he once came to absolute starvation and some of the readers of his florid filth almost wish he had quite arrived." He did not deny the Frenchman's talent but agreed with his book reviewer that Zola's mistake was "to find his subjects in the slums of social and moral life, while he possesses the power to delineate its higher and nobler phases."

This was a formidable challenge. Pulitzer's reporters had yet to unearth any high and noble phases of slum life.

Pulitzer's scorn for the French could partly explain his anti-Zola stance, but certainly not why the *World* joined the bandwagon in panning Mark Twain's homegrown *Huckleberry Finn*, headlining the piece:

WIT AND LITERARY ABILITY WASTED ON A
PITIABLE EXHIBITION OF IRREVERENCE AND VULGARITY.

An incongruous complaint from a newspaper whose owner, after all, was in the business of irreverence and one of its leading exponents, and frequently accused of printing a vulgar rag. Yet he okayed the review that damned the book as "careless hack-work" and a cheap and pernicious account of "the scrapes in which a wretchedly low, vulgar, sneaking and lying country boy" gets involved. It only needed the Public Library of Concord, Massachusetts, to agree and ban the book from its shelves as "trash" to make it a best-seller, sales topping 50,000 by early summer and climbing steadily.

Eventually he came to appreciate Twain and Zola. His own reporters' accounts of New York's slum life persuaded him that Zola had not exaggerated the horrors inflicted on the poor, but told it like it is. Their reports enraged Pulitzer and moved him to contrast the Vanderbilts and the Goulds sailing in their "floating palaces" and feasting in their megamansions in which the doors alone cost fortunes, while, within shouting distance, New York's poor were reduced to eating dogs and cats and died like flies. In fact, 11 people perished in one year from a building on Baxter Street, and 633 over three years in two adjoining blocks.

Infant mortality in these slums mocked Chauncey Depew's view of New York as a "splendid society." According to biographer George Juergens, only a solipsist or someone with tunnel vision could deny that it was "a divided city: uptown a center of wealth, culture and sophistication, and downtown, a Dantean vision of purgatory." Pulitzer agreed with this view and was all for tearing down the tenements, saying that the health if not the survival of the community outweighed the selfish interests of greedy slumlords and the temporary inconvenience of the "inmates" until rehoused.

When typhus fever struck a tenement on West Thirty-second Street, killing several, including a visiting priest there to comfort the dying, Pulitzer blazed the news on page one, telling how ambulances had been busy all day transporting "filthy, dirt-incrusted people" to Blackwell Island's hospital, while workmen shoveled cartloads of filth from a nearby flat factory roof onto which tenants had thrown their garbage. They did not use their toilets in the cellar. To reach them meant wading through foul waste matter, and the janitor, whose wife had died of typhus, refused to clean it up.

Pulitzer warned the rich that it was in their own interest to get involved because the sewers connected their homes with the tenements of the poor, and typhus was no respecter of persons. He also blasted the Board of Health and its sanitary inspectors for tolerating such pestilential squalor. They metaphorically moved upwind and ignored his advice.

Nevertheless, the *World* persisted in exposing the awful conditions of the desperately poor. It revealed, for example, that in the colorful tenement-district street markets the food for sale was mostly contaminated, the poverty-stricken boys and girls dressed alike in material made from old bedclothes, and "one of the families subsisted for nearly a week upon the carcass of a big Newfoundland dog. The father said that the children eagerly ate the flesh and cried for more, although they knew whence it came."

A report by the Sanitary Aid Society confirmed the *World*'s horror stories. To enter what inspectors called "pestilential human rookeries," they had to walk though alleyways reeking with poisonous and sickening gases caused by a river of sewage, then to climb rotten stairs into dark and dirty passages swarming with rats. "Then, if you are not driven back by the intolerable stench, you may gain admittance to the dens in which thousands of human beings herd together." In the attics, where inspectors hoped to open windows and breathe fresh air, they gagged as they stepped among the putrefying carcasses of cats, birds, and "viler abominations still."

During the recent presidential election campaign Pulitzer had blamed twenty years of Republican rule for such obscene conditions and implied that the only way to create a just society was to kick them out. He had mocked Whitelaw Reid's *New York Tribune* for trying to convince workingmen that they were enjoying a carefree, comfortable life thanks to the Republicans—when many were barely surviving on near-starvation wages and thousands were without work or hope for a better future.

A crusading and effective muckraker, forerunner of Lincoln Steffens, Upton Sinclair, and George Seldes, Pulitzer kept up the pressure, not only revealing the suffering but also suggesting a partial remedy: to bring the slumlords and neglectful authorities to account. He sent his reporters to visit the homes of working women and describe their straitened lives. On an average wage of seven dollars a week, with food and lodging costing five dollars, and transportation and other necessary expenses another two dollars, it left nothing for medicine, clothes, or heating during the winter, not to mention unexpected expenses. Pulitzer challenged the nation's leading financiers to explain how to live on such a budget.

No answers coming from the financiers, Pulitzer encouraged readers to contribute to the Working Girls' Vacation Society, which enabled poor workingwomen to take a break from work.

He endorsed any humanitarian effort to help those in want but did not encourage massive government intervention. Nor did he expect it—because, although a Democrat was in the White House and Democrats had a majority in the House, Republicans still ruled the Senate. Many of them were million-aires, Pulitzer pointed out, who voted for bills in which they had big financial stakes. Reform would have to wait, he wrote, until the Senate "had some poorer and more honest men" in it.

Strangely, although he was revolted by how the vulgar, self-indulgent rich made and spent their huge fortunes, he praised William Henry Vanderbilt, who, with some two hundred million dollars to play with, had done little to alleviate the conditions of the less fortunate. Pulitzer explained in an editorial that what he liked about him was that he didn't flaunt his wealth, "own yachts or put on aristocratic airs. We do not believe that the coat-of-arms on his car-riage is as big as a full-sized hand. His servants do not wear yellow tags and cockades. We never saw Mrs. Vanderbilt nursing a poodle. He has not sought to buy European gingerbread titles for his daughters, as he could have done with his large wealth, and as many of our vulgar moneyed aristocrats do. The young Vanderbilts, male and female, have all married plain Americans."

Perhaps the five hundred thousand dollars Vanderbilt gave in 1884 to establish a medical school associated with the College of Physicians and Sur-geons in New York got him off Pulitzer's selfish-rich blacklist.

Pulitzer's competitor, the *Tribune*'s Whitelaw Reid, asserted that the poor were either moral degenerates or ignorant and indolent immigrants, with only themselves to blame for their wretched condition. Not so, said Pulitzer; large numbers applying for assistance "are now more intelligent and of a better class. Many of them are American born, others of the better class of German. Hereto-fore neither of these sought relief. This unmistakeably shows that the pinching has begun to be felt by those who never dreamed of such a thing as asking for alms."

Pulitzer gave one reason why: the wages of nonunion laborers had plum-meted, while the profits of manufacturers had soared. Miners in Ohio got fifty cents for every ton of coal they dug up. When they struck for a raise, the mine-owners called out the state militia and threatened to replace them with foreign scab labor. The *World*, sympathizing with the miners and their families, started a fund to aid them.

And Pulitzer was quick to counter an attempt by Republicans to evade the result of a referendum that overwhelmingly opposed using convict labor in pri-vate industry. Their bill, he said, "shows how eager the Republicans are to return to a system which was a mine for State Prison officials, go-betweens and favored contractors, to the injury of honest labor."

Pulitzer won that one: a vote in May killed the bill.

But there was always someone or something else to deplore. He despised both the self-indulgent rich and the relatives of political icons who "sold" them-selves to big-money interests, especially a direct descendant of President Adams "given over to money-making, embarking on railroad corporation schemes with Jay Gould, and while denying that he is that tarnished operator's tool, boasting that he is in general harmony with his venal associate and fellow director! This is a materialistic age. Family renown, personal character, a high sense of honor are more or less suspended and this is why we find a Charles Francis Adams, the great-grandson of Washington's successor and grandson of another President, bent on making money with apparently as much eagerness and 'in general harmony' with Jay Gould."

At times Pulitzer muddied his message by ridiculing fellow reformers, such as the Ladies' Health Protective Association. Despite his respect for their reducing cruelty to animals, he approved a page one headline describing them as vigilantes, and mocked them as "five fashionably dressed middle aged ladies and five young men setting out from a good address on East 51st Street, the women pausing to fuss with their wraps and Easter bonnets," and whose approach to the stockyards was announced by a small boy yelling, "'Here comes the Smelling Committee!'"

What Pulitzer took very seriously was the recent gift to America from French workingmen and workingwomen. They had contributed $250,000 for a magnificent statue of a woman symbolizing liberty, and representing the enduring friendship between the two peoples. But the 225-ton statue lay languishing in France, because Congress refused to pay $100,000 to construct a pedestal for it.

Pulitzer told his readers that "it would be an irrevocable disgrace to New York City and the American Republic to have France send us this splendid gift, emblematical of our attainment of the first century of independence, without our having provided even so much as a landing place for it." And he urged them to pay for the pedestal: "Take this appeal to yourself personally. Give something, however little." He gave $250.

Tens of thousands of positive replies poured in, including:

"I am a wee bit of a girl, yet I am ever so glad I was born in time to contribute my mite ($1) to the Pedestal."

"The inclosed dollar comes from a party of poor artists."

"Inclosed please find five cents as a poor office boy's mite toward the Pedestal Fund. As being loyal to the Stars and Stripes, I thought even five cents would be acceptable."

"I am a young man of foreign birth and have seen enough of monarchical governments to appreciate the blessing of the Republic. Inclosed please find $2 for the fund."

Though the World covered New York high and low life exhaustively, and much of the rest of the country, foreign affairs in which the United States was not actively concerned got short shrift. In the spring, when Britain and Russia were on the verge of a war that never happened, Pulitzer's concern was the welfare of the American farmer. And he suggested that if war became inevitable, "the British Navy cannot proceed to pay its respects to the great Russian seaports too soon. And the sooner they are closed the better the price of American wheat."

His attitude toward Cuba's future did an about-turn in the course of a year. When the *World* enthusiastically reported the imminent sale of Cuba to the United States by its Spanish overlords, two Cuban newspapers that reprinted the *World* account were suspended. At this threat to press freedom, Pulitzer announced his support of a revolution to free Cuba, though his idea of a free Cuba seemed to imply American control. He was all for the sale until he suspected that much of the rumored $150 million purchase price would go to sleazy speculators, and then he opposed it, predicting "that it is only a matter of time when Cuba will fall into our hands naturally without any great cost."

His aim to inform and reform was often on target. But he knew that an unrelieved diet of plague-ridden slums, crime-ridden streets, and aggressive tin-pot dictators south of the border would stampede readers to his rivals. So he often gave them a break from horror stories and let loose his writers with a penchant for puns and reporters attuned to the wild and wacky side of life. This gave his highbrow critics more ammo to fire at him. In an age when puns were not automatically greeted with groans, Pulitzer used such beauties as: "Cyrus H. McCormick invented a great reaper, but the Reaper whose name is Death cut him down, and now he is no mower." And, "A paper has been started in Memphis bearing the primitive title of Adam. Of course it is issued in the Evening and it is also Adam poor newspaper."

He followed the enduring fashion in alliteration, too; even a report of the previous day's storm could raise a smile with this headline:

BOREAS ON A BENDER.

Also in the lighter vein, sketches of different-shaped noses illustrated a feature promoting the "science" of "noseology." The headlines told the thrust of the piece:

NOSEOLOGY.
HUMAN CHARACTER ILLUSTRATED
BY THE HUMAN PROBOSCIS.
SOME MEN WHO ARE FAMOUS AND
SOME WHO ARE NOT.
DISTINGUISHED NEW YORKERS WITH
CELEBRATED NOSES.
HOW THAT ORGAN INDICATES STRENGTH AND
MENTAL PECULARITIES.
A SOLEMNLY SCIENTIFIC SUBJECT ARTISTI-
CALLY ANALYZED.

Female noses were featured the following week.

W. G. MacLaughlin, the new editor of the no-nonsense trade magazine the *Journalist*, claimed that "people of refinement dropped the paper in disgust and held their own nasal organs—figuratively speaking." But unrefined readers must have loved the feature, because Pulitzer gave them a similar treat in the spring: illustrations of eyes and lips as clues to character and personality.

Kissing couples—a mother kissing a child good night, a skinny man locked in a tight embrace with a stout woman, a young woman snatching a kiss from a surprised male, a fashionable couple doing it with aplomb, and a woman kissing her dog—illustrated another article for the romantic or the curious, headed:

THE PAROXYSMAL EPOCH
KISSES IN EVERY KNOWN AND UNKNOWN
LANGUAGE
How It Is Done, and Generally
What Is Thought of It.

The feature reported that there were kissing clubs, kissing teachers, that a kissing journal was in the offing, and described kissing a ballet dancer as like [kissing] "cold corn starch," or "early cucumbers without any vinegar or any salt."

"Kissing is indeed part of the life of the modern man and woman," said the *World*, and went on to explain that because kissing rehearsals between the sexes were verboten, in the best society people practiced on their pets!

Having catered to men with sports, politics, and crime, Pulitzer made sure women also clamored for his paper. Those writing to the *World* were advised on how to handle men, and men were advised to break the ice with women by complimenting them on their complexion or dress, after which "the conversation will drift pleasantly." On Sundays the *World* published fiction, usually love stories, and romantic poetry to appeal to women, and flattered them outrageously. New York City women were assured that they were more cherished, respected, independent, self-assured, sophisticated, and better-looking than their European counterparts. The *World* accounted for this by the women's Saxon ancestry and the domestic and political freedom they enjoyed in America. How Pulitzer got away with this without antagonizing his many non-Saxon and especially his Jewish and Celtic Irish readers is a mystery.

Just as New York City women outclassed foreigners, said the *World*, so their style and complexions surpassed those of women in the boondocks and other American cities. Why? Because of the sea air and their sensible way of life and diets. The *World* anticipated the smart aleck who might point out that Boston women enjoyed the same Atlantic air. Sure, the Boston women looked attractive at first glance, but they were spoiled by their passion for "culture," and susceptibility to fads and intellectual pursuits. Fortunately, New York women were not "burdened with scholarship," said the paper. Their great quality, the *World* concluded, was their wonderful "tact, the jewel of the feminine soul." Among those who bought this baloney was the circulation manager, who persuaded Pulitzer to do a follow-up feature during a circulation drive in Brooklyn. The paper then suggested that Brooklyn women were more naturally attractive than New York City's beauties, who achieved their effect with cosmetics and corsets, driving "away the bloom of nature for the artificialism of the toilet chambers."

Early in the year, Kate saw that her husband was becoming exhausted from overwork, and soon after their fourth child, Joseph Pulitzer Jr., was born on March 21, 1885, talked him into a long vacation abroad. Typically, his last thought before he set sail was about the paper. He told Cockerill to gradually cut down on the use of illustrations while he was away, until they were entirely eliminated, because he felt they lowered the tone of the paper. Then, assured that their servants and doctor would care for the children and that Kate's brother, William Davis, would keep an eye on Joseph's business interests, they set off for Europe, reaching Paris in May.

A vacation for Pulitzer was always a working vacation, with emphasis on work. After he and Kate had congratulated Auguste Bartholdi, the sculptor of the Statue of Liberty, attended art sales, and decided on which cases of wine to have shipped home, Joseph resumed his irresistible workaholic practices. He eagerly scoured the *World* and other U.S. papers mailed to him, received reports from several of his staff, and sent them frequent instructions—and got little sleep from worrying about who should replace him in overall control of the *World* while he was in Congress.

When they went to spas in Aix-les-Bains and Bad Kissinger, Kate tried to get him to take it easy, but a relaxed Pulitzer was an oxymoron.

The Pulitzers were still in Europe when Victor Hugo died in Paris on May 22, and so were aware of the enormous reaction there to his death, which accounts for the unexpectedly long and glowing *World* obituary for a man who was surely unknown to most readers. It doubted "whether a writer has ever lived who rivalled him in capacity for doing great work in every department of literature. In poetry, in romance, in drama, he has taken the highest honors." Yet few men had known such personal tragedy. "At the time of his marriage his brother's mind became clouded. His daughter, Leopoldine, and her husband Charles Vacquerie were drowned together when boating. He buried his son Charles, carried off by an attack of cerebral congestion on the day that the Communist outbreak took place in Paris; his other son, François, died two years later, after a lingering illness." He left half his fortune of 4 million francs to his daughter Adele, the inmate of a lunatic asylum.

The *World* could not have published a more sympathetic obituary of a great American author. But Pulitzer's affection and respect for the French had blossomed recently, especially since their generous gift of the Statue of Liberty.

In England he kept up his frenetic activity, met old friends, popped into the U.S. consulate in London, visited several newspaper offices including the *Times* of London, and had discussions with members of Parliament.

Back home he encouraged Cockerill to give wide play to crimes by the police, and to stress that some cops, such as Sergeant David Crowley, were simply thugs in uniform.

Crowley had raped a young woman, yet he freely walked the streets boasting that influential political friends would clear him—while his distraught victim was kept in a cell awaiting the trial. The *World* bailed her out, raised money for her impoverished widowed mother, and covered every day of the trial on page one, with editorial comments on page four. In mid-May the jury found Crowley guilty, and he got seventeen years at hard labor in Sing Sing. The *World* alone had shown continued interest in bringing the rapist to justice, and Pulitzer justifiably claimed to have acted in the public interest.

All of this intense activity was taking its toll on Pulitzer. Dillon, still his editor on the *Post-Dispatch*, was one of the first to sense that something was seriously wrong. He had recently complained he was Pulitzer's puppet, but now he was told he was in complete charge. The boss didn't want to be bothered with the *Post-Dispatch*'s problems. It was so out of character that Dillon guessed Pulitzer was heading for a nervous breakdown and wrote to warn him: "You are suffering from something more than mere overwork. You have been overworking the creative mental power, that faculty which in man is the type of the highest or divine creative power. Not one man in ten thousand has it at all. Now please excuse the apparent flattery of all this. I mean it seriously and I have been trying for a long time to make up my mind to say it. The faculty which creates, you possess to a rare degree. You have overstrained it. But if you can do as the rest of us do, go six months without creating an idea, and get cured thereby, the cure will be worth the sacrifice. If you wish you can do the work of a lifetime in five years—and break down; or you can do the work of a century in a lifetime, and live while you do it, which is much better."

It was well meant, but like asking an alcoholic to stop drinking.

Back home, Pulitzer found that Cockerill had disobeyed orders. At first he had used fewer illustrations in the paper, but when he realized that circulation was dropping, instead of reducing the illustrations, he increased them. Then, according to the *Journalist*, "the circulation rose like a thermometer on a hot day, until it reached over 230,000 on the day of [General] Grant's [heavily illustrated] funeral [in July]." Pulitzer didn't argue with such success and approved Cockerill's decision.

On August 11 Pulitzer told his readers that he had the money for the Statue of Liberty's pedestal. With the exception of his own contribution, $1,000 from a Pierre Lorillard, and $250 from Secretary of the Navy William C. Whitney, the rest had come from 120,000 workingmen, workingwomen, and children, while the wealthy, he wrote, "looked on with an apathy that amounted to contempt. Yet in the opulent city of New York more than enough money is wasted every day in licentiousness, folly and shame to build this Pedestal."

In October the Pulitzers moved to 616 Fifth Avenue, in an area known as Millionaires' Row. But neither the European vacation nor the new home calmed Joseph's nerves. He frequently lost his temper over nothing, once over misplaced underwear. Kate had usually been able to talk him into a good mood. But now nothing would placate him, and their quarrels escalated. Kate recorded in her diary what must have been one of the most painful of these occasions—when he told her she was a failure as a wife.

Her entry for October 16, 1885, read:

"He said that all the little things that go to make a man comfortable, that I failed in. I told him that there was no servant in his house who had worked harder than I had. That I put him first, have sacrificed the children and myself to him. I lost my temper, and said I had made a slave of myself, that he was utterly spoilt, that with his disposition he must have something to criticize. He said that I did not understand, had never been taught to understand the duties of a wife. He then ordered me out of the room saying that these scenes left a blot on me in his mind that he never forgave. When will these scenes end or when will I be at rest?"

In his first love letter Pulitzer had warned her that he was self-absorbed and difficult. She had since discovered he was also an impetuous, hard-driven, high-strung, hot-tempered, and demanding perfectionist—or, as his business manager and biographer Don Carlos Seitz had characterized him in two words, "forever unsatisfied."

A clue as to what Pulitzer expected and wasn't getting from her had once appeared in his editorial about a Brooklyn woman who defied a court order giving an elevated railway company the right of eminent domain to her property, and who had to be forcibly removed from her home. As Pulitzer wrote at the time, "It is doubtful if a woman ever understands how to fight the inevitable. She always expects a grand-trunk railroad to change its time-table so that she can fix her hair, and she always tells her husband, who has the affairs of the universe on his shoulders, that if he does not lay them aside and come to the matinee with her he does not love her."

Pulitzer was surely taking on more than his share of the affairs of the universe. And Kate must have had mixed feelings in December 1885 when he left their Manhattan home for Washington, D.C., to take his seat as a congressman in the Forty-ninth Congress. Although he had unchained Dillon to edit the Post-Dispatch without his supervision, he still expected to edit the World while undertaking his new political duties.

On December 19, 1885, soon after his arrival in Washington, he offered attorney Roscoe Conkling, a former Republican congressman, ten thousand dollars for defending the World in twenty-one libel suits it had incurred since June 1883. Conkling apparently accepted.

According to cartoonist Walt McDougall, Pulitzer was so obsessed by the fear of libel suits "that he nightly read most every paragraph in the paper." But this belies the provocative material he continued to print, exposing powerful, corrupt individuals.

Pulitzer devoured the paper because he was obsessed with his work and wanted everything to be perfect, just as he wanted Kate to be perfect. In his angry outburst at her he seemed at the end of his tether, which was hardly surprising. Trying to do the work of two men, he, like the Brooklyn woman, was fighting the inevitable. Something had to give.

CHAPTER 10

Haymarket Square
Massacre

1886

—

38 to 39 years old

Having spent Christmas with his family in Manhattan, Pulitzer left for Washington, D.C., soon after to assume his duties as a congressman. But he didn't stay long. Despite his passion for politics, he couldn't let go of the paper, constantly riding the railroad back to Manhattan to make sure it maintained his imprint. He spent more time between the two cities than in Congress. And even in the nation's capital he almost hibernated in his rooms at John Chamberlain's Hostel at Fifteenth and I Street. There, with his secretary, Edwin Grozier, he dealt with a constantly replenished pile of correspondence.

Many were begging letters, and he responded generously—to the New York Sanitary Aid Society, to his financially strapped librarian friend Udo Brachvogel, to a Catholic charity, and to the Parnell fund. He also endowed a bed for sick journalists in Roosevelt Hospital, and after the death of William Patrick, who had helped him become an attorney, Pulitzer paid for the education of Patrick's two sons. He gave his close friend Thomas Davidson a hundred dollars a time to write for the *World*, which was really charity because his scholarly style was so obviously inappropriate that his efforts rarely saw print.

It wasn't all one-way. In the new year, grateful St. Louis newsboys sent Pulitzer a gold-headed cane as a token "of the high esteem in which we hold you personally, and of our appreciation of your many kindnesses."

Dana, of course, grabbed the chance to expose Pulitzer's apparent neglect of his congressional duties. But Pulitzer believed his newspapers were engaged

110

in more relevant issues than the current windy debate over a bill to regulate oleomargarine sales, punctuated by drunken congressmen suffering from altered states of consciousness or snoring in their seats.

For instance, he welcomed bureau chief Theron Crawford's plan to use a whistle-blower to flush out Collis Huntington from his cover as an honest businessman. The whistle-blower revealed that in recent years Huntington, a Union Pacific Railroad lobbyist, had spent some five hundred thousand dollars at every congressional session. He swore that it wasn't to bribe congressmen, but the *World* proved him a liar and spurred the first law to regulate interstate commerce. Pulitzer also okayed stories of more earthy appeal: of a Cabinet member's son seducing a hotel chambermaid, then hotfooting it to Arizona, and of a Democratic politician entrapped and blackmailed by his enemies because of his starring role in a sex scandal.

Despite these preoccupations, Pulitzer made his brief House appearances count, introducing a bill to give a pension to the family of the late General Hancock, a Union Army Civil War hero, and serving on the Interstate and Foreign Commerce Committee. He called at the White House for friendly conversations with the man he'd helped put there. Then he sent for his cartoonist McDougall to ridicule some of the clowns in Congress. McDougall saw Pulitzer in a new light, surprised to find that a few drinks made him boyishly boisterous, especially the night he left the Capitol grounds after a few cocktails. Then, in the cartoonist's words, Pulitzer "was lit up to the seventh magnitude."

It took Pulitzer only three months in Washington to realize that he couldn't run the *World* and try to run the country. So he resigned from Congress on April 13, assured by bureau chief Crawford that "you have a much better position as editor of the *World* than any official in Washington." Judging by the plan he okayed on returning to Manhattan, his new motto was "The Sky's the Limit." The idea was to place a huge billboard in New Jersey with greetings to the inhabitants of Mars, and recommending the *World* as their news source when they landed. But the proposal was spiked when some killjoy asked, "What language shall we print it in?"

Pulitzer quickly came down to earth to fire a young *Post-Dispatch* clerk who had embezzled some seven hundred dollars from the paper. But he decided not to prosecute him, having bigger crooks to pursue in Manhattan, especially Jacob Sharp and Henry Jaehne. Sharp, owner of the Seventh Avenue streetcar line, had bribed city officials to give him a 999-year franchise to operate another line, on Broadway. Alderman Jaehne, also a real estate broker, accepted Sharp's twenty-thousand-dollar bribe, which topped the bribes offered by rivals for the franchise. All but two of the other twenty-two aldermen also accepted Sharp's bribes. This explains why he got what he wanted, with only two dissenting votes and despite the mayor's veto. Though the crooked deal had not yet been exposed, and *World* reporters came up with only circumstantial evidence, Pulitzer dared to charge that "the Broadway Railroad job was carried through the Board of Aldermen by bribery. It is a piece of vandalism, another illustration of the helplessness of the public when unscrupulous capital organizes to plunder."

His demands for an official investigation led to the appointment of a grand jury in April. Then detectives confirmed his charges and more. Alderman Jaehne, they said, was a fence who did a big business in stolen goods. Caught with the loot in his home, Jaehne admitted to taking Sharp's bribe. Three other aldermen also confessed, hoping for light sentences. Six others escaped to Montreal, Canada.

Sharp was arrested outside his home as his coachman in a green suit with silver buttons opened his carriage door and Sharp ordered, "Central Park, James."

"Sorry, sir," interrupted one of the three waiting detectives, "but you've been indicted for bribery and you're wanted downtown."

"All right," said Sharp, confident he could bribe his way out of anything. "Jump in, gentlemen. Never mind Central Park, James. Drive to police headquarters."

That evening, the somewhat deflated streetcar magnate returned to his mansion on Twenty-third Street—free on fifty thousand dollars bail.

At the trial, the thirty-two-year-old prosecutor, De Lancey Nicoll, impressed Pulitzer as talented and incorruptible. The *World* applauded his forceful handling of the case and his resistance to strong political pressure and a fortune in bribes. All the men on trial were convicted. Jaehne got nine years in Sing Sing. Sharp, who got four years and a five-thousand-dollar fine, appealed the sentence. His ultimate fate would greatly affect Pulitzer.

During that same summer of 1886, Pulitzer was appalled by the deadly confrontation between police and striking workers in Chicago—known as the Haymarket Square Massacre. It followed on the heels of a terrible winter when thousands of the unemployed crowded bread lines and soup kitchens, which ran out of food. Labor leader Mary Jones recalled how, on Christmas Day, "hundreds of poverty stricken people in rags and tatters [protested by parading] on fashionable Prairie Avenue before the mansions of the rich and carrying the black flag [of anarchism]." This was an almost certain warning of violence.

"Mother" Jones, as the labor leader was affectionately known, feared as much, especially in a city she saw "divided into two angry camps. The working people on one side—hungry, cold, jobless, fighting gunmen and police clubs with bare hands." And on the other, wealthy and ruthless businessmen. Strikes recently organized by labor leaders had been brutally suppressed by Chicago's police chief, John Bonfield, and denounced by conservative newspapers as the work of traitors.

Anarchists fed the seething resentment of the poor by stressing the cruel inequities of capitalism at highly charged meetings that attracted thousands. On May 3, 1886, anarchist August Spies addressed some six thousand striking workmen outside the McCormick Harvester plant. Spies was a leader of the

International Working People's Association, which advocated using dynamite and assassination to achieve its aims. Now he simply encouraged the strikers to hold fast to their goal—an eight-hour workday. But as he spoke, scab laborers who had replaced strikers emerged from the plant, inciting some of the crowd to chase them back into the building, to smash windows, and to exchange gunfire with the police there to keep the peace. The skirmish left one striker dead and six badly wounded. Six policemen were also seriously injured.

The next evening, a few hundred people assembled in Chicago's Haymarket Square to protest the shooting. August Spies, the first speaker, stood on a wagon to address the crowd. He blamed Cyrus McCormick for "murdering our brothers," in the mistaken belief that six strikers had been killed the previous night, and called on the crowd to "destroy the hideous monster that seeks to destroy you."

He was followed by Albert Parsons, editor of *Alarm*, a journal advocating violence. Facing a crowd that had grown from hundreds to thousands, he warned them to arm themselves if they did not want their wives and children to die of hunger, or to be "killed or cut down like dogs in the street."

At 10:00 P.M., when a third speaker, English-born teamster Samuel Fielden, took over, it began to rain. Many of the crowd ran for shelter, leaving only two hundred or three hundred to hear him yell, "You have nothing more to do with the law! Throttle it, kill it, stab it, do everything you can to wound it!" Fielden continued to harangue the crowd until he saw a police captain at the head of 180 policemen moving toward him and ordering the crowd to disperse. Then he morphed into a peacenik, exclaimed, "We are peaceable," and jumped from the wagon.

Almost as he hit the ground, someone in the crowd threw a dynamite-filled bomb. It exploded among the police, killing one immediately, mortally wounding seven, and seriously injuring sixty-seven.

This devastating first use of dynamite as a weapon in the United States stunned and scared every survivor on the scene. But it was not enough to end the bloodshed. After a few moments, the police rallied and charged the crowd, firing their revolvers as they went, killing one civilian and wounding at least thirty-three.

Pulitzer's response was fast and frantic. He excoriated "foreign Anarchists who, having been forced out of Europe come to the United States bringing with them the insane passion for incendiarism, rapine and anarchy which they have cherished and fostered for years at home under a sense of tyranny and oppression. These pests of civilization have for some reason made their headquarters at Chicago. Mercy would be misplaced towards such men and none should be shown them. They [should be treated like] the savage Indian who invades a Western settlement with brand and tomahawk to burn and kill."

Afraid that Americans would not distinguish between these "foul" anarchists and honest workingmen seeking to better their conditions, he urged labor organizations to shun the anarchists and other radicals "as they would avoid contact with poisonous reptiles," and only go on strike as "a last resort and when sanctioned by enlightened public opinion."

Calling anarchists "dynamite demons," he blamed Illinois governor Richard J. Oglesby for "failure to promptly meet the uprising of the mob with military force." Finally, he assured his New York readers that the well-disciplined police and military would protect them from a similar fate.

Two days later a McDougall cartoon headlined "The Common Enemy—To Jail or the Gallows With Him!" appeared on page one. It showed a policeman grabbing what looked like a heavily armed minimaniac waving a flag marked "Down with Property!" and wearing a belt marked "Anarchist." At his feet were a burning brand and a dynamite bomb. A symbolic working woman looked on. The cartoon was captioned "AMERICAN LABOR—'Take Him Away, Officer. He's No Child of Mine.'"

When the *Chicago News* charged Pulitzer with libeling its governor and police, he fired back on May 11: "For fully ten years the Chicago police were threatened by these miscreants with dynamite bombs, and yet when moving last week to disperse an unlawful gathering of Anarchists a platoon of police exposed itself to an assault which killed or mangled fifty of its members. No police force ever behaved with more courage, but when we say that it was not equal to the emergency we mean that it did not profit by the knowledge that it ought to have possessed, and did not kill enough of the enemy to have a salutary effect on the country. The lesson of Chicago is that it is a fatal mistake to temporize with an organized body which openly proclaims that its interest is to destroy property, murder policemen and root out every vestige of law."

An unexpected attack on Pulitzer came from British newspapers, which had the gall to use the Chicago riot to discredit Gladstone's and Pulitzer's sympathy for the Irish cause. Quoting several of these slanted pieces in his editorial, Pulitzer wrote: "Nearly every English journal treats the outbreak as one for which the Irish-American portion of our population is responsible, and points to the Anarchists in this country as specimens of the sort of people to whom it is proposed to extend Home Rule." The *London Standard,* he continued, damned the rioters as part of "'the motley crowd that have fled from prisons in their own countries to find in America, pending the construction of an Irish Parliament, a secure resting place.'"

The *London Morning Post* conceded that the Chicago violence had no connection with Irish politics, but thought it might "'open the eyes of servile worshipers of Mr. Gladstone to the dangers of making any terms whatever with those who openly resist the law and employ dynamite in order to secure submission to their demands.'"

To exonerate the Irish and refute the British press, Pulitzer pointed out that in Chicago three of the "brave officers who lost their lives in the fight [later, five more died of injuries]—Deigan, Reddin and Shannon—were all Irish by birth or extraction." And that of fifty-one severely wounded policemen, thirty-two had unmistakably Irish names. While "among thirty-four wounded rioters and bystanders only seven names bear any evidence of Irish nationality. Let justice be done to all. So far from Ireland being a nest of Socialism, a recent investigation showed that there was only one Socialist organization in the country. That was in Dublin, but it had not a single Irish member." In this and future editorials Pulitzer did not distinguish among anarchists, Communists, and socialists, perhaps because in those days extremists in all three camps were inclined to violence.

The *World* continued to cover the riot's aftermath, noting that eight known anarchists had been held for trial. When it began in June, Pulitzer hoped that the law would "deal with them, sharply, justly. To send them to the gallows for murder would be a lesson that would save hundreds of lives."

Although the bomb thrower was never identified, seven were found guilty of "inflammatory speeches and publications" that incited the mob to violence. Judge Joseph E. Gary sentenced them to death, giving the eighth man, Oscar Neebe, fifteen years in prison. The sentences were upheld by the Illinois and U.S. Supreme Courts.

On November 11, 1887, four of the anarchists were hanged: August Spies, Adolph Fischer, George Engel, and Albert Parsons. Louis Lingg, the youngest and most fervent of the group, had already beaten the rope by exploding a dynamite cap in his mouth. Death sentences of the remaining two, Michael Schwab and Samuel Fielden, were commuted to life. Five years later the new Illinois governor John P. Altgeld, a Democrat, pardoned them, saying that a fair trial had been impossible with a prejudiced judge and a jury selected to convict, and that the "state had never discovered who threw the bomb which killed the policemen, and the evidence does not show any connection between the defendants, and the man who did throw it." Some papers branded Altgeld an anarchist-sympathizer and used the bloodshed caused by a small group of violent radicals as an excuse to attack all labor unions; employers used it to smash or discourage unions in their plants, and both state and federal courts used it to harass labor organizations.

Pulitzer had demonstrated an impetuous rush to judgment. Though calling for a fair trial, he had prejudged the accused men guilty. But he had not deserted the workers and gone over to the plutocrats. He proved it through his lifelong campaign launched—the summer of the Haymarket Square Massacre—against John D. Rockefeller and his monolithic company, Standard Oil.

After making a killing during the Civil War speculating in grain prices, Rockefeller had switched to oil, driving out or absorbing rivals until his Standard Oil trust had a virtual monopoly in oil production. Pulitzer predicted that when people looked back on the nineteenth century they'd be astonished to find that the United States had "tolerated the presence of the most gigantic, the most cruel, impudent, pitiless, and grasping monopoly that ever fastened upon a country."

President Cleveland had other things on his mind, briefly interrupting his workaholic routine to marry his ward, Frances Folsom, in the White House.

He was forty-nine, she twenty-two. Frances was the daughter of his deceased law partner, the likely father of the son whom Cleveland had acknowledged as his own during the scandal-ridden presidential election campaign. The Pulitzers didn't attend because Kate was expecting her fifth child any day. Two weeks after the president's wedding, she gave birth to a girl they named Edith.

Just one day later Pulitzer joined his friend Thomas Davidson for a month's sea voyage. Kate apparently was all for it, because he had worked himself to a frazzle. Getting away from it all was just what he needed. The insatiably curious publisher welcomed Davidson's company because, as Pulitzer had once implied, Davidson was the nearest thing to an encyclopedia, who knew all about everything.

As Pulitzer sought to get at the truth through his reporters, Davidson had pursued it through philosophers. Disappointed with philosophy, he switched to religion, spending a year in Greece studying and finally discounting the teachings of the Greek Orthodox Church. In Rome, after meeting the pope, he told a priest: "If you can prove to me that your church is the organ of the Divine, and the pope its mouthpiece, I will go to the Vatican and kiss his slipper." No kissing occurred. In England, Davidson helped to found the Fellowship of the New Life, an offshoot of the Socialistic Fabian Society of which playwright George Bernard Shaw was a prominent member.

Pulitzer had prepared for his departure by hiring two men to cover for him, enticing William Merrill, from the *Boston Herald*, as an editorial writer, and the socially connected and somewhat imperious Ballard Smith from Bennett's *New York Herald*, giving him the ominous title of acting editor—ominous, that is, for editor in chief Cockerill, who felt threatened with a man breathing down his neck who might be after his job. This was the start of Pulitzer's provocative practice of pitting one man against another—hoping to get the best out of both in their efforts to come out on top. It achieved mixed results, leading some to thoughts of homicide and in one case a mental breakdown.

Although Pulitzer was not around for the next month to witness the high tension he had caused in the newsroom, he continued to contribute to it from afar. He constantly cabled both of his newspapers with orders, admonitions, and questions, sending Cockerill, Smith, and Dillon into a flurry of anxious activity above and beyond their normal deadline duties. Even Davidson's stimulating conversation failed to distract Pulitzer from working while on the sea voyage.

In August he briefly joined his family on vacation at Lenox, Massachusetts, leaving them to attend Samuel Tilden's funeral in Yonkers, New York, and then was off to St. Louis to check on the progress of the *Post-Dispatch*. Dillon had done well. And there was no shortage of important news to fill both papers, including, in September, the end of the last major Indian war, when federal troops captured the Apache chief Geronimo.

The big sporting event of the year, also given prominent coverage in the *World*, was the first international polo match at Newport, Rhode Island, in which the Americans lost to the British, 10 to 4 and 14 to 2.

The hot political news was the closely contested mayoral race. Three men were running for mayor of New York City in 1886: a former cattle rancher from North Dakota, Republican Theodore Roosevelt, aged twenty-seven; a highly principled Democratic former U.S. congressman, Abram Hewitt, aged sixty-four; and the United Labor [Workers'] Party candidate, a reform-minded economist and author, Henry George, aged forty-seven. Not a dud among them, but Pulitzer dismissed Roosevelt as a wealthy young man "who is something of a reformer, a very good lecturer and a first-class bear hunter."

Many workers supported George as their champion. And Pulitzer admired him as humane and well-meaning, but thought Hewitt the better man. At the risk of alienating most of his readers, he backed Hewitt. The rest of the New York press were terrified of George, fearing, with recent memories of the Chicago riot, that he would encourage bomb-throwing radicals. The *World* alone treated George as a decent man and viable candidate, to such an extent that Davidson, who favored him, wrote to Pulitzer: "You are doing excellently well by George, better than if you openly supported him."

When it seemed George might win, Roosevelt was asked to withdraw to avoid the horror of the city being ruled by George, the "anarchist" and a mob of revolutionaries. He refused. But enough of Roosevelt's Republican supporters switched to Hewitt the Democrat to put him over the top.

Hewitt won with 90,552 votes. George followed with 68,110, and Roosevelt came last with 60,435.

Since taking over the *World*, Pulitzer had been a major factor in electing the president of the United States and the governor of New York State, and now his man ruled New York's City Hall: three in a row.

Late in October Pulitzer prepared to celebrate his fourth triumph: the Statue of Liberty. Only his persistence had made it possible. Bennett of the *Herald* had suggested leaving the statue in France and erecting instead a small statue of Lafayette, the French nobleman who fought beside the colonists against the British in the American Revolution. The *New York Times* had called the "bronze female" too expensive even for a "true patriot in the present state of our finances."

But Pulitzer had prevailed.

A steady drizzle descended on Manhattan on the morning of October 28, but as one reporter noted, "human joy has rarely been so bright." Some twenty thousand people marched south from Madison Square past President Cleveland's reviewing stand, to celebrate the unveiling of the Statue of Liberty on Bedloe's Island (renamed Liberty Island in 1956). The U.S. Marine Band, the Sons of Lafayette, New York's National Guard—"The Gallant Seventy-first"—led the way, followed by the drill team escorting the coach that carried George Washington to his inauguration. Almost anyone with a French connection joined the parade, members of the Alsace-Lorraine Union, three culinary societies, and several marching bands playing the "Marseillaise." There were so many marching groups—Freemasons, Columbia University students, black bands, firemen pulling the city's oldest fire engine, a small boy in full-dress naval uniform escorting a model of the *Monitor* (the iron warship used by the U.S. Navy in the Civil War), and wagons carrying wounded veterans—that Cleveland hurried off before he'd greeted them all, to make the unveiling ceremony on Bedloe's Island on time.

As the island was too small to contain the huge crowd expected, Pulitzer had hired two steamboats for his staff and their families to watch from offshore. They were joined by hundreds of other boats, yachts, steamers, fishing boats, ferryboats, and rowboats crammed with people with the same intention. Pulitzer's family watched the ceremony from aboard a yacht, while he, the man who had made this day possible, sat beneath the statue, listening to the speeches. Said Frenchman Ferdinand de Lesseps, engineer and promoter of the Panama Canal now under construction: "In landing beneath its rays, people will know that they have reached a land where individual initiative is developed in all its power." A sentiment Pulitzer surely shared.

An inevitable mishap made the day even more memorable. Standing 302 feet on its pedestal, the statue was too immense to be completely covered. Instead, a red, white, and blue tarpaulin had been draped over the head alone (for which the sculptor's mother had been the model, while his mistress had modeled for the body). A man stood ready to pull the rope unveiling the rest of the statue's head the moment the keynote speaker, a U.S. senator, finished his speech. However, when the senator paused for dramatic effect, the man on the rope mistakenly thought he had finished—and pulled. Liberty was prematurely revealed in all her glory. Cannons fired, and ships let rip with a cacophony of horns, an orchestral version of bedlam. Despite the chatter and guffaws that followed, the senator continued to produce what seemed to be a filibuster. Eventually he resumed his seat, order was restored, and more speakers took their turn.

Pulitzer applauded Cleveland's speech, which concluded, "We will not forget that Liberty has here made her home." But it was little more than a polite gesture. In future editorials, disappointed in the man he had elected, Pulitzer berated him as a misinformed and poorly educated man, masquerading as a Democrat while pandering to Republicans and their business lobby on Wall Street.

Pulitzer was permanently recognized for his vital role in bringing the Statue of Liberty to America—in the statue's toe. A golden rivet engraved with his name was driven into it, like a giant splinter, an honor he shared with the sculptor, Bartholdi. Later, a Pulitzer postage stamp came out with the statue in the background.

A Philadelphia friend, George Childs, had once called Pulitzer "the Napoleon of journalists." Now, fearing that an overworked Pulitzer was heading for his Waterloo, Childs wrote to Kate: "What is fame and fortune without health?" and urged her to persuade Pulitzer to take it easy, to leave the details to others while remaining in overall charge of his papers. "Then we can see him enjoy the results of his wonderful brain and energy."

But Pulitzer seemed less concerned with fame and fortune than with his mission. His friend Henry Watterson had defined a good newspaper as one that gives a true account of yesterday. Pulitzer took that for granted. To him, a paper's highest mission was to render public service, concerning itself with what should happen in the future and trying to make it so.

With such a goal how could he—the greatest journalist on earth, according to the Texas Newspaper Union—think of resting?

Even Kate failed to persuade him to relax, writing in despair to a friend that Joseph "is pushing his body in a manner no human being can stand."

Kate herself was part of the problem, at times driving him crazy by her extravagance and by responding to what he saw as his tolerance and generosity with indifference or anger. Too agitated or preoccupied to confront her, he sent her a memo expressing his complaints and suggesting six rules to help her curb her spending. It must have been a terrific shock. Up to now she had seen herself as the complaisant one in their partnership, subject to his high-strung, perfectionist personality and unexpected fits of rage.

The rules, he wrote, "are just intended to bring you to your senses and possibly to the appreciation of my intelligence and forbearance in the past, and also to an appreciation of the very large dividends I have given to you with pleasure on my part for your pleasure. The least you could have done would have been to give me a few words of appreciation, [but] instead of getting them I have received only blows, and hurts and injuries."

He pointed out that he gave her an allowance of a hundred thousand dollars a year for her "clothes and finery, and that of the youngest two children," and agreed to continue paying her traveling expenses and stays at Aix-les-Bains "or anywhere else you go for your health strictly." But he refused to finance her trips to Paris, where, he complained, she had run up "large dressmakers' bills kept unpaid for a year or two and then dumped upon me."

At the end of his memo to Kate, Pulitzer took most of the sting out of it in a remarkable about-face. "Strictly speaking," he concluded, "you can do with your own money just what you like and disregard my wishes."

Putting his complaint in writing seemed to have cooled him off.

CHAPTER 11

Nellie Bly Goes Crazy

1887
—
39 to 40 years old

How Pulitzer's vindictive rivals Dana and Bennett would have mangled and misinterpreted his memo to Kate if they had gotten hold of it, portraying him, no doubt, as a weakling afraid to criticize his wife—except in print or at a distance. As it was, they seized every chance to humiliate him personally and to discredit the *World* as a lying scandal sheet. When Bennett got wind of a fistfight between Pulitzer and a reporter, he published a mocking account in the *Herald*.

Disappointed when Pulitzer pulled him from a choice assignment—covering the Montreal winter carnival—the reporter, Joseph Howard, had vainly tried to argue his way back on to it. An exchange of expletives was followed by an exchange of punches that sent both men's glasses flying. Unable to see his opponent clearly, each went on hands and knees to feel for his glasses. Pulitzer found and replaced his first, lifted Howard—who was quite hefty—by his collar and the seat of his pants, and tossed him from the room. Howard then continued out of the building and of Pulitzer's employ to pursue a successful journalistic career elsewhere.

According to the *Herald's* savagely satirical version of February 9, 1887, the fight erupted because Pulitzer had cut Howard's salary for refusing "to fill a vast area of vacant space in the journal of 'brag, swagger, inflation and mendacity.'" Pulitzer wore "the spangled tights now so familiar through exhibitions in his great feat of jumping from one side of the fence to the other." And, during their fistfight, when Howard swung, "as the room is small the blow necessarily landed on Mr. Pulitzer's smeller." During the second round, "Howard let out and Mr. Pulitzer dodged—he learned the trick during the few weeks he served

Joseph Pulitzer
at forty in 1887.

in the rear ranks of the Lincoln cavalry" (a false implication of cowardice in the Civil War).

In March Pulitzer was shocked to read what he thought was a false report in his paper of trouble in the marriage of the American beauty Jennie Jerome and Lord Randolph Churchill, leader of the British Conservatives. It was too late to kill it, but he cabled his London correspondent on March 28, 1887: "Jerome-Churchill story very wrong. Let them alone. Be careful avoid scandal gossip."

Soon after, he got a letter from Jennie's irate father, Leonard Jerome, founder of the American Jockey Club and part owner of the *New York Times*. "It is not the first time the World has published similar dispatches & not the first time you have sent me your regrets," he wrote. "I know you would not willingly publish scandalous articles about me & my children even if true [he was wrong there!], but when it turns out that they are manufactured, I think you will agree that something more than 'regrets' is in order. Imagine a perfect stranger calling on you half a dozen times &, finally getting in, states his business to be to ascertain how you were getting on with Mrs. Pulitzer! That's your

London correspondent. I should like you to ask Mrs. Pulitzer what she thinks of him."

It hit home: Pulitzer apologized to Jerome, had Ballard Smith apologize, too, and even published a retraction of the story.

In fact, the story was accurate. The marriage had been on the rocks for years, and the two lived virtually separate lives. Randolph Churchill had contracted syphilis before their marriage from an alcoholic-induced encounter with a prostitute. He had his first paralytic attack in 1881. And Jennie was so notorious for her interest in other women's men that she was nicknamed "Lady Jane Snatcher." Among her slew of mostly royal or aristocratic lovers were Count Kinsky, Baron Hirsch, Lord Dunraven, Herbert von Bismarck, American politician Bourke Cockran, William Waldorf Astor, and the prince of Wales, later King Edward VII. "The future king frequently took Jennie to lunch in a private restaurant, one wall of which opened up to reveal a double bed." Yet the Churchills, like most of their circle, considered adultery preferable to divorce and were still married in 1895, when Lord Randolph died insane.

Surprisingly, though Pulitzer despised Americans who married off their daughters to English aristocrats, he handled the Jerome-Churchill situation with kid gloves. Perhaps it was because Churchill as a working aristocrat had made something of his life and, better still, as a moderate Conservative supported Irish home rule.

That cause took Pulitzer and his wife to England in the spring to present a bronze bust to the Liberal prime minister, William Gladstone, for his role in advocating home rule for Ireland. Contributions from more than ten thousand *World* readers had helped to pay for the award. But first the couple did Paris, buying paintings, attending a charity ball, and attending a fete to benefit the ambulance service. At Tiffany's, Joseph bought Kate a diamond necklace and jewelry for their seven-year-old daughter Lucille. Then they moved on to the health spa at Aix for two weeks. During much of June they toured England with James McLane and his wife. McLane, their family doctor in America, had become a family friend.

Pulitzer and Kate finally met Gladstone at his suburban London home on July 9, 1887. Presenting the bust to him, Pulitzer said: "10,689 people of the first city of America ask the first citizen of England to accept this gift as a tribute to your determination that the principles of liberty and justice, which have made England so free and great, shall no longer be denied to Ireland. Americans know how your people have sympathized with every struggle against tyranny in Europe. Why then refuse a parliament to Ireland? It will never be possible to convince true Americans that your demand for an Irish parliament for Irish affairs is not right and just."

The Tory British press went ballistic in reporting the event, damning Gladstone and demeaning Pulitzer, who gleefully reported the reaction he had aroused in a page one story on July 12, 1887, headed:

IT ROILS THE BRITISH SOUL.

THE GLADSTONE TESTIMONIAL RAISES A
BIG RUMPUS IN LONDON.

Savage Attacks upon the Grand Old Man
and His American Friends by All the
Tory Organs—The Irish Cause Ridiculed
and Its Supporters Classed as Fenians—
Cut to the Quick by Gladstone's Speech

"The Gladstone testimonial presentation has made a great sensation. The *Times* [of London] in particular is enraged. It gives this morning over five columns to the subject in an ugly, angry editorial, and says, 'The graven image which Mr. Gladstone accepts in the great Irish cause was the happy thought of Mr. Joseph Pulitzer, a Bavarian, who conducts a New York newspaper largely dependent upon the Irish for support. Conceive the depths to which a man must have sunk before he can contemplate such an offering as this with anything but repugnance and disgust. Conceive the insult to the American people conveyed in the assumption that when they wish to honor a man they can do nothing better than scrape together 600 pounds by months of frantic adjuration in the New York *World* and by charging for the admission to dancing and fireworks!'"

The *World* editorial continued, quoting the English *St. James Gazette*: "'The intensity of the American editor is equalled by his perseverance, and he is now repaid for all his labors. He had succeeded in extracting from Mr. Gladstone a speech more furious, unscrupulous and shameless than any which he has previously uttered [supporting Irish home rule] and it is the duty of the Government to redouble its efforts to crush the treasonable organization which has gained so unscrupulous a recruit.'"

The liberal *Pall Mall Gazette* ridiculed the *Times* as "silly and too enraged in its editorial opinions to be tolerated by people of any common sense. We probably know a thousand times more about Mr. Joseph Pulitzer in this office than all the *Times* staff put together. We could write a detailed biography of him from the time he began to live in St. Louis up to the day on which he addressed Mr. Gladstone and we say that the *Times* account of the testimonial is mostly bosh."

Pulitzer had good reason to despise the *Times*, which had recently shown its bile and bias by publishing a letter purportedly written by the Irish leader Charles Parnell approving the murder of an English politician in Dublin's Phoenix Park. The letter proved to be a forgery.

Energized by his European trip, Pulitzer considered starting a publishing empire on both sides of the Atlantic. Already toying with the idea of buying a controlling interest in the *Chicago Times* for three hundred thousand dollars, he told his London correspondent to keep him informed of a likely English newspaper up for sale.

Though he didn't buy an English paper or the *Chicago Times*, he copied Dana, who had come out with an evening *Sun*, by publishing a four-page evening edition of the *World*, matching Dana's price of a penny a copy. Then Pulitzer followed up with a supplement for the Sunday *World*. Both were financial successes but, wrote biographer Allen Churchill, "he cared little for the Evening and Sunday editions beyond expecting them to prosper. He reserved all his interest and affection for the Morning edition. The others were commercial ventures. The Morning contained his soul."

Early in September a distraught young woman named Elizabeth Cochrane, desperate for work after someone had stolen her purse containing her life savings of a hundred dollars, confronted Cockerill in his office. The vivacious twenty-three-year-old explained how as a reporter on the *Pittsburgh Dispatch*, using the pen name Nellie Bly, she wrote about her personal experiences—her life in Mexico; what it was like to work in a factory; and how, at fourteen, during her mother's divorce trial, she had testified against her drunken stepfather. This was not her first attempt to work for Pulitzer. Previously, having heard that he was sponsoring a balloon flight from St. Louis, she had written to him repeatedly, offering to join the flight crew and report her experiences, but never received a reply. Now she handed Cockerill a list of other story ideas. Sympathizing with her plight, he gave her twenty-five dollars to tide her over and promised to consider her proposals.

Her timing was perfect. Pulitzer had been wondering how to investigate a tipoff that mental asylum nurses on nearby Blackwell's Island (renamed Welfare Island in 1921 and Roosevelt Island in 1973) mistreated their helpless patients. Among Bly's suggestions passed on to him was for her to feign insanity, get hospitalized, and then report her experiences as a patient. A great idea, said Pulitzer. It would test her reporting prowess and, if she pulled it off, might shame public officials into reforming the place. Realizing that once inside as a certified lunatic Bly might have trouble getting out, Pulitzer promised to rescue her after a certain time.

She prepared for the assignment like a method actress, reading ghost stories to scare herself into the role, and rehearsing before a mirror by making grotesque faces. Then she put on old clothes, mussed up her hair, and went to live in a home for women at 84 Second Avenue. Her mad act, to get used to the role, terrified the other residents, one whispering, "I'm afraid to stay with such a crazy being in the house." Another said with a gasp, "She'll murder us before morning!" And she featured in a third woman's nightmare. The next day, someone called a cop, who took Bly before Judge Patrick Duffy in Essex Market police court.

Despite her attempt to appear unappetizing, she looked so attractive that Duffy assumed she must be, in his words, "somebody's darling." This unjudicial remark caused titters in the courtroom, and Bly, a great giggler, almost broke up. But she managed to hide her amusement. She answered the judge's questions in an Hispanic accent picked up during her trip to Mexico, saying that she came from Cuba but knew nothing else about herself. Though he didn't think she was insane, he assumed from her distracted manner that she had been drugged, and sent her to be examined by experts in Bellevue Hospital. Then he asked court reporters to publish her description, hoping their accounts would reach the "somebody" in her life, who would then claim her.

Rival papers delighted Pulitzer by obliging the judge and giving his imminent exposé great advance publicity.

Dana's *Sun* splashed it on the front page for September 25, 1887, headed, "Who Is This Insane Girl?" and described Bly as a "comely" young woman with a pleasing voice and cultivated manner whose mental state baffled Bellevue doctors. "The most peculiar case," they agreed, "that ever came into the hospital." Bennett's *Herald* interviewed the head of the hospital's insane division, Dr. William Braisted. He discounted drugs or poison as the cause of her apparent dementia, and concluded that "her delusions, her dull apathetic condition, the muscular twitching of her hands and arms and her loss of memory, all indicate hysteria." The next evening's *Telegram* got Braisted to confirm his diagnosis that the mystery woman was undoubtedly insane.

Only one of the five experts who examined her was not fooled. William O'Rourke, Bellevue's warden, called her a humbug. But he was outnumbered, and the others committed Bly to the mental asylum on Blackwell's Island, in the East River.

Her first shock, as she later wrote, was the sight of the monsters who held her fate in their hands: "coarse, massive" females who "expectorated tobacco juice about on the floor in a manner more skillful than charming."

A few days later a rival investigating reporter appeared, and during his escorted tour of the hospital he came across Bly, recognized her, and almost blew her cover. In a frantic whisper, she begged him not to. He was either a good sport or realized he'd eventually get a better story by letting her keep up the pretense, so he pretended not to know her.

After Bly had spent ten days in the hellhole, Pulitzer, as promised, sent an attorney to get her out. He assured the authorities that he had located friends to take care of her, and they let her go.

World cartoonist Walt McDougall, who went to the asylum with the attorney, planning to illustrate Bly's upcoming exposé, got a vivid picture of her fellow inmates, which he later described. While waiting in a courtyard, he was almost stripped naked by "a raging crowd of female maniacs, idiots and plain bugs. The way the mob rushed me, one would have thought I was the first train out after a subway hold-up."

Bly's impassioned account of the cruelties inflicted on women lunatics impressed Pulitzer. He admired her guts and colloquial style, and approved the headlines that told how, by fooling judges, reporters, and medical experts into believing her mad, she had been able to expose the asylum's awful conditions.

The first of her two articles appeared on October 9, 1887, headed simply:

BEHIND ASYLUM BARS.

Calling the place "a human rat trap," Bly told how vicious nurses goaded helpless patients and dragged demented old women into closets, where their cries were forcibly stifled. One of her own ordeals was having to share towels with "crazy patients who had the most dangerous eruptions all over their faces."

She came across sane foreign women treated as lunatics because no one in authority spoke their language, so couldn't understand that they were completely rational. The treatment—enough to drive anyone balmy—included the dreaded cold bath which Bly endured when a nurse suddenly poured "one after the other, three buckets of water over my head—ice-cold water, too—and into my eyes, my ears, my nose and my mouth. I think I experienced the sensation of a drowning person as they dragged me, gasping, shivering and quaking from the tub. For once I did look insane."

Two days before Bly's second and final piece appeared in the *World*, Dana's rival *Sun* took up the story and went to town with it, using six columns on the front page, headlined:

PLAYING MAD WOMAN

Nellie Bly Too Sharp for the Island Doctors

Nine [Ten in fact] Days' Life in Calico

The Sun Finishes Up its Story of the "Pretty Crazy Girl"

The account included the reactions and rebuttals of the asylum physicians and staff to Nellie Bly's exposé.

The next day Pulitzer responded to the *Sun's* account with the following headlines:

ALL THE DOCTORS FOOLED
THEY TRY TO EXPLAIN NELLIE BLY'S STAY IN THE INSANE ASYLUM
Six Columns of Excuses, Apologies, Defenses—Somebody Ought
to Have Found Out that the Plucky Representative of "The World"
Was Not Insane, Of course, but Nobody Is to Blame, as Usual.

Newspapers throughout the United States and Canada lauded Bly's work, and expressed dismay that so many experts could be fooled. It reminded the *Hamilton Times* of Canada of the days when "men and women were sent to insane asylums by doctors in collusion with relatives interested in having them put out of the way."

Columnist Bessie Bramble, a former colleague of Bly's at the *Pittsburgh Dispatch*, believed that Bly had boosted the prospects of female journalists by showing "that cool courage, consummate craft and investigating ability are not monopolized by the brethren of the profession. By her clever woman's wit she has shown how easily men can be humbugged and imposed upon—and men hitherto deemed smart and experts at their business at that."

In November, two weeks after Bly's story had appeared, Assistant District Attorney Vernon Davis headed a grand jury to investigate conditions at the Blackwell's Island asylum, and Bly accepted his invitation to join them.

She wasn't surprised to find that the authorities had cleaned up the place, improved the food, and fired or hidden the sadistic nurses and foreign patients. Yet it was still a hellhole.

After their inspection, the grand jury recommended: more money to care for the insane; better food; to reduce overcrowding; to stop locking the ward doors, which created fire hazards; and to hire a more qualified staff, including women doctors to care for women patients.

On December 18, 1887, the authorities approved a 57 percent increase in the appropriations to improve conditions on Blackwell's Island, prompting Bly to report: "On the strength of my story the committee of appropriations provides $1 million more than ever given before, for the benefit of the insane."

Pulitzer's approval of the outcome was reflected in his paper's headline "The *World* Their Savior . . . How Nellie Bly's World Will Help the City's Insane."

He readily accepted Cockerill's proposal to hire Bly permanently and welcomed her as "a very bright and very plucky new member of the staff." After rewarding her with "a handsome check," he said: "She is well educated and has a great future before her."

McDougall, the cartoonist who accompanied her on all future assignments, explained why Pulitzer found her so valuable: "Her appearance was at the precise moment when sensations were coming so fast and so plentiful as to begin to pall and a fillip was needed. This was supplied by femininity. A voyage through the Minetta sewer or a fake bomb attack on a British man-o'-war no longer stirred the jaded sense, but done by a girl with a name like Nellie Bly any live story was bound to register."

Pulitzer's perpetual cry was for someone to suggest and produce great new story ideas. Nellie Bly provided both, which naturally exasperated his rivals, especially Dana.

As implacable enemies, he and Pulitzer stuck to Dr. Johnson's dictum that to treat your adversary with respect is to give him an advantage to which he is not entitled. Yet they had similar tastes and political views. Both were antislavery, supported Horace Greeley's reform movement, favored Tilden over Hayes, and regarded Hayes's election as a dirty fraud. Both were highly intelligent, well educated, spoke several languages, and believed that newspaper writing should be simple, arresting, and clear. But in competing for the same readers they descended to such childish exchanges as Dana claiming he had never told a lie and Pulitzer responding, *"That's a lie!"*

Their sneers turned to snarls during the fall election campaign for New York district attorney. Pulitzer favored the incumbent, De Lancey Nicoll, who had triumphed in prosecuting crooked alderman Jaehne and financier Jacob Sharp. Though Nicoll was a Democrat, he had been rejected by Tammany Hall as beyond their corrupt control, so Republicans and independents had nominated him. Dana also had favored Nicoll until a week after Pulitzer came out with his competing *Evening World*. Then Dana had dropped Nicoll to back Tammany's choice, John R. Fellows, who was also supported by President Cleveland and Mayor Hewitt.

After reproving Cleveland and Hewitt, men he had helped to victory, Pulitzer challenged "the vicious editor of the *Sun*" to explain why he had changed sides. Dana shot back on October 18: "We have withdrawn from our support of Mr. Nicoll because we distrust the *World* and its motives, and more than suspicion exists to indicate what these motives are. Col. Slayback was shot and killed, under shocking circumstances, in the editorial rooms of Mr. Pulitzer's newspaper, by Col. Cockerill, then as now Mr. Pulitzer's editor. It has been charged that the reason why the St. Louis Grand Jury failed to indict Col. Cockerill for murder, was that such was the degree of Mr. Pulitzer's hold upon the District-Attorney of St. Louis and his administration that the indictment was frustrated. It is our manifest duty to take account of these facts in the light of the unprecedented, frantic and astounding effort which the same men are now making to obtain what is virtually the control of the District Attorney's office and look with horror upon the contingency that an enmeshed captive of the *World* should fill an office which would give it any peculiar power over the criminal prosecutions of New York County."

"Malicious lies," Pulitzer replied. "About what might be expected from Charles Ananias Dana. A mendacious blackguard who is capable of any amount of distortion of facts in an effort to avenge himself in a journalistic rivalry in which, aided by his own supreme folly, he had suffered destitution. The revival of the St. Louis affair is worthy of an assaulter of women and a mortgaged, broken-down calumniator in the last agonies of humiliation. Two grand juries, composed of citizens of every shade of opinion, thoroughly investigated the case of Mr. Cockerill and refused to return a bill. The public will judge this unscrupulous performance as it has judged his other acts of cowardice, malice and mendacity."

There was a brief pause in the mutual recriminations until Pulitzer's *Evening World* began to outsell Dana's *Evening Sun*, when Dana took another potshot at his enemy by inflating a minor mishap into a calamity. "How odd it was," he wrote in the *Sun* of October 28, 1887, "for that truck load of unsalable *Evening Worlds* to break down in front of Newspaper Row! News of it set the whole town roaring with laughter yesterday. The bluster and brag of our contemporary mystified a great many persons who see how tame and tedious the *Evening World* is and could not understand what gave it the circulation its owner boasted it possessed."

Next day, referring to the ongoing election campaign, Dana began a series of anti-Semitic jibes: "The boss behind Nicoll is Judas Pulitzer, who exudes the venom of a snake and wields the bludgeon of a bully. He has accepted the candidacy of Nicoll from the Republicans with as much thankfulness as in the days when he cringed for a nickel on the barroom floor. This Dick Turpin of journalism, this contemporary Judas has not even the sensibility of his prototype."

Soon after, when Dana attended a mass meeting to support the Democratic–Tammany Hall candidate, his paper reported that Dana was greeted with enthusiastic cheers.

Not so, according to a *World* reporter who covered the affair: he was hissed. Pulitzer took his reporter's word for it, calling the sixty-eight-year-old a dotard and finding nothing strange in Dana being hissed: "They know Dana's record as a Republican, a tool of Jim Fisk [a crooked financier shot to death by a business associate] and Jay Gould. How humiliating it would be to Ananias, if he had even the sensibility of an armadillo, to know that the men he seeks to serve despise him. Hissed in the home of his supposed friends! Poor, despised, disgraced, old Ananias!"

Early that summer Dana had written that Pulitzer "came to this country, not to promote the cause of his race or his native land, but to push the fortunes of that part of Jewry which is situated over the soles of his boots and under the hat that covers his head." On election day, Dana reprinted an article from the *Hebrew Standard* that supported Fellows and attacked Pulitzer. It read: "We Jews have a special interest in this would-be 'Sahib' of the Bohemian tribe. He happens to be of Jewish extraction, which he denies. The man who will deny his race and religion for the sake of ambition, social standing, or whatever motive, will betray his political friends, will betray his party, if his aspiration is served thereby."

Dana's comment followed: "The Jews of New York have no reason to be ashamed of Judas Pulitzer if he has denied his race and religion. The shame rests exclusively on himself. The insuperable obstacle in the way of his social progress is not the fact that he is a Jew, but in certain offensive personal qualities. His face is repulsive, not because the physiognomy is Hebraic, but because it is Pulitzeresque. Cunning, malice, falsehood, treachery, dishonesty, greed, and venal self-abasement have stamped their unmistakable traits. No art can eradicate them. Jewish citizens have the same interest as all other intelligent, self-respecting and law-abiding people in the defeat of Pulitzer and his young dupe, Nicoll. The Jewish vote will contribute very largely to that."

Pulitzer was reluctant to discuss his religious beliefs even in private. His wife and children were Episcopalians. If he felt allegiance to any religion, he kept it to himself. He did not doubt that his father was a Jew, but it is possible he mistakenly thought his mother, Louise Berger, had always been a Catholic. Previous biographers believed her to be a Catholic, but recent research by András Csillag, a Hungarian scholar, shows she was Jewish.

One of Pulitzer's secretaries, Harold Stanley Pollard, believed he shared Disraeli's view that all sensible men have the same religion, and sensible men never tell. In fact, Pulitzer appears to have been an open-minded agnostic, critical at times, for example, of the Mormons, but on political, not religious grounds—for being unpatriotic.

Ignoring Dana's attempts to bait him with religious slurs, Pulitzer put his heart into the local political fight, which, even excluding the mud slung by the two feuding editors, was one of the dirtiest in the city's history.

On November 8, the night of the election, Dana waited in his office, relishing the early reports that his man, Fellows, was winning. Meanwhile, Pulitzer was a whirlwind in his newsroom, feverishly energetic, interrupting an editorial he was composing to rush to pick up AP copy with the latest results, and giving almost nonstop instructions to his staff.

Shortly after midnight he knew the worst: his man had lost.

The final vote was: Fellows, 99,798; Nicoll, 77,556.

Dana had triumphed, and wasted no time in moving in for the kill. Even the *Sun*'s headlines that morning were aimed at Pulitzer:

DEMOCRACY TRIUMPHS

Traitors and Renegades are Swept
From the Board.

JOHN R. FELLOWS ELECTED.

He Beats Pulitzer's Dude
by 20,000 Plurality.

THE PEOPLE REBUKE THE LIARS

"Liar" was the least of the epithets Dana flung at Pulitzer: he was also a "treacherous, venomous, greedy, junk dealer."

Dana compared him to the Old Testament character Haman, an enemy of the Jews who ended on the gallows he had prepared for someone else. And suggested that, like Haman, Pulitzer be given "no more rope than is necessary for the final act of his career." Then he addressed his defeated opponent directly:

"And now, Pulitzer, a word with you!" he wrote. "You stand before this community in the same startling light that you stood in some years ago in St. Louis when your career of scandal and blackmail culminated in murder. You have reached the apogee of remunerative infamy here without having had to resort to any form of homicide. That you are here is indisputable, and that the public has found you out is obvious. Perhaps your lot will be like that of the mythical unfortunate of the same race you belong to and deny, that weird creation of medieval legend, a creation, by the way, far more prepossessing than you are—we mean, The Wandering Jew! [strangely prophetic words]. In that case it may shortly please the inscrutable Providence, which has chastened us with your presence, to give you that stern and dreadful signal—'Move on, Pulitzer, move on!'"

Pulitzer's editorial response was bolstered by the news that the World's circulation had reached 317,940 daily, "the largest ever printed by any newspaper in the world, so far as our knowledge extends," while the Sun's, of barely 100,000, was declining.

The next day, Pulitzer wrote: "For nearly three weeks, the New York Sun, arrayed upon the side of the worst elements in our politics, after a career of unparalleled treachery, has teemed with the vilest abuse of the World and its editor. The editor especially appreciates the agonized heart-cry of Mr. Dana, which appears in yesterday's issue of the Sun, in the midst of a literary muckheap. 'We wish, Pulitzer, that you had never come.'

"From his innermost soul the broken and humiliated editor of the Sun wishes that the regeneration of the World had never taken place. That the discriminating public should prefer the World to his vile sheet he has held as a case for a quarrel with the editor of the World—such a quarrel as only a jealous bankrupt can make with the successful rival around the corner.

"Sad, no doubt, Mr. Dana is, that somebody came who could provide the New York public with the newspaper which it wanted. But the man is here, and he will remain. The World has never advocated a bad cause nor proved recreant to a good one. It will continue to war against corruptionists with renewed vigor. It rests upon a solid foundation of Honesty and Public Service and against it the disappointed, malice-cankered, envious sons of darkness cannot prevail."

Nicoll went on to be a high-priced corporation lawyer. Fellows proved to be an honest and effective district attorney.

Pulitzer regretted having turned his paper into a political organ during the recent election, and was deeply disappointed when his man lost. As he emerged from his office, the newsroom staff looked up to note his mood.

"Gentlemen," he said, "we have been getting out a fine political paper. From now on I want a fine newspaper every day!"

Even more distressing to Pulitzer than Dana's vitriolic contempt and the failure of his political favorite was the recent death in jail while awaiting a retrial of crooked financier Jacob Sharp. Many blamed Pulitzer for putting him there and even held him responsible for the man's fatal heart attack. Pulitzer took the criticism hard. He was still disturbed about it years later when he told his secretary Alleyne Ireland that he suspected the incident had triggered his subsequent breakdown and the onset of his blindness.

As Ireland recalled in his memoirs, Pulitzer said to him: "'The World had been conducting a vigorous campaign against municipal corruption in New York—a campaign which ended in the arrest of a financier who had bought the votes of an alderman in order to get a street railroad franchise.' At this point Pulitzer paused. His jaws set and his expression became stern, almost fierce, as he added: 'The man died in jail of a broken heart, and I . . . and I . . . I was, of course, violently attacked; and it was a period of terrible strain for me. What with the anxiety and overwork I began to suffer from insomnia, and that soon produced a bad condition of my nerves. I always read every line of editorial copy. When I picked up the sheets I was astonished to find that I could hardly see the writing, let alone read it. I thought it was probably due to indigestion or some other temporary cause, and said nothing about it.'"

He returned to the two-hundred-thousand-dollar three-story mansion he had recently bought at 70 East 55th Street. Next morning his sight was no better.

As he later told his secretary Ireland, "On my way downtown I called in at an oculist's [Dr. Herman Knapp]. He examined my eyes and then told me to go home and remain in bed in a darkened room for six weeks." He took the advice.

News of his illness spread to Washington, and Secretary of the Navy Whitney wrote to Kate: "Is it true that Mr. Pulitzer is seriously ill? I heard from a mutual friend in strictest confidence. I sincerely hope not." Pulitzer dictated a reply: "I am not quite dead yet. It is simply a bad case of overwork. You had better take heed yourself and take things easy."

Dr. McLane, his affectionate friend who was also the family doctor, kept him company on many dark days and nights. When the six weeks were up the oculist reexamined Pulitzer, diagnosed a ruptured blood vessel in one eye, and ordered him to stop work entirely and to take it easy for six months in the California sun.

To Pulitzer that seemed almost like a death sentence.

CHAPTER 12

Tries to Save His Sight

1888

—

40 to 41 years old

Hoping to save his sight and his sanity, Pulitzer, with his wife, children, and a small entourage, sought respite in Monterey, California. They traveled by train in a private coach, and stopped at New Orleans en route to visit Kate's relatives. In California, ensconced in a suite at the Hotel Del Monte, Pulitzer put his secretary Charles Merrill to work sending crates of oranges to his friends and dictating replies to the many letters of sympathy and advice. His doctor friend McLane wrote to say how much he missed their conversations and to thank him for the gift of a clock, the striking of which "reminds me of your generous loving-kindness to me." And the *World*'s business manager, George Turner, begged him to stop worrying about the paper and recommended a long sea voyage to isolate him from the paper's problems.

But even the sunshine and sea breezes failed to divert Pulitzer from his work. He worried that Cockerill might be neglecting the paper to entertain his recently acquired wife, Leonara Barner, an actress young enough to be his daughter. And when he heard that his London correspondent, Tracy Greaves, had splurged on cables and sent a reporter to Berlin on his own initiative, Pulitzer fired him. Back came a letter from Greaves explaining his "mistakes" and recalling that during their face-to-face conversations, Pulitzer was always "kind and considerate." Just the right touch: Pulitzer rehired him.

In February, partly due to pressure from Pulitzer, the New York Senate Committee began investigating John D. Rockefeller and his Standard Oil trust. According to the World, he faced the group, immaculately dressed in a frock coat, looking at them with "sad and dreamy" eyes, answering the toughest questions in "a manner which now seemed mildly reproachful and now tenderly persuasive, but which never betrayed the slightest vexation."

In reporting the hearing on February 28, the *World* denounced Rockefeller as "the father of trusts, the king of monopolists, the czar of the oil business, the $15-a-week clerk of fifteen years ago, the autocrat of today, who handles a business worth $20,000,000 per annum, and relentlessly crushes all competitors into the slough of failure and bankruptcy."

While the committee's attorney, Roger Pryor, shook an accusing finger at him, striding around the room like a boxer in the ring, repeatedly moving in for the attack, Rockefeller played the slightly confused innocent, winning the sympathy of spectators. "It was a glorious picture which this prince of philanthropists presented," said the *World*. "Ah, how he glowed as he told of the glorious missionary work which the trust has accomplished! Beginning with $70,000,000 capital, which by thrift and care it has increased to $90,000,000, the charity has paid from 7 to 10 per cent a year of profits, while it has improved the plant, has steadily reduced the price of kerosene (it may be said parenthetically that the price of crude has dropped correspondingly), has improved upon the quality of its products, has never undercut antagonists in the way of freight discriminations or price, has never done anything to injure the business of competitors, and is on the best of terms with refining companies outside the trust. In tones so gentle that the wild birds of the wood would not be frightened this gilded monopolist told all this and more."

Bennett's *Herald* also took a cynical view of Rockefeller, who "proved conclusively that [the Standard oil monopoly] is the greatest philanthropy of the age, a sort of missionary society engaged in spreading the evangelical light of kerosene oil over the dark places in a naughty world."

Though well aware of the terror tactics used by his people to kill the competition, Rockefeller denied any knowledge of it and dodged and weaved his way through the rest of the hearing. Despite his skillful subterfuge, the committee finally agreed with Pulitzer that Rockefeller was a menace, concluding in its fifteen-hundred-page report that Standard Oil was "the most active and possibly the most formidable moneyed power on the continent [and] almost the sole occupant of the field of oil operations, from which it has driven nearly every competitor." The report scared many states into enacting antitrust laws, and the U.S. Congress began to consider following suit.

Pulitzer was not finished with Rockefeller, who joined Jay Gould as one of the unenlightened financial titans on the publisher's growing list of enemies of the people.

Luckily, Pulitzer was still in California in March, because the great blizzard that struck New York on March 11, 1888, might have finished him off. For thirty-six hours, transportation and communications were paralyzed, and thousands of stranded passengers slept in Grand Central Station. Messages to Boston and other cities had to be relayed via England. All stores and offices closed, and no coal, milk, or newspapers were available.

When Pulitzer learned that his attorney, Roscoe Conkling, had collapsed after battling his way from his office through the blizzard and snow drifts to reach his home three miles away, he sent a sympathetic telegram. After receiving it days later, Conkling replied: "Would gladly face greater storms to make your eyes strong enough to be squandered reading newspapers." Though Pulitzer's well-paid employees might be suspected of toadying, many, including Conkling, felt genuine admiration and affection for him—as well as, at times, the urge to strangle him. Conkling had once confided to District Attorney Nicoll that of the many prominent men he had met, including U.S. presidents and European big shots in and out of politics, Pulitzer was the ablest of the lot. Conkling showed no sign of recovering from his exposure to the blizzard, and Pulitzer, greatly concerned, asked for daily reports of his condition.

Meanwhile, Nellie Bly was proving every bit as effective as the best male reporters. After her undercover triumph at the women's lunatic asylum, her second success, published on April 1, was to expose an Albany lobbyist, Edward Phelps, for bribing politicians.

Bly's account captured the colorful, direct, and sometimes playful style Pulitzer encouraged, starting with this bit of doggerel:

"For I'm a Pirate King!
 I'm in the Lobby Ring!
 Oh! what an uproarious,
 Jolly and glorious
 Biz for a Pirate King!"

She continued: "I was a lobbyist last week. I went up to Albany to catch a professional briber in the act. I did so. The briber and lobbyist whom I caught was Mr. Ed Phelps. I pretended I wanted to have him kill a certain bill. Mr. Phelps was cautious at first and looked carefully into my record. He satisfied himself that I was honest and talked very freely for a king." She reported that he asked her for $1,000 to pay off six assemblymen to get her bill killed, naming the men as he checked off their names on a printed list which she kept.

Next day the World published Phelps's letter, calling the report "a romance" together with the paper's persuasive point-by-point rebuttal of his denial.

Six politicians Bly had named as on the take proclaimed their innocence and demanded an investigation, which was granted. When Bly appeared before the Assembly Judiciary Committee investigating her charges, according to the Albany Argus "the giggling, rather pretty witness" attracted more interest than anything else that had occurred in the assembly all winter. "Nellie Bly evinced an uncontrollable desire to laugh all through her testimony. She swore to the story as printed in the New York World, producing in corroboration the committee list which she said Phelps had marked." The politicians were exonerated, but Phelps left town and did not return the following year.

For her exposé of the lobbyist, the Journalist gave Bly a positive plug, profiling her as "the most beautiful reporter in this city," who, though "she comes from Boston does not wear eyeglasses."

A muckraker before President Teddy Roosevelt popularized the term, Bly's exposés were becoming remarkably effective in fulfilling Pulitzer's goal to reform the system: her firsthand account of the disgusting way male guards treated women in city prisons caused the appointment of women matrons to guard female inmates. She also visited free dispensaries pretending to be ill to check on the medical care of the poor and, acting as a decoy, exposed a bartender who spent his leisure time driving a horse and carriage through city parks, picking up women new to the city to seduce and turn into prostitutes. Her report, revealing how he bribed police with beer to let him get away with it, ended his outdoor career.

Encouraged from afar by Pulitzer, one week she unmasked a famous mind reader as a phony and the next dramatized in vivid, emotional language the misery of starving slumdwellers. Pulitzer's delight in Bly's work was muted by news that Conkling had died on April 17. Too sick to return for the funeral, Pulitzer sent a huge wreath and approved a glowing obituary.

That spring Pulitzer enjoyed a belated but spectacular revenge. He bought French's Hotel—the place he'd been kicked out of in 1865—paid $630,000 for it in cash, then had it demolished to make way for the tallest structure in Manhattan, with a golden dome, his *World* headquarters.

The new building was to be directly opposite the *Sun* building and would literally put his archenemy's *Sun* in the shade. The *World* rubbed it in with this editorial comment: The *Sun* "dreads being overshadowed architecturally by the *World*, as it already has been overshadowed by us in circulation, influence, character, enterprise and all that makes a newspaper successful and powerful."

But despite ambitious plans to build the tallest building in New York, if not the world, to house his flourishing paper, Pulitzer was more focused on restoring his health and saving his sight. Because California had not been the answer, he returned to New York, making a brief, and what would be his final, visit to St. Louis en route.

On June 9 he crossed the Atlantic to consult specialists in England and on the Continent. Dr. McLane went with him as friend and doctor. From now on Pulitzer would never be without a doctor at hand. In London he consulted Scottish Harley Street specialist Sir Andrew Clark, like himself a workaholic. Clark had suffered from consumption in his youth but had outlived all his colleagues. The novelist George Eliot (pen name of Marian Evans) had been one of Clark's patients. She had suffered a nervous exhaustion similar to Pulitzer's. Discussing her with the specialist, he resolved to reread Eliot's novels, which he had enjoyed in his youth. But that was the only benefit from the consultation. The specialist's advice, a repetition of McLane's to give up his work completely, was tantamount to recommending suicide. His work *was* his life.

Kate joined him in Paris, where he consulted several more specialists, including famed neurologist Jean Martin Charcot, whose hypnotic experiments on hysterical women had impressed Freud. Pulitzer was not impressed because Charcot repeated the same unacceptable advice as all the other doctors: to lead the life of a vegetable, and above all, to avoid excitement. Instead, he returned to New York to direct the *World*'s handling of the upcoming state and national elections. Kate, six months pregnant, continued on to Lenox where Joseph would join her later.

With failing sight and nerves on edge, he avoided most of the staff—but still made his presence felt. A twenty-three-year-old Princeton graduate, George McClellan Jr. (son of the Union Army general), who had recently been hired to write for the *World*, never saw Pulitzer but, wrote Swanberg, McClellan Jr. "heard him frequently. When anything went wrong, and things seemed to go wrong with him very often, there would come from his office a stream of profanity and filth that almost overwhelmed even that expert blasphemist [sic], John A. Cockerill."

Cartoonist McDougall confirmed in his autobiography that Pulitzer went to the *World* offices every working day even though the noises he once loved— the roar of the presses, yells for copy boys, and commotion in the city room— almost drove him crazy. "He came against his doctor's orders," McDougall recalled, "and aggravated his afflictions by efforts to attend to details. Only death could repress his energy and insatiable curiosity. His invariable inquiry was, Why? I heard it the first time I knew him, and the last."

In the early stages of the presidential election campaign, Cockerill undercut the *World*'s campaign to support President Cleveland for reelection by turning Republican and producing a pro–Benjamin Harrison slant in the news reports. Pulitzer tolerated this as his contribution to freedom of the press. Besides, he was disappointed in Cleveland for not living up to his promise to reform the system, and gave him only halfhearted support in his editorials.

Nellie Bly's contribution was to interview the presidential candidates' wives, all former first ladies, and female attorney Belva Lockwood, a presidential contender. Only Cleveland's young wife, Frances, escaped. Sighting Bly's approaching carriage, she sprang from a hammock and hurried into the White House, where she remained incommunicado.

Though not as dirty as the previous one, the presidential campaign had its moments. Cleveland, "the Beast of Buffalo," was falsely accused of being a drunk who beat his young wife. And the naive British ambassador, Sir Lionel Sackville-West, was tricked into expressing his approval of Cleveland when a Republican posing as a former British subject wrote to ask how he should vote. "For Cleveland," replied the ambassador. "The Democratic Party wants to maintain friendly relations with Great Britain." When Sackville-West's letter was published it brought cries of "foreign interference!" from Republicans and was almost as effective in arousing Irish voters against Cleveland as the "Rum, Romanism, and Rebellion" goof of 1884 had helped him.

In the final tally nationwide, Cleveland still got 98,000 more votes than Benjamin Harrison, but lost in the Electoral College, 168 votes to 233.

In New York, Governor David Hill, a Democrat and promising presidential candidate, was reelected governor with Pulitzer's support. Hill had recently signed a bill to use electrocution rather than hanging to kill prisoners sentenced to death. A *World* reporter would soon write a gruesome eyewitness account of the first such execution.

Electricity had been found useful for illumination as well as for extinction. Pulitzer had it installed in his new lavish country home, Chatwold, on the ocean at Bar Harbor, Maine, where he and his family were to spend many future summers. And there Pulitzer would build a soundproof tower to shut out the noisy world he could no longer tolerate—which included the cries of Constance Helen, his daughter and sixth child, born on December 13, 1888.

At year's end, despite expert treatment and advice, his shattered nerves and failing eyesight had not improved. According to his business manager and biographer Don Carlos Seitz, Pulitzer had not only inherited defective eyesight but also "long hours of reading in poor light and in bed while a boy in St. Louis had laid the foundation of weakness; longer hours writing and poring over proofs in the dim hot gaslight of the day had complicated the preparations for disaster."

CHAPTER 13

"An Instrument of Justice, A Terror to Crime"

1889
—
42 years old

In the new year, Pulitzer did the unthinkable: he quit the *World*. He had decided to devote his time to an all-out effort to cure his frazzled nerves and fading sight. Meanwhile, he appointed a triumvirate to run the *World* and supervise the building of the paper's extraordinary new headquarters that would cost a whopping $2.5 million and tower above every building in the city. The three men he entrusted to these tasks were Cockerill; business manager George Turner; and Kate's brother William Davis, a mining engineer. Although Davis knew nothing about newspapers, Pulitzer trusted him to referee the inevitable squabbles between Cockerill and Turner. Managing Editor Ballard Smith, presumably, was thought to have his hands full putting out the paper.

Pulitzer then sailed for Europe with Kate, nine-year-old Ralph, eight-year-old Lucille, and four-year-old Joseph Jr., leaving newborn Constance to the care of nurses.

After stopping briefly in Paris at a hotel on the Rue de Courcelles, he moved almost immediately to St. Moritz, with a newly hired secretary-companion, Claude Ponsonby, and a handful of servants, while his family remained in Paris. Ostensibly he was in Switzerland to recuperate from his various illnesses, but he spent much of the time listening to Ponsonby read copies of the *World*—which arrived in batches—and then dictating detailed criticisms and plaudits.

Pulitzer was also on a recruiting drive. His cable to Julius Chambers, editor of the *Herald*, persuaded him to join the *World* with a three-year-contract at $250 a week, and another cable lured George Cary Eggleston from the *Commercial*

139

Advertiser to write *World* editorials under Pulitzer's direction. This staff "stealing" was a common practice among newspaper publishers of the day.

Delighted with his choice of Chambers, he wrote to him through Ponsonby: "Never fear of troubling me with any suggestion concerning either the welfare of the paper or your own; and nothing, looking to the elevations and improvement of the paper, is too small to mention."

Left behind in Paris, Kate had not been able to resist a shopping spree, which prompted Pulitzer to dictate a sharp rebuke: "I decidedly object to your buying any more jewelry out of the large dividends you receive. Very decidedly. It is unbecoming in a woman whose husband is practically blind, a wretched invalid and has a certain public character and position." At least he didn't tell her to return the jewelry. His ambivalent attitude toward his wife and children was described by one secretary as "the strangest mixture of deep affection, anxious solicitude, arbitrariness and caprice."

Pulitzer moved from Switzerland to Wiesbaden, Germany, where a leading oculist, Dr. Hermann Pagenstecher, examined him and confirmed the depressing diagnoses of the other experts.

Thinking he must miss the children, Kate proposed to send them to keep him company. Pulitzer declined her offer, affectionately but firmly: "My Dearest, I am really much better—at least compared with a week ago. But remember again all my statements of improvement are *comparative*. If you want to send them [the children] on my account, there is no necessity for it. The time passes easily enough and I can't yet see that the children will be happy here. Between drinking waters, taking baths, driving out in the afternoon, I can kill time easily enough. *Don't* send me any newspapers until I ask for them. I want to experiment being without them for a fortnight, but the letters (any+all) please see that I receive promptly. With sincere love, ever your devoted husband, JP."

Ponsonby wrote to Kate soon after, saying Pulitzer's nerves and insomnia had improved, that he walked for at least an hour a day and even seemed to enjoy it. He no longer complained of dullness, as he had in Paris, and he wrote, "I am sure you will be glad to hear that he *scarcely ever* alludes to his health."

Pulitzer was also cheered by news that largely thanks to Nellie Bly's daring investigations, the Sunday *World*'s circulation had zoomed to a record 285,860 in March and a whopping 345,808 in May. Recently, to show how the police mistreated innocent people under arrest, Bly had managed to get herself imprisoned on a false charge of grand larceny. Then she wowed readers with lurid details of her humiliating experiences: strip search by a homeless woman, and lockup in a cell with male prisoners. A lawyer later tried to bully Bly into hiring him, and a detective on the case made a pass at her. Her report pressured the prison to employ women to supervise female prisoners. She also warned readers of swindlers peddling worthless washing machines, and, to illustrate the tricks of the trade of private detectives, posed as the wife of a man who was having her tailed. Interviewing boxing champ John L. Sullivan, she felt his muscles and asked him how much money he made. And Bly gave readers a review of her first ride on one of the latest bicycles with same-size wheels now rapidly replacing the risky one-big-wheel-one-small-wheel type.

Twelve nights with McDougall ghost-hunting in Connecticut's reputedly haunted houses turned out to be "a dreadful fizzle," according to the cartoonist. But her trip to Boston was more productive. There, at the Perkins Institute for the Blind, she met a nine-year-old girl the director predicted would be "the marvel of the age." Her name was Helen Keller.

Readers lapped up Bly's dramatic account of the tempestuous lives of a former New York State legislator, Robert Hamilton, grandson of the famous Alexander Hamilton; his wife, Evangeline; and a nurse. It ran in the World for weeks, further boosting the already booming circulation. Promoted as "one of the most astounding stories of conspiracy, of turpitude, of plot and counterplot, ever revealed outside the realms of improbable fiction," the hype wasn't far from the truth. What appears to have been the truth is as follows: Evangeline had been a prostitute. Not knowing this, Hamilton made her his mistress while she continued a curious close relationship with a Mrs. Anna Swinton. Evangeline tricked Hamilton into marrying her by pretending to be expecting his baby, then got Swinton to buy one for her. The baby soon died, though this was kept from Hamilton. Swinton provided a second baby to replace the first. Easily fooled, Hamilton believed it was his. When this baby also died, Evangeline bought a third child but, because it looked so different from the first, she gave it away. Finally she bought a fourth baby, named Mamie, which the incredibly gullible Hamilton, still unaware of the switches, accepted as his.

During the Hamiltons' summer vacation in 1889, when they stayed in an Atlantic City hotel, the baby's nurse, Mary Donnelly, argued with her mistress. She knew about Evangeline's past, and at the height of the quarrel shouted out the sordid secrets within Hamilton's hearing.

Moments later, startled hotel guests at lunch in the dining room heard a woman's screams from above and the sound of furniture being smashed. According to the World report, a waiter rushed upstairs to find a wild-eyed blonde "striking out in all directions with a blood-stained dagger" while her husband tried to disarm her. A scared six-month-old baby was crying on the bed, and her nurse lay bleeding on the floor. The waiter helped Hamilton get the weapon from Evangeline, and the police arrested her.

The nurse recovered in time to testify at the trial. Evangeline, found guilty of atrocious assault and battery, got two years in Trenton Penitentiary. Her close associate, Mrs. Swinton, was charged with fraudulent production of an infant under false pretenses. Bly now showed why she was so valuable to the World: she sustained readers' avid interest in the scandal by interviewing Evangeline in her cell, and also investigating the baby-buying racket by posing as an eager customer. In the interview, Evangeline told Bly that Mrs. Swinton, who knew of her past, had been blackmailing her. She also claimed that Hamilton had made her end two pregnancies and only married her when she threatened to leave him. She insisted that baby Mamie was really hers and that Swinton had bought the four babies for someone else. Obviously the court had not believed her. In her account, Bly remained the impartial reporter, letting Evangeline give her version of the affair and allowing readers to judge for themselves.

As for the baby-selling racket, Bly had no trouble finding four places where anyone willing to fork out ten to twenty-five dollars could walk out with a baby. It was as easy, she said, as buying a hat.

Before the year was out, Bly reported another arresting story in the paper that gave seven doctors heartburn. A longtime sufferer from migraine head-aches, she decided to search for a cure, using herself as the guinea pig, and to share the outcome with *World* readers. She went to seven doctors. Each gave her a different diagnosis—including dyspepsia, malaria, eye problems, neural-gia, nerves—and a different prescription. None worked. As a result of the fea-ture, in which she embarrassed the doctors by naming them, some seven hun-dred readers wrote to her with their remedies for migraine. She responded in the paper: "Two weeks ago, I had seven physicians who charged large fees. Today I have 700 physicians who diagnose my case and prescribe without charge."

Most advice from readers was to change her diet or to take a long rest. But one who signed himself "A Jerseyman" advised her to "eat a raw onion every night before you retire, and you will feel as fresh as a lily in the morning. You must not dread any smell from your breath, for an onion will sweeten it. If you should take a nice mild one every night for a week, I will bet my last crop of celery against a decayed apple that you will have no more headaches. Those doctors know all that, but there is no money in writing 'onions.' Please do not look on this as a joke, for it is a fact." Bly ended her report: "Confidentially, I have tried the onions. Three nights I have eaten onions and for three days my head had not ached."

If Pulitzer followed the onion advice, it failed to work for him. He didn't even feel up to returning to lay the cornerstone for the new *World* building on the day he had chosen, October 10, obviously with his lucky number ten in mind. Instead he stayed in Wiesbaden while his family returned to New York and his youngest son, four-year-old Joseph Jr., represented him at the cere-mony. Dressed in a sailor suit, the boy took his task seriously, tapping the stone with a trowel and saying three times: "It is well done."

The ailing publisher did rouse himself to send a stirring cable, which was read out at the ceremony: "God grant that this structure be the enduring home of a newspaper forever unsatisfied with merely printing news, forever fighting every form of wrong—forever Independent—forever advancing in Enlighten-ment and Progress—forever wedded to truly Democratic ideas—forever aspir-ing to be a moral force—forever rising to a higher plane of perfection as a Pub-lic Institution. God grant that the *World* may forever strive toward the highest ideals—an instrument of Justice, a terror to crime, an aid to education, an expo-nent of true Americanism. Let it ever be remembered that its every stone

Joe Pulitzer Jr., age four, representing his father in the cornerstone-laying for the *New York World* building in Manhattan on October 10, 1889.

comes from the people and represents public approval for public services rendered. God forbid that the vast army following the standard of the *World* should ever find it faithless to those ideas and moral principles to which alone it owes its life and without which I would rather have it perish. Joseph Pulitzer." Among those listening were New York mayor Hugh Grant; New York governor David Hill; inventor Thomas Edison; and former U.S. president Grover Cleveland.

In November Pulitzer took his doctors' advice to go on a long, leisurely sea voyage—but on his terms. Even before he set off, it was obvious he was going to stay in charge of the *World* by remote control, especially when he asked his brother-in-law William Davis to send pleasant mail to him at various places he intended to visit in India, China, and Japan, and only to forward annoying mail if vitally important. He added: "If it is an extraordinary thing of real importance, you need not hesitate, and I want you to cable me fully, even if it costs four dollars a word or forty. Of course, anything concerning the paper and our people will interest me just as much in the Himalayas as in St. Moritz, perhaps even more, and regular, full and, I trust, favorable reports will be specially agreeable."

On November 28, five days after Pulitzer sent that keep-me-informed cable, Nellie Bly reached England, on the first leg of her own trip around the world that would make her and the *World* international superstars.

CHAPTER 14

Nellie Bly Races
around the World

1889–1890
—
42 to 43 years old

Pulitzer not only had a nose for news but also was a pioneer in creating news—or stunts, as his critics called them. They were often entertaining, sometimes educational, and invariably attracted more readers. The most wildly successful aroused international interest and made Nellie Bly the world's most famous reporter. It began when Pulitzer decided to challenge the record of Phileas Fogg, the fictional hero of Jules Verne's novel *The Tour of the World in Eighty Days* who, to win a bet, went around the world in that time. And Pulitzer chose Nellie Bly for the job. Then he upped the ante by inviting readers to guess how long she'd take: the one who came closest to guessing the time would get a free trip to Europe and $250 spending money. Almost a million submissions poured in.

Bly traveled light, even declining a revolver for her protection, though she feared as a young woman traveling alone that she might not survive the journey through dangerous territory.

Pulitzer's London correspondent, Tracy Greaves, met her at her first stop, the English port of Southampton. He had arranged for her to visit the almost legendary Jules Verne himself, but at a price. She'd have to lose two nights' sleep to make up for lost time, as the author's home, in Amiens, north of Paris, was out of her way. More than willing, she crossed the English Channel to France, then took a train to Verne's hometown. He and his wife were enchanted with the young American. Verne thought her extremely modest, quiet, and ladylike, and "the prettiest girl imaginable." After her visit he said he'd been delighted to see her and that "Madame Verne has never ceased speaking

144

Nellie Bly dressed and equipped for the record-breaking race around the world that made her famous.

of her since." He had another reason to be delighted. A few years before, he had been shot in the leg by a nephew who had gone mad. Since then, the injury had kept him housebound, unable to travel to do research for future books. News of Bly's projected journey had so excited the French public that ten new editions of his book had been printed and a Parisian stage version was in the works.

Leaving Amiens, Bly headed by train for Brindisi, on Italy's southeast coast. Told that the previous week the train had been held up by bandits, she said she wished she'd taken a gun. Fortunately the bandits were otherwise engaged, and she arrived intact and unmolested.

Armed, she might have been tempted to wipe out the mostly English passengers and crew of the *Victoria*, which then took her from the Adriatic coast and through the Suez Canal. She hated them all, despised their "much talked about prejudices," and found the food revolting and the captain and crew rude. She seemed blithely unaware of her own prejudice, describing the Lascar sailors, according to her biographer Brooke Kroeger, as "a grim, surly-looking set, climbing about over the ship like a pack of monkeys." At Port Said, when hordes of beggars confronted the passengers, "fighting, pulling and yelling" to take them ashore in various boats, the male passengers brandished canes to keep them at bay. When that failed, the captain ordered his crew to beat off the most persistent beggars with long poles.

She reached Ceylon on December 8, overjoyed to be two days ahead of schedule and expecting a brief stopover. Instead she was forced to stay put for five days because her new ship, the *Oriental,* had to wait for a slow old clunker to deliver more *Oriental* passengers before it left for Singapore. To keep readers hooked, she cabled a day-by-day report of her experiences. She had resisted the offer of a boy for sale in Port Said and a girl in Ceylon, but when she reached Singapore she fell hopelessly for a monkey on sale there.

By now almost the entire English-speaking world was rooting for her—and her pet monkey.

A monsoon hit the ship en route to Hong Kong. To Bly it was the most beautiful thing she'd ever seen. Not a bit scared, she left her monkey safely in the cabin and went on deck. A wacky male passenger joined her, suggesting they embrace and jump together into the raging sea—because, he shouted, "Death by drowning is a peaceful slumber!" Just in time, a ship's officer came to the rescue.

She also told how someone inadvertently opened the door to the cabin of another passenger, the most stunning woman aboard, and glimpsed her—bald and toothless!

Despite the monsoon, the ship reached its destination two days early. Waiting for her next connection, Bly took a ferry to Canton on the Chinese mainland, where she spent Christmas and visited an exhibition of Chinese instruments of torture. The exhibits included the heads of executed prisoners preserved in jars, and a lifelike model of a man subjected to the bamboo punishment, in which he was forced to stand upright, legs astride, over a bamboo shoot that in time would grow straight through him. On Christmas morning she visited a leper colony and had lunch in the Temple of the Dead, returning to the ship with a sick headache.

After another stormy voyage she landed at Yokohama, Japan, on January 3. Four days later, aboard the *Oceanic,* she headed across the rough Pacific Ocean for the United States.

On January 20, with San Francisco in sight, Bly was almost certain she would beat Phileas Fogg's time. She shared her excitement with the purser, who suddenly looked seasick. "My God!" he said with a gasp. "The bill of health [showing she had no infectious disease] was left behind in Yokohama!" He told her they'd have to wait for the document to arrive on the next ship from Japan—at least two weeks. Bly became hysterical, threatening to cut her throat if she couldn't go ashore as soon as they reached port. The purser believed her, and promised to search again just in case it was still aboard. He found it stuffed in the ship doctor's desk.

No longer suicidal, she hurried aboard a waiting tug to take her and her monkey ashore, but as it moved away from the ship the quarantine doctor leaned over the ship's rail and shouted: "You can't leave until I've examined your tongue!"

He kept shouting, so she just stuck out her tongue at him—a double entendre if there ever was one.

Stymied, he made the best of it and yelled, "All right!"

Pulitzer had a special train awaiting her on the West Coast, in which she traveled with flags flying, eager crowds and reporters greeting her at every stop. Near Gallup, New Mexico, the train approached a bridge under repair. When the workmen saw it moving toward them at fifty miles an hour, it was too late to flag it down. Horrified, they watched the approach of what seemed certain disaster: the structure supporting the rails over a deep ravine was held in place only by jackscrews. Almost miraculously, the train reached the other side safely.

Her journey from San Francisco to Chicago in a record-breaking sixty-seven hours made up for all the delays.

Though still at sea on his own more leisurely journey, Pulitzer had arranged for a ten-gun salute (again, his lucky ten) to welcome her to Jersey City from her extraordinary 24,899-mile trip around the world. And he devoted much of the paper to her exploits, beginning with:

FATHER TIME OUTDONE!

———

Even Imagination's Record Pales Before
the Performance of 'The World's'
Globe-Circler

———

Her time: 72 days, 6 hrs. 11 mins, 14 secs

———

Thousands Cheer Themselves Hoarse
at Nellie Bly's Arrival

———

Welcome Salutes in New York and Brooklyn

———

The Whole Country Aglow with Intense Enthusiasm

———

Nellie Bly Tells Her Story

———

Pulitzer was inundated with congratulatory cables. One from Jules Verne read: "I never doubted the success of Nellie Bly. She has proved her intrepidity and courage. Hurrah for her and the director of the *World*. Hurrah! Hurrah!"

A dice game to keep *World* readers interested in Nellie Bly's race around the world.

Verne thought her achievement fantastic, especially since she had traveled in the dangerous winter months. More tributes followed. A racehorse was named after her. Her photo was distributed with the Sunday *World*. Games were named after her, and songs were written about the queen of stunt journalism.

Her exploits would lead the way for other women to crash the male-dominated newspaper world.

Allan Forman of the *Journalist* concluded that "a young woman sent around the world for no practical purpose will work to greater advantage in booming a newspaper than a dozen men sent out after the facts." However, he conceded that "it has proved the immense resources of the *New York World* and the vigor and intelligence with which they are utilized; and it has proved that the great majority of the American people dearly love a sensation—no matter how flimsy—so long as it gives them something to gabble about. It has been a great advertisement for the *New York World* and Miss Nellie Bly."

F. W. Stevens of New York City, who came closest to guessing the time of her trip, was right to within two-fifths of a second. One hundred sixteen others guessed to within fifteen seconds.

Meanwhile, Pulitzer was making his own momentous journey. Leaving Kate in Paris, he set off with his doctor friends James McLane and George Hosmer, friend Charles Fearing, and secretary Ponsonby, almost following Bly's route to India, through the Aegean Sea to Constantinople, then through the Suez Canal.

For the rest of his life he took extraordinary precautions not just to survive, but also to continue his life's work. Warned, for example, not to bend over for any reason in case it caused a brain artery to rupture, he had his cabin washbasin raised to chin level and never again tied his own shoelaces.

Approaching Aden, on the Red Sea, Ponsonby wrote to Kate: "He is *certainly* better than when we left, but is inclined to take a despondent view of his health and pitches into Fearing and myself when we try to cheer him up by telling him he has already improved. His appetite is *first class*. He sleeps very fairly. Coughs only a little, very little. But that very little seems to annoy him greatly and still excited a certain amount of nervousness. I can conscientiously say that you would be pleased were you here, at the change for the better."

Pulitzer disagreed, writing to her the same day in a huge scrawl: "I am certainly no worse than when I came on ship, though. I still have that cough in spite of every precaution and for several days felt very miserably . . . I still continue to lose flesh. Can't wear things that were already taken in 2–3 times and my bones absolutely become melancholy, literally painful. Still I manage to preserve a little spirit and humor and hope. I write this solely because I think you may like it. But it is horrible scrawling I know. It hurts my eyes and is written under electric light.

"P.S. Make the children write often."

In a brief note to her from Bombay on New Year's Day, he said the voyage could not have been more pleasant and nearly everybody was happy but he was still sleeping poorly, hadn't been able to shake the cough, and was suffering from rheumatism.

Though it had been a boyhood dream to visit India, and what little he had seen of it had been fascinating, he wrote to Kate that he had decided not to see any more because he couldn't face long train journeys and noisy Indian hotels. "I really feel that my health is broken . . . and that I cannot in reason expect to regain it without either that freedom from all business worry and care and the enjoyment of that domestic care and peace which seem beyond my reach. Travel will not cure me. I am miserable. I cannot trust myself to write more. Whatever I feel however, you are still the only being in this world who fills my heart and mind and hope and receives my love and tenderness and affection."

On his return journey, a cable from his brother-in-law Davis that Cockerill and Turner were fighting made him overwrought for hours. But there was no apparent physical reaction until one afternoon when the ship had docked outside Constantinople. He and Ponsonby were at the rail of the ship when Pulitzer said: "How suddenly it has gotten dark."

His secretary hesitated before saying: "It's not dark."

"Well it's dark to me," was Pulitzer's disturbing response.

It wasn't a stroke, but McLane believed the retina of his worst eye had become detached, leaving him with only faint vision in the better one. In something of a panic they headed back to Europe to have specialists examine him. At Naples he was left to rest in a darkened hotel room, while the others spoke in whispers so as not to disturb him.

Suddenly guns from a nearby fort opened up for artillery practice. For a man who could no longer tolerate even the crunching of toast the gunfire was unbearable torture.

Frantic, Ponsonby rushed to the Italian authorities and explained the situation. His being the nephew of an English lord and Pulitzer an American millionaire proved a winning combination. "All his life thereafter was spent in evading noises," remarked biographer Allen Churchill, "though with unerring ill luck he invariably managed to be at the center of whatever clatter abounded."

The guns were silenced for the rest of their time in Naples. They stayed until he was fit enough to stand the journey to St. Moritz, Switzerland, where they hoped he would benefit from the fresh mountain air, but instead it gave him bronchitis. He rested for several weeks in Lucerne, and in August Kate joined him.

Dr. Hosmer, who took care of him through the illness, had been both a physician and a lawyer before switching to journalism, working first for Bennett as head of the *Herald*'s London bureau, and after a fight with his boss had joined the rival *World*. He augmented rather than replaced Ponsonby, advising Pulitzer on medical and legal matters as well as becoming one of the growing band of secretary-companions required to keep Pulitzer alive, entertained, informed, and in good spirits.

At least one story in the *World* that month was hardly likely to calm a sick man in a highly agitated state. A *World* reporter had defied a gag order, to report the first execution ever in an electric chair. It took place at Auburn Prison on August 6, when William Kemmler was electrocuted for killing his mistress with an ax. The execution had been horribly botched, and Kemmler had been burned alive rather than shocked to death, as the *World* headline indicated: THE FIRST ELECTROCIDE . . . A Roasting of Human Flesh in the Prison — Strong Men Sickened and Turned from the Sight.

The doctor who examined Kemmler's corpse confirmed that parts of his body had been charred black.

Hosmer tried to shield Pulitzer from such horror stories after finding him, as he noted in his diary, "in a state so feeble that he could scarcely get around on foot. He passed days on a sofa. It was a physical strain for him to cross the room and sit at the table. Physical collapse had assumed the form of nervous prostration, directly due to his intense efforts in building up The World. He had previously compromised his health by his labors on the St. Louis Post-Dispatch which he had also raised from the dead."

Pulitzer was driven to the pleasant seaside resort of Trouville, where he recovered from bronchitis and, as Hosmer recorded in his diary, "to some degree from his great physical debility. With this small recovery, however, he listened to the telegrams from home which urged him to new activities." His return to America in October 1890, ostensibly to consult a Philadelphia neurologist, Dr. Silas Weir Mitchell, was also due in part to the conviction that The World needed him.

Mitchell's advice, backed up by other doctors, was shattering. Pulitzer must have absolutely nothing more to do with his newspapers. They must not even be read to him. He must never communicate with his staff, nor they with him. Furthermore, he must rest after meals, take daily exercise, and have massages every evening to help him to sleep. Meanwhile, he should consider taking another long sea voyage away from all causes of stress.

To almost everyone's surprise, Pulitzer agreed and approved the following announcement in the World on October 16, 1890:

"Yielding to the advice of his physicians Mr. Joseph Pulitzer has withdrawn entirely from the editorship of The World. For the past two years Mr. Pulitzer has been unable, by reason of a misfortune to his sight, to give a personal supervision to the conduct of his journal. The entire control of The World has been vested in an Executive Board of its principal editors who have been long in its service, and have conducted it in the absence of its chief. The change is thus more nominal than otherwise. It involves no change of men, of methods, or principle or policy. The World will continue to be guided by the ideas of the man who made it what it is. It will follow lines marked out by him in dedicating this journal to the public service—to the cause of justice, of good morals and good government."

The response of his rival, Bennett, was hardly less unexpected than Pulitzer's submission to his doctors' advice. Bennett wrote: "A great vacuum is made in the present actuality of American journalism. What the Greeleys and the Raymonds and the Bennetts did for journalism thirty years ago, Pulitzer has done today. As for us of the Herald, we droop our colors to him. He . . . has succeeded all along the line; has roused a spirit of enterprise and personality, which, up to this time, has not been known. We have not always agreed with the spirit which has made his ideas a journalistic success, and we cannot refrain from regretting that he did not encourage us in the new departure which he has made, instead of merely astonishing us, frightening us, and we may add—now that it is past—perhaps a little bit disgusting us. But, *le Roi est mort, vive le Roi! The New York World* is dead! Long live *The World. Pacet!*" Pulitzer was so moved by that tribute that he ordered his staff never again to attack Bennett or the *Herald*.

The Texas Newspaper Union hailed Pulitzer as "the greatest journalist on earth," called his failing health "a calamity of national import," and his career "phenomenal—and honest. He stands as a monument of what a strong will with a definite purpose in view can accomplish. The *World* is known, admired and quoted wherever the English language is spoken. The secret of his success is his ability to surround himself with the best intelligence obtainable, to pay for services rendered like a prince and by personal good will and his own peculiar ability retain not alone a man's services but his friendship." The *Buffalo Weekly Gossip* believed Pulitzer's "tireless energy and love of justice have made the New York *World* the foremost paper of the world. There is not a working journalist in the United States who does not regret the cause of his retirement." The *New York Saturday Review* stated that "The *World* has become the journal of greatest circulation, of widest influence and of largest wealth on this continent. [Pulitzer] announced that it would serve the many instead of the few, that it would denounce wrong and defend right, strive earnestly to advance the public interest without fear or favor and . . . with all its might. He kept that solemn pledge [and] has partially lost his sight in the service of the people: he is, in fact, a martyr to public duty."

Harper's Weekly remembered how "thirty years ago [Pulitzer] landed in this country without a friend or a dollar or the ability to speak the language of the people among whom he found himself. In that time he has made for himself a reputation as a writer and speaker of English, he has been elected to Congress, and he is the proprietor of a newspaper from whose sales he has erected a building on the site of the hotel which refused him hospitality in the days of his poverty." The *Asheville Citizen* of North Carolina recalled that "the reception of Mr. Pulitzer at the hands of the leading New York newspapers was about such as might have been extended by as many famished polar bears. He was derided, caricatured, libeled and maligned. Here was a man with a tremendous burden on his shoulders, forced to originate paying ideas where hundreds of bright men had preceded him and failed, and all this to do in the face of scores of predictions from friends as well as enemies that his efforts were doomed to failure. He bought the best talent in the market and was so successful a manager of men that he drew from this brilliant staff the best work they had ever done. The result is known wherever there are readers of newspapers. Mr. Pulitzer has written his name across the face of the history of journalism."

Novelist Henry James had a more jaundiced view of Pulitzer, partly based on gossip he shared with his sister Alice, who was visiting him in England in November 1890. Years before, James had been asked to write fiction for the *World* but had declined when Pulitzer told him to avoid "anything literary." Asked what he would advise a friend who had once considered working for

Pulitzer, James replied, "I would rather sweep the dirtiest [street] crossing in London!" He added that Pulitzer had made a fortune editing "the vulgarest conceivable newspaper." Had Henry James been less uptight, he would have found in Pulitzer a great subject for a novel.

After announcing his retirement, Pulitzer spent much more time with his family, often looking at them with his faint and fading sight, as if to imprint their looks on his memory. At times he lightly moved his hand over their faces to augment by touch what he could barely see. He continued to spoil all his children outrageously. As his daughter Edith explained, he did this until they were twelve, when he expected them to behave as adults. At this time Ralph, his eldest son, was just eleven. Pulitzer visited friend and neighbor William Whitney, a presidential hopeful for 1892, whose three-year-old daughter Dorothy sat on Pulitzer's lap and pulled his beard, and ever after he showed an interest in her career because he remembered her as one of the last of those he could see.

Still clinging to the lucky ten, he chose December 10, 1890, for the official opening of the new World building. Its sixteen stories reaching 309 feet (it is surprising he didn't go for 310) made it the tallest in the country, towering six floors above any other building. The printing plant was in the basement, business offices on the first floor and mezzanine, office space to be rented out on floors two to ten, and news offices above them all. For editors and reporters working so late that they couldn't get home, Pulitzer had provided bedroom apartments on the eleventh floor.

His own semicircular office was appropriately on top, in the golden dome itself, with three windows giving a wonderful view he could never enjoy of Governor's Island, Brooklyn, and Long Island. Inspired by visits to Venice, the architect, George B. Post, had supplied frescoes on the ceiling and wainscoted the walls with embossed leather. Next to Pulitzer's office was a smaller one for his brother-in-law William Davis, a library, and a conference room. Almost putting Kubla Khan to shame, it was an appropriate building for what Pulitzer considered *the* profession and that the World headlined as "THE GREATEST NEWSPAPER BUILDING IN THE WORLD" and "A People's Palace Without a Cent of Debt or Mortgage." It was true. He had paid millions in cash for the whole thing—lock, stock, and Hoe printing presses. Crowds invited to the ceremony gazed at the golden dome of burnished copper topped by a flagpole, and crushed into the six elevators for rides to Pulitzer's office on the top floor and stops in between. A notable antivice crusader, Reverend Charles Henry Parkhurst, was among them, and said that when he looked out of the sixteenth-floor windows he felt like Christ being tempted by the Devil. Another man followed him off the elevator and asked, "Is God in?"

Fearful of heights, Managing Editor Ballard Smith did not look down from the windows for almost a year.

Dana of the *Sun*, now literally in the shadow of the *World*, sneered that the golden dome looked like a brass head tack. In response, according to a jaunty

The *New York World*
building (center right)
on lower Broadway.
It literally put Dana's
Sun in the shade.

New York Times report, "Mr. Pulitzer had issued strict orders that no brick-
bats should be dropped into Mr. Dana's chimneys, no matter how great the
temptation."

Because of a feud between two of the triumvirate, Cockerill and Turner,
over who was in charge, chief editorial writer William Merrill gave the welcoming address on Pulitzer's behalf. Three governors—of New York, Pennsylvania, and Connecticut—responded, as well as General Taylor of the *Boston
Globe*; Murat Halstead, editor of the *Cincinnati Enquirer*; and St. Clair McKelway, editor of the *Brooklyn Eagle*.

The noise and excitement would have been too much for Pulitzer, especially the explosion caused by a photographer's flash powder, which a policeman said must have been dynamite and gunpowder. According to a hyperbolic
New York Times subhead, "THE PULITZER CELEBRATION COMES NEAR BLOW-
ING UP THE CITY HALL."

The explosion did cause a heavy stone to fall from City Hall across the street
and broke fifty or so of its windows. It also smashed one window in the *World*
building. But Pulitzer was unaware of it. He and Kate had left for Europe the
previous day, sailing on the White Star steamship *Teutonic*, and it would be
weeks before the accolades of the country's newspapers caught up with him.

Had his achievements justified calling him the world's greatest journalist?
When he first took over the paper, his announced intention to "serve and bat-

tle for the people" and to "eradicate evil from high places" had sounded like a dream of Don Quixote's. Yet, in 7½ years, he had worked wonders. And the *World* proudly listed some of his achievements. Among them, apart from making Cleveland president, were:

- Frustrating "scheme after scheme of the corporate and plutocratic planners at Albany and Washington because the light of publicity was turned upon them in the columns of the *World*."
- Exposing political corruption in Connecticut and New Jersey.
- Preventing a Louisiana lottery from continuing to swindle the nation out of ten million dollars a year, and stopping its operators from spreading the scam to Dakota.
- Revealing how Henry Hilton had turned a home intended to be a charitable institution for poor workingwomen into the Park Avenue Hotel for his own financial gain.
- Showing John D. Rockefeller to be a mercenary mogul who made his fortune by destroying rivals, and (like the Mafia) by enforcing a code of silence.
- Establishing that Bell Telephone had become a monopoly through fraud.
- Funding a scientific investigation of New York's food supply.
- Improving the working conditions of Pennsylvania miners.
- Pressuring authorities into the arrest and imprisonment of a pseudoastrologer for trading in young girls.
- Encouraging insane asylum reform through Nellie Bly's undercover reporting.
- Persuading the New York State legislature to modify the medieval law that sent debtors to Lydlow Street jail.
- Solving Connecticut's Stony Creek murder mystery, which led to the conviction of the killer, Peter Coffey.
- Having extortionist "Fatty" Walsh dismissed as warden of the Tombs (the New York City prison).
- Finding janitor Titus, the killer of Tillie Smith of New Jersey.
- Freeing a poor workingman imprisoned in Connecticut for asking at a farmhouse for a cup of coffee.
- Warning the poor about fraudulent insurance companies.
- Backing an expedition that rescued a dozen "shanghaied" men and boys from the "oyster pirates."
- Shaming corrupt lobbyist Edward Phelps by sending Nellie Bly to Albany, New York, to trap him.
- Defeating Senator William Mahone in his bid to be Virginia's governor by revealing his financial shenanigans.
- Providing evidence that convicted the owners of New Jersey's gambling dens.
- Contributing twenty thousand dollars from *World* readers to Johnstown flood victims.

- Getting a law passed to hire women factory inspectors.
- Organizing an expedition to the Yutacán that rescued twenty-four white slaves from bondage.
- Twice defeating efforts of Wall Street bankers and big corporations to overturn the Saturday half-holiday law.
- Exposing Georgia's slave-gang system.
- Persuading the treasury secretary to overhaul the immigration system.
- Urging reform of the law committing children to institutions; the reform resulted in children being returned to their parents. Previously a police magistrate had decided the fate of a child without any right of appeal, even when new evidence was available. After the *World's* campaign New York State allowed an appeal to a higher court.
- Defeating the corrupt Washington, D.C., lobbyists for the Pacific Railroad who were trying to smuggle bills through Congress that would have concealed the past crooked management and gained future advantages at public expense.
- Denouncing Matthew Stanley Quay, U.S. senator from Pennsylvania and the Republican "boss" under whose leadership Benjamin Harrison was elected president; "He was exposed, not because he was a Republican, but simply because he was a public rascal. THE WORLD is against embezzlers of any stamp."
- Sending Walter Buddensiek to prison for ten years for constructing jerry-built houses that collapsed soon after the owners moved in.
- Financing a Free Doctors Corps for the Sick Babies of the Poor. Partly from readers' contributions, some 35 first-class doctors were hired and in one year visited 19,764 houses and treated 12,821 children, free. Food and clothing were also given to the destitute.
- Successfully proposing the establishment of free lectures, free public baths, and the creation of more city parks.
- Discovering that Stuyvesant Park had for thirty years been almost "an aristocratic preserve," and "the rich man's back yard," when it was really public property—and after a struggle having it opened for the public to enjoy.
- Giving free Thanksgiving dinners, Christmas trees, and parties to poor children, and providing the needy with free ice in summer, free coal in winter, and free medical care.
- Informing readers in "damning detail" of the corrupt Brooklyn lobbyists who cost the public hundreds of thousands of dollars.
- Agitating for better streets, better libraries, better art galleries, and more and better schools.
- Investigating and publicizing the African slave trade.
- Making possible the Statue of Liberty in New York Harbor.
- "Introducing a new, entertaining and effective feature into American journalism," consisting of interviews with notable individuals, illustrated

with photos "showing the distinguished [subjects] interviewed in their characteristic postures."

- Sending reporter Thomas Stevens to Africa, where he was the first to meet fellow reporter Henry Stanley emerging from the wilderness.
- Breaking into the Brooklyn Navy Yard at night to show that Uncle Sam's property was at risk.
- Equipping reporters with snowshoes to continue working during the great blizzard of 1888, which also allowed them to bring relief to passengers on stalled trains.
- Sponsoring Nellie Bly's race around the world to beat the record of the imaginary Phileas Fogg.

The record of his triumphs and innovations had a note of finality about it. And those who compiled it must have suspected that the new building was to be his memorial, rarely if ever to contain his living presence, and that the paper would never again reflect his ideas nor follow his orders.

Further evidence came when, after reaching Paris with Kate, Pulitzer asked his European correspondents to find a new home for him—an ocean-going yacht that could be adapted to his special needs. It looked as if Dana's jibe about "The Wandering Jew" had been prophetic, that Pulitzer's crusade had come to an end, and that he would live out what was left of his life as an invalid at sea with no fixed destination.

Here he was at forty-three, a physical and mental wreck, almost totally blind, and plagued with insomnia, "asthma, diabetes, and great swings in mood that at times made him seem to be on the verge of suicide." He also suffered frequent savage headaches and was moved to uncontrollable rage or hysterical tears by "sounds that others would disregard as the hubbub of daily existence."

But those who thought they'd heard the last of Pulitzer didn't know the man.

Despite his awesome physical and mental problems, he remained in constant charge of the *World* and his own destiny. He managed this remarkable and unique feat by creating an almost totally noise-free environment and by hiring a coterie of talented men as his eyes, messengers, and traveling companions. A doctor, and a male nurse doubling as his guard and majordomo, were always on hand. He succeeded so magnificently that the twenty-one tempestuous years that lay ahead would be the years of his greatest achievements.

The spirited and determined "Wandering Jew" would stay at the center of the action to become an even more vital force in his nation's destiny.

The phoenix had nothing on Pulitzer.

CHAPTER 15

Running the *World* by Remote Control

1891–1892

44 to 45 years old

I n the new year Pulitzer, Kate, Ponsonby, and a few friends left Paris for Menton on the French Riviera, where they boarded the chartered steam yacht *Semiramis*. They planned to sail from Nice to Barcelona, down the Spanish coast to Gibraltar, east along the coast of North Africa, and on to Greece. "Mrs. Pulitzer," Hosmer noted in his diary, "had determined to accompany Mr. P. on this cruise but soon made the discovery that nature had not intended her for a sailor and she reluctantly withdrew." This was the start of their frequent separations, with Pulitzer at sea and Kate with the family at their homes in America or on European vacations.

Leaving Kate behind in France, Pulitzer and the rest of his party continued on to Tunis to visit the ruins of ancient Carthage before sailing through a tremendous storm to Greece. Though there was a telegraph office in a small coastal town there, Pulitzer resisted sending his normal barrage of questions and instructions to his staff in New York. Having proved himself a better sailor than Kate, and finding shipboard life more tranquil than city life, he cabled New York agreeing to buy the yacht *Katerina*, formerly owned by the duke of Sutherland. Being among the top 1 percent of affluent Americans, he easily managed the asking price of a hundred thousand dollars and renamed it *Romola*, after a favorite George Eliot novel. Back on the *Semiramis*, he resumed his Mediterranean trip from port to port for almost four months: Athens . . . Alexandria . . . Smyrna, then on to the Dardanelles. While some played cards or chess, others entertained Pulitzer by reading to him a Walter Scott adventure, George Eliot's *The Mill on the Floss* and *Felix Holt,* Hall Caine's *The Deemster* and *The Bondsman,* and Thackeray's *Vanity Fair.*

Shielded from disturbing news, Pulitzer knew nothing of the lynching, led by prominent New Orleans citizens, of eleven Sicilian immigrants suspected of murdering the city's Irish police chief, David Hennessey. But the *World* made it a front-page story with a somewhat premature headline: "HENNESSY AVENGED . . . NEW ORLEANS STRIKES MAFIA A DEATH-BLOW." This was possibly the first time the Mafia presence in the United States was mentioned in an American newspaper.

In May Pulitzer rejoined Kate in Paris, but when he heard that Dr. Silas Weir Mitchell was in Rome, he hurried there to discuss if his anxiety about his "long-continued separation from concerns of great importance" might be the cause of his "cerebral irritation." In other words, inactivity was driving him nuts. Mitchell was adamantly opposed to Pulitzer returning to his previous frenetic lifestyle, warning him that the stress would endanger what little sight he had left. Then an unidentified individual broke through the protective barrier around him to tell Pulitzer that his paper was going to the dogs. It was true. The top executives were partly to blame, fighting each other for power and neglecting their work. Both morale and circulation had suffered.

Defying his doctor's warning, Pulitzer sailed for New York on June 3, arriving at his house on Fifty-fifth Street during a heat wave. From there he began to crack the whip. He fired his business manager, George Turner, who had demanded a hefty share of the profits, and replaced him with John Dillon from St. Louis. Pulitzer promoted Managing Editor Ballard Smith to replace Cockerill as editor in chief and made twenty-seven-year-old George Harvey managing editor, answering only to Pulitzer himself—an arrangement that infuriated older hands, especially Ballard Smith. Perhaps Pulitzer saw Harvey as his heir apparent and a younger version of himself, with, wrote Swanberg, "a tendency to asthma, a genius for conversation and an infallible memory." Pulitzer's toughest task was to handle Cockerill, who had been his brilliant partner for years, during which they called each other "John" and "Joe," and conversed with no holds or expletives barred. Now they were equally frank. Cockerill, like Turner, wanted a greater financial stake in the paper's profits and more recognition for his contributions to its success. Pulitzer was unwilling to give him more cash or credit. When their fights became too disruptive, Pulitzer told him to return to St. Louis and resume charge there. Cockerill refused and resigned. The great partnership was over, unfortunately, because, in Seitz's opinion, "no one ever came into the editorship who fitted in so well with Mr. Pulitzer and at the same time was able to rally men to himself and inspire them with his zeal and energy." Two weeks later Cockerill became editor of the morning edition of New York's *Commercial Advertiser.*

With Cockerill gone, Pulitzer initiated a system that would give him overall control of the paper wherever he was in the world. His top men were to meet every Monday at three in the afternoon to suggest story ideas, tackle problems, and respond to Pulitzer's cabled questions. He called the group his World Council.

That settled, Pulitzer took a test run in his newly acquired yacht, *Romola*, intending, if all went well, to sail her back to Europe. But during dinner on board, the heat in the main cabin almost cooked him, and he returned to Europe by steamship, ordering the yacht to join him at Leghorn. He hoped the stifling heat had been due to the unusually hot weather and that things would be cooler in European waters.

But it was as bad in Leghorn. Pulitzer spent one miserable night on board, then ordered the *Romola* returned to New York to be sold, before he headed for Paris. The yacht had no takers for several years until Venezuela bought it as a gunboat for twenty-five thousand dollars—seventy-five thousand dollars less than it cost him. And he chided Kate for her extravagance!

Pulitzer continued to defy his doctors' warnings by getting Ponsonby or Hosmer to read the *World* to him. A few weeks after he had settled in Paris, he cabled to Ballard Smith asking who had written the recent arresting page one report of a railroad wreck. Told it was a new man, Charles Chapin, Pulitzer sent his compliments, told Smith to give Chapin a large cash bonus, and made him city editor of the *Evening World*.

To protect the little eyesight he had left, he spent the rest of the summer in Wiesbaden under treatment, his days and sleepless nights relieved by smoking mild cigars while his secretaries read him the novels of Scott, Trollope, and the Brontë sisters. But he hardly relaxed, often urging them to skip the dull parts and get to the point.

On August 10, 1891, he cabled his World Council to suggest what public service or popular agitation the *World* should cover in the upcoming issues.

They gave him plenty to consider, such as:

1. Should we send a correspondent to Russia to report on the persecution of the Jews?
2. If, as seems likely, we could prove Police Captain Brogan was in the pay of brothelkeepers, should the *World* expose him?
3. The *World* has published a story based on a confidential report from a doctor who had analyzed James C. Blaine's urine and concluded that he was unfit for the Republican presidential nomination in 1892. Dana's *Sun* and other papers have scoffed at the report as fraudulent. How can we show the report was genuine and still protect the doctor's anonymity?
4. Propose recommending a children's playground be included in the [city's] East River park project.
5. Suggest combating the anti-*World* slurs of rival newspapers by taking the high road and praising their best work.

Eventually Pulitzer exposed anti-Semitism in Russia but did not approve using Blaine's urine test against him. As for Police Captain Brogan probably being on the take, Pulitzer was always eager to name crooked cops. He himself paid for a children's playground.

But what neither he nor his World Council ever appear to have suggested was whether to try to rehire star reporter Nellie Bly. She had quit the paper soon after her around-the-world triumph, saying that Pulitzer had failed to reward her as promised. Afterward, she had lectured, written a mildly successful novel, and then became deeply depressed. Pulitzer had a reputation for generosity and for keeping his word. His failure in Bly's case is puzzling. Yet she knew she would be welcomed back if she chose to return. There was certainly no prejudice against women reporters on the *World*. The daring and dashing twenty-three-year-old Elizabeth Jordan, for one, was encouraged to repeat Bly's exploits: write accounts of her visits to prison, a lunatic asylum, and—armed with a dagger—to a lonely mining camp in the mountains where no other woman had ever set foot. When the Koch Lymph treatment for consumption was being tested on Blackwell's Island volunteers, Jordan went to investigate. She was holding the hand of a patient at 3:00 A.M. when the woman died. Three hours later, her report of the incident landed on Ballard Smith's desk.

Jordan's big scoop for the *World* was her exclusive report of a murder charge against twenty-three-year-old medical student Carlyle Harris for poisoning eighteen-year-old Helen Harris, whom he had secretly married while she was still in boarding school. He was eventually executed. Jordan also wrote editorials and, in 1892, was promoted to assistant Sunday editor of the *World*, a job she held for seven years, when she left for *Harper's Weekly*.

She probably never met Pulitzer, who remained abroad until October 1891, when he felt up to another trip to New York just in time to oversee the handling of shocking news from Chile. On October 16, a mob in Valparaiso killed two American sailors and wounded others from the USS *Baltimore*. America threatened to go to war until the Chilean government apologized and paid seventy-five thousand dollars to the injured and to relatives of the dead men.

The following month, *Town Topics* printed a rumor that Pulitzer was desperately trying to persuade Cockerill and Turner to return to the *World* because Acting Editor in Chief Ballard Smith "wobbles about in his editorial chair in a truly ridiculous manner, and keeps everybody wondering what the *World* will do next to stultify itself." The magazine was on to something. But neither Turner nor Cockerill was tempted to return.

Soon after, Pulitzer hired Ballard Smith's probable replacement, Arthur Brisbane, a talented former London correspondent of the *Sun*. Brisbane's job also entailed confidentially evaluating his coworkers and sending Pulitzer regular reports about them. They in turn were expected to let Pulitzer know their views on Brisbane. This system of spying, perhaps necessary for a blind man directing the enterprise by remote control, inevitably became known to the victims.

None of the staff defended the practice, which caused "suspicion, jealousy and hatred," said cartoonist McDougall, and "a maelstrom of office politics that

Arthur Brisbane,
a workaholic, left
Dana's *Sun* to join
Pulitzer.

drove at least two editors to drink, one into suicide, a fourth into insanity, and another into banking [almost as tragic to newspapermen]. Even those of his employees who were naturally kindly and of generous instincts were compelled in self-protection to resort to unseemly tricks."

Although *World* reporter Charles Russell knew that backstabbing went with the territory in most city newsrooms, he found it worse under Pulitzer's regime, noting that "the news editor and the city editor were engaged in a savage effort to ruin each other" and that because Pulitzer valued new ideas so highly everyone kept a record of his own ideas "so that none might steal the credit."

Business Manager Don Carlos Seitz believed that he fomented competition to inspire workers to greater efforts in trying to outdo one another. But this never worked, according to Seitz: either the competitors became hopelessly deadlocked or "divided their domain and lived peacefully."

Yet despite Pulitzer's Machiavellian tactics, which he could have justified as an earnest effort to be well informed for the sake of the paper, McDougall, Russell, Seitz, Chambers—and even Cockerill—continued to admire him.

Cartoonist McDougall especially had reason to feel that way. Pulitzer had never criticized him nor discouraged his sometimes wild ideas. And when he was tempted to quit and work for Bennett's *Herald* for seventy-five dollars a week, Pulitzer told him, "I'll make it a hundred and ten dollars. You go away and be a good boy and don't bother about Bennett!" McDougall stayed, happily, for sixteen years.

During December, Pulitzer got an exasperated warning from Dr. Silas Weir Mitchell: "I want to say for the hundredth time what I think in regard to your present condition, not that it ought to need repetition," that continuing to direct the *World* newspapers, even from a distance, "will inevitably result in

Don Carlos Seitz,
Pulitzer's business
manager and
biographer.

destruction of what remains of your eyesight." Not only that, "but it is quite impossible for you to carry on your paper under present conditions without total sacrifice of your general health. The course on which you are now engaged is one of physical disaster."* The only concession Pulitzer made was to keep away from his majestic new building. Otherwise he defied his doctor's warning by continuing to indulge in his passion for politics. He was even preparing to promote a friend, David Hill, as a presidential contender, but when Hill advocated dropping the gold standard in favor of silver, he lost Pulitzer's support.

As usual, Pulitzer spent Christmas with his family, spoiling the children on the days when he wasn't bedridden with asthma. Some attacks were so bad, he began to work on his will.

In mid-January 1892 he was off to Washington to get a firsthand picture of the political situation, but on January 25 he had a near-fatal attack of asthma. To recuperate, he went south to Jekyll Island, Georgia, an exclusive resort limited to a hundred millionaires—among them J. P. Morgan, William Rockefeller, John Jacob Astor, and E. H. Harriman, many of them Republican robber barons Pulitzer continually lambasted in his papers.

The Pulitzers had been in the *Social Register* for a year, but as one of his secretaries remarked, "most wealthy socialites seem to look upon any sort of connection with J. P. as a very malignant from of leprosy and yet they have nothing definite to say against him." Some, obviously, were stung or humiliated

---

* Dr. Mitchell, a psychiatric pioneer, was also a novelist, and had been an army surgeon during the American Civil War, famous for his "rest cure."

by the way they were portrayed or exposed in his papers and had reason to shun him. He regretted losing some potential friends because of this but refused to compromise his "without fear or favor" principles. Wanting to educate a new generation of newspapermen and newspaperwomen to such rigid standards, he offered to fund a school of journalism at Columbia College—but that, like the social snubs, was rebuffed with a thanks but no thanks.

In early April 1892, after Pulitzer recovered from another asthma attack, he took his family to Paris, with the exception of Ralph, who stayed behind in his prep school. If his doctors hoped that distance would "cure" his obsessive interest in the imminent presidential campaign, they were mistaken. He was soon cabling suggestions to bring Cleveland back into the picture as the Democratic candidate, if only because Cleveland favored sticking to the gold standard.

Suspecting that Ballard Smith, the World's acting editor in chief, was not completely absorbed in the paper, Pulitzer considered replacing him with one of three contenders: the up-and-coming young dynamo George Harvey; his loyal chief editorial writer, William Merrill; or the triple threat Solomon Carvalho, who was said to resemble the Russian wolfhounds he raised as a hobby and who had proved equally adept as editor, reporter, and businessman.

Pulitzer first put Harvey to the test, by asking him to respond to the following:

"Suppose Ballard Smith should take his favored trip around the world, or for any other reason should make you and me unhappy by retiring from the paper; and suppose that all his functions were to fall upon your young, delicate and inexperienced shoulders, and you had entire responsibility—What difference would such change make in your work, your hours, and the general progress of the paper? What lines, ideas and faults would you alter? In short, would the paper be run differently if you had the chance? And how? What methods and men would you change? Please be specific, suggestive and fearless as possible; and please remember that this is only a hypothetical case; that I do not wish to promise anything; and that I remain with kindest wishes, always your friend, J. P."

Harvey's fearless reply was not fearless enough to eliminate the competition, so Pulitzer summoned Carvalho to Paris to grill him as Ballard Smith's possible replacement, intending to interrogate Harvey in person later.

Meanwhile, Pulitzer was leading Merrill to believe he was destined for the top job, asking him, like Harvey, to assume an hypothesis: "Please assume this hypothetical case, subject to change. J. P. dead [and] old Merrill the only trustee supposed to know anything about newspapers."

While Carvalho sailed for Europe at Pulitzer's bidding, Ballard Smith was making the hypothetical a virtual certainty by the way he was handling the summer's biggest news: a violent strike at a steel plant near Pittsburgh.

Despite its enormous profits, the Carnegie Steel Company at Homestead paid slave wages, especially to the imported Slav laborers. When Carnegie's deputy Henry Clay Frick announced a pay cut, the workers struck. Frick then announced he would reopen the plant the following month with scab labor if necessary. Enraged strikers drove out the Pinkerton guards Frick had employed and seized the plant. He countered by hiring a private army of three hundred armed Pinkerton detectives from New York and Chicago.

On July 6 the private army slowly approached the plant in two barges towed up the Monongahela River by the tugboat *Little Bill*. As they got within range, strikers peppered them with bricks and bullets, wounding a Pinkerton captain. The Pinkertons returned fire, killing two strikers, who responded with yells of "Kill the hired thugs!," and increased their firepower with sticks of dynamite, and even cannonballs from an ancient cannon. The barges moved relentlessly forward until strikers set some rafts alight and aimed them at the barges. The Pinkertons held out against the flames and smoke until midnight, when they raised the white flag and requested safe conduct out of Homestead. This was granted. But as they marched toward the railroad station, a mob beat two of them to death and wounded dozens of others. All told, ten men were killed and sixty-five injured in the fighting.

As expected, the *World* took the workers' side. In his editorials, William Merrill described "capitalist" Carnegie as "a foreigner" living "in a baronial castle in Scotland, his native land." As his "millions have increased from year to year, so have the wages of his employees decreased." Now, as "the foe of organized labor," he had hired "Pinkerton Hessians" (mercenaries) to convert his plant into a fortress against American workers. Ballard Smith had sent several reporters to cover the strike, and their accounts of the bloody confrontation— three pages of text and illustrations sympathetic to the strikers—supported the editorials and justified the subhead "The First Fruit of the Ironmaster's Resolve to Crush his Men."

Still occupying a rented villa in the Paris suburbs, Pulitzer was horrified when he learned of the violence from European newspapers Carvalho read to him, and noted that there were as many casualties as in many a South American revolution.

Because the edition of the *World* reporting the battle would not reach him for several days, he cabled New York, ordering a summary of the paper's coverage. When he heard it, he deplored the *World*'s apparent support of anarchy. His subsequent cable modified without completely reversing the paper's stand: he believed the strikers had been wrong in using force to seize and defend the plant. And Merrill was persuaded to include this Pulitzer suggestion in his July 12 editorial: "There is but one thing for the locked-out men to do. They must submit to the law. They must keep the peace. Their quarrel is with their employers. They must not resist the authority of the State. They must not make war upon the community."

Obviously Pulitzer had not anticipated that Governor Pattison would eventually answer Carnegie's call for troops by sending the state militia, which broke the strike and consequently destroyed the steelworkers' union.

Carvalho presumably agreed with Pulitzer's views on the strike. During his stay in Paris he had been bowled over by Pulitzer's intelligence. When he left to return to the States he was convinced that his boss had the most brilliant mind he'd ever known, and that a few days' conversation with him were as good as years of formal education. In his turn he impressed Pulitzer, who promoted him to vice president and chief financial officer of the company and gave him an embarrassing first assignment: to fire Ballard Smith as acting editor in chief while not offering him any other position, and to replace him with George Harvey.

Biographer Seitz suggests that Ballard Smith was not fired because of his partisan handling of the Homestead strike but because he was acting like a man on the verge of a mental breakdown. And Pulitzer was in no state to deal with that. In fact, he himself became depressed without Carvalho's stimulating company, and obsessed with saving his sight. Seeking reassurance, he went to Wiesbaden to be reexamined by Dr. Pagenstecher. The oculist had grim news, which he chose not to share with his patient. He wrote to Kate, instead, warning her not to reveal the "real character of the disease of the left eye, because it would take away every hope from him and would have a great and unfavorable impression on his total nervous system. In his present state of health every thing should be avoided that might affect his nervousness."

Not yet knowing he was a hopeless case, Pulitzer took the cure in Baden-Baden, where his sons Ralph and Joe spent a few days with him and where Hosmer finished reading *The Life of George Eliot* to him. He had recovered his spirits enough to be amused when an Englishwoman at the spa found out who he was and sent a note to him that read: "Dear Mr. Pulitzer, I hate to force myself in this way but honestly I should die if I couldn't get books and I will, with the greatest delight, read whatever you like—on the terrace—in the reading room—anywhere. Tomorrow at three if you like an hour's reading command me." Pulitzer forwarded the letter to Kate with his comment scrawled in large letters: "My dear Kate, The enclosed shows the terrible danger I am exposed to. Save me! Come quick! So far still faithfully & devotedly J. P."

Perhaps to escape from the willing woman, but mostly because Baden-Baden was too noisy to get much sleep, he investigated Egypt as a "land of possible tranquility" but quickly found it was even noisier than Germany.

Back in Paris, he began to show indecision if not ambivalence in writing to George Harvey. In the same letter, of July 22, he invited and disinvited Harvey to meet him. Shortly before, Harvey was so certain Pulitzer wanted him in Paris that he sent his wife on ahead, while he attended to pressing work at the *World* that kept him so late that each night he slept in one of the newspaper's bedroom suites.

Now Pulitzer was asking Harvey to bring all the dope on the presidential hopefuls (Democrats Cleveland and Adlai Ewing Stevenson, Republicans Harrison and Whitelaw Reid), as well as "about 200 cigars, the very lightest that exist and, of course, the best, regardless of price. Have every box opened and examine them so as to make sure that each is the lightest shade existible. Of course I assume that you will sail, but this is based on the assumption that you would not sail if, by so doing, any great opportunity were neglected. I want to see you very much, but I must say frankly that it is not about the 'Paper' half so much as because I think the trip will be a pleasure to you and its loss a disappointment. You are personally sympathetic to me, and I would enjoy your visit, you must know by this time. But I always sacrificed my pleasure for the paper, and I would like you to feel the same way."

Knowing a test when he saw one, Harvey stayed in New York, which meant his wife spent their much-anticipated European vacation on her own. Despite what a visitor called Pulitzer's very melancholy state, he did rouse himself to apologize to Harvey's wife for her husband's absence, adding disingenuously, "My regard for you is so high that I cannot for a moment believe you would allow your private wishes to interfere with your husband's public duties." Soon after, he cabled Harvey encouraging him to devote twelve hours a day to the job, quickly following it with a message begging him to take care of his health and not to regard the "twelve-hour" cable too strictly. On the other hand, he said, he was as anxious for Harvey to succeed during this trial period as if his own son were up for the job.

Incredibly, for a sick man tormented with insomnia Pulitzer was brimming with detailed ideas on how Harvey should proceed: "Perhaps fifty different essentials for improving the paper, none might be more immediately felt than if you were to be your own City Editor for a month, going into every detail and minutia with utmost vigor. If you could for a month so arrange your work as to have two or three hours every night to teach the different copy readers how to condense, how not to pad, how to eject all water, padding, rot, rubbish, etc., you would do the most necessary work. Every night you ought to go to bed feeling that you have condensed at least one page, if not two. Every night you ought to go to bed feeling that you have taught the other fellows something that will save you trouble in the future. Every night you ought to go to bed feeling that you are yourself developing as a great condenser. Every night you ought to go to bed feeling that the great work of an editor after all is not what he does himself, but what he teaches and trains others to do for him."

Harvey was tempted to reply: Every night I won't have time to go to bed. But he wanted the job.

Pulitzer's treatment of Ballard Smith, which at first seemed callous, turned out to be generous and sympathetic. On August 24 he gave him a farewell dinner at Delmonico's and cabled: "Grateful memories for loyal services, sorrow for parting and confident hopes for happy career. The *World* will always be a tender Alma Mater, proud of your talents, watchful of your fame and helpful of your high aspirations."

They were not empty words. Pulitzer made him the *World*'s London correspondent. Ballard Smith lasted there a year, until he had the anticipated nervous breakdown, and returned to the United States. He died seven years later in a Waverly, Massachusetts, sanitarium.

* * *

In the fall of 1892 Pulitzer increased the competitive tension among his top executives. Instead of choosing one man to run the paper, he appointed a tri-umvirate under his overall direction: Harvey as acting editor in chief in charge of news; Merrill, the editorials; and Carvalho the finances, with orders, because of increasing costs, to cut expenses to the bone, especially the generous staff salaries.

Harvey still appeared to be the leading contender for the top job as Pulitzer's eventual successor, judging by Pulitzer's efforts to test his resilience and whip him into shape. Instead of giving him time off after covering the exhausting presidential election campaign, for example, Pulitzer advised him to put in more time: six hours a day reading newspapers, from which to extract ideas, suggestions, and criticisms; several more hours sharing his discoveries with other executives; and two or three additional hours reading books to culti-vate and equip his mind! And, of course, he also had to get the paper out.

Pulitzer told Harvey that if his criticisms seemed harsh or unjust after the honeymoon period, he should take it as a reassuring sign: "Remember that fault-finding is perhaps both my privilege and my weakness, that correction is the only road to improvement, and that my quick temper and illness are enti-tled to some consideration. As long as I find fault with you, I hope and believe in the use of trying to train, teach, and perpetuate you. When I find it hopeless to improve a man, I always quit the job and never criticize."

If this was the honeymoon period, Harvey must have had second thoughts about the marriage. But, at least, unlike many of his colleagues, he still had his job.

By October 22 Carvalho had obeyed Pulitzer's orders to cut costs by firing twenty-five reporters, sending jitters through the rest of the editorial staff. According to the *Journalist*, because of these Friday night massacres, even the survivors felt like "jelly-fish, with the possible exception of Carvalho (the exe-cutioner). The men are today on salary, tomorrow on space, now doing night work then assigned to day work and, of all the press men, they are really the most miserable." Now, instead of comparing him with his Russian wolfhounds, disgruntled newsmen said that Carvalho's limp—he had an artificial leg—and swarthy complexion made him look like Satan.

Assured that his paper was in good hands, Pulitzer cabled Cleveland his congratulations when he won the presidential election, pleased at least to have a Democrat back in the White House, then left for Monte Carlo to spend the winter in a milder climate. But he was out of luck. He caught a cold while attending the opera in Nice and was bedridden for two weeks. Even so, he con-tinued to handle an avalanche of cables. One especially agitated him. It reported that Zebulon Brockway, warden of New York State's Elmira Prison, despite instituting several reforms, was still flogging difficult prisoners. Pulitzer called for a sustained campaign to get rid of Brockway. Harvey complied, dubbed Brockway "The Paddler," and repeatedly demanded his removal.

CHAPTER 16

Pulitzer's
"Satanic Journalism"

1893–1894
—
46 to 47 years old

As a tribute to Pulitzer's ten years at the helm, the Sunday *World* printed a huge hundred-page issue, which sold a record four hundred thousand copies. Three days later, on May 10, 1893, he arrived in Manhattan, having crossed the Atlantic aboard the liner *Majestic* in a specially soundproofed stateroom. But he couldn't soundproof Manhattan. Bracing himself for loud voices and clattering cutlery, he invited his top twenty men to celebrate the paper's birthday at Delmonico's.

As if to designate his heirs apparent, he sat his chief editorial writer, William Merrill, on his right and Publisher Solomon Carvalho on his left. Managing Editor George Harvey responded to this implied demotion by getting sloshed. He, John Dillon, and George Eggleston then became a competitive trio who raised the spirits and lowered the resistance of everyone by repeatedly proposing toasts. Past midnight, Harvey stood for probably the tenth toast, glass in hand, and tipsily proposed, perhaps in jest: "To the . . . ah . . . er . . . King!"

Pulitzer was not amused. "Damn it!" he protested. "No kings! No kings!"

During his three days in New York, Pulitzer had reporter David Graham Phillips to dinner at his Fifty-fifth Street home. The charming Princeton graduate, who had trained on the *Sun*, proved such an informed and agreeable guest that Pulitzer offered him the job of London correspondent. Phillips accepted and traveled back to Europe with Pulitzer and his entourage on May 13.

A month later, in his search of an ideal summer home for his family, Pulitzer again crossed the Atlantic, to Mount Desert Island near Bar Harbor,

Maine. There he took a three-month lease on a fifteen-acre oceanside estate called Chatwold. The main house had twenty-six rooms and seven bathrooms. Most bedrooms and several guest suites were on the second floor. There was room on the third floor for twenty or more servants. The place also had separate servants' quarters, a caretaker's cottage, a large stable, and two greenhouses.

At Chatwold, Pulitzer pondered Harvey's fate. Pulitzer had quickly become disillusioned with the boy wonder after office spies told him that Harvey was often a no-show at the Dome and tried to edit the paper by phone from various clubs. Harvey had also toyed with an offer to be consul general in Berlin, though he had finally rejected it. Was this a man he could rely on as his possible successor?

When Harvey contracted pneumonia, Pulitzer was forced to act. Carvalho seemed a sure thing, but Pulitzer decided to find an outside man to take over—bitterly disappointing long-term and loyal men on the staff who had hoped for a crack at the job. He finally chose forty-five-year-old Colonel Charles H. Jones, former editor of the Democratic *Missouri Republican*, who had raised its circulation and the blood pressure of political opponent David Francis, Missouri's equally feisty governor. The two had eventually abandoned words for a fistfight—Pulitzer's kind of man, reminding him of Cockerill, perhaps, or even himself. But he still had to grill him to make sure, which he did almost nonstop for a week, when Jones came as his guest at Chatwold. He more than passed the test: he was as good as anointed.

In July, to the astonishment and chagrin of other executives, Jones arrived at the Dome waving a blue envelope containing Pulitzer's instructions putting him in complete editorial charge of the *World* and making triumvirate members mere figureheads. But Jones got off to a bad start. Resenting his promotion over them, the old-timers scoffed at his side whiskers—then out of fashion— and mocked his "ladylike manners." But Jones plowed ahead, with the panache of a confident dictator—until he overplayed his hand.

In August, President Cleveland called Congress into emergency session to repeal the 1890 Silver Act, which he believed had caused the financial depression that now had Wall Street in a panic. All other leading nations were on the gold standard, he said, while the federal government was frittering away gold to buy almost the entire silver output of the United States. As Pulitzer agreed with Cleveland, the Washington bureau chief, John Tennant, confidently reported that repeal of the Silver Purchase Act was assured. To Tennant's dismay, Colonel Jones unexpectedly turned up at the Washington bureau, where he wrote a long editorial opposing repeal. Then he ordered Tennant to send it to Carvalho for publication—which he did, reluctantly.

On getting it, Carvalho informed Pulitzer in Bar Harbor, who naturally killed an editorial counter to his views. When it didn't appear in the paper, Jones accused Tennant of not sending it and of substituting his own report. Tennant proved him wrong by taking him to the telegraph office, where they confirmed that Jones's message had gone out and that nothing of Tennant's had been sent that day. Jones returned to New York furious and humiliated, to the delight of the rest of the staff.

The *World* continued to oppose the silver-buying spree and to support the bill that became law later in the year, letting the government maintain its gold reserves. While Jones still remained in charge of the paper, he had lost some of his bark and most of his bite.

By August Harvey had recovered from pneumonia, and Pulitzer summoned him to Bar Harbor to recuperate and to discuss his future. There, Harvey shocked him by saying that, unable to stomach the thought of Jones as his boss, he had already resigned. Anxious not to lose him, Pulitzer asked Harvey to help him write a book about journalism, but he declined. The book was never written, though Pulitzer later spelled out his journalistic principles and practices in conversations with secretary-companions, which appear in their books about him.

Meanwhile, Phillips, the recently appointed London correspondent, complained that he was not getting a byline—as promised—not even for his recent dramatic scoop: an exclusive account of the accidental sinking of a British battleship, *Victoria*. "It's because I'm not yet satisfied with your work," Pulitzer explained. "The *Sun* and *Herald* have formed a rather more favorable impression," Phillips replied and handed in his notice.

But Pulitzer persuaded him to rejoin the paper on an irresistible assignment—leading the *World*'s campaign against Rockefeller's Standard Oil and other monster monopolies. Phillips set to with enthusiasm. He established that the Sherman Antitrust Act was a dud and that, despite attempts to break up Standard Oil, it was still intact and ruled by Rockefeller. Phillips took on Attorney General Richard Olney for not enforcing the law aggressively, ending each published exposé with the same: "Such, Mr. Olney, are the facts, and here, sir, is the law," which he then quoted.

President Cleveland tried to silence Phillips by twice writing to Pulitzer insisting that the *World* was misinterpreting the antitrust act. In fact, the act was so riddled with legal loopholes that some lawyers for giant trusts got away with the argument that their companies were protected by the Fourteenth Amendment—meant to protect the rights of ex-slaves as persons. They claimed that corporations were also persons who could not be deprived of their property without due process of law. In this Alice-in-Wonderland atmosphere, instead of taming tycoons, the antitrust law was enforced to emasculate labor unions, using the argument that unions restrained trade.

Far from obliging Cleveland by silencing Phillips, Pulitzer backed up his reporter when he supported striking workers at Henry Havemeyer's sugar refinery in Brooklyn. The refinery was part of a gigantic sugar trust which Attorney General Olney had made no attempt to break up. And when Havemeyer called for police protection from the strikers, the *World* attacked him and the federal government: "Havemeyer knows that this Sugar Trust of his is a lawless, criminal conspiracy, that its very existence is a crime, and that the only reason those who maintain it were not long ago brought to trial is that there has been an era of inefficiency in the Attorney-General's office during which only those criminals who wear shabby clothes and have no social position have been prosecuted."

Four railroad companies fueled the financial panic of 1893 by going bust and putting three million more men with shabby clothes out of work. The federal government went into shock, and the *World* started a bread fund to feed the hungry. Fearing that anarchists would seize the opportunity to throw bombs, the police cracked down on potential threats, among them twenty-five-year-old Emma Goldman. As editor of *Mother Earth*, an anarchist magazine that as good as promised bloody revolution, and as a lover of fellow anarchist Alexander Berkman, who had tried to assassinate Henry Clay Frick during the Homestead Strike, Goldman was on the most-wanted list. The police arrested and imprisoned her on a charge of incitement to riot.

Who better to interview her than star reporter Nellie Bly, welcomed back at the *World* after time out to recover from a long bout of depression?

The *World* felt partly responsible for Goldman's arrest, having reported her rabble-rousing speech to a mass rally in Union Square, and which the police cited as damning evidence.

In her report of the interview, Bly, who was captivated by Goldman, disputed the *New York Times* description of her as a "fire-eating anarchist," and other views of her as a "property-destroying, capitalist-killing, riot-promoting agitator with a red flag in one hand, a burning torch in the other, and murder continually on her lips." Instead, Bly called her a neat, immaculate, and modestly dressed "modern Joan of Arc . . . a little bit of a girl, just five feet high, with a saucy, turned-up nose and very expressive blue-gray eyes."

Bly's piece on Sunday, September 17, 1893, was prominently displayed on page one, above the fold and across seven columns. It was headed—with Bly in the starring role:

NELLIE BLY AGAIN

———

She Interviews Emma Goldman
and Other Anarchists

In the interview, Goldman decried murder, being satisfied, she said, "to agitate, to teach, and I only ask justice and freedom of speech." At her trial Goldman claimed she had not incited the hungry and unemployed to violence, but had merely urged them to demonstrate in order to obtain their rights. And she blamed her plight on the *World* for printing a garbled account of her speech.

Not wanting to keep an innocent woman in prison by misquoting her, Pulitzer gave her the benefit of the doubt and offered to print a speech she had not been allowed to read in court—an offer she accepted. But it didn't help, nor did Bly's sympathetic portrait of a gentle idealist. She got a year in the Blackwell's Island prison.

Either Goldman had snowed Bly or had revealed only one side of her volatile personality, which she dramatically demonstrated after leaving prison. Goldman, who had two concurrent lovers, Johann Most and Alexander Berkman, both anarchists, was attending a lecture by Most. Forewarned that he meant to denounce her other lover, Berkman, for trying to kill Henry Clay Frick, Goldman was prepared to protest. She hid a whip under her skirt. And when Most began criticizing Berkman for his assassination attempt, the "little bit of a girl . . . with a saucy, turned-up nose" leaped onstage, whipped him across the face, then broke the whip over her knee and threw the pieces at him. Perhaps her idea of free speech.

The *Journalist* welcomed Bly back as an improved model: "When through her indomitable pluck with the assistance of the *World*, she awoke to find herself famous, she forgot that her successes were only in the line of doing odd things and that literary merit had little to do with them. Now she comes back to the *World* to make her name over again. Her command of language is improved; she is more of a woman of the world; and she has a better idea of what the public will read."

Her work encouraged Pulitzer to hire another attractive woman reporter, Dolores Marbourg, and to give her similar "stunt" assignments. For one, she stood outside the Union Club posing as a flower seller, leading to an account of how an unnamed distinguished married man had propositioned her. The magazine *Town Topics* went to town in expressing moral indignation against a paper that printed such stuff, suggesting, "There is only one more step for Joe Pulitzer's crew of editors to take, and that is to employ a virtuous girl to go into a house of ill repute and write the story for the Sunday issue. Everything else has been done."

One can imagine a simultaneous laughing response from the *World* editors: "Great idea! But the boss won't go for it." In fact, Pulitzer had a puritanical attitude toward sex, although he approved almost any other type of story that might entertain readers—but only on Sundays. The daily edition remained sacrosanct and held to much higher standards. However, Pulitzer's definition of an unforgivable sin was to produce a dull paper—any day of the week.

Dartmouth graduate Morrill Goddard, editor of the Sunday edition, was rarely guilty of sinning. He persuaded a leading Episcopal clergyman to live in a Hell's Kitchen tenement for six weeks and report his impressions, which started with a sizzling: "I would rather live in hell than Hell's Kitchen."

Goddard also chose a shopgirl to write a provocative review of a play about an English shopgirl, which began: "Can it be possible that such a stupid specimen as Ada Smith could get a situation in any of the London shops?" Considered the leading practitioner of the "crime, underwear and pseudo-science school of journalism, [Goddard] illustrated a science feature on anatomy with the shapely legs of actresses and showgirls."

Pulitzer applauded Goddard's golden touch, and when circulation topped five hundred thousand, promised that if the next week's circulation rose he'd give him "two weeks salary instead of one." From then on, Goddard's pay was frequently doubled.

In October 1893 Pulitzer and his entourage left Maine for Paris, which he found unendurably noisy, so he headed south, for Nice. There he began to plan an extraordinary, unique lifestyle that would allow him to resume complete control of his *World* without going near the place. This would have been a challenge for a healthy man with all his faculties, yet, at forty-seven, Pulitzer was an asthmatic, rheumatic, neurotic, diabetic, insomniac, pathologically sensitive to noise, and virtually blind. Without his millions and almost manic drive he could never have pulled it off.

First he hired George H. Ledlie, Dillon's assistant on the *Post-Dispatch*, as a real-estate scout, with orders to find a place in the south of France free of barking dogs, courting cats, traffic of any kind, and noisy neighbors.

When Ledlie found such a rarity—a villa with a large garden leading down to the Mediterranean—Pulitzer had the building completely soundproofed before moving in. Then Ledlie had to hire several secretary-companions to entertain Pulitzer around the clock, read him to sleep with novels, provide music and intelligent conversation, keep him informed of national and international events as well as the daily contents of the *World*, and relay his orders, comments, and ideas to his staff thousands of miles away in the golden Dome.

One candidate for secretary-companion was eliminated when he made a nervous gesture and broke a valuable Persian vase. The noise, not the value of the piece, lost him the job. The first man he did hire in Nice was Alfred Butes, a capable and discreet Englishman, a sign that Pulitzer was beginning to lose his anti-British bias.

Soon after, Pulitzer's chief editorial writer, William Merrill, joined his boss for what he recalled as "the longest and most delightful vacation of my life." Pulitzer also treated subeditor Arthur Brisbane to a few weeks in the southern sun. Brisbane repaid his generosity by persuading him to resume horseback riding—which he had given up because of his poor sight. Astride a gentle horse, with Brisbane at his side, he regained his confidence and enjoyed riding for the rest of his life.

Pulitzer continued to regret losing Harvey, to whom he wrote sadly of "the apparently pangless severance of our relations," and even offered to send him money if he needed it. Forgetting that Harvey had resigned, not been fired, he followed up with: "I am not afraid to go even a step further and to say that while the lamp still holds out to burn, my favorite prodigal may return." Urged by Pulitzer, Brisbane also wrote to Harvey: "If you send Pulitzer the right sort of cable, you can have your job back, if you want it." Harvey didn't, although he and Pulitzer stayed friends for life. He went on to make a small fortune assisting financier William C. Whitney, and afterward became president of the book publishing company Harper & Brothers.

Those who stayed with Pulitzer, especially his secretary-companions, vied with one another to win his approval or to cheer him up when he was down.

Hosmer, who also doubled as his doctor, resented Butes's outstanding success at this and once tried to top him at dinner with a joke that fell flat. Instead of laughing, Pulitzer remarked ominously that it was sometimes dangerous to be too funny. After the meal Hosmer wrote to Kate like a jealous suitor, complaining that "when a little pet-secretary of the amusing variety gets absolute control of a great man's mind—the old serious donkey style of secretary must take a back seat & shut up. It seems to me impossible to stay the winter in the difficult circumstances & I may have to get out. In that case I shall ask for a position on the paper. Will you support my application with your illimitable influence?" In Hosmer's periodical report to Kate of Pulitzer's health he again revealed his sour grapes: "J. P.'s mind is perfectly normal—as to his getting into a rage & being wrong—he has probably done that all his life. But his immeasurable fondness for his new friend is a symptom worth attention."

Hosmer proved useful in March 1894, when Kate arrived with their son Ralph in St. Moritz, Switzerland, where the boy was to recuperate from pneumonia and an asthma attack. Pulitzer joined them and sent Hosmer first to Davos in Switzerland and then to Colorado Springs to search for a good doctor to treat Ralph's asthma. Although he proposed several suitable doctors in Colorado Springs, Pulitzer turned them all down and ordered a disgruntled Hosmer back to Switzerland. Pulitzer then took Ralph with him to enjoy the mineral water at Ragatz, Switzerland, where he rented a villa for the rest of the spring, leaving Kate in St. Moritz.

In a note to Kate from Ragatz, Pulitzer explained his infrequent letters to her: "Writing to me is 'headachey,' such sweet sorrow, that in the language of Shakespeare I always say 'Goodbye till 'tis tomorrow'—and thus no letter. I had a long séance with Dr. Holland about his bill [for treating Ralph] and of course he is perfectly convinced that he is perfectly right and I perfectly wrong." He surprised her with another letter next day: "A line to tell you we are well, that this is my day off, my mood corresponding with the dark cloudy rainy dismal weather outside, that Ralph is very well and that I am thinking of you probably a great deal more than you are entitled to, sorry for you if you are still abed [with a minor ailment], and hoping for you to be up soon. Now I think this is really after all a pretty good letter considering that I am very ill-tempered and only started to send you 'a line.' Give me credit for it for I do not intend to write you for another month now. As ever, affectionately, J. P."

Though his family rarely mentioned their own illnesses, they sometimes couldn't resist it, which inevitably induced him to match or top them. So when Kate mentioned her rheumatism, he replied: "I have frightful rheumatism and have had it for six weeks more than in the last six years together. This morning I could hardly sponge my face or eat my bread—rheumatism of the joints of my right hand. I can now fully sympathize with you if you have the thing as badly."

Back at Bar Harbor in June, Pulitzer hired Felix Webber as secretary/piano player. Webber saw the worst of Pulitzer almost immediately, describing him in a letter to relatives in London as "a coarse, bloated millionaire, who thinks that by paying people he can buy immunity from the little self restraint that comes natural to most people (thank goodness)."

At dinner with the family, Webber witnessed a quarrel between Joseph and Kate over money. "It is incredible that any man could be so horribly selfish as he is," Webber wrote. "We've been going through stormy days partly because it is the beginning of the month and accounts have to be settled up. Mrs. P. says she cannot and will not run the house on $6,000 a month, that she cannot make ends meet on less than double that sum and so when a cheque was given to her for that amount [$6,000] for this month through the business secretary, she returned it and left the task of making conversation to J. P. at meal time to the unfortunate secretaries."

Resenting the triple chore of playing for, reading to, and conversing with his boss, Webber grumbled that Pulitzer could tire out twelve secretaries in twenty-four hours by his ceaseless demands to be entertained or enlightened. "It takes me every moment of my time to devour literature enough to keep J. P.'s mind occupied and even then my stock of conversation runs out before we get to the end of the drives and I am barely one novel ahead of him. I have to have two or three in hand to feel comfortable."

Webber was most disgusted by Pulitzer's callous treatment of his fourteen-year-old daughter Lucille. She had lost a lot of blood from throat surgery, Webber told his relatives, and "after hours of torture fainted away when the second operation was made and then was given morphia to spare her more pain. Mrs. P. was terribly upset with all this—never left the girl, came to meals in a peignoir with hair uncurled (a sign of terrible anxiety with her), couldn't eat anything and began to look very ill herself. Meanwhile the great J. P. never even went up to see his daughter, and at dinner Mrs. P. asked him why this was, and if he did not pity her. 'Pity Lucille!' he shouted. 'No! I'm the only one to pity—has no one any pity for *me!*—does no one realize what I suffer! My own house turned into a hospital! Doctors coming at all hours! You rushing upstairs in the middle of meals, without a word of conversation for me. No one pities me and you ask me to pity Lucille!' After this outburst of eloquence Mrs. P. could not bring herself to speak to him for a long time. The next day she gave me instructions that J. P. was not to be allowed upstairs, that he was to be kept down by main force if he should want to go up, 'but,' she added ferociously, '*he* won't want to come up, he won't even ask after her.' And she was right. The next day J. P. seems to have realized that he had shown what a brute he is when a message came from Lucille asking why he had not been to see her. He went up to her and promised her a pair of cobs and a carriage for her to drive herself as a reward for the pluck she had shown. By her bedside he saw piles of flowers, and when he was told that they had been sent by different friends, he got quite jealous (jealousy of the most intense kind is the only symptom of anything approaching affection he can feel for anyone, even his own children) and so he told me to go and order the handsomest basket of flowers I could get, regardless of price, and have it sent up to her. But having done so much he thought he had quite made up for everything and began patting himself on the back for his wonderful generosity and again lost all interest in the child and seemed bored when I asked him if he had any preference as to the sort of flowers. 'Oh, any sort,' he said impatiently, 'as long as they are the handsomest in New York.' So I obeyed instructions and spent $25 on a basket of roses."

At the time Pulitzer was interrogating another potential secretary named Harbord, whom Webber believed stood a good chance "because he never stops talking. Dull as ditch water he is, but he somehow manages to keep the ball rolling and that's the chief thing that's wanted so that at times when J. P. and Mrs. P. are not on speaking terms—should be less apparent at meals." A disgruntled employee from the start, Webber resented Pulitzer's "way of keeping all your nerves on the bristle and even if some time he doesn't say or do anything disagreeable, there is always the fear that he will. If 100 difficult things are done and well-done and one little slip is made he will forget the 100 things but remember and rub well in the one slip. Leaving him is just like getting up from the dentist's chair and letting all one's nerves relax again."

Pulitzer justified his angry outbursts by saying that all men who amounted to anything, including Napoleon, were ill tempered and that a good temper "was entirely incompatible with greatness in any line." Lord Randolph Churchill, who appeared in Chicago that summer, was a case in point, supporting Pulitzer's contention. Here was a man of moment with an imperious manner and fierce temper, exacerbated now by a fatal illness that was driving him insane. The *World* report was headlined:

CHURCHILL IN RETREAT
The Brilliant Young Tory Leader Is
Under Treatment in Chicago for
the Morphine Habit.
TO AMERICA AS A LAST RESORT.
He Had Vainly Sought Relief in Africa,
in Italy, in Spain, in Russia and
in France.

W. R. Gilbert, a famous English cricketer and friend, was quoted as saying: "Lord Randolph Churchill's break down in the House of Commons led to his placing himself under the doctor's charge. Eyewitnesses aver that nothing has been seen in that house as pitiable as the once brilliant statesman's collapse. So great, indeed, was it that old friends shed tears of sympathy. The break down was not, as many claimed the result of liquor."

Not even the *World* knew that the cause of Churchill's collapse was a syphilis-induced incurable disease, general paralysis.

Coincidentally, Nellie Bly was in Chicago at the time, not to interview Randolph Churchill but to cover a catastrophic railroad strike that had started there against the Pullman Company and now paralyzed much of the nation.

George Pullman, coinventor of sleeping berths in railroad cars and owner of the company making them, had planned to protect himself from business reverses caused by strikes and the bombs of angry anarchists. His solution was to build a personal fiefdom south of Chicago, with some twelve thousand workers and their families as his serfs, over whose minds, money, and hearts he had almost godlike control. And he named the town Pullman. As one worker put it: "We are born in a Pullman house, fed from the Pullman shops, taught in the Pullman school, catechized in the Pullman Church and when we die we go to the Pullman hell."

Despite the continuing financial panic in 1894, George Pullman was in great shape, living in a mansion with its own pipe organ and swimming pool. That same year, though his company had made a twenty-five-million-dollar profit, he began a mean-spirited economy drive, laying off workers, then rehiring them at wage cuts averaging 25 percent. In the town of Pullman, their rents, deducted from their pay, were 25 percent above the going rate in nearby communities. But when three workers asked Pullman to reduce rents to compensate for their wage cuts, he fired them—and sparked a devastating strike, shutting down railroads throughout much of the country.

At the end of June, President Cleveland sent twelve thousand federal troops to Chicago—about half the U.S. Army—to break the strike, ostensibly because it prevented delivery of the U.S. mail. Railroad officials had given him this contrived excuse by hooking up mail trains to Pullman cars. Strikers retaliated by torching and looting the trains, and twelve were killed in the riots that followed.

The *World's* Colonel Jones responded to the troop deployment with a provocative editorial, damning Cleveland as a strikebreaker and supporting strike leader Eugene V. Debs for defying the government. The *World* was almost a lone voice in its prounion stance. The *Washington Post* called the strike a "social pestilence brought here from abroad by the criminals and outcasts of European slums." And according to the *Chicago Tribune*, Pullman's employees were happy and uncomplaining until "dictator Debs and his dupes ordered them to strike."

When his own paper's editorial written by Jones was read to him, Pulitzer was furious. Though he sympathized with the workers, as he did during the Homestead strike, he abhorred their violent tactics and defiance of the federal government. Summoned to Bar Harbor, Jones refused to acknowledge he had made a mistake. Unable to fire him because of his watertight contract, Pulitzer hoped to "exile" him to St. Louis with the offer of a half interest in the *Post-Dispatch* for three hundred thousand dollars, but Jones wasn't buying. He stayed at the *World*, but with clipped wings—banned by Pulitzer from writing any more editorials.

Sent to Pullman to cover the story, Nellie Bly was at first against the strikers until she saw their deplorable conditions. They told her how Pullman's "paradise" was more like purgatory, where he charged "50 cents for every nail we drive in the house and a tax of 50 cents a month on houses with shutters. Shutters are taxed just the same as water. One man didn't want to pay the tax and had them remove the shutters but they charged him just the same because the shutters had been on the house. And if you break a pane of glass the company won't let you repair it for yourself, but they do it and charge double what we could have done it for."

After a half day at Pullman, Bly reported that she was "the most bitter striker in town." Taking a line at odds with Pulitzer's editorials, she wrote that the strikers "are not firebrands; they are not murderers and rioters; they are not Anarchists. They are quiet, peaceful men who have suffered beneath the heel of the most heartless coward it has ever been my misfortune to hear of."

Later, she said, she "went in fear and trembling" to interview John Altgeld, the tough Illinois reformist governor with a "hair-raising" reputation for hating the press. His pardoning of three anarchists serving life terms for murder during the 1886 Haymarket Square riots had raised storms of protests and accusations that he, too, was an anarchist.

She dared to ask him straight out if he was an anarchist. He flatly denied it, and astonished her when, despite his fearsome reputation, her account of the strikers' pathetic conditions brought tears to his eyes. But he doubted that any Chicago newspaper would publish anything against capitalists, and was sure Pulitzer would kill her prostriker report. "It's already been printed," she replied, explaining that Pulitzer hired "people to find out and publish the truth about everything, regardless of all other considerations, and if the truth is not given it is solely the fault of the writer, not the paper."

When Bly left, although the governor told her he still hated reporters, it was obvious that he liked her—so much so that on his next trip to New York he sought her out. Pulitzer was then campaigning against cruelty to zoo animals. So, mixing business with pleasure, Bly persuaded the governor to join her to investigate conditions in the Central Park Zoo.

Pulitzer's main concern was still the Pullman strike, and he applauded Cleveland's decision to appoint a commission of inquiry. It exonerated Debs and his American Railway Union from the charge of provoking violence and panned Pullman and the railroad owners as selfish dictators. But the damage had been done: Debs had spent six months in prison—where his reading of history converted him to socialism—and his union had been all but destroyed.

Pulitzer's support of the underdog did not impress his jealous rival the New York Times, which was losing readers in droves and threatened with extinction. It accused him of irresponsibility in pandering to the public's low tastes. When, for example, a young couple committed suicide in New York's Central Park and a clipping from the World was found in the dead man's pocket, the Times blamed Pulitzer for the tragedy. The clipping, part of a World series titled "Is Suicide a Sin?," had contained a letter from atheist colonel Robert Ingersoll advocating suicide under certain extreme circumstances. The Times implied that the letter encouraged the couple to kill themselves, and, even worse, that it was a fake letter concocted by a *World* reporter from an interview. He had "called on Col. Ingersoll," according to the *Times*, "and asked him several hypothetical questions on suicide and Col. Ingersoll answered them. But when the interview was published, all the questions had been eliminated and the article made to look like a letter [from Ingersoll] in favor of suicide as a way for a person to get rid of his troubles. Had the questions been printed as they were given there would have been no such idea conveyed. Col. Ingersoll is highly indignant and has already prepared the papers in a libel suit which he will bring against the newspaper."

When asked to comment Ingersoll demolished the *Times* account, calling it completely untrue.

Instead of apologizing, the *Times* launched a counterattack—with scurrilous letters purporting to come from readers blaming the two suicides on Pulitzer's "satanic journalism" and asking, "Is there no law by which the leprous Jew can be punished?" Others reproved Pulitzer for clamoring for beer, baseball, and music on the Sabbath; for making "police spies of young women" by sending them to investigate social crimes; and for commanding "a young woman of education to attend the cruel flagellation of a thief in Delaware in order that she might describe 'piquantly' the spectacle of his agony and shame." By straining after sensationalism, concluded the *Times*, the *World* may have caused several other suicides besides the Central Park couple, and the penalty for encouraging such a crime was up to twenty years in prison.

Failing to fault the *World* for inaccuracy, *Times* scribes tackled the man who had turned the tables on them. They berated Ingersoll as an "infidel" for his ungodly views, especially his suggestion that Christ himself had virtually committed suicide. Several follow-up features, attempting to discredit him, backfired: they gave "infidel" Ingersoll's "sensational" views free publicity.

However, the subject of suicide soon paled beside the war that broke out between China and Japan over which country should enslave Korea. Pulitzer persuaded James Creelman to leave Bennett's *Herald* to cover the war for the *World*. To commemorate the occasion, Bennett showed extraordinary magnanimity in publishing in his rival paper a picture of Pulitzer captioned "The Great Editor" alongside one of Creelman as "The Great Reporter." A daredevil Canadian, Creelman soon made international news and burnished his reputation in his account of atrocities committed by the Japanese (who won the war) during their capture of Manchuria's Port Arthur. According to Creelman, he refused a Japanese bribe to whitewash their savagery, and his cable appeared in the *World* verbatim: "The Japanese troops entered Port Arthur on November 21 and massacred practically the entire population in cold blood. The defenseless and unarmed inhabitants were butchered in their houses and their bodies were unspeakably mutilated. There was an unrestrained reign of murder which continued for three days. The whole town was plundered with appalling atrocities. The Japanese in this instance lapsed into barbarism. All pretence that circumstances justified the atrocities are false. The civilized world will be horrified by

James Creelman
covered the war
between China and
Japan for the *World*.

the details. The foreign correspondents, horrified by the spectacle, left the
army in a body."

Some American newspapers denounced his report as false, including,
strangely, the *Herald*, which had previously called him a great reporter. Creelman could hardly be accused of partiality, because he also reported: "The Chinese fired on the Red Cross, violated hospitals, beheaded sick soldiers, tortured
prisoners to death, and used the white flag of peace to cover treachery, while
the Japanese tenderly nursed Chinese captives and risked their lives to rescue
enemy wounded."

Pulitzer stuck by Creelman. Fellow war correspondent Julian Ralph, of the
London Daily Mail, later confirmed his account of Japanese atrocities. The
report in the *World* eventually came to be accepted as true and radically
changed American public opinion, which at first had favored the Japanese.

That fall a visitor at Bar Harbor to discuss politics was disturbed by Pulitzer's
imperious treatment of his staff. He recalled how the publisher entered the
room on the arm of his secretary Claude Ponsonby, then told him to fetch
some cigars, and, when he brought in the wrong brand, Pulitzer "cursed him
up hill and down dale." The visitor concluded that "Pulitzer always had as his
private secretary some poverty-stricken gentleman whom he always treated
abominably. He paid one hundred dollars a week, a large salary in those days,
in return for which the secretary was required to take smiling the lashings of
Pulitzer's very active tongue."

The shared life of luxury was one inducement for them to stay, but several,
it seems, actually enjoyed the experience—with reservations. Perhaps his intellectual curiosity and charismatic personality compensated for the pain, as
well as his high principles and dogged devotion to humanitarian causes.

Theodore Dreiser at
twenty-three, when he
briefly worked as a
reporter for Pulitzer.

In November twenty-three-year-old Theodore Dreiser, a reporter from the *Pittsburgh Dispatch*, joined the *World*. But this great novelist in the making was intimidated by the "snarling savage" of a city editor (probably Chapin) and disappointed by his pay, which depended on his reports getting into the paper — and amounted to less than the "going rate for street sweepers." Sent to report a street fight, he found it was only a noisy quarrel between drunks, so he wrote a fictional account of a spirited battle between a man and a neighbor whose piano playing had interrupted his sleep. Taking fiction for fact, the editor bought it and rewarded Dreiser with a promising assignment: to interview Russell Sage, a Jay Gould associate worth at least sixty million dollars.

Three years before, a man had burst into Sage's office and demanded money. When Sage refused to oblige, the intruder exploded a dynamite bomb, killing himself and Sage's secretary and badly injuring a clerk. But Sage was unhurt.

The assignment was no favor to the timid Dreiser, who assumed that Sage would be leery of strangers and thought: "They might as well have asked me to interview St. Peter." And when he failed even to get a foot inside the multimillionaire's front door, his disappointed editor relegated him to Bellevue Hospital and the morgue. At both places he was disgusted by the cynical and sadistic staff. Once, when an accident victim was brought into the hospital, Dreiser saw two surgeons "wager over his condition. One said, 'Fifty that he's dead,' the other, 'Fifty that he isn't.' A stethoscope was applied, the man was found dead and $50 changed hands."

This was the kind of inhuman-human-interest vignette that Pulitzer craved, but Dreiser didn't see a story in it and returned to the *World* that night empty-handed, saving his account of the incident for his autobiography *Newspaper Days*. To Pulitzer, a timid reporter was an oxymoron and had no future on his *World*, but before Dreiser got the inevitable boot, he quit. It was no loss to the *World*, which continued to lead the New York pack, unlike the *St. Louis Post-Dispatch*, which was sinking fast.

Pulitzer decided to solve the problem in St. Louis by turning troublemaker Colonel Jones into a troubleshooter. Jones must have seen it as an opportunity to both redeem himself and put Pulitzer in his debt; Pulitzer, as a chance to use Jones's wasted talent. And Pulitzer was careful not to make it sound like an order. Would Jones be willing to go to St. Louis for ten days to investigate the trouble and to recommend solutions? The pompous and peppery colonel said yes.

Pulitzer was more diplomatic in his dictated letters than in face-to-face encounters, when his fierce invective often rattled even hardened newsmen. By mail, Dr. Jekyll; in personal confrontations, the irascible Mr. Hyde. This may explain why, when Colonel Jones returned to Manhattan from the *Post-Dispatch* with his answers to the paper's problems, Pulitzer listened to him briefly but made no decision.

Instead, he wrote to him a few days later:

"I have accepted your advice about St. Louis, and must seriously ask you to go out there (again), at least for a time, to help in the new departure and to carry out your suggested changes in the character of the paper. There are obvious reasons in our difficulties and your present environment in the World office which to my mind should make this an agreeable change and opportunity, especially if you return here with fresh laurels of Western success."

This Dr. Jekyll on paper and Mr. Hyde in person was only too evident to his wife, Kate, and her criticism during one of their frequent separations brought his plaintive defense: "You like to emphasize the word 'order,' my order or your order, when you refer to my wishes, or when I refer to them, especially a wish that is habitually trampled upon and disregarded. I wish you would not do that, because it reminds me how utterly ignored my wishes are."

Again, when railroad magnate Chauncey Depew wrote to complain of his treatment by the *World*, what might have been a "Go to hell!" or worse, in person, on paper became: "It is, I hope, not necessary to say that I had nothing to do with some very stupid paragraphs relating to you which have appeared in my beloved *World*. I have knocked the perpetrators down with a little cable club, and hope there will be no further lunacies in this line."

After a brief stay in his Manhattan home, Pulitzer headed south, for the milder air of Jekyll Island, while Jones entrained for St. Louis, a hatchet man disguised as an efficiency expert, a guise even Pulitzer hadn't yet seen through.

CHAPTER 17

Prevents War between the
United States and Britain

1895

―

47 to 48 years old

O n January 1, 1895, while in St. Louis, Colonel Jones resigned from the
World, to the delight of almost everyone on the paper. Then he made an
offer he thought Pulitzer couldn't refuse. He agreed to rescue the floundering
Post-Dispatch if he was made its owner, as majority shareholder with 5,003 of
10,000 shares. How would he pay for those shares? He expected Pulitzer to buy
them for him or at least to lend him the cash. Daylight robbery springs to
mind. Desperate, or spellbound by the colonel's chutzpah, Pulitzer continued
to negotiate, finally agreeing to sell him 1,667 shares for $80,000—paid for by
the colonel himself. Pulitzer also placated him with the titles of president, editor, and manager of the *Post-Dispatch*, a triple threat with as much control as if
he *were* the majority stockholder. Jones signed the agreement at Jekyll Island
on February 3. When Pulitzer expressed concern for the welfare of the *Post-
Dispatch* staff, Jones promised to judge them on their merit and treat them
with consideration.

He intended no such thing, and Pulitzer got wind of it from early reports
soon after Jones took over, sending Carvalho to St. Louis to restrict Jones's control by amending the agreement. The colonel adamantly refused and immediately fired several men Pulitzer wished to protect, replacing the business manager with his own brother, George Jones. Colonel Jones also thumbed his nose
at Pulitzer by expressing his pro-silver views in the paper's editorials. Pulitzer
responded by giving all the dismissed men jobs on the *World* and began legal
proceedings to rescue his *Post-Dispatch* from Jones' clutches.

Adding to his concerns, Pulitzer was facing unexpected competition — from what had once been his brother's paper. When he owned the *New York Journal*, Pulitzer's estranged, gross, and apparently mentally unbalanced brother Albert had been no threat. He had catered to less discerning, apolitical readers. But then John McLean, a wealthy and active Democrat, bought the *Journal* from Albert for a whopping million dollars, upgraded the paper, and introduced his political views, competing for the same readers as Pulitzer's *World*.

In the spring, needing a suitable environment to take on this new challenge, Pulitzer bought Chatwold in Bar Harbor, the house he had previously rented, and hired notable architect Stanford White to design an adjacent four-story building. In this building he required a steam-heated swimming pool in the basement, filled with water pumped in from the ocean; an almost forty-foot-square living-room-study on the first floor; and above it, bedrooms for himself and his secretaries. Pulitzer insisted that the entire structure must have foot-thick granite walls to shut out the noises of his lively young family and other unbearable distractions in the main house. While "The Tower of Silence," as his staff called it, was being built, Pulitzer escaped from the racket to England with his family and a handful of secretaries. They stayed at Moray Lodge until Pulitzer was driven berserk by the cries of peacocks in nearby Kensington Gardens. Stymied in his efforts to move or muffle them, he leased another house, where he found the cooing of pigeons and the twittering of sparrows less maddening.

In London he met dynamic fellow publishers Henry Labouchere and Alfred Harmsworth. Labouchere, a sardonically witty liberal member of Parliament for Northampton, owned a muckraking magazine, *Truth*, devoted to exposing frauds. He had helped to unmask Richard Piggott as the forger of a letter published in the *Times* of London, falsely incriminating the Irish leader Charles Parnell. As ardent an antiroyalist as Pulitzer, Labouchere had vainly campaigned to cut Queen Victoria's allowance. A century ahead of his time, he advocated abolishing the House of Lords and once remarked of the prime minister, "I don't object to Gladstone always having the ace of trumps up his sleeve, but merely to his belief that God Almighty put it there."

He had also accused the up-and-coming Winston S. Churchill of homosexuality and race-fixing! When someone repeated the libel, saying that at Sandhurst Churchill participated in "acts of gross immorality of the Oscar Wilde type," Churchill sued and won, getting an apology and five hundred pounds in damages. In fact, the "gross immorality" was simply roughhousing or hazing at the military academy.

While still in England, having afternoon tea with the latest publishing wonder, Alfred Harmsworth, later Lord Northcliffe, Pulitzer confided, "I am the loneliest man in the world. People who dine at my table one night might find themselves arraigned in my newspapers the next morning." But he did not

Pulitzer's summer home, Chatwold, in Maine, was on fifteen acres, with a swimming pool in its basement, a servant's building, a caretaker's cottage, and a stable for twenty-five horses.

mention how he tried to retain such friends by blaming his staff and not himself for the public pummeling.

Apart from losing newsworthy friends through his refusal to "protect" them from the *World*'s ridicule or condemnation, he was too obsessed with his work, or as Kate would say, "enslaved" by it, to stay in touch with other friends. However, he had recently made time to renew a lapsed friendship with Thomas Davidson, writing to him: "When I did not hear from you for eight years I did worry a great deal about your silence, thinking it most strange. I did suffer more during those eight years by loss of sleep, sight, health and activity than in all my previous existence. I do feel very much like seeing you and talking over those happy days of poverty."

They met and corresponded more frequently after that, but work remained Pulitzer's chief preoccupation. With a secretary always on tap, Pulitzer kept in contact with the *World* around the clock, to dictate or oversee its editorials and to keep tabs on his staff. Even so, Nellie Bly's second departure was a surprise. She left the *World* to work for the *Chicago Times-Herald*, apparently unable to resist the higher salary. Then, when its owner died unexpectedly, 30-year-old Bly quit that paper and married a millionaire old enough to be her grandfather. As the *World* headlined it:

MR AND MRS.
NELLIE BLY

———

the World's Famous Reporter Marries an Aged New
York Millionaire.

———

THIS IS NOT AN EXPOSE THIS TIME.

———

Mr. Robert Seaman, the Happy Husband
Is Seventy-two Years Old and
Never Married Before.

With Pulitzer's approval, the story was given positive play, with romantic overtones: "Miss Bly has been greatly admired by many, and has had more than one opportunity to become a bride before this. Mr. James Metcalfe, one of the editors of *Life* has been very persistent and devoted in his attention for several years. It has in fact, more than once been reported that they were engaged. Cranks, too, wrought up to a state of frenzied adoration by her brilliant work, have thrown themselves at her feet with offers of marriage. But it remained for the aged millionaire to be made happy in his declining years."

The *World* concluded: "Miss Bly becomes the mistress of a metropolitan residence, a magnificent country seat, a whole stable of horses and nearly everything the good fairy of the story books always pictures. Few women have had more world experience at the age of 30 than Miss Bly, and few are more capable of enjoying the pleasures of 'a millionaire existence.'"

Despite the *World*'s denial, *Town Topics* took it as another of Bly's stunts, asserting, "Such is the degradation of the press that nobody would be surprised to see a sensational article headed: 'Is Marriage a Failure? Nelly [sic] Bly Tries It With a Good Old Man! Her Experience and His!! A Divorce Applied for. Full Details by Seaman's Journalistic Wife!!!'"

The success of Bly and other women reporters had persuaded Pulitzer to hire several more, so the *World* was not short of gutsy women to replace Bly, all willing to do almost anything for a story. But none achieved her fame. They also had to share the same byline, Meg Merrilies. (Did no one notice that the name ends as—lies?)

In the Bly tradition, Meg Merrilies slept among the "tortured inmates" of Chambers Street Hospital; saw a surgeon remove a cataract from a baby's eyes; rescued a child from a burning building; steered a ship in a gale; and leaped into the path of a speeding trolley car, to show the need to equip the city's public vehicles with better brakes.

Meanwhile, Pulitzer was struggling with how to respond to the recent appointment of Theodore Roosevelt as the city's police commissioner. Having ridiculed his early political pretensions, Pulitzer now conceded that Roosevelt was trying to clean up the corrupt police department from the top down. He had fired the city's police chief, Thomas F. Byrnes, who had amassed a questionable fortune; his deputy, Inspector Alexander Williams, who owned a yacht and a Connecticut estate; and hundreds of other cops on the take. The *World* responded with rave reviews, including this vivid picture by Arthur Brisbane of Roosevelt intimidating cops charged with dereliction of duty.

The account was headed:

ROOSEVELT AS JUDGE

The Reform Commissioner Tries
Nearly One Hundred Policemen in One Day.

NOVEL METHODS AT HEADQUARTERS

Then the *World* gave the sort of detailed report Pulitzer encouraged. It read in part: "Think what must be the poor policeman's feelings when he comes up for trial before a man like Roosevelt! Roosevelt speaks English accurately. He does not say 'I done it' or 'I seen it.' He talks much more like a Boston man or an Englishman than like a New York Police Commissioner. . . . When he asks a question, Mr. Roosevelt shoots it at the poor trembling policeman as he would shoot a bullet at a coyote [and] shows a set of teeth calculated to unnerve the bravest of the finest."

Convinced that Roosevelt was on the right track, Pulitzer turned his attention to the U.S. Supreme Court's 5-to-4 decision declaring the Democratic-sponsored national income-tax law as unconstitutional. This delighted the likes of Senator John Sherman, brother of General Sherman, to whom the tax was "socialism, communism, devilism," and leading lawyer Joseph Choate, who called it "a communistic march on private property." Pulitzer would have been among those paying the 2 percent tax on incomes above $4,000, yet true to his principles he supported the tax and damned the decision to kill it as "another victory of greed over need."

Late that summer of 1895, President Cleveland was in something of a panic—the U.S. Treasury's gold reserves were disappearing so rapidly that the country was in imminent danger of going bankrupt. Early in the year, banker J. P. Morgan had come to the rescue, but at a cost. He headed a syndicate that bought $64 million worth of government bonds at a bargain price of $104.50 apiece, then sold them to the public—making a whopping profit estimated at $1.5 million to $18 million. With Morgan's money the government bought enough gold to partly replenish the Treasury. In August the *World*'s Washington correspondent warned Pulitzer that the Treasury again needed more gold and said that another bond issue was to be floated. After sending more than ten thousand telegrams of inquiry to banks and other financial institutions, Pulitzer received overwhelming evidence that the public was eager to buy the bonds at $120. He immediately set his publicity machinery into action. In two editorials he urged Cleveland to offer the bonds to the public and not at a cut rate to Morgan and his syndicate. Pulitzer promised personally, as his patriotic duty, to buy $1 million worth of bonds, however high the price. Because of the *World*'s campaign, Cleveland was embarrassed into making the bond offer public, and the issue of $100 million was oversubscribed six times. Pulitzer had won the day—and unexpectedly made $50,000 on the deal. What should he do with it? After he had consulted with all the wise heads in the Dome and rejected one useless suggestion after another, his business manager finally said: "Why not keep it?" Which Pulitzer did.

After several months it became clear that the anticipated competition from John McLean's *New York Journal* would not materialize. McLean had lost so many readers by doubling the paper's price to 2 cents that he practically gave it to William Randolph Hearst on September 25, 1895, for $180,000, which was $820,000 less than he paid for it!

A week after Hearst bought the *Journal*, Pulitzer went to court in St. Louis to try to regain control of the *Post-Dispatch* from the cocky and feisty Colonel Jones, who was driving it into the ground by vicious editorial attacks on advertisers. But his five-year contract was solid: Jones won the case and remained in charge.

Distracted by the problem of how to handle Jones, Pulitzer ignored the much bigger threat just arrived from San Francisco. He had brighter news on November 30, when Kate gave birth to their seventh child. They named him Herbert. Because his son was only a misty shape to Pulitzer, he commissioned an artist to sketch the boy in thick black lines on very white paper.

Pulitzer soon became preoccupied with the imminent danger of war between the United States and Britain over, amazingly, a fifty-year-old border dispute between Venezuela and British Guiana (now Guyana). During that time the British government had played a delaying game, declining to discuss the problem and, in fact, not even acknowledging that a problem existed.

Since the border had been established, Venezuelans had complained that it unfairly favored the British. When gold was discovered in the disputed area, they were ready to fight for it. Being outmatched, the Venezuelans sought support from someone with more firepower—President Cleveland—and gave him a rationale, the Monroe Doctrine. This held that the United States would regard any attempt by European powers to extend their control in the Western Hemisphere as an unfriendly act. Richard Olney, the pugnacious U.S. secretary of state, agreed, warning British prime minister Lord Salisbury that flouting the Monroe Doctrine could have deadly results. To scare Salisbury into negotiating, Olney claimed that "the United States is practically sovereign on this continent and its fiat is law . . . because . . . its infinite resources combined with its isolated position render it master of the situation and practically invulnerable as against any or all other powers."

As historian Barbara Tuchman remarked, "Lord Salisbury . . . was no more disposed to respond to this kind of prodding than he would have been if his tailor had suddenly challenged him to a duel." And far from accepting Olney's view that America was almost invulnerable, Salisbury didn't even consider it a world power. When he did reply, after several months, he asserted that British Guiana "belonged to the Throne of England before the Republic of Venezuela came into existence."

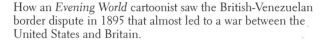

"THE REAL BRITISH LION"

How an *Evening World* cartoonist saw the British-Venezuelan border dispute in 1895 that almost led to a war between the United States and Britain.

Salisbury ridiculed the Venezuelans' claims as "exaggerated pretensions" and implied that Olney was stretching the Monroe Doctrine to allow the United States to intervene in *any* international disputes within the Western Hemisphere.

Salisbury's supercilious response made Cleveland "mad clean through," he later admitted. In that mood he addressed Congress on December 18, 1895, denouncing Britain as a threat to America's "peace and safety." Consequently, he declared, America would fix the boundary line, and both the British and the Venezuelans would have to accept the decision. Reacting perhaps to those who had mocked him as a fat coward for not immediately declaring war, Cleveland made it clear that his were fighting words, concluding his speech: "I am fully alive to the full responsibility incurred and keenly realize all the consequences that may follow." The House gave him unanimous support, the *Tribune* called his opponents "peace-at-any-price cuckoos," the *Sun* denounced anyone reluctant to fight Britain as "an alien or a traitor," and eagerly anticipated heroic naval battles "in the British Channel and the Irish Sea." Police Commissioner Theodore Roosevelt, hoping to widen the prospective war, looked forward to "the conquest of Canada," gleefully adding, "If there is a muss [squabble] I shall try to have a hand in it myself!"

Pulitzer stood almost alone in his opposition, calling Cleveland's militant message to Congress a dangerous mistake and asserting that "to interfere in

South America and bring on a war between two great, free and highly civilized nations on any account less serious than a menace such as the President described would be the monumental crime of the century."

And again on December 21: "This Venezuelan boundary dispute in no way touches the Monroe Doctrine. The doctrine looks solely to the defense of our institutions and of our national safety. There could be no greater absurdity than the assumption that a threat to either is involved in a dispute between the miners of British Guiana and the miners of Venezuela as to the ownership of certain gold-bearing lands in a region so pestilential that the deaths there outnumber the births by two to one. The ripest scholars of our time in constitutional history declare that the Monroe Doctrine is in nowise involved in the controversy. The greatest statesmen of our past—Calhoun, Webster, John Quincy Adams, Clay, Benton, Jefferson and Madison—have left upon record their interpretations of the Monroe Doctrine, and not one of them so interprets it as to fit it to this case."

Congress was not moved by the words of the ripe scholars, of Pulitzer, or even of Monroe himself. On December 22 the House unanimously authorized a commission to taunt the British by investigating the disputed boundary without consulting them. Cleveland signed the bill the same day.

The threat of war gave Wall Street the willies, and stocks tumbled. Yet the brokers almost to a man supported the government's gung-ho stance. A rare exception was broker Charles Smith, who persuaded a handful to sign his peace petition, which bought this scornful *New York Times* response: "Under the teaching of these bloodless Philistines, these patriots of the ticker, if they were heeded, American civilization would degenerate to the level of the Digger Indians, who eat dirt all their lives and appear to like it. We should become a nation of hucksters, flabby in spirit, flabby in muscle, flabby in principle, and devoid of honor."

Many Irish American readers, ever eager to twist the British lion's tail, could be expected to oppose Pulitzer's peaceful editorials, stirred by the recent Irish national convention in Chicago, where using force was proposed to free Ireland from British rule. Every South American republic except Chile supported Cleveland's war cries.

As Christmas approached, the British fleet prepared for action and Americans strengthened coastal defenses.

Pulitzer now launched his own personal peace offensive, what biographer Swanberg called "a master stroke of journalistic propaganda." He sent scores of cables to movers and shakers among the potential enemy, to politicians, prelates, and publishers, and members of the royal family, inviting each to cable collect his "feeling as to the existing difficulty between the two countries." Cables went to Britain's prime minister, Salisbury; two former prime ministers, Gladstone and Rosebery; the prince of Wales; the duke of York; bishops and archbishops; and his recent British acquaintance Henry Labouchere. Pulitzer's urgent personal message to Gladstone on December 20 read: "American sentiment is at the turning point. Once turned the wrong way, no power on earth will hold it back. In the American mind you, more than any score of other men and more than the Government, epitomize the British people. A word of peace and fellowship from you today will aid to check the clamor, to soothe passion, to encourage sober thought, and may avert calamity."

Gladstone replied on December 21: "Dare not interfere. Only common sense required. Cannot say more with advantage."

Grasping at that one straw—common sense—Pulitzer relayed the message to papers worldwide and wrote in the *World* on Christmas Eve: "This morning the whole world knows that the aged and honored man who is the foremost of living statesmen thinks that all that is required to avert war between Great Britain and the United States is COMMON SENSE."

Pulitzer published facsimiles of all the replies to his cables on the front pages of the *World* for several days. They were overwhelmingly declarations of friendship and pleas for peace. A typical response, from Lord Rosebery, Liberal leader and former prime minister, read: "I absolutely disbelieve in the possibility of war between the United States and Great Britain on such an issue as this for it would be the greatest crime on record. History would have to relate that the two mighty nations of the Anglo-Saxon race at a time when they appeared to be about to overshadow the world in best interests of Christianity and civilization preferred to cut each others' throats about a frontier squabble in a small South American Republic. The proposition only requires to be stated to demonstrate its absurdity. All that is wanted is a level head and cool common sense in our governments. I congratulate you on the good work that your paper appears to be doing in this direction."

The most unequivocal response came from the provocative publisher and parliamentarian Labouchere, who cabled: "Would prefer Venezuela and Guiana consigned to the bottom of the sea rather than war with the United States."

The archbishop of Armagh deplored the prospect of an American-British conflict as tantamount to a civil war—"unnatural strife between mother and daughter." And Cardinal Vaughan, archbishop of Westminster, thought: "We are too closely bound to America by blood, respect and affection for her people to tolerate the idea of bloodshed."

With Queen Victoria's approval, the prince of Wales (later King Edward VII) and the duke of York (later King George V) sent a joint reply. They earnestly trusted that "the present crisis will be arranged in a manner satisfactory to both countries and will be succeeded by the same warm feeling of friendship which has existed between them for so many years."

Pulitzer also published the disappointing response from John Redmond, Irish member of Parliament for Waterford. Because the British had rejected home rule, he said, the Irish did not regard them as friends. As a representative of Irish opinion, he predicted that "if war results from the reassertion of the Monroe doctrine, Irish national sentiment will be solid on the side of America." With that exception, the cables Pulitzer gathered and prominently displayed throughout the Christmas season, unanimously for peace, won the day—but not the thanks of the U.S. secretary of state. Furious at being outmaneuvered by Pulitzer, Olney tried to punish him for it. He resurrected a century-old statute that threatened any private American citizen who communicated with another government to influence foreign policy with up to three years in jail and a five-thousand-dollar fine. Pulitzer shot back: "The statute cited is aged, obsolete, moldy, moth-eaten, dust-covered. It is true, furthermore, that the more modern laws, notably anti-trust laws and anti-monopoly laws, are not enforced. The World will not descend into the dungeon and put out its million-candle-power torch of liberty and intelligence without a struggle."

Theodore Roosevelt backed Olney, more than willing to douse Pulitzer's torch of liberty. As Roosevelt confided to a friend: "It would give me great pleasure to have the editors of the World put in prison the minute hostilities began." But the many British messages, now published worldwide, advocating a peaceful resolution, took the wind out of the warmongers.

To Pulitzer's relief, he said, "[T]he war clamor ceased. Publicity had done its work. Truly 'peace hath her victories no less renowned than war.' Benjamin Constant [a Franco-Swiss novelist and political writer] was right: 'The press is mistress of intelligence, and intelligence the mistress of the world.'"

In the less bellicose atmosphere, Britain and Venezuela agreed on independent arbitration, which eventually ruled in favor of the British—granting them almost all of the disputed area.

Although many historians have failed to mention Pulitzer's vital contribution, Britain's colonial secretary Joseph Chamberlain credited him for the peaceful outcome, saying: "The World led public thought when it secured expressions and opinions from leading men and performed an inestimable service to the English-speaking people of the whole world. War between the two countries would have been a terrible calamity, and the World performed a patriotic service to its country. It did not wait for a leader, but led the people."

If the Nobel Peace Prize had existed in 1895, Pulitzer would surely have been a contender. It was first awarded six years later.

Pulitzer played exactly the opposite role in a war that was threatening in Cuba, where guerrillas had attacked their inept and corrupt Spanish rulers.

Most Americans sympathized with the rebels and were eager for news of the fighting. Not yet having their own men in the field, the World published an eyewitness report by a twenty-year-old lieutenant in the British army, Winston S. Churchill, son of the late Lord Randolph Churchill. He and a friend were ostensibly on vacation in Cuba as guests of Marshal Martinez Campos, head of the Spanish army ordered to smash the rebellion.

Churchill had seen a battle at La Reforma plantation on December 2 and despite his youth and inexperience described it with the confidence of an old hand: "The country is open and the battlefield, half a mile broad, was flanked by dense forests," Churchill cabled from Havana's Gran Hotel Inglaterra. "The enemy was behind hedges with a forest in the rear. The Spanish infantry proceeded slowly to within thirty yards of the enemy's position, whereupon the latter retired. Gen. Suarez Valdes, in full uniform and on a white horse, rode up close behind the infantry. He was a conspicuous target. Gen. Garcia Navarro, commanding the advance, exposed himself in a manner no comman- der is justified in doing.

"The insurgents are bad shots. It appeared to me that tons of lead passed over the heads of Gen. Valdes' staff, with whom I was. Three orderlies were wounded. The Spanish loss would have been heavy had the enemy's shots told, for the troops marched in close order through the open country towards the protected position held by the insurgents. I was much impressed by the patience, the courage and, I may add, the indifference of the Spanish infantry. The men laughed and sang under fire. Their obedience was like that of the Russian soldiers—implicit. Twenty-five sharpshooters . . . were the only good shots the insurgents had."

When Churchill and his friend arrived in Manhattan en route back to England, they were interviewed by a *World* reporter whose jaunty report read: "Two young English warriors . . . who have just taken their baptism of fire in the Cuban war set sail for England yesterday. Both are in the Fourth Hussars. . . . The *Bungtown Bird of Freedom* and the *Kalamazoo Daily Celery Stalk* printed many flaming editorials on the conduct of these gentlemen, declaring that they were emissaries of the British Government sent to teach Campos how to whip the secessionists, and that England was throwing more bricks at the Monroe doctrine. Of course this was nonsense. Churchill is not yet twenty-one years old, and knows only the amount of strategy necessary for the duties of a second lieutenant. He and [Lieutenant (later Major General) Reginald] Barnes went on the trip actuated only by youthful enthusiasm."

Whatever their real names, those papers were on to something. Churchill was not what he seemed to be. He had taken advantage of the Cuban trip to produce his first serious journalistic effort—a remarkably sophisticated five-part series published in London's *Daily Graphic*. But he was also in Cuba as a spy, assigned by Colonel Edward Chapman, director of British military intelligence, to report the effectiveness of a new bullet used in the fighting. Though the *World* account mentioned that "Mr. Churchill had in his pocket a rough insur- gent bullet that struck and killed a Spanish soldier standing quite close to him," no one outside the intelligence community discovered his successful under- cover operation until David Stafford revealed it in his 1998 book *Churchill and the Secret Service.*

In the *World* interview Churchill mentioned a problem that would bedevil Pulitzer when his war correspondents covered the rebellion: "While the Span- ish are masters of the art of suppressing the truth, the Cubans are adepts in inventing falsehoods."

Churchill had a decidedly ambivalent view of the *World* and other New York papers, telling his mother: "I have been civil and vague to the reporters and so far I can only find one misstatement in the papers." And to his brother

Jack, "The essence of American journalism is vulgarity divested of truth. Their best papers write for a class of snotty housemaids and footmen and even the nicest people here have so much vitiated the style. I think, mind you, that vulgarity is a sign of strength. Picture to yourself the American people as a great lusty youth who treads on all your sensibilities, perpetuates every possible horror of ill manners, but who moves about his affairs with a good hearted freshness which may well be the envy of other nations of the earth. Of course there are here charming people who are just as refined and cultured as the best in any country in the world. This is a very great country but there seems to be no such thing as reverence or tradition."

At year's end, as Churchill was sailing for home, he stared "at ships off the English coast, wondering which would be our transport to Canada" to defend the country from American attack. He didn't yet know that Pulitzer's peace campaign had already made such a journey unnecessary.

Even so, what a bloody year! As Pulitzer reminded readers, "From Japan westward, bloodshed has encircled the globe. When the year 1895 dawned the Italians were engaged in a bloody war with Abyssinians; Haiti was overrun by rebels, who had burned the capital, Port-au-Prince, and slaughtered many people; the French were preparing for their disastrous if victorious war in Madagascar; the Dutch were slaughtering the natives of Lombok, one of their dependencies in southeastern Asia; and rebellions were in progress in several of the South American countries."

CHAPTER 18

Fighting Crime and William Randolph Hearst

1896
—
48 to 49 years old

William Randolph Hearst, the spoiled only child of George Hearst, a mining multimillionaire and U.S. senator, was expelled from Harvard for a prank involving chamber pots. Then, in what should have been his senior year at college, he worked briefly for Pulitzer's *World* as a cub reporter. Hearst's father also owned a newspaper, having acquired the *San Francisco Examiner,* which he used to advance his political career. Though it was on artificial life support—infusions of George's almost limitless cash—his ambitious son determined to revitalize it by transforming it into another *World* in all but name. He raved about the *World* to his father as the best and most popular in its class, "in that it appeals to the people and depends for its success on enterprise, energy and a certain startling originality." He also applauded its crusading spirit, support of the underdog, and unrelenting attacks on corruption.

While working at the *World,* Hearst tried to tempt managing editor Ballard Smith into leaving Pulitzer to join him. But Smith declined the offer. So Hearst went to California without him. Having learned the tricks of the trade from Pulitzer, he put them to spectacular use as the new owner of the *San Francisco Examiner,* making it a West Coast wonder as a virtual carbon copy of the *World.* And beat all the competition. Flush with success, he headed back to New York hellbent on being number one there, too, and at any cost. Because Pulitzer already held that spot, Hearst was ready and willing to sink his old boss and shanghai his staff. As James Melvin Lee, author of *History of American Journalism,* saw it: Hearst "broke into New York with all the discreet secrecy of a wooden-legged burglar having a fit on a tin roof." He already had a foot in the

A cartoonist's view of Pulitzer's formidable rival, William Randolph Hearst, in 1896.

door—an office, ironically, in the *World* building, the Dome, for his *Examiner*'s East Coast correspondent. Soon after reaching New York, he leased more offices in a building a block south of the Dome and, with the skeleton staff he'd brought with him, he began to realize his invasion plan.

When his one-cent-a-copy *New York Journal* hit the streets, a lively near-clone of the *World* but half the price, it found a huge instant audience.

Up in his Silent Tower in Maine, Pulitzer waited for Hearst to go broke, unaware that he had an almost unlimited cash flow from his willing, wealthy mother. Now, not content with picking Pulitzer's brain, Hearst prepared to steal his staff.

As he glanced through the *World* one morning, Hearst found the kind of surefire circulation-builder he wanted for his new venture. It was a hilarious account of a raunchy stag party thrown by architect Stanford White, in which, for dessert, a naked model "covered only by the ceiling," as the *World* put it, stepped from a papier-mâché pie. Hearst liked the way the *World* put it, and chuckled over how Editor Morrill Goddard had spread an eye-catching sketch of the shapely dessert across two pages. Though Pulitzer sometimes balked at such wild ideas, he gave way when shown they sent sales skyrocketing.

Goddard's pale, unprepossessing appearance belied his almost diabolic daring, especially in his reporting days. Then, as a recent Dartmouth graduate, he crashed President Grant's funeral with a black suit and sad expression, slipped into the first car in the procession, and sat himself next to the grieving Mrs. Grant. Having duped both the widow and the police into thinking he was an undertaker's assistant, he wrote a widow's-eye-view of the funeral for the Sunday *World*.

As its editor he had initiated a stunning pseudo-scientific series, including "The Suicide of a Horse," "Cutting a Hole in a Man's Chest to Look at His Intestines and Leaving a Flap That Works as if on a Hinge," "Experimenting with an Electric Needle and an Ape's Brain," and "Science Can Wash Your Heart."

Always on the lookout for a compelling new feature, Goddard had once noticed a crowd glued to a store-window display of the cross section of a ship with a shark swimming below, all in dazzling colors. He adapted the idea in a series showing the innards of a chorus girl, a murderess, prehistoric animals, and patients undergoing surgery—all in colored cross sections. Both Pulitzer and "some of the staff objected," Goddard admitted, "but circulation jumped four or five thousand a week. On the day I printed a full-page cross section of a gorilla, it jumped ten thousand. All I had to do was cite those figures and all objections disappeared."

Pulitzer rewarded him with two Grecian urns, a bonus check, and a pat on the back: "I knew when I appointed you that you were just the man for the Sunday job." And now he was just the man for Hearst.

Hearst believed he could buy anything and anybody and was rarely disappointed. Touring Europe at ten with his indulgent mother, he had asked for the Louvre in Paris and was incredulous when told it wasn't up for grabs. But he soon discovered that almost everything else had a price—and one he was able to pay—especially after the death of his mining millionaire father. Though his mother inherited the millions, she was a soft touch, and when Willie, at thirty-two, already owner of the *San Francisco Examiner*, a gift from his father, asked her to buy him a New York newspaper, she didn't say no. Nor did Goddard when Hearst made an astonishing offer—to hire him and his entire staff for double what Pulitzer paid them.

Goddard, his editors, reporters, and artists resigned en masse, walking the short block south to work for Hearst, even taking the office cat. Goddard's secretary, Emma Jane Hogg, alone remained with Pulitzer.

Informed of the sudden desertion of his Sunday staff, Pulitzer told Carvalho to get them back whatever the cost. Carvalho persuaded Goddard to meet him in the Dome, where he offered to top Hearst's bid. The offer was accepted. Again Goddard and staff walked the short block—this time heading north.

It was a short-lived victory. They "only remained in their nest in the Dome for twenty-four hours," said Seitz, "when Mr. Hearst, resuming his checkbook argument, prevailed and the young men vanished, as it were, in thin air. The most extraordinary dollar-matching contest in the history of American journalism had begun." The desertion was hardly a question of disloyalty. At most, as on other papers, important staff members had a one-year contract. Colonel

Jones was an exception. Almost everyone else was on sufferance, as insecure as day laborers. Pulitzer had his own idiosyncratic reasons for hiring and firing. James Gordon Bennett Jr., owner of the *New York Herald,* was said to promote only those editors approved by his Pekingese pet dogs. A grating voice was enough for Pulitzer to fire an offender.

What most infuriated Pulitzer was that Hearst had used his *San Francisco Examiner* office in the Dome to talk *World* men into joining him. Damned if I'm going to have my "building used for purposes of seduction," he said, kicked Hearst out, and leased the office to the *Boston Globe.*

Then he called for an emergency meeting with Carvalho. Reporter Albert Payson Terhune happened to witness the rare sight of Pulitzer entering the Dome escorted by a servile circle of sycophantic senior executives. Guided by two of them, he took the elevator to his office on the eleventh floor. Cartoonist McDougall glimpsed him at his desk discussing the emergency, surprised that after such a humiliating blow from Hearst he showed no sign of being upset or angry. He struck him more like a chess player about to make a critical move.

That move replaced Goddard with Arthur Brisbane as the Sunday *World*'s editor, with a scratch staff snatched from the morning and evening editions. Pulitzer also promoted City Editor Richard Farrelly to managing editor of the morning edition and then announced a banquet in his honor. But Hearst had not completed his raid. He also wanted Farrelly. To Pulitzer's chagrin, Farrelly went over to Hearst—the day before the banquet. The banquet, of course, was canceled.

As Pulitzer headed south to Jekyll Island for his annual retreat—now the word had an ominous ring—Carvalho and Norris huddled with him in his private railroad car to discuss battle plans. Although the *Morning World* sold a healthy 185,000 copies, Hearst's daily *Journal* had already reached almost 150,000. Pulitzer decided to level the battlefield by cutting the price of the *World* in half to match the *Journal*'s one cent.

Then Pulitzer suffered another desertion. Business manager Carvalho succumbed to Hearst. Pulitzer immediately replaced him with John Norris.

The good news was that thirty-year-old Arthur Brisbane, now editor in charge of the depleted *Sunday World,* was every bit a match for the departed Goddard. Like Pulitzer a social radical who supported the underdog, he cut his teeth as a cub reporter in London for Dana's New York *Sun* when he covered parliamentary debates, and horrified readers with his gory accounts of the gruesome, still unsolved Jack the Ripper killings. He knew that murder, mayhem, and mystery sold, and despite Pulitzer's pleas to tone down and upgrade the features to attract discerning readers, Brisbane, like Goddard, usually got away with gee-whiz stuff by proving it paid.

It was the sort of material Nellie Bly had provided, so Brisbane was delighted when she asked for her job back. Disenchanted in her marriage to the jealous old coot, who suspected her of two-timing him (she wasn't) and had put a tail on her, she decided to provide for her own financial future—especially after she found that his will would leave her three hundred dollars while three other women got ten thousand dollars apiece.

Brisbane told Business Manager John Norris to inform Pulitzer that Bly was back on board, but not to let the news leak to Hearst. Because Pulitzer suspected that Hearst had spies in the *World* offices, he had created code names for various individuals and institutions to guard his plans. Some appear to reflect his view of them.

Hearst was known as GUSH; Pulitzer himself as ANDES; Morrill Goddard as GUIDELESS; John Dillon as GUESS; Theodore Roosevelt as GLUTINOUS; the Democratic Party as GOSLING; the Republican Party as MALARIA; Tammany Hall as GREYHOUND; Morning *World* as SENIOR; Evening *World* as JUNIOR; Sunday *World* as SENIORITY; all three *Worlds* as GENUINE; the managing editor, GRUESOME; the *St. Louis Post-Dispatch* as GRASPING; a combination of advertisers was code-named RAT; financial loss, PIGEON; and financial gain, PIGGERY.

In the early days of the code, Pulitzer didn't always remember who was who and what was what. And because Bly had no code name, when Norris tried to inform Pulitzer of her return in a secretive manner he impatiently cabled back: "Please don't write in Delphic phrases. Name person re-employed." The great news was repeated to him unscrambled.

The timing was bang on. Pulitzer needed Bly to blow the whistle on Police Commissioner Roosevelt's latest outrage: he was about to abolish shelters for homeless women in police stations. To dramatize the need for them, Bly spent the night in the Oak Street station house, with fifteen mostly immigrant Irish women brought low by "misfortune and whisky." Her empathetic account took a full page in the new Sunday magazine, a supplement to the Sunday *World*.

Pulitzer's early enthusiasm for Roosevelt had taken a nosedive when he began to arrest saloonkeepers for selling booze on Sundays. Roosevelt admitted to his friend, Henry Cabot Lodge: "The outcry against me is tremendous. The *World, Herald, Sun, Journal* and *Advertiser* are shrieking with rage; and the *Staats-Zeitung* is fairly epileptic." Pulitzer's shriek touched a nerve when he accused Roosevelt of continuing to harass saloonkeepers while dangerous crimes went unsolved—and he backed up the charge by publishing a long list of criminals on the lam. Roosevelt shot back that Pulitzer was a liar because only a few of the crimes he had listed had occurred and that he'd obviously fabricated the rest.

Roosevelt's enraged response got prominent play in the *New York Times*: "Of the forty-five highway robberies, burglaries etc. reported by The World just four were genuine; in other words The World's statement contained a little less than 9 per cent of truth; a somewhat unusually large percentage of truth for The World as most of its accounts of burglaries, robberies, and the like do not even have this slender foundation in fact. Mr. Pulitzer's paper does not even do well its own disreputable business. There is always a risk, where the reporters of a paper are paid to lie . . . they will finally grow to think it easier to invent untruths than to seek facts."

Roosevelt insisted that crime had decreased substantially "in spite of the industrious service rendered to the criminal classes by The World in its efforts to persuade all of its readers who are crooks to take up their abode in New York." As his *coup de grâce*, Roosevelt brought up a *World* report on December 16. It had featured the mug shots, bios, and MOs of twenty-six great professional criminals, and claimed they were all still at large in New York City, which an accompanying editorial described as a "Paradise for Crooks." According to Roosevelt, eight of the men were dead, one was dying, seven were in jail in Europe, three had reformed and were leading reputable lives, and of the remaining seven, not one was in the city.

Pulitzer reminded him, said Roosevelt, of a line from a Macauley essay: "As soon as he ceases to write trifles he begins to write lies; and such lies!" But he cunningly preempted Pulitzer's inevitable response by saying that in the future he wouldn't bother "to deny any unsupported statement whatever that may appear in The *World*."

Pulitzer struck back with a triple whammy: in the news columns, in a cartoon showing Roosevelt destroying police reports, and in an editorial: "We present a simple statement of facts today which must compel an apology on the part of Commissioner Roosevelt if he is an honest man or one who cherishes self-respect. He called many of the statements [in the *World*] 'fakes,' and indulged in much vituperative language of the barroom sort, falsely assuming that this journal was the author of the statements. He knew perfectly well that almost every one of the reports which he characterized as 'fakes' and falsehoods was published by other newspapers in New York, including those that made indecent haste to publish his untruthful assault upon The World under heavy headlines. [Roosevelt also knew] that these reports were mainly taken by the newspapers from official [police precincts'] blotters. If they were false the falsehood was officially certified by the police under his own control."

The news report headed ROOSEVELT ATTACKS THE WORLD counterattacked: "The victims of the crimes that he designates as 'pure fakes' have been interviewed by The World, and without exception they have declared that the reports of the crimes published in The World were correct, while they brand Mr. Roosevelt's explanations and denials as false and an outrage upon them." Pulitzer's rebuttal restored the *World*'s credibility, at least in this case.

Of course, its reporters were not paid to lie, but they were called upon to risk their reputation as serious journalists by clowning around. After using Bly to expose the plight of homeless women, the *World* featured a front-page sketch of her atop a huge elephant, headed "Nellie Bly As An Elephant Trainer," and quoting the real trainer's "She performed feats that professional trainers would have feared to try," and her reply, "I hadn't the courage to say I was afraid."

If Bly was ever afraid, she did a good job of hiding it, especially when she proposed leading a regiment to fight on the side of the rebels in Cuba battling against the occupying Spanish forces.

Nellie Bly atop an elephant in the *World's Sunday Magazine*,
February 23, 1896.

Early in the year, Spanish general Valeriano Weyler had been sent to Cuba
to put down an intensifying rebellion against Spanish rule. Sympathizing with
the rebels, Pulitzer approved a four-part series by David Graham Phillips titled
"The Hideous History of Old Spain." It was updated with illustrated accounts
of Spanish troops clubbing or garroting unarmed Cubans to death.

The massacres galvanized Nellie Bly into extraordinary action, according
to this Sunday *World* report a month later:

NELLIE BLY PROPOSES TO FIGHT FOR CUBA

Women Have More Courage Than Men
and Would Make Braver
Officers.

READY TO RECRUIT VOLUNTEERS FOR
HER FIRST REGIMENT.

"Nellie Bly is arranging to add a new terror to war! At first thought you
could say that it would be impossible for a slender, comparatively frail young

woman to do such a fearsome thing. But that is because you are not thoroughly acquainted with Nellie Bly. It is very difficult to get her to talk about her plan. She is so busy arranging details that she has 'no time for chat,' as the gentleman said to his friends on the corner who called to him when he was being towed down the street by a wild steer." Despite the tongue-in-cheek approach, Bly seemed deadly serious. She designed a uniform for her regiment, sought to recruit calm, intelligent women officers with personal magnetism who would inspire males under their command "to do and dare," and suggested that soldiers led by woman would never even flinch on the battlefield. "Do you think," she asked her interviewer, "that if a woman drew her sword and said, 'Come on!' there would be a single soldier in the whole army who would not come on, until his wounds made it impossible for him to crawl any further? No, indeed. With women leading the way there would be no such things as drawn battles. Every battle would be fought to the bitter end, and wars would be brief and decisive and less destructive. If the United States goes to war with Spain, this woman's regiment will go to the front, and you will see war such as there never was before. And I shall raise up such friends for poor, harassed Cuba as no nation fighting for liberty ever had before."

That was the last word she wrote on the subject. Was it a case of Brisbane going too far with a gimmick and Pulitzer yanking his chain? Though Pulitzer supported the Cuban rebels, he certainly wouldn't risk his star reporter's life emulating Joan of Arc. Bly avoided explaining her aborted mission by quitting the paper and going to live with her husband in Europe, induced to return to him after he had changed his will to leave her most of his property.

Pulitzer was even reluctant to send male reporters to Cuba—fearing for their safety—though other papers had correspondents on the spot reporting how the insurgents were dynamiting trains and torching sugar cane fields.

Sylvester Scovel, a recent Wooster College graduate, and the seasoned James Creelman kept agitating Pulitzer to let them go to Cuba, until he changed his mind. He first sent Scovel to report rebel action and then Creelman to cover the Spanish response. His caution seemed justified when Scovel, mistaken for a legendary mercenary, El Inglesito, was arrested by Spanish soldiers and sentenced to death by firing squad. The very day he was to die, he established his true identity and was freed. Scovel's first report described his travels with a rebel army of fifteen hundred Cubans harassing a force of three thousand Spanish soldiers. During one skirmish he had been shot in the leg. Under Spanish military law, for a journalist to contact the rebels was a crime punished by a long prison spell. But Scovel avoided capture a second time by disguising himself as a businessman suffering from tropical fever and boarding a ship to Key West, where his wound was treated.

When Creelman arrived in Havana in March, he presented his credentials to Cuba's new military governor, General Valeriano Weyler. Weyler bawled him out, angrily complaining that half the American correspondents in Cuba were spying for the rebels and the other half were liars "who poison everything with falsehood."

Creelman denied Weyler's charge that American newspapers were fanning the flames without which the rebels would long since have run out of steam, and pointed out that "American papers did not stir up Mexico and Peru to rebel, and the American newspapers were not in existence when the Netherlands fought against the Spanish crown for independence." As they were arguing, Weyler's secretary entered the room. Creelman froze, anxious not to give the man away. He had recognized him as a rebel spy and instantly sensed that Spain would inevitably lose the fight.

Exhausted by the heated discussion and shaken by the appearance of the spy, Creelman left Weyler's headquarters for a much-needed drink in the nearby Inglaterra Café, full of Spanish soldiers. To his astonishment, the stranger who joined him with a polite "Nice evening" was his colleague Scovel, in disguise. Scovel confided that after the *World* published his interview with rebel leader Gomez on February 23, Weyler offered a five-thousand-dollar reward for the reporter dead or alive. Since then, for the past six weeks, he had been traveling undetected between Florida and Havana by growing a mustache, plucking his bushy eyebrows, and assuming the identity of Harry Brown, a retired *World* reporter living in Key West. The atheist son of a Presbyterian clergyman, Scovel was an active rebel sympathizer, though handicapped by not speaking Spanish.

Stymied by Spanish censorship, he had been unable to send hard news of the fighting. Instead he reported a wild rumor about a rebel regiment of Amazon women who "show no mercy" as they "hack, hew, with their machetes, and shout in such a way as to alarm any opponent, and yet, when the fight is over, they are as tender to their foes as to their friends." Another tall tale had the rebels destroying sugarcane fields by pouring kerosene on snakes and setting them on fire. The burning snakes then slithered along the rows of cane, setting many alight before they, too, turned to ash. Scovel explained to Creelman that Pulitzer ran such stories only to ridicule them and was anxious to get well-documented investigations into alleged atrocities by Spanish troops. What Pulitzer did not want was more blatant propaganda about them butchering wounded prisoners, raping Cuban women, poisoning food and water, and cutting off the ears of their victims as trophies. The most horrific tale in this vein featured a drunken Spanish major who slaughtered fifty old men and boys, then sliced them up to feed to dogs.

Creelman believed he could get the documentation Pulitzer demanded. Having been tipped off about Spanish soldiers killing unarmed civilians in the village of Campo Florida, he headed for the place on horseback after dark, with two Cuban guides who led him to mounds of earth outside the village. There they dug into the earth and uncovered the bodies of thirty-three civilians, their hands tied behind their backs. Creelman was so disturbed by the sight that he vowed "at that moment, that I would help to extinguish Spanish sovereignty in Cuba if I had to shed my blood for it." His cable appeared in the

World on May 1, with the names of all thirty-three victims. On that same day he handed General Weyler a copy of his report, saying that if the general wanted to know "the real cause of the war" he should investigate "the crimes against civilians."

In response, Weyler had Creelman deported.

That left Scovel, still at large and with a price on his head, to check if Creelman's discovery was an isolated incident or if such massacres were widespread. With eleven bodyguards he set out one day in May shortly before dawn for what he had heard was the site of a recent mass killing near Havana.

A flock of vultures feeding on human corpses in the village of San Pedro convinced him that he was on the right track. Throughout the summer he collected 196 affidavits confirming 212 individual cases of civilians murdered by Spanish troops, including locales, names and ages of witnesses, and often the names of the death squad commanders. To protect them from reprisals, Pulitzer withheld witnesses' names in the published accounts but used Scovel's poignant plea for American intervention: "Blood on the roadsides, blood in the fields, blood on the doorsteps, blood, blood, blood. Is there no nation wise enough, brave enough, and strong enough to restore peace in this blood-smitten land?"

Scovel's earlier gunshot wound became badly infected after a three-day walk through a polluted swamp. Friends at the American consulate in Havana saved his life by smuggling him out of Cuba in disguise. When he reached *World* headquarters in New York, his haggard appearance so alarmed Brad Merrill that he gave him all the time off he needed to recover.

How viable were the documented atrocities? General Weyler as good as admitted that he was not playing by the marqess of Queensberry rules, saying: "How do they want me to wage war? With bishops' pastorals and presents of sweets and money?"

But even rebel leader General Maceo refused to confirm Scovel's charge that Weyler was waging a war of extermination, downplaying the horrors Scovel had exposed by dismissing them as occasional. In his book *Facts and Fakes About Cuba*, Scovel's friend and rival correspondent George Rea, a Brooklyn-born Irish American, exposed scores of fake horror stories reported by American correspondents. And he also challenged Scovel's modus operandi in trying to satisfy Pulitzer's demand for hard facts. Rea, the conservative son of a wealthy banker, had spent a long time with the rebels as a correspondent for the *New York Herald*, which was mildly supportive of the Spanish regime. And he swore he had never seen one dead civilian.

He concluded that the well-meaning Scovel had been bamboozled by his bodyguards who interviewed witnesses and translated their remarks. But he was not able to disprove any of the cases.

With Scovel on sick leave and Creelman deported, Pulitzer sent a small cadre of reporters to replace them in Cuba. Then he set off for England to augment his staff depleted by Hearst's raids. He had his usual entourage of servants and secretaries with him as well as his seventeen-year-old son Ralph. They again stayed at Moray Lodge in Kensington. Apparently the previous problem of noisy peacocks had been solved.

Meanwhile, Hearst, his biggest rival now, kept a high profile, literally, floating in a balloon over New York to show his reporters he wouldn't ask them to risk anything he wouldn't do, while his gossip columnists publicized his charity contributions for slum kids and disaster victims.

Pulitzer launched his recruiting drive in London at ground level by inviting Ralph Blumenfeld, a former *New York Herald* editor, to lunch. During the meal Pulitzer discussed a slew of subjects, from spiritualism to murder trials. Although impressed by Pulitzer's wide-ranging and well-informed ideas, Blumenfeld was put off by his petulance when the ever-present Dr. Hosmer "refused him permission to eat certain foods." Driving in a cab after lunch, Pulitzer asked Blumenfeld how Bennett, the *Herald*'s owner, ran his paper. Blumenfeld resisted. When Pulitzer said he expected him to be more communicative after he joined the *World*, Blumenfeld replied that he never said he wanted to join the *World*.

Pulitzer's face flushed a vivid pink. "Why not, please?" he asked.

"Because I do not choose to be on the *World*. At least not at present."

"Stop, please," Pulitzer said, poking the coachman with his cane. "The gentleman is getting out here." And he dropped Blumenfeld off in Chelsea, leaving him to find his own way home. In his diary, Blumenfeld penned this picture of the American phenomenon: "Tall, cadaverous, reddish beard, piercing but dead eyes, long bony hands; a fascinating yet terrifying figure. He is not quite blind, but cannot see to read even with the most powerful glasses."

Any hope of rehiring his feisty former partner John Cockerill was dashed by news of his death in an Egyptian barbershop. He had been working as a foreign correspondent for the *New York Herald*. Pulitzer gave him a warm sendoff, called him the "Custer of Journalism," and described him as "handsome and intellectual, a fighter if there was fighting to be done [and] infinitely proud of being a newspaperman." Despite their past quarrels Cockerill evidently had retained his respect for Pulitzer, having appointed his old partner executor of his will.

Pulitzer sought his next recruit in Wiesbaden, Germany, where he also took the cure and consulted with eye doctors. They did not raise his hopes. He had gotten over his contempt for the English to the extent that he progressively hired more of them. On this trip his quarry was a twenty-five-year-old Englishman, Wickham Steed, a freelance reporter in Germany who had just been offered the job of Berlin correspondent for the *Times* of London. Steed knew the *World* as a popular, mass-circulation paper and applauded Pulitzer's role in preventing war over Venezuela. But he wanted to write for the fewer, better-educated, and informed readers of the *Times*.

Pulitzer stressed the importance of being able to influence the minds and votes of millions at critical moments and offered to triple the amount the *Times* would pay.

Steed said he'd prefer to reach a few enlightened readers than a million idiots.

"Pulitzer let me see that he thought me a young fool," Steed recalled, "but he did it so kindly that he won my heart."

Steed went on to become a great editor of the *Times* of London.

A disappointed Pulitzer returned to England to be feted by politicians and peace groups for averting a war between the United States and Britain.

On June 5, 1896, representatives of Britain's peace societies gathered at Pulitzer's London residence to thank him for his role in preventing war between their country and the United States. After several eulogies, Pulitzer stepped forward to loud applause. "I am deeply touched," he said, "but am, unfortunately, an invalid under doctor's orders, and I ask permission that my response be read by a young American friend—my son." Seventeen-year-old Ralph, his eldest boy, then read Pulitzer's reply, titled "The Reign of Reason versus the Reign of Force." Highlights included: "I know of no purely moral sentiment that has been advanced in England since the abolition of slavery that appeals to the mind and heart as this idea of substituting civilized methods of peace and reason for barbarism and needless war." Here the critical word was "needless." Far from pandering to the peace-at-any-price advocates in his audience, he told them that Americans regarded "war against a cruel despotism or slavery as not only just, but as inevitable," leading them to sympathize "with the uprising of any people against despotism, whether in Greece or Hungary or Poland in the past, or in Cuba today."

Those who had known him in the days when he wrote off most foreigners as little better than apes would have been amazed to hear him concede that "Jingoism is found in England as well as in America, in Germany as well as in France, in Russia as well as in Japan. Jingoism is an appeal to national vanity, national prejudices, or national animosities. Every day there rests upon the conscientious press the responsibility of combating these prejudices."

Presumably his frequent travels in Europe and especially the intelligence and compatibility of some of his English secretary-companions had converted him from Anglophobe to Anglophile. That seems to explain these concluding comments:

"One of England's greatest glories is that for a century she has been for all Europe the strong place of refuge for political offenders. She has protected all alike, whether anarchist or monarchist, whether rebel or pretender to the throne. And since England has shown this devotion to political freedom, Englishmen will understand a similar spirit in America. We speak, we read, we think, we feel, we hope, we love, we pray—aye, we dream—in the same language. The twentieth century is dawning. Let us dream that it will realize our ideals and the highest destiny of mankind. Let us dream not of hideous war and butchery, of barbarism and darkness, but of enlightenment, progress and peace."

Back in Maine for the summer, Pulitzer chose Creelman to cover the presidential election campaign of thirty-six-year-old William Jennings Bryan, the passionate and eloquent champion of the "toiling masses"—especially small farmers devastated by persistent deflation—against Wall Street. He blamed the gold standard under which the U.S. Treasury minted dollars containing both gold and silver, the number of grains of each reflecting the commercial value of the respective metals. In 1894, when the price of silver had tumbled, the ratio of silver to gold in the dollar coin became much higher: thirty-two grains of silver to one of gold. Now, fearing their dollars would be further devalued, concerned citizens and foreign investors traded them in for gold, rapidly depleting the Treasury's gold reserves. Bryan believed he could solve the problem by making the ratio of metals in the dollar sixteen of silver to one of gold—thereby doubling the value of silver and flooding the country with these coins. The inevitable rampant inflation that followed, he claimed, would cause workers' wages to rise astronomically and bring general prosperity.

As a fellow Democrat, Pulitzer agreed with Bryan's colorful comment on trusts—"One of the most important duties of government is to put rings into the noses of hogs"—and supported many of his liberal and populist views. But he saw the fiscal flaw in Bryan's "silver" plan. Although inflation would raise workers' wages, it also would raise the *price* of everything and exacerbate the country's already deep depression.

Creelman was at the Democratic national convention in Chicago when Bryan wowed and won the crowd with an astonishing performance in the sweltering Coliseum. As he leaped to the platform two steps at a time, the crowd of twenty thousand greeted him with thunderous applause. Then he held them spellbound for forty minutes with his resonant voice and flawless diction.

Toward the end of his bravura performance, he brought the crowd to their feet yelling hoarse encouragement, then silenced them by touching his forehead with both hands as if in pain, and saying in words that still echo down the years, "You shall not press down upon the brow of labor this crown of thorns!" Assuming the attitude of the crucified Christ, he concluded: "You shall not crucify mankind upon a cross of gold!" And the crowd went berserk, yelling and raving, waving flags, throwing hats in the air, and acting "like wild men."

Bryan's antics drove the *New York Times* to ask "Is Bryan Crazy?," conclude that he was, and bolster its diagnosis by interviewing psychiatrists and publishing letters from laymen who overwhelmingly agreed.

Hearst's *Journal* was one of the few major papers to endorse Bryan. Pulitzer accused him of a selfish motive: his family's fortune came from silver mines, and increased silver production would benefit him personally. Hearst's mother, Phoebe, believed that privately her son, too, supported McKinley and the gold standard and vainly tried to persuade him to change his mind.

Though torn by his decision to support a Republican, Pulitzer was totally absorbed in the details of the political struggle—a race between a sluggish tortoise and a hyperactive hare.

Republican tortoise McKinley mostly campaigned from his front porch in Canton, Ohio, giving the same well-rehearsed speech to the converted. One day, without taking a step from his home, he made sixteen speeches to some thirty thousand people, a few thousand at a time. In the meantime, Bryan, the energetic Democratic hare, tore around the country on a whirlwind tour of some eighteen thousand miles, making more than six hundred speeches to a total of at least five million people who all but worshiped him. Some climbed trees and lampposts to catch a glimpse of him in passing. Creelman, with him every foot of the way, spent the final six weeks, day and night, eating and sleeping in Bryan's private railroad car.

Pulitzer spent those same months, said Seitz, "in unceasing labor, never for a waking moment out of touch with the telegraph, dictating, urging, informing [Creelman]. The fever of the fight revived his bodily strength and he labored as few in the fullness of their powers could do, sustained by his devotion to the right."

As well as exchanging detailed messages with Creelman about the campaign, Pulitzer sent orders, ideas, questions, advice, and criticism to his staff at the Dome. Because Hearst's people seemed to know of these confidential communications the same day, Pulitzer tried to plug the leaks by creating and using more code words. The new owner-editor of the *New York Times*, Adolph Ochs, became "Glucose"; net profit, "Nelson"; circulation, "Curate." Code words for the months all began with a T. January was "Toilet"; August, "Tomato"; and December, "Tonic." By using code, Pulitzer also met his own demands to "Condense! Condense!" A general criticism he had previously expressed as something like "On the first of the month there was an article, the tone of which I did not like on the subject of . . . " now shrank to one word, "Uneasy." Judging by his frequent use of it, "Sedentary" was his favorite code word, which, decoded, meant "A prompt reply is required."

Here is a sample of coded messages Pulitzer sent that fall:

Geranium [Hearst's *Journal*] is never to be mentioned in the pages of the *World* except as "the silver paper."

Why such a failure about colored potash [advertisements]? Everybody here agrees that last magazine disgracefully printed.

Why does Geologist [Bennett's *Herald*] with much lower circulation than Senior [Morning *World*] have as much Mustard [Want Ads]? Request more Mustard.

Mr. Pulitzer is sorry to complain but 80,000 returns on Seniority [Sunday *World*] is enormously wasteful and must be cut down.

Pulitzer also asked Business Manager John Norris to watch Horace (code name for Brisbane, the newly appointed editor of the Sunday *World*) and to "report on the hours he spends daily at his desk and whether he shows signs of flagging interest."

Initially Pulitzer had been so taken with Brisbane that he had given him complete control of the evening edition except for the editorial pages. Was his faith in him wavering? Or had he heard through his intelligence service that Brisbane was thinking of jumping ship and joining Hearst?

The fear of a Bryan victory so discombobulated *New York Times* writers that, not satisfied with calling him insane, they had readers scurrying for dictionaries or Latin lexicons by saying he suffered from "paranoia querulenta, graphomania and oratorical monomania."

Bryan kept his cool and sense of humor, quipping at one meeting while addressing farmers from a manure spreader: "This is the first time I have ever spoken from a Republican platform."

Discounting Bryan's charisma and mass appeal, Pulitzer was certain he'd lose, predicting in a *World* editorial: "There is no doubt as to the result of the election, except as to the size of McKinley's popular and electoral majorities. To question this is to doubt the intelligence, the underlying honesty and the public morality of the people. The *World* is absolutely confident that the proposal to debase the currency to the standard of a few semi-civilized countries, against the standard and the experience of the most enlightened and prosperous nations, cannot stand the trial of a four months' discussion."

Hoping to win him over, Bryan sent an emissary to warn Pulitzer that as he was a shoo-in, the *World* would suffer if it didn't support him. When editorial writer George Eggleston relayed the threat to Pulitzer, he simply laughed. And then he made an even more daring and precise prediction.

"As we sat there on his little private porch at Bar Harbor," Eggleston later wrote, "Mr. Pulitzer named every state that would give its electoral vote to each candidate, and the returns of the election. 'You may embody that,' he said, 'in an editorial predicting that the result of the election four months hence will be very nearly, if not exactly, what those lists foreshadow. Let that be our answer to Mr. Bryan's audacious message.'"

To finance a massive attack on Bryan, McKinley's campaign manager, Mark Hanna, shook down big corporations to contribute 1 percent of their wealth. With the millions of dollars collected, $250,000 from Standard Oil alone, he distributed 250 million pieces of campaign literature in 12 languages, and hired 1,400 speakers to swamp the country with anti-Bryan oratory.

By supporting Bryan, Hearst had lost many big advertisers. Yet he seemed not to care. Even though his *Journal* was losing more than $100,000 a month, he gave Bryan's campaign $40,000, and in September launched an evening edition of his *Journal* to compete with Pulitzer's Evening *World*. He also made another raid on Pulitzer's staff, coming away with Richard Felton Outcault, creator of a wildly successful cartoon series called "Hogan's Alley." It starred a mischievous street urchin with a gap-toothed grin and a gleam in his eye. He wore what looked like a yellow nightshirt, which explained his nickname, the Yellow Kid. Every Sunday, *World* readers eagerly riffled through the pages to see his latest high jinks or mocking imitations of New Yorkers' foibles.

But on the morning following a rally for Bryan in Madison Square Garden, they couldn't find it. The Yellow Kid cartoon had disappeared from the *World*. It reappeared on the front page of Hearst's *Journal*. Many subscribers quit the *World* to follow their favorite cartoon character. But it wasn't a complete defeat

OPENING OF THE HOGAN'S ALLEY ATHLETIC CLUB.

The Yellow Kid (*at bottom right*) in a panel from R. F. Outcault's popular "Hogan's Alley."

for Pulitzer: he still owned the cartoon's title, "Hogan's Alley," forcing Hearst to adopt the less catchy "McFadden's Row of Flats."

Pulitzer then adopted one of Hearst's tactics—copying the competition. He told staff artist George Luks to produce the Yellow Kid's identical twin, including yellow nightshirt and perky personality. Now each paper had a Yellow Kid. And billboards throughout the city advertised the rivalry.

Searching for a metaphor to characterize the mass appeal of the *World* and the *Journal, New York Press* editor Ervin Wardman found it in the competing Yellow Kid cartoons. So he dubbed the Hearst-Pulitzer exploitation of horror and scandal "yellow journalism." The innocuous phrase became a slur that has come to represent all exponents of the creed "If it bleeds, it leads."

Interest in the battle of the Yellow Kids gave way to election night fever on November 7, 1896. Then, thousands cheered in City Hall Park when a magic lantern projecting the results on a wall of the *World* showed that McKinley had won.

Amazingly, the results varied from Pulitzer's prediction of four months earlier by only 2 electoral votes of 447. McKinley 271, Bryan 176. Popular vote: McKinley 7,102,246, Bryan 6,492,559.

After 120 days of unrelenting work, without a day off, Pulitzer was at the end of his rope. So he left Maine for rest and recreation in Europe. Someone goofed in booking his passage on the liner *Colombia*, which had a brass band that seemed to play nonstop. Neither pleas nor entreaties could silence it. Seeking respite when he reached Monte Carlo—he was driven frantic by the constant chiming of ships' bells in the harbor—he urged his secretaries to find him a soundproof refuge.

He settled for an isolated country hotel in Cap Martin, between Menton and Monaco, just across the French border in Italy, an idyllic area of small farms, pine woods, and olive groves. The hotel's noises had already been subdued to suit the nerves of a royal resident, the empress of Austria.

On December 11 he cabled Business Manager John Norris not to send him any newspapers or letters, and to give all his editors Christmas presents of overcoats lined with Persian lamb. Brisbane was also to get a four-hundred-dollar bonus for boosting the Sunday *World*'s circulation to a record 623,000. For some reason, Pulitzer omitted from the overcoat list a former secretary, Frederick Duneka, recently appointed editor of the *Evening World*. The one letter that got through Pulitzer's embargo was from Duneka, who had the nerve to write that because he had not yet received his coat, he assumed Pulitzer intended to send him a more luxurious model with a sable collar. And wished him a happy Christmas.

"Damn your impertinence!" Pulitzer replied. "Coat will arrive by New Year's." Fortunately, impertinence was not a firing offense. Duneka stayed with Pulitzer for several more years.

CHAPTER 19

War Fever

1897

49 to 50 years old

Deeply depressed by his failing health, while in Europe Pulitzer sought help from Dr. Ernest Schweininger, celebrated for his successful treatment of Otto von Bismarck, chancellor of the German Empire. He charged accordingly, which, of course, didn't lighten Pulitzer's mood. Under this forceful doctor's orders, he followed a rigorous regime, but it was no help. Kate had remained in the United States, and he wrote to her from Cap Martin that although he had quit smoking cigars and drinking claret and had never exercised so much, he had never been so miserable. He slept better in America, he said, found the Riviera a dreadful bore, and was counting the hours for the ship that in two weeks would carry him from Genoa back to her. He complained that he had expected his older children to write to him regularly, which none had, and so was sending his love to the younger ones, Herbert and Constance, but not to Edith, Joseph, Lucille, or Ralph.

It also was a love letter. With it went a bouquet of orchids and his assurance that "I have thought of you every day. I have thought of you every hour of every day. I have thought of you many an hour of the night while awake. I have intended to write every day but could not because I was determined not to write more complaints and felt I could not write anything else."

Pulitzer came home to find that Hearst's *Journal* was threatening to outsell the *World*. Hearst had recently scooped the *World* with a shocking story about the strip-searching of three young Cuban women by male Spanish detectives aboard an American ship in Havana Harbor. The women were being sent into exile for helping the rebels.

Journal reporter Richard Harding Davis, also aboard the ship bound for Key West, later interviewed one of the women, Señorita Clemencia Arango.

Expecting "a woman of the people, with a machete in one hand and a Cuban flag in the other," he found "a well-bred, well-educated young person who spoke three languages and dressed as you see girls dress on Fifth Avenue after church on Sunday." He explained that all three women had been searched twice before boarding the ship, as they were suspected of carrying messages to rebels in Key West and Tampa. Then he reported that "when the young ladies stood at last on the deck of an American vessel, with the American flag hanging from the stern, the Spanish officers followed them there and demanded that a cabin should be furnished them to which the girls might be taken, and they were then again undressed and searched for the third time."

Davis asked: Would the captain of any British ship, even a coal barge, tolerate such an insult?

The *Journal* published the front-page story beneath a provocative banner headline DOES OUR FLAG SHIELD WOMEN? and—so that no one missed the point—with an illustration by famed artist Frederic Remington of a naked young woman being examined by three male detectives.

Outraged readers of the *Journal* persuaded New York congressman Amos Cummings to urge the secretary of state to investigate.

Meanwhile, the three women had landed in Tampa, where they called the *Journal* report false: they had been searched only by women and never with men present. In fact, Davis's report had been ambiguous. He had not stated the sex of those who had searched the young women, but the *Journal* had simply assumed they must have been men.

The *Journal* ignored its mistake, even though Davis said he was misquoted and would never write for Hearst again. But the *World* blazoned the distortion on page one, headlined THE UNCLOTHED WOMEN SEARCHED BY MEN WAS AN INVENTION OF A NEW YORK NEWSPAPER. Pulitzer also seized the chance to contrast *his* source, "Harry" Sylvester Scovel, now back in Cuba—admired for his "devotion to duty, accuracy, graphic descriptive power, absolute courage and skill"—with Hearst's fabricators.

An early proponent of the theory that a lie frequently repeated will be mistaken for the truth, Hearst ran distorted versions of the same story for three more days and, as *Journal* reporter Willis Abbot recalled, "I never heard [him] in public or private express the slightest regret for the scandalous 'fake.'"

As the naked women had become the *Journal's* brief *cause célèbre*, Scovel became the *World's*. Shortly after his return to Cuba, Scovel was imprisoned for possessing a fake police pass under an assumed name. Pulitzer then encouraged mass meetings and politicians to demand his release.

He became even more insistent on Scovel's release when a Cuban-born American dentist, Dr. Ricardo Ruiz, arrested as a rebel fighter, died in his Cuban prison cell. The Spanish authorities called it suicide. But Hearst reporter George Bryson saw the body and believed Ruiz had been murdered. The *Journal* printed a distorted version of his account under the emphatic but inaccurate headline AMERICAN SLAIN IN SPANISH JAIL. It was inaccurate be-

Frederic Remington's misleading illustration for Hearst's *New York Journal* of how Spanish detectives searched Señorita Clemencia Arango, a young Cuban. The *World* blazoned this distortion on its front page.

cause it had not been established how he had died. Nevertheless, the *World* jumped at the chance to use the story to fuel its own campaign to free Scovel, declaring that "The murder of Dr. Ruiz—an inoffensive American citizen in a Cuban cell, sharply illustrates the peril in which Scovel is placed" and claiming that he was "in imminent danger of butchery." Scovel's fate was continually dramatic front-page news in the *World* throughout February. The warning that SCOVEL MAY DIE BUT HIS DEATH WILL FREE CUBA hinted at an imminent American invasion and brought statements supporting Scovel from more than a hundred American newspaper editors and reporters. Seventeen state legislatures called for his release, and the U.S. Senate unanimously requested the State Department to persuade Spain to transfer Scovel from a prison in the sticks to Havana, where the U.S. consulate could monitor his welfare.

Meanwhile, Hearst's *New York Journal* and *San Francisco Examiner* never mentioned Scovel's existence.

Though Hearst and Pulitzer were political allies in supporting the Cuban rebels, they remained bitter and scornful rivals as publishers eager to denounce the other's flaws. In one instance, the *Journal* quoted Ohio senator John Sherman saying, "If the facts are true and American citizens are being murdered in cold blood, the only way to put an end to the atrocities is to declare war on Spain." When the senator denied he had said any such thing, the *Journal* chose to ignore him. But the *World* gladly printed Sherman's charge that the *Journal* report was "a lie from beginning to end."

Although the soldiers who arrested Scovel had thought of shooting him on the spot, they reluctantly let the "fucking Yankee" live. Once in prison he was treated like a celebrity, perhaps thanks to Pulitzer's campaign. His carpeted cell contained a comfortable bed, nightstand, desk, and rocking chair, gifts from Señora Madrigal, wife of a U.S. consular official. During her frequent visits she noticed that his cell was filling with presents from other prisoners: leather belts, paper flowers, and decorated toothpicks. Another visitor who attempted to talk with Scovel was constantly interrupted by excited delegations of giggling groupies.

Scovel wrote a daily account of his life datelined "Calaboose #1," which, smuggled out by Señora Madrigal, regularly appeared in the *World*. One described how, while he sat in the rocking chair steadied by two chunks of wood and smoked a cigar, he had a tooth extracted without anesthetic by an old, long-retired American dentist. After the operation he, the dentist, and Señor Madrigal had breakfast together in his cell on buckwheat cakes provided by Madrigal's wife. Because of his wife's delicious cooking Madrigal was so enormously fat, said Scovel, that he could only be weighed on factory scales.

In a more serious report Scovel denied a charge by Spain's ambassador in Washington that he was both an American spy and a colonel in the rebel army. Pulitzer supported his denials. In fact, as Scovel later admitted, he had tried to help the rebels—a capital offense in Cuba punishable by death.

Though Scovel treated his captivity as a joke, it was strictly gallows humor. Given many chances to escape, he suspected a setup, afraid that if he fell for it he'd end up like his Cuban guide whose mutilated body had been discovered shortly after Scovel's capture.

On February 28, "Butcher" Weyler, the Spanish general charged with putting down the rebellion, went to see Scovel for himself. The *World* had once described Weyler as a remarkably energetic and intelligent man who did not deserve his reputation for cruelty. Pulitzer had allowed this fair assessment to be printed. But as the fighting intensified, so did Weyler's repressive measures, and the *World* reassessed him as a ruthless monster. Weyler glanced with pursed lips at Scovel in his cozy, gift-filled cell, walked away without a word, then demoted the prison warden and forbade any more visits from female groupies. Apparently this did not include Señora Madrigal, because Scovel was still able to smuggle out a report that ridiculed Weyler's "fierce face" and "sloppy form."

Soon after, Scovel was freed and deported from Cuba—by orders of the Spanish government—pressured, according to Pulitzer, by the *World's* publicity campaign.

Back in the United States, Scovel was feted like a national hero. As a dinner guest of honor at Pulitzer's Fifty-fifth Street mansion he entertained his boss with stories of derring-do in Cuba and the eccentricities of his father, a Presbyterian minister. He got a big laugh from quoting his father's letter to the effect that now that Scovel was expelled from Cuba he could quit reporting and work at something worthwhile.

Recently inaugurated President McKinley was anxious to discuss the Cuban crisis with Scovel, and they got together on April 3. Scovel then went directly from the White House to St. Louis to marry Frances Cabanne, an attractive and spirited brunette to whom he had been unofficially engaged for several months. He expected Pulitzer to send him to cover the war that had just broken out between Greece and Turkey over who controlled Crete, and hoped to take Frances with him on an extended honeymoon behind the front lines.

Pulitzer had other ideas, which he expressed in this telegram to editorial executive Brad Merrill: "Give Scovel my kind regards and say I hesitate about sending him to Greece because I do not wish to disturb honeymoon or interfere with his domestic relations yet feel convinced a war correspondent exactly like a soldier must be entirely free from trammels or distracting thoughts, perhaps even more than a soldier because soldier is bound by discipline and *compelled* to move like a screw while a war correspondent is left to his individual freedom of action. That state of mind is everything. I cannot ask him to leave Mrs. S. behind and positively do not ask him, but he must assume for his own good that he positively cannot go without leaving his bride on this side of the Atlantic."

Pulitzer aficionados knew what this meant: Send Scovel to cover the Greek-Turkish war minus his missus.

Ironically, Scovel's wife, Frances, wanted the newspaper's readers to think he was unmarried. As Scovel confided to Merrill, Frances so despised the *World* that her "one condition to become my wife was that, in the pages of the *World*, Mr. Scovel is to be treated as a bachelor." Because she realized that Scovel's dream of becoming the paper's chief European correspondent depended on his pleasing Pulitzer, she let him go alone, without protesting. Some two weeks after their wedding she returned to her parents' home in St. Louis, and Scovel sailed for Europe.

To get closer to the political action, Pulitzer spent the spring in Washington, D.C., with Kate in a mansion owned by the widow of a General Logan. This was an unhappy choice for a man in Pulitzer's grim mood, as the widow had turned a wing of the house into a museum to memorialize her dead husband. Pulitzer called it "the mausoleum."

While defeated presidential contender William Jennings Bryan was in Washington he called on Pulitzer "to exhibit his hoofs and horns, so to speak," as Seitz put it. From his colorful account, Seitz was a fascinated witness of the occasion, writing that "the interview was prolonged and argumentative, Mr.

Pulitzer seeking to persuade his brilliant visitor to see the error of his ways and the latter standing his ground. Toward the close of the interview Mr. Pulitzer remarked that his guest had made 'a great deal of trouble' for him, and asked permission to pass his hand over Bryan's face. The latter took the delicate fingers in his own heavy fist and passed them over his adamantine jaw. 'You see, Mr. Pulitzer,' he observed, 'I am a fighter.'

"Mr. Bryan's jaws were clean shaven; Mr. Pulitzer's well upholstered. He asked the former to lend him his hand. This he passed over the foundation of his whiskers. 'Yes, I am one, too,' he commented." To Seitz, Bryan seemed to agree.

While in Bar Harbor for the summer Pulitzer became agitated about the cost of maintaining his homes and yacht, and paying his high-priced doctors, especially Dr. Schweininger—not to mention what he considered Kate's extravagance. His personal income for that year was $348,040.57, of which $72,000 went to Kate. But, having to provide for their baby Herbert, she found it difficult to cope and wanted Pulitzer to pay several of her outstanding bills on top of her allowance. He could hardly ask her to follow his example. He was about to buy a $350,000 mansion near Tarrytown owned by William Rockefeller, who eventually decided not to sell. And despite his pleas to Kate to economize, he continued to fund scholarships for forty-seven students at Columbia Teachers' College, to support relatives in Hungary, and give Kate's sister Clara Davis $5,000 a year.

To avoid the inevitable fight, Kate had learned not to approach him directly about money. Instead, while she was in Bar Harbor and he was briefly in New York, she wrote to his secretary, Alfred Butes, asking him to bring her plight to "Mr. Pulitzer's attention immediately, or the baby & I will be thrust into prison. Seriously, do get Mr. Pulitzer to attend to this *at once*, & send me a check *at once*. Don't let the paper, in this instance, come before his family. I hate to owe money. When I had probably nothing, I owed nothing. Now that I am supposed to have much, I owe much. This seems unfair & I will not consent to it. J. P. told me to pay all bills whether rightfully included in my allowance or not & let him have the totals. I hope there will be no brouhaha about this, but in any event I will not suffer any further worry. Money is such a contemptible thing to so constantly fight about. I wish there was no such thing as money in the world. Do make him careful in avoiding high winds, bright lights, glare, and sudden violent movements. As long as his eyes trouble him he should not go into the pool, nor ride horseback. These things, at least, he can do, even though it is impossible for him to stop worrying."

Pulitzer's attempts to economize crippled his coverage of the Greco-Turkish war. Short of ready cash and being the only *World* reporter in Greece, Scovel faced tough competition from several Hearst correspondents, including two women and their large support staff. So he resorted to trickery. He cabled Brad Merrill to send him two hundred dollars fast, then offered to slip the anticipated money to the man in the Athens cable office as an inducement to send his war reports immediately and to hold up the *Journal*'s for twenty-four hours. The man agreed. But because Merrill delayed sending the bribe money, the cable operator reneged on his promise. And even worse, when Scovel left the front to straighten out the problem in Athens, he missed the one important battle of the war, in which an overwhelming Turkish force of ten thousand defeated the Greeks at Velestinon.

Reaching the battleground when the fighting was over, he was reduced to interviewing witnesses. Even then, because the *World* was slow in sending his expenses, he had to borrow from the American ambassador to cable the secondhand story.

Frustrated, he wrote to his wife: "I wonder how Mr. Pulitzer is satisfied. It is too bad that I should come out here expressly to see a battle and miss the only one likely to happen. But it was distinctly not my fault."

His urgent cables to Merrill for money to cover the last days of the fighting were ignored. Instead Merrill said there was little interest in the battles and suggested he interview the Turkish commander, Edhem Pasha, or King George of Greece. Hoping to compensate for his failures, he arranged for an exclusive interview with the king. But His Majesty canceled because of "cardiac spasms," caused, according to Scovel, not by losing the thirty-day war, but by a subsequent encounter with James Creelman, now working for the rival *Journal.* In fact, the king had been so irritated by Creelman, said Scovel, that he swore he would never again speak to an American newspaperman.

Pulitzer decided to make Scovel his European correspondent, but based in Madrid rather than London, and when Scovel reached Spain, Pulitzer asked him to interview the prime minister, Antonio Canovas. As the Spanish press reporting the situation in Cuba had already blown the whistle on Scovel as a rebel sympathizer, it would have been political suicide for anyone in the Spanish government to cooperate with him. However, Scovel did send his impression of the Spanish view of the Cuban crisis. "They would quietly rejoice," he wrote to Pulitzer, if the United States took the problem out of their hands. And if the Americans persuaded the Cubans to accept home rule while still under the Spanish flag, because that was what Spain wanted "but is ashamed to ask for." Although there would be "a thunderous amount of clamor," Scovel said, and some Americans in Havana might be killed, he believed that outright war was unlikely.

Afraid that Scovel himself might be in danger in Spain, Pulitzer called him back to cover the home front.

That summer of 1897 a gruesome story made the front pages: a headless male corpse, also missing arms and legs, had been discovered in the East River. Hearst determined to outwit Pulitzer and the New York police in solving the crime, by forming a "murder squad" from the best of his street-smart reporters— and offering a thousand-dollar reward for information that led to the arrest of the guilty party. Days later, when arms and legs were washed ashore and placed with the torso in the morgue, George Arnold, of Hearst's murder squad, paid a visit. Arnold worked out at the Murray Hill Baths in midtown Manhattan, and there was something about the unusually calloused hand of the dismembered corpse that reminded him of a masseur there named Charles Guldensuppe. Hearst then challenged *Journal* reporters to find the seller or buyer of the oilcloth in which the body parts had been wrapped. Armed with similar pieces of oilcloth, scores of them questioned storekeepers throughout the city and nearby areas.

In Astoria, a Mrs. Max Riger recalled selling a bolt of similar oilcloth to a Mrs. Augusta Nack, a midwife. Before anyone else could reach Mrs. Nack, Hearst leaped onto a bicycle and, a gaggle of his reporters pedaling after him, raced to the tenement where Nack lived. Hearst then rented all the building's vacant flats, into which he moved his reporters like an occupying army, with guards posted in the hallways and at the entrance. His aim was to flush out Mrs. Nack while keeping rivals at bay, especially *World* reporters.

It worked like a charm. Convincing Mrs. Nack that they had the damning evidence, *Journal* reporters persuaded her to go with them to police headquarters. There she admitted that she and Guldensuppe had been lovers, but she had dropped him for a handsome barber named Martin Thorn. When Guldensuppe objected, they killed and dismembered him, wrapped the pieces in oilcloth, and threw them into the East River. His head was found floating there, while she was still being questioned. Thorn was eventually electrocuted, and Mrs. Nack got fifteen years in prison. It was a great triumph for the *Journal*, which justifiably ran this eight-column headline:

MURDER MYSTERY SOLVED BY THE JOURNAL

The report was illustrated with sketches of the body parts, the murder knife, and the principals. Hearst claimed that the crime was solved "under the direction of the best editorial brains in the world."

Hearst reporter George Arnold, who identified the murdered man by his calloused hands, got the thousand-dollar reward.

Meanwhile, Scovel had hardly landed in New York from his brief spell as European correspondent when Pulitzer sent him to cover a coal strike in West Virginia, with instructions to "breathe the breath of truth into every line you write." He didn't get the chance. Stopping en route in Pittsburgh, where his wife joined him, Scovel received new orders to forget the coal strike because there were no signs of present or potential bloodshed and to join the Klondike gold rush, now in full flood, where thousands were headed and violence was inevitable. His wife, Frances, insisted on going with him. Told to follow the crowd, Scovel led instead, with Frances at his side, spending seven hundred dollars of his expense money on dynamite to widen a passageway through a gap between two mountains that had been a bottleneck for the frantic would-be gold miners.

Scovel proudly wrote to Pulitzer that the reporter's wife, Frances, was "no ordinary woman" and "should not be judged by ordinary rules." And then explained how her skill and "quickness of nerve" had prevented a tragedy: on a mud-slicked mountain trail she had proved a daring, resourceful companion, saving herself and two horses at the last moment from a fatal five-hundred-foot drop.

As for Hearst, having shown the New York police how to bring criminals to justice, he now tried to shame the U.S. government into a war with Spain over its treatment of eighteen-year-old Evangelina Cisneros. She had been imprisoned in Cuba, said the *Journal,* for resisting a Spanish colonel who tried to rape her.

The paper's George Bryson interviewed Evangelina and reported, "This tenderly nurtured girl was imprisoned among the most depraved Negresses of Havana, and now she is about to be sent in mockery to spend twenty years in servitude that will kill her in a year. This girl, absolutely ignorant of vice, unconscious of the existence of such beings as crowd the cells of the Casa de Recojidas, is seized, thrust into a prison maintained for the vilest class of abandoned women of Havana, and shattered in health until she is threatened with an early death." Hearst greeted the news with an exultant cry of, "We've got Spain now!"

Pulitzer greeted it with strong reservations. Suspecting Hearst of toying with the truth, he cabled General Weyler, who replied that Evangelina was on trial for luring the military commander of the Isle of Pines to her house, where she had men hidden, who tied him up and tried to kill him. "No sentence has been passed nor approved by me," Weyler said. "I answer the World with the frankness and truth that characterize all my acts." But in its accompanying report the *World* confirmed rather than exposed the *Journal*'s version. It stated that Evangelina, together with her father and sister, had been exiled for rebellion to the Isle of Pines. Its governor, Colonel José Berriz, the Spanish prime minister's nephew, fell in love with her, wrote to her often, "and finally imposed a condition worse than death on the young and delicately reared girl." She later invited him to her home, where several of her men friends were hiding, and when the colonel appeared, they attacked him. A passing patrol heard his cries and rescued him. Then they arrested Evangelina, her father, and her friends.

To arouse worldwide public support, especially from women, Hearst launched a campaign that at least matched Pulitzer's efforts to prevent war with Britain over Venezuela.

Pulitzer remained cautious, writing that "the Spanish in Cuba have sins enough to answer for, as The World was first to show, but nothing is gained for the Cuban cause by inventions and exaggerations that are past belief."

The *World* exposed one of its rival's wildest distortions about Evangelina's confinement in prison by publicizing the informed views of the American consul in Cuba, General Fitzhugh Lee. He said: "I wish to correct a stupid impression which has been created by some newspapers. Evangelina has two clean rooms in prison and is well clothed and fed. It is all tommy-rot about her scrubbing floors and being subjected to cruelties and indignities. She would have been pardoned long ago if it had not been for the hubbub created by American newspapers. That she was implicated in the insurrection on the Isle of Pines, there can be no question. She herself, in a note to me, acknowledged that fact, and stated she was betrayed by an accomplice named Arias."

The facts did not discourage Hearst. Nor did he make any attempt to embrace them. His campaign was gaining ground, and circulation was soaring. When the queen of Spain suggested moving Evangelina to a convent, Hearst had a more exciting idea. In early October he sent one of his rugged reporters, Karl Decker, to organize Evangelina's prison break and escape from Cuba.

Pulitzer apparently got wind of Hearst's plan and decided to beat him to it. In September he recalled Scovel from the Klondike and gave him the assignment. The mission was so secret that even Scovel's wife didn't know what he was up to. But he was out of luck. Soon after he set foot in Havana he was recognized, arrested, and deported.

Decker had better luck. He bribed her guards to free Evangelina and smuggled her to New York. There Hearst put her up at the Waldorf, gave her a banquet at Delmonico's, a parade on Fifth Avenue, and organized a spectacular Madison Square Garden reception for her with two bands playing, searchlights illuminating the scene, and a fabulous fireworks display.

Hearst proclaimed his triumph in exuberant headlines: "MISS EVANGELINA CISNEROS RESCUED BY THE JOURNAL . . . An American Newspaper Accomplishes at a Single Stroke What the Best Efforts of Diplomacy Failed Utterly to Bring About in Many Months." Perhaps the *Journal* was justified in lying about how Evangelina was rescued—to protect the guards who had accepted the bribe to let her go. But readers were given the cover story: an exciting, exaggerated account of rescuers in disguise climbing onto the prison roof at night, using hacksaws to free her, then smuggling her aboard a ship dressed as a sailor and smoking a cigar.

Though Pulitzer decried Hearst's lies and distortions, he admired his innovations and creative staff, many of whom had once been his. Despite their intense rivalry Pulitzer considered Hearst's *Morning Journal* "a wonderfully able and attractive and popular paper, perhaps the ablest in the one vital sense, of managing to be talked about; of attracting attention, of constantly furnishing something which will compel people to talk about something they saw in that paper."

This is why he asked Seitz to "find somebody in the Journal's office with whom you can connect, to discover exactly who furnishes their ideas, who is dissatisfied and obtainable. If it would be helpful, get some tactful and discreet man to assist you in getting information." Pulitzer authorized Seitz to spend at least twenty-five dollars a week as a "'luncheon fund' to promote sociability!—a secret service, diplomatic fund, as it were." Today we'd call it industrial spying.

Suspecting that Hearst was on another recruiting raid, he asked Seitz to determine "the precise degree of accuracy in the statements recently sent to me. You might also give me your personal impression as to what has been the

The *New York Journal's* front page about Evangelina, October 10, 1897—a cover story in both meanings of the term.

effect of these offers on the gentlemen named, whether they are really to be depended upon or are to be regarded as insecure. Advise how Horace [Brisbane's code name] talks and acts. Whether disgruntled."

Brisbane *was* disgruntled. Despite his handsome salary of fifteen thousand dollars a year as editor of the *Evening World*, he felt that Pulitzer was wrong in trying to make the paper respectable. But what most exasperated Brisbane was Pulitzer's refusal to let him write signed editorials. When Brisbane persisted, Pulitzer replied: "You may do features or news stories. You may travel to any part of the globe on assignments. But these newspapers belong to me, and as long as I live, no one (other than myself) will express an independent editorial opinion in my newspapers."

Ambitious and confident, Brisbane decided to put Pulitzer's resolve to the test. For several days, while Pulitzer was out of town, Brisbane tapped out a signed column on his old Remington typewriter and placed it prominently on the front page of the *Evening World*. Tipped off that Brisbane was disobeying orders, Pulitzer suspended him for a week and asked Seitz for back copies of the paper and "your judgment about the character of the Evening World generally, how low, how objectionable has it been." After the papers were read to him, Pulitzer cabled Brisbane: "Stop [your] column at once. I don't want the Evening World to have an editorial policy. If you want good editorials, rewrite those in the Morning World."

Even so, it was Brisbane's assistant George Edward Russell who, lured by a pay raise, led the new exodus to Hearst. Soon after, Brisbane invited Russell to his Long Island home where, talking far into the night, he tried to get him to return to Pulitzer's employ. Brisbane warned him he was "committing journalistic suicide" by joining "an unknown upstart" and that he just had to compare the two men's heads—Pulitzer's "as long as a horse's"—to know that "Pulitzer will lick Hearst in short order." Apparently Russell was not into phrenology, and stayed with Hearst.

Rethinking his own advice, Brisbane now considered journalistic suicide a good career move. And his timing couldn't have been better. He learned that Hearst was on the verge of closing down his *Evening Journal*, which was on the skids. Pulitzer's *Evening World*, with a circulation of 325,000, was outselling it eight to one. Brisbane assured Hearst that he could save the *Evening Journal* and offered to accept a salary cut from his current fifteen thousand dollars to eight thousand dollars. In return, he asked for a thousand-dollar bonus for every extra ten thousand copies sold after he took over. Hearst agreed.

Brisbane even swore he'd drink nothing stronger than tea until he had raised the *Evening Journal*'s circulation to equal the *Evening World*'s, which he expected would take seven years. To everyone's amazement, his especially, he quit drinking tea after seven weeks. Six months later he had made twenty-three thousand dollars and was on his way to becoming a multimillionaire.

The loss of Brisbane must have stung Pulitzer, but he had more serious concerns. His oldest daughter, Lucille, was dangerously ill. The seventeen-year-old had contracted typhoid fever at her coming-out party at Chatwold, but seemed to be making such a good recovery that Pulitzer had invited his old friend Thomas Davidson to visit. After Davidson left, she suffered a relapse and, as Pulitzer explained to him, "Poor Lucille is still very ill and I need not tell you that I have been worried almost to death. You never wrote me from Boston—never gave me your address—ran off like a bad boy. Yet here I am thinking of you and proposing to you a trip to Naples if I am able to get off, which is still very doubtful, depending not only on Lucille's condition but on other things."

Pulitzer hired the country's leading medical specialists for Lucille, but she died on December 31. Her father, who began the year depressed, ended it distraught. Of all his children, noted his biographer Seitz, "she was most like him, with the same eager mind, the same restless energy, and the same desire for accomplishment." The *New York Times* obituary called her "one of the most beautiful of the debutantes of last summer."

A Pulitzer secretary, William Fitts, wrote to Davidson, saying that the Naples trip was canceled, and "I hardly dare think how this loss will affect Mr. P., & doubt if there is anyone who appreciates or understands the depths of his nature. Of course Mrs. Pulitzer is prostrated with her grief."

What helped Pulitzer was that he could bury himself in his work. He and Hearst, the nation's giants of journalism, were about to engage in the biggest battle of their lives—competing with each other as promoters and cheerleaders of a war against Spain over Cuba.

CHAPTER 20

Americans at War in Cuba

1898
—
50 to 51 years old

T wo headlines dominated the *World*'s front page for January 14, 1898:

THE RIOTS IN HAVANA MEAN **REVOLUTION,**

with the last word in bold type as shown, and

TO TRY ZOLA FOR
AIDING DREYFUS.

Vying for readers' attention on the same page was a lighthearted account of a trivial pursuit: William K. Vanderbilt entertaining friends in his Fifth Avenue mansion with a "New 'Coon' Song." Accompanying himself on the banjo, the multimillionaire sang what was reported as "I Want Yer, Ma Honey!" When the song title was repeated in the report, it was called "I Want Yer, Ma Money!" An inattentive or politically incorrect proofreader?

Between the news of revolution in Havana and bigotry in France was a story headed:

FROM SKIRTS TO TROUSERS

It told of a prisoner arrested as Christina Becke and placed in the woman's ward who was found through "her masculine arms" to be a cross dresser and rebooked into the men's section of the jail as Christian Becke. But, although Pulitzer encouraged variety in his paper, he left no doubt that the world's hot spots were France and Cuba and that cruelty and injustice were their common themes.

In France, a closed military court had sentenced Alfred Dreyfus, a Jewish French army captain, to life imprisonment for spying for Germany. Novelist

Émile Zola had gathered evidence that would exonerate Dreyfus. Zola then deliberately provoked the French General Staff by accusing them of knowingly sending an innocent man to prison, hoping they would charge him, Zola, with libel. If they did, he intended during his trial to plead for another trial for Dreyfus, but this time an open one. It worked: they charged him with libel.

Pulitzer was undeterred when the French government refused his request to interview Dreyfus on the dreaded Devil's Island, off the coast of French Guiana, South America, where the broken and humiliated prisoner was serving a life sentence in solitary confinement. He then asked Zola himself to undertake the interview as the World's special correspondent.

Zola replied, "I am greatly indebted to The World. It champions the oppressed the world over, but I can undertake the fight better in Paris. No one could get within a league of Devil's Island under present restrictions. To see Dreyfus would be impossible. He is too well guarded. The fight will be won here." Zola was elated, he told the World, "at the prospect of being prosecuted or persecuted [at his libel trial]. I did not deliver my challenge lightly. I resolved to force the hands of the Government to expose the atrocious injustice and I have succeeded. Now I am certain of the liberation. Our proofs are overwhelming."

Pulitzer's Paris correspondent spoke with the prisoner's "beautiful, pale, and agitated" wife, who said it was a lie "to state that my poor husband confessed his guilt. He always protested his absolute innocence both to me and to everyone. A fair, open inquiry is all we need to establish this."

The World also published a London report stating, "Outside of France all Europe believes Dreyfus is the victim of a villainous conspiracy, and prosecution of Zola has broadened the question, for the whole French Army is now virtually placed on trial. The gravity of the situation is enhanced because the whole of France is in a state of growing hysterical excitement." The London correspondent mentioned something the Paris correspondent avoided: that being a Jew, Dreyfus "was chosen as a convenient scapegoat. A monster manifestation is preparing in Paris for tomorrow. Allegedly it is anti-Dreyfusian. Really it is anti-Semitic."

While the World did not report the rampant anti-Semitism in the French Army and among much of the French population, its headlines made clear that it was rooting for Dreyfus:

FRANCE REFUSES TO ALLOW ZOLA
TO SEE DREYFUS FOR THE WORLD.

———

The Solitary Prisoner of Devil's Island
Cannot Now Speak Even to His
Guard—His Friends in Paris
Persecuted.

———

VICE-PRESIDENT OF FRENCH SENATE DEMANDED
"PUBLICITY" AND LOSES HIS OFFICE.

_____

Trial in the Full Light of Day All that He Asked;
It Is Now the Most Important Question Before
Europe—Zola's New Message and Mme.
Dreyfus's Statement in The World.

The *World* reported that as Zola went to and from the court to answer the charge of libeling the French Army General Staff, "bands of students paraded the streets shouting incessantly: 'Spit on Zola!' and 'Death to the Jews!' The windows of a house mistaken for Zola's were broken."

Hearst also sympathized with Dreyfus and asked Decker, who had spirited Evangelina Cisneros from Cuba, to prepare a plan to rescue Dreyfus from Devil's Island, but it proved too difficult. Neither Hearst nor Pulitzer lost interest in Dreyfus's fate, but more pressing events in Cuba commanded their attention.

Although predicting revolution in Cuba, the *World* stressed that Americans were safe in Havana and that the Spanish government—with which the U.S. government was still friendly—was doing its utmost to restore peace.

By contrast, Hearst's *Journal*, in a mix of lies and wishful thinking, and a hint of spins to come, falsely reported that the riots were "aimed against American citizens in Havana, rather than a brawl between rival Spanish and Cuban factions and predicted United States military intervention within forty-eight hours."

The *World's* Sylvester Scovel, twice banished from Cuba, was allowed to return because General Weyler had been replaced by the more amenable General Ramon Blanco. Nevertheless, Scovel still found conditions there desperate. So many Cubans were dying, often of starvation, he reported, that "in many towns the supply of coffins had long been exhausted. Homeless rural vagrants begged in the Havana streets. U.S. Vice Consul John Springer estimated that a third of the city's fifty thousand people were 'absolutely without food and clothing, and 11,000 without homes or shelter.' Appalled by the suffering, President McKinley made a special appeal for Red Cross donations, himself giving five thousand dollars anonymously."

Representing a new, liberal Spanish government, General Blanco's offer of autonomy had been refused by the Cuban rebels, who demanded complete self-government. On the other hand, Scovel reported that the pro-Spanish faction, called "the irreconcilables," wanted to maintain complete control of the country. Their rage, he said, was directed "against Blanco's policy of moderation, rather than against Americans. The Spanish irreconcilables have an undying hatred of anything smacking of autonomy for Cuba and cling to Weyler's policy of 'Exterminate the Cuban breed.'" U.S. Consul General Lee walked freely about in Havana's Central Park at night during the rioting, attended to his official business as usual next day, and dined in the evening at the Hotel

Inglaterra. He did not ask for a U.S. warship to be sent to Havana, but knew that if Americans were at risk he could rely on a squadron of fighting vessels at Key West, only six hours away, to rush to the rescue.

Scovel warned that if the pro-Spanish volunteers who called Americans "fat pigs for Spanish bayonets to stick into" acted on their threats, then "no citizen of the United States will be safe." But, in that event, Scovel assured readers, the American consul "will ask for United States warships—and he will get them." He was proved right a few days later when the consul heard Spanish soldiers shouting "Death to Blanco!" and feared that Americans were now in danger. He made a secret call for help that brought the battleship *Maine* to Havana Harbor on January 25. The official cover story described it as a friendly visit, and General Blanco took it in that spirit, sending a case of sherry to the crew, some of whom went ashore to watch a bullfight.

On the night of February 15 Scovel was dining with his wife in a café within sight of Havana Harbor when an enormous explosion shook them in their seats. He hurried to the scene, guided by the screams and groans of dying and injured men. He saw the shattered *Maine*, corpses floating on the water and rescuers already at work—but he had no idea of the immensity of the tragedy, that the explosion had killed 266 American sailors. His first report to the *World* was fair and factual: "The United States battleship *Maine* was blown up in Havana harbor shortly before 10 o'clock this evening. Many of those on the *Maine* were killed and many more injured. The injured do not know what caused the explosion. There is some doubt as to whether the explosion took place ON [sic] the *Maine*. The battleship was practically destroyed, but little of her being above water."

Scovel's report next day published under the headline:

MAINE EXPLOSION CAUSED BY BOMB OR TORPEDO?

was full of rumors and speculations: of a doctor overhearing a plot to blow up the ship; of a dynamite expert's theory that it was no accident; and that the captain's dispatch to the U.S. State Department, blaming the enemy for the explosion, had been suppressed.

Hearst's front-page headlines for the same day emphatically declared:

DESTRUCTION OF THE WAR SHIP MAINE WAS THE WORK OF AN ENEMY
Assistant Secretary Roosevelt*
Convinced the Explosion of
the War Ship Was Not
an Accident
NAVAL OFFICERS THINK THE MAINE WAS DESTROYED BY A SPANISH MINE

---

* Theodore Roosevelt had resigned as New York City police commissioner to be assistant secretary of the navy.

863,956

863,956

WORLDS CIRCULATED YESTERDAY

WORLDS CIRCULATED YESTERDAY

The 🌐 **World.**

VOL. XXXVIII. NO. 13,356.   NEW YORK, THURSDAY, FEBRUARY 17, 1898.   PRICE

MAINE EXPLOSION CAUSED BY BOMB OR TORPEDO?

Capt. Sigsbee and Consul-General Lee Are in Doubt---The World Has Sent a Special Tug, With Submarine Divers, to Havana to Find Out---Lee Asks for an Immediate Court of Inquiry---Capt. Sigsbee's Suspicions.

CAPT. SIGSBEE, IN A SUPPRESSED DESPATCH TO THE STATE DEPARTMENT, SAYS THE ACCIDENT WAS MADE POSSIBLE BY AN ENEMY.

Dr. E. C. Pendleton, Just Arrived from Havana, Says He Overheard Talk There of a Plot to Blow Up the Ship---Capt. Zalinski, the Dynamite Expert, and Other Experts Report to The World that the Wreck Was Not Accidental---Washington Officials Ready for Vigorous Action if Spanish Responsibility Can Be Shown---Divers to Be Sent Down to Make Careful Examinations.

The *World*, February 17, 1898, vividly reporting the *Maine* explosion.

The *Journal* account was slanted if not false. Charles Sigsbee, the captain of the *Maine*, who escaped injury, had advised U.S. navy secretary John Long, "Public opinion should be suspended until further report. Many Spanish officers including representatives of General Blanco are now with me to express sympathy." In fact, General Blanco cried when he heard the news, and sailors from a Spanish cruiser had joined in the rescue work even while ammunition was still exploding. President McKinley also asked the public to suspend judgment and promised to let them know the truth about the cause of the explosion as soon as he did. The Spanish government, in an effort to express its horror at the event, offered to stop fighting the Cubans.

While Pulitzer implied in his headlines and news columns that the Spanish might be the perpetrators, he ridiculed Hearst editorially, saying that nobody outside a lunatic asylum believed that the Spanish had blown up the *Maine*. To find out for himself, he hired five divers to examine the wreck, but Spanish authorities stopped them.

To compete with Hearst in arousing the public's appetite for war, Pulitzer quickly abandoned any pretense of impartiality. On February 17, for example, two days after the event, both men published a "secret" cable from the *Maine*'s

Captain Charles Sigsbee to Secretary of the Navy Long saying the explosion was not an accident. The message later proved to be a fake.

Not all New York newspapers lost credibility. For the past two years the *New York Times* had been directed by Adolph Ochs, who promised readers a straightforward approach to the news. With a circulation of barely ten thousand he had to rely on AP dispatches while Pulitzer and Hearst had the money to send their own correspondents to every major crisis spot. Even so, Ochs was living up to his promise to supply unbiased, unsensational coverage. Obviously not yet aware of Hearst's views, Ochs wrote on February 17: "Nobody is so foolish as to believe that the Maine was destroyed by Spaniards with the knowledge and connivance of their government. A fanatical partisan of BLANCO might have done the deed at the prompting of his own private hatred of the United States, but the crime of an irresponsible wretch cannot be justly charged against his Government. Spain has just too many reasons [to avoid offending us to think] that she would not exercise due diligence to protect a ship of our navy visiting her waters."

To this day no one has conclusively proved if it was deliberate or an accident. A U.S. court of inquiry concluded that a submarine mine applied externally caused the explosion but did not determine who did it. Later evidence suggested the ship's magazine exploded internally, perhaps accidentally.

Hearst never wavered from his charge that the Spanish were to blame. From the start he had been an unabashed propagandist for the Cuban rebels, reflecting the views of many of his readers. His *Evening Journal* of February 20 featured a Brisbane-inspired illustrated feature headed: "How the Maine Actually Looks as It lies, Wrecked by Spanish Treachery, in Havana." All pure fantasy, but the public loved it and sales of the paper for the three days following the sinking of the *Maine* totaled a record 3,098,825.

Hearst even had the gall to publish a fake interview with Theodore Roosevelt in which he was purported to have said: "It is cheering to find a newspaper of the great influence and circulation of the *Journal* tells the facts as they exist and ignores the suggestions . . . from sources that cannot be described as patriotic or loyal to the flag of this country." When Roosevelt called the interview a complete invention, Pulitzer rubbed Hearst's nose in it by printing the disavowal and dismissing the *Journal* as a paper "written by fools for fools."

Edwin Godkin, the respected editor of the *Evening Post*, blasted both men. He regarded their "gross misrepresentation of facts, deliberate invention of tales calculated to excite the public, and wanton recklessness in the construction of headlines which even outdid these inventions, the most disgraceful behavior in the history of American journalism. . . . Every one who knows anything about 'yellow journals' knows that everything they do and say is intended to promote sales. No one supposes a yellow journal cares five cents about the Cubans, the *Maine* victims, or anyone else. A yellow journal is probably the nearest approach to hell, existing in any Christian state. It is a crying shame that men should work such mischief in order to sell more papers."

Selling papers and competitive fervor surely played a large part. But Pulitzer and Hearst also genuinely deplored the suffering of the Cuban people—400,000 held in ghastly concentration camps in which some 210,000 perished. Furthermore, millions of Americans never exposed to their propaganda were "on fire" for war with Spain. The war fever had a traumatic effect on the *Evening World*'s workaholic managing editor, Ernest Chamberlin. Even Pulitzer's spy system failed to anticipate this tragedy. One evening in late February when the paper had gone to press and most of the editorial staff had left, he raced up the stairs to the composing room yelling: "War! War! We must get out an extra!" Then he hurried down and sent telegrams to his staff ordering them back to work. He greeted them calmly, saying, "The war has begun, boys. We must get out an extra," and showed them a massive one-word headline: WAR! spread across the entire front page. They asked for the reports to justify the headline, but he simply murmured repeatedly: "War! War! War!" Charles Chapin and others sensed that "Poor Chamberlin had gone stark mad from overwork and worry and had manufactured the war declaration from the raving of his crazed brain."

They sent him home by cab and ordered several boys to retrieve the few copies headlined WAR! already on the street.

Pulitzer was fond of Chamberlin and distressed when told what had happened. The messenger who brought the news to him returned with orders for another editor, Foster "Curser" Coates, to replace Chamberlin. Coates was an affable, warmhearted, and kindly man, "though superlatively profane," said Chapin, who worked with him. In this he seems to have topped even Pulitzer, because, according to Chapin, "There is no word in blasphemous vocabulary that wasn't on the tip of his tongue. He ripped out oaths that fairly made the windows rattle, but it was habit more than temper, for otherwise he was almost without fault."

Chamberlin developed pneumonia a few days after his mad outburst and died shortly before his "declaration" of war was proved prophetic. (Coates also eventually worked himself to death, dropping dead as he entered his home after a hard day at the office.)

Soon after Pulitzer's majordomo, Jabez Dunningham, suffered a slight nervous breakdown, his secretary Butes became ill, and Kate left to spend the spring in England. Her secret informant, his secretary George Ledlie, wrote to reassure her that although Pulitzer was "wildly absorbed" in the paper and the possibility of war, he seemed in good shape. Ledlie also thought her husband was anxious to join her in England, though "this probable war may delay his departure. He had hoped it would be fought and ended before he started—but that now is impossible."

Ledlie's letter to Kate crossed with hers to Pulitzer in which she sent greetings for his fifty-first birthday on April 10 and a present of lilies.

Pulitzer celebrated his birthday by publishing his first prowar editorial: "Spain is a decaying, ignorant and well-nigh bankrupt nation. No Spanish ship could stand an hour before the Americans. [He was right.] Havana is at our mercy [Right again.] and this is a nation that talks of war with the United States. Now fifty-four days have passed since the Maine was destroyed by a stationary mine. God forbid that The World should ever advocate an unnecessary war! That would be a serious crime against civilization. The first duty of the President and Congress is to order the navy to proceed to Cuba and Puerto Rico without delay. No declaration of war is necessary. Send the fleet to Havana and demand the surrender of the miscreants who blew up the Maine."

The next day an exhausted President McKinley, having taken sleeping pills to get some rest, reluctantly caved in to public pressure and private insults, such as war hawk Theodore Roosevelt's crack that he didn't have "the backbone of a chocolate éclair." On April 11, 1898, McKinley urged Congress to approve armed intervention to free oppressed Cubans. Three hundred eleven congressmen voted for war and only six opposed. It was closer in the Senate, with forty-two for and thirty-five against.

The United States officially declared war against Spain on April 25, 1898.

Pulitzer and Hearst were already selling their papers in record numbers with the distorted news that had made war all but inevitable. Ostensibly, at least, Pulitzer still tried to keep the World on the straight and narrow. But it was like demanding chastity in a whorehouse. He told Brad Merrill to read all editions of the paper, "criticizing, complaining, stopping bad tendencies, killing bad schemes, vetoing sensationalism, suggesting, proposing, curbing, stimulating." Obviously Merrill did not complain enough.

By April 26, 1898, the World had a daily sale of 1.3 million, neck and neck with the Journal. No one complained about that.

Engrossed in the conduct of the war, Pulitzer was enraged when instead of attacking Cuba—as he would have done—the United States adopted Theodore Roosevelt's plan and headed for the Spanish-occupied Philippines, on the other side of the world. There, soon after daylight on May 1, Commodore George Dewey led six U.S. warships into Manila's fortified harbor. The ten antiquated Spanish ships didn't have a prayer. Dewey's men destroyed them all and killed 381 Spanish sailors. The only American fatality died of heat stroke.

World correspondent Edward Harden, aboard one of the U.S. warships, had the bright idea of going ashore at Hong Kong. There he paid the highest "urgent" rate of $9.90 a word to cable the news to his paper. It was even transmitted ahead of the official government report and scooped the Journal and all other New York papers by several hours. In announcing the victory on the front pages of the World and the Journal for May 2, 1898, the text and headlines were, for a change, almost entirely accurate, except that Hearst's THE MAINE IS AVENGED! perpetuated as fact what remains only supposition.

Hearst was in such a state "of proud ecstasy" for having, as he believed, forced war on the reluctant president, that he appointed himself commander in chief, asking his readers, "HOW DO YOU LIKE THE JOURNAL'S WAR?"

Hearst's ego swelled with his skyrocketing circulation, and Pulitzer, playing follow the leader, put "Accuracy! Accuracy!! Accuracy!!!"—and honesty—on hold for the duration.

Anxious not to be beaten by their rival, World editors sometimes stole and rewrote Journal stories. Journal editors were alert for this, having themselves been caught stealing World material. So the Journal set a trap, printing a completely phony report from Cuba that read in part: "Colonel Reflipe W. Thenuz, an Austrian artillerist of European renown, who, with Colonel Ordonez was defending the land batteries of Aguadores was so badly wounded that he has since died. Col. Thenuz was foremost in the attempt to repulse the advance and performed many acts of valor."

The World did the minimum of rewriting: "Colonel R. W. Thenuz, an Austrian artillerist well known throughout Europe, who, with Colonel Ordonez, was defending the land batteries of Aquadores, was so badly wounded that he has since died." Attempting to disguise the theft, the World attributed it to an impressive bogus source: "On board the World dispatch boat Three Friends, off Santiago de Cuba, via Port Antonio, Jamaica."

One can imagine the roar of triumph in the Journal newsroom when the World swallowed the bait. The letters of the Austrian colonel's name were an imperfect anagram for: "We pilfer the news." For the next month the Journal relentlessly mocked the World, with a proposal to erect a monument for Colonel Thenuz, funded by readers sending "Confederate notes, Chinese cash and repudiated bonds," with a cartoon of the imaginary colonel captioned, "Specially taken for the World by the World's special photographer," with a comic poem honoring the colonel, and letters from other newspaper editors damning the World for dishonesty. Finally, on Sunday, July 10, Hearst printed a full-page cartoon depicting frantic World editors stealing the phony story.

Meanwhile, Scovel had been producing great, exclusive stories for the World. As a secret agent for the U.S. military—scouting the strength and location of Spanish defenses and going into the interior to discuss with rebel General Gomez potential joint action against Spanish troops—he was privy to information hidden from other correspondents.

Scovel was joined by the brilliant young novelist-reporter Stephen Crane, who had been a Hearst correspondent in the Greco-Turkish War. Now, having failed the medical for the U.S. Navy, he had accepted Pulitzer's cabled offer to work with Scovel. Before he ever witnessed a battle, Crane had produced literary alchemy in The Red Badge of Courage, a vivid and seemingly authentic account of men at war. He still had to use his imagination working for Pulitzer because, as he said, "editors demanded hair-raising dispatches, bombastic scoops on heroism, and urged [us] to remember that the American people were a collection of super-nervous idiots who would immediately have convulsions if we did not throw them some news—any news."

Sick and dosed with quinine, Crane landed with the U.S. Marines in their invasion of Guantánamo on June 7. In his report to the World headed "In the

1,011,068
Per Week-Day April Average.
GAIN In One Year - - 338,748   "Circulation Books Open to All."

The

WORLD. 1,011,068
Per Week-Day April Average.
"Circulation Books Open to All."   GAIN In Three Years - 461,205

VOL. XXXVIII. NO. 13,404.   NEW YORK, MONDAY, MAY 2, 1898.   PRICE

DEWEY SMASHES SPAIN'S FLEET

VICE-ADMIRAL MONTOJO.

Great Naval Battle Between Asiatic Squadron and Spanish Warships Off Manila.

THREE OF THE BEST SPANISH VESSELS WIPED OUT, OTHERS SUNK.

The Damage Done to the American Boats Engaged Only Nominal---Hundreds of the Enemy Slain in the Encounter.

CONMODORE DEWEY.

The Defeated Commander of the Spanish Fleet.

Winner of First Great Victory for New American Navy.

LISBON, Portugal, May 1, 11 P. M.----The Spanish fleet was completely defeated off Cavite, Philippine Islands, according to trustworthy advices received here.

WASHINGTON, May 1, Midnight.---President McKinley expresses entire satisfaction over the reported battle between Commodore Dewey's squadron and the Spanish fleet. He accepts the news as true, but believes it is worse for the Spanish than they will admit. There has been no official confirmation of the news. Nothing official is expected for forty-eight hours.

THE THREE SPANISH CRUISERS COMPLETELY DESTROYED.

CASTILLA.   DON JUAN DE AUSTRIA.

FLYING SQUADRON STRENGTHENED.

SPANISH FLAG SHIP "REINA MARIA CRISTINA"

ADMIRAL MONTOJO ADMITS HIS UTTER ROUT.

In His Report to Spain He Says Many Ships Were Burned and Sunk and the Losses in Officers and Men "Numerous."

MADRID (via Paris), May 2.—The time of the retreat of the American squadron behind the merchantmen was 11.30 A. M. The American squadron forced the port before daybreak and appeared off Cavite. Night was completely dark.

The Naval Bureau at Manila sends the following report, signed "Montojo, Admiral:"

"In the middle of the night the American squadron forced the forts, and before daybreak appeared off Cavite. The night was completely dark. At 7.30 the bow of the Reina Christina took fire and, soon after the poop also was burned.

"At a lighter o'clock, with my staff, I went on board the Isla de Cuba. The Reina Maria Christina and the Castilla were then entirely enveloped in flames.

"The other ships having been damaged retired into Baker Bay. Some had to be sunk to prevent their falling into the hands of the enemy. The losses are numerous, notably Capt. Cadarso, a priest, and nine other persons.

"The Spaniards fought splendidly, the sailors refusing to leave the burning and sinking Don Juan de Austria. There is the greatest anxiety for further details.

MADRID'S FORLORN HOPE.

LONDON, May 2.—The Madrid correspondent of the Financial News, telegraphing this morning, says:

"The Spanish Ministry of Marine claims a victory for Spain because the Americans were forced to retire behind the merchantmen. Capt. Cadalso (or Cadarso), in command of the Reina Maria Christina, went down with the ship.

MADRID OFFICIAL REPORT ADMITS DISASTROUS DEFEAT

MADRID, May 1, 8 P. M.—The following is the text of the official despatch from the Governor-General of the Philippine Islands to the Minister of War, Lieut.-Gen. Correa, regarding the engagement off Manila:

"Last night, April 30, the batteries at the entrance to the fort announced the arrival of the enemy's squadron, forcing a passage under the obscurity of the night.

"At daybreak the enemy took up positions, opening with a strong fire against Fort Cavite and the arsenal.

"Our fleet engaged the enemy in a brilliant combat, protecte

How the *World* reported a U.S. victory against the Spanish fleet off Manila in May 1898.

First Land Fight 4 of Our Men Are Killed," he wrote that though most of the marines had never before been under fire, none flinched.

Soon after, seventeen thousand Americans left Key West, Florida, to invade Santiago de Cuba, on the island's southern shore.

Despite the twenty-six-year-old Crane's fragile physique and shy, sensitive disposition, a fellow correspondent judged him to have "the highest and truest courage, the courage of a man of keen imagination, and he proved it on more than one stricken field." When Hearst reporter Edward Marshall was shot during the fighting on June 24, Crane helped to carry him to a field hospital, where the wounds were pronounced fatal. Crane asked if there was anything more he could do, and Marshall replied, "Well, you might file my dispatches. Not ahead of your own, old man—but just file 'em if you find it handy." After Marshall had dictated what he thought would be his last words to his rival reporter, Crane trudged in the intense heat some five miles to Siboney to transmit Marshall's account of the battle destined for the pages of the *Journal*, a generous act for which he would soon pay. Crane's own report was somehow delayed and not printed in the *World* until July 7.

He was in the thick of the Battle of San Juan exposing himself to enemy fire on July 1 and 2, when his colleagues argued whether he was incredibly brave, suicidal, slightly nuts—or all three.

In his July 5 *World* report, Crane told of white-aproned American surgeons treating fifty-two wounded Spaniards in a Catholic church. He noted that the kindness of American soldiers amazed the thousands of refugees and that "Spanish sharpshooters picked off our ambulancemen and surgeons. They bowled them over at every chance. Yet three of the miscreants who fought among the trees, wearing clothes stripped from our dead, have been set to work about headquarters." On July 8, Crane was half delirious with malaria when a *World* colleague, George Bronson Rae, helped him aboard the *City of Washington*, taking the sick and wounded to a Virginia hospital.

After being discharged from the hospital in the sweat-soaked clothes he had worn in Cuba for several months, Crane bought a new outfit for twenty-four dollars. Then he showed up at *World* headquarters to ask for his next assignment, and expense money to pay for his new clothes. But Business Manager Seitz refused to give him another cent, because he regarded Crane as disloyal for helping rival Hearst reporter Marshall transmit his report.

Seitz even accused Crane of robbing Pulitzer by taking three thousand dollars for his three months' assignment and sending just one worthwhile dispatch—a lie, repeated by historian Walter Millis in his 1931 book *The Martial Spirit*. In fact Crane sent at least twenty dispatches, some of which were judged by fellow war correspondents as among the best of the war.

In its report of the fighting, the *World* described New York's Seventy-first Regiment as being demoralized and retreating while Theodore Roosevelt courageously led "Rough Riders" in a victorious charge up Kettle Hill.

Unable to resist discrediting Pulitzer, Hearst resorted to his now customary elephantine headlines:

SLURS ON THE BRAVERY OF THE BOYS OF THE 71ST
The *World* Deliberately Accuses Them of Rank Cowardice at San
Juan

Calling the accusation a "dastardly lie," Hearst countered that the men had suffered heavy casualties. And although he hadn't witnessed the battle, he had the nerve to write his firsthand testimony to the courage of the men of the Seventy-first on the day in question, headed:

Stephen Crane, the
brilliant novelist,
was also a *World*
war correspondent.

EDITOR OF THE JOURNAL'S PERSONAL EXPERIENCE OF THE SPLENDID
HEROISM OF THE SEVENTY-FIRST

When Pulitzer challenged his claim to have seen the battle, Hearst cited
his correspondent Edward Marshall as a witness. But Marshall had been seriously wounded before the battle and in no shape to say what happened. For a
week the rival publishers made their fight seem more important than the war.

Margaret Leech (second wife of Ralph Pulitzer) wrote in *In the Days of
McKinley* (1959) that New Yorkers "were especially touchy about their gallant
Seventy-first, whose prowess the newspapers had glorified without regard to the
facts. The *World*, in an inadvertent moment, had printed a truthful account of
the panic in the regiment under fire." Excoriated for telling the truth, Pulitzer
tried to placate his critics by printing individual accounts of bravery by members of the Seventy-first and by raising money for a joint memorial to the regiment and New York members of the Rough Riders.

Hearst "jeered at this repentance of a defamer," wrote Swanberg, and reported that the men of the Seventy-first refused to accept any memorial from
Pulitzer. Embarrassed, Pulitzer returned the contributions he had collected for
the memorial.

But Theodore Roosevelt proved Pulitzer right and Hearst wrong. Infuriated by the dispirited Seventy-first Regiment, which had impeded his attack on

San Juan Hill, he swore that "no Rough Rider could sleep in the same grave with the cowardly dead of the 71st."

Who wrote the *World* report about the Seventy-first Regiment that caused Pulitzer so much trouble? Surely not Crane. On July 15, when the story was sent from Cuba, he was in a Virginia hospital. Yet Seitz chose to make Crane the scapegoat. Too proud to argue the point, and perhaps thinking he was protecting Scovel, Crane quit Pulitzer to rejoin Hearst briefly. But then, seeing no future with Hearst or Pulitzer, he rejoined his wife in England to concentrate on fiction, befriended and idolized by such literary luminaries as Joseph Conrad, Henry James, and H. G. Wells. Two years later, at thirty, Crane died of tuberculosis, when Pulitzer made belated amends, or at least corrected Seitz's lies—in a laudatory obituary. There, under the headline "Madcap Genius Stephen Crane," the *World* admitted that his Spanish-American War reports "were masterpieces of description. If he had a fault as a war correspondent it was that his enthusiasm took him too deeply into the thick of the fighting."

This was equally true of Sylvester Scovel, who was getting himself into hot water in Cuba at a military victory parade. By now he, like Crane, was in terrible shape, having lost fifty pounds in a few weeks. He suffered from chronic insomnia and intermittent nausea. Still he arrived at a victory ceremony in Santiago de Cuba on July 17 eager to get a good view and maybe get into the official photograph. He climbed onto the roof of the governor's palace near the flagpost on which the U.S. flag was to be raised. Ordered to get off the roof by a couple of army brass, he played around for a time, moving from the roof to a nearby tree and then back.

An eyewitness recalled: "At this spectacular moment in the histories of Spain and the United States, what more natural and to be expected than that Scovel should be in the center of the stage? This was journalism, as his career had interpreted it. Behold him, then, defying martial edict, conspicuous upon the hoary palace roof, ready to assist in hoisting the American flag, while the commanding general and his staff glared in blank amazement."

The gout-ridden head of the U.S. Army in Cuba, sixty-three-year-old General William Shafter, so overweight he sometimes had to be carried on a door, was not a man to be trifled with. Almost falsetto with rage, he ordered Scovel thrown off the roof, a humiliation Scovel avoided by quickly jumping to the ground. The victory ceremony followed with the lowering of the Spanish flag, the raising of the U.S. flag, a twenty-one-gun salute, and the playing of "The Star-Spangled Banner." Scovel then walked to Shafter to explain or justify himself. But the general interrupted him to yell, "You son-of-a-bitch! You and your tribe are goddamned nuisances!" In shock, Scovel replied: "You shouldn't use such language to me, sir."

Shafter later explained that what he had intended to be a "flamboyant gesture of dismissal" inadvertently struck Scovel in the face, knocked his hat off, and sent him staggering back. When Scovel recovered his balance he shouted, "You! A major general of the United States Army! You ought to be ashamed of yourself!" And then he took a swing at him. Though the blow never landed, the general yelled back, almost hysterically: "Let no one see that man! Let no one speak to him! He ought to be shot down in his tracks!"

"Next thing I knew," Scovel recalled, "about 281 marines were all over me. For the first time since I came to Cuba, I was really scared." That night he found himself in a Cuban jail—for the second time—where he learned he was to be shot again for the second time—although, on this occasion, by his own side for defying a military order.

The next day, several reporters pleaded with General Shafter to have Scovel deported rather than shot. He agreed. But he was not finished with Scovel. Interviewed by *New York Herald* reporter Thomas Millard, Shafter put such an anti-Scovel spin on the fracas that Pulitzer fired him. But the story didn't stop there.

The "splendid little war," as Roosevelt called it, ended with the conquest of Puerto Rico. Historian Thomas A. Bailey speculates that "had the Spaniards held out a few months longer the American Army might have melted away" through "malaria, typhoid, dysentery and yellow fever." The figures support him: fewer than four hundred were killed by bullets, while more than five thousand died from disease, which is why Roosevelt demanded a speedy evacuation of the army before the rancid rations known as "embalmed beef"—sold to the army by crooked contractors—finished off the survivors. For a change, the president and publisher agreed, and Pulitzer ordered editorial writer William Merrill, "Make your demand to send soldiers home stronger. The cry for investigation is secondary. The instant, immediate, urgent necessity is to break up the pest camps and disband volunteers. Not slightest necessity for this immense army. The navy has force enough to take care of remote contingencies."

With the war over, Pulitzer resumed his scrutiny of John D. Rockefeller, but, in line with his resolve to upgrade the paper, the coverage wasn't always cutthroat. He listed him as one of the country's biggest benefactors to higher education after Rockefeller gave two hundred thousand dollars to the University of Chicago, and seventy-two thousand dollars to Wayland Academy. The *World* even gave front-page prominence to news that an assessor had maliciously raised Rockefeller's taxes on Rockwood, his palatial gray-stone mansion in Mount Pleasant, and publicly boasted that he intended to reduce the taxes of the poor by raising the taxes of rich suckers like the Rockefellers. Consequently a referee had reduced the taxable value of John D.'s house from a whopping $2,189,555 to $343,775, saving him taxes on almost $2 million.

That August, Pulitzer beat Hearst to the punch in expressing patriotic fervor. He welcomed home the victorious North Atlantic Fleet—that had destroyed a Spanish fleet in Cuban waters—by sponsoring a naval pageant, with a parade of warships on the Hudson River, and had a line of wooden arches erected on Park Row decorated with red, white, and blue bunting.

Tentatively considering his own armistice with Hearst, he told Merrill: "There is a proposition before me to stop all unfriendly utterances between the

World and the Journal. In the meantime you might suspend such utterances until there is provocation. You might tell the others also, but very discreetly, as I doubt whether the thing will finally go through."

He already regretted his contest to outsell Hearst during the war. Despite the popular view that both men were war profiteers, they had in fact lost heavily. Although they sold more papers, their costs in covering the war rose astronomically and wiped out their profits. Pulitzer had hired eighteen war correspondents and financed three "dispatch" press boats that carried the correspondents to and from the scenes of battle and delivered dispatches from Havana to Key West to evade the Spanish cable censorship. The charter for each boat cost some nine thousand dollars a month. Newspaper dealers did not cut their orders during lulls in the battles when there was no war news—and then the World had been swamped with thousands of unsold copies.

In keeping with his new goal not to sensationalize the news, Pulitzer relegated the Sing Sing execution of gruesome murderer Martin Thorn to page three but still gave it extraordinary coverage. The killer's last hours were described in detail, including his discomfort on discovering that a keeper who had befriended him was named Croak. To investigate the claim by some that electric-chair victims were still alive when disemboweled during autopsies, Pulitzer persuaded Warden Omar Sage to allow him to make a unique experiment. He hired a Dr. J. A. O'Neill, who witnessed Thorn's execution. Then, armed with a phonendoscope, thermometer, and ophthalmoscope, O'Neill tested Thorn for signs of life. Finding none, he tried to revive him by injecting brandy, strychnine, and nitroglycerin. The doctor concluded that death had been instantaneous and painless.

A three-column illustration showed Thorn strapped in the chair, with Warden Sage on his right and Father Manselman, prayer book in hand, on his left, the instant before the fatal shock. What must have disappointed Pulitzer was the inadequate description of Thorn: "a big, strong man, with a well-nourished body." Even the illustration failed to show his face, because it was completely obscured by a mask.

To cut costs, Pulitzer had vetoed using illustrations unless they were both exceptional and newsworthy (which Thorn obviously was), explaining that "the picture that does not make a new impression, or give a new idea, or tell a new story, is space wasted."

But he never economized on his traveling, taking an entourage with him to England in October, including David Graham Phillips, a current favorite. In Phillips he thought he had finally found the editorial writer to meet his rigorous demands. Phillips, however, had his own agenda. Annoyed by this irascible semi-invalid who wouldn't let him smoke cigarettes in his presence, he planned to leave him the moment he'd saved enough to devote almost all his time to writing novels.

While in London, Pulitzer hired a new permanent secretary, Arthur Billing, a bishop's son. On his return to New York in early November Pulitzer received a hard-hitting memo, probably from Bradford Merrill, squarely putting the blame for the controversial Seventy-first-Regiment story on someone other than Crane or Scovel. It read in part: "I do not discount the talent of Mr. Nelson Hersh, but I do think the man who is responsible for the 71st Regiment blunder, the man who faked the page on Mrs. Ladenburg and the man who recommended that THE WORLD should tie up to Pat McCarren [a disreputable Tammany Hall politician] is not a safe character for the conduct of the newspaper which must regain and retain the confidence of the people. I would put handcuffs on every arm and leg of him [Hersh]. Coming to the other gentleman, Mr. [William] Van Benthuysen, there is no alchemy which would transform him from an ox-like genial man willing to obey, but inert and inactive, who plods along, strong enough to take his medicine in case of blunders but not strong enough or alert enough to prevent them."

It's astonishing, if the memo was accurate, that Pulitzer hadn't already fired Hersh and Van Benthuysen. Instead, he called them and other senior staffers to his home and told them he wanted the World to resume its prewar principles of fairness and accuracy. Consequently, on November 28, all members of the news staff got pep talks from Van Benthuysen, Hersh, Bradford Merrill, and Seitz.

Van Benthuysen told them: "Every bit of copy you write, every line you edit and send to the copy desk, every picture you draw, every bit of news given, make it absolutely accurate so that it is not to be denied the next day. We must all work unceasingly together to produce the greatest newspaper in the land. Sensational? Yes, when the news is sensational. But it must never be forgotten that every story which is sensational in itself must also be truthful."

Nelson Hersh, a faker according to the recent memo to Pulitzer, now urged others to practice "condensation, punctuality, and accuracy."

Bradford Merrill said: "Mr. Pulitzer holds that the foundation of everything in life which is worth having, the only success which can possibly endure, is the success built on honesty to convictions and fidelity to truth. In strenuous competition a man may do a thing for a newspaper which he would not do as an individual.

"It is Mr. Pulitzer's desire that no man should ever do anything as a member of the staff of the World which he would not do or believe in doing as a man. The great mistakes which have been made [and] I have made a number of them myself—have been caused by an excess of zeal. Be just as clever as you can. Be more energetic and more entertaining than any other man if you can, but above all, be right."

Don Carlos Seitz concluded: "In the spirit of competition there has been engendered a disposition which has worked to the injury of the paper. This disposition has to be overcome."

In December Spain signed an armistice handing over Cuba, Puerto Rico, and Guam to the United States, and including the Philippines—for twenty million dollars. Meanwhile, Sylvester Scovel awaited his fate in the Waldorf-Astoria, where he and his wife, Frances, were recovering from malaria contracted

in Cuba. She had been an unpaid volunteer nurse during the war, taking care
of wounded members of the press corps.

Realizing he had been unfair to fire Scovel without thoroughly investigating the facts, Pulitzer asked three *World* correspondents who had witnessed the
Shafter-Scovel confrontation to give him their independent accounts of what
happened, as if under oath. All three—George Rae, Louis Seibold, and Adolph
Koelble—confirmed Scovel's version. Pulitzer then asked Scovel to put it in a
letter, which was syndicated throughout the country, together with witnesses'
supporting testimony. Many papers ran it, and public opinion began to veer to
Scovel.

War correspondent Richard Harding Davis sent a searing dispatch to his
paper, the *Herald*, describing General Shafter as "this gross Falstaff [who] knew
when he struck Mr. Scovel that he had 16,000 men behind him to protect him
and that if Scovel struck him in return he did so at the risk of being legally shot.
And yet knowing this, this officer and gentleman struck the civilian in the
face." Too hot for the *Herald* to handle without checking it out, they delayed
publishing it until December 1.

The *Washington Chronicle* denounced the *World* as cowardly for not
immediately coming to Scovel's defense: "The moment it was informed [of his
arrest] it should have turned its bitterness upon Shafter and portrayed him as
he is—a pudgy [330-pound], featherbrained, irritable old granny; a bully and a
blackguard. It would have been the natural and manly thing if Scovel had *shot
him down* instantly when Shafter struck Scovel in the face."

Scovel was finally saved by the intervention of President McKinley, to
whom he wrote on December 22, thanking him "for your kindness in looking
into the case of my answering the general's blow. You have raised from me the
stigma of being officially barred from the army and the navy of the United
States. You have reopened for me the possibility of advance in my profession.
And for all this and more, I am profoundly grateful."

Pulitzer reinstated Scovel, sent him to report on life in Cuba under American control, and asked him to consider heading the *World*'s European bureau.

Despite Pulitzer's efforts to regenerate the *World*—to make it fair and reli-
able—it was still banned from exclusive Manhattan men's clubs as hazardous
to the members' mental health and moral equilibrium, though it's a safe bet
that the more daring members smuggled the "immoral and defamatory" sheet
home wrapped in a copy of the *New York Times*. Even the high-minded owner
of the *Times* acknowledged that neither Pulitzer nor Hearst was the devil incar-
nate, as their most vehement critics implied. Though he had once dismissed
their work as freak journalism, now, interviewed by a trade paper, Adolph Ochs
changed his tune. "Such papers as *The World* and *The Journal* exist," he said,
"because the public wants them. I hold that some of their features are open to
criticism, but each of them has done infinitely more good than harm."

What the public wanted was certainly not Pulitzer's main concern; otherwise he would have supported popular war hero Theodore Roosevelt, a Repub-

lican, when he ran for New York State governor. Instead he gave a Democrat, Judge William Gaynor, his editorial accolades. But it was a wasted effort. Gaynor wasn't interested, and Roosevelt got the job.

In their strident attempts to arouse Americans to fight with the Cuban rebels against their Spanish occupiers, Hearst and Pulitzer had used disreputable tactics that branded them as the leading exponents of what became known as yellow journalism. Some said their motives were strictly mercenary. Others applauded them as patriots, humanitarians, and defenders of democracy.

Veteran correspondent James Creelman, who had left Pulitzer to work for Hearst and would eventually return to Pulitzer, was among the most informed defenders of their work. "How little they know of 'yellow journalism,'" he wrote, "who denounce it! How swift they are to condemn its shrieking headlines, its exaggerated pictures, its coarse buffoonery, its intrusions upon private life, and its occasional inaccuracies. How blind to its unfearing warfare against rascality, its detection and prosecution of crime, its costly searching for knowledge throughout the earth, its exposure of humbug, its endless funds for the quick relief of distress!"

A less partial critic defined the yellow journalist as someone who "can work himself into quite as fiery a fever of enthusiasm over a Christmas fund or a squalid murder, as over a war or a presidential campaign. He sees everything through magnifying glasses and can make a first-page sensation out of a story which a more sober paper would dismiss with a paragraph inside."

Hearst and Pulitzer would argue that a sober paper was a dull one and that they were out to shock, entertain, and inspire as well as to aid and inform their readers. Yet, in their relentless quest for increased circulation, as historian Thomas Bailey put it, they both "stooped, snooped and scooped to conquer."

Unlike Pulitzer, who generally admired Hearst's positive achievements, Hearst unfairly characterized Pulitzer as "a journalist who made his money by pandering to the worst tastes of the prurient and horror-loving by dealing in bogus news, such as forged cablegrams from eminent personages, and by affecting a devotion to the interests of the people while never really hurting those of their enemies, and sedulously looking out for his own."

Even if partly true, it applied more to Hearst, and Pulitzer eventually rose above it.

CHAPTER 21

For the Boers,
against the British

1899
—
51 to 52 years old

Pulitzer's first move on New Year's Day was to send Scovel back to Havana to report on America's formal occupation of Cuba. Soon after he landed in the city, the self-styled bishop of Havana put the bite on him to feed starving Cubans, and Scovel smelled a rat. When he described the man to his father, a Presbyterian minister, he identified the "bishop" as a phony who had pulled similar scams in America.

Having done the locals a favor by getting a con man off the streets, Scovel surveyed the political situation. Cuba's peaceful future seemed assured, because rebel leader General Gomez had promised to disband his army, and both loyalists and rebels had agreed to support a free and independent country. Scovel told Pulitzer there was no further need for the U.S. occupation of Cuba. The fact, he wrote, that "Cubans have been able to preserve order and not wreak revenge is ample proof that present combination of all nationalities in Cuba [will be] permanently successful. This means Cuban independence now, or bad faith United States. When Spanish businessmen and property owners [are] willing to trust to Cuba Libre, the annexation jig's up." Pulitzer agreed. But the U.S. government didn't, preferring to wait and see. However, the jig was up for Scovel. Pulitzer decided there was not enough hard news out of peacetime Cuba to keep a man permanently on the spot. He offered him the plum job of chief correspondent in Europe. But Scovel preferred to work as an engineer—his other talent—for the U.S. occupation government in Cuba. It was the end of a dazzling reporting career.

244

Instead of seeking replacements for Crane and Scovel, Pulitzer concentrated on cleaning up the *World* while allowing the evening or Sunday editions some discretion in catering to the mass market. He soon faced the challenge with the first execution of a woman in Sing Sing's electric chair. In a jealous rage, Martha Place had blinded her stepdaughter with acid before strangling her, and then tried to ax her own husband to death. The new governor of the state, Theodore Roosevelt, refused to commute her sentence.

Unlike Pulitzer, Hearst had no qualms about his sensational handling of the news during the Spanish-American War and obviously intended to keep at it for peacetime stories. He sent his ace woman reporter, Kate Swan, to cover the Place execution, and she suckered Warden Sage into letting her be photographed in the electric chair beforehand. An etching of the photo appeared in the *Journal* along with an interview with the executioner, who vowed I WILL KILL NO WOMAN — a promise he broke days later.

On March 21, 1899, the *New York Times* gave Place's execution modest play on page three with these one-column headlines:

MRS. PLACE PUT TO DEATH

———

The Brooklyn Murderess Goes to the
Electric Chair Calmly — Current
Killed Instantly

The *World* gave the event almost as much coverage as if she were the country's first woman president, with prominent page-one treatment spilling over to page two. But instead of a sketch of the doomed woman dying in the chair, the *World* showed a copy of her prayer book. And, to restore the paper's former reputation for accuracy, it told how Martha Place "bravely" went to her "instantaneous and seemingly painless death," refuting "an afternoon newspaper which says that Mrs. Place died in agony and amid torture." As evidence, the *World* quoted a witness who claimed Place's pulse was regular to the last and that she showed not the slightest sign of suffering.

Although Pulitzer treated the *Morning World* like a favorite child, he also felt responsible for keeping the Sunday paper in line. But he didn't want to knock the stuffing out of it. Afraid that instead of cleaning it up, his staff was dulling it down, he fired off these superheated comments: "Amazing stupidity. I forbid emphatically that dullness and politics on the Sunday pages. I forbid more than one article on national politics any day. I forbid editorials to exceed a single column. This is the way you drive me to distraction."

Another way was to remind him of the unfair state tax system. Tammany boss Richard Croker had assessed Pulitzer $500,000 for "personal taxes" alone, from two to five times the amount charged Carnegie, Rockefeller, or the Astors, who were far more wealthy. Rather than challenge the assessment Pulitzer paid up, then led a campaign to reform the system. He pointed out that while individuals were heavily taxed, huge corporations paid next to nothing, and he proposed a state law to remedy the situation. When it was allowed to die without a vote, Pulitzer hired a special train to take a committee of 100 concerned citizens to Albany. There they demanded that the Assembly vote on the proposal. Under Pulitzer's pressure the politicians revived and passed the bill by 104 to 18.

He hailed it as "a notable victory for justice through publicity," because "it will reduce by $15,000,000 the burden upon the present taxpayers of this city and increases the bond-issuing capacity of the city by $100,000,000. But greater than this is the demonstration that when the people will do so they still rule."

More and more his travels abroad were becoming recruiting drives. Although several secretaries stayed for years, many couldn't take it, so he often had to seek new men. The main recruiter was London bureau chief James Tuohy, a forty-one-year-old Irishman who sardonically referred to the task as "the pursuit of the White Mice." Presumably Pulitzer was the boa constrictor with the insatiable appetite. Americans were generally ruled out as temperamentally unsuitable, which meant they were unlikely to tolerate Pulitzer's imperious demands and ferocious temper. Grace under pressure from Pulitzer was a must. The ideal prospect was patient, tolerant, witty, healthy, highly intelligent, well-read, musical, and entertaining. Preferably an upper-middle-class or aristocratic Briton whose voice wasn't grating, made no noise when he ate— and was strapped for cash.

Before Pulitzer met a likely prospect, Tuohy and his wife usually invited him to dinner, watched how he handled the celery and other noisy foods, and tested his conversational prowess, his ability to handle stress, and his staying power. Only about one in ten made it.

Anticipating Pulitzer's arrival on a recruiting drive, Tuohy put this personal ad in the *Times* of London: "Gentleman, with somewhat indifferent health, who travels a good deal, wants as companion a cultivated, well-read gentleman of about 40, who is a bright, ready, well-informed talker, with literary tastes and knowledge. The principal desideratum being agreeable, intellectual companionship, exceptional conversational gifts essential. Musical accomplishments (not singing) and riding are both highly desirable also. Liberal salary. Unexceptionable references as to character and attainments required."

Pulitzer reached London in May with his inevitable entourage, including his son Ralph and his friend and former partner John Dillon. Tuohy had goofed in choosing Maitland House, in Kensington, for Pulitzer to live in. It was one of the noisiest spots in the area. But despite his constant complaints, he stayed there to set the traps for his White Mice and to put them through their paces.

No potential spy or worker on a top-secret project was subjected to such an emotional and intellectual obstacle course. For days, even weeks, the candidate's every word, move, glance, bite, and gesture would be discussed and analyzed by Pulitzer and his assistants.

Montague Wood, one of the first, "a tall gentlemanly young fellow," according to Tuohy, did not play any musical instrument but was polite and charming, and Pulitzer warmed to him. His only obvious disadvantage was a slight lisp that, apparently, Pulitzer could tolerate. Tuohy meant to recommend him for a trial period when, to his dismay, he discovered that Wood had been involved in a messy divorce case, and wrote him off. Then Tuohy found he'd made a mistake: a Marmaduke Wood, not a Montague Wood, had played a role in the divorce scandal. But by then it was too late to reopen negotiations.

Walter Leyman, another promising candidate, decided after two weeks with Pulitzer that he couldn't take it and bowed out. In a letter of explanation, Leyman wrote that on the positive side Pulitzer had taught him a lot about American life, politics, and journalism. But he found it a heartbreaking task to try to sustain a conversation when Pulitzer lapsed into silence yet expected him to keep talking in a nonstop monologue.

"You have become so used to command," Leyman wrote, "that any other position with regard to those always with you became impossible for you. Friends and interesting acquaintances outside your daily life you like & possess, but an intimate friend always with you who would treat you as such & speak freely and intimately would be an annoyance and irritation. It is not a question of your health and nerves but of temperament and disposition. . . . The qualities which command great success mitigate against intimacy. Like all very successful men you have to a degree a contempt for those whose lives have been to some extent failures. You cannot help letting them feel that you regard them as inferior."

At least Pulitzer's relationship with his son Ralph was improving. Pulitzer had recently complained to Kate that he had never "received a line of affection [in letters] from Ralph in my life. I never received even one kind word of inquiry or sympathy—nothing but shallow commonplaces—considering his age [twenty]—cold and dull and unfeeling."

But things were better in London, he told Kate: he and Ralph were getting on well. Ralph filled his days boxing, fencing, and riding in Hyde Park. They hadn't had one row, even though Pulitzer insisted on an early curfew for his son. Not that everything was perfect. He still hadn't found the quiet he craved. The house Tuohy had leased for him had now become unbearable. It was an almost unbelievably bad choice for the noise-sensitive Pulitzer, being near three churches and four clocks, including one belonging to an army barracks next door "every stroke of which I hear day & night, with chimes thrown in, bugles from six in the morning till a quarter to ten at night, relieved only by drums and fifes and the bellowing tones of the drill sergeant."

He returned from London to the tranquillity of his Tower of Silence in Bar Harbor, where he invited David Graham Phillips to join him, setting tough ground rules for their meeting: Phillips must insist on Pulitzer giving him a no-holds-barred critique of his—that is, Phillips's—work over the past three years and an assessment of his prospects. Pulitzer claimed that he, himself, was "so cowardly about criticizing sensitive and delicate, likeable persons, that I am sure to run away from it unless you use a club, with the understanding that it is for your own good, and for the sake of your future. Mine is behind me, as you know."

This was absolutely not true, but rather a bid for sympathy, or the mood of the moment. He remained a vital force for the rest of his life.

Phillips survived the ordeal, still his heir apparent.

That summer Pulitzer promoted an international conference to stop the arms race and the building of "terrible engines of destruction." Proposed by the Russian czar, Emperor Nicholas II, it prompted a cynic to scoff at the idea of a peace conference headed by "the ruler of the most backward of the peoples commonly called civilized." Rudyard Kipling shuddered at the idea and tried to scare his readers from supporting it with an allegorical poem titled "The Bear That Walks Like a Man." This told of a hunter who, "touched with pity and wonder," holds his fire—to have the bear rip his face away, leaving him maimed and blind! The prince of Wales dismissed the conference as a trick thought up by the czar's foreign minister, Count Muraviev.

Skeptics failed to discourage Pulitzer from urging an American presence at the conference, which may have moved President McKinley to appoint a former history professor, Andrew White, as the American representative. But White proved a dead loss. Along with the British, he even vetoed a proposal to outlaw the god-awful dumdum bullets, which expanded in the victim's body. Of the twenty-four delegates, only two voted against their use. It was more like a meeting of arms dealers. They even failed to delay the war brewing between the Boers and the British in South Africa.

There, the descendants of Dutch, German, and French settlers, the Boers (Dutch for farmers) saw the influx of mostly British foreigners as a threat to their way of life. To weaken British influence, the Boers' messianic leader, Paul Kruger, refused to give them any political rights until they became citizens, for which there was a fourteen-year waiting period. In April 1899 more than twenty thousand British subjects in South Africa protested that Kruger was treating them like slaves. The seventy-year-old Kruger countered that the British were trying to capture his country and turn the Boers into slaves.

The *New York Times* backed the British, called Kruger a dictator, and predicted the certain "triumph of the foreign element, represented mainly by the British. [The Boers'] is not a tenable position. It is the position which the North American Indians took when they insisted upon pursuing a mode of life which required some thousands of acres for the support of every adult male, which the Mormons [also] took until civilization caught up to them, and they had to abandon it. It is the position which every 'peculiar people' has to take, which is resisting the assimilating influences of modern civilization. But in every case it is futile. There is no room in the world for 'peculiar peoples' who insist upon nonconformity, and upon taking up more room than belongs to them. Superficially they may seem to be, and may be, in the right. But essentially they are in the wrong, and they are doomed. They must conform, like the Mormons, or else they must be extinguished, like the North American Indians."

These views were completely at odds with those of the pro-Boer Pulitzer, who offered Kruger a chance to state his case in the *World*. Kruger's reply on October 11 "electrified the chancelleries of Europe," according to Seitz, "roused England and sent a thrill through the United States." It read: 'Through the *World* I thank American friends most sincerely for their sympathy. Last Monday the republic [of South Africa] gave England forty-eight hours' notice within which to give the republic assurance that the present dispute will be settled by arbitration or other peaceful means and troops will be removed from the borders. This expires at 5 p.m. today. The British agent has been recalled and war is certain. The republics [South Africa and the Orange Free State] are determined that if they must belong to England a price will have to be paid which will stagger humanity. Have, however, full faith that the Sun of Liberty shall arise in South Africa as it arose in North America.'"

Kruger asserted that mining moguls and prospectors were determined to destroy the republic, make it part of the British Empire, and seize control of the world's richest gold mines. He concluded: "Though we have no such powerful friend as you proved to be to Venezuela and other republics, we have strong faith that the cause of freedom will triumph in the end." Being reminded of Venezuela stirred Pulitzer to resume his role of peacemaker. He organized a massive propeace public meeting in Manhattan and got many big names to sign a petition imploring President McKinley to intercede.

The *World* summarized McKinley's response: First, the United States, having been the recipient of moral support from England during the war with Spain, will do nothing distasteful to England. Second, while the sympathies of the president and his cabinet are, to a certain extent, with the Boers, yet their love for England is stronger and outweighs their friendliness for the Krugerites. Third, the president will not intervene, believing, as he does, that intervention might enable some foreign power to take a hand in the Philippine war.

Pulitzer agreed that the United States was morally obligated to England for her support the previous year, but asked McKinley to "deepen that obligation. Show for England that higher friendship, that higher love, which is not inconsistent with your duty as a civilized man and as a representative of the great republic—love of peace, love of justice, love of the American principle of arbitration!"

As for McKinley's point about the Philippines, the *World* was totally opposed to the U.S. annexation of the country, describing the proposal to "establish a military despotism over remote and forever alien Malay millions" as coming from "the inner temple of Mammon," a blatant attempt to monopolize the markets through conquest, "which will rob us of our unsullied character as the friends of liberty, the advocates of government only with the consent of the governed."

When the Boer war began on October 12 the Boers were armed to the teeth with the latest German Mannlicher and Mauser rifles and outnumbered the British two to one. Like other pacifists, once the war started, Pulitzer took sides, cheering on the Boers, much to the despair of his English majordomo, Dunningham, and several English secretaries. In one excited outburst, when Pulitzer said he hoped every English soldier in South Africa was killed, his English secretary Alfred Butes quietly remarked that another English secretary, Arthur Billing, who was in the room with them, had a brother in the British Army in South Africa. Pulitzer immediately—though briefly—changed sides. "My God!" he exclaimed. "The poor fellow may be dead!"

"Very likely, sir," Billing said with the sangfroid one might expect from a bishop's son. It turned out that Billing's brother had been killed in battle.

Kate had welcomed Pulitzer home to Bar Harbor after his return from England, but they were together only briefly. In the fall she went to Hot Springs, Virginia. She was there when he wrote to her of his plans to improve the *World*, adding, "With all its faults I think it has done some things that will be remembered after I am gone—if anything is remembered that a daily newspaper does."

His old, ailing friend Thomas Davidson kept him company for a few days at Bar Harbor. Pulitzer was distressed to find that the once lively and stimulating companion was now an invalid. Pulitzer booked a comfortable stateroom for him on his homeward-bound train, and Davidson was touched by this thoughtfulness, which spared him considerable pain.

Throughout the fall Pulitzer had been increasingly agitated by the failure of his editors to carry out his ideas. Letters and cables didn't do the trick. So he called one of his top men to Bar Harbor, who returned to the Dome with what amounted to twelve commandments. In a nutshell they were: Thou shalt not bore nor lie to readers.

To spur his staff to greater effort he offered a "$500 reward with utmost pleasure to the reporter who will discover beyond peradventure the author of the recent murder—the woman cut up. Please keep this very secret or THE JOURNAL will have it." The editor who got this message noted at the bottom: "Received Nov. 2. Understood: yes. Executed: Quietly." But apparently no *World* reporter solved the crime.

The day after Pulitzer offered the reward he sent an SOS to Kate in Hot Springs: "Utterly alone here [except, of course, for his servants, majordomo, doctor, and secretary-companions], weather blusteringly cold, nervous as a cat, everything going wrong, when do you get back?"

Among things going wrong was his editors' failure to satisfy his rigorous standards. But he never stopped trying to whip them into shape. On December 5 he berated an editor for giving too much play to a contemporary bigamy case because it "distinctly tends to lower the tone of the paper and to revive the idea of sensationalism, the giving of the foremost place and extraordinary headlines to what is after all, a salacious story and not an important or serious matter."

A few days later he asked: "Who wrote that asinine story about the Hungarian banquet? Why allow a reporter to be used by a faction? It so happens that Baron Hengelmuller [a Austro-Hungarian diplomat] is a friend of mine and stays in my house. Even if he were not you ought not to allow somebody to make use of the paper in this way. I want you to read this story. Is this a fair report or chronicle without bias or prejudice? Is this a real mirror of events? Someone should see Baron Hengelmuller and present the apology of the paper for the blunder and give the Baron the chance to correct the matter."

As Christmas approached, Pulitzer announced three prizes to the editors who produced the most intelligent condensations of long reports. He warned contestants to use a light touch, because "it can be done to death, killing the very essence of the story." He also offered three prizes for the most striking and succinct nonsensational headlines that described the story and attracted attention "without repelling belief and good taste." And four prizes for reporters: one for the best, clear use of English; another for the most effective use of humor; a third for the most vivid and picturesque description of an event; and a fourth for the best, lifelike, detailed, and analytical pen portrait of a face, figure, or character.

For sports fans he ordered his editors to hire the foremost experts on forty different sports to become regular contributors.

For intellectual readers he suggested contacting the brightest editors of newspapers throughout the United States, including the religious press, to join with World editors in expressing their views about timely subjects of general interest. Write to them, Pulitzer advised, something like this: "Do you favor a national divorce law? If not, why not? If yes, why yes? Please state your reasons succinctly."

Pulitzer became keen on the subject after learning that 5 percent of the Kansas population was suing for divorce (a lot for those days) and decided that the World itself should advocate a national divorce law. To put a human face on the statistics Pulitzer also called for an account of the moral standards of different European countries, with historical examples of famous Europeans who defied the conventions, such as "George Eliot living with Lewes as husband and wife without being married; George Sand living with everybody; Byron living not with his wife but Countess Guiccioli, and with everybody else's wife; Goethe with housekeepers; Voltaire the Marquise du Chatelet. Even Gambetta, the greatest political genius produced in France since Talleyrand, lived with a mistress."

To balance the accounts of people "living in sin," he ordered a regular Sunday feature from outstanding religious leaders. Was this a masterstroke? By providing a paper that was both risqué and morally uplifting, catering to the pious and the promiscuous, was he making sure that no one could resist it? Thoughtful views on timely subjects, the sex lives of the famous, sports news by forty experts, and words of wisdom from men of God. Didn't that cover the interests of everybody?

Or as someone said years later to the editor of a pious but racy tabloid that also published racing results: So your readers are the religious nuts, the gamblers, the gossips, the starstruck, the sex-crazed, and the perverts. My God! You've cornered the market in EVERYONE!

CHAPTER 22

"Accuracy! Accuracy!! Accuracy!!!"

1900

—

52 to 53 years old

Pulitzer hardly needed to express his New Year's resolution. It was peren-
nial: to produce a better paper. And he never let up. Even while ostensibly
relaxing with his fifteen-year-old son Joe on January 5 in the bucolic atmosphere
of his Lakewood, New Jersey, retreat, Pulitzer found a flaw in a recent *World*
report and cabled Bradford Merrill: "The story 'How Standard Oil manages a
Bank' is exaggerated, sensational and objectionable because inaccurate in one
single point, although excellent otherwise. . . . Accuracy! Accuracy!! Accuracy!!! More effective."

Early on the bitterly cold morning of January 9, while Pulitzer was still in
New Jersey with Joe and Ralph was at Harvard, his Manhattan home caught
fire. The rest of his family were asleep in the blazing building at 10 and 12 East
55th Street. A workman saw smoke pouring from its windows and rushed to
the basement of the four-story house, yelling "Fire!" His cries woke houseman
James Kane, who raced up the stairs, activating fire alarms that rang bells
throughout the house.

Kate woke in her front bedroom on the second floor, choking from acrid
smoke, and hurried to the third-story bedrooms where her children, Constance,
fourteen, Edith, twelve, and three-year-old Herbert, were already up. The girls
and their servants were terrified, and one servant, in hysterics, was about to
jump from a window. Kate yelled for them all to follow her and led the way
through the thickening smoke toward the circular staircase. Kane, the houseman, met her in the hallway, and seeing she was in her nightdress and barefoot,
grabbed a curtain and threw it over her shoulders. Almost asphyxiated from the

smoke, when they reached the sidewalk they almost froze—until a neighbor welcomed them into his house. Other servants climbed down a fire escape to join them. There were two fatalities. Firemen couldn't save Kate's companion-housekeeper, Mrs. Morgan Jellett, or governess Elizabeth Montgomery.

The *New York Times* ran the story for a column and a half on page three, headed:

PULITZER HOME DESTROYED

———

Narrow Escape of Family of the
Proprietor of the World

———

TWO WOMEN BURNED TO DEATH

———

Companion of Mrs. Pulitzer and the
Governess the Victims—Valuable
Art Collection Ruined

The *World* also ran the story on page three. Its more specific headlines read:

MR. PULITZER'S HOME
BURNED; 2 LIVES LOST.

———

Mrs. Jellet, Private Secretary to
Mrs. Pulitzer, and Miss
Montgomery, Governess,
Perish in Flames.

———

ESCAPED, RE-ENTERED HOUSE.
[Refers to the two women who died.]

———

Mrs. Pulitzer Rescues Her Daughters
And Carries Her Infant Son
from the Nursery.

———

AWAKENED BY ELECTRIC ALARM.

———

The two papers hardly differed in their accounts except that the *World* emphasized Kate's role in rescuing her children and had her carrying three-year-old Herbert to safety, while the *Times* had him carried by a nurse. The *World* also printed an illustration of the house after the fire.

In Lakewood, New Jersey, Pulitzer did not hear about the fire until he got a telegram that afternoon. His majordomo, Dunningham, read it aloud, careful to first assure him that all his family were safe. Pulitzer wanted to join them, but Dunningham insisted that his boss was too fragile to travel and went in his

MR. PULITZER'S HOUSE AFTER THE FIRE.

The *World* account of a fatal fire in Pulitzer's home, January 10, 1900.

place. Already on his way to the city when his father received the telegram, Joe didn't learn about the fire until he reached the Dome.

Dunningham took charge when he arrived in Manhattan. He delivered loving messages from Pulitzer, then moved the family to the Netherlands Hotel and the seventeen servants to a boarding house on East Sixtieth Street.

Fire battalion chief Binns believed that faulty wiring caused the fire that destroyed paintings by Franz Hals and Millet; a bronze Buddha seated on a lion, brought by Creelman from China; priceless Gobelin tapestries; and antique oriental rugs. Pulitzer most regretted the total loss of his library. The now gutted oak-paneled dining room had been considered the finest in the city. Kate's jewelry, kept in a safe, survived. It included a diamond necklace bought at a sale of the French Crown jewels that cost Pulitzer $120,000 and a pearl necklace valued at $150,000. Pulitzer estimated his losses at $300,000, but his insurance covered all but $50,000 of it.

The deaths of the two servants were initially kept from Pulitzer for fear they would cause him to break down. When told, he paid for their funerals and sent $500 to the fire department pension fund and $250 to the police pension fund. Then he wired David Graham Phillips: "Please take five o'clock train this evening. I need you to cheer me up."

In February, Pulitzer leased a home at 9 East 72nd Street and the following month paid $240,000 for a site on East 73rd Street for a new five-story house of fireproof limestone and granite. At first he told his architects not to include a "ballroom, music room, or picture gallery under any disguise," nor "French rooms requiring French furniture," because he wanted a home for comfort, not for show or entertainment. Kate changed his mind, or twisted his arm: the final plans called for a ballroom, music room with a pipe organ, and an indoor swimming pool.

Two months after Pulitzer's fiery $50,000 loss, fifteen-year-old Joe had the nerve to write from his prep school, St. Mark's, in Massachusetts, asking for $1,300 for a "knockabout" boat to sail in the summer at Bar Harbor, plus enough to hire a skipper. Joe reminded Pulitzer that he had already given Ralph a boat. To soften up his father he showed that he at least glanced at the *World*. "I notice," he wrote, that the editorials "have been quoting or mentioning other papers a good deal. For instance [one] said something like this: 'We congratulate the Times and Herald in their fight against gambling dens.' Is this not a new idea?"

The soft soap failed, since Pulitzer had just learned of Joe's failing grades. He replied in a fury, expressing his disappointment, and sent an equally heartfelt but less enraged letter to Joe's headmaster, the Rev. Dr. William Thayer: "The World is to me far more than a property. I regard it as a public institution, capable of exercising daily influence on public thought, watching and safeguarding public morals and the public interests. It is my fervent hope that, when this inheritance falls to my sons, they will fully realize their public responsibilities, and be so equipped as to exercise for the public good whatever influence may be theirs. But Joseph is as yet destitute even of the elementary knowledge he ought to have by this time." Fortunately, Joe's mother acted as a buffer between father and son, and recommended extra tutoring for Joe—which Pulitzer accepted as a temporary solution.

His father's anger may partly explain why Joe was unable to confide in him. For example, Joe was shocked and puzzled when fellow students called him "sheeny" and hissed when he walked by, but he didn't mention it to his father. Strangely, Pulitzer had never discussed anti-Semitism at home, even though he had often been taunted as "Jewseph Pulitzer." It is possible that he mistakenly believed that his mother, Louise, was a Roman Catholic, as did previous Pulitzer biographers. (Recent research shows that both his mother and his father were Jewish.) He was also nominally an Episcopalian, a faith in which all his children were raised. Consequently, perhaps, he did not regard himself as Jewish. He may have taken what were meant to be racial slurs as misdirected and hardly deserving response.

In any case, young Joe eventually confided in his WASP mother, Kate, who doubtless discussed his Jewish heritage—at least through his Jewish grandfather. She did tell him that the Jews were a great people and named several distinguished and respected New York Jews. She lost no time in complaining about the hissing and "sheeny" incidents to Joe's headmaster, who assured her that such bigoted behavior would not be tolerated and who apparently kept his word.

In the meantime, Pulitzer had to tackle a more pressing problem than his son's scholastic failures—the loss of several top men.

His former partner turned editorial writer, John Dillon, left to work for the *Chicago Tribune,* and the ever-generous Pulitzer gave him a farewell gift of a diamond pin. Another editorial writer, George Cary Eggleston, retired to devote the rest of his life to literary work. He called Pulitzer the most hospitable man he had ever known. Pulitzer's greatest loss was Frederick Duneka, editor of the *Evening World,* who, despite inducements to stay, joined *Harper's Weekly.* Early in his career with Pulitzer, Duneka had had the chutzpah to ask him for a fur-lined topcoat—and gotten it. On leaving, Duneka thanked Pulitzer for the privilege of knowing him.

Despite Pulitzer's well-established spy system, the easygoing, unenterprising William Van Benthuysen surprised him when he spoke of plans to retire because of a heavy workload. Instead of gladly letting him go, Pulitzer wouldn't hear of it, gave him a bonus, and sent him on an all-expenses-paid vacation in California.

Pulitzer had second thoughts about his generosity when Business Manager John Norris reported sinking profits. He ordered Norris to economize. Norris, in turn, told Charles Chapin, editor of the *Evening World,* to cut his staff. Soon after, Pulitzer phoned Chapin at his home before six one morning asking him to stop in on his way to the office. When he arrived, Pulitzer was breakfasting alone and immediately asked what was going on. Presuming that Pulitzer wanted news of the economy drive, Chapin said he had fired a dozen reporters the previous day.

"Were there any good ones among them?" Pulitzer asked calmly.

"Some were promising and might have developed into first-class men," Chapin replied.

"Then why fire them?"

"I was ordered to by Norris."

Pulitzer's face twitched, he frowned, he compressed his lips: "I know what I would have done had I been in your place," he said, almost to himself. He didn't elaborate, but Chapin got the message: Pulitzer would not have fired promising reporters.

When next Norris told him to cut down on the staff, Chapin refused, and although Norris "fumed and fussed and ripped and snorted and even threatened," Chapin recalled, "I stood pat and never again did I discharge competent men for no other reason than that I was ordered to" (although later, Chapin earned his reputation as a hatchet man). Norris quit soon after the other executives, telling Pulitzer he was not temperamentally equipped to get along with him. Yet Pulitzer gave him a great recommendation, which got him a job on the *New York Times*.

Having lost so many top men, Pulitzer put even more faith in his favorite, David Graham Phillips, as the man to lead the *World* into the twentieth century until his own sons could take over.

Now his goal was to elect the next president of the United States. Assured by Cleveland himself that the *World* had made *him* president, Pulitzer determined to unseat McKinley and put another Democrat in the White House. He began by sending Phillips on a tour of the United States, to assess the political mood of the people.

With input from Phillips, Pulitzer picked Admiral Dewey, the hero of Manila, as a possible candidate and asked his Washington bureau to feel him out. The *World* gave prominent play to Dewey's response. He said he was eager to serve if the people wanted him to, "because I am convinced that the office of the president is not such a very difficult one to fill, his duties being mainly to execute the laws of Congress. Should I be chosen for this exalted position I would execute the laws of Congress as faithfully as I have always executed the orders of my superiors." Amazingly, when asked what party he belonged to, the admiral took the Fifth. And his relatives didn't help: his brother said Dewey was a Democrat; his nephew, a Republican.

Pulitzer must have felt foolish at the prospect of promoting a rubber stamp who refused to declare his political allegiance and whose statements made him look ridiculous. Some said he was simply obeying the wishes of an ambitious wife; others joked that having spent his life at sea, he was still all at sea, adrift with neither party nor platform. Pressured, he said he was a Democrat. But it was too late for Pulitzer to arouse enthusiasm for a man who had been so evasive and was married to a Catholic.

Depending on Phillips to keep him abreast of American politics, Pulitzer sailed for England in April with his usual servants, secretaries, doctor, and several guests. He chose a White Star steamship because its crew deadened the noise of strolling passengers by laying a thick rope carpet on the deck above his cabin. He paid for everything, including the cost of transporting his horse and those of several guests.

When Pulitzer arrived in London and moved into a mansion in Chesterfield Gardens for a three-month stay, he heard that Chapin was in town and about to sail for the States after a summer vacation touring France and England by car. Pulitzer phoned him and told him to cancel his passage so they could lunch together the next day.

At lunch Pulitzer insisted that Chapin stay for another week to visit the House of Commons and the National Portrait Gallery as his eyes and ears and then to describe everything of interest. They met again three days later. Then, as they drove in a carriage through Hyde Park, Chapin gave him the highlights of Joseph Chamberlain's speech in Parliament. As colonial secretary, Chamberlain had represented the British cabinet in the failed negotiations with Kruger. Although Chamberlain had supported British interests in South Africa, he had been attacked by both factions for being too reasonable. Pulitzer also listened avidly to Chapin's account of his conversations during "tea with lords and their ladies on the broad portico overlooking the Thames, [and] of being shown the wardrobe of the King and his Queen in the House of Lords." He was enthralled by Chapin's description of the paintings in the portrait gallery. And when Chapin finished, tears were running down Pulitzer's cheeks. "'What wouldn't I give to see what you saw,' he sobbed, as he sank back into the cushions of the carriage and remained pensively silent throughout the remainder of our drive."

While Pulitzer remained in London, Kate was taking a separate vacation in Europe and being treated for sciatica. When Pulitzer sent her an affectionate message, she replied: "Darling, your telegram gave me great pleasure, as any word of tenderness from you always does. I slept with it under my pillow. I think I forget I am an old married woman with five great children. Never you *dare* say I can't go *any* where again. Acknowledge you are mistaken in what a woman can do, if she is as high headed as I am."

Absence did seem to make their hearts grow fonder. They were never more affectionate than when apart. Long separations made their marriage work, and, of course, the cash that made possible their luxurious lifestyles. Pulitzer called for Kate's company when in despair but seemed able to exist tolerably well when they were apart for months at a time. Having intellectually stimulating and entertaining secretary-companions at his command around the clock was vital for a blind, hypersensitive, insatiably curious, driven perfectionist running major newspapers by remote control. He justified his extreme care in choosing them by saying it was like selecting a wife. Kate may have taken comfort from the fact that he needed six secretary-companions but only one wife.

That summer, when twenty-one-year-old Ralph graduated from Harvard, Pulitzer told Seitz to teach him the rudiments of the newspaper business. He was to treat him like a clerk at the bottom of the ladder or an ignorant schoolboy, to see he worked at the *World* from nine to six, and to "note infractions daily." After a few months, Seitz reported that Ralph had been on time every morning but one and was generally doing well, except that he couldn't remember when the various editions went to press. Answering a question about Ralph's health, Seitz said he weighed 142 pounds and had an excellent appearance, although perhaps he needed more sleep.

Pulitzer was disappointed in his two older boys, seeing his fragile, asthmatic son Ralph as timid and lazy, and Joe, though a scrapper who liked boxing, as lacking ambition. Dumont Clarke, a friend who was also his financial adviser, assured Pulitzer that "[Ralph] is a good boy, my dear J. P. and only wants to be handled right, and you will be proud of him some day."

Pulitzer shared his concerns with a cousin in Vienna, Professor Adam Politzer [sic], who replied: "What you tell me about Ralph and Joseph proves that you claim too much from these young men. Do not forget that they were born and brought up under quite different circumstances than we. Self-made men like you and myself come to maturity in the hot battle for existence. I have seen more than once that [the sons of wealthy parents], having grown out [of] a certain stage, and particularly when no pleasure was denied to them in their youth, the gravity of life suddenly takes hold of them [and] ambition awakes."

As Chapin saw it, Ralph and Joe were "fine chaps, the best types of rich man's sons, but full of the joy of youth and their father seemed to expect them to grow into sedate, serious men before nature intended they should." At least Ralph had a sense of humor, responding to his father's desire for precise, detailed information, by describing a recent Saturday evening: "I then went up to the house (it being 5.45) took a bath, changed my clothes, and joined Phillips at the Manhattan Club at 7."

Pulitzer was still in England in May, when the British were celebrating a victory against the Boers. However, there was no need for him to feel uncomfortable in expressing his pro-Boer views. Quite a few British people, especially Liberals, also sympathized with them. Still, it was surprising that he could sustain a friendship with the militantly anti-Boer Alfred Harmsworth, owner of the million-circulation *Daily Mail*, whose paper ran such headlines as:

Unarmed English at the Mercy of the Boers
and
Englishmen in Danger Sing "God Save the Queen."

Harmsworth hailed the relief of Mafeking on May 17, 1900, as a glorious British victory and portrayed Colonel Robert Baden-Powell (who later started the Boy Scouts) as a hero. He had defended the besieged town for 217 days with such sangfroid against Boer attacks that he regularly played cricket on Sundays while surrounded by the enemy.

Despite their support of opposing sides in the Boer War, Pulitzer and Harmsworth stayed friends. In fact, in June, a month after the relief of Mafeking, they spent the day together. However, Pulitzer had not been persuaded by Harmsworth or other British friends to support their cause, but he did publish an accurate account of their ecstatic response to the war news. On May 19, 1900, it was:

MAFEKING RESCUED:
LONDON GOES WILD.

Siege Raised After 211 [217] Days —
Heavy Shelling of Laagers
and Forts Before Boers
Were Driven Off.

And next day:

BRITAIN DELIRIOUS OVER MAFEKING
WHILE AMID RECORD BREAKING POPULAR JOY
QUEEN WIRES PRAISE TO BADEN-POWELL.

————————

Whole British Empire Mad
with Joy at Raising of Siege.

————————

BADEN-POWELL ADORED

————————

Londoners Give Themselves Up to
Most Extravagant Demonstrations of Delight

————————

HERO'S HOME A MECCA OF MOBS

Alongside the report was a dramatic sketch of a dashing group of armed Boers on horseback galloping past one of their own felled by a shell burst. Pulitzer only spoke his mind in that day's editorial:

THE RELIEF OF MAFEKING

Mafeking besieged for 211 [217] days, has been relieved at last. Col. Baden-Powell and his 1,200 men, stubbornly standing their ground through seven weary months, sorely pressed by sickness and hunger within and hard pressed by the bravest and sternest foes without, have written a new page in the annals of human heroism. The moral merits of the cause for which the garrison of Mafeking stood are not improved by the devoted courage with which they defended their flag. But the hearts of all brave and chivalrous men quicken with a sympathetic thrill wherever unflinching and dauntless courage shows itself. We believe that the Boers themselves being brave and courageous men, will not grudge Baden-Powell and his unyielding little garrison the tribute of respect and admiration which will be everywhere awarded them. In an age of gloomy speculations on the decay of the virile virtues the Mafeking episode comes like a blast of north wind, to give assurance that the saving salt of utmost daring and supreme sacrifice still abides among civilized men.

On a brief trip back to New York that summer, Pulitzer stayed with his family in the rented house while his new home was under way. One morning he asked Chapin to call in on his way to work, and launched into an exasperated complaint about an editorial writer not following his instructions. The carelessness or deliberate disobedience drove him to explosive profanities. "And how shockingly that blind old man could swear!" Chapin recalled. "He swore so passionately and so loudly and grew so choleric and red in the face, that I feared something inside of him might snap. Suddenly he checked himself and pricked up his ears. There were angry voices in an adjoining room.

One of his young sons [Joe probably] was having a run-in with his tutor and was forcibly telling what he thought of him. A mixture of annoyance and amusement came over my employer's countenance. 'Dear me,' he said, 'I wonder where that boy learned to swear.'"

While Pulitzer made small economies, paying only $1,350 of a $1,400 bill, which he thought excessive, for redecorating the rented house, and putting off settling a $39 bill for coal, he bought a motor-driven delivery truck for $2,000, before any other New York newspaper had one—followed by twenty more, which meant seventy horses could be retired to pasture. Then he paid $250,000 for his new house at 7–15 East 73rd Street, and ordered more than a thousand bottles of wine from abroad. Yet unlike William Randolph Hearst, who eventually seemed compelled to buy up Europe and relocate much of it in warehouses, Pulitzer turned down the offer of a European castle worth $1.8 million and going for a mere $100,000.

That was one point in McKinley's favor: Americans generally were prospering, after winning the war and sticking to the gold standard. Now he was up for reelection, with the dynamic and charismatic war hero Theodore Roosevelt as his vice president.

While McKinley stayed home, Roosevelt raced through the country, making 673 speeches, often with a bodyguard of former Rough Riders. He handled hecklers like a pro, responding to a Democrat who yelled "What about the rotten beef in Cuba?" with "I ate it, and you'll never get near enough to get hit by a bullet!"

The Democrats fielded William Jennings Bryan, with Adlai E. Stevenson of Illinois as vice president. They agreed with Pulitzer in opposing the Republicans' colonial policy—the acquisition of Puerto Rico, Guam, and the Philippines, and the annexation of Hawaii. But Bryan persisted in his call for silver to replace gold, a rickety platform, because silver was now a dead issue with the discovery of gold in Alaska and South Africa, which lowered its cost.

Passionate as he was about politics, Pulitzer had little enthusiasm for any candidate. But, being a Democrat, he gave Bryan his reluctant support. So did Hearst, while applauding the Republican colonial policy. Knowing how agitated Joseph became as election day approached, Kate, to her own surprise, managed to persuade him to get away from it all. In October he headed for Wiesbaden, Germany, whose healing waters attracted people with dyspepsia, rheumatism, gout, nervous disorders, female disorders, and weight problems. Pulitzer suffered from at least half of them.

Stopping en route in London, he invited two journalists to join him on the journey, as companions to augment his paid staff. But they declined, one writing to the other that Pulitzer "appears quite unable to battle with the malady of the century—unrest—why can he not settle down peacefully to the soft music of Hungarian bands?"

He surely wished he'd taken that advice. In Belgium his train stopped because of a train wreck ahead, and Pulitzer had to walk through rain-soaked fields to board another train ahead of the accident. As usual, Dr. Hosmer kept Kate informed of Pulitzer's moods. Now, he wrote, "everything was wrong all the time & the world was full of damn fools." Apparently this included people in Wiesbaden: as soon as he arrived, he wanted to leave.

Did Kate fear that his restlessness was a sign of an imminent mental breakdown? That would explain her uncharacteristically threatening telegram, sent to him at the Hotel and Pension, Wiesbaden: "You are not to leave Baden until you hear from me. Otherwise blood & murder certainly will be in the future."

Presumably he got the green light: he was back in London by early November. Still restless, he moved to the fashionable seaside resort of Bournemouth on the south coast, where he rented a house and told Hosmer, Butes, and Billing to find him some good company. Journalist Charles Jerningham, who had turned down the trip to Germany, suggested Ronald Scarlett and Lord Frederick Bruce. Neither met Pulitzer's rigid requirements, but he sent Jerningham a case of liebfraumilch (a good white wine) for his efforts. Butes suggested six men. None panned out. Pulitzer's Viennese professor cousin heard of his unsatisfied search for company and recommended Kurt Leitner, a fellow Austrian. Leitner spoke four languages, had known Wagner, Liszt, and Brahms, and shared Pulitzer's love of music, art, and literature. For nine years he had been Baron Anselm Rothschild's secretary, and then for ten years, the secretary of the duke of Bielitz, an eccentric insomniac. Leitner himself added to the enthusiastic letter of recommendation: "I beg to tell you I have not lost my energy and my good humour in spite of some unfortunate experiences. I am not nervous. I am accustomed to accommodate myself to others." He didn't mention that his last employer, the duke of Bielitz, had spent his declining years in a mental asylum. Come at once, Pulitzer wired this erudite paragon. But Leitner was felled by a long bout of bronchitis and never made it.

When he was giving up hope, a former secretary-companion, Claude Ponsonby—the first one he had hired, eleven years earlier—turned up for an unexpected and very welcome visit.

While he was still in Bournemouth, Pulitzer's fourteen-year-old daughter Edith sent him a bill for several novels by Alphonse Daudet—a Gallic Dickens. But Pulitzer complained to Kate that Daudet was too shocking for their daughter, adding, "I would as soon give her strychnine as let her read the average French novel at her formative, impressionable age. You should watch this sharply and tell the governess to do the same." That same day, December 12, he wrote to the headmistress of Edith's school, saying that he wanted her "to be a good rather than a society woman, with high ideals and intellectual tastes and inclined to interest herself in the serious things of life." Of all his surviving children she alone displayed something of his brilliance, but he never indicated any wish for her to join him and his sons in the newspaper business.

After a few weeks in Bournemouth, Pulitzer hired a special train to take him and his staff to Liverpool, from which they sailed for New York on December 19.

On board, he renewed his acquaintance with newspaper publisher Alfred Harmsworth and his wife. Pulitzer became so bowled over by the thirty-four-year-old Englishman's ideas that he made an extraordinary suggestion. To commemorate the birth of a new century, how would Harmsworth like to be in complete charge of the *World*'s January 1 issue? Harmsworth said he would like nothing better.

Though famous as a provocative press tycoon in Britain, Harmsworth was surprised to be greeted as a celebrity in New York, writing to his mother, "People say that no young man's coming has stirred up the United States so much before." Hearst, after a brief meeting, described him as looking like a mixture of Napoleon, Edison, and one of Raphael's cherubs.

While Harmsworth was preparing the first issue of the *World* for the twentieth century, Pulitzer gave readers an uncannily accurate glimpse into the future by publishing an artist's impression of how New York City would look in 1999—a century hence. At a quick glance it looks like the real thing today—except that Central Park is missing.

Pulitzer had also persuaded Émile Zola, who was still trying to free and vindicate Dreyfus, to answer this question: "What is the outlook for the new century?"

Zola replied: "I look forward into this pregnant new century with joyful confidence. I believe that we will soon abolish the abnormal privilege of inherited wealth; it will be abolished on the same principle that made us republicans already deny the inheritance of the sceptre. The two things are one. In fact, it is much more absurd that a young Vanderbilt . . . with a possible commercial value of $25 a week should inherit millions than it would be to permit the sons of [President] McKinley and Loubet to rule us because their fathers did.

"Humanity can now produce exactly twenty times what it can possibly consume. I firmly believe that the outrageous anomaly of human beings wanting food, clothes and shelter will disappear early in the twentieth century. The twentieth century will also find means to eradicate the corruption that disgraces the public life of all countries and probably reserve capital punishment for political knaves alone, sending other criminals to curative establishments and the care of specialists."

Meanwhile, the British were still killing Boers and vice versa, Americans killing Filipinos and vice versa, and nearly all nations were deploring the savagery of Belgian King Leopold for supporting the slaughter of the natives of the Congo to build *his* empire.

While Pulitzer remained in his Manhattan home, he gave Harmsworth a free hand with the New Year's issue. As if the Englishman were royalty or the head of state, the entire *World* staff working for him at the Dome wore formal evening dress, with one exception. Pomeroy Burton, the city editor, refused to take part in what he called an affectation. Yet, a few years later, he quit the *World* to join Harmsworth's staff, became a British citizen, and in 1923 was knighted as Sir Pomeroy Burton!

The *World*'s remarkably prescient idea of how New York City would look a hundred years in the future—in 1999. Note how the tallest skyscrapers resemble Pulitzer's golden Dome.

Saying that he doubted if any other great newspaper proprietor except Pulitzer would have entrusted his plant to a young foreigner, Harmsworth produced in his one special edition what he called "The Busy Man's Paper"—nine by sixteen inches—that could be folded and stuffed in the pocket. It was handy for those still ashamed to be seen reading the *World*.

Pulitzer had dared to surrender control of his paper for a day because he saw Harmsworth as a British version of himself, with similar goals and gifts. Both were volcanic, high-strung men, driven at times to the brink of madness (Harmsworth died insane). And both were all but impossible to please. Pulitzer trusted Harmsworth with his paper but not with his staff. Forewarned of Harmsworth's cutthroat business practices, he feared the Englishman might

Alfred Harmsworth.
Pulitzer trusted him
only so far.

emulate Hearst and "steal" his best men, so that when Harmsworth asked for a staff directory, Pulitzer made sure no directory was available. He also declined Harmsworth's offer to take the staff to dinner. But he did send Harmsworth a box of choice cigars and a bouquet of flowers for his wife—together with his thanks and congratulations. Then he went back to publishing a full-size newspaper.

CHAPTER 23

President McKinley Assassinated

1901

—

53 to 54 years old

At midnight of December 31, 1900, the first Harmsworth-edited pocket edition of the *World* came off the press, and fifteen minutes later a messenger rushed it to catch a Washington-bound train. It was in a race against Hearst's *Journal*, to be the first twentieth-century newspaper perused by President McKinley. Gamblers were betting on Hearst as the favorite, because he had hired a special express train to take his paper—enclosed in a silver box—to the commander in chief. The box arrived at the White House well ahead of the *World*. But then fate took a hand.

McKinley's secretary, who knew about the race between the two rivals, was still steaming from the shellacking Hearst had given his boss during the election campaign, and pleased with Pulitzer for pulling his punches. He ignored the *Journal* resting in its splendid silver box in the anteroom and waited for the tiny tabloid *World* to hand-deliver to the president. It not only won the race but also became a collector's item, selling an extra hundred thousand copies.

"Today's *World*," Harmsworth wrote in his prophetic editorial, "closely resembles the newspaper of the future."

It may have been the future for Harmsworth but not for Pulitzer, who never again went tabloid, bolstered perhaps by a reader's response: "The best thing about Mr. Harmsworth's experiment is that Mr. Pulitzer limited it to one day." Yet Harmsworth's publish-and-be-damned British tabloid *Daily Mirror*, launched in 1903, would become wildly successful and is still going strong. In fact, that one reader's negative response was atypical. Pulitzer published paeans of praise for Harmsworth's experiment the day after it appeared, including

Thomas Edison's: "Your idea of the 20th Century, as carried out in The New York *World* of today is in my opinion an innovation that all great newspapers must adopt." Pulitzer obviously didn't agree.

In the special issue Harmsworth's editorial headed WHERE AMERICA BEATS THE WORLD glorified the United States as second to none in almost everything, especially ingenuity and compassion. "In the great matter of surface transit— you are leading the universe. You gave us the Morse telegraph, the telephone, the phonograph, the incandescent lamp, the Maxim gun, the Hoe printing press, the Linotype typesetting machine, the electric automobile, the typewriter, the sewing-machine, the model office building . . . which testify in every land to the force of American genius. Those who are too prone to criticize surface faults in the United States should witness, as I have, the landing at Ellis Island of the hordes of illiterate foreigners fresh from the tyranny and misrule of the Continental countries, and should remember that Americans stand exposed to the criticisms of the whole world on events and actions largely brought about by the swarms of newly arrived immigrants. The kind of American news that comes to Europe consists chiefly of strike riots and other crimes too frequently committed by this same foreign element. No other people in the world would assimilate and in a single generation make a man of the kind of human derelict dumped down daily on your shores from Europe."

High on Pulitzer's agenda in the new year was the design of his new home, a long-delayed masterpiece in the making and about which Pulitzer was driving his architect, Stanford White, up the soundproofed walls. After carefully exploring several models with his fingers Pulitzer had rejected them all, inciting White to complain that he "had made twice as many studies and done twice as much work on this project as we have ever done on any interior work before." Pulitzer finally approved the next best thing to a Venetian palace. Its elaborate facade mimicked the Rezzonico and Pesaro palaces created by the great seventeenth-century Venetian architect Baldassare Longhena along the Grand Canal.

It rivaled one of Manhattan's most famous domiciles, the Astor mansion, which had been strictly off-limits to the press. No lowly reporter had set foot inside it until the *World*'s Nixola Greeley-Smith broke the barrier. Pulitzer had recruited this granddaughter of publisher Horace Greeley after Nellie Bly's triumphs. Nixola's forte was to get "impossible" interviews with people no one had dared to question before. An attractive, dark-haired woman with a confident and complex personality, a competitor described her as having "the smile of a happy child, the inscrutability of a sphinx: she has wisdom and philosophy, yet behind the sweetest smile she hides a disdain and a bitterness that can surpass anything I have ever known."

"Her questions," said another woman reporter, "were intelligent, amusing, surprising, and sometimes impertinent, so that people were blown off guard."

Mrs. William [Caroline] Astor, the queen of Newport and New York society, was certainly blown off guard when Nixola faced her, armed with a letter of introduction from railroad tycoon Chauncey Depew. Invited into the mansion, she had a long conversation with the woman, whose inaccessibility to the press was legendary. Back at the Dome, when she wrote it up, Nixola had a pang of conscience. Perhaps Mrs. Astor hadn't realized that their conversation was to appear as an exclusive interview in the *World*. So Nixola returned to 842 Fifth Avenue to get permission to publish it. A maid kept her waiting at the door, then said Mrs. Astor wasn't available and handed Nixola $2. "Mrs Astor sends you this," said the maid, "because she knows that you work for a living and that you have been put to some trouble coming here."

Nonplussed, Nixola Greeley-Smith showed that she could outsnub New York's top snob. "Tell Mrs. Astor," she said, "that she not only forgets who I am, but she forgets who she is. Give her back the $2 with my compliments and tell her that when John Jacob Astor was skinning rabbits, my grandfather was getting out the *Tribune* and was one of the foremost citizens of New York." When Nixola returned to the Dome and told her editor of Mrs. Astor's message and $2 tip, he laughed. "Look at the check for $250 that Mary Baker Eddy [the founder of Christian Science] once sent me," he said, pointing to the wall (presumably to "buy" a puff piece). "It tickled me so much I had it framed."

Unappeased, Nixola rewrote the article less sympathetically, and posters were plastered around town announcing the *World*'s first-ever interview with Mrs. Astor—which brought her son storming into the office to threaten a lawsuit if the interview ran. It ran. There was no lawsuit.

Pulitzer rewarded Nixola with more plum assignments, and in the coming months she interviewed Mrs. George Keppel, mistress of Britain's soon to be King Edward VII, and the wife of Dr. Charles Parkhurst, head of the Society for the Prevention of Vice. For a change of pace, she got a dead man to talk to her—through a medium.

The *World* devoted two full pages, one and two, to Queen Victoria's death on January 22, after sixty-three years on the throne, with condolences from President McKinley and William Jennings Bryan. Pulitzer usually made her an exception in his antiroyalist diatribes. Now he eulogized her as the noblest and best of Britannia's rulers, a sharp contrast to his opinion of her grandson Wilhelm. Pulitzer was amazed that the Germans tolerated this paranoid, saber-rattling emperor of Germany's Second Reich.

In March, while dedicating an army barracks in Berlin, Kaiser Wilhelm astonished his troops by warning them to "be ready day and night to spill your blood, if ever this town should rise against me. Devotion to king and fatherland must be sealed with blood and life. We shall always be victors for there is a mighty ally, that is the eternal God in Heaven." The kaiser's friends tried to explain his remarks as due to an attack of nerves after a lunatic in Bremen had tried to kill him. Others considered that he was the crazy one to raise the subject when no revolt was brewing. Pulitzer thought it ludicrous "that 56,000,000 as intelligent, sensible, and self-respecting people as the Germans should acknowledge as their 'sovereign' a person wild enough to give vent to such nonsense in the twentieth century. And the culminating touch of humor is the formation of a committee of high officials in Berlin to wait upon this madman and assure him that 'no one in Berlin entertains a thought of impudence or insubordination.'"

"Impudence" and "insubordination" may also have sprung to Pulitzer's mind and a few choice expletives to his tongue when he heard that his son Joe had been expelled from school. When he learned why, he hit the roof. Joe and several other boys had broken out of school to buy beer in the nearby village of Southborough, Massachusetts. On their return they found they were locked out. Daredevil Joe led the way back in, climbed an ivy-covered wall, and entered through an open window—surprising the headmaster and his wife in their bedroom.

Pulitzer was not amused, explaining in an angry letter to Kate: "It's not the incident but the cause, the character, the loss of moral sense and loss of honor. He has very little mind, very little intelligence, very little head but a great deal of animal instinct, a great deal of passion for pleasure and nothing else. No respectable aims, no high ambitions, aspirations, ideas, so far as I can see, except for physical pleasures."

His harsh reaction to his son's escapade might be explained by his own disciplined disposition and history: to him the work ethic was almost a religion. At Joe's age, alone in a foreign land and fighting in the Union Army, he had been forced to take life seriously simply to survive. He blamed Kate for spoiling Joe and insisted on taking full charge of his upbringing, but only if she didn't interfere, and cooperated with him "to help save the boy so that he will have an honorable, happy, useful career, and not disgrace my name. . . . No amount of school will reach the root of the trouble [caused by one who has] committed a crime against his father, his mother, his sisters and his own good name and future. This should be rubbed into him. That might, with the other circumstances, make a real man out of him."

From then on he monitored Joe's life hour by hour, from morning to night. On vacations, escorted by his tutor, Mr. Sheafe, Joe went horse riding in Manhattan's Central Park and visited Washington, D.C., where, he dutifully reported to his father, "we spent a good deal of time in the House and Senate but unfortunately heard no good speeches. We also went to Mt. Vernon. I found the place most picturesque and absorbingly interesting. I saw my cousin, Varina, Mrs. Jeff Davis, has given several old Washington relics to the place." Joe also exchanged a few words with boxer Jim Corbett: "He is not as one might suppose, a loudly dressed cheap sport. Instead he dresses quietly and well and has a pleasant manner." After glimpsing Theodore Roosevelt's sharp-tongued daughter Alice, Joe described her as "rather attractive." Then he crossed out "rather" and added "very."

The summer season ended and fall began with a national tragedy. It might have been avoided had President McKinley taken threats on his life seriously. Instead he seemed indifferent to his physical safety. There had been no big shakeup after a Secret Service agent supposed to be guarding him in the White

House had been found sleeping on a sofa. When the *World* reported rumors of a plot to assassinate him by pro-Spanish Cubans, his guard was augmented by one fat, flat-footed Secret Service agent, George Foster, assigned to accompany him whenever he left the White House. But McKinley often gave him the slip. Fearful for McKinley's safety, his secretary, George Cortelyou, advised him to cancel his appearance at Buffalo's Pan-American Exposition on September 6. "Why should I?" the president replied. "No one would wish to hurt me."

On that day, George Foster and two other Secret Service agents joined McKinley in the exposition's Temple of Music. A Bach sonata could be heard faintly just above the noise of the crowd. Buffalo detectives mingled with them, prepared to stop anyone who looked suspicious from reaching the president. Foster and another agent faced him and the third agent stood on his right, ready to spring forward at any sign of danger.

Inconspicuous among those waiting to shake hands with the president was a short, lean young man with a blank expression. But he was on fire, he said, to kill a great ruler. He grasped a short-barreled .32-caliber Iver Johnson revolver in his right hand, wrapped in a handkerchief as if covering an injury. It fooled all the guards. As they later explained, it was a hot day, and many of the crowd were holding handkerchiefs to fan themselves or wipe their faces.

When his turn came, the self-professed anarchist held out his left hand to take McKinley's right, pressed the hidden gun against the president's stomach, and fired two quick shots.

The crowd groaned, gasped, and screamed, wrote historian Margaret Leech, as they watched the assassin "knocked down, pinioned under a heap of assailants, and then dragged to the center of the hall. As McKinley was assisted to a chair, his eyes followed that other man. A blow landed on his vacant face. 'Don't let them hurt him,' the President said. A few men stood about, fanning him with their hats. Cortelyou bent close, while the President fumbled at his breast and belly. There was blood on the hand he raised to Cortelyou's shoulder. 'My wife,' he whispered, '—be careful, Cortelyou, how you tell her—oh, be careful.'"

His concern for his wife was emphasized in the *World*'s headlines:

M'KINLEY [SIC] SHOT . . . ASSAILANT CONFESSES . . .

PRESIDENT'S FIRST THOUGHT
IS OF HIS INVALID WIFE.

First Bullet Strikes Mr. McKinley's Breast Bone and
Is Readily Extracted, but the Second Goes
Through the Stomach and Lodges in His Back
and Gives the Surgeons Grave Anxiety.

PRESIDENT THE CALMEST OF ALL THOSE
WITHIN SOUND OF THE REVOLVER

The paper also revealed that although six members of an anarchist group called the Free Society had been arrested and charged with plotting to kill the president, Leon Czolgosz claimed he had acted alone.

Pulitzer sent his personal physician, Dr. Hosmer, to join *World* reporters in Buffalo to provide expert information about the president's condition and medical treatment. His first message was hopeful: the attendant physicians believed McKinley would survive the two bullet wounds. But when gangrene set in, Hosmer's second message was: "President dying. Respiration said to be 40. Does not respond to treatment. Cannot survive." He died on September 14, aged fifty-eight, eight days after the shooting. His killer was electrocuted a month later, in Auburn Penitentiary.

Comparing anarchism to a fatal disease, Pulitzer proposed an effective antidote: to require all immigrants to provide evidence that they were not carriers. He believed that McKinley's assassination would have been "incredible" but for the similar fate "that befell the great and gentle Lincoln and the genial Garfield. As in their cases, too, there was no motive for the crimes."

Some blamed Hearst for McKinley's death, citing a vicious editorial in which he had called the president the most hated creature in America. Another Hearst editorial even encouraged assassination. It read: "If bad institutions and bad men can be got rid of only by killing, then the killing must be done." Few doubted that Hearst meant McKinley. Even more damning was that after the fatal shooting of Kentucky governor William Goebel, Hearst had printed this provocative verse by Ambrose Bierce:

The bullet that pierced Goebel's breast
Can not be found in all the West;
Good reason, it is speeding here
To stretch McKinley in his bier.

Rival newspapers accused Hearst of being an accessory to murder. Some of his best advertisers left him, and former New York mayor Abram Hewitt urged a boycott of the Hearst press. New Yorkers snatched bundles of his *Journal* from newsboys and burned them. When demonstrators in New York and other cities hanged or burned Hearst in effigy, he armed himself with a pistol and for a time didn't open packages that came in the mail.

But Pulitzer was not inclined to kick a man when he was down. He told his staff to go easy on Hearst and to stick to factual reporting. When they went too easy, he explained that "ignoring Geranium [the *Journal*] and personalities did not mean suppression of current legitimate news like Hewitt's speech chamber of commerce meeting or even burning anybody in effigy if facts absolutely correct, true, and the thing is not displayed maliciously."

In the late fall, with President Roosevelt now in office, Samuel Blythe, the *World's* Washington correspondent, wrote several satirical pieces about the slowness of the White House renovations for the new occupant. The architects had put their work for Pulitzer on hold to accommodate the president but were still behind schedule. "If you have no compassion for the architects," Pulitzer wrote to Blythe, "please have some for me. I am an old man and hope to pass my few remaining years in a house I am building here. These architects are my architects and unless you allow me to show them more respect in my own paper they will never finish the house for me."

When White House renovations were completed, Roosevelt had Booker T. Washington to dinner—and caused an uproar. Washington was black and a former slave. He had worked in a salt furnace at age nine and later in a coal mine. To save for his education he had slept under a boardwalk, eventually becoming a college principal. Now, at forty-five, he was the leading spokesman for black Americans. But the thought of his dining at the White House gave much of the press, especially in the South, conniptions. The *Memphis Scimitar*, suffering from historical amnesia, called it "the most damnable outrage ever perpetrated by any citizen of the United States." And the *Richmond Times* screamed that Roosevelt was promoting white-black intermarriage! Roosevelt called his critics crazy. Pulitzer agreed, and risked a circulation plunge in this editorial response: "One of the most learned, most eloquent, most brilliant men of his day—the President of a college [Tuskegee Institute]—is asked to dinner by President Roosevelt and because the pigment of his skin is some shades darker than that of others a large part of the United States is convulsed with shame and rage. The man is a negro. Therefore in eating with him the President is charged with having insulted the South. This man may represent us in the Senate Chamber, he may educate us, but not eat with us; preach our Gospel [and] die for us but not dine with us. Truly Liberty must smile at such broadminded logic, such enlightened tolerance. Or should she weep?"

Pulitzer was off to London soon after, where he sought the advice of tea tycoon and yachting enthusiast Sir Thomas Lipton about buying a yacht. However, he returned in late November without one, pleased to find that his choice for mayor of New York City, Columbia University president Seth Low, had unseated the incumbent, Tammany Hall puppet Robert Van Wyck.

As always, he maintained a keen interest in his staff. By getting them to assess or squeal on each other—take your pick—Pulitzer continued to monitor their lives in and out of the office. But, his heir apparent, David Graham Phillips, remained a mystery. While others usually went for a drink and a chat after work, he invariably went straight home. In fact, he was turning the tables on Pulitzer. Instead of assessing his colleagues, Phillips secretly assessed the publisher, recording his words and actions for a novel to be based on the *World*, with a Pulitzer-like tycoon as the controversial protagonist.

Phillips had an odd writing habit. Because of an irrational fear that continuous bending to write while seated at a desk or a table would give him appendicitis, he worked at his novel, often all through the night, while standing upright at what looked like a pulpit. Titled *The Great God Success*, the book was published in 1901 under a pseudonym, John Graham. The main character, based on Pulitzer, was named Howard.

When critics praised it as a convincing account of the newspaper world, Phillips acknowledged he was the author. Pulitzer, who was in the French Alps at the time, was naturally curious and got his secretaries to spell one another in reading it to him. Some of it was a true picture of Pulitzer's earlier days, such as this statement by Howard [Pulitzer]: "'We are going to print the news, all the news and nothing but the news. No favours to anybody; no use of news-columns for revenge or exploitation. The only questions a news-item need raise in your mind are: Is it true? Is it interesting? Is it printable in a newspaper that will publish anything which a healthy-minded grown person wishes to read?' . . . Every day he came down town planning for a better newspaper the next morning than they had ever made before. And his vigour, his enthusiasm pervaded the entire office. He went from one news department to another, suggesting, asking for suggestions, praising, criticizing."

Things soon got very embarrassing for the secretaries. As they read farther into the *roman à clef*, its idealistic publisher became progressively more despicable. He began to sacrifice everything to his work, including his family. He invested heavily in railroad stocks and refused to use his paper to expose crooked dealings of railroad companies in which he had invested. What started out as his genuine sympathy and support of the underdog eventually became a cynical ploy to make money. The Pulitzer-like character ended up rich, powerful, and miserable, knowing he had betrayed his youthful ideals.

The effect was deadly because much of it was an accurate portrait of Pulitzer. He had indeed sacrificed everything for his work. He was rich and powerful—and often miserable. Being close to Pulitzer, Phillips knew that much of the book rang true. But Pulitzer had not betrayed his ideals. He continued to support the underdog. He had never prostituted his papers to protect his investments. In fact, Pulitzer had once exposed a company in which he had stock. As his financial adviser Dumont Clarke had recently reminded him, "My experience has been that you have always led attacks upon the coal combination, although the Lackawanna (in which you are largely interested) was the most important of the [coal] companies affected."

Long after Pulitzer's death, former editor Charles Chapin testified in a memoir written in his Sing Sing cell: "I was never once asked to withhold or suppress or color a news article. Pulitzer was the last man who would have suggested such a thing." Had he done so, particularly for his financial advantage, his many enemies surely would have unearthed it. For Phillips to have implied otherwise, even under the cover of fiction, was a dirty trick. But Pulitzer didn't fire him. Though deeply wounded by the distorted picture of himself, he hid his distress from the cause. He even sent him a fan letter from Aix-les-Bains saying he had enjoyed the novel "very much with one single reservation." No need, of course, for him to spell it out. Instead he praised Phillips for a book that "showed undoubted talent, imagination, and skill in constructing dialogue." Then he advised him to read Dostoyevsky's *Crime and Punishment*: "It is the greatest novel I have ever read." In it Dostoyevsky suggests that the most degraded people can redeem themselves through suffering. Was Pulitzer telling Phillips that he needed to atone for defaming his boss?

Don Seitz knew Pulitzer well and observed that he was "keenly hurt when he discovered the author [of *The Great God Success*] was Phillips. He was very fond of him and had striven hard to develop in him a fitness for first place on the paper."

If Oscar Wilde's "Every great man nowadays has his disciples, and it is always Judas who writes the biography" didn't spring to Pulitzer's mind, it surely occurred to his equally well-read secretaries. But in a sense, Phillips [code name Gumboil!] did Pulitzer a favor, reminding him that he was human: he might one day be tempted to whitewash a corrupt company in which he had a big financial stake. Pulitzer even raised this possibility with his editors, and made it clear that if it ever happened they *must* ignore his instructions.

CHAPTER 24

"Find a Man Who Gets Drunk and Hire Him"

1902
—
54 to 55 years old

Pulitzer continued to cater to his many immigrant readers eager for news of "the old country" and to justify the name of his paper, with regular accounts of foreigners' fights, fashions, and foibles, even reporting the sexual depravities of high society—though couched in phrases fit for family firesides. The *World's* issue for January 5 devoted half a page deploring and detailing the rampant divorce rate "and epidemic of scandal" among European royalty "since Victoria's restraining hand was removed by death."

While supposedly resting at Lakewood, New Jersey, in January, Pulitzer sent for Business Manager Seitz to discuss ways to enliven the paper. Seitz suggested that shifting the staff around might do the trick. Pulitzer disagreed. The paper was dull because none of you gets drunk, he complained, then named all the nonalcoholics on the staff, one by one, including Seitz himself. "When I was there someone always got drunk," Pulitzer said, "and we made a great paper. Take the next train back to the city, find a man who gets drunk and hire him."

As he crossed Park Row returning to the Dome, Seitz met Esdaile Cohen, a first-rate word wizard. Cohen confided that he'd just been fired from Hearst's *American* because "I couldn't let the hard stuff alone." Amazed at his good luck, Seitz immediately put him on the payroll.

It was just what the paper needed. Cohen's copy made lively reading, and his presence enlivened the office, especially when he had delirium tremens. In its hallucinatory grip, he once saw, as he stared through the glass door of the managing editor's office, a blue attack dog about to make mincemeat of his boss. Cohen rushed to the rescue, smashed the glass with his fist, and cut a vein.

An emergency room surgeon saved him from bleeding to death. Despite his d.t.'s, his job was never in danger, and he remained on the staff even through Prohibition until he was killed in a barroom brawl.

In February, while wintering on Jekyll Island, Pulitzer discovered that he was only at his peak mental efficiency for an hour a day, usually during the editorial meetings at breakfast. So he called for William Merrill to join him and work out how to make the most of the time when the group came to Jekyll Island. Merrill returned to the Dome with their solution: to tell Bradford Merrill (no relation)—discreetly—not to talk or interrupt so much at editorial meetings, and Seitz not to speak with his mouth full and to crunch his toast less loudly. Merrill advised Seitz to keep a bread crust at the side of his plate as a reminder. With those aggravations removed, Pulitzer expected to make more efficient use of his peak hour.

Normally he kept his religious views under wraps, except when a religious controversy made the news and he felt bound to comment—such as the German kaiser's current "crusade" against Christian Science. This belief, advanced by a fragile eighty-one-year-old American woman, Mary Baker Eddy, that disease could be eliminated by spiritual rather than medical means, had spread to Europe. The kaiser feared that his court officials and army officers were being duped by ideas that would "sap the foundations of the Christian faith." As a fervent Christian, he vowed to stamp them out by banishing everyone from his court connected with Christian Science, Spiritualism, or other cults. He defined cults as "outgrowths and diseases" of Christianity, and believed that the practitioners were duped by charlatans or were victims of their own misdirected religious feelings. Although Pulitzer had recently ridiculed the kaiser as paranoid, he was inclined to agree with him about Christian Scientists, asserting, "There is a strong leaning toward the view that the misguided religious people are hysterical women and weakminded men."

He would eventually try to investigate the elusive Mary Baker Eddy, but now turned from religion to a subject that had more impact on readers—the high cost of meat. He blamed the beef trust, another monopoly, for ripping off the public. Under the headline "Prices That Stagger Humanity," he called the retail sale of beef for eighteen to twenty-four cents a pound "daylight robbery."

Not all the news was negative. Ecstatic Cubans, celebrating on the eve of their freedom from U.S. occupation, got prominent play in the paper. So did an exclusive account of conditions on the island by Governor General Wood, the U.S. government representative. He boasted that he was leaving Cuba free from all contagious diseases, with efficient, well-equipped schools, good hospitals, charities and jails, a reorganized Rural Guard and court system. It sounded too good to be true. And it was. But without a full-time correspondent in Cuba, Pulitzer couldn't challenge the excessively overoptimistic report.

The death on May 21 of Edwin Godkin, the founder of the *Nation* and editor of the *Evening Post*, gave Pulitzer a chance to savage a man who had once damned the *World* as "the next thing to hell" and Pulitzer, presumably, as the next thing to the devil. However, Pulitzer loved the *Post*, a small but influential paper aimed at the intelligentsia, and told William Merrill that the obituary should stress Godkin's unflinching integrity and intelligence, "all the more because he has never failed in fifteen years to abuse the *World*, and no doubt hated me. I think the profession has lost the ablest mind since Greeley. It is a great loss to the independent thought of the press."

While Pulitzer and Kate were spending the summer in London, at 21 Kensington Palace Gardens, a British veteran of the Boer War, Lieutenant Colonel Norman Thwaites, turned up unexpectedly. He wanted a job and had heard that Pulitzer's overworked secretary, Alfred Butes, needed an assistant. Butes invited him in and told him some of the rigid requirements: a pleasant voice, wide knowledge of literature, great patience, ability to ride a horse, tolerate rough seas, breathe and eat quietly, and keep fit. After a while, Pulitzer joined them, explained to Thwaites that he was blind, and suggested they get some air. Pulitzer took the visitor's arm as they strolled in the garden and asked, "What's in the papers?"

By chance, Thwaites had read an amusing editorial in that morning's *Daily Telegraph*. Pulitzer asked him to read it aloud when they returned to the house. Meanwhile, they talked about books. Thwaites had a wide knowledge of European literature, and was able to discuss German philosophers, Spanish poets, and the works of Shakespeare and Molière. When they returned to the house, Thwaites read the funny *Telegraph* editorial with unrestrained guffaws. He had not yet learned, as he later remarked, that "to interrupt a reading with noises indicating one's own enjoyment was not tolerated; nor had I learned that this man was a martinet of terrifying sternness. However, on this occasion, Pulitzer was pleased to join in the humour of the situation, and within a few minutes he told me I might come over to New York to see whether I should remain, subject, of course, to being found suitable on closer acquaintance." Before Thwaites left, he submitted to Pulitzer's extraordinary scrutiny: first being peered at in the light from a sunny window, then having Pulitzer's fingertips tour his face. Now describe yourself, he said. Thwaites tried, but Pulitzer needed more objective views and asked everyone in the room to describe him, "down to the last detail, height, figure, colour of eyes—a very important matter in Pulitzer's opinion," and then to judge his character from his appearance.

That afternoon Pulitzer had a painting of the actress Mrs. Siddons, by John Hoppner, carried into the still sunlit garden for his consideration. With his left eye, Pulitzer could dimly distinguish enough colors and contours in the painting to buy it for his still unfinished New York mansion.

But nothing absorbed him as much as his work. He believed with a passion that at its best, journalism was a great intellectual profession of vital importance to the nation's welfare. He had wrestled for a long time with effective ways to recruit, train, and sustain the right people. In late summer he made an offer to Nicholas Murray Butler, Columbia University's president. Pulitzer would bankroll a journalism school on campus staffed with outstanding journalists and

Norman Thwaites.

thinkers and award annual prizes for outstanding journalism. Years before, Columbia had turned down a similar offer. Butler, who knew that many academic colleagues still had a jaundiced view of the *World*, stalled and said he'd think about it.

But not all intellectuals scorned the *World*. Émile Zola was among a minority of intellectuals who thought highly of the paper. It had vigorously backed his campaign to get a second trial for Alfred Dreyfus, the French Jew found guilty of spying for Germany. He had succeeded: in 1899 Dreyfus had been brought home from Devil's Island for a retrial, during which the French military judges were shown overwhelming proof of his innocence. To save face they again found him guilty with extenuating circumstances, leaving it to French president Émile Loubet to cancel the order to ship him back to Devil's Island and then to grant him clemency. Dreyfus had been free for two years when on September 28 Zola died in mysterious circumstances. Having admired Zola for his ardent defense of Dreyfus, Pulitzer gave his strange death detailed coverage. The death, at first, was attributed to suicide, then to accidental carbon dioxide poisoning, but some believed he was murdered by sore losers—the anti-Dreyfus faction.

The *World's* headlines told the story:

ÉMILE ZOLA
FAMOUS WRITER
FOUND DEAD.
Great Novelist Asphyxiated
by Gas in His Bed Chamber
in Paris, and it is First
Thought He Committed
Suicide by Taking Poison.

———

HIS WIFE OVERCOME
BY THE SAME AGENCY.
Investigation Satisfies the Com-
missary of Police That Death
Was Accidental—Mme. Zola's
Condition So Dangerous that She
Is Not Told Her Husband is Dead.

His wife survived. So did the two pet dogs that slept in their bedroom. If Zola was murdered, his killer or killers were never brought to justice.

After their annual stay in London, Kate and Pulitzer returned together to Chatwold, where John Dillon, his former partner on the *Post-Dispatch*, was among their first guests. Riding a horse on Pulitzer's estate, Dillon fell and cracked a rib. Pleurisy set in and he was attended by doctors for a month before he died on October 15. He was fifty-nine. Pulitzer paid all medical expenses and funeral costs, including transporting Dillon's body to St. Louis.

That fall, in covering the sensational trial of an abortion ring in Dresden, Germany, Pulitzer's biggest headache was how to avoid the appearance of pandering. He came up with two solutions: to use euphemisms, and to treat it as a sociological study of the human condition. On October 2 he cabled Seitz an outline of the story and his okay to run it, but so cautiously that he must never use the word "abortion": "If you will send for the German papers and especially the Dresden papers since Sept. 15 and pledge yourself to be conscientiously careful in printing the story with utmost delicacy and cleanness I will suspend the rules and allow publication of one of the most terribly shocking stories I have ever heard of. It will certainly make a sensation but you must [print it] for its human interest, as a study of modern morals and German character. No matter how interesting any point may be it must not be published in an indelicate or offensive form. Nearly anything can be said if only the right words are chosen although these are often very difficult to find. The word 'abortion' must be avoided. 'Criminal operation' is better." Pulitzer's orders were obeyed to the letter: abortions were euphemized as "criminal operations," "systematic iniquity," "criminal practice," "the evil," and "criminal doings."

At the time, twenty-five thousand prostitutes were plying their trade in Manhattan, catering to every vice imaginable. According to writer Richard

O'Connor, "No other city on earth—not even Port Said, the Marseilles water-front, San Francisco's Barbary Coast, New Orleans's French Quarter or the Casbah of Algiers—could boast of so much wickedness per square mile [where] every whore, pimp and madam operated virtually under license of the [corrupt] New York Police Department." And New Yorkers knew it. Why, then, as a sophisticated sin-city resident, didn't Pulitzer call an abortion an abortion? Apart from his own sensibilities, he was anxious to maintain the paper's restored reputation.

Pulitzer's desire for the *World* to regain its reputation and influence explains his "take care" directives. But it hardly explains why he didn't blow the whistle on archrival Hearst when he had the chance.

Hearst's Napoleonic political ambitions had persuaded him to seek the aid of corrupt Tammany boss Charles Murphy to get a sure seat in Congress. Hearst celebrated on November 4 by financing a massive fireworks display near Madison Square Garden. A firework exploded prematurely, igniting scores of others. The explosion killed eighteen onlookers, decapitated a policeman, and seriously injured more than fifty people. The next day's press, the *World* included, splashed the disaster on their front pages, with one exception. Hearst's *Journal* carried it on page five and omitted his connection with the disaster as sponsor of the fireworks display to celebrate his political victory.

Seitz called Hearst a coward for not admitting his responsibility for the tragedy. Pulitzer was more cautious. He kept any reference to Hearst out of the detailed and dramatic report on pages one and two, though it was obvious whom he meant when he editorialized: "Perhaps some day intelligent man will be able to express his more ebullient emotions of joy or patriotism without resort to the barbaric noise and sputter of uncertain pyrotechnics."

As winter approached, Pulitzer followed with great concern a strike by Pennsylvania's 140,000 coal miners, many of them illiterate immigrants. Earning less than $2 a day for a ten-hour workday, they had demanded a 20 percent pay raise and a nine-hour workday. The mineowners refused, bolstered by the view of their spokesman, George Baer, a multimillionaire, that "the rights and interests of the laboring man will be protected and cared for—not by labor agitators, but by the Christian men to whom God in His infinite wisdom has given control of the property interests of the country."

Assured that God was on their side, the mineowners hoped that the prospect of millions freezing to death in their homes would force the miners back to work. President Roosevelt, who believed in a "square deal" for everyone, met with the mineowners, who remained inflexible. Exasperated by the "extraordinary stupidity and bad temper" of the "wooden-headed gentry," as he called them, he was tempted to take one "by the seat of his breeches" and chuck him out of a window. At first Roosevelt claimed he was powerless to get the two sides together. Then he did just that. On October 3 John Mitchell, president of the United Mine Workers of America, met with Baer in the president's office, where Roosevelt appealed to their patriotism to end the strike. Mitchell agreed to arbitration, but Baer refused. He accused Roosevelt of "negotiating with the fomentors of anarchy" and objected "to being called here to meet a criminal even by the President of the United States." Infuriated, Roosevelt warned Baer's banker, J. P. Morgan, that unless the mineowners agreed to arbitrate, he would order federal troops to seize and operate the mines. The threat worked. The mineowners agreed to arbitration. The miners settled for a 10 percent pay raise and a nine-hour workday. Pulitzer supported Roosevelt's aggressive role, noting that it was the first time a U.S. president had helped to settle rather than to break a strike.

At year's end, David Graham Phillips quit the paper to concentrate on his novels full-time. Despite Phillips' unjustified implication in *The Great God Success* that he was a hypocrite, Pulitzer remained fond of him and respected his talent. James Creelman's return to the *World*, after briefly working for Hearst, was some compensation for losing Phillips. Although Creelman had recently published a novel, *Eagle's Blood*, at least it didn't feature a demonized newspaper publisher.

CHAPTER 25

Euphemisms for Abortion

1903
—
55 to 56 years old

Anyone trying to pull a fast one on Pulitzer usually wished they hadn't. When Seitz tried it by sending him an artificially inflated paid circulation figure, Pulitzer replied on January 7, 1903, in a surprisingly benign mood: "I return this to you in the best of humors believe me — in the *kindest* spirit, wishing however to teach you a lesson against optimism, which is not a mere harmless vanity but, in serious matters of business, a *great danger*. Exact knowledge and foresight are essentials to success. What you call the *increase* means nothing but a number of papers distributed free under my direction and to your knowledge. If we keep 15,000 or even 10,000 you should be satisfied. Can you blame me if, applying the illustration to other information sent me, I am so often in doubt? With kind regards, JP."

Having recently sent Joe to work on the *Post-Dispatch* while Ralph worked at the *World*, Pulitzer made sure his son was not treated with kid gloves. He advised the various department heads that Joe must "cultivate the habit of concentration and accuracy and learn to make small calculations in his head." He must be "polite to everybody down to the officeboy [and] consider himself not the proprietor's or the rich man's son, not entitled to luxury, but like any other worker." He should "study, watch, learn what workers and particularly managers are doing [until he understands that] the life and blood of the property are in circulation, which springs from the news and advertising, which springs from the circulation." Pulitzer asked his son to keep a daily diary of his work in shorthand and to write to him twice a week.

After two months Pulitzer called Joe back to New York from St. Louis to work on the *World* and on March 21 gave him a yacht for his eighteenth birthday. It had a cabin, two staterooms, crew's quarters, and a galley with a stove up forward. Joe thanked his father "a thousand times" for it. Several weeks later, in April, Pulitzer financed a trip for Ralph to Japan to expand his horizons. But he wasn't generous only to his family. That same spring, at his expense, he sent ailing staffer James Clarke to recuperate in England for two months. However, he couldn't resist telling him how to spend the time if he got bored. He should study the latest hot topic, socialism, though not "if it will interfere with your brain and mind but if you feel perfectly fresh and need some reading."

Columbia University hadn't rejected or accepted the idea of the first ever School of Journalism, and on April 10 Pulitzer made it more enticing by putting a big dollar figure on his proposed endowment: two million. When this became public, skeptics ridiculed the idea of teaching journalism, citing the well-worn maxim that journalists are born, not made. Pulitzer challenged them to "name some great editor born full-winged like Mercury, the messenger of the gods. The only position that occurs to me which a man in our Republic can successfully fill by the simple fact of birth, is that of an idiot."

A major obstacle was Columbia president Nicholas Murray Butler's reluctance to accept Harvard president Charles W. Eliot on the proposed Journalism School's advisory board. Eliot had been Pulitzer's enthusiastic choice, as a man "worth twenty editors," and he believed that Butler's resistance was personal and petty—jealousy of an academic peer.

While advocating higher journalistic standards, Pulitzer was in danger of being discredited and humiliated by Pomeroy Burton, the World's managing editor. Burton, who had been investigating the shenanigans of the Metropolitan Street Railway Company—operated by a syndicate headed by William C. Whitney and Thomas Fortune Ryan—tipped off a friend that Metropolitan stock would take a tumble when the World exposé was published. And he expected, Burton wrote, to share in any profit made from this inside information. Instead of taking his advice, the so-called friend showed Burton's letter to Ryan, who copied it and threatened to publicly charge the World with manipulating stocks for its own financial gain.

Burton apologized to Pulitzer, claiming that his mistake "would harm no one but himself." Pulitzer valued Burton too much to fire him. Instead, he demoted him to the Sunday World, replaced him with Caleb Van Hamm, who continued the investigation of the railway company, and ordered Seitz to find out if anyone else on the staff was involved in insider trading. Apparently Burton had done it alone.

Before sailing for his customary European trip, Pulitzer explained exactly how he wanted the World to cover its twentieth anniversary. The 136-page issue of May 10, 1903, following his instructions, celebrated the paper's spectacular triumph, restated its political and moral imperatives, and revealed its financial secrets. In those 20 years the World had earned a total income of more than

$67 million, had expenses of some $46 million, and its daily circulation had skyrocketed from 9,669 to 518,707.

But, to Pulitzer, "The highest satisfaction felt by the director of the World in its success comes from the reflection that it has not been won by any sacrifice of principle, any surrender of conviction, any appeal to party spirit or class prejudice." Among the published congratulations was one from ex-president Cleveland, who conceded that although he had "quite often differed with The World very broadly, I would, however, be ashamed if any difference between us made it difficult for me to cheerfully testify to the notable service which this great newspaper has rendered within the last twenty years, to the cause of democracy." Including, of course, getting Cleveland elected. It was a generous tribute to a paper whose reporters had hounded him mercilessly on his honeymoon! Pulitzer also reminded readers: "Mr. Blaine himself [Cleveland's Republican opponent] had no doubt and freely said that the use instantly made by The World of the millionaires' banquet [which it cartooned as Belshazzar's Feast] and of the "Rum, Romanism and Rebellion speech of Dr. Burchard influenced far more than enough voters in his city to decide the result."

The anniversary issue featured "Twenty Years' History of the World: Its Aims and Some of Its Achievements" by James Creelman; "Twenty Typical Fights in Which the World Has Battled With Earnest Sincerity"; "Opinions of the World from Richard Croker, John F. Carroll, ex-Mayor Van Wyck and other men whom it has always opposed from principle"; "Twenty Memorable World Cartoons that have helped to Make History"; "Twenty great criminals whom the World has helped to bring to justice"; "The Press Today" by U.S. Supreme Court Justice David Brewer; "Twenty Years of the Army and Navy" by Nelson Miles, commander of the U.S. Army, and George Dewey, admiral of the U.S. Navy. Among the "experts in almost every field of human endeavor" writing specially for the World were airship inventor Alberto Santos-Dumont; Pierre Curie; Alexander Graham Bell; Columbia University's professor Michael Pupin; and British prime minister Arthur Balfour, who celebrated Anglo-American brotherhood.

Pulitzer was in Bad Homburg, Germany, when Arthur Billing, who had put in five high-tension years as one of his secretaries, asked for a less arduous position. Pulitzer agreed to his request to leave the secretariat and work at the World—a rest cure by contrast. London correspondent James Tuohy then had to find a quick replacement. It wasn't easy. He wrote to Pulitzer that a man named Foggo "was very pleasant, intelligent, and good-humored, plays the violin, has been all over the world, has excellent references, but he frankly admitted that reading had not occupied much of his time. He rides well [but] as to his capacity to gut a magazine or book satisfactorily I am much in doubt. [A second prospect] impressed me most favorably as to his intelligence, agreeableness and conversational capacity, but unfortunately he is flat-footed to such an extent that makes him almost hobble along, turning out his toes markedly [presumably making him a noisy walker]. [A third applicant] drank nothing but diluted wine, and didn't appear to care much for the pleasures of the table. He is undoubtedly a man of ability and cultivation, but he is not what you would call festive, and has an anxious, worried look. He doesn't dress very well and has something of a slouchy gait, with very high shoulders. His temperament, possibly, has been affected by overwork when he was at University."

Pulitzer had briefly settled in Etretat in July when several of Tuohy's screened nominees arrived to be put to the final test, including a German baron who claimed to be a brilliant musician well versed in European literature. Only one, Lindsay Bashford, survived and he lasted just over a year.

The restless Pulitzer had moved to St. Moritz, Switzerland, when Brad Merrill cabled him that Columbia's president Butler was still reluctant to have Harvard's president Eliot on the board of advisers for the School of Journalism. Instead Butler suggested that they simply get Eliot to endorse the school.

But Pulitzer was through with negotiating. Exasperated, he cabled Merrill: "Understand jealousy. Telegraph Butler my insistence. Unalterable. Final."

Butler caved. Five days later the *World* announced on page one: SCHOOL OF JOURNALISM FOR COLUMBIA UNIVERSITY. The *New York Times* also carried the news on its front page.

Apart from Butler, seven advisory board members were listed: Hon. Whitelaw Reid, Greeley's successor as editor of the *New York Tribune*; John Hay, secretary of state; St. Clair McKelway, editor of the *Brooklyn Eagle*; Andrew D. White, founder and first president of Cornell University; Charles W. Eliot, president of Harvard University; Victor F. Lawson, editor of the *Chicago Daily News*; and Charles H. Taylor, editor of the *Boston Globe*. Pulitzer's careful choices were among the most brilliant and accomplished men in the country. Hay, for example, was not only Theodore Roosevelt's secretary of state but also had been Abraham Lincoln's assistant private secretary and McKinley's ambassador to Britain. Hay was also a lawyer, poet, novelist, and historian, who had written for the *New York Tribune*, and had coauthored with John Nicolay a twelve-volume Lincoln biography. Pulitzer's justification for the school seemed irrefutable: "The lawyer, who may imperil your fortune by ten lines of erroneous legal advice; the doctor, in whose opinion, good or bad, may repose all the possibilities of life or death for those whom you love—from these men the State exacts, as a rule, from eight to ten years of arduous preparation; but the newspaper men, who are in many directions the informers and teachers of the people, the exponents and to some degree the makers of public opinion which rules communities and governs states and the nation, have hitherto received no special preparation for their delicate and important tasks."

Pulitzer was giving five hundred thousand dollars of the two million dollars for a journalism school building on Morningside Heights. He asked for the building to bear his name after his death and to contain a tablet inscribed "To the Memory of My Daughter Lucille."

At midsummer, Pulitzer told Joe to take a two-week vacation at Bar Harbor and then get back to work in the *World*'s New York business office, advising him to study "particularly what other men are doing. If you could simply learn to know who is really doing the real work of direction, suggestion, initiative, from whom the ideas emanate, you would be doing capital work."

Late in August, now in Carlsbad, Germany, Pulitzer got a letter from Seth Low, former president of Columbia University, congratulating him for endowing a journalism school. In his reply (headed "Private and confidential except as noted") Pulitzer reminded Low that he had proposed a similar school to him eleven years before, when Low was Columbia's president—and been turned down. Now Pulitzer expressed his feeling that the project was doomed:

"I have already doubts whether Columbia as at present represented will do the best with it. I fear President Butler is not the right man. He has shown a spirit of jealous objection to the most eminent men on the Advisory Board; and a desire to fill their places with small incompetent men disqualified under our agreement. I say this with reluctance and regret [but] the thought is now seriously upon my mind that Harvard could do much better in carrying out my trust. President Butler has not uttered one word or thought indicating any comprehension of the subject beyond the fact that it may add to his and Columbia's prestige. . . . As I am anxious to do no man injustice, and as President Butler may make a satisfactory explanation you are at liberty to show this letter to him."

Fortunately, Pulitzer had an escape hatch. He had agreed to provide one million dollars up front but would only hand over the other million if the school lived up to his expectations. This, of course, was a strong incentive for Butler to placate him. But Pulitzer was rapidly losing faith in Butler's enthusiasm for the project and ability to direct it.

He also had little faith in his own architects when told, on arrival back in Manhattan, that his new home on East Seventy-third Street was ready. No home was ever ready until he put it to the test. And what a test! Two of his secretaries were recruited as noisemakers. A third stood in for Pulitzer, stationing himself in the master bedroom, and listened intently while the others went into the street and yelled. The two then took the elevator to the floor above the bedroom, stamping all over it as if trying to break through. Didn't hear a thing, said Pulitzer's stand-in. Assured that his bedroom was soundproof, Pulitzer spent the night there. He emerged yelling almost as loudly as the two secretaries had done in the street. Their tests had completely missed some excruciating noises: vibrations from a pump used to get rid of water in the cellar, and the opening and closing of an elevator door in the hall outside Pulitzer's bedroom.

Architect Stanford White was called to account and hired an acoustical expert from Harvard to solve the problems. He moved the sump pump to under the sidewalk and muffled the noisy elevator door so effectively that one night when firemen arrived to douse a small fire, Pulitzer slept through the entire operation. Yet he still wasn't satisfied. Although the three thicknesses of glass on each bedroom window killed the noise of passing traffic, on windy nights all three panes beat a tattoo like a kettledrum. And when that was fixed,

Pulitzer's home on East 73rd Street in New York City designed by distinguished architect Stanford White.

he was agitated by the strange sounds of the house settling and its woodwork creaking, so he hired another architect to find a solution. White's replacement designed a building attached to the rear of the main house by an enclosed soundproof passageway, the floor of which rested on ball bearings to prevent the wood from creaking when anyone walked on it. To reach Pulitzer, visitors, family, and staff had to open and close three doors hung on well-oiled hinges.

Nevertheless, he still complained that inside this cocoon he still heard factory whistles and trolleycar bells. The architect was called back and found the culprit—the chimney was acting as a funnel for street sounds. He came up with an ingenious sound trap, hanging thousands of silk threads inside the chimney to absorb the noises. It worked like a charm—so well, in fact, that his secretaries called the place the vault or the mausoleum. But it gave Pulitzer the silence he craved.

CHAPTER 26

Breaking In Frank Cobb

1904
—
56 to 57 years old

B y age fifty-seven Pulitzer, now a blind invalid for fifteen years, had arranged
his life to make use of every waking minute. At sea or on land, at home or
abroad, he always had at his command at least four secretaries, his personal
physician, his majordomo, and invariably members of his news staff. Tall and
emaciated, with a high brow, prominent hooked nose, and well-trimmed Van
Dyke beard, he often intimidated people, behaving more like an imperious
king than a commoner. Despite various illnesses he had the clear, pink complexion of a healthy girl, dressed impeccably, and was always meticulously
groomed. Although totally blind in his right eye, he could still distinguish light
and shadow with the left. It was a bright, deep blue, and gave some the uneasy
impression that he not only saw them but saw through them. Kate and the children joined him wherever he was, but only occasionally and briefly, because
the family's squabbles and noisy exuberance caused him, wrote author Allen
Churchill, "sleepless nights, savage pain, and desperate weariness." Still, he
wanted to hear from them—by mail—as often as possible.

His day began at 9:00 A.M. when his Cockney valet and confidant Jabez
Dunningham helped him to dress. During and after breakfast a secretary read
the *World*'s major stories to him, Pulitzer's body language indicating his response. If he approved, he gently stroked his nose or beard. Disapproval was
indicated by wriggling in his seat, often followed by a series of verbal rockets
such as "Story wretchedly written and edited with pitchfork. Example of bad
tendency, worse workmanship. Evidently sensationalized, badly arranged, full of
reporter's slapdoodle, diffuse and verbose. This tendency must stop."

When Pulitzer had finished dictating the critical cables, leavened by occasional words of approval, a second secretary took over. He read out highlighted
clippings from rival New York papers and major U.S. and European news-

Though blind, Pulitzer still rode. Here he is (left) in New York City's Central Park with secretary Arthur Billing beside him and coachman Eugene Stewart following.

papers, which gave Pulitzer ideas for *World* stories and editorials. Then a third secretary read Pulitzer's mail to him and recorded his replies.

Before lunch he went horse riding with a secretary alongside, and coachman Eugene Stewart bringing up the rear, or he walked arm-in-arm with a secretary or two—on deck if at sea, expecting to be at most enthralled and at least diverted by their nonstop conversation. Secretary Alleyne Ireland prepared for this task by stuffing "human interest" news clips into his left-hand coat pocket. Pulitzer invariably held the man's right arm as they walked together, leaving Ireland free to dip into his left pocket whenever he ran out of ideas and needed a new one. The clips, he recalled, "covered every imaginable topic—small cases in the magistrates' courts, eccentric entertainments at Newport, dinners to visiting authors in New York, accounts of performing animals, infant prodigies, new inventions, additions to the Metropolitan Museum, announcements of new plays, anecdotes about prominent men and women, instances of foolish extravagance among the rich. [Once] when he had complained of feeling utterly tired out mentally I asked him if he would like me to stop talking. 'No, no,' he replied at once; 'never stop talking or reading.'"

All the secretaries on duty joined him for lunch, competing to impress him with their verbal jousting and gymnastics. When the definition of "chaperon" was up for grabs, Thwaites topped the lot with: "A social instrument to defeat the ends of nature." Pulitzer got a kick out of that. He also enjoyed their good-humored badinage, particularly one exchange between a British and American secretary when they were relaxing with him on a boat deck. The American called the British an unenterprising lot, to which the Brit replied: "You are typical of a species of American. There you sit in a rocking-chair chewing gum. One is movement without progress and the other is mastication without nourishment."

Getting Pulitzer to take his daily siesta was quite a production. A secretary had to talk him to sleep. As Pulitzer lay on his bed, sometimes in pajamas, usually after just removing his boots and coat, the assigned secretary, said Ireland, began reading "in a clear, incisive voice. After a few minutes Mr. Pulitzer would say 'softly' and the secretary's voice was lowered until, though it was still audible, it assumed a monotonous and soothing quality. After a while the order came 'more softly.' At this point the reader ceased to form his words and commenced to murmur indistinctly. If, after ten minutes of this murmuring, J. P. remained motionless it was to be assumed that he was asleep; and the secretary's duty was to go on murmuring until Mr. Pulitzer awoke and told him to stop or to commence actual reading again. This murmuring might last for two hours, and it was a very difficult art to acquire, for at the slightest change in the pitch of the voice, at a sneeze, or a cough, Mr. Pulitzer would wake with a start, and an unpleasant quarter of an hour followed."

The afternoon was spent much as the morning. Dinner was at seven and then serious subjects, especially politics, were discouraged. However, should anyone dare to state something as a fact, Pulitzer would put him through a rigorous, minutely detailed cross-examination until he had justified his assertion or been proved wrong. At nine Pulitzer retired to his library, when a secretary read for an hour while Mr. Mann, the German secretary, played Liszt, Wagner, Beethoven, Brahms, and Chopin on the piano nearby. At times the reader had to raise his voice to be heard, in competition with the piano and Pulitzer himself, who whistled softly along with the music and beat time with his hand. Despite his usual hypersensitivity to noise, Pulitzer reveled in this medley of words and music, and when the reader was drowned out would ask him to "please read that last passage, and do try to read it distinctly."

Early in the year, Pulitzer decided his chief editorial writer, sixty-four-year-old William Merrill, had grown too tired and timid for the job and began a search for his replacement. Pulitzer's son Ralph, who had joined the five-man editorial writing team under Merrill along with Mark Twain's nephew Samuel Moffett, was not even in the running. Pulitzer wanted a laconic, lively, and lucid writer well versed in foreign affairs, especially as Japan, resenting Russia's influence in the Far East, had just made a sneak attack on the Russian Fleet. The replacement also had to pass the soup test. As Pulitzer biographer James Barrett remarked: "If a candidate for an editorial position on the *World* guzzled, smacked his lips, or tried to mix soup with air, using his mouth as a carburetor—he was lost." To be hired or avoid being fired, "every *World* man must be able to truthfully say: 'I eat soup but I do not inhale it.'"

Having considered and rejected every editorial writer in New York, Pulitzer told reporter Samuel Williams to tour the country to find the right man. He was to read the editorials in local papers and then to interview likely prospects. Eventually Williams cabled Pulitzer: "Think I have found editor, Frank Cobb, Detroit Free Press. Knows American history and biography. Has a passion for politics. Only handicap is he over-admires Theodore Roosevelt. Writes with punch in last paragraph."

That was not enough for Pulitzer. What did Cobb know about American history? Had he read historians "Rhodes, McMaster, Trevelyan, Parkman? What works on the constitution and constitutional law? Has he read Buckle's history of civilization? Where did he stand during Bryan free silver campaigns? What about the state of his health? How tall is he? Is his voice harsh or agree-able? My ears are very sensitive. Take him to dinner and note his table manners. Is his disposition cheerful? Sound out his ambitions; whether satisfied or looking for a larger field. Be very careful to give no intimation I am interested. Describe minutely his appearance, color of eyes, shape of forehead, manner-isms, how he dresses, search his brain for everything there is in it. JP."

Williams reported that the thirty-four-year-old "Cobb was joyously candid and innocently revealed himself." He was tall, muscular, bright-eyed, and clean-shaven, and had worked in a sawmill and as a schoolteacher, reporter, and political correspondent. He had read all the books on Pulitzer's list, was against Bryan and free silver, admired Roosevelt but had written some anti-Roosevelt editorials. He was cheerful, had a pleasant voice, good table manners, eating "his soup without a gurgle."

Pulitzer complained that the sample Cobb editorials read to him were "not incisive, terse, and direct enough," but still summoned him to Jekyll Island in March for the usual third degree. Afterward Pulitzer expressed cautious opti-mism: "Cobb knows American history better than anyone I have ever found. [Yet] he has that damnable Roosevelt obsession and he must learn to be brief. But in time, we can make a real editor of him."

Merrill got the news that his eventual replacement was to start on a trial basis in May at a hundred dollars a week and under the code name Gram-marite. "I hope you will maintain your position as chief of writers for a very long term, to your satisfaction and my own," Pulitzer told Merrill, who surely knew his days were numbered. "I will forgive dullness in all other articles, if you will only manage to have one leader strong, striking and respect-commanding. After a while people will be educated to look for that leader, and therefore the man who writes it should touch no other thing the same day. Indeed, I will give him forty-eight hours, making him rewrite it sixteen times. Do please take a little pains with Ralph. Talk to him on topics and questions of the hour. Also show him all my notes, directions, cables and perhaps, this too. And don't for-get the clippings."

Pulitzer soon became absorbed in the looming presidential election. Roosevelt was trying for a second term. Bored by his duties in Congress, William Randolph Hearst also announced his bid for the top spot at the White House, a prospect Pulitzer found unnerving if not unbearable. Anxious for Pulitzer's support, Roosevelt invited him to lunch or dinner at his convenience. Pulitzer used his ill health as an excuse to decline. He had soured on Roosevelt since the trust-buster, whom he had applauded, now welcomed the trust's directors as his financial backers. Hearst being out of the question, Pulitzer supported Alton Parker, chief judge of the New York State Court of Appeals, as the Democratic nominee. So did Ochs in his *New York Times*.

Despite his interest in the outcome, Pulitzer accepted the advice from Kate and others to escape to Europe to avoid the nerve-wracking excitement of the election campaigns. He told Brad Merrill: "I am going away really to escape thought. I have no rest if my mind is to be disturbed." But by the time he reached Ireland the news blackout was killing him and he gave instructions to have Hearst's editorials sent to him every day.

Alarmed by Hearst's successful self-promotion in his eight newspapers, Pulitzer ordered Creelman to call on the lethargic Judge Parker and encourage him to "say some manly ringing words on such paramount issues as trusts, Philippines, tariff reform, shocking extravagance in Washington . . . etc."

His brief cables to Kate were mostly complaints about his health and indications that he was hopelessly engrossed in the coming election. She wrote to him once a week, and on May 13 "wished there was more sunshine in your life—worry & wearisome work are dull companions. If you could only take pleasure in things outside your work it would be a Godsend. I thought of the 21st anniversary of the paper! Twenty-one long years of slavery for you—we will pass over what it has been to me—and my heart was so full of conflicting elements of pride & pain, that I could not speak of it."

When Pulitzer reached Carlsbad he gave in totally to what he called his foolish weakness for politics, and demanded a weekly report on the political situation. It wasn't enough. He summoned Samuel Williams to join him to give a blow-by-blow account of the fight between Parker and Hearst for the Democratic nomination.

By chance Pulitzer met Adolph Ochs, publisher of the *New York Times*, in Carlsbad, and they hit it off. For hours the rivals discussed national and international politics like old friends. In eight years Ochs had increased his paper's circulation from nine thousand to a hundred thousand and had just moved into a new building—even taller than the Dome—on Forty-second Street. His success had persuaded the city to rename Longacre Square, Times Square.

Pulitzer amazed him, he wrote later, as "a man of great strength and great intellectual power, and of education and culture. He is a man among thousands. He is positive, well informed on current topics, truly a philosopher. It is a great and tragic misfortune that he is virtually blind. If he had not that affliction he would be a tremendous figure in national affairs." Pulitzer told Ochs

Hearst's presidential
bid ridiculed as a
comic-strip parade.

that he was an invalid and suffered continually from severe headaches. Ochs
noticed for himself that he was so nervous and sensitive to noise "that he
objected to the scraping of the brakes of the carriage wheels. He was very cordial, and very cordial to The New York Times. He spoke disparagingly of his
own New York World."

After moving to the Hotel Splendide at Aix-les-Bains, France, Pulitzer
wrote to Ochs: "Do give me the pleasure of seeing you again if you come to Bar
Harbor, and let me congratulate you upon the splendid growth and success of
The Times. I have the Times sent to me abroad when the World is forbidden
and most of the news I really receive from your paper. You have a very, very
able editorial page."

What a contrast Pulitzer was to Hearst: Ochs's success seemed to have irritated Hearst into a venomous anti-Semitic signed editorial, hardly rational in a
presidential candidate, which appeared in the *Morning American* and the *Evening Journal*. In it Hearst repeated the false rumor that the *Times* was controlled by Jewish bankers, and caricatured Ochs as an "oily little commercial
gentleman with obsequiously curved shoulders."

Although thousands of miles away in Europe ostensibly taking it easy,
Pulitzer was fully engaged in the presidential race. On June 15, a week before
the Republican Party Convention in Chicago, he advised editorial writer Samuel
Moffett, "Shut yourself up for two or three days; at home, if you prefer, and
write one editorial on Roosevelt, reviewing his career apropos of his nomination

and presentation for re-election. It may be hung upon the unquestionable shouting, yelling, yellow plush eulogisms brought out by his nomination. These, very crudely and hurriedly, are the main points: 1. Absolute fairness. Put together all that can possibly be said about the wonderfully interesting career of the young man, who less than ten years ago only had a little local office—noted for his teeth. Do him full justice for whatever he has done, whatever courage, physical or moral, he has displayed. For instance, his treatment of negroes— the Booker Washington incident, the Northern merger decision [Roosevelt had successfully prosecuted the Northern Securities Company, controlled by J. P. Morgan, using the Sherman Antitrust Act against monopolies], etc., etc. Then, having done him full justice, unroll the indictment. I will not trouble you by giving you the specifications. [Then he did!] My idea is that his real weakness and vulnerability lie in his jingoism, blatant militarism, unconstitutionalism, in the personal Government he has substituted for that of *law*, in what [William] Nelson [editor of the *Kansas City Star*] very well termed, his lawless mind— Panama, Philippines, Wood, pensions, the Cuban letter. You must remember other instances. Don't forget, guardedly, to indicate that in spite of all his follies, even political crimes, his re-election seems probable unless the Democrats act with considerable wisdom both in presenting the opposition candidate and putting him on the right platform. But, in that case, intimate that Roosevelt could be beaten."

In June, as Pulitzer expected, presidential incumbent Theodore Roosevelt was named the Republican choice for a second term. The following month, to Pulitzer's relief, his own choice, Judge Parker, was voted the Democratic nominee for president, knocking Hearst out of the running. Now in the battle to beat Roosevelt, Pulitzer smelled corruption in George Cortelyou's role as Roosevelt's national campaign manager. As he had suspected, Cortelyou was still collecting big campaign contributions from the very trusts Roosevelt had been praised for busting—from railroad companies that had been charged with violating interstate commerce laws; from the Standard Oil Company, which had previously opposed Roosevelt's actions in curbing its power; and from many other big corporations.

Cobb's early editorial attempts to expose Cortelyou for accepting what appeared to be bribes disappointed Pulitzer, who cabled William Merrill from aboard the SS *Baltic*: "I hope Cobb will improve with age, but the first two editorials you sent as excellent specimens of irony (one on Cortelyou's selection as chairman of the Nat. Committee; the other on Rockefeller's wife going to church) were to my mind or taste, very poor. Flippancy, dear old fellow, triviality, frivolity, are not irony—please underscore these few words and put them in Cobb's brain. Irony requires a delicacy of touch which triviality does not supply—indeed, destroys. The Cortelyou article should not have been treated in any except the most serious spirit. No more shameless offense against public morality was ever committed by Mr. Roosevelt."

THE COUP d'ETAT.

New York World, November 9, 1903.

The *World*'s view of Theodore Roosevelt as a blatant militarist.

Because the latest political news was taking too long to reach him, Pulitzer returned to Bar Harbor in August, welcomed by Kate shortly after their twenty-sixth wedding anniversary. She had written to him that she hoped he would be "in a very good humor, very tender, in fact the man of 26 years ago." But he was too aggravated by the weakness of his candidate and the inadequate performances of his *World* staff to fulfill her hopes. He spat out a memo to Seitz telling him to stay at the office every day until the last issue of the paper had left on the last truck, and to investigate every department, "watching, observing, reforming wherever possible every screw, every man, exactly as if [he] had just begun as a new man."

When Kate saw how obsessed he was with his work, she took off for Europe with her secretary-companion, Maud Macarow, and two servants. Despite her generous eight-thousand-dollar-a-month allowance, she asked him for more, explaining, "My only extravagance, if it could be called that, has been automobiling to Geneva and back. I have bought a few furs there for Edith—I am chuckling at your despair at this statement. I can hear you say she would find something to buy were she in a forest untrodden by civilized man, but you are quite mistaken, I never buy anything save the strictly needful. You should consider yourself very fortunate that you have such an economical wife. My own feeling is that you should be a little ashamed of my parsimony. Had I any spirit of enterprise I should collect things, pictures, objets d'art, priceless fans, price-less snuff boxes, have a hobby, such as a self-respecting wife of a very rich man should have."

Pulitzer more likely swore than chuckled over her letter, then cabled her the cash. She had a point, of course. He spent a fortune on himself.

No one marveled more over Pulitzer's abilities than fellow workaholic Charles Chapin. He later recalled in his Sing Sing cell (he had killed his wife in a failed mutual suicide attempt) that "we had youth, health and numbers on our side, yet this man, aged by suffering, tormented by ill-health, loaded with responsibility, kept pace with our united labors. We brought a thousand offer-ings to his judgment; many of them he rejected with an impatient cry of 'Next! Next! For God's sake!'" He illuminated what came to him "as crude material for conversation [until it] assumed a new form, everything unessential rejected, everything essential disclosed in clear and vigorous English."

Chapin remembered most vividly "the capaciousness of his understanding, the breadth of his experience, the range of his information, and set them side by side with his blindness and . . . shattered constitution. [Then] I forget the severity of his discipline, I marvel only that his self-control should have served him so well in the tedious business of breaking a new man to his service."

Cobb, the latest man on trial and under fire, was included in Pulitzer's overall critique of one issue of the paper: "Good lead on the Kaiser Wilhelm story—tell Cobb not to indulge in fancy guesswork—does he know the situation between France and Germany getting worse? Get the facts. Rest of page weak—bank robber described as short—what is short? Four feet? Five feet? Be exact. Electric power utility scandal written too vague—I know the name of every man involved and so do you. Put them in. The World protects no one. Editor-ial on Philippines good—keep it up—the World favored war with Spain but should have given [the Cubans] independence immediately afterward—call it right name—Teddy Roosevelt imperialism—woman suffrage article poor—ridicule not effective."

Another man Pulitzer was breaking in and on whom he was equally tough was his son Joe. His younger son had been agitating to get out of the Dome business office to become a reporter. Pulitzer refused, but when they were horseriding together at Bar Harbor he listened to Joe's plea to attend Harvard in order to prepare for a career in journalism and politics. Without a college edu-cation, he said, he felt handicapped. Kate supported Joe, telling her husband to "remember that nature does not make us all alike and that there never was a more loyal, honest nature than his." Suspecting that Joe merely wanted to have a good time, Pulitzer imposed strict conditions. If Joe passed the Harvard entrance exam he would finance him for a six-month trial period, paying doc-tors' bills and for his room furnishings and giving him an allowance of nine hundred dollars to cover all other expenses. He must account for every cent spent, keep a daily diary recording the times he got up and went to bed, plus any original thoughts and newly acquired information beyond the banal. He'd

Fortunately, Frank
Cobb could eat "his
soup without a gurgle."

be expected to read and review both editions of the *World* every day except Sundays. And he must keep in mind that having been expelled from St. Mark's for a stupid prank, doing well at Harvard was his chance to redeem himself. Any slipup of any kind during the six-month trial period would mean the end of his Harvard education; there would be no second chance. Joe agreed to the conditions.

To ensure that there was no misunderstanding, Pulitzer persuaded him to write down the conditions he'd accepted and mail the agreement to him. This Joe did, signing the letter "Your loving son."

With his family out of the way, Pulitzer showed his staff how to attack a political opponent, defying his own demands for brevity by filling an entire page and a half of the *World* to roast Roosevelt. Part of it read: "You know that these corporations which are determined to govern the Government itself are the real enemies of the Republic. You knew it before you began to understand how strongly secret alliances with the corporations would make for your political advancement. You have not kept the faith, Mr. President, in your promise of publicity in the interests of the public as to the affairs of the corporations. Why have you turned your back on your splendid promises?" Pulitzer suggested that Roosevelt could make amends by telling the country how much the following had contributed to his campaign: the beef trust, paper trust, coal trust, sugar trust, oil trust, tobacco trust, steel trust, insurance trust, the national banks, and the six great railroad trusts. Pulitzer noted that money was still pouring into Roosevelt's campaign from such men as Morgan, Harriman, Rockefeller, and Gould, who previously "were clamoring for your political life [but] now believe that the best interests of the country will be served by your election." Pulitzer challenged Roosevelt to deny that they were filling his campaign chest because they expected him to submit to them after his election.

To keep up the pressure, Pulitzer told William Merrill to hammer away at "the great scandal involved in Cortelyou collecting millions from Corporations he was appointed to investigate . . . and do this day after day with fresh examples."

Roosevelt was enraged by Pulitzer's implication that he could be bought and that the trusts supported him because they expected a quid pro quo after his anticipated November triumph. Yet he did nothing to discourage the influx of corporate cash until a reporter revealed that Rockefeller's Standard Oil trust had sent him a check for $100,000 (in fact, for $125,000). Roosevelt then ordered it returned, but Cortelyou chose to ignore the order and kept it in the campaign treasury. Had Pulitzer known, he would have gone ballistic. Years later, when he made a proposal—yet to be enacted—to ban the use of corporate funds for political purposes, Roosevelt conceded that Pulitzer was right to suspect the corrupting influence of big money.

As election fever grew, Pulitzer again tried to avoid catching it by escaping to London. There, one crisp winter morning, he and secretary Norman Thwaites were chatting as they walked their horses in Hyde Park. Suddenly a boy threw his cap into the air, spooking Thwaites' horse, which raced off with him to the end of Rotten Row, leaving Pulitzer far behind. As Thwaites rode back, Pulitzer was still talking but had changed the subject to having his portrait painted by the fashionable American artist John Singer Sargent and comparing him favorably with French artists. When Thwaites "drew alongside him rather breathless," Pulitzer asked for his opinion. "I quite agree," he replied with a gasp, then, when he had recovered his breath, he explained his absence. "'I thought you were rather silent,'" Pulitzer said.

While in London he became frustrated by reports of Judge Parker's listless campaign. Repeatedly, Pulitzer urged him to go on the attack and expose the huge, suspect funding of the Republican candidate. Parker finally responded, calling Republican donations from corporations "blackmail." But it was too little, too late to affect the outcome. Roosevelt won the election with 7,628,834 popular votes to Parker's 5,884,401—the overwhelming victory astounding even the victor. Parker lost, Pulitzer concluded, because he "acted the perfect dolt during the whole campaign in pompous . . . overdignity and silence on this very question of campaign contributions. The World alone hammered and howled about them all during the campaign."

CHAPTER 27

Unmasking Corrupt Insurance Companies

1905

—

57 to 58 years old

At age 29, James Hazen Hyde was a majority stockholder of the Equitable Life Assurance Society. A Harvard-educated Francophile, he dressed in silk shirts and eye-catching red-heeled shoes, and rode around town as if he owned it. But what caught the *World*'s attention was a fabulous costume party he threw in Manhattan's Sherry Hotel. On January 31 Hyde had its ballroom converted into a replica of Versailles' Hall of Mirrors during the reign of Louis XVI, and hired the Metropolitan Opera orchestra and a French actress to entertain guests coming from all over the world. One local guest was young Franklin D. Roosevelt. The *World* report made the event seem outrageously extravagant but avoided the excesses of other papers, which called it an orgy and implied that the French actress was Hyde's mistress. What alerted the *World* to a potential blockbuster was the suspicion that Hyde was milking the insurance company and defrauding the public to sustain his self-indulgent lifestyle.

Meanwhile, at Harvard, Joe seemed to be emulating Hyde the big spender—though on a smaller scale. He startled his father with the news that he had only 65 cents in the bank, 29 cents in his pockets, and debts of $149.43. Pulitzer reacted with surprising moderation: he sent Ralph up to Cambridge to straighten Joe out, settled his debts, and even offered him a $250 fur coat for the winter, which he declined. When Pulitzer pressed his chastened son to include more substantial comments about the *World* in his letters, he obliged with: "For Heaven's sake stop all Cuticura ads. 'Baby's Face a Mass of Pimples' and 'Itching all day long' are some of the fascinating little bon-mots. A paper can hardly be called high toned when it prints such filth as this." Pulitzer ignored the advice, although he doubtless agreed, but medical ads were a big source of income.

Instead of explaining the business reality behind the ads, Pulitzer changed the subject: he feared that his son was being led astray by a young woman he met on weekend trips to New York. "You are wrong," Joe replied. "Although of course she doesn't know it, she encourages me to work faithfully and to keep straight. A darn sight more, in my opinion, than you can say for the average girl and especially the average N.Y. girl!'"

But his grades that semester justified Pulitzer's fears that Joe was out of control. He had a B− in government, a C+ in English, a C in French, and a D in American history, which, at least, he said, wasn't an F. Joe warned his father that his grade in European history, yet to be disclosed, might be his worst, because the professor, "old McVane is such a sleepy, uninteresting old ass," and the course covered too much territory. Looking on the bright side, he mentioned that "eight of the nicest lads in the class have just been dropped out of college for poor marks," and he, at least, was "hanging on by his teeth."* Instead of pulling him out, as was justified by their agreement, Pulitzer ordered Joe to stay at Harvard throughout the summer and to take additional courses in algebra, archaeology, and architecture.

On Jekyll Island for what was left of the winter, Pulitzer frequently turned his thoughts from family affairs to the Russo-Japanese War. Since February 1904 the two countries had been fighting over territory and influence in the Far East. Not having correspondents in either country or with either battle fleet, Pulitzer was getting secondhand and second-rate war news. So he ordered his bureau chief in Paris, Stephen McKenna, to restrict his cables to news of extraordinary importance and then to be brief. McKenna was also to try for interviews with newsworthy Russians such as Tolstoy, Gorky, "the czar himself describing [his] features etc. all by mail." In the same cable Pulitzer characterized AP war news as "exaggerated and fakey" and required his London bureau chief, Tuohy, to pay less attention to the mostly phony French accounts of the Russo-Japanese War and instead to watch German papers for both news and pictures.

For weeks Pulitzer had been baffled by the mysterious maneuvers of the Russians' Baltic fleet, commanded by Admiral Rojestvensky. Setting out for Japanese waters, it had fired in panic into a group of English fishing vessels in the North Sea, mistaking them for Japanese torpedo boats. The shortsighted or trigger-happy Russians killed several fishermen and almost caused a war with

---

* Joe's contemporaries at Harvard included Walter Lippmann and Heywood Broun, who later had distinguished careers on the *World*. Others included T. S. Eliot, already writing poems, and the future radical journalist, John Reed. Maybe Harvard president, Charles W. Eliot, encouraged Joe's attitude: He had advised students that the purpose of a Harvard education was to allow each man to do and think as he pleased.

Britain. After that fiasco, the Russians, barred by international law from using the Suez Canal, took the long route around the Cape of Good Hope, stopping for repairs at Madagascar before moving on. Then, expected any day to launch an attack on the Japanese fleet commanded by Admiral Togo, the Russians dropped out of sight. And no one seemed to know where they were.

"Find the Russian Baltic fleet," Pulitzer ordered a newly hired editorial writer, L. R. E. Paulin, "and publish a daily report on its progress."

"I thought the old man had lost his mind," Paulin, a former Colorado cattle rancher, admitted later. "The only thing I knew about naval affairs was what I learned on the Staten Island ferryboat. But there was a job to do and I had to do it. Every day I studied maps intently. Every day I put out an editorial, surmising that Rojestvensky might be here, there, or somewhere. I had one assurance — as long as [he] remained in hiding nobody could contradict me. Luckily, in one of my daily guesses, I placed the Russian fleet near the Straits of Singapore. Suddenly, after three painful weeks, the Japanese Admiralty announced that Rojestvensky's fleet had been sighted. Guess where? In the Straits of Singapore! I relayed the news to JP and breathed a sigh of relief — 'I hope the old man is satisfied now.' But in a very few hours, another message came from JP: 'Have Paulin say for me that Togo will wipe the Russians off the sea when, where he chooses to meet them.' I was dumbfounded. I talked to Frank Cobb, John Heaton, and other editorial writers. We thought the old man must be upset. We tried to dissuade him by telegraph, but his only answer was: 'Follow directions.' So, I wrote the editorial; Rojestvensky's fleet was plunging into the China Sea to its doom! How foolish and wicked of the Czar to insist upon this Russian sacrifice! That was the tenor. Events proved that JP was right. Just as the Chief predicted, Togo did fall upon Rojestvensky [on May 27] and he did wipe the Russians off the sea."

Nobody has ever explained how Pulitzer pulled it off.

While Paulin had been speculating about the Russians, World reporter David Ferguson had been investigating Wall Street rumors sparked by James Hazen Hyde's lavish party in January. The result appeared on February 12, with the insurance company's president, James Alexander, accusing Hyde of tapping the Equitable treasury to pay for the party. Hyde denied the charges and threatened the World with a libel suit. Ferguson responded by disclosing a round robin signed by twenty-six Equitable officials who had agreed to resign en masse if Hyde remained in control.

A director of the insurance company, hardheaded Henry Clay Frick — who'd survived an assassination attempt by anarchist Alexander Berkman — chaired a committee of fellow Equitable executives to interrogate Hyde and Alexander. The committee concluded that they should both be dismissed. The two quickly reconciled and gathered a majority of "dummy directors" or rubber stamps to defeat the Frick report by 24 to 15.

"Rejection of the Frick report was not surprising," the World commented. "A grand jury can hardly be expected to indict itself. The fact remains, nevertheless, that the committee pleaded guilty on behalf of Equitable to the charges of corruption."

Ferguson continued to dig. He discovered that major insurance companies were controlled by a few individuals who were reaping vast fortunes from speculations with insurance funds—not a cent going to their small stockholders. Ferguson also found that these same insurance companies "kept a huge fund for corruption, employed to buy or suppress laws, with [lobbyists] who kept their eyes on the legislation all over the land, and used money lavishly to carry out the mandates of the management." Any reforms proposed were quickly quashed by bribing state legislatures and congressmen. The Big Three—Equitable, New York Life, and Mutual—had bloated the coffers of the Republican Party during presidential elections between 1896 and 1904 to keep in power the men who protected the racket.

Until the *World* broke the story, small stockholders had not the slightest suspicion they were being robbed, because many company bigwigs, such as Astor, Vanderbilt, Depew, Frick, and Harriman, were respected if not revered as pillars of society.

Pulitzer was in Carlsbad, Germany, in the early spring when he caught up with the latest news of the insurance probe and criticized his staff for being overzealous. To their dismay he urged them to concentrate on other scandals, especially the street railway system in St. Louis and the gas corporations in New York. "Nothing short of revolution can mend these evils," he wrote to Cobb. "I consider the bribery of Senators to prevent remedy and reform an infinitely greater evil morally and politically than oppression of the people by excessive charge."

But his staff were eager to pursue the insurance scandal. Was Pulitzer's order to put it on the back burner and then proceed with caution because he was—incredibly—trying to protect a friend, or—even more incredibly—trying to protect his own financial interests? Had Phillips' *The Great God Success* been prophetic and was life imitating art?

In June there must have been a spontaneous sigh of relief in the Dome editorial office when Pulitzer approved several editorials denouncing Equitable Life Assurance corruption.

Earlier in the year, Pulitzer had arranged to be immortalized by portrait painter John Singer Sargent, reigning favorite of the rich and the famous. He was said to reproduce what he saw with astonishing accuracy and even to capture the soul of his subject. Someone had jokingly tried to discourage Pulitzer by warning him that Sargent exposed his sitters' "inner weaknesses as well as their strengths." Undeterred, when he arrived in London in late June, Pulitzer had agreed to a six-day sitting. He told Sargent of the warning he had received but said he was not afraid of exposure and "wanted to be remembered just as I really am, with all my strain and suffering there." Contrary to his reputation, Sargent made no claim to psychological insight. He didn't even guarantee that

John Singer Sargent's striking painting of Joseph Pulitzer in 1905, when he was fifty-eight and blind.

the result would be pleasing. "I paint what I see," he said. "I don't dig beneath the surface for things that don't appear before my eyes."

Each morning, Pulitzer rode in Hyde Park with secretary Thwaites before heading for the artist's studio. Warned that Pulitzer might prove a difficult customer, Sargent was surprised, he told Thwaites, to find him "delightful." Pulitzer had, in fact, become a much more benign presence, even tolerating Sargent smoking Egyptian cigarettes without a murmur of protest. Had a secretary dared to light up in his presence he would have yelled bloody murder. But Pulitzer couldn't maintain his nonchalance for long. When a man who bored him called at the studio, hoping to renew their acquaintance, Thwaites saw "a look of fury and impatience" entirely change Pulitzer's expression as he refused to see the visitor. And Sargent saw Pulitzer living up to his reputation.

Did Sargent capture what was there? Pulitzer biographer Swanberg called it "a remarkable portrait of duality, showing the character, intellect and intensity blended with a touch of the Mephistophelian." To Seitz, "the pain and invalidism of years show on his face, blended with high intellect, energy of character and fierceness of temper. It is Joseph Pulitzer as Time and Trouble moulded him." Pulitzer biographer Barrett believed that "the left side of the face expresses tenderness, the right side, with the totally blind eye, is full of anger, and a touch of cruelty. Put a piece of paper over one side and then the other and you can easily see the contrast." Or consider Louis Starr's view that it shows "the fierce determination with which Joseph Pulitzer alternately inspired and terrorized his employees to editorial greatness." Pulitzer himself, of course, could appraise neither it, nor the painting Sargent did of Kate Pulitzer.

Returning to New York on the liner *Cedric*, Pulitzer cabled to Cobb: "How dreadfully slow all these state officials have been to catch on and how terribly strong and firm in trying really to defend, bolster up or hush up the Equitable business."

Learning that Senator Chauncey Depew, with whom he was on friendly terms, had a twenty-thousand-dollar annual retainer from Equitable, he instructed Cobb to "review him but not without giving him a chance to explain his position. I hope he may possibly set himself right or only half wrong. What a spectacle! A Senator of the United States! Extraordinary coincidence that so many Republican politicians had their fingers in the Equitable pie. Be careful. Only the real truth, if possible." Followed by: "I don't want to stifle the paper in its duty, don't want favoritism and am suggesting no suppression. But I don't think it necessary to kick him too hard. When a man is down we may show a little charity—especially towards an old man of seventy-two, who has some good qualities and who has been polite. Don't misunderstand me. I have not a word to say in criticism of the hard criticism of him. But don't be unnecessarily cruel."

When the *New York Times* and other papers joined the *World* in demanding an investigation of insurance scandals, Francis Hendricks, the state insurance superintendent, belatedly held one—in private. Hendricks then kept it secret by locking the only three copies of the report in his office safe and refusing to let Governor Higgins, New York district attorney William Travers Jerome, or the press even catch a glimpse of it. It was a challenge Pulitzer's man in Albany, Louis Seibold, couldn't resist. "Every newspaperman in Albany was after that report," he recalled. "The *Herald* was offering five thousand dollars for a copy." Luckily Seibold had a friend in the Insurance Department who said that although it would be a tough job, he'd try to help. They met for dinner in New York's Central Park Casino a week later, on a Saturday, when the anonymous friend handed the six-hundred-thousand-word report to Seibold, who promised to return it by six o'clock Monday morning. Several *World* stenographers were standing by to make handwritten copies of the report. They spelled one another through Saturday night, Sunday, Sunday night, and until five-forty-five Monday morning, when the job was completed. Seibold returned the original copy to his friend, who smuggled it back to the safe in Albany.

The report was dynamite. Highlights filled eleven pages of the *World* on July 11, 1905. The *New York Times* picked it up the next day, giving the *World* credit for breaking the story.

Pulitzer arrived back from England a few days later and, fearful that the *World's* campaign might destroy public confidence in life insurance, he told

Seitz: "If there is anything I most specially would urge you, Cobb and Speer to take to heart, it is to feel personal responsibility for words spoken, a scrupulous anxiety to weigh every word before it is irretrievably too late, and it goes out to the world to be found wanting in truth and to injure the reliability of the paper; to diminish its power for good, make it distrusted, and make me sick when I read it."

During the Atlantic crossing he had dictated ninety-nine pages of notes for an editorial about the insurance scandal in which he stressed that a few bad apples did not reflect on the companies as a whole, and urged a more moderate approach. He felt that Seibold had gone overboard in his efforts to expose the entire industry. Cobb disagreed and refused to use Pulitzer's material as an editorial, running it instead as a letter a few days later and disguising its source by signing it P. J. Furious, Pulitzer ordered Cobb to be suspended for three weeks, but Cobb ignored the order and no one tried to enforce it.

Frustrated, Pulitzer called Seibold to his Seventy-third Street annex to fire him and raged: "My God, Seibold, you made a lot of trouble for me. I spend four days on shipboard writing an editorial and you do something that makes me look foolish. You deserve to be punished, Seibold; and, Great God, you shall be punished. Go down to the office and report to Bradford Merrill." To Seibold's surprise the punishment was more like a prize. At the Dome, Merrill handed him a check for one thousand dollars and a note from J. P. praising his work and concluding with: "Don't use the money to start a rival newspaper." There was no need. Pulitzer soon rehired Seibold, who eventually won a Pulitzer Prize for an interview with Woodrow Wilson.

Less than a week after firing Seibold, Pulitzer had a change of heart and urged his staff to "carry on the fight in far less space but even more vigor [and] more accuracy and less sensationalism. Sharpen attack on [Governor] Higgins. He is now really responsible as head of state." He followed up nine days later with a cautionary message: "The news columns both morning and evening must be absolutely non-partisan and the tendency to play politics for or against one or another faction by falsified headlines or in any other way is a crime that will be severely dealt with. I attach the greatest importance to nipping this tendency in the bud. It must be clear to every reporter that for any infraction of this rule he will lose his place."

Under Pulitzer's direction Cobb now produced a series of editorials that pressured Governor Higgins into a public investigation of the major insurance companies. With Charles Evans Hughes as counsel to the investigating committee, the hearing lasted from September 6 to December 30. Hughes was superb in handling the reluctant witnesses. Patient, polite, but persistent, he persuaded them to reveal the inner workings of Equitable Life Assurance and its competitors and to concede that massive sums were spent to bribe politicians, pay executives excessively high salaries, and provide them with luxurious offices.

When one witness refused to divulge "confidential" information, Hughes remarked, "There is nothing confidential about the insurance business now," and made him spill the beans. When Richard McCurdy of Mutual Life called his company "a great beneficent missionary institution," Hughes quipped, "The question comes back to the salaries of the missionaries"—which were enormous. Over sixteen years McCurdy had paid his son, Robert, $1.7 million and a son-in-law $145,687 for one year's work. The *World* calculated that McCurdy and his relatives had taken Mutual for a total of $15 million while dividends to policyholders dropped from $110 to $7.

Hughes's relentless questioning brought out that the $300,000 Mutual Life paid its chief lobbyist, Andrew Fields, for "legal expenses" was in fact to bribe politicians and entertain them in an Albany mansion called the House of Mirth, where they got free bed and board and the chance to play risk-free poker—they always won.

Lobbyists were in remarkably short supply at the hearing. Several had skipped town, as had some of the insurance executives. To avoid testifying, Equitable's James Alexander went abroad, where he died in a sanitarium. James Hazen Hyde also left the country, with enough cash to live it up in Paris for more than thirty years, only returning to the United States after Hitler invaded France. McCurdy followed Hyde overseas, where he died, but his family returned $815,000 to Mutual Life Insurance. New York Life's George Perkins returned $48,000 plus interest to the company, money that had fueled Theodore Roosevelt's election campaign. Insurance Superintendent Hendricks, who had been suspiciously reluctant to hold a public hearing and then opposed punishing the guilty, resigned.

Hughes recommended two bills to reform the insurance companies: to ban their use of lobbyists, and to make it illegal for them to bankroll politicians. And when Governor Higgins signed the bills, Pulitzer hailed it as crowning "with complete victory The World's long struggle against life insurance corruption." Seitz, less sanguine, concluded that "Republican influence of the highest order kept [the committee] from sending anyone to prison, where not a few deserved to go." Nevertheless, he believed that unmasking insurance corruption, reforming the practices of gigantic corporations, and starting Charles E. Hughes upon an exalted career—he became chief justice of the U.S. Supreme Court—were the *World*'s greatest feats.

In October, William Randolph Hearst ran for New York City's mayor against the corrupt Tammany machine. Pulitzer didn't think he had a prayer, but he admired his guts and almost supported him, advising his editorialists Heaton and Cobb to treat Hearst "without a particle of prejudice, if this be possible, judicially, concentrate on the one point that while as a matter of conviction we sincerely detest most of his professions, principles [and] purposes . . . the same conviction compels an expression of respect for his courage in accepting a candidacy which cannot lead to his election and must appear as devotion to his principles." But, to Pulitzer, the main questions were "who teaches more independence in voting, who awakens more indignation against corruption and misgovernment, who comes nearer presenting the real truth, who is more against party humbug, who against fooling the people?"

Pulitzer was right: Hearst didn't win—but largely because his opponents beat up his supporters and stole ballots likely to favor him. As the *World* reported: "Men battered and bruised were helped by friends into [Hearst's headquarters]. One man had a broken arm dangling in his sleeve. Another's head was cut and the blood was trickling through his bandages. Tammany thugs in the Lower East Side district had all but killed him. From many parts of Manhattan reports poured in of the greatest violence and crimes at the polls that New York has ever known."

Hearst demanded a recount, but it didn't help. Tammany printed new ballots and had them marked for their favorite, George McClellan, a Princeton graduate and son of the Civil War general—who turned out to be an honest mayor.

Since the spring, Pulitzer's attention had not entirely focused on the insurance scandal or other *World* affairs. At twenty-six, Ralph had fallen in love with Frederica Vanderbilt Webb, granddaughter of William Henry Vanderbilt. Pulitzer had pilloried him in the *World* twenty years earlier for avoiding taxes on a two-hundred-million-dollar fortune by claiming his expenses exceeded his income. Frederica's mother, Vanderbilt's fourth daughter, had inherited ten million dollars; her father, William Seward Webb, was a retired doctor. The Webbs lived on Fifth Avenue, wintered in Palm Beach, and summered at their thirty-five-hundred-acre estate near Burlington, Vermont.

When Pulitzer first became aware of Frederica's existence, earlier in the year at Chatwold, he put her through a rigorous interrogation to make sure she was not one of the frivolous Vanderbilts and would make a suitable partner for the future editor of the *World*. Then he gave the couple his blessing, provided they waited a few months before getting married.

He was in Carlsbad when Kate wrote to say that Ralph wanted money for an expensive engagement present for Frederica—and suggested that Pulitzer buy the young woman (code name Destiny) a piece of jewelry on his way through Paris.

Ralph, not Kate, got his response: "It was a great mistake to take shelter behind your mother. I beg you not to do it again because we have practically no communication whatever except when she wants money and if she interferes on your behalf would only prejudice your case." But he sent the money and assured Ralph, who thought his father would not be interested in hearing about Frederica: "I am interested, always have been in love affairs. My imagination is in flames & my thirst for news covets even the smallest trifle. Is there any possibility of her coming to Bar Harbor in July or August? I need hardly tell you how deeply interested I am in the young lady & how very glad I should be to have a talk with her—not frightening her as I did last time. Give her my real sincere love."

Pulitzer had another chance to test her worth when Frederica and Ralph again visited Chatwold in August. Afterward she wrote to thank him "for your kindness, and hoping that someday I may prove myself less frivolous and unambitious than you now think me."

Ralph Pulitzer and his wife, Frederica Vanderbilt Webb.

On October 14 Ralph married Frederica Vanderbilt Webb in the little Trinity Episcopal Church in Shelburne, Vermont, near her family's country estate. Eight hundred guests attended the wedding breakfast, but there was room for only 157 of them in the small church. The *New York Times* reported that his brother Joe was best man, his sister Edith a maid of honor, and that Pulitzer's wedding present to the couple was a house. It did not mention that the house, at 17 East 73rd Street, adjoined his own, nor if he and Kate were at the wedding—though both were. The *World* account of the wedding mentioned Kate but not Pulitzer—obviously what he wanted. He also gave the couple five thousand dollars for a honeymoon in the Adirondacks and Europe, made Ralph a *World* vice president, substantially increased his five-hundred-dollars-a-month salary, and upped his monthly allowance to two thousand dollars. He skipped the reception, unable to face the crowd or the music—played by an orchestra and a military band.

While the couple were still abroad on their honeymoon, Pulitzer cabled Ralph: "I wish for nothing more than that by some divine inspiration and imagination both you and Destiny could really feel in your hearts how much I have thought of you and am thinking of you. Not to speak of the tears that were in my eyes during the ceremony, when I came very near to breaking down. God bless you both."

Ralph sent an affectionate reply, wishing "I could give you some of my happiness. I looked at you as we walked down the aisle, in fact yours was the only face I saw, and I felt a lot of things that I probably would not have been able to express to you."

Pulitzer's sentimental mood didn't last long, judging by the apoplectic cable he sent to William Steigers, advertising manager of the *Post-Dispatch*, on October 25: "Please tell the editors apropos of clipping in *World* today that I have one hundred times forbidden the use of the word CATER also the word PATRON or PATRONAGE. All three words are vile, vulgar, abhorrent, absolutely forbidden. The man who wrote CATER should commit suicide."

In November Pulitzer learned that Joe was improving at Harvard. Helped by a tutor, he even got an A in German. He'd also changed his mind about having a fur coat, telling his father he now wanted one, but only for watching sports and not for classes, which would appear ostentatious. Pulitzer must have wondered if the fur coat was only for watching sports, because in his next letter Joe rhapsodized over girls he'd seen on a trip to Baltimore. By contrast, he wrote, Boston girls were, with few exceptions, "homely, stupid and dead." As Boston girls were closer to hand, perhaps it was meant to reassure his father that he wasn't having too much fun.

Pulitzer was in his usual giving mood that Christmas. He had already sent Cobb a check for his good work in writing scores of hard-hitting editorials against the corrupt insurance companies, and when Cobb declined the money, saying he was adequately paid for his work, Pulitzer insisted that he take it. He also gave editorial writer Samuel Moffett several hats, his mentor Carl Schurz a box of cigars, sent $100 to Booker T. Washington, and donated $5,000 for Jewish victims of Russian pogroms. Secretary Butes got $380; Dr. Hosmer, $160; and his valet, Dunningham, $100.

CHAPTER 28

"I Liked the Way He Swore"

1906
—
58 to 59 years old

Despite Pulitzer's generosity and occasional praise, Cobb was exasperated by his more frequent criticisms, and wrote to him that he'd as good as accepted an offer to return to the *Detroit Free Press*. His letter crossed with Pulitzer's cable—another crack across the knuckles—panning his recent editorial as "a crazy page" that made him sick. In it Cobb had attacked the city's rapid transit board. It's a "splendid" board, Pulitzer insisted, and ordered Cobb to apologize in the next editorial for his "intemperance of language." Cobb's response was a one-sentence letter of resignation.

Frantic at the thought of losing Cobb, as soon as he returned to New York, Pulitzer called Seitz to his home. Seitz arrived in a raging snowstorm. Instead of inviting him to discuss the problem in the comfort of his soundproof annex, Pulitzer ordered a cab to drive them through Central Park despite the storm. Seitz sympathized with Cobb and advised against trying to hold him against his will. Pulitzer seemed to agree by not replying until they had almost circled the park, when he said, as if to himself, "I like that young man. I liked the way he swore." Then he relapsed into silence until they approached the Seventy-second Street exit. They had almost reached Pulitzer's home when he ordered the driver to stop and in a burst of fury yelled at Seitz: "Go back to the office and tell that goddamned young fool I will *not* let him resign, goddamn him!"

Seitz delivered the message verbatim but without the fury. Cobb thought it over and agreed not to break his contract. Pulitzer sent for him the next morning, and Cobb arrived expecting angry recriminations. Instead, Pulitzer playfully pulled Cobb's ear—a habit Napoleon, apparently, had also displayed when pleased—and said ruefully: "My dear boy, don't you know you quite spoiled my Easter?" They agreed not to get mad at each other at the same time. Cobb resigned many times after that, and it became customary for Pulitzer to remark casually, "I suppose you know Cobb has resigned again." It wasn't the frequent raises that kept him, Cobb later explained: "My tastes are rather simple. What I care about money is not having to think about it." And Pulitzer made that possible. No one ever got Pulitzer's wholehearted approval, but Cobb came close to it. He and Pulitzer often disagreed. Their fights were fierce, profane, and short-lived. But fundamentally they were close political allies sharing an almost identical political philosophy, epitomized in this extract from a Cobb editorial: "There is seldom more than one issue in American politics—government for Privilege versus government for the People. That is the beginning and end of the trust question, of the tariff question, of the financial question, of the conservation question, of the boss question."

While Pulitzer had been pacifying the rebellious Cobb, he had also been trying to steer his son Joe toward a less self-indulgent life. To solve the problem, he again chose a cab ride in Central Park, though in balmier weather, with Joe as a captive audience and Kate as a witness. He said that if Joe had a natural bent for learning or intended to be a lawyer, doctor, or scholar, then he needed a Harvard education. But he had shown little interest in reading books, or the *World*, and, if anything, his mind was less mature now than when he started college two years before. Instead of wasting time at Harvard, Pulitzer told his silent son, he should be taking over some of the responsibilities on the St. Louis paper.

Joe insisted that he was learning something at Harvard, especially in English literature, and asked to be allowed to stay there, promising to improve his grades, and to maintain a detailed diary that would confirm he was keeping his promises.

Probably encouraged by Kate, Pulitzer gave Joe one last chance. But on returning to Harvard he seemed determined to sabotage himself. Having assured his father that he was learning something in English literature, he now admitted in his diary that what he was learning was to hate it! But what finally did him in was a report from Harvard dean B. S. Hurlbut that over the past six months Joe had cut college classes thirty-seven times. So Pulitzer whipped him out of Harvard, intending to hand him over, as a cub reporter, to the no-nonsense workaholic city editor of the *Evening World*, Charles Chapin.

Pulitzer had taken to augmenting his cables with use of the newfangled telephone. The day before he sailed for Europe, he phoned Chapin to say that he must treat Joe just like any other beginner. "There is no partiality to be shown because he is my son," Pulitzer insisted. "Do you quite understand?" Chapin promised to follow Pulitzer's instructions.

"Good, I shall rely on you," Pulitzer replied. "Don't forget about the discipline. I know how you handle young men and I wish you to do the same with him that you do with them."

When Joe turned up next morning eager to start work as a reporter, Chapin sent him to the Criminal Courts Building under the wing of veteran reporter

Bob Wilkes. For two mornings running, Joe arrived at eight on the dot. But on the third he was more than an hour late, casually explaining to Chapin as he strolled in, "The butler neglected to call me."

All newsroom conversations stopped. Chapin savored the moment, mouth agape, temporarily speechless, then slowly swiveled in his chair, and in a voice colleagues recalled as a mixture of a snarl and whine, told Joe that reporters were not supposed to rely on butlers to get them out of bed. "On your way home this evening, stop at a department store," he suggested, "and invest in an alarm clock." Joe took the advice and arrived on time for almost a week, writing enthusiastic letters to his father, saying in one that he found reporting so natural and interesting that it hardly seemed like work, and in another that he had surprised himself by not fainting when witnessing an autopsy in a morgue. "I think I must be cold blooded," he added.

Then he went AWOL for an entire working day.

When Chapin asked him why, he said he'd spent the morning at his dentist's and the afternoon at a ball game. Chapin explained that nobody was allowed time off unless they were ill or had been excused. Joe apologized, and promised it wouldn't happen again.

The following day he asked for time off to meet a girlfriend arriving from the West. Chapin let him go. The day after that, Joe wanted to spend the weekend with the young woman's relatives in the country. Chapin repeated Pulitzer's strict instructions but gave in. A week later, eager to attend another weekend party, Joe swore it would be his last request and he'd work extra hard on his return. Though he felt guilty about betraying Pulitzer's trust, Chapin again let him go. The following week, when Joe pleaded for a few more days off, Chapin finally put his foot down. Joe went anyway and didn't return for almost a week. When he did appear, Chapin fired him.

"The office gasped with astonishment when it got noised about that I had discharged 'Prince Joe' as they called him," Chapin related in his memoir. "But Joe good-naturedly treated it as a joke and took the night train for Bar Harbor, where he fitted out his yacht and sailed it in all of the regattas until his father returned from Europe."

This time, father and son had a conference in a launch rather than in a horse-drawn cab. Pulitzer decided to give him one more chance to make good—by working on the St. Louis paper with the goal of taking it over. If he accepted the offer, he should tell his boss there, Frank O'Neil: "I am out here to learn something in case something happens to my father. Teach me as much as possible without my becoming a bore." Joe accepted.

While dealing with Frank Cobb and Joe, Pulitzer also faced a renewed attack from New York district attorney William Travers Jerome. The ongoing feud between Jerome and the *World* was over priorities, with the paper charging that he went after petty crooks and ignored the big-time operators.

Jerome hit back by resurrecting the incident in which *World* city editor Pomeroy Burton had tried to enrich himself by insider trading. In a scorching after-dinner speech to the Delta Upsilon Club on March 23, Jerome said that the city editor of "a great paper in the city, the walls of which are decorated with large printed placards, 'Accuracy, Terseness, Accuracy,'" had intentionally published a lying report in his paper.

Pulitzer defended the accuracy and integrity of his paper with a challenging letter to Jerome that read in part:

"With your knowledge of the facts, your charges constituted a deliberate falsehood. THE WORLD assures you that a retraction of your false statements will buy you no immunity from deserved editorial criticism in the future. Neither will a refusal alter the policy of this newspaper to commend you when it believes you are doing your duty. THE WORLD is merely offering you a chance to wash the bad taste of that speech out of your mouth, and to make your peace with your conscience."

The letter was published in the *New York Times*, but Jerome wisely chose to hold his fire. Pulitzer had the facts on his side.

Earlier in the year, on a brief visit to Germany, Pulitzer had consulted Dr. Pagenstecher. The oculist had previously suggested that an operation might restore partial sight. But now, when Pulitzer agreed to go through with it, the doctor changed his mind and said it was impossible. Pulitzer was devastated. When she got the news, so was Kate, who wrote to him: "My poor dear, I wish I could do something for you. If the knowledge that you have my tenderest sympathy and constant thoughts helps you at all you may be assured of that."

As if compensating for his blindness, Pulitzer had extraordinarily acute hearing, which often drove him to distraction but also had a positive feature. He demonstrated this on a visit to Carlsbad, when a former U.S. postmaster general, John Wanamaker, was also there. Walking in the woods, Wanamaker saw four horsemen approaching, recognized Pulitzer among them, and shouted in a friendly way, "Mr. Pulitzer of the New York World, halt!" The two men had met briefly only once before, twenty-two years earlier. Yet, to Wanamaker's amazement, Pulitzer immediately replied, "Wanamaker of Philadelphia, is that you?" They met and chatted several times after that, and Wanamaker concluded that Pulitzer's ability to identify him instantly after so long was because he had "sight in his ears."

Back in New York City on June 24, 1906, the biggest news seemed to be the fate of John D. Rockefeller's powdered wig, imported from France for a ball and held up at customs—until the evening, when a story broke that would hit the headlines for months.

World reporter Albert Payson Terhune wrote the first report. Waiting in the canopied Madison Square Roof Garden to cover the opening night of a musical comedy, he noticed Stanford White among the audience sitting alone at a nearby table. White was the famous architect who had designed Madison Square Garden and Pulitzer's home, and whose wife had attended Ralph Pulitzer's wedding. At a nearby table, Terhune spotted millionaire playboy Harry Thaw and his attractive showgirl wife, Evelyn Nesbit.

Evelyn Nesbit, the motive
for the murder of Pulitzer's
architect, Stanford White.

Thaw seemed particularly restless during the show, and as the chorus girls
pointed fencing foils at the audience and sang

I challenge you,
To a duel, to a d-u-e-l,

Thaw walked over to White, drew a revolver from his breast pocket, and fired
three shots at him. The first missed. The other two got him in the back.

After interviewing the few onlookers who hadn't panicked and run for it,
the muscular Terhune rushed down the red-carpeted stairs to the only phone
booth on the floor below. It was occupied by a man talking to a young woman.
When he refused to hand over the phone, Terhune dragged him from it and
took over. He was still trying to get the operator to put him through to the
World when the man returned with a pal brandishing a chair. With one arm
and one leg Terhune fought off the two men as he phoned in the story.

Terhune's report began, "Harry Kendal Thaw, the young Pittsburg millionaire, shot and instantly killed Stanford White, the noted architect, last night in
the Madison Square Roof Garden. Thaw said to several bystanders, 'He ruined
my wife and deserted her, and I got him. It's all right.' . . . [Evelyn] was a noted

World reporter Irvin S. Cobb covered the sensational Thaw murder trial.

show girl and artist's model when Thaw married her a few years ago. His family disapproved." (Eventually Terhune became famous as a writer of dog stories.)

Just how Stanford White had ruined the showgirl, Thaw's murder trial, and the lurid sex lives of both men were to keep readers enthralled and appalled for months. As noted by another *World* reporter, Irvin S. Cobb, who covered the trial: "The story had everything, 'wealth, degeneracy, rich old wasters, delectable young chorus girls and adolescent artists' models; the behind-the-scenes of Theaterdom and the Underworld, the abnormal pastimes and weird orgies of over-aesthetic artists and jaded debauchees. In the cast of the motley show were Broadway toughs, Harlem gangsters, Tenderloin panders, Broadway leading men [including Evelyn's first lover, actor John Barrymore, who skipped town to avoid a subpoena], Fifth Avenue clubmen, Wall Street manipulators, uptown voluptuaries and downtown thugs—a bedaubed, bespangled Bacchanalia.' And the whole country was yearning to learn just what went on in wicked New York among the rich and beautiful and famous."

Pulitzer took a special interest in the upcoming Thaw trial, knowing both the prosecutor, his *bête noir*, William Travers Jerome, and the murdered man, his architect. Thaw was obviously off his rocker and a sadist, while White was a sexual predator who seduced or raped his victims after doping them with drugged champagne in his mirror-ceilinged love nest. This may explain why the trial ended with a hung jury, a second trial being set for 1908.

In the meantime, Pulitzer had more significant news to handle—a report that "Alfred Dreyfus was completely vindicated today by France. The Supreme Court of the Republic announced its decision annulling the conviction of Dreyfus by the court-martial of Rennes in 1899. To wipe every stain from Dreyfus' reputation and to emphasize the condemnation of the false evidence that was tried against him the court orders that he need not stand trial again. In conclusion the court noted that Dreyfus had committed no offense." In an interview afterward Dreyfus said: "'I am inexpressibly thankful to all who have assisted in the maintenance of truth.'"

On the same front page across four columns, the *World* printed scenes from Dreyfus's life and portraits of those who fought for and against him. It was captioned:

MARTYR OF DEVIL'S ISLAND, HIS PUBLIC DEGRADATION, HIS WIFE,
SOME OF HIS FOES AND STEADFAST FRIENDS.

On page two the paper explained how an innocent man had endured twelve years of horror.

The *World*'s lead editorial, headed A TRIUMPH OF JUSTICE, told how public opinion had "worked a tremendous change in France. There was no resisting its weight. M. Mornard, Dreyfus's counsel, stood in no danger of being called the enemy of public peace. The Government itself was [now] on the side of the disgraced Captain. . . . The day of a rehearing was bound to come. . . . When the scoundrel Esterhazy was whitewashed by a court-martial Zola rose in his wrath of an honest man and pointed the finger of scorn straight at the conspirators. His defiant 'j'accuse' rang around the world. Never since Voltaire pilloried the priests of France for driving the innocent Calas to a criminal's death and forced the rehabilitation of his memory by the Parliament of Paris has a man of letters won such a triumph."

Readers more concerned with justice closer to home were treated two days later to Pulitzer's latest attacks on monopolies, headed:

SUGAR TRUST SLAVERY
OF ITS MEN WORSE THAN
THAT OF THE "JUNGLE."

The *World* revealed that the principal owners of the Sugar Trust refineries, the Havemeyer family, lived in luxurious homes while the people they employed lived in squalor, that U.S. senators profited from investing in sugar trust stock, and that a broker once went to jail for "refusing to tell the Senate who of these men were his customers in sugar speculations when favored legislation was being enacted."

"Jungle" in the headline referred to Upton Sinclair's recent book *The Jungle*, exposing the meat trust and describing the nauseating practices in meatpacking plants of grinding poisoned rats in with moldy sausage meat for public consumption. The exposé galvanized Theodore Roosevelt into promoting, then signing into law, the Pure Food and Drug Act and the Meat Inspection Act.

In August, the *World* editorialized about another trust, Standard Oil, being indicted on 6,428 counts involving possible fines of $125 million, and praised Roosevelt for accepting "the trust's challenge. After years of popular agitation his is the first Administration to drive this arrogant corporation into the criminal courts. He has proved that in vigorous hands the law shall be respected."

The *World* also applauded Roosevelt's decision to adopt reformed spelling in government documents but was cautious about its wider use: "Just as the 'e' has been largely discarded from ax and wo, a superfluous 'l' from skilful and the 'u' from armor, the order may help in the transformation of the 'ed' of past particles into 't.' We may some day have 'kist' and 'curst,' 'leapt,' &c. [But] to carry out the phonetic reformation of the language to a logical conclusion would be to plunge into a morass of inconsistencies. As between 'you' and 'ewe' and 'yew,' what shall the 'simplified' spelling be? or between 'feat' and 'feet,' 'fare' and 'fair,' 'read' and 'reed' and the thousands of other homonymia which a uniformity of spelling would hopelessly confuse?"

Pulitzer's approval of Roosevelt followed Roosevelt's approval of Pulitzer. When *World* reporter Samuel Williams had recently interviewed the president, he said, "The *World* and I stand on the same ground. Your paper is magnificent and strong. It is ably edited, it is courageous in its views and its editorial page is the finest in the country. Your showing up of [D.A.] Jerome, for example, was magnificent. Then there are your attacks on men of wealth and power, the class of predatory wealth. The way you went after them was magnificent. That is a magnificent phrase of Mr. Pulitzer's—'Predatory wealth and predatory poverty,' I wish I had thought of its complement 'predatory poverty.'"

William Randolph Hearst was still Pulitzer's most ferocious rival. Despite a growing newspaper empire, Hearst's lust for more of almost everything had not been satiated. Since September he had fervently campaigned as the Democratic nominee for New York State governor, making some hundred speeches—sixteen in one day—in a wispy voice that nevertheless carried his message and highly quotable disdain for his critics. Judge Parker was "a political cockroach from under the sink," and Theodore Roosevelt had "sold himself to the devil and lived up to the bargain." Most Manhattan newspapers ridiculed Hearst and revived the charge of assassin, with reference to the McKinley killing. Pulitzer, however, told Cobb "to treat Hearst without a feeling of prejudice, if this is possible," while encouraging Republican attorney Charles Evans Hughes—straight from his triumph over the insurance companies—to run against him.

"We are trying to treat Hearst 'without prejudice,' as you say," Cobb replied, but "it is a damned hard job. I am prejudiced against Hearst. Some day I shall consider it a precious privilege if you will lift the lid and give me permission to scatter his intestines from the Battery to the Bronx." When Cobb's pro-Hughes editorials went over the top, Pulitzer admonished him: "Please don't call Hughes a political and intellectual giant. It is an exaggeration and hurts him and the paper. He is an honest, able man. That, the people will believe and that is enough. Accuracy, Accuracy, Accuracy!"

As usual, unable to stand the excitement of the election, Pulitzer sailed for Europe with Kate and Herbert. He and his eleven-year-old son then headed for Wiesbaden while Kate and her companion, Maud Macarow, stayed at Divonne-les-Bains to take the cure. Pulitzer had high hopes for Herbert, confiding to Kate: "He is the brightest of your children—by far the brightest and most promising of all. He ought to be a public man of great distinction if properly educated and trained. I see no reason why he might not be President of the United States." This was hardly a fanciful dream: with the World behind him, any viable candidate had a fighting chance. Then Pulitzer made a remarkable admission: "I want the child about me as an idea or feeling, with sense, or sentiment, not as a reality (because I scarcely ever see him) but he is the only thing I love about me & my nature is so constituted & always has been, that I must have someone to love about me. [Kate presumably wasn't in the running.] It is not that he loves me, but he is useful to me because I can love him. That is why I have carried him around like a woman who wears a crucifix or talisman."

Herbert had already been tutored in French and English, and Pulitzer's secretaries had screened dozens of applicants to tutor him in German. None was found suitable.

While in Wiesbaden, Pulitzer was delighted to get pages of Joe's diary showing he was working well in St. Louis, but not at all delighted by the accompanying letter in which he complained about phony medical ads in the Post-Dispatch and taunted his father: "When I see you, please be ready to receive a strong kick on the disgraceful medical ads that we print. They are not only disgusting but are a mean deception of an ignorant public that can in no way be justified." Ten days later Joe sent a batch of the ads with this contentious comment: "You don't need the money. Why then do incalculable harm by accepting such filth? I think it is positively criminal. I beg you to read the enclosed, which are comparatively mild, and act accordingly. Or else place the matter in my hands and let me act."

Too angry to respond directly, Pulitzer got his secretary Alfred Butes to bring Joe to heel:

"You were sent out to learn your profession—not to kill the medical ads. Leave disagreeable problems of management alone. Even, if your judgment were correct, you would be doing the grossest wrong to your father in laying the responsibility upon him. You know very well that the paper is in charge of competent managers who have the fullest control, and are men of character. The responsibility is *theirs*. Mr. P. says that when the time comes—if it ever comes—for *you* to take charge of the paper you will be able to kill these ads. He would be glad if that time could come *soon*. But it will not be brought nearer by irritating letters. Besides studying the business he suggests also thorough self-examination. Your letter, he says, shows deplorable self-deception. You assume that you have made but *one* mistake, ignoring all that has happened in the past four years—broken promises, pledges and obligations which have caused him grief a thousand times greater than you will ever know. Your father is also grieved to notice a train of coarseness that comes into your writing, and, he fears, into your mind. For instance, frequent slang like 'Hearst's old man'—too frequent oaths and hells. Remember your age and to whom you are writing. *Absolutely and positively* you must write *no more disagreeable letters*."

It was a disingenuous defense: Pulitzer could have ended such ads with a couple of words. And Joe was not intimidated. He replied to Butes, sorry for irritating his father but insisting that he had raised the matter in the interest of Pulitzer and the paper, knowing that none of the managers "would feel justified in killing such valuable business. I still believe that what I did was right and you or anyone else can't dissuade me from this belief. I still contend that my view of this class of business is the only upright, honorable, and *refined* one. I hope you will note this word 'refined.' I shall not worry about his views as to my refinement. It's very probably another case of self-deception, either on my part or his. And I am satisfied that it is on his." He welcomed Butes's letter because it was "not only sane and logical in expression, but between the lines I could read indications of your apparent liking for me and your desire to smooth things over." [Joe must have been psychic!] "I shall do the same for you whenever I get the chance." He gave Butes permission to read the letter to his father verbatim or edited, as he felt fit.

Joe sent a more conciliatory letter to his father and concluded: "When I shut my eyes for a while, as I often do, and the full realization comes over me that you actually are blind, I feel how utterly selfish and inconsiderate I often am. I shall gladly welcome any line from you that will tell me that you have forgotten this new trouble that I have caused you and that you love me."

Having recently become the grandfather of Ralph Pulitzer Jr. put Pulitzer in a more benign mood. In late September he gave Joe four days off plus travel time to visit his brother, sister-in-law Frederica, and newborn nephew at Shelburne Farms in Vermont. Despite a fall from a horse on the first day that sprained his left wrist, Joe wrote to his father that he had "never enjoyed four days more in *all my life*."

Joe continued to enjoy life, especially after meeting the "decidedly clever and attractive" Nellie Wickham at a dinner party in St. Louis, but assured his father that he was not "letting work come after play." However, he added, "One of the strange differences between us two is the fact that you have never come anywhere near learning how to enjoy life, whereas I, I fear, have learned the lesson too well." Joe went on to recount his pleased surprise that St. Louis girls were allowed to go to the theater and parties without chaperones: "In spite of this unusual liberty, which to a N.Y. girl would seem incredible, the girls here are extremely well behaved and not a bit foolish or giddy. I tell you this realizing that it's very frivolous but hoping that it will interest you."

"Your letter certainly did not bore me as you seem to expect," Pulitzer replied, encouraging Joe to report the course of what seemed a budding romance and relieved to know his son no longer regarded St. Louis as a place of exile and of men who spat in the streets.

Pulitzer got more good news to celebrate when Hughes defeated Hearst, and predicted that he'd be the best New York State governor since Tilden.

Hearst, infuriated by the *World*'s support of his opponent, called Pulitzer "a coward, traitor, sycophant and pimp," inciting Joe to promise his father, "The next time I happen to meet [Hearst] I shall sail in and knock hell out of him." He soon got the chance. After the election, Hearst set off for Mexico with his wife, family, and a group of friends, stopping en route at the *Post-Dispatch* building to send a message through the AP correspondent who had an office there. Told that Hearst was in the building, twenty-one-year-old Joe introduced himself and asked Hearst if he meant what he had said about Pulitzer.

"I usually mean what I say," Hearst replied.

Joe tried to "knock hell" out of the heavyset publisher, but others intervened and his first punch never landed, to his eternal regret. But news of the encounter was published nationwide and even in a Belgian newspaper, the accounts often elaborating the scuffle into a fistfight, with Joe's fist connecting with Hearst's belly. Even biographer Swanberg went with this false version and had "the lovely Mrs. Hearst" separate the two men. Pulitzer's pleasure at Joe's loyalty was overshadowed by the news that Bradford Merrill, one of his most valued men, had left him to work for Hearst.

Kate returned to New York in November to attend a memorial service for Pulitzer's mentor Carl Schurz, who had died that summer at seventy-seven. "It was a meeting," Kate wrote to her husband, "that must do men's souls good to feel that a man's upright life even more than his splendid mind commanded such respect. You would have been proud of your chief."

To Pulitzer's despair, Joe seemed unable to keep out of trouble. He had gone AWOL from the *Post-Dispatch* for five days to attend the Harvard-Yale football game. But he felt so guilty about it when he learned his father was giving him five hundred dollars and a week's vacation at Christmas that he admitted taking the trip to New Haven. Pulitzer cabled back: "Amazed. You must certainly stay [in St. Louis over Christmas] and recover your lost confidence. Had just intended to raise your pay, position, powers, title, handsomely, but first importance I must depend on you. Grieved."

Joe spent his first Christmas away from home, in St. Louis, visiting "Poor Children's Festivals" sponsored by his father and was so moved by the children that at times he was on the verge of tears. The ever-restless Pulitzer went from

Germany to Cap Martin on the French Riviera for Christmas, taking his son Herbert and entourage with him, including Dr. Hosmer. But Hosmer had to leave suddenly after falling sick, and Pulitzer was left without a resident doctor. Then his fierce headaches recurred with a vengeance.

Yet Pulitzer rallied, to cable Frank Cobb: "The last message sent was on this point of exaggeration and slopping over. You do not heed my injunctions and do not weigh words carefully. Instruct Heaton urge strongly raising President's salary to one hundred thousand dollars a year. Favor additional twenty-five thousand dollars for Roosevelt's travelling expenses." And then he critiqued several more Cobb editorials with such comments as: "Railroad rate question, dry technical—should have left it out that day anyhow for the sake of variety." And "Good!—but missed central, burning point (i.e.) defeat of Gas Bill by corruption. Should have been leader, overshadowing all other points." And on and on, including his recommending Roosevelt for the 1906 Nobel Peace Prize for persuading the warring Russians and Japanese to sign a peace treaty. The Nobel committee agreed and gave it to him.

CHAPTER 29

Protesting Jingo Agitation

1907
—
59 to 60 years old

In January, Pulitzer sailed through the Mediterranean with his son Herbert and a depleted staff, stopping briefly at Taormina, Athens, and Alexandria. At one port Pulitzer got a letter from Frank O'Neil, an editor at the *Post-Dispatch*, with the welcome news that Joe was turning out to be his father's son after all. "Joseph is becoming more censorious," O'Neil wrote, "and I am glad to report his criticisms are mainly on behalf of good journalistic standards. He would edit the advertisements from Manhood Restored to 98 Percent Pure Silk Shirtwaists, until they fooled nobody; and he would hunt all forms of crime and misconduct into deep, deep holes, with the editorial pitchfork. All of which is admirable." Because O'Neil felt that his account, "barren as it is of black marks," might challenge Pulitzer's credulity, he admitted that "the young man has surprised, and in a measure disappointed, me in his failure to disclose some really reprehensible or barbaric characteristics. Every boy has 'em, and I'm waiting."

Joe soon met O'Neil's expectations when he shocked his father with an apparent ultimatum. He wanted a pay raise sufficient to afford a "flat (2 rooms and a bath); a servant, probably a Jap (for they are cheap and good), and a horse," and to stay in St. Louis for at least three years. If his father refused to comply, Joe would expect a year's paid leave of absence, after which he would make his own way in the world. And they'd never again communicate with each other except in an emergency such as a serious illness. Could they meet and talk it over?

Three weeks later, getting no reply, Joe again wrote to his father, concerned that the earlier letter might "cause you to think that I wrote it in a dissatisfied, resentful and ungrateful spirit." His main fear, he explained, was being sent back to the *World* because everything about New York was distracting: the very air full of amusement, frivolity, and dissipation. "But in St. Louis, no matter whether a fellow is so inclined or not, he *has to work* to occupy his time. And that is why I think you should keep me in St. Louis and away from New York. . . . Won't you as a great favor, on receipt of this letter, dictate a few lines, telling me that you have not misunderstood my motives and telling me what your plans for me and my immediate future are?"

For two months Joe waited for a response. In the meantime Pulitzer announced his retirement—for the second time—to take place on April 10, his sixtieth birthday. Joe hosted a banquet in St. Louis and Ralph in Manhattan to celebrate the event. Pulitzer remained in Europe but sent telegrams.

Commenting on how the telegrams contained the familiar high-minded phrase "to sacrifice everything to the public interest," Joe asked Ralph, "How can anyone believe that he and the paper are sincere when we carry this fraudulent, deceptive stuff and make ourselves every day parties to the crime of ruining the fortunes and health of scores of ignorant people who believe in the paper they read? If I thought I should never be able to run a successful newspaper without that class of stuff, I'd say To Hell with Journalism. Why don't you do something about it?"

Ralph, the more cautious of the two, responded: "It's ridiculous to maintain that a paper should pander to paternalism by constituting itself the protector of its readers against their own foolishness." He maintained that the only way to protect readers would be to hire a "prohibitively costly staff of experts in innumerable different lines of business from mines through medicine to metaphysics" to screen out phony claims, and consequently the only ads to get in the paper would be death notices.

Weeks had gone by and still his father had not replied to Joe's two letters. Hoping to shock him into a response, he wrote: "To whomsoever it may concern: Please urge Andes [Pulitzer's code name] to write me immediately! I'm tired of this one-sided correspondence! He need expect no more letters from me until I have received one from him."

While Pulitzer continued to give Joe the silent treatment, he sent letters of advice and encouragement to Ralph at the *World*. On February 10, aboard the yacht *Honor*, docked in Alexandria, despite a sleepless night and a "terrible headache," he dictated a long letter to Ralph, urging him not to "be too much influenced by the financial prosperity of their paper. I care comparatively little for that. A permanent satisfactory organization, the development of men of brains & character for the future interests me more. Indeed, I beg you again and again to use your influence in spending money liberally on the paper, and checking the tendency of managers simply to conduct the paper for money-making." He said that although Ralph had not yet the experience or energy to take over any department of the paper, "this in no way limits your right to criticize every single edition of the paper, morning, evening, Sunday, and make a name for [yourself] outside the paper—as a representative of the paper. You can't do this unless you take more interest in public matters. Remember you will be 28 years of age in June and Octavius Augustus was only 19 when he became master of Rome and Alexander 22 when he conquered all Asia. Tell Frederica [Ralph's wife], if you please, she is spoiling you dreadfully instead of stirring you up. With a great deal of love, as ever Your affectionate Father.'"

In New York, Kate gave a dinner party to seventy upper-crust guests, including the Vanderbilts, Fishes, and Choates, then entertained them with a Russian play starring the celebrated actress Nazimova. But Kate was distracted by recent disconsolate messages from Joseph.

She suggested that she and their girls meet him in Europe. He vetoed the idea, yet accused his family of deserting him. Afraid something was desperately wrong with him, she replied, "You refused to let me or me & the children join you, then cable that it is a reflection on the family that they are not with you. All this worried me greatly & makes me extremely anxious as to your nervous, as well as physical condition. Please have your doctor write to me as to how you are. If you knew how miserable I feel about you, how many wakeful nights I spend thinking of you, you would give me definite information."

Dr. Hosmer couldn't help her. He was still ill and had returned to the United States for treatment. Pulitzer reassured Kate to some extent by changing his mind and inviting her to join him. But first he wanted her to line up several possible Hosmer replacements for him to interview when back in Bar Harbor. He also needed more secretaries to replace recent defections. Kate asked friends to help and advertised in New York papers. There was a big response, she told Pulitzer, but only from "impossible people—such as valets, masseurs & even gardeners."

Pulitzer returned from his Mediterranean cruise to the Villa Cynthia in Menton on March 26 to be immortalized by the great sculptor Auguste [*The Thinker*] Rodin. In no mood to charm or entertain as he had the portrait painter Sargent, Pulitzer refused to talk directly to Rodin, and their strained communications were relayed by their respective secretaries. Rodin wanted Pulitzer to remove his shirt to see the set of his head on his shoulders. Pulitzer refused. Rodin threatened to walk out and Pulitzer compromised, agreeing to remove his collar and undo one shirt button, but only if no strangers were in the room. After the ordeal, with Pulitzer maintaining a sullen silence, Rodin wrote to a friend: "I have just done the bust of a man who was *un diable!*" A Rodin biographer described the bronze version as "a remarkable portrait capturing all the intensity, *yet serenity,*" of the blind man! Today it is in the hallway of the Columbia School of Journalism.

Pulitzer moved on to Aix-les-Bains, where Kate joined him and listened to his complaints about Joe. Eventually she persuaded her husband to let her reply to the unanswered letters. "Your father," she wrote, "is still smarting from" you deserting your "post to go to a ball game." But what infuriated him and "cut him to the heart" was your threat to leave him and not to communicate with him unless you got "a flat, a Japanese servant and a horse. When he is hurt, he cannot forget. His mind revolves around and around the hurt during all the long hours of night and headachy days. [But] he still loves you and has tried what he considers best for you. With a heart full of love, your devoted Mother."

Relieved and encouraged, Joe wrote to his father that he had originally expressed himself in an asinine way. He had not meant the flat, horse, and Japanese servant to be a demand. It was simply his view of the ideal situation. He promised to make up for the desertion by working hard all summer without a vacation except for a few days to meet his father on his return home.

The peripatetic Pulitzer was in Carlsbad when he sent Joe his reply: "There is not one scintilla of a shadow of reason for the thought that I ever contemplated your coming to New York last year, this year or next year. [He had in fact told him to contemplate the possibility of working for the World in New York sometime in the future but with no specific date.] But what has it to do with the regular threat that unless you could have a horse, a flat and a Japanese servant, you would not only leave St. Louis, not only shift for yourself, but have *no communication with me for a year?* . . . I want some love and affection from my children in the closing short span of life that remains. If I cannot have that love and affection, I may expect to be spared wilful deliberate disrespect, disobedience and insult."

Two days later Pulitzer sent an abject apology: he had misinterpreted Joe's original letter as a threat. "I quoted from memory and was wrong," he admitted. "I am glad I was wrong because it is in your favor." He now wanted Joe to meet him in New York and for them to travel together to Bar Harbor. In a postscript, Pulitzer touched on something that explains Joe's reluctance to leave St. Louis. "Of course I hope you will be glad to go to Bar Harbor," he wrote, "and not show the smallest anxiety about returning to the young lady in St. Louis until I tell you to do so. Perhaps it is of some importance for you to [see me] before you see her."

Despite his formal retirement, no one close to Pulitzer expected him to surrender control of his papers—and he didn't. After all, it was his life.

Even while strolling through the Carlsbad woods, he asked his secretary Norman Thwaites to keep him informed of the latest news. Thwaites read out a three-line newspaper report: Maximilian Harden, editor of the *Die Zukunft*, had been sued for libel by the kaiser's closest friend, Prince Philipp Eulenburg. As Thwaites recalled, Pulitzer "stopped dead in his tracks, said, 'There is a big story behind that'" and immediately sent him to Berlin to interview the prince and chief of police. The libel case developed into an international scandal in which Eulenburg and other members of the kaiser's personal circle were charged with engaging in homosexual orgies.

Even before the trial, the kaiser panicked and fired three of his aides-de-camp and Count Kuno Moltke. The kaiser then followed the trial closely, terrified that he, too, might be implicated. Eulenburg's wife testified "with passionate fervour" that they had been married thirty-four years, had eight children, "and I have never perceived the smallest sign of anything but a perfectly normal emotional life or even manner of life." She explained the charge as an invention of the prince's enemies eager to destroy him. Eulenburg became so ill from thrombosis that he was carried to court in a hospital bed; then, when he showed no signs of recovery, his trial was postponed indefinitely. He spent the rest of his life as a semi-invalid, dying fourteen years later.

Thwaites concluded that "whatever may have been true of the Eulenburg menage, a hideous scandal was uncovered by the [trial], resulting in the banishment of several officers of the Guard—men who bore names of honour in the Reich—and the disclosure of practises which shocked the world. No longer were Germans able to point the finger of scorn at what they had, since the Oscar Wilde crime, referred to as the 'English vice.'" Especially after Count Hulsen-Haeseler, chief of the military cabinet, dropped dead while dancing for the kaiser's entertainment. "Rigor mortis having set in by the time the doctors came, the general's body could only with the greatest difficulty be divested of [a pink ballet skirt] and restored to the propriety of military uniform."

Just before sailing home to Bar Harbor, Pulitzer told Ralph to expect to join him there for several days when he would teach his son how to run the *World*. During that time Pulitzer also hoped to find a replacement for his ailing personal physician, Dr. Hosmer, and he urged Ralph, "to wake up and show intelligence and energy in arranging with [secretary Alfred] Butes as to which of the candidates now pending I am to see first, second and third. Even seeing a man on the strict understanding that it is a trial & a test is a terrible strain for me—a nervous tension, almost equal to a blind man walking the rope and if it can be avoided for God's sake see that I do not have to try any impossible or unpromising men." He said that he could no longer depend on Dr. Hosmer nor his own family to take care of him on his necessary travels and needed to employ someone nearer his own age, because it made him look ridiculous "in the sight of people all over the world to be seen travelling with only young men in my employ, when they wonder why my wife and some of my grown children are not with me. I cannot tell you how grateful I am that you have kept so well physically. [Ralph suffered from asthma.] This really is the best point in the whole situation—the main consolation. With heartfull of love, Your Father."

When Joe arrived at Chatwold shortly after Ralph, instead of the expected warm reception, his father bawled him out, reminding him of all his previous mistakes, including the "hold-up" letter. In a memo of their conversation, Joe noted that Pulitzer said he dared not be generous, because "it might ruin me, and but for my bad record at Harvard, trip to watch the football game, and misunderstood letter, he would have been only too happy to have [given] me some title, position, prestige, like Ralph." Having appointed Ralph both the *World*'s acting head and president of the *Post-Dispatch*, Pulitzer assured Joe that "when I feel sure you'll not run away" and have regained "my confidence and affection you can have the very first place in St. Louis." But, he said, confidence was much more easily destroyed than regained. And Joe must bear this in mind before he again saw "the young lady in St. Louis."

Being a romantic himself, Pulitzer had soon grasped that Joe's reluctance to leave St. Louis was not to avoid the temptations of Manhattan but to enjoy the company of Elinor Wickham. To distance his son from that temptation Pulitzer told him he was too young for a serious relationship. Then, having insisted that he had no intention of moving Joe to New York for several years, he reassigned him there immediately. He was to be Pulitzer's editorial watchdog, observing others at their jobs, and reading and comparing the competition. Joe reluctantly agreed.

Having tamed his rebellious son, Pulitzer turned his attention to agitators in San Francisco protesting the flood of Japanese immigrants to the labor market. The local school board tried to placate them by segregating Oriental children in a special school. Japan protested. President Roosevelt at first denounced the board's action but was persuaded to moderate his language by San Francisco's bigoted mayor, Eugene Schmitz.

When, on July 8, Roosevelt was reported to be sending battleships to the Pacific coast to intimidate the Japanese, Pulitzer suspected it was an attempt to create a situation that would compel Roosevelt's nomination for a third term. So he told Cobb to make the entire editorial page a daring, fearless expression against such jingo agitation. He mentioned how public fervor had helped to launch the Franco-German War, the Boer War, and the Spanish-American War. And he suggested quoting verbatim the English music hall song "We don't want to fight, but by Jingo if we do, we've got the ships, we've got the men, we've got the money, too," because the song had "carried the country away and forced savage, unjust and ruinuous conflict" during the Boer War. Pulitzer recalled how Bismarck and Moltke were desperate because their plans to fight France seemed doomed, so Bismarck had altered an innocent telegram to make "it read like an insult to the Emperor and the nation, and by this forgery so excited Germany that [the Franco-German] war became inevitable." Referring to the Spanish-American War, Pulitzer pointed out that "Spain had granted to Cuba all that we demanded, but passion in Spain and here forced the hands of the government." [Had Pulitzer forgotten that he was among the most passionate?!] In case Frank Cobb had missed the point, Pulitzer told him to emphasize in the editorial "these illustrations of danger of Jingo agitation."

Rather than send the fleet to San Francisco or the Philippines, Roosevelt solved the problem by a "gentleman's agreement" in which Japan agreed to restrict Japanese immigration to the United States, and the San Francisco school board repealed their segregation decision.

Soon after, the *World* reproached Roosevelt for naming his secretary of war, William Taft, as his choice to succeed him as president. Pulitzer sprang to his defense. "Attack on Roosevelt for preferring Taft and trying to secure his nomination preposterous," he cabled from Bar Harbor. "Jefferson selected Madison. Madison selected Monroe. Jackson nominated Van Buren as his successor. What more natural than Roosevelt should feel anxiety and ambition to have his work finished in his own spirit as far as possible? He would make a more statesmanlike, just, law-respecting chief magistrate than Roosevelt, though lacking latter's amazing initiative in everything."

Alfred Butes, the man in charge of handling such messages to and from the *World* staff, as well as Pulitzer's private correspondence, was probably his favorite secretary-companion. He was also Kate's confidant. Butes had survived thirteen roller-coaster years in the employ of a difficult and demanding invalid. Expecting him to remain to the end and assured of his integrity, Pulitzer named him in his will as both a trustee of his estate and to receive a large legacy.

Another secretary, Norman Thwaites, who had been with Pulitzer for five years, was at Chatwold that summer when Butes said he was quitting to work for Lord Northcliffe in England. "It was my unfortunate lot," Thwaites recalled, "to try to console Pulitzer when Butes finally decided to leave his service." Thwaites rode with Pulitzer through the woods at Bar Harbor, hoping to keep his mind otherwise engaged by bits of news from the day's papers. But he did not respond at all, and, as Thwaites later wrote, "I gradually sank into silence." Then Pulitzer came to life. "Why don't you talk?" he shouted. "Is there no news in the papers? Dammit, man, talk!" And he swung at Thwaites with his riding crop, hitting him several times. "I have been talking steadily for an hour," Thwaites replied. Pulitzer immediately apologized, then asked why he was treated so cruelly—for which, of course, Thwaites had no answer.

Pulitzer struck Butes from his will, and sent a bitter telegram to Lord Northcliffe blaming him for Butes's defection.

Several candidates to replace Butes failed the customary Pulitzer interrogation. One, John McNaught, was engaged but lasted only a few weeks. In a letter to him afterward, Pulitzer revealed that he was looking for more than a secretary, saying that he had learned to respect and like McNaught, but added, "how much I would give if I could only deceive myself with the thought that my anxiety to attach you to me as my long lost and longed for friend is not entirely unappreciated."

Pulitzer took the loss of Butes hard, but was diverted to some extent by a manhunt. The "fugitive" was the father of the world's richest man—John D. Rockefeller. Rumor had it that he had led a scandalous life as bigamist and con man and was now virtually in hiding. Only his immediate family seemed to know where he was, and they weren't talking. But someone gave reporter Ida Tarbell a hint that he was a senile old codger living somewhere out West. She led the hunters but never found him.

To Pulitzer, this was a thrilling mystery that would grab readers, and he assigned one of his most resourceful reporters, W. J. Slaght, to track down the old man. The search took him to Iowa, Indiana, and Alaska. He even peddled razors from "door-to-door trying to pry information from suspicious German farmers. 'I'll bet I shaved myself ten or fifteen times a day, till my face was sore, selling the blamed razors,'" said Slaght. Despite his persistence and ingenuity he returned to the *World* exhausted and empty-handed.

When Hearst set his reporters on the hunt, Pulitzer offered an eight-thousand-dollar bonus to any *World* or *Post-Dispatch* reporter who found old man Rockefeller.

That same month, U.S. judge Kenesaw Mountain Landis (who later became the first baseball commissioner) fined Rockefeller's Standard Oil Company twenty-nine million dollars for violating the antitrust law by granting unlawful freight rebates. Pulitzer enthusiastically welcomed the decision and telegraphed the *World*, "The greatest breeder of discontent and socialism among the masses of the poor is not only lack of confidence in the justice of the law, but popular belief that the law is one thing for the rich and quite another for the poor. Landis's [decision] is a really terrible blow at past Administrations, which did not enforce the law. If Roosevelt had never done anything else except to start the majesty of the law in the direction of prosecuting these great offenders despite their huge campaign tributes, he would be entitled to the greatest credit for the greatest service to the nation. The one initiative impulse and persevering instinct must be held as offsetting a hundred wrong impulses of a minor character."

It was a hollow victory. The Standard Oil Company didn't pay a penny of the twenty-nine-million-dollar fine, the verdict being reversed on appeal. And when the company was "dissolved" in 1911, "each of its parts became richer and stronger than the original whole, and lived to more than double the cost of their products to the public."

In the fall Pulitzer called Joe to Bar Harbor to act as his temporary secretary. Trying to control his sons—which Joe especially resisted—he still expected them to send him their diary entries from time to time. Recent ones from Ralph spurred Pulitzer to complain that too many dealt with "trouble, vexation and annoyance [which] I am impotent to deal with." Joe took down the message but before sending it south, added: "Dear Ralph, One cold day and one rainy day have kept the great mogul indoors most of the time. Hence his bellyaching tone. He apparently doesn't want to be told anything unless it is that Hearst, Brisbane, Carvahlo [*Journal* men] have all jumped in the river, that no one in N.Y. is reading anything except the morning Sunday and evening *World*, and that the price of white paper has dropped to nothing. Anything else he considers unnecessary and indicating a particular desire on everyone's part to hound him down."

For months Pulitzer had been eagerly looking forward to the delivery of his custom-built $1.5 million yacht. That winter, in New York about to leave for Europe to pick it up, Pulitzer must have somewhat nervously calculated the enormous cost of maintaining it and its sixty-man crew. Which explains why he asked Frank Cobb, his chief editorial writer, to join him in his soundproof

Manhattan home to discuss his finances. "Boy," he said, "I am, as you probably know, a large owner of stocks. Some of them are bound to be affected by public action. I am not sure of myself when I see my interests in danger. I might give way to such a feeling and send you an order that would mean a change in the paper's policy. I want you to make me a promise. If I ever do such a thing, swear you will ignore my wishes."

Cobb swore. But there is no evidence that Pulitzer ever put him to the test.

CHAPTER 30

Secret Double Life
of Rockefeller's Father

1908

—

60 to 61 years old

Arriving in Nice in early January, Pulitzer stayed at the Villa Lisberg, which Queen Victoria had occupied during her visits to the French Riviera. There he impatiently awaited the delivery of his spectacular yacht built in Leith, Scotland, under the supervision of Arthur Billing, his favorite secretary since Butes had left him. With it he could travel the world in quiet comfort— almost everything aboard was muffled—whenever the mood took him. He called it *Liberty*, which was what it meant to him. To his personal staff, at his command around the clock, it would become known as *Liberty Ha! Ha!* But Jane Tuohy, daughter of the *World*'s London bureau chief, knew who buttered her father's bread and simply cried out "Liberty!" as she doused it with champagne before it hit the water.

At 304 feet from stem to stern and 36.5 feet wide, it was one of the world's biggest private yachts, able to travel six thousand miles without refueling. When it arrived at Nice at the end of the month, Pulitzer immediately took it for a trial run—and was overjoyed. Everything about it delighted him. There were no structures on its smooth teak decks to trip him. Only faint outside noises reached his cabin because of its double bulkheads, double doors, and double portholes. And the insomniac was assured that when he slept no one would disturb him thanks to a prominent notice outside his cabin forbidding anyone to enter unless summoned. He could do that without moving from his four-poster bed by pulling bell cords—identified by their varying lengths—to bring to his side in seconds his majordomo Dunningham; his yacht's captain;

At 304 feet long, Pulitzer's *Liberty* was one of the world's biggest private yachts.

the chief steward; or his personal physician Hosmer, recovered from his illness. Forward were a gymnasium and quarters for his personal assistants. Aft were twelve staterooms for family, guests, and secretaries. The main deck contained the dining room, music room, and Pulitzer's sitting room, within easy reach of a five-hundred-volume reference library. Having explored the ship, to Billing's relief, he raved about it: "I love it. Here I am at home and comfortable. In a house I am lost in my blindness, always fearful of falling on stairs or obstacles. Here the narrow companionways give me safe guidance and I can find my way about alone. Nothing in all my life has given me so much pleasure."

His joy spread to Joe, when Pulitzer had a change of heart and gave him permission to leave New York to work in St. Louis on the *Post-Dispatch*. Learning that Elinor Wickham's parents would be sending her on a six-month world tour may have influenced his decision. But he had also been charmed by Joe's description of her and his assurance that she came from a good family. Pulitzer even gave her the flattering code name "The Divinity," to use in correspondence.

Kate and Herbert joined him in Nice, as did the latest additions to his team of secretaries, both British: Randall Davies, a curate's son, and William Elmslie, an Oxford graduate who doubled as Herbert's tutor—and eventually became Pulitzer's son-in-law by marrying Constance.

Back in Manhattan, the second trial of Harry Thaw for killing Stanford White, Pulitzer's architect, had just begun. It was called "The Crime of the Century"—though the century was not yet ten years old—and the *World* had compelling evidence that the public wanted all the salacious details. During the first hung-jury trial, when the *World* carried the uncensored testimony, circulation had soared by a hundred thousand.

The paper was again well represented among reporters crowding the tables in the center of the courtroom, with feature writers in a row of seats in the corner known as the royal pew. Nixola Greeley-Smith and Samuel Hopkins Adams covered the trial for the *World's* morning edition, feature writer Irvin Cobb for the evening. Nixola was to provide the woman's angle or sob stuff, as male reporters scornfully called it. But, obeying Pulitzer's perpetual cries for colorful details as well as accuracy, Adams's and Cobb's accounts were sometimes hard to distinguish from Nixola's. For example, Irvin Cobb described Evelyn Nesbit as "the most exquisitely lovely human being I ever looked at— [with] the slim, quick grace of a fawn, a head that sat on her flawless throat as a lily on its stem, eyes that were the color of blue-brown pansies and the size of half dollars; a mouth made of rumpled rose petals." She was certainly enticing enough to receive 122 marriage proposals should her husband, Harry Thaw, get the electric chair.

At first Nixola saw Evelyn as a hard-bitten gold digger. "I have no illusions about her," she wrote. "I think merely that she was sold to one man [by her mother] and later sold herself to another, and that most of her troubles were due to the fact that the [Stanford] White benevolence was a family affair [including her mother] while the Thaw golden shower was not so inclusive but fell on Evelyn alone." But when Evelyn testified, Nixola had a change of heart: "Looking at her I almost fancied myself in the children's court. It did not seem possible that this pale child could be the grown-up cause of Stanford White's alleged drugging of her, with such genuine and terrible shame that sitting there listening to this baring of her besmirched child's soul I felt myself almost as great a criminal as she made him appear, when, broken and trembling, still less moved than those before her, she ceased to talk of White and began the story of her life in Pittsburgh, the tension relaxed. The horror had been too great even for strangers to endure, and they found relief in hearing her tell of days when they only had biscuits to eat."

A mob greeted Nesbit when she arrived at the court in a new electric brougham to face a relentless two-hour cross-examination by New York district attorney William Travers Jerome. During the questioning he suggested that Stanford White had not needed drugged champagne to seduce her, and even got her to admit that she had had sex with White some time after the drugging incident.

Nixola sat with three other women reporters at tables in the center of the room. The sight of these young women writing about the "vices of man," as someone put it, astonished onlookers. According to Nixola they didn't write for long, but "writhed and bowed their heads before this hideousness," then fled from the courtroom. The next day she reported that her flight was no criticism of Jerome's methods, but "I simply feel that compared with the ordeal to which the frail young woman is subjected, a prize fight must be an elevating spectacle, and a day at the Chicago stockyards a pastoral delight."

Unlike its competitor the *Sun*, which referred to "conditions which cannot be described in a family newspaper," the *World* gave all the lascivious details provided by its male reporters. When President Roosevelt complained that Pulitzer was printing dirt, the *World* responded with: "It is easy enough to rail at newspapers for printing stenographic reports of the case, but what ought they to do? Garble the testimony? Suppress the evidence upon which Thaw's life depends? Or print without color and without elaboration the verbatim testimony of the material witnesses, as English newspapers are compelled to do by law, if they undertake to print anything at all?"

Irvin Cobb was disgusted by the psychiatrists on both sides, scornfully discounting their testimony as a "scurvy, sweated smear of pseudo-scientific poppycock which was spread all over the fraud-tinged transcript." The self-proclaimed experts eventually agreed that Thaw was a manic-depressive with "delusions of being an avenging angel, armed with whip and gun, with a mission to punish the wicked." The jury bought their conclusion, which prompted Cobb's cynical comment that the "former Poo Bahs of the popular lunatic asylums along our eastern seaboard" avoided each other's gaze "for fear of betraying a giggle."

After the jury verdict of not guilty by reason of insanity, the judge sentenced Thaw to be indefinitely confined in the State Asylum for the Criminally Insane at Matteawan. There his therapy was said to consist mainly of giving him all the vanilla éclairs he demanded. His wealthy, doting mother appealed to the U.S. Supreme Court for his release, which was denied.

On February 2, the day after Thaw was sentenced to the asylum, the *World* revealed in front-page headlines that it had another sensational tale to tell:

SECRET DOUBLE LIFE OF

ROCKEFELLER'S FATHER

REVEALED BY THE WORLD.

Mystery of Years Cleared—Old Dr. William A. Rockefeller and "Dr. William Levingston," Who Lived as a Bigamist Thirty-Four Years, Proved to Be the Same—He Deserted Mother of John D. in 1855, and Married Margaret L. Allen in Canada.

Following Pulitzer's dictum, the lead paragraphs told the story in a nutshell: "The body of Dr. William Avery Rockefeller, father of the 'Oil King,' John D. Rockefeller, lies in an unmarked grave in Oakland Cemetery, Freeport, Ill. He died in that city May 11, 1904, aged ninety-six years five months and twenty-eight days. For fifty years he led a double life. Under the assumed name of Dr. William Levingston he farmed and sold medicine of his own decoction in Illinois and North Dakota."

During thirty-four years of the fifty he was a bigamist, with two wives. One was Mrs. Eliza Davison Rockefeller, the mother of John D. Rockefeller. The other was Mrs. Margaret L. Allen Levingston. He had married his first wife, the mother of the world's richest man, in New York State in 1837. (She had died in New York in 1889, aged seventy-five.) He married his second wife, Mrs. Levingston, in Ontario in 1855, while his first wife was living with their five children in Cleveland, Ohio. His second wife apparently never knew until just before he died that her husband was a bigamist. "We lived happily together for fifty years and I shall be a true woman to the end," she said.

During the last twenty-five years of his life Dr. Rockefeller's whereabouts and the existence of the other wife were known to his sons, John D., William, and Frank Rockefeller, and to his son-in-law, Pierson D. Briggs of Cleveland. But to no one else.

The exposé spilled onto page two under these subheads:

Life of Mystery and Deceit
From Early Years to Grave.

———

Career of John D. Rockefeller's Father Traced From First
Marriage, Through Wanderings and Hiding—An
Eccentric Character, Shrewd and Tricky.

The report concluded that William A. Rockefeller, under the name of "Levingston," was well cared for by his sons but that his second wife was never acknowledged by them and that they made efforts to induce him to live apart from her as much as possible.

A neighbor who lived in a shack across the road from Levingston said: "We all took him for a great fraud. He was very 'schemish.' He wanted to make money fast and easy. The field was alive with prairie chickens then and he used to shoot them and take them over to Grafton and sell them. He was a great man for telling stories, and he'd lie when the truth would do just as well. He was as streaked as a gopher." Pressed for details, the neighbor continued: "He cured all kinds of diseases from the same jug, and he charged high for it, too. There weren't many doctors here then and he did a lot of business. He had an old screw kind of thing for pulling teeth, and people would come for miles to get a tooth pulled. He'd yank them out and charge a $1 apiece."

The *World* account acknowledged that reporter Ida Tarbell had already exposed the shenanigans of the Standard Oil Company in *McClure's* magazine, in which she proved that John D. Rockefeller's companies had corrupted politicians, extorted favors, and crushed competition. But the paper justifiably claimed that it had found his father's grave and revealed his secret life.

The *World* characterized Rockefeller Sr. as a colorful con man who had pretended to be deaf and dumb when selling goods on Indian reservations because, he told a friend, the Indians believed it was a sign of his supernatural powers. Later he posed as a physician at camp meetings, handing out handbills that claimed "Dr. William A. Rockefeller, the Celebrated Cancer Specialist, Here for One Day Only. All Cases of Cancer Cured unless too far gone and then they can be greatly benefited."

True to form—still using silence or evasion as his modus operandi—John D. Rockefeller did not refute the picture of his father as a con man and a bigamist—probably because he knew it was true.

On April 10, Pulitzer's sixty-first birthday, as was his custom he *gave* lavish gifts to friends and family. They included ten thousand dollars to Ralph to buy paintings for his home. A month earlier he had sent Joe twelve hundred dollars for his twenty-third birthday, to which Joe added eight hundred dollars of his savings and bought a secondhand 1906 Packard runabout.

That spring Kate and Herbert moved from Nice to Aix while Pulitzer, still enchanted with the *Liberty,* sailed to Naples and Syracuse. Then, to Kate's dismay, he became as elusive as old man Rockefeller. When he did contact her, she complained, "My dear Joseph, You have been as impossible to locate as a criminal hiding from justice."

He rejoined her in Aix, where he took the usual cure and showed his continued passion for politics. Driving from Aix to Annecy a tire exploded, and as he wrote to Ralph, "my nerves [were] nearly 'busted'" by the sudden loud report. While the tire was being repaired he sat in the car at the side of the road dictating to secretary Arthur Billing a nineteen-page letter to his eldest son, part of which read:

My dear Ralph,

[Here are] rough, unhewn notes for the leading editorials the day after Taft's nomination [which Pulitzer anticipated as certain]. Subject to the great unknown & the possible unexpected: 1. Provided the democrats nominate Bryan, Taft is the next president of the U.S. without ifs or buts. 2. Treat Taft absolutely with impartiality & fairness, The World will continue to treat him throughout the campaign exactly as if the World were the Supreme Court of the U.S. Unquestionably able, honest, intelligent & outside of Roosevelt's domination, independent. For this choice at least Roosevelt deserves special credit. There seems to be no conceivable chance for Bryan. He cannot possibly escape from his own record of free silver, government ownership of railroads & all sorts of populistic, half-baked, semi-socialistic false reforms. Say all this with moderation, with philosophical tolerance, with regret, even with humor.

Pulitzer suggested headlining the editorials "President Taft" with a subhead "Roosevelt's Reign of Terror Over," [but] "if Cobb has scruples of conscience about his friend Theodore he can leave out the word 'Terror.' In fact, as a mark of my warm regards I will make him a present of the word 'terror,' and it can read, 'Roosevelt's Reign Over.' I'd like to add Thank God!

"Now I beg of you, *my dear boy*, to attach the greatest importance to this. My stay in Bar Harbor will be *terribly, terribly* short & I have a great many things on my mind that I ought to make productive. So I will give no further minute details but will leave it to you that I have reports covering the last half of May, all June & July up to the day & hour of my arrival."

Rather than protest his father's excessive demands, Ralph was in awe of his passion for accurate detail and *le mot juste*, remarking at the *World*'s quarter-century celebration, "I have in my mind's eye the picture, seen many and many a time, of a man in the throes of sightlessness and suffering, insisting on a paragraph or phrase, just dictated, being read and reread to him over and over again, listening with painful attention to catch and correct any slightest suspicion of misstatement in fact, any slightest shade of overemphasis in an adjective, and possibility of conveying an impression that was not altogether accurate and scrupulously just."

Kate left Europe ahead of Pulitzer to spend the summer at Bar Harbor. He joined her soon after, having crossed the Atlantic on the *Liberty* with a shipload of guests she hadn't expected. When his guests had gone, Pulitzer relaxed on a small balcony behind the Tower of Silence overlooking Bear Brook, his favorite spot—until the foghorn at nearby Egg Rock Lighthouse opened up and drove him frantic. He even importuned the authorities to silence it, who naturally refused.

In late July he made what would be his third and last visit to the *World*'s editorial offices in Manhattan. The great man was already sitting on a couch in the reception room attended by a swarm of sycophants when someone on the staff first announced his presence. Despite the summer heat he wore a three-piece business suit, dark glasses shielding his sightless eyes, hair graying at the temples, reddish beard neatly trimmed.

On the arm of secretary Arthur Billing, he walked through the twelfth-floor newsroom to the office of night editor Robert Lyman. Told the room was fifty feet from the copy desk, he snapped, "That's damned foolish. Idiotic! Why not put it over in City Hall Park? The night editor must be near the copy desk. No nonsense about it. Swear you will change it!" Several voices swore in chorus.

Pulitzer greeted an editor, George Carteret, with: "I have wanted to meet you for a long time. You show promise." And by questioning him, he discovered that Carteret was married, thirty-five, lived in Brooklyn, was 6 feet, and weighed 250 pounds.

"My God!" Pulitzer exclaimed. "Better train down. Do you mind if I place my hands on your head and face?"

Carteret didn't mind and Pulitzer explored his face, stopping with a surprised: "My God! You have a big head, Mr. Carteret. Now, tell me, what is in that big head for tomorrow's paper?"

Carteret stuttered a few inadequate answers and Pulitzer demanded: "What did you have in the *World* this morning that the other papers didn't?"

Carteret hadn't had time to read all the other papers, and Pulitzer, when told that it was eleven-thirty, exploded, "Great God! What kind of editors are running this paper? When I was on Park Row I had all the papers read by eight."

Billing, who had previously worked as an editor, tried to ease the situation by saying, "I had them read before five!"

"Yes," replied Pulitzer, "but you read them on the way home from some all-night party. You didn't know that the papers were twenty-four hours old!"

Everyone laughed but Carteret.

"Mr. Carteret, you have spoiled my morning!" Pulitzer complained. "I beg you go back to your desk and get all the morning papers. Someday soon I shall invite you to Bar Harbor to talk to you some more. And for God's sake when you come, please be prepared. I shall ask you many questions—for your own good. Now swear you will read the papers early every morning."

Carteret obliged and Pulitzer left him with, "It was a pleasure to meet you."

On the way out, Pulitzer questioned Arthur Clarke about his health—he had recovered from a recent illness—then asked him, "What are you preparing for tomorrow morning's paper?"

Again, Pulitzer was not pleased with the answer. "There isn't one good, bright Monday morning feature!" he said. He touched Clarke's head. "What have you in there, Mr. Clarke? That is where your Monday morning feature should be. You must cudgel your brain all week for it." Clarke agreed to cudgel his brain all week.

Having shaken up the World staff, Pulitzer put the Post-Dispatch's managing editor, Oliver Bovard, on the spot. He sent him a letter marked STRICTLY AND MOST ABSOLUTELY CONFIDENTIAL in which he told him that Joe wanted to take his [Bovard's] place during his August vacation, and although Pulitzer had told Joe he was "utterly unfit and that it was ridiculous," would Bovard express his "impartial, unprejudiced, fearless opinion" of Joe's fitness for the position and name who on the staff was the fittest? Pulitzer promised Bovard to keep his response a secret.

When Bovard named Joe as up to the job with experienced men willing to help him, Pulitzer gave his twenty-three-year-old son the go-ahead. Joe subsequently did a good job, writing to Pulitzer, "I have been in heaven for the past week." He replied, "I am only too glad to express immense satisfaction and surprise about your general success. [I liked most] the enthusiasm, ambition and love of work you showed. No man can do much without the latter no matter what his talent and no man can help doing something and perhaps considerable with it."

In August Pulitzer gave Frank Cobb ten points to follow in editorials on the presidential race. Among them were:

"4. Don't say an unnecessary unkind word about Taft. Treat him fairly. Not a word of untruth under any circumstances against him or Bryan; or anybody else, not even Hearst.

5. Don't hesitate to criticise Taft politically as Roosevelt's proxy or dummy until he disproves it.

6. Don't defend Bryan on any charge made against him which you know to be founded.

8. Don't comment on everything Bryan says. Don't be afraid to ignore his speeches and talk. Don't forget that you are not compelled to write and express an opinion on anything; *silence, silence, silence* is peculiarly wise at times.

9. Don't, whatever happens, ever say that Bryan will or should be elected or that he is even fit and qualified."

Pulitzer promised Cobb a present of several hats if he observed these "rules," especially number 9. But he also warned him that if "the news and facts should change," then all the rules were subject to change.

Pulitzer then sailed in the *Liberty* from New London to England. Although Dr. Hosmer had recovered from his illness and had rejoined Pulitzer, being on the brink of eighty, he was thinking of retiring, so Tuohy met the yacht at Cowes on the Isle of Wight with Hosmer's possible replacement.

At dinner that evening, each time the candidate sliced an apple, his knife hit his plate noisily. Aghast, the other diners watched Pulitzer's face grow progressively more stormy, but before he could protest, his secretary Thwaites quipped: "If you cannot break that plate with your knife, I will send for the ship's ax." Pulitzer led the laughter that followed, but it didn't last long. Though the man was under consideration to be his doctor, Pulitzer also expected him to share his interests and be stimulating company. At the very least, he had to be well versed in literature. Pulitzer's probing soon found his weak spot. Asked to name his favorite novel, he cleared his throat and then lapsed into silence. Trying to help him out, a secretary surreptitiously wrote *The Ordeal of Richard Feverel* on a scrap of paper and handed it to him. Then the *applicant's* ordeal began. The crib didn't help because Pulitzer asked him about the plot and characters, and he hadn't a clue, irritating Pulitzer into a muttered, "I suppose you *can* read." The man finally left the yacht in a huff, saying he wouldn't accept the job for ten thousand a year.

Tuohy came up with several other doctors, but all were unsuitable, especially the one who wore scent—which Pulitzer hated.

While the doctor with the noisy knife and others thought Pulitzer was impossible, secretary James Barnes reported that Pulitzer always treated him with kindness and courtesy and said, "I actually looked forward with eagerness to the companionship of his mind. The study of his mental processes—was interesting to the point of enchantment. It was against his nature to be thoroughly trusting; his blindness made him doubly suspicious; possessing ideals, he had few beliefs. Insistent and dominant though he was, he could be intimate, kindly and—I use the word advisedly—affection compelling. His personality was full of contradictions. Depending so much upon others he had at his beck, the arts of flattery and cajolery; but also an ugly method of expression that ranged from sarcasm to downright invective. Never would I have stood what some of the others were forced to swallow and probably he knew it. [Son of a railroad tycoon, Barnes had a substantial private income.] But no man could be so bitter against himself as he was, in respect to what he called his own 'constant and manifold failures.' He could pity himself in more varied terms of speech than anyone I ever knew."

Barnes got used to Pulitzer stating his views frankly and clearly, followed by the inevitable, "In all of which I suppose you do not agree with me in the least. However, we will not argue about it."

Eventually Barnes rated Pulitzer as "the most fearless, astute and remarkable newspaper head living. Northcliffe, in his heyday, was not to be mentioned in the same class."

Still anxiously searching for a doctor to replace Hosmer, Pulitzer sailed for Amsterdam, then took a train to Wiesbaden, where twelve-year-old Herbert stayed with him while Kate took the cure at Divonne. He had become almost obsessed with his young son, interviewing some sixty potential German tutors for the boy, several times collapsing with the strain in mid-interview before settling for one. He wrote a *mea culpa* letter to Kate of his terrible initial mistake in not teaching Herbert foreign languages when he was younger. Now Pulitzer was making up for it by hiring a riding teacher instructed to speak only German with Herbert, and taking him to the opera to hear Caruso in *Rigoletto*.

Only then could he focus on his own work. Returning to his continuing battle against corruption in presidential election campaign financing, he ordered his editors to examine the background of an influential attorney, William Nelson Cromwell, "especially his relations with corporations and trusts. Is it true that he gave $50,000 to the [Republican] campaign fund? If so, why? What great devotion to public purity and public morality has he contributed?" The investigation would soon lead Pulitzer into a bitter confrontation with Theodore Roosevelt.

In early October, when Pulitzer reached Amsterdam to board the *Liberty*, Herbert rejoined his mother, but Pulitzer was so miserable without him that he persuaded Kate to send the boy, his tutor, and his governess to meet the yacht at Cherbourg. At Southampton on October 9, Pulitzer cabled Frank Cobb: "Don't fail to show wherever honestly possible, and only when honestly possible, the utmost Democratic sympathy both before and after [presidential] election should I not be home, which, of course, does not mean puffery for anybody, including Bryan."

Ten days later, before sailing for home, Pulitzer again cabled Cobb: "One thing I insist upon most particularly whatever the result: *The paper after election must be Democratic in tone, temper, sympathy and principles.* . . . The logic of events and circumstances make the *World the* great Democratic paper of the country and the only one in New York City [a fact, not a boast]. This does *not* impair in the least its freedom and independence. As long as I live I shall be far more anxious to make it independent and *non-partisan* than Democratic."

The rough crossing didn't bother him: he was a good sailor, and arrived on November 1 to stay in his soundproof Manhattan home.

On election day, despite a "thick headache," Pulitzer dictated a message to Frank Cobb: "I honestly declare that I want you to say nothing that your conscience, carefully examined, does not approve as really true. Impartiality, entire dismissal of prejudice or personal dislike alone can discover the real truth. I know this is difficult, especially to a gentleman of your ardent temperament, but I pay you the compliment of supposing that you [will] at least try."

When he learned that Taft had been elected president, Pulitzer finally concluded that Bryan "never can, never will be elected President. He is an agitator, not an administrator. Let us hope he will realize the final verdict of the people, drop the Presidential bee and devote himself to real Democratic ideas."

Before taking a cruise to the West Indies on the *Liberty*, Pulitzer gave Ralph permission to spend a couple of weeks "roughing it" in the woods of New Brunswick, Canada, which doctors had recommended to toughen him up.

Some three weeks later Pulitzer briefly disembarked at Havana. He expected Ralph to be back from Canada, but when he tried to contact him at the Dome he was told that he hadn't returned. Furious, Pulitzer cabled to the *World's* treasurer, Angus Shaw, to dock Ralph's December salary and to ask for his resignation as the paper's vice president.

In fact, Ralph had been snowbound in Canada, unable to get or send messages, and returned to work several days late, on December 4.

Told of Pulitzer's orders, he immediately cabled him, resigning as vice president, then wrote to express his dismay and disappointment and "that you did not await the explanation before inflicting the punishment (a course of common justice which you would ordinarily not have denied the humblest groom in your stable) distresses me greatly. I do sincerely hope that the week's cruise of which you cabled Mother has in the meantime greatly improved your health and spirits, and that when you now read the following explanation you will agree that I was not so much to blame as you originally considered me."

Almost as tall as Pulitzer but weighing only 140 pounds, Ralph was a sensitive twenty-nine-year-old in thrall to a brilliant, domineering, and demanding father always on his case. He had a wife and a child to support, two homes to maintain, and a career and an inheritance of millions at stake. Despite or because of Pulitzer's hypercritical attitude, Ralph had acknowledged that a word of praise from his father made him feel "happy and exhilarated, and as if I could surmount any obstacle or perform any task."

After blaming the snow for his late return to the Dome, Ralph reminded Pulitzer that four physicians had agreed it was critical for him to take time off for his health—he shared many of his father's illnesses—and that Pulitzer had agreed. Then he appealed to him as his father rather than as his employer not to cut his pay for December, which would "deprive your son of the means of supporting himself and his family." Pulitzer restored Ralph's salary but asked him to look around for another vice president to replace him.

Ralph fell seriously ill a few days later, and Pulitzer paid for him and Frederica to take a European vacation. Joe reluctantly obeyed the call to quit the *Post-Dispatch* to fill in for his brother on the *World*.

Pulitzer still hadn't found a doctor to take over from Hosmer. But he was about to face a much tougher problem—an infuriated President Theodore Roosevelt hell-bent on putting him in prison.

CHAPTER 31

Roosevelt Tries to Send Pulitzer to Prison

December 1908

—

61 years old

P ulitzer's suspicion of a payoff to William Nelson Cromwell for his hefty
contribution to the Republican Party appeared to be panning out. He had
not yet returned from his Caribbean cruise when his probing reporters concluded that President Theodore Roosevelt might be in cahoots with Cromwell—
ominously described by U.S. representative Henry Rainey as "the most dangerous man this country has produced since the days of Aaron Burr," although he
hardly looked the part. To one *World* reporter, Cromwell was a charming
lawyer in his fifties with brilliant blue eyes, "clear as a baby's and as innocent-
looking as a girl's," who could "smile as sweetly as a society belle and at the same
time deal a blow to a business foe that ties his opponent in a hopeless tangle."

The *World* soon unearthed and published details of Cromwell's question-
able past. With a hot tip that the United States meant to buy from a bankrupt
French company the rights to build a canal linking the Atlantic and the Pacific,
Cromwell had jumped the gun. Apparently he had formed a syndicate that
bought the canal rights for $3.5 million, then sold them to the U.S. govern-
ment for $40 million, pocketing the difference. Roosevelt's brother-in-law
Douglas Robinson and Taft's brother Charles were somehow involved. But a
Senate investigation into the transaction had stalled when Cromwell clammed
up and had finally fizzled out when its chairman died.

Now, two years later, the *World* claimed that Cromwell's syndicate had
made a huge fortune at public expense. The *Indianapolis News* picked up the
World exposé and demanded an official explanation. Roosevelt's friend William
Foulke read the *News* account and mailed it to him, saying that the report was

Aboard the soundproofed *Liberty*, Pulitzer walks between Don Seitz *(left)* and son Joe *(right)*.

damaging Republican prospects in the Indiana campaign that the public should know if the charges were true, and if not the paper should be exposed for lying. Roosevelt shot back with an angry letter—which was released to the press— denying everything, and calling the editor of the *Indianapolis News* "a lying blackguard and I have no doubt a corrupt crook."

On the morning of December 7, 1908, Seitz and Joe arrived by train at Charleston, South Carolina, following Pulitzer's order to meet him aboard the *Liberty*, docked in the harbor. When Seitz read him a local newspaper carrying Roosevelt's complete denial of the *News* story and told him that the *World* was also implicated, Pulitzer nervously exploded, "I knew damned well it must be! If there is any trouble you fellows are sure to be in it."

It was too late to douse the flames. Armed with what he thought were the undisputed facts and afire with righteous indignation, *World* editorialist William Speer had already sent the next morning's editorial to press. Headed "The Panama Scandal—Let Congress Investigate," it committed the *World* to the battle, called the president a liar, and demanded that Congress make a "full and impartial investigation of the entire Panama Canal scandal." The editorial reminded readers that when Cromwell had been questioned about the canal's financing in 1906 his silence had incited the Congressional Committee's chairman, Senator Morgan of Alabama, to quip, "You seem to be suffering from professional lockjaw!" Since Morgan's death soon after, no one had taken his place "to reveal the truth about Panama corruption."

There was no corruption, Roosevelt insisted—at least by Americans—and the *World* was dead wrong, because, as he wrote, "the United States did not pay a cent of the $40,000,000 to any American citizen," but paid it all "direct to the French Government [and] has not the slightest knowledge as to the particular individuals among whom the French Government distributed the same. So far as I know there was no syndicate; there certainly was no syndicate in the United States that to my knowledge had any dealings with the Government directly or indirectly."

To which the *World* replied—in italics for emphasis: *"To the best of* The World's *knowledge and belief, each and all of these statements made by Mr. Roosevelt and quoted above are untrue, and Mr. Roosevelt must have known they were untrue when he made them."*

Under the subhead WHO GOT THE MONEY? the editorial continued: "As to the details of the Panama loot only one man knows it all. And that man is William Nelson Cromwell. The two men who were most in Mr. Cromwell's confidence are Theodore Roosevelt, President of the United States, and Elihu Root, former Secretary of War and now Secretary of State." According to the *World*, Roosevelt and Root helped Cromwell to stage a Panama revolution to obtain territory from Colombia through which the canal would run, and then agreed to pay $40 million for the canal properties, plus an additional $10 million for a manufactured Panama Republic. The money was paid by check on the U.S. Treasury to J. P. Morgan & Co., not to the French government, as Roosevelt claimed.

The *World* even charged that Cromwell had used bribery to effect a revolution in Panama—to make sure the canal was built there—and under the provocative subhead HOW THE REVOLUTION WAS MANUFACTURED quoted Señor J. Gabriel Duque, who said, "Mr. Cromwell made the revolution. He offered to make me President of the new republic [of Panama] and to see me through if I would raise a small force of men and declare a secession from Colombia. He made promises that we should have the help of his Government. It was accomplished by a liberal use of money. We bought this general and that one, paying $3,000 to $4,000 per general. The Colombian officers were all paid off and the Colombian general, who was sent to stop the revolution, was also paid off."

The editorial concluded that whether or not Douglas Robinson, who was Mr. Roosevelt's brother-in-law, or any of Mr. Taft's brothers associated themselves with Mr. Cromwell in Panama exploitation, or shared in these profits, was incidental to the main issue of letting in the light. Even if all the profits went to Cromwell, the fact that Theodore Roosevelt as president of the United States issued "a public statement about such an important matter full of flagrant untruths, reeking with misstatements, challenging line by line the testimony of his associate Cromwell and the official record, makes it imperative that full publicity come at once through the authority and by the action of Congress."

The editorial created a sensation and sparked the rumor that before hunting big game in Africa, Roosevelt was first out for Pulitzer's blood. On the heels of this editorial challenge an agitated Pulitzer arrived at his Manhattan home, sent for Managing Editor Caleb Van Hamm, and asked, "What proof have you that Douglas Robinson and Charles Taft are involved in this matter?"

"None at all," he replied.

"My God!" Pulitzer said with a gasp. "No proof? You print such stories without proof?"

Van Hamm explained that his source was Cromwell himself, who had named both men.

Anticipating trouble from Roosevelt, Pulitzer prepared for it. He sent Van Hamm back to the Dome and then dictated instructions to Frank Cobb: "Turn over the files to refresh your memory. After years of discussion it was assumed that the Nicaragua Canal was an accomplished fact, and all of a sudden it was dropped. Roosevelt and Root recommended the Panama route, forcing it through under the usual pressure of administration patronage etc. That was a mystery too just exactly as the mysteriously large contributions of Cromwell to the campaign fund. Try to put the whole thing . . . upon the pivot of asking questions instead of making definite charges . . . questions that could not possibly exist if either Cromwell or Mr. Pierpont Morgan or Mr. Roosevelt would take the public into their confidence and make a clean breast of it."

Instead of coming clean, Roosevelt went on the attack. On December 11 a Pulitzer secretary read a front-page *New York Times* story to him. Headlined ROOSEVELT TO PROSECUTE FOES, it reported that Roosevelt might sue the *World* for criminal libel and referred to Pulitzer and his editors as "creatures of the gutter so low that they envy the eminence of the dunghill."

Despite the provocation, Pulitzer did not reply in kind. Instead he dictated a memo directing Cobb to accept the claims of Taft and Robinson that they were not involved in the scandal, then to concentrate on Cromwell, asking, "Who got the money? How much did Cromwell keep himself? Finally and running through the whole article, of course, the red thread should run: 'Let there be light. Let us have the facts.'"

After the memo was cabled, Pulitzer sent a messenger with more ideas for Cobb to consider, including the fact that Roosevelt had been bullying and terrifying the House and Senate, abusing judges, and the courts, and now threatened the freedom of the press. Pulitzer believed that, intoxicated by his power and popularity, Roosevelt mistook himself for a king and took all criticism as *lèse-majesté*. Cobb should make fun of him while treating "him and the office with perfect dignity and respect." However, if Cobb couldn't be satirical or good-humored, Pulitzer told him to drop the idea entirely.

William Jennings Bryan and virtually the entire U.S. press were in Pulitzer's corner, demanding an inquiry into Panama. An exception, the *Springfield* (Mass.)

Republican, blasted the *World* for its "inadmissible license" in insulting the president "by calling him a liar." A second rare exception, the pro-Roosevelt *Raleigh News and Observer,* observed: "The New York *World* evidently covets a place in the Ananias [Liars] Club."

On December 15 Roosevelt sent a blistering message to Congress insisting that the statements in Pulitzer's paper were "infamous libels. No shadow of proof has been, or can be, produced in behalf of any of them." Roosevelt charged that Pulitzer had tried "wantonly and wickedly" to blacken the character of reputable private citizens and to persuade the world that the government was guilty of wrongdoing "of the basest and foulest kind." He announced that the attorney general was considering what legal steps to take against Pulitzer.

Pulitzer was ill and resting on a couch under a blanket in the Vault, his soundproofed refuge, when Norman Thwaites anxiously read the president's words to him. Braced for an outburst, he was relieved when he came to the end and Pulitzer calmly asked him to read out other news items. But the outburst was merely delayed. Thwaites was still reading when Pulitzer punched the blanket off him, got to his feet, and fervently declared, "The World Cannot be Muzzled! The World Cannot be Muzzled! That's the headline!" There followed a stream of excited instructions to Frank Cobb. Among them were: "Assume hypothetically that the entire editorial page will be given up to article called 'The Truth About Mr. Roosevelt—Government by Denunciation,' or something of that sort [with] quotations from Roosevelt's messages, speeches, addresses, letters, but more particularly speeches of the most violent intemperance, the most violent denunciation of everything he has touched. His own words only. I think it might not be a bad idea to print extracts from the World showing that we were friendly to Roosevelt whenever he deserved it. Very friendly indeed . . . Tell the editorial gentlemen to dine downtown at my expense and have a good bottle of wine. Let them stay down till midnight. I consider this an emergency. Put your whole brain into it although it is mere quotation."

When that same day a *Times* of London reporter named Porter asked to see Pulitzer, he replied in a friendly note that he was in bed and preparing for jail, telling Porter he was astonished that Roosevelt was so mad at him—but would continue to criticize the president, if necessary from jail. He assumed that Roosevelt's threat was an attempt to squash the paper's criticism, just as Congress had been shut up. Pulitzer also told Porter he very much hoped to meet him for lunch soon because, when abroad, he had enjoyed every word of his dispatches. Meanwhile, he advised him to read next morning's *World* editorial.

Headed LESE-MAJESTY, it was a good example of the Pulitzer–Frank Cobb combination. Cobb led off with, "Mr. Roosevelt is mistaken. He cannot muzzle The World." Then he pointed out that "*The World* fully appreciates the compliment paid to it by Mr. Roosevelt in making it the subject of a special message to the Congress of the United States. . . . This is the first time a President ever asserted the doctrine of lese-majesty, or proposed . . . the criminal prosecution by the Government of citizens who criticised the conduct of the Government. Yet Mr. Roosevelt, in the absence of law, officially proposes to use all the power of the greatest government on earth to cripple the freedom of the press on the pretext that the Government itself has been libelled—and he is the Government. If The World has libelled anybody we hope it will be punished, but we do not intend to be intimidated by Mr. Roosevelt's threats. So far as The World is concerned, its proprietor may go to jail, if Mr. Roosevelt succeeds, as he threatens; but even in jail The World will not cease to be a fearless champion of free speech, a free press and a free people.

"It cannot be muzzled."

While the *World* editorial defied the president, its front-page headlines ridiculed his efforts:

ROOSEVELT'S BITTER
ATTACK ON WORLD
CAUSES MERRIMENT.

———

Senate in a Roar and House in Giggle
as President's Message Denouncing
This Newspaper and Its Proprietor
for Seeking Light on Panama
Affairs Is Read, and Everybody
Laughed but "Little Father."

According to the report, eight Democrats and twenty-four Republicans had delayed their lunch to hear the president's State of the Union message on the Panama scandal, and all but one "roared and laughed with gusto and enthusiasm like a bunch of children at a first minstrel party" when Roosevelt said "the statements in that paper [the *World*] will be believed by nobody." The president's message was also received in the House "amid roars of laughter."

Questioned by the *New York Times* about Roosevelt's attack, Pulitzer replied that because of ill health he had mostly been at sea for the past two years and for almost the whole of October and had been in Europe during the entire presidential campaign. "I never read a word or syllable of [the original] Panama story [written by Speer], was not in connection with the paper, and had nothing to do with it. Mr. Roosevelt knows all this perfectly. He knows I am a chronic invalid and mostly abroad yachting. I think his anger is simply due to the sharp attacks made by The World on him politically. For that perhaps I am responsible. The World is really the only Democratic paper in the city, and it objects strongly to Mr. Roosevelt's policy of imperialism, militarism and jingoism."

Most of Pulitzer's version was accurate, but it was wildly untrue to at least imply that he had been out of touch with his paper for about two years. His memos discount that. He also omitted to say that he initiated the Panama story in an October 1, 1908, memo to his son Ralph and Frank Cobb, telling them to investigate corrupt political campaign funding "by another broadside (perhaps the entire editorial page will do) on William Nelson Cromwell. What [is] he doing in the campaign for the Republicans? Examine his Panama record and his relations with Corporations and Trusts."

Unexpected and amusing support for Pulitzer came from his St. Louis rival the *Republic*, which said, "Mr. Joseph Pulitzer must be a very proud man today. Not since Charles A. Dana used to give mellifluous expression to his views about Mr. Pulitzer, has he been subjected to such castigation as is administered by Mr. Roosevelt in the message transmitted to Congress. Compared to the Dana outpourings, however, Mr. Roosevelt's excoriation is gruff and cruder and unpolished. Yet it is really a tremendous compliment."

On Christmas Eve Pulitzer had a memo phoned to Frank Cobb telling him not to print another editorial about Panama unless new facts emerged, and then Cobb should use Pulitzer's favorite weapons—irony, wit, and restraint. Pulitzer added: "If you swear to be witty you might have one [editorial] on Lese Majesty every day for a few days. . . . But dig, dig, dig and don't print until you have something proven."

When, as Pulitzer expected, New York district attorney Jerome brought charges against him, he asked Cobb to write an editorial asserting that Roosevelt was hounding Pulitzer merely to gratify his resentment against the paper for its long criticism of Roosevelt's "jingoism, his centralization, and his cowboy policies"—that Jerome had turned against the *World* because it had "pitched into him" for doing nothing about wealthy lawbreakers. However, Pulitzer said he would take responsibility for his paper and Cobb should stress that neither Jerome nor Roosevelt nor anyone else could "muzzle the *World*. But make it dignified," Pulitzer insisted.

In an effort to discredit Pulitzer, many of the staff of the *World* were tailed by an extraordinary number of secret agents, who opened their mail in the post office and examined the portfolios of its messengers between New York and Washington. The Pulitzer Building itself had been "filled with spies."

Had Pulitzer not been an invalid, his secretary James Barnes felt sure he would have stayed on land to face the music, "but he disliked discomfort and, old war horse that he was, he decided that he would rather direct the battle from a safe distance; so he took to the high seas," waiting for Roosevelt or Jerome to strike.

The *Liberty* spent the winter months outside the three-mile limit of the United States, from the semitropical Gulf of Mexico to the snowstorms and windstorms of Long Island's Montauk Point. Occasionally the launch would be sent ashore to pick up the mail and send out letters. Many messages were for Frank Cobb, telling him to keep defending press freedom and questioning the motives of Roosevelt and Jerome.

CHAPTER 32

"The Big Man of All American Newspapers"

1909
—
61 to 62 years old

C hicago Daily Journal publisher Charles Clark had inside information about the Panama Canal rip-off. Or so it seemed from this confidential letter he sent Ralph Pulitzer on January 2, 1909: "This Panama deal was begun before the De Lesseps company [which started to build the Suez Canal] quit the isthmus in 1887, and any attempt to investigate from this end will be very difficult to carry through, because Americans didn't get into the game until the fertile Frenchmen had planned it. If we patiently gather up all the clues in Frisco and Central America, use them as a wedge in Paris, and finally deal with America, we can open the oyster, which is undoubtedly in a bad state of decomposition."

Pulitzer already had L. Paulin investigating in Paris. A member of the *World's* editorial staff who spoke French, Paulin happened to be vacationing there at the time, until Pulitzer had asked him instead to spend twelve hours a day digging into the Panama mystery to find out who got away with what.

The day the Chicago publisher wrote to Ralph, Pulitzer was aboard the *Liberty* off Charleston warning Frank Cobb in a memo to "please be very, very moderate about Roosevelt and above all don't *overdo* things. Of course his message you must criticize, analyze *sharply* but fairly." He also asked Cobb to go to Washington, D.C., to try to persuade Democratic House members to introduce a resolution to "expunge at least the personal point of Roosevelt's message." He was uneasy, to say the least, with prison looming in his future. Justifiably. In the White House, Roosevelt told lunch guests that he and his brother-in-law Douglas Robinson, whom the *World* had originally implicated in the Panama scandal, were confident they could put Pulitzer away for criminal libel.

When Frank Cobb had failed in his Washington assignment, Pulitzer invited him aboard the *Liberty* to plan how to keep out of prison. As they cruised along the New Jersey coast, Cobb urged a tough counterattack, which Pulitzer resisted. They argued fiercely late into the night until, with an impressive exchange of expletives, they broke their promise never to get mad at the same time.

Pulitzer ended the argument by ordering the captain to throw his "indegoddampendent" editor off the yacht. The English captain, A. E. Caws, reared on the marquess of Queensberry rules, protested that Cobb would have great difficulty in returning to New York from the deserted shore. "I don't care how much trouble he has!" Pulitzer yelled. "The more trouble he has the better I'll be pleased." How Cobb got back remains a mystery. So does why he didn't quit. Perhaps he understood that Pulitzer was under almost unbearable stress—or considered a night alone on a New Jersey sandbank a vacation compared to the divorce he, Cobb, was going through. Or he recalled the good times. Less than a year before, after working for Pulitzer for four years, he had told him, "I would not barter those four years for any other years of my life."

Meanwhile, Paulin's search in Paris proved futile. The men with information were dead or had run for cover. In a statement to Congress, Roosevelt had said that Panama Canal Company records were kept by Crédit Lyonnais of Paris and he was sure "that on the request of our Ambassador in Paris the Lists of individuals [stockholders] will be shown him." He was wrong: the head of the Crédit Lyonnais refused to show the records to anyone, even to President Roosevelt, because, under French law, such records could not be examined even to provide evidence of fraud and after twenty years would be destroyed. As Seitz quipped, "The French have perfected the art of preserving mysteries. Who has ever identified 'The Man in the Iron Mask'?"

Frank Cobb had somehow returned from New Jersey to his desk at the Dome, and Pulitzer had gone ashore to hole up for a few days in his Manhattan mansion, when Irvin Cobb (no relation to Frank) was asked to help out. For someone who had never met Pulitzer, Irvin had a vivid and compassionate sense of him. In Irvin's words, Pulitzer was "a giant intelligence eternally condemned to the darkest of dungeons, a caged eagle furiously belaboring the bars." Now that Pulitzer was literally faced with prison—which would probably kill him—Cobb was called into Seitz's office and told, "Mr. Pulitzer is in a very depressed, very harassed state. The possible consequences to his health are dangerous." Pulitzer feared that District Attorney Jerome, fresh from his triumph at the Thaw trial, would jump at the chance to prosecute him for criminal libel on Roosevelt's behalf. Irvin Cobb's mission was to find out if this was so; time and expense no object.

He didn't need much of either. It cost him a nickel for the trolley ride to Jerome's Centre Street office, where he asked him straight out if he meant to prosecute Pulitzer. Jerome replied: "I don't like a hair of that man's head. He has attacked me viciously, violently, and, as I see it without due provocation. The *World* has had their crepe-heeled flunkeys dogging my steps and shadowing my people. So, because of all that and nothing else, I've let King Pulitzer and his gang of sycophants—stew in their own juice. Whereas, if any properly accredited reporter from the *World* had come to me, I'd have told him." As good as his word, Jerome revealed to accredited reporter Cobb that, as he hated both Roosevelt and Pulitzer, he had decided not to help one by prosecuting the other.

Who would be the prosecuting attorney was still unknown on February 17 when a District of Columbia grand jury indicted Pulitzer, his managing editor Caleb Van Hamm, and his night editor Robert Lyman for criminally libeling Theodore Roosevelt, J. P. Morgan, Charles Taft, Douglas Robinson, Elihu Root, and William Nelson Cromwell.

Frank Cobb responded in the *World* the next day, "These libel proceedings have no other object than to enable Mr. Roosevelt to employ the machinery of the United States Government to satisfy his personal desire for revenge. Whatever indictments Mr. Roosevelt may [bring] against *The World* or against Mr. Pulitzer or against editors of *The World*, he will not intimidate this newspaper or swerve it in the slightest degree from the performance of its public duty. Mr. Roosevelt is an episode. *The World* is an institution. Long after Mr. Roosevelt is dead, long after Mr. Pulitzer is dead, long after the present editors of this paper are dead, *The World* will still go on as a great independent newspaper, unmuzzled, undaunted and unterrorized."

In freezing winter weather the *Liberty* took Pulitzer from New York Harbor to Charleston, where he stopped to pick up and send mail, nervously aware that U.S. marshals might be on the dock waiting to arrest him. Anticipating the worst, he tried to find out what kind of jail to expect should Roosevelt prevail.

To compound Pulitzer's problems, Caws, the yacht's captain, caught pneumonia, from which he died in a New York hospital, to be succeeded by Brooklynite Hiram Dixon. Pulitzer also fell seriously ill, and as Dr. Hosmer had retired and no permanent replacement had been found, a temporary took over.

In fact, Pulitzer could only be prosecuted before a Washington, D.C., grand jury if he set foot in that city, so Taft's inauguration in a howling blizzard on March 4 was not that day's big news to Pulitzer: to him it was the day Roosevelt persuaded U.S. attorney Henry Stimson to assemble another grand jury, this time in New York—Pulitzer's home ground, where he would be more vulnerable to arrest.

Frank Cobb was an early witness. Fresh from being dumped by Pulitzer on the New Jersey shore, was he a witness for the prosecution? Not at all: Cobb gave his boss rave reviews. He testified, "Mr. Pulitzer conducts a school of journalism in regard to me. He often says he expects that I shall be able to carry on the principles of *The World* for the next 20 years." But Cobb also claimed to feel free to ignore Pulitzer's instructions with which he disagreed. Asked if he regarded Pulitzer "as the Big Man of The World," Cobb replied, "I regard Mr. Pulitzer as the Big Man of all American newspapers."

During the grand jury testimony, Pulitzer dared to leave the *Liberty* to make a brief visit to his Seventy-third Street home. By then his nerves were so badly frayed that he exploded and yelled at his twenty-two-year-old daughter Edith when she scraped her dinner plate while carving a squab. She burst into tears. Joe leaped to his feet and angrily told his father, "I won't allow you to speak to my sister in this way! I'm not going to stand any more of your bullying! I'm pulling out!" Joe then took off for St. Louis, where he tried to get a job on competing newspapers. When that failed, he returned to Manhattan, where Pulitzer ordered him out of the house—the lowest point in their often stormy relationship.

Back on the *Liberty*, Pulitzer had second thoughts and sent Joe a conciliatory telegram. But Joe was in no mood for compromise, replying in a frank, even brutal letter he must have known would devastate his father: "For years I have resented the realization that I was nothing but a rich man's son of no market value in this world and dependent for everything I had on you. I am so selfishly constituted that I am unable to make allowances for your many afflictions. I feel that I was acting the part of a hypocrite in swallowing my resentment and simulating demonstrations of affection." He hoped to get married but not "on an allowance that I might be deprived of any day. Perhaps I am ruining my life by writing this letter, but I am young and foolish and optimistic and I prefer to believe that instead of ruining it I am beginning it. I shall not go to hell as you fear." He predicted that in the process of making something of himself his affection for his father would grow rather than diminish—which, in fact, happened.

Pulitzer ordered his new captain to head for Portugal, then changed his mind and had the *Liberty* anchor off Greenwich, Connecticut. There he called for a lawyer to come aboard to formalize a new codicil to his will. In the 1904 version Joe was to receive 60 percent of the income from stock in the two newspapers, with Ralph and Herbert each getting 20 percent. Joe would pay dearly for opposing his father. His inheritance was drastically reduced, to 10 percent; Ralph's remained unaltered at 20 percent; but Herbert's was tripled, to 60 percent. Principal editors and managers were to share the remaining 10 percent. Pulitzer allowed for the sale of the *Post-Dispatch* with the trustees' approval but never wanted the *World* to be sold. As he put it, in a cry from the heart, "I particularly enjoin my sons and my descendants the duty of preserving, perfecting and perpetuating The World newspaper."

Eventually, after reconciling with his father, Joe agreed to work at the *World* in New York if he could spend a week each month in St. Louis—but only until Ralph was fit enough to return to the *World* full-time, "when I shall go back to St. Louis for good."

Having updated his will to Joe's great disadvantage, Pulitzer headed for Portugal, his mercurial mood matched by the rough seas through which his yacht rolled, sometimes at a dramatic angle of forty-five degrees. The new young ship's doctor, O. E. Wrench, was baffled by an illness that kept Pulitzer bedridden. When they reached port, the Pulitzers' family doctor, Frank Kinnicut, located in Pau, France, rushed to Lisbon to give a second opinion. He diagnosed whooping cough, a dangerous illness for a patient of Pulitzer's age and frail constitution.

Another threat to Pulitzer's life was a new secretary, William Paterson, a Scot, who, soon after boarding the *Liberty*, came down with smallpox. He was taken to a Gibraltar hospital, where he slowly recovered. The yacht was fumigated and everyone aboard vaccinated. Pulitzer then went ashore at Marseilles and took a train to Aix-les-Bains to recuperate from whooping cough. Weeks later he returned to his comparatively germ-free yacht.

Pulitzer hoped that President Taft would drop the libel prosecution now that Roosevelt was out of office and expending his energy on eliminating African wildlife. That hope was dashed when the new president appointed Attorney General George Wickersham to lead the attack. America now represented a threat to Pulitzer, and instead of spending the summer at Bar Harbor he ordered the *Liberty's* skipper to take him north, to Norway.

After stopping at Oslo to pick up and send messages, the yacht lay at anchor in a Norwegian fjord. Pulitzer stood on deck beside secretary James Barnes and said, "Tell me what you see." Barnes tried, but Pulitzer impatiently broke in with, "But where are we? What is it like? Where are the shores? Where are these hills you talk about? How far away are they? What are the points of the compass?" And on and on. Then he paused, pressed Barnes's arm, and in a quieter voice said, "Forgive a poor blind man. Please take me to my cabin."

There he dictated a message for Frank Cobb, beginning, "Are you tired? I hope not," and asked for an editorial panning President Taft's decision to appoint no black in the South without the approval of southern whites. "We cannot agree in drawing such a skin color or race line," Pulitzer declared, calling it a nullification of the Fifteenth Amendment.

He also asked Cobb for a feature on Reno as a divorce resort, calling Nevada "an utterly farcical state." Finally, referring to the ongoing grand jury investigation, he said, "I think you can impress people with our fairness when we say we acquit Roosevelt of having any knowledge of Robinson's connection with the syndicate. [But] the attack he made on me was undignified and lowering to the dignity of the Presidency. We hope the day may come that even he may be ashamed of himself for what he has done."

While Pulitzer dictated his notes for Cobb, James Barnes had a bright idea. He commandeered a cork mat from one of the bathrooms and stuck different-size pins into it, representing the shoreline and the little town off which the yacht was anchored. He added islands and hills—crumbled paper held in place with sticking plaster—made a compass from cardboard, and whittled the hull of a miniature yacht.

The next day, while Pulitzer sunned himself on deck, Barnes placed the makeshift three-dimensional map in his lap. Then he guided Pulitzer's finger to follow the shore, the hills and island, the position of the yacht, and, as Barnes wrote in his memoir, "he entered into the game like a child with a new toy."

Some twenty minutes after Barnes had taken the "toy" away, another secretary came on deck, and Pulitzer led him to the ship's rail. Pointing at the shore, he began, "We are headed north by east; the harbor lies over there [and] you can see the spire of a church against the dark, pine trees. We are a quarter of a mile from shore. Over here is a rocky island and beyond it, about a mile, another smaller one; the cliffs come almost straight down to the water and are a thousand feet in height. There is a herd of cows grazing in a pasture up on the hillside at the head of the fjord; in the shadows are some fishing boats."

"My God!" the secretary muttered to others on board. "He can see!"

In good weather the *Liberty* cruised north beyond the Arctic Circle, then returned to Oslo, where Pulitzer and his staff intended to go ashore for a few days while the yacht was refueled.

To ensure a peaceful stay, Harold Pollard went in advance, and money being no object, he took over a small hotel a few miles out of town. The occupants were moved to nearby cottages so Pulitzer and his staff would have the place to themselves. To get Pulitzer from the harbor to the hotel, Pollard stopped at a private livery stable, where he hired an elaborate coach and four white horses used by the king of Norway on state occasions, and two smaller open carriages for Pulitzer's entourage. As Barnes recalled, "No funnier or more astonishing visit was ever paid to Norway by a private citizen than Mr. Pulitzer's. As we neared the royal boat landing, where crowds of people were assembled, I could see the equipages waiting on the dock; the drivers were in white uniforms with gold braid and knee-high boots. In the stern of the big launch sat the chief himself—a most picturesque figure. He had on a wide-brimmed black hat of a style known as 'a brigand,' a long blue cape with silver clasps; with his height of nearly six foot three, and his long, reddish gray beard, he looked more than distinguished—he was overpowering."

Many curious onlookers doffed their hats as he was helped up the gangway to the pier, and when he drove through the city, shopkeepers and pedestrians, seeing the white horses pulling the royal coach, also raised their headgear.

Driving through open country, Pulitzer dictated a memo to Frank Cobb while laborers left the fields, lined the roadside, and gawked at the colorful procession. The hotel wasn't ready for the party, so they killed time by a trip along a driveway through nearby fields, where haymakers dropped their rakes and pitchforks to stare openmouthed at Pulitzer and the royal carriage. After reaching several large buildings, the travelers turned around and returned to the hotel.

When Barnes told the hotel proprietor where they'd been, he said that they had gone through the grounds of a private lunatic asylum. Barnes gave the news to Pulitzer at lunch, and he threw back his head and laughed as if he'd never stop. "A lunatic asylum!" he exclaimed at last. "Oh, my God! Why didn't you leave me there?"

On land or at sea Pulitzer never let up in his memos to Cobb, pointing out that despite Roosevelt's criticism of "malefactors of great wealth," he had sent none to jail, and instead was persecuting the only Democratic newspaper in New York City, not unlike the situation in Germany, where "hundreds of editors are always being locked up." He repeatedly stressed that the great question about Panama the public must never forget was "Who Got the Money?"

In the early fall, after the trip to Norway, Pulitzer left his yacht to stay at a house in Berlin, near the Tiergarten. Typically, the house had been specially prepared to meet his needs. Three layers of glass in all the windows; thick rugs on all the floors; a new bathtub with no sharp edges; the best-quality bed and table linen; silver, porcelain, and glassware for at least twelve people. Curtains of the heaviest, sound-deadening material were hung over the doors and windows of Pulitzer's bedroom, and electric bells installed to ring in the valet's room. All doors, windows, and locks had to be carefully adjusted and oiled to be as noiseless as possible.

Soon after moving in, he approved two ideas Joe sent him to show the vulnerability of the U.S. Navy to attack: by dropping a make-believe bomb—a bundle of *Worlds*—on a battleship in New York Harbor, and to offer a twenty-thousand-dollar prize to the first pilot to fly from New York to St. Louis.

He was in good spirits, attending the opera and dining with friends, until a reporter phoned to tell him that his brother Albert had committed suicide. The *New York Times* reported that he had suffered from incurable neurasthenia for twenty years "through overwork, causing an unbearable sensitiveness to the slightest changes in temperature and light [a version of his brother's supersensitivity to noise]. Lately his malady developed into persecution mania, a sudden attack of which may have prompted the suicide. A rumor that his fortune had been left to the Vienna Voluntary Aid Society is incredible, as, according to his secretary, Mr. Pulitzer's fortune consisted chiefly of a life annuity, which expired at his death."

The *World* account was headed:

ALBERT PULITZER A
SUICIDE IN VIENNA.

Founder of Morning Journal Took
Poison, Then Sent a Bullet
Into His Brain.

It read in part: "He first swallowed poison, then, standing in front of a mirror, shot himself in the right temple. Mr. Pulitzer is said to have had a nervous breakdown and to have been greatly depressed at the failure of his physicians to benefit him." The five-paragraph account on page seven, next to a cigar ad, did not mention that he was Joseph's brother.

In his "brigand" hat, Joseph Pulitzer walks between his daughter Edith and secretary Harold Pollard outside the Café de Paris, Monte Carlo, in 1909.

Though the brothers had been estranged for years, Pulitzer sent Thwaites to Vienna with fifteen thousand dollars to give Albert a decent burial. He found his body in a cheap box, destined for a pauper's grave, and arranged for a burial with Jewish rites. Thwaites watched the flower-covered casket lowered into the ground in a snowstorm as a choir sang the Jewish prayer for the dead. "The exquisite service moved me greatly," he told Pulitzer, which begs this question: If Pulitzer—mistakenly—believed his mother was Catholic, and didn't think of himself as a Jew (he would eventually be buried as an Episcopalian), why did his brother consider himself Jewish? The puzzle remains unsolved.

In late October Pulitzer joined his daughters Edith and Constance aboard the *Liberty* at Menton, France, for a cruise to the Greek islands, during which they discussed Joe. Pulitzer was all for his son marrying Elinor Wickham if he settled in New York and worked "steadily for six months." He failed to recognize that what irked him most—Joe's independent spirit—was a reflection of his own character. And when his son determined to live in St. Louis, Pulitzer dismissed it as "a provincial town" that "affords far less scope than New York for a man ambitious for honor, importance, power and prestige." But Joe was beginning to buckle down to his father's demands, judging by his promise to devote himself to a recent assignment Pulitzer gave him: to critique the *World*. Joe vetoed a proposal to run ads on pages two and three, and criticized a cartoon

of J. P. Morgan emphasizing "his diseased nose," because of "my natural instinc-
tive horror of hurting a man's feelings." He disagreed with his father's opposition to building U.S. embassies in Europe. "It is undignified to say the least,"
Joe wrote, "for ambassadors to have to operate out of hotels."

After the Mediterranean cruise, Pulitzer moved into the Villa Arethusa at
Cap Martin, with a breathtaking view of Monte Carlo across the bay—but lost
to him, of course.

One day, as he was being driven on the Corniche road, the car stalled and
his secretary, Pollard, left to get help from the nearby village of Roquebrunne.
Sitting beside Seitz in the stalled car, Pulitzer said, "You see how quiet I am.
Real troubles never bother me. It's only the small annoyances that upset me."
Then he added, "We will not have many more rows." Seitz jokingly replied that
he hoped that pleasure would not be denied them. "No I am serious," Pulitzer
insisted. "I am not going to live long. I have had warnings. Besides I am no
longer equal to thinking or deciding [refuted by his ongoing avalanche of
memos]. You will have to get along without me more and more from now on."

While on the yacht one evening Pollard was so overwhelmed by a spectacular sunset that he persuaded Pulitzer to try to get some sense of it. Pulitzer
strained his eyes in the direction Pollard indicated, then said regretfully, "It's no
use, my dear boy, I cannot even get a glimmer of light."

CHAPTER 33

Roosevelt Seeks Revenge

1910
—
62 to 63 years old

Pulitzer was briefly elated after Democrat William Gaynor was elected New York's mayor, especially as the profane and peppery judge beat Hearst, still thirsting for office, by a hundred thousand votes. But Pulitzer then faced the grim prospect of Roosevelt returning from his African safari to fight for a third presidential term, and continuing to pursue the criminal libel case against him with all the power and prestige of the White House. Yet, not wanting to handicap Roosevelt by boosting Taft unfairly, he warned Frank Cobb's editorial partner, Horatio Seymour, to avoid any distortion in his anxiety to "make a phrase or show brilliant, rhetorical style." Instead, he must stick to the facts and use "moderation, reasonableness in every word whether criticizing or praising."

It would be fair, he wrote, to criticize Taft's "absurd" talk about war because it showed his "ignorance of European conditions." (Hardly absurd—World War I was only four years ahead.) It would also be fair to attack his "preposterous advocacy of the old military cries of Roosevelt that we must have a bigger army and a bigger part in European politics, while reasonable to praise him "*warmly and strongly*" for his "policy for economy and retrenchment." Pulitzer admitted that if Seymour wanted Roosevelt nominated, the best policy would be to "tear Taft to pieces. That is, if I allow you, which I don't."

Yet Pulitzer required "every editor to write only what he conscientiously believes, and if he disagrees with the policy of the paper [i.e., with Pulitzer] to remain simply silent. *But I do ask you to be silent* when you disagree with me."

A few months later he complained, "I have never known the *World* to come so near to being muzzled, afraid of saying anything about Taft or his weaknesses. If there is anything under the sun I hate, and that I believe the *World* was never guilty of before, it is trimming or sitting on the fences or the failure to do its duty about men in the highest places. Taft has made a lot of mistakes perfectly obvious to everybody, and yet the World remained silent. Please—Why?—Frankly?"

Any editor at the Dome who hoped to avoid Pulitzer's scrutiny over the Christmas season was quickly disillusioned with his: "Who made up the paper, putting the stories of Mrs. Belmont, Pinkerton's break with the banks, and Mrs. Astor's estate, all inside? Who put Mark Twain's arrival from Bermuda under small heading on last page? Who made up the paper of Dec. 26? Death of Sheldon put inside. Seymour remarks it was worth first page but was placed by Lyman and Adkins. When was Lyman put back again at night and why, how, and was it with your *consent*? If such imbecility reigns after [my] cable I simply must be consulted much as I dislike it. Why is there not some man solely in charge of pictures? The suggestion has been made at least 100 times in the course of the last twenty years."

He asked Ralph if Roosevelt's criminal libel case against him, now under way with Taft's blessing, was vigorous or nominal, and to compare the spirit, honesty, and reliability of Pulitzer's own defense attorney, De Lancey Nicoll, with the government's legal big guns. Before Ralph could reply, the trial had taken place. Nicoll had argued that the law of 1898 had been enacted to protect national defenses, not to cover libel against an individual, had failed when used against Dana of the *Sun* some years previously, and "as for libel against the government, [it was] utterly absurd!" The judge agreed. Pulitzer was exonerated. He would not, as he had feared, die in prison.

American newspapers cheered with one voice regardless of political sympathies. "A victory for freedom of the press," said the *Sun*, adding that "it signified absolutely nothing as to the truth or falsity of the statements printed in the *World* about the disposition of the Panama Canal money." Hearst reminded readers that his *American* had been "on record in protest against this prosecution and all like attempts to make the law of libel an instrument of political repression." To the *New York Times* it was "a very appropriate ending for an action most unwisely begun and prosecuted upon the theory, which the Court declares to be quite baseless, that the libel was 'against the dignity of the United States.'" The *Philadelphia Record* asserted that "if one hurt the President's feelings by insinuating that he 'blabbed' among his familiars, and that these familiars turned the information thus given to good and profitable account, that is a strictly personal matter; and the President is no better than any other citizen and has no greater right of redress for an injury to his individual susceptibilities. To speak disparagingly or even libelously of the President's brother-in-law or the President's secretary's brother has not yet become a crime against the United States. Mr. Roosevelt made the mistake of confounding the majesty of his office with the majesty of himself." The *Springfield* (Mass.) *Republican* regretted that the judge tried the case so quickly, because, had it "gone to a jury, the details of the Panama revolution would have been exposed in a way to startle the country."

In February, apparently free from the threat of prison and enjoying a Mediterranean cruise on the *Liberty*, Pulitzer sent reminders to Ralph of stories to cover and editorial ideas to follow. He believed that Taft's secretary of state, Philander Knox, known as "Sleepy Phil" when McKinley's attorney general because of his weak-kneed prosecution of the trusts, was confirming his reputation as a tool of big money. "Knox's foreign policy [is] foreign indeed," Pulitzer wrote. [He is] acting as agent to Morgan, Kuhn Loeb and other financiers." Pulitzer also suggested a series on how extravagant American women increased the cost of living, "which everybody knows [is true] and yet no paper seems to have the courage to admit." He recommended sending Greeley-Smith to Europe to compare the spending habits of the European wives of laborers, average men, and the wealthy, with their American counterparts. "A nice trip," he added, "for anyone who will work." Despite the outstanding work of his female reporters, Pulitzer had the typical contemporary male view of women. He urged Ralph to argue against women suffrage "without fear, but satirically, sardonically, perhaps humorously. But don't be afraid—idol worship has been abandoned for some thousands of years. Women worship might at least be subjected to truth, that would be a devilish good and entertaining analysis."

When symptoms of Pulitzer's whooping cough returned, Thwaites sent a medical SOS to Tuohy in London to find a first-rate physician willing to spend a month on the yacht calling at Constantinople, Athens, Egypt, and the Red Sea. His job would be to study and diagnose Pulitzer's "peculiar history and conditions of nervousness, insomnia and recently recurring complications of whooping cough." Other than that, it should be a great vacation. A vital proviso was that the candidate had to be seasickproof. "It is quite different from anything he has asked before," Thwaites explained, "in that it distinctly eliminates the point of intellectual companionship [and] he may stutter, or be a hunchback, but, of course, not preferably so."

A few days later a secretary read a recent *World* to Pulitzer that galvanized him from his sickbed into dictating a response: "My dearest [Frank] Cobb, I nearly fainted when reading your editorial. It is a dreadful example of over zeal—good intentions carried to excess. What is the use of writing a whole column containing not a single new point? Why this dreadful repetition? Please forgive me. You know I mean well and, incidentally, whether I mean well or not you will have to come over here and talk over the political situation and general semi-comatose condition of the editorial page."

Pulitzer believed that 1910 offered a great chance for the *World* to become even more famous by backing the Democratic cause, by stressing the need for a dynamic opposition party "for the sake of the party in power itself, an idea admirably readapted and expressed by Taft but ignored by the *World* at the time. I want the *World* to lead with vigor and force and courage and yet retain its independence and never expose itself to the charge of partisanship." In the upcoming November elections he expected several states, including Ohio and New York, to elect Democratic governors, for the Democrats to become a majority in the House of Representatives and to gain seats in the Senate. Then he wanted readers to know "that it was the World's fight and the World's victory."

A week before Joe's twenty-fifth birthday on March 21, Pulitzer invited him to Cap Martin, where he gave him a thousand dollars and his blessing to marry Elinor. Homeward bound, at first by train, Joe glanced at the distant villa and, as he wrote to his father the next day, "it made me realize more keenly than I have realized in all my life under what deep obligation I am to you and how very much at fault I have been in the past in not feeling this obligation. In a way I hated to leave you back there and even now with the happy prospect that I have before me I feel very selfish in going away. The thought of that letter I wrote you a year ago has haunted me. It fills me with shame." Joe promised to do all he could to help his father, even to give up "my contemplated visit to St. Louis, if it will please you. I ask only that you put me to the test."

Late in March, Pulitzer felt well enough to tour the Mediterranean coast with his new physician, a Dr. Guthman. Kate was also in Europe and in a reversal of their roles, he lost track of her. It wasn't clear whether she was at Cap Martin, Paris, or Aix. Concerned, he wired all three places, asking her to say where she was immediately. At Athens almost everyone went ashore to see the Acropolis. Pulitzer remained on board with Dunningham, and as biographer Swanberg relates, "this was one of the few times when his blindness and his self-pity brought him such despair that he gave way to tears."

After returning from the cruise, Pulitzer moved to Wiesbaden for the usual treatments, which apparently gave some relief from his chronic illnesses, but nothing interrupted for long his work to improve the World.

He had some of his best ideas in his car, dictating as many as twenty pages of notes at a time as he was driven to or from a musical evening or a restaurant. One bright suggestion was to encourage the embryonic aviation industry by offering ten thousand dollars to the first pilot to fly the 137 miles from Albany to New York in a day. Trying for the prize, Glenn Curtiss took off from Albany in a biplane at 7:03 A.M. on May 29. New York Times editor Carr Van Anda outmatched and embarrassed the World by hiring a special train with Mrs. Curtiss aboard to follow her husband's flight and report her reactions. Crowds watched all along the route, gasping when the plane bounced up and down fifty or sixty feet in the treacherous air pockets. Flying at an average fifty-four miles per hour, Curtiss landed, after two hours and thirty-two minutes, at Isham Farm at Broadway and 214th Street.

The Times outdid all the competition by giving the most complete and colorful coverage of the flight—almost seven pages. But the World still got the plaudits from, among others, President Taft, who said; "It seems that the wonders of aviation will never cease." The World immediately offered thirty thousand dollars for the first flight from New York to St. Louis, or vice versa.

Spending much of his time afloat or in Europe, Pulitzer had not yet met Elinor, but he had been captivated by Joe's glowing accounts of the "Divinity."

Joe Pulitzer *(left)* with
his father's secretary,
Harold Pollard.

And as the marriage date approached, Pulitzer made sure Joe could support
such—an enchanting woman by giving him a yearly $20,000 personal allow-
ance on top of his salary. He also authorized a $10,000 wedding present for Eli-
nor and amended his will to leave her $250,000.

Too sick to attend the wedding in Elinor's St. Louis home on June 2,
Pulitzer sent the couple a $50,000 solid-gold dinner service. Joe's sister Edith
was a bridesmaid and Ralph his best man. The bride's uncle Daniel Catlin
gave her away. He had been one of the first friends Pulitzer had made in St.
Louis some forty years before.

In late July, former secretary James Barnes was Pulitzer's guest at Bar Harbor. They took long walks together on the deck of the *Liberty* discussing the
joys of Shakespeare, which Pulitzer quoted by the page, and speculating on
Theodore Roosevelt's plans after his recent triumphant return from big-game
hunting in Africa. Talking politics reminded Pulitzer to cable Cobb to keep
an eye on Roosevelt, to endorse Woodrow Wilson as Democratic candidate for
governor of New Jersey, and to help Democrats everywhere. He also urged
Cobb to make "the *World*'s Democratic sympathies plain and unmistakable,

while retaining full measure of honest independence. The *World* should be more powerful than the President. He is fettered by partisanship and politics and has only a four-years term. The paper goes on year after year and is absolutely free to tell the truth and perform every service that should be performed in the public interest. Be fair. If Roosevelt, for example, should come out in favor of a great reform like tariff revision, I'd praise him for that one thing and support him on that one thing, without altering a word of criticism as to his follies."

Soon after, he called Cobb to Bar Harbor for a pep talk. "You must seize every opportunity to right a public wrong," he said, "to denounce injustice and oppression, to strike a blow for humanity. I want The *World* every day to champion the people's interest from whatever quarter they are attacked."

The next morning Chapin, editor of the *Evening World*, sent a reporter and a cameraman to cover Mayor Gaynor's departure for Europe. As Chapin recalled, "[They] were aboard the ship when one of the most sensational news happenings of the year took place, a crazy assassin shooting down the Mayor because of a fancied grievance he had been brooding over. It so chanced that the shot was fired at the very instant the photographer clicked his camera. The film showed the wounded Mayor sinking into the arms of those closest to him." Within an hour the photo and story made the *World*'s front page.

Before he returned to Europe in the fall, Pulitzer wrote to Gaynor in Hoboken's Saint Mary's Hospital to congratulate him on his "narrow escape and excellent prospect of complete recovery. If I have not expressed my sentiments before it was because I was ill. The news of the dastardly attempt upon your life caused me the same sickness of heart as when the news of the assassinations of Lincoln, Garfield and McKinley reached me. I regarded it as a special calamity to the City of New York; a threatened loss to the Republic, the cause of Reform, and the great masses of democracy who yearn for a leader."

Ensconced in the Hotel Quisisan, Wiesbaden, in October, Pulitzer cautioned Frank Cobb against calling Glutinous (Roosevelt's code name) a liar. "Would it not be better," he asked, "to prove [him a liar] without rather than with the use of that word? Compliment him, flatter him about his wonderful veracity, love of truth etc. etc. In deadly parallel, however, quote his own words proving the contrary, respectfully submitted. The point is: to prove him a liar by his own words—*his own words*." Soon after, in a letter to James Barnes, Pulitzer said, "My feeling about T. R. [Roosevelt] is purely political. Personally, I admire his genius and agree with much of what is good in him."

The incredible attention Pulitzer gave to detail is shown in a request from secretary Thwaites to Joe. "Your diary states: 'Corrected grammatical error on the editorial page.' Andes [Pulitzer] would like you to send him this instance of error with your correction."

Disturbed by Ralph's latest diary entries about office animosities, he asked him rhetorically, "What can I do about Lyman and Spurgeon not hitting it off?

A *World* photographer took this remarkable picture of New York
mayor Gaynor moments after he was shot by a disgruntled worker.

And as for Seitz making "ironical remarks about me. You might misunderstand
him. Second: He might have made these remarks in his usual hurry and without intent. Third: He makes them anyhow to you privately, certainly not knowing that they would come to me and it is a question whether you have the right
to report them. *And fourth: Anyhow, I do not want to receive one single word
that is unpleasant or irritating or hear a single complaint or criticism that I cannot remedy.*" Instead, he asked his son to send weekly summaries of his diary,
eliminating all the problems and complaints Pulitzer couldn't solve. He also
asked Ralph to meet him at Menton in early December—with Frederica if she
cared to come—to discuss important changes in the paper, a meeting that he
said he anticipated "with very great pleasure."

Ralph was ultrasensitive to his father's disapproval, but Seitz relished Pulitzer's
"delightfully pungent" criticism. Typical was this, fired at new managing editor
Charles Lincoln: "The man who wrote the enclosed story on 'Why Tennessee
will elect a Republican Governor' certainly ought to be discharged and the

copy reader and the man who passed it. Who is Hooper? Banker, cow puncher, astronomer, or what? The story does not say, except that he was an orphan found in the streets. Somebody ought to be ashamed of himself. . . . Apropos the destruction by explosion of the Los Angeles *Times* [which killed twenty people] the story is put on the 13th page of the main news section. I wonder it was not put on the 87th page. It was worth first page position, more than that it was a dreadful story. Whose fault? Whose judgment?"

If Lincoln feared his job was in jeopardy, he was reassured by a November message from Pulitzer, now in Cap Martin and recovered from a deep depression. He thanked Lincoln for his "effective work," then added disingenuously, "You certainly cannot complain about my having interfered or being disagreeable."

Having recently invited Ralph and Frederica to visit him, Pulitzer changed his mind and tried to discourage them, because "The place here is damnable for a woman and your mother and Edith ought to explain it to you. The Villa is too small. The big hotel where your mother and the girls stopped not yet open. The place perfectly dead before January." If that didn't put them off, Pulitzer's additional comment may have, namely: "You can't mean it! that when you last saw me I 'was more cheerful' and that 'the improvement in my spirits delighted you beyond words.' Good God! What are you talking about? When you last saw me I was nearly dead, certainly collapsed beyond precedent."

A week later, in a happier mood, he replied to Joe's account of life in St. Louis: "Delighted to hear of your house and home—appetizing description. I am interested in every detail, not of course on account of the d——d [he had recently stopped swearing!] money but because the money is simply an indication of kind and character. Any particular handsome furniture you would like to have or need?"

Pulitzer's happy mood was short-lived. He had not anticipated Roosevelt's fighting spirit. The ex-president had just killed seventeen lions in Africa and was out for more blood. Having lost his libel suit against Pulitzer in a lower court, he took another final shot at him by bringing the case to the court of last resort—the U.S. Supreme Court.

The *World's* angry response disturbed Pulitzer and he warned Lincoln to go easy: "There is another [*World*] article on Panama bordering on showing animus besides exaggeration. But most of all because there is an undertone of hostility toward the Panama *work* itself. *That must not be.* It would show additional animus at least, as we have fought the Panama scandal in accepting the *route* by Congress and Glutinous [Roosevelt]. But the question of suspicious motives in the adoption of the route is a totally different thing from throwing suspicion of corruption and dishonesty into the *construction* and *building* of it. . . . It is a great work—the greatest work of the century in the way of construction."

Despite the countless repeated memos from and many personal conferences with Pulitzer, Frank Cobb also got things wrong, especially when he stated that the *World's* main objective was to elect a Democratic president.

"No!" Pulitzer corrected him: "The chief work is to make it an interesting, independent page full of truth, moral courage and thought-making talk—educating the people in sound principles. Teaching, teaching, teaching, not only the truth per se but puncturing the falsehood, humbug, demagoguery etc. President-making may be a *consequence* of this, but it must not be a primary object."

Pulitzer often seemed schizophrenic in his advice. Two days later he told *Post-Dispatch* editor Johns to conduct the editorial page "with the uttermost impersonality, accuracy, judicially personal detachments, as if the editor were on the bench under oath," but to "build up Woodrow Wilson on every suitable occasion showing the greatest possible sympathy for and appreciation of his remarkable talents and character. I think he is an abler man than Tilden was—and I admired Tilden." The next day Pulitzer asked Johns to "put in the word 'perhaps' he was an abler man than Tilden. Inject that word 'perhaps' simply because I want to be accurate. I think [Wilson] is ten times more intellectual than Cleveland and I knew both Tilden and Cleveland personally. Tilden had intellect beyond question. Cleveland had little but his great force was *moral courage*. Yet while strongly building up Wilson don't commit yourself without reserve or against all other possibilities."

When Johns sent Pulitzer an editorial Joe had written, he pronounced it "Not bad for a beginning" and told Johns to encourage Joe to keep writing.

One of the *World's* biggest mistakes had been prematurely reporting the death of Mary Baker Eddy, founder of Christian Science, the fault of overzealous reporters and the secretive nature of her organization. Even her actual death from pneumonia, at ninety, was kept secret until the next day, December 4. So the *World* didn't report it until December 5, with quotations from her work in which she called death "an illusion." The paper did not mention it had mistakenly reported her death from cancer some time before, when it had also instigated a next-of-kin "suit by her son, George Glover, to gain possession of her vast properties." Glover, according to biographer Barrett, "made a private settlement [for $250,000] and left the *World* holding the bag"—and embarrassed.

In its harsh but accurate editorial the *World* called her "perhaps the most extraordinary woman of her century who spent more than half her life in poverty and obscurity, a commonplace, neurasthenic woman. Yet she founded a religious sect that had shaken the foundations of every evangelical church in the United States. While maintaining the forms of a pure democracy it is ruled as despotically as the Russian Church. It may be said of Mrs. Eddy's work that what is true in it is not original and what is original is not true." As for her views in her book *Science and Health*, the *World* maintained that "such elementary ideas have been floating around the world since the dawn of time. Mrs. Eddy herself had only a vague and indefinite comprehension of them, but nevertheless she built a new church out of them [and] framed the structure of a religion that is one of the unmistakable influences of the century. That it should be the work of a woman is still more amazing. . . . In all respects Christian

Science has blazed a new trail for itself. It is a church without a charity, a mission or a martyr."

A Christian Science spokesman explained to the *World* that Mrs. Eddy "never preached that there is no material death" but "has predicted the ultimate conquest of death in times to come." Pulitzer's attitude to all such movements was informed skepticism, and he encouraged the *World* to follow his lead.

In November, Pulitzer had been surprised to hear from George Hosmer, his former doctor-companion for twenty-one years, now retired in Summit, New Jersey, on a generous Pulitzer pension. Pulitzer was even more surprised that the eighty-one-year-old had launched into writing a Pulitzer biography. "Just read your letter and nearly fainted when I came to the '25,000 words and still at it'!!!," he informed Hosmer. "I wish you could write 2,500 words of synopsis. Now for God's sake don't do this unless it gives you pleasure, and unless you are quite well. All I can wish is that you should know how often and, in fact, how constantly I think of you." To protect Hosmer from the New Jersey winter, Pulitzer sent him a fur-lined overcoat.

Hosmer thanked him and Pulitzer replied: "I never dreamt of your ever attempting anything like a sketch of my life. . . . You are the only man living who can speak from actual knowledge about my connection with the editorial page. As Mary Stuart said about her heart being left in France as she sailed for Scotland, my heart was and still is in the editorial page and will be in spirit. If you do anything more, please concentrate on the last twenty years of your own personal memory."

When Hosmer's twenty-five-hundred-word summary was read to Pulitzer, he was amazed that he'd forgotten so much of his own life and at Hosmer's wonderful memory. "If you go over the last twenty years, I think you ought to tell *the precise truth* as you remember it," he advised Hosmer. "The story of my invalidism may explain many errors which I could not possibly prevent . . . may also be a lesson in adversity and the fight against disadvantage. I hate the idea of passing away known only as the proprietor of the paper. Not property but politics was my passion—politics in the sense of liberty and freedom and ideals of justice. . . . With my cordial wishes for a very HAPPY New Year to you and yours. Affectionately, J. P."

Hosmer died in 1914, and Seitz took over the material, adding his own memories and publishing it ten years later as *Joseph Pulitzer: His Life and Letters*.

Shortly before Christmas Pulitzer again changed his mind and reinvited Ralph and Frederica to join him, not in the cramped French villa but aboard the spacious *Liberty* on a cruise to Athens, during which he hoped to give Ralph detailed instructions for the coming year. Meanwhile, he had arranged for Joe to take over from Ralph on the *World* as Charles Lincoln's assistant. Joe went without complaint, surprised to find New York City much less fearsome than he remembered, perhaps because Elinor was with him.

Pulitzer was pleased to hear that David Lloyd George had arrived for a vacation in nearby Monte Carlo. A charismatic, bright-eyed radical of high principles but less lofty practices—at least where women were concerned—as chancellor of the exchequer he had overcome the powerful opposition of the House of Lords to push through Britain's first national health and unemployment insurance programs. Apparently Pulitzer knew nothing of his wild way with women, whom Lloyd George picked up and dropped with equal fervor. Impressed by his political acumen, Pulitzer offered him the use of his car. If he accepted the offer he must have been amazed by the quiet ride: to meet Pulitzer's needs the Renault's thirty-five-horsepower engine was fine-tuned to a purr.

From Cap Martin on December 25 Pulitzer sent a bittersweet cable to his employees: "Sincere wishes for pleasant Xmas, Happy New Year, and better paper, and much better reporting." He also sent hundreds of presents, including several gramophones. But he kept to himself his fears that Theodore Roosevelt might win his case now before the U.S. Supreme Court. If that occurred, he knew that his failing health would make it impossible for him to survive prison. The alternative was the life of an exile, on the run, or perpetually sailing in international waters—a modern Flying Dutchman.

CHAPTER 34

Victory!

1911

—

63 to 64 years old

I n the new year, the U.S. Supreme Court justices ruled unanimously in Pulitzer's favor and against Theodore Roosevelt.

Overjoyed, the *World* staff and the vast majority of the nation's newspapers celebrated Pulitzer's victory as a triumph for press freedom. Had Roosevelt won, no American newspaper would have been safe from overwhelming government pressure. As one Chicago paper put it, "Roosevelt's legal lackeys [used] this engine of despotism for the destruction of the freedom of the press and of the citizen." Roosevelt's aim seems to have been to kill an investigation into who inspired the Panama revolution, how active a part he played in seizing the isthmus, and who, if anyone, made illegal millions in buying the Panama Canal Company. In preventing the answers from coming to light he ultimately succeeded, because someone destroyed the vital documentary evidence.

However, historian Walter LaFeber confirms that Pulitzer was on the right track. He writes that a U.S. commission had recommended a canal route through Nicaragua as far cheaper than one through Panama. But lawyer-lobbyist Cromwell, "father" of the Panama Canal, "miraculously prevented the inclusion in the Republican Party platform of a plank favoring the Nicaraguan canal. His means for working the miracle were direct: he contributed $60,000 [Pulitzer thought it was $50,000] to the party. Cromwell later charged this and other expenses to the Canal Company and apparently collected nearly a million dollars in fees." Justifying his decisions regarding the Panama affair to his cabinet, according to LaFeber, Roosevelt had "demanded to know whether his explanation would silence his opponents. 'Have I defended myself?' he asked. 'You certainly have,' replied a brave Elihu Root [secretary of war]. 'You have shown that you were accused of seduction and you have conclusively proved that you were guilty of rape.'"

Although Joe reported jubilation in the Dome over the Supreme Court verdict, he told his father he was "not in sympathy with this enthusiasm, for the question of whether we have grossly libeled several citizens remains quite unanswered." *

In the same letter Joe persisted with his own pet project, warning his father that "before we are exposed" he should kill the ads in the *World* by "unscrupulous moneylenders [who] suck the life out of the ignorant poor" and that no other reputable New York newspaper carried. Joe also complained of cures for hemorrhoids and stomach gas alongside a "high class" feature on new Democratic governors. He suggested junking such "fraudulent and disgusting" ads because they undermined "whatever elevating influence the paper derives from the tone of its high-class editorial page and from the much improved tone of its news columns."

Thwaites began reading Joe's complaints to Pulitzer, who, anticipating more of the same, told him to stop, and dictated a furious reply: "For the tenth time I forbid you sending annoyances like potash [code for advertising]. You should realize my condition and need for repose. The first thing any God-damned fool can do is to criticize something he could not possibly correct if he tried and which I certainly cannot. [Of course he could.] Many years ago at Bar Harbor you almost broke me up by one tactless, gross letter. What on earth is the matter with you? Now don't answer, don't refer to the subject."

He cooled off on a cruise to Corsica with Ralph, Frederica, and his old friend Henry Watterson, the lively, charming editor of the *Courier-Journal*. He had been one of Pulitzer's strongest supporters in the Roosevelt libel suit, calling the Panama affair "a confidence game" and "a great robbery." When he went ashore at Ajaccio to visit Napoleon's birthplace, Pulitzer stayed behind to have a batch of recent *Worlds* read to him. Watterson overdosed on wine in Corsica. Returning to the yacht in maudlin tears, he flung his arms around the embarrassed Pulitzer and "began to sob out a mournful monologue on the misfortunes of the Emperor."

Pulitzer's secretaries disentangled Watterson and helped him to his cabin to sleep it off while the yacht continued on to Naples.

---

* Had the *World* libeled Douglas Robinson, Roosevelt's brother-in-law? Or was he in fact involved in the Panama Canal Scandal? According to John Gable, executive director of the Theodore Roosevelt Association, Roosevelt had entrusted all his financial affairs to Robinson—until Pulitzer raised questions about the canal's investors—then, while publicly asserting Robinson's innocence, Roosevelt quietly dropped him, transferring his funds to a bank run by the president's cousins, Roosevelt and Son.

On reaching port, Pulitzer caught up with the latest news, shocked to hear that former *World* reporter turned novelist David Graham Phillips, who had unfairly portrayed him as the hypocritical publisher in *The Great God Success*, had been fatally shot. The murderer, a young, mentally disturbed violinist, Fitzhugh Goldsborough, believed that his sister had also been disparaged as a character in a Phillips novel. He stalked the novelist to Manhattan's Gramercy Square, where he shot him, then killed himself with a bullet through the head.

The *World* had given the tragedy page one prominence, headed:

DAVID G. PHILLIPS
DIES IN BELLEVUE
OF HIS WOUNDS

———

Novelist Who Was Shot Down
by Crazed Violinist Near
Princeton Club Expires at
11.07 P. M.—Sister and
Brother at Bedside—"The
Odds Are Too Great Against
me," His Last Words.

The odds were the six bullets in his body, the fatal one penetrating a lung. The *World* also revealed that hundreds attended his funeral, millions had read his books, and some rated him the most distinguished American novelist of his time, but did not mention that Phillips had been one of the paper's top reporters. By chance, Pulitzer had recently suggested a running feature about the most interesting of the 180 homicides in New York during 1910 from a moralistic rather than a sensational view, revealing killers' motives, social rank, ages, and nationalities, and to compare them with European murderers. Phillips's violent death was certainly among the most bizarre.

All such news reports were relayed to Pulitzer through his various secretaries. In fact, he was now so dependent on them that when they left to pursue other careers he was desperate. He was outraged when one quit to marry, and the inevitable cry went out to find a replacement. So Tuohy put the usual ad in the *Times* of London.

Forty-year-old Alleyne Ireland was among thousands to apply. Tuohy and Ledlie screened him, then Ralph Pulitzer traveled to London to interview him over lunch in the Café Royal. Ralph was impressed but asked for a two-thousand-word life story for Pulitzer to consider.

Ireland complied—educated in Manchester and the University of Berlin, a skilled sailor, senior civil servant, *Times of London* correspondent, much-traveled expert, and lecturer on the British Empire.

He had almost given up hope after several weeks of silence, when Tuohy called him to his office and handed him a ticket and traveling expenses to Menton, where Pulitzer waited anxiously to put him through the final test.

At Menton a car took him up the winding road to Pulitzer's Cap Martin hillside villa. Dunningham, the majordomo, led him to the drawing room, where Pulitzer greeted him in a high-pitched, strangely challenging voice: "Well, here you see before you the miserable wreck who is to be your host; you must make the best you can of him. Give me your arm into dinner."

Ireland had, of course, been told that Pulitzer was blind, but he was surprised to see that though one eye was dull and half closed, the other, a deep, brilliant blue, gave the impression of a searching, eaglelike glance. In the dining room the butler motioned for Ireland to sit on Pulitzer's right. Several secretaries in tuxedos stood at their places and nodded in a friendly manner as Pulitzer announced in a bantering tone: "Gentlemen, this is Mr. Alleyne Ireland; you will be able to inform him later of my fads and crochets; well, don't be ungenerous with me, don't paint the devil as black as he is."

Quizzed about his recent reading, Ireland cited Meredith Townsend's *Asia and Europe*, which Pulitzer asked him to discuss. "I left my dinner untasted," Ireland recalled, "and for a quarter of an hour held forth on the life of Mohammed, on the courage of the Arabians, on the charm of Asia for Asiatics." Suddenly Pulitzer interrupted with: "My God! You don't mean to tell me that anyone is interested in that sort of rubbish. Everybody knows about Mohammed, and about the bravery of the Arabs, and, for God's sake, why shouldn't Asia be attractive to the Asians? Try something else." They settled on *Caesar and Cleopatra*, Shaw's take on "Julius Caesar as the psychological woman tamer." Ireland's account had Pulitzer's rapt attention until he reached the scene where Britannus objects to Cleopatra's marriage to her brother, Ptolemy. But when Caesar responds "Pardon him, Theodotus; he is a barbarian, and thinks that the customs of his tribe are the laws of nature," Pulitzer broke into an uncontrollable fit of laughter. Ireland tried to continue, but Pulitzer, still laughing, begged him: "Stop! Stop! For God's sake! You're hurting me!" The candidate soon found that it was as important "to avoid being too funny as it was to avoid being too dull," for, while the latter "hurt his intellectual sensitiveness," prolonged laughing gave him headaches.

An eerie silence followed the laughter, the secretaries handling their food so cautiously that their eating utensils never touched the plates, while a footman moved behind them silently on rubber-soled shoes. Pulitzer's dinner had been cut up in advance, and he skillfully found the pieces with his knife and fork. Before long Ireland saw for himself that "the sudden click of a spoon against a saucer, the gurgle of water poured into a glass, the striking of a match, produced a spasm of suffering" in Pulitzer. At times a barely audible sound made him turn pale, tremble, and break into a cold sweat.

As the evening progressed, Ireland was astonished by how quickly and dramatically Pulitzer's expression changed. One moment lively and genial, giving way to "a cruel and wolf-like scowl," followed in a flash by a look of deep depression. As if he'd met the real Jekyll-and-Hyde prototype, Ireland noted,

"No face was capable of showing greater tenderness; none could assume a more forbidding expression of anger and contempt."

After dinner the butler lit Pulitzer's cigar for him. He took a few puffs, then left the room on the arm of his Scottish secretary William Paterson, long since recovered from smallpox. The others told Ireland he had done well, that Pulitzer was deliberately provocative with new applicants to make sure they were worth further testing.

The next morning, as a chauffeur drove the two men along the Corniche road above the Bay of Monaco, Pulitzer told Ireland, "You'll find this business of being a candidate a very trying and disagreeable one. Well, it's damned disagreeable to me, too. What I need is rest, repose, quiet, routine, understanding, sympathy, friendship, yes, my God! the friendship of those around me. Now I must explore your brain, your character, your tastes, your sympathies, your prejudices, your temper; I must find out if you have tact, patience, a sense of humor, the gift of condensing information, and, above all, a respect, a love, a passion for accuracy."

As they continued the drive, Pulitzer said: "I can do everything for a man who will be my friend. I can give him the reputation, the power, the wealth, which comes to a man who speaks to a million people a day in the columns of a great paper. But how am I to do this? I am blind, I'm an invalid; how am I to know whom I can trust? I don't mean in money matters; money's nothing to me; it can do nothing for me; I mean morally, intellectually."

Without waiting for a response, he went on: "I've had scores of people pass through my hands in the last 15 years—men of so-called high family, men of humble birth, [from] a dozen universities, self-taught men, young men, old men, and, my God! what have I found?" His voice became scornful as he listed what he had found: "Arrogance, stupidity, ingratitude, loose thinking, conceit, ignorance, laziness, indifference; absence of tact, discretion, courtesy, manners, consideration, sympathy, devotion; no knowledge, no wisdom, no intelligence, no observation, no memory, no insight, no understanding. My God! I can hardly believe my own experience when I speak of it."

To Ireland, Pulitzer seemed to be acting in a highly emotional play, especially when he raised his arms with fists clenched, or threw back his head and flung his outstretched arms in front of him, as though "appealing to the earth, to the sea, to the air, to hear his denunciation of man's inefficiency." But not of his secretaries. "Mind!" he said, raising a cautionary finger, "I'm not making any criticism of my present staff. You will do well to try to model yourself on them." At times Pulitzer paused and fixed his eyes upon Ireland as if he could read his mind. Then Ireland could hardly believe this astonishing man was totally blind—until he asked him to look outside and describe "every cloud, every shadow on the hillside, every tree, every home, every dress, every wrinkle on a face, everything, everything." He seemed pleased with Ireland's descriptive powers but not when he suggested writing for the *World*.

"You mustn't think that because you've written articles for the London *Times* you are competent to write for the *World*," Pulitzer replied. "Why should I accept you at your own estimate? My God! You're too cocksure of yourself!"

Pulitzer's face was damp with perspiration, he clasped and unclasped his hands, his voice veered from loud to higher-pitched, as he described in detail what was demanded of a *World* reporter. Then he suddenly calmed down to say, "You shouldn't let me talk so much. Well, Mr. Ireland I'll let you off for the afternoon: go and enjoy yourself and forget all about me. Come up for dinner about 7 and try to be amusing. You did very well last night. I hope you can keep it up. It's most important that anyone who is to live with me should have a sense of humor. I'd be glad to pay a man a handsome salary if he would make me laugh once a day."

Ireland understood he was to be on trial until Pulitzer was absolutely sure of him, and that providing a laugh a day was less vital than protecting him from friendly strangers when he was walking near them.

This occasionally occurred after the customary morning drive to Menton or Monte Carlo. Pulitzer would then leave the car and, grasping a secretary's arm, walk for a while. As he was well known locally, someone invariably called out his name in greeting, which drove him frantic. He would stamp his foot, raise a clenched fist menacingly, and cry, "My God! What's this? What's this? Tell him to go away. I won't tolerate this intrusion! Tell him I'll have him arrested!" When strangers ignored Pulitzer's distress and closed in, Ireland had to push them away or warn them off with a ferocious look. To avoid similar disturbances at concerts in Monte Carlo or Nice, Pulitzer took friends or secretaries along as buffers to sit on either side of him.

Spring as usual meant a trip to Wiesbaden for a regimen of baths, massage, and the water cure. On the first leg of the journey Pulitzer sailed to Genoa, where he waited while his secretary, William Paterson, went ahead to find a suitable hotel in Milan for lunch and a siesta. After narrowing the choice to three hotels, Paterson spent hours in each to determine if Pulitzer's prospective room was near any noise source. When he found a quiet, well-ventilated hotel room, he booked it for Pulitzer. The problem of noisy guests in adjoining rooms was easily solved. Paterson also took rooms on each side, three rooms facing it, and a room above and one below. He still had to determine the quietest route from Genoa to the hotel, avoiding bustling street markets, children in playgrounds, and rough roads. Only then was Pulitzer willing to continue his journey.

After lunch and a siesta in the tranquil Milan hotel, Pulitzer was driven to a villa in Wiesbaden. There, curiously, noise did not always prove excruciatingly painful, even in crowded restaurants. For some reason his intense curiosity about people seemed to overcome its effects. His secretaries, however, had little time to eat because he would ask them to select the most interesting-looking person in the room, try to imitate how they spoke, then describe them in minute detail. Or, according to Ireland, he "might say: 'I hear a curious, sharp, incisive voice on my right. There it is now—don't you hear it?—s s s s s, every s like a hiss. Describe the man to me; tell me what kind of people he's talking to; what you think his profession is.' Or he might say: 'There are some gabbling women over there. Describe them to me. How are they dressed, are they painted, are they wearing jewels, how old are they?'" To test the accuracy of the descriptions he asked them to describe his children or others he knew well, their features, hair texture, expression in their eyes, "and every little trick of gait or gesture."

One night he went to Frankfurt to hear Richard Strauss's new opera *Der Rosenkavalier*. Strauss was then the most famous living composer. Pulitzer endured the modern music until the middle of act two, when he stood abruptly and exclaimed, "My God, I can't stand any more of this! I want to go home!"

Back at the villa, he was curious to know why Ireland only read the *World*'s editorial pages. Because there was too much crime and disaster, he replied, and not enough foreign news in the rest of the paper. "Go on," Pulitzer said, "your views are not of any importance, but they're entertaining." Ireland, well prepared, took a clipping from his pocket and read a verse about the *World*:

> A *dual personality is this,*
> *Part yellow dog, part patriot and sage;*
> *When't comes to facts the rule is hit or miss,*
> *While none can beat its editorial page.*
> *Wise counsel here, wild yarns the other side,*
> *Page six it's Jekyll and page one it's Hyde;*
> *At the same time conservative and rash,*
> The World *supplies us good advice and trash.*

"Clever, but absolute nonsense," Pulitzer said, "except about the editorial page. Always read me anything of that kind. Anything that is bright and satirical. Now I'm going to give you a lecture about newspapers, because I want you to understand my point of view.

"I do not say that *The World* never makes a mistake in its news columns. What I say is that there are not half a dozen papers in the United States which tamper with the news, which publish what they know to be false. But if I thought I had done no better than that I would be ashamed to own a paper. You have to make everyone connected with the paper believe that accuracy is to a newspaper what virtue is to a woman." Having studied every important French, German, or English newspaper for a quarter of a century, Pulitzer concluded that the American press generally was more accurate than its European counterparts, although he conceded that some European "newspapers, chiefly English, are as accurate as the best newspapers in America." On the other hand, he said, no American newspapers were "so habitually stuffed with fake news as the worst of European papers."

"A newspaper," he went on, "should be scrupulously accurate, it should avoid everything salacious and suggestive, everything that could offend good taste; but within these limits it is the duty of a newspaper to print the news. When I speak of good taste I do not mean the kind of good taste that is offended by every reference to the unpleasant things of life, but the kind of good taste which demands that frankness should be linked with decency, the kind of moral tone which is braced and not relaxed when it is brought face to face with vice."

Those opposed to long and dramatic accounts of murders, train wrecks, "fires, lynchings, political corruption, embezzlements, frauds, graft, divorces" were wrong, he said, because "we are a democracy and there is only one way to get a democracy on its feet—by keeping the public informed about what is going on." He concluded his eloquent defense of the *World* with his somewhat overoptimistic view of its considerable power: "There is not a crime, there is not a dodge, there is not a trick, there is not a swindle, there is not a vice, that does not live by secrecy. Get these things out in the open, describe them, attack them, ridicule them in the press, and sooner or later public opinion will sweep them away."

Ireland was with Pulitzer for only a few months but experienced several of his conflicting personalities: the driven workaholic, the charming and erudite sophisticate, the self-pitying invalid, the demanding autocrat, the concerned humanitarian, and the enraged tyrant. Once, after Pulitzer had blown a fuse over some triviality, he put his hand on Ireland's shoulder and asked, "What do you feel when I am unreasonable with you? Do you feel angry? Do you bear malice?"

"Not at all," Ireland said. "I suppose my feeling is very much like that of a nurse for a patient. I realize that you are suffering and that you are not to be held responsible for what you do at such times."

"You never said anything which pleased me more," Pulitzer replied. "Never forget that I am blind and that I am in pain most of the time."

Pulitzer's rebellious son Joe also was reconciled to his father's behavior, writing to him in May, after one year of marriage, "The past year has been far and away the happiest year of my life and one that I shall, I hope, always remember that I have you to thank for."

It was a sentiment Pulitzer's wife, Kate, hardly shared. From the Hôtel Vendôme in Paris she wrote to Ralph about his three-year-old son Ralph Jr.: "I don't believe that child has a drop of J. P.'s blood or it could never go on making things so pleasant for everyone." Unusually harsh coming from Kate, who generally lived up to her reputation as a resilient woman who handled Pulitzer's moods with good humor. Apart from mutual affection, what apparently saved their marriage was their mobility. If things got too explosive when they were together, one or the other could always make a quick getaway to other homes or foreign parts.

When Pulitzer decided to return to Bar Harbor in June, Ireland asked for a few days off to visit London. Pulitzer suggested that he stay even longer to take in some plays and art galleries—then tell him all about them. But most important, he wanted Ireland to get speech lessons to soften his harsh voice.

Having been hired despite this impediment, his other attributes must have been outstanding. However, Ireland had been in London only two weeks—not long enough to change his voice—when he got an urgent message to go straight to Liverpool. From there he was to sail back to America with Pulitzer, his wife, and daughter Edith aboard the SS *Cedric*. The *Liberty* would make the same journey without them.

Crew members put heavy mats outside Pulitzer's suite and a rope surrounding it to prevent other passengers from promenading outside. But they hadn't anticipated babies crying around the clock. Remarkably, Pulitzer tolerated them as a natural disaster, commenting to Ireland with scientific detachment, "I really think one of the most extraordinary things in the world is the amount of noise a child can make. Here we are with a sixty-mile gale blowing and some ten thousand horsepower engines working inside the ship, and yet that child can make itself heard from one end of the boat to the other. I think there must be two of them; the sound is not quite the same at night." Pulitzer asked Ireland to find out, "just for the fun of it. But don't let the mother know. I wouldn't want to hurt her feelings. Ask one of the stewards about it." He was right: there were two.

When Pulitzer and his party reached New York they transferred to the waiting *Liberty* and headed for Bar Harbor.

During the mostly tranquil summer Pulitzer made several trips in the *Liberty* from Maine to New York and back.

Ashore at Chatwold, the extended family sometimes gathered to join him on the veranda overlooking the sea. His curiosity about them was inexhaustible, especially those like Ralph Jr., born after Pulitzer became totally blind. But he could only take them for short periods before his nerves shrieked, stomach protested, or head ached. Then he would head for the yacht for a few days of rest.

Ireland noticed that getting Pulitzer on or off the *Liberty*, during even the gentlest ocean swell, was always a tense occasion. To leave the yacht and board the launch that took them ashore, Dunningham went first and backward. Pulitzer followed facing Dunningham, one hand on his majordomo's shoulder, the other on the gangplank handrail. A secretary walked behind Pulitzer to steady him if he slipped. The dangerous time came when Dunningham moved aside and positioned Pulitzer to step from the gangplank to the bobbing launch into the arms of the officer in charge. Waiting until the best moment, Dunningham would say, "Now, step please, Mr. Pulitzer." But Pulitzer invariably hesitated until the launch had moved dangerously out of reach. Then he would step into the space, only to be grabbed and held back while yelling, "My God! What's the matter? You told me to step!" This was followed by an argument about what word should have triggered Pulitzer's step from gangplank to launch. Should it have been "Now"? "Step"? "Please"? or perhaps "Pulitzer"? Apparently this was never resolved. And each time, embarking or disembarking, it took several similar scary attempts before Pulitzer finally made it. Mor-

Ralph Pulitzer walks with his father on New York City's Fifth Avenue.

bid curiosity, Ireland admitted, led him and many of the yacht's crew, whenever they got the chance, to lean over the side watching the "nerve-wracking exhibition" undertaken by a "blind man with a will of iron and a nervous system of gossamer."

No wonder Pulitzer sometimes preferred to take the launch instead of the yacht, cruising for hours in Frenchman's Bay, sitting in an armchair, while Ralph and Joe read to him or discussed business. Once, Ireland went along and concluded that, tough as it was, it was easier to be his secretary than his son. Never before had he seen men put through such severe tests of industry, concentration, and memory while responding patiently and with affectionate concern. Ireland believed that the burdens Pulitzer imposed and the "strictness of the account to which you were called were the truest measure of his regard" and that, next to politics, nothing interested him more than molding "the people around him. His activities in this direction ministered alike to his love of power and to his horror of wasted talents; they gratified his ever-present desire to discover the boundaries of human character and intellect, to explore the mazes of human temperament and emotion."

At long last Pulitzer's persistence paid off. The U.S. Supreme Court justified his years of protest by ordering the split-up of the Standard Oil Company for unreasonable restraint of trade—another triumph for the public. Encouraged, but knowing other illegal trusts still flourished, he urged John L. Heaton, Frank Cobb's editorial page deputy, to write a "comic history of the Beef Trust litigation—the most iniquitous of all the trusts."

Believing that Heaton needed to feel more independent to get the best work out of others, Pulitzer told him to imagine "that I am abroad, in the grave, not in existence, certainly not in Bar Harbor." But how the devil could Heaton think of Pulitzer in the grave when he immediately peppered him with lively comments and suggestions? Such as: "Perhaps you will forgive me a few criticisms which I will send you from time to time really in a friendly spirit." Immediately followed by: "The editorial on [Mayor] Gaynor was a mistake, palpably unfair. Every reader knows that a man with a bullet in his neck and [who] is overwhelmed with work and trouble, cannot be expected to lead a political movement requiring aggression, fresh mind, time and energy—foolish! Above all, below all, behind all and first of all cultivate scrupulously a terse, trenchant, caustic, ironical style."

Two days later came the by now customary appeal: "Condense to the uttermost, rewrite and refurbish; file and polish the form remembering that style is the highest art and I would rather have a ten-lines paragraph that will arrest attention and make a point than ten columns or more a week more or less average but not original. Quality, quality, quality! Irony, irony, irony! Terseness, terseness, terseness! Trenchant, trenchant, trenchant!"

And again: Speculating about presidential hopefuls to succeed Taft, Pulitzer took a shine to the Democratic New Jersey governor Woodrow Wilson, and asked Heaton to send all Wilson's remarks about the Standard Oil decision: "Should prefer essence to verbosity," he said. "Ditto Bryan's opinions in essence. But brevity, brevity!"

Soon after, Ralph wrote to Heaton from the *Liberty* of his father's amazement that no editorial had appeared about the U.S. Senate's bill to publicize election campaign contributions. "Passed almost unanimously by a senate which did not believe in it, [the bill] is a wonderful moral object lesson of the power of public opinion. Father has advocated this measure all his life. Indeed till a few years ago the World was [its] only supporter. [It's] probably the most important bill in a generation so far as real progress and purification of politics [are] concerned. Work up a strong editorial. [Take] even the whole page, though the shorter the better. You might go back and quote from the World showing how consistently and persistently we have advocated this. Refer to the 1908 campaign in which Roosevelt refused to publish contributions before the election. Andes [Pulitzer] has just read today's and yesterday's pages and is delighted with your editorial on [George] Wickersham [Taft's attorney general]. Even that is too mild, still thanks, thanks."

In August, Pulitzer called several of his staff to Bar Harbor for conferences, then took them back south on his yacht. On the way Frank Cobb took notes of his conversations with Pulitzer, who wanted him to ask Heaton if he'd like to write a book about Pulitzer's "Thirty Years of Journalism." And he told Cobb to prepare an optimistic article titled "Forty Years Ago," comparing the corruption in the Tweed and Grant administrations with today, and to show "business is booming, despite Wall Street pessimism." Pulitzer also urged him to suggest "the idea that no New York politician should be President, until party is purged of corrupting influence." Cobb's notes from Pulitzer continued: "Taft is more than halfway thro' his term. Amazing extravagance of the government ought to be kept in mind. Emphasize our regret that [Taft] could not now detach himself from all other issues and be a candidate for re-election on the simple issue of peace and arbitration."

Peace became a hot issue when Germany sent a gunboat, *Panther*, to the Moroccan port of Agadir, to which France had territorial claims, and some thought war was imminent. Pulitzer didn't. He told Frank Cobb to review the facts of the Moroccan question "without flapdoodle, speculation or conjecture, simply informatory to enlighten readers. It seems to come down to a plain case of blackmail. It says: '[We] have no land in Africa. We [Germany] have come too late and if you don't give us a slice of Morocco we want some land on the Congo.' Of course there will be no war, yet the fact that English and French are not only in sympathy, but possibly have an understanding against Germany, is interesting [and also a premonition of the lineup in the great war three years ahead]. Ridicule our jingo friends but also the apprehension and alarm of our friends who see war."

Pulitzer was right. There was no war over Morocco. Germany blackmailed France into handing over French territory in Africa and in exchange recognized a French protectorate in Morocco.

Exhausted by the editorial conference, Pulitzer briefly escaped from work by cruising with Kate, Joe, and Joe's wife, Elinor. Then, dropping them off at Bar Harbor, he sailed south and soon began to miss them. "I am hungry for him [Herbert] or somebody," he cabled Kate. "I am dreadfully tired and unfit. Miss you. Love to all. Father." He rallied enough to send two messages. One rewarded Frank Cobb with a hundred first-class cigars for recent editorial pages, "But don't smoke more than three daily for your health." The other, to give cartoonist Ketten an extra week's pay for good work.

Kate arranged for Herbert and his tutor to join the *Liberty* at either Marblehead or Greenwich, Connecticut. At Greenwich on September 18, Pulitzer also waited for Ralph and other *World* executives to arrive. But his two-hour discussion with Ralph exhausted him. The ever-attentive Dunningham insisted that he stop working and immediately sail home to Bar Harbor.

The trip north revived him sufficiently to tackle an interesting problem. After the *World* had published an interview with Attorney General Wickersham, he claimed to have spoken off the record to a man who had not identified himself as a *World* reporter. He vigorously disavowed two quotes attributed to him: "The United States Steel Corporation is a combination in violation of the law" and "The men under indictment in the Beef Trust cases in Chicago would go to prison if I had my way." He did concede that the interview

Joseph's favorite
and youngest son,
Herbert Pulitzer.

was otherwise substantially correct. Pulitzer, the political junkie, called Wickersham's objection "perfectly natural. Old trick to say did not know he would be published [and] only spoke privately though he knew he spoke to a reporter of *World*." Pulitzer told his editors to give Wickersham the benefit of the doubt and to publish the interview again minus the contested quotes.

In the fall, he and Kate returned to their New York City residence. There, in a soundproof octagonal room with slender columns of pale-green Irish marble reaching up to a glass dome, he entertained many visitors and discussed with Ralph and Seitz the rising cost of newsprint. They finally persuaded him to spend two million dollars to buy his own paper mill at Pyrites, New York.

Pulitzer had recently put writer Clark Firestone through the usual intellectual wringer before he was considered fit for the *World*. His first reaction was disappointment, and he vented it by ridiculing Firestone to Frank Cobb. But on further acquaintance he realized he had misjudged the man. Always quick to admit and try to remedy his mistakes, he made amends in a confidential note to Cobb: "Please expunge my foolish and unjust remark about Firestone not having read anything or whatever I said. I find, on the contrary, that he has read some very good books, although also some queer ones. Nevertheless, whatever my remark, I consider it unjust and you must not mention it to him or anyone."

CHAPTER 35

The Last Days

October 1911
—
64 years old

Although Theodore Roosevelt had denounced many violators of the Sherman Antitrust Act of 1890, Pulitzer complained that none had gone to jail. But when Taft gave a tough speech against trusts, Pulitzer advised Cobb on October 2, 1911, to praise him but not to harp "*too* heavily upon sending [J. P.] Morgan or somebody to jail. Perhaps at the very end you ought to have a reaffirmation of our shibboleth that one man (say Mr. Morgan) or Swift or Armour, particularly the Beef Trust fellows, in prison for twenty-four hours, would do more to help the law and make it respected than all the monopolies dissolved and a hundred prosecutions by [Attorney General] Wickersham." Make the piece ironical and sarcastic, Pulitzer added, and mention that the "public welfare would be more affected by the example of [Morgan] being in jail for twenty-four hours, than by one thousand speeches by the most illustrious demagogues in the land. . . . But the Morgan idea is an example, not expectation; a hypothetical expectation, not an illusion."*

The next day Pulitzer received an Associated Press report that the Italian Navy had bombarded Libya's capital, Tripoli, occupied the city, blown up the Turkish governor's house, and destroyed the Turkish fleet in the Dardanelles. Convinced it was merely a rumor, he cabled Frank Cobb and Charles Lincoln to ridicule the war reports because not a single fact had been confirmed: "There has been no bombardment. No occupation of Tripoli. Make the thing funny. There will be no war. Turkey will surrender. The great powers will stop

---

* To be fair to Roosevelt, according to John Gable, robber baron Henry Clay Frick complained of the president: "We bought the son-of-a-bitch, but he didn't stay bought."

the nonsense. Turkey will lose Tripoli, just as she has lost Sardinia, Roumania, Crete, Egypt, Tunis, Bulgaria, Montenegro and Greece [all once part of the Ottoman Empire]. Tripoli is a tempest in a teapot. Every false story and report ought to be punctured from the beginning."

Pulitzer, however, had seriously misjudged the situation. Italy's urge for an African empire led to fighting that would last for more than a year and in which thousands of Italians, Turks, and Arabs would be killed or die of cholera before Turkey surrendered to Italy. At least Pulitzer had been right about the final outcome.

On October 5 Frederica gave birth to Pulitzer's second grandson, Seward Webb. On their mother's side, the boy and his brother Ralph Jr. were great-great-grandsons of Commodore Vanderbilt, the railroad magnate Pulitzer had once called a vulgar, ruthless tax evader. The *World* later praised Pulitzer's children for "marrying plain Americans," rather than European nobility.

In mid-October Pulitzer invited a former secretary, James Barnes, to join him on a trip south, to Jekyll Island. When Barnes boarded the *Liberty* at New York he was greeted by Dunningham, several secretaries, and Pulitzer's sixteen-year-old son Herbert. Pulitzer was attended by the ship's new physician, Dr. Guthman, and nurse Elizabeth Keelan. Barnes was shocked to see how pale and fragile Pulitzer had become since their long, peripatetic conversations on deck the previous year.

On October 19 Pulitzer sent the last of his thousands of messages to Frank Cobb: "The editorial in the Tribune today is a good peg on which to have a few reflections and, if possible, ironical and witty. The charge that the *World* is apparently inconsistent is perfectly correct but circumstance and circumstance alone is accountable. We are in favor of fusion [the coalition of political parties] as a principle, just as much as in favor of repudiating [Tammany boss] Charles Murphy's power. We shall do our duty to the limit of our poor ability in appealing to the people to wipe him off the slate as a boss-general over the legislature, helping to defeat every one of his creatures. As to the local ticket, nobody cares a rap who is sheriff but everybody ought to care a great deal indeed who is to be Surrogate and Judge of the Supreme Court. Everybody should select his own judges on absolutely non-partisan grounds. The big fight must be on the legislature. There is no other way [to destroy corrupt Democrat Murphy's power than by electing] a Republican legislature."

As the *Liberty* headed south, for Jekyll Island, Pulitzer still expected his secretaries to feed him the latest news and record his notes, to discuss with him prospects for the 1912 presidential election, and to tell him everything they knew about Woodrow Wilson's personality and politics. He asked Ireland, no longer subjected to his searching interrogations—having passed the various tests—to keep him entertained with light reading. From the well-stocked library Ireland chose Lorimer's *Letters of a Self-Made Merchant to His Son;* some of Frank Stockton's stories—Stockton was famous for his *Lady or The*

Joseph Pulitzer
spent most of his
last months at sea.

Tiger; and a book by humorist George Ade, who often used slang. Pulitzer usually hated slang, but he enjoyed Ade.

Whatever the subject, Pulitzer was still a critical and demanding audience. It was not unusual, Ireland recalled, "that after I had told J. P. one of the best tales in my collection he would say: 'Well, go on, go on, come to the point. For God's sake, isn't there any end to this story?'"

On October 25, 1911, after five days at sea, he was eager for the latest news, so the *Liberty* anchored in Charleston Harbor, and a secretary went ashore to collect the mail and newspapers. The next day *Charleston Courier* editor Robert Lathan boarded the yacht to lunch with him and discuss the likely prospects of a Democratic victory in 1912. Ireland had never known Pulitzer to be so genial and in such high spirits.

Perhaps the visitor was too much for him, for on October 27 and 28 he stayed belowdecks, resting and suffering from chest pains. A Dr. Robert Wilson, sent for from Charleston, diagnosed acute indigestion and gave Pulitzer Veronal. Sedated, he had slightly less pain. But Barnes, who spoke with him briefly, thought he was dangerously ill, and when the intense chest pains recurred, Kate was summoned from New York.

At 3:00 A.M. on Sunday, October 29, Dunningham woke Ireland to say, "Mr. Pulitzer wishes you to come and read to him." Five minutes later Ireland was at his bedside, and for two hours read an essay by British historian Thomas

Babington Macauley. He listened attentively, but moved restlessly from time to time and twice left his bed to sit for a while in a chair. The pain intensified at 5:30 A.M., when Pulitzer called for Dr. Guthman. He did all he could to help. At about six Pulitzer thanked Ireland and told him to "have a good rest, and forget all about me." Then he asked him to send for the German reader Friedrich Mann.

Even in pain, he had been unusually calm and uncomplaining, more concerned with Ireland's welfare than his own. It would be his secretary's last memory of him.

After six hours' sleep Ireland woke at noon and went on deck, where he asked how the boss was doing. Told that Mann was still with him, Ireland joined the others in scanning that day's newspapers in anticipation of Pulitzer's questions.

At lunchtime, Mann was still in Pulitzer's cabin, now reading to him *The Life of Louis XI*—an odd choice for a man who had no time for living kings. He appeared to enjoy it, however, asking Mann to reread several passages. As Mann reached the end of the chapter recounting the death of the French king, Pulitzer murmured the customary "*Leise, ganz leise*" (German for "Softly, quite softly"), as a sign that he was drifting off to sleep. He was whispering the words when his wife and son Herbert arrived to replace Mann at the bedside.

The secretaries were lunching together at 1:40 P.M. when Jabez Dunningham appeared, tears streaming down his face, to say that Pulitzer was dying. A few minutes later the *Liberty*'s flag was lowered to half staff.

"*Leise, ganz leise*," had been his last words.

He had died of heart failure at sixty-four.

The death of the most interesting man on the planet, as one contemporary called him, was front-page news in every daily newspaper in the United States and reported in every European capital.

Dr. Hosmer heard the news of his death the same day and advised Florence White, the *World*'s general manager, to "say all that is possible concerning him as a great force in public life, great voice in politics, always for the cause of people, great intellectual and moral force. The last time we talked he spoke as fearful that he would be most considered as having made a great fortune rather than as having done, or endeavored to do good in the fight for good government and honest politics. The news knocks me over a little. I cannot go on."

The *World* celebrated his life and mourned his death on its two front pages for October 30, 1911, with Sargent's portrait of him prominently displayed. Its lead editorial, simply headed JOSEPH PULITZER, called him "A man of wide culture, commanding intellect and compelling genius. . . . That he was much more than this by reason of his tireless zeal in the public service, The World is the imperfect but sincere witness. This paper is his chief life work. It has been his absorbing passion not as an end but solely as a means to the expression of his ideas and ideals for human welfare."

The *World* (left) and the *New York Times* (right) of October 30, 1911, report Joseph Pulitzer's death.

Just as a doctor misdiagnosed Pulitzer's fatal heart problem as indigestion, so no physician he consulted had ever correctly diagnosed the underlying cause of his hyperactive mind and emotional outbursts. Biographer Swanberg discussed this with psychiatrist Dr. Henry Wexler. He concluded that while medical specialists treated Pulitzer for failing eyesight, frazzled nerves, asthma, crippling headaches, diabetes, and chronic insomnia, they missed what had tormented him much of his adult life: "the demons of depression and mental anguish."

Pulitzer was embalmed to look as if enjoying a peaceful sleep and his body returned to his cabin, where sixty crewmen walked past the open coffin. Then it was put on a northbound train for the funeral service at St. Thomas's Episcopal Church on Fifth Avenue and Fifty-third Street. He was nominally a member of the congregation, but no one recalled him having previously entered the building.

More than six hundred people attended his funeral service, and some two thousand stood outside, on Fifth Avenue. Pallbearers included Columbia University president Nicholas Murray Butler; Colonel George Harvey, whose friendship with Pulitzer had survived their fights; Seth Low, former New York mayor; St. Clair McKelway, editor of the *Brooklyn Eagle*; and the family doctor, James McLane. A group represented hundreds of students Pulitzer had aided with grants since 1893. Dr. Hosmer was there along with secretaries Billing, Ireland, Pollard, and Mann, and valet-confidant Jabez Dunningham. The once-famous Nellie Bly mingled with several former *World* reporters and editors, excited to see one another. Among officials present was state Supreme Court justice Leonard Geigerich, who, noted biographer Swanberg, doubtless "had not read that morning's World which charged that he had paid $9,000 for his nomination."

Kate was there with Herbert, and Ralph and Joe with their wives. But his daughters Constance, traveling from Colorado Springs, and Edith, en route from Paris, arrived too late for the service.

While Rev. Ernest Stiles, who had married Ralph and Frederica, read the service, the presses were stopped, lights extinguished, and phones disconnected at the *World* and the *Post-Dispatch* for five minutes of silence—a silence no one would have appreciated more than Pulitzer.

That afternoon he was buried next to his daughter Lucille Irma in the family plot at Woodlawn Cemetery in the Bronx.

After his death editors, politicians, and friends attested to his extraordinary character, courage, and generosity. The *New York Times* called his career astonishing and his spirit unconquerable. Its publisher, Adolph Ochs, considered Pulitzer "one of the greatest men of this time." Even William Randolph Hearst, who had once defined his career as that of "a coward, a traitor, sycophant and pimp," now eulogized him as "a towering figure in National and international journalism. A mighty democratic force in the life of this Nation and in the activity of the world. Not the great success which Joseph Pulitzer achieved nor the great wealth which he accumulated, nor his association with men of selfish purpose and class prejudices, ever deprived him of his essential democracy or calloused him to the requirements of the democratic masses."

Attorney De Lancey Nicoll believed that "Mr. Pulitzer's death removes from American affairs probably the greatest individual force among us." William Kellogg, a former U.S. senator from Louisiana, called Pulitzer "One of the most delightful persons I ever knew. I lived with him at the Willard [Hotel] in the seventies. He was a born newspaperman, with a pungent, forceful style, outspoken and bold as a lion." John Henderson, a former U.S. senator from Missouri, regarded him as "a man of transcendent ability and a conscientious conductor of the greatest newspaper in this country." The editor of the *Boston Globe*, Charles Taylor, rated him "One of the giants of journalism, not only of this country but of the world. His career was one of the most brilliant, inspiring, and successful that has ever been known in the journalism of the world. When Mr. Pulitzer bought the New York World party organs were the fashion among American newspapers. He did more to abolish them than any journalist the country has ever known. Though a strong Democrat, he criticised his own party as savagely as he did the opposition. He reported Republican conventions and meetings as fully and as impartially as he did those of the Democrats." To Oswald Garrison Villard, editor of the *New York Evening Post*, "the evolution of The World into a fearless, outspoken, independent newspaper, with a trenchant editorial page, has made it an invaluable force on the side of the people in their battle against special privilege and that form of 'legalized graft' known as the protective tariff."

Years later, secretary Ireland wrote in *An Adventure with a Genius:* "When I recall the capaciousness of his understanding, the breadth of his experience, the range of his information, and set them side by side with the cruel limitations imposed upon him by his blindness and his shattered constitution, I forget the severity of his discipline, I marvel only that his self-control should have served him so well in the tedious business of breaking a new man to his service."

One *World* reporter remembered how highly he had rated his boss. Once, while covering a revival meeting, he had been invited by the preacher to join the converts up front. Explaining that he was "a reporter here on business," he declined. "There's no business as momentous as the Lord's business," said the preacher. "Maybe not," he replied, "but you don't know Mr. Pulitzer."

Secretary Norman Thwaites, who lasted eight years with Pulitzer, recalled that "my early fear of him was replaced by affection and immense admiration, not only for his amazing talent but for his idealism and his desire for public service through journalism. Few have been more misunderstood and misjudged. The abuse hurled at Pulitzer has made me very reluctant to believe ill-natured gossip of public men."

Pulitzer exemplified the journalist's creed of comforting the afflicted and afflicting the comfortable—and the crooked and the contemptible. In his frantic circulation battle with Hearst during the Spanish-American War he betrayed his own high standards, which he regretted and remedied. He went on to fulfill his early promise to "expose all fraud and sham, fight all public evils and abuses, and to battle for the people with earnest sincerity." As a devoted though independent Democrat, he exhorted his staff always to ask themselves: "Is this a fair report without bias or prejudice? Is this a real mirror of events?" And he practiced what he preached: never to kick an opponent when he's down, nor pull your punches when he's up. Against incredible odds—blind and in pain from various ailments for much of his working life—he kept an iron grip on his world to the end. And he is not forgotten. Even today, almost a century after his death, Pulitzer's three commandments, "Accuracy!" "Brevity!" "Persistence!" remain the watchwords of his journalistic admirers.

Pulitzer himself, a few years before he died, had defined a journalist's role. It was that of "the lookout on the bridge of the ship of state. He notes the passing sail, the little things of interest that dot the horizon in fine weather. He reports the drifting castaway whom the ship can save. He peers through fog and storm to give warning of dangers ahead. He is not thinking of his wages or of the profits of his owners. He is there to watch over the safety and welfare of the people who trust him."

CHAPTER 36

The Aftermath

THE PROPERTY

Pulitzer's $18,645,249.09 estate, excluding his homes at Bar Harbor and Jekyll Island, was divided according to his will as follows: $2 million to create the Columbia School of Journalism, which opened on September 30, 1912, and for the annual Pulitzer prizes. Also, $1 million each to the Metropolitan Museum of Art and for the Philharmonic Symphony, hoping that it will "recognize my favorite composers, Beethoven, Wagner and Liszt." He left money for scholarships to worthy high school students; $25,000 for a statue of the much-admired Thomas Jefferson, now in the inner courtyard of the School of Journalism; and $50,000 for a fountain at the Plaza Hotel entrance on Fifth Avenue near Central Park. He gave $5,000 to the Children's Aid Society.

He provided his widow, Kate, with the income from a $2.5 million trust fund, daughters Edith and Constance with $750,000 apiece, and daughter-in-law Elinor with $250,000. (Frederica would eventually come into a family inheritance through Ralph.) Among his staff, his valet-nurse-confidant Jabez Dunningham was most richly rewarded, receiving $100,000 for his twenty years of devoted service. Another $100,000 was equally divided among his secretaries and his London correspondent James Tuohy. Dr. Hosmer, who already had a generous Pulitzer pension, got $20,000.

In his will Pulitzer urged his descendants to preserve, perfect, and perpetuate "the World newspaper (to the maintenance and upholding of which I have sacrificed my health and strength) in the same spirit in which I have striven to create and conduct it as a public institution, from motives higher than mere gain, it having been my desire that it should be at all times conducted in a spirit of independence and with a view to inculcating high standards and public spirit among the people and their official representatives, and it is my earnest wish that said newspaper shall hereafter be conducted upon the same principles."

It was up to his three sons Ralph, Joe, and Herbert to carry out his wishes. Each had something of their father's personality—Ralph his idealism, Joe his guts, Herbert his stubbornness—but none matched his incredible drive, curiosity, and intelligence. Who could?

His favorite, Herbert, was left 60 percent of the income from stock in the *World* and *Post-Dispatch*; Ralph, 20 percent; and Joe, penalized for often infuriating him, a mere 10 percent. The remaining 10 percent was earmarked for those editors and managers the trustees felt most deserving. Four trustees, including Ralph, were in control of the destiny of both papers.

Pulitzer's retreat, The Tower of Silence at Chatwold, was demolished in 1936. Ten years later, Chatwold itself, the family home, was torn down. Pulitzer's golden Dome, the *World*'s headquarters, was razed in 1955 to make room for a new approach to the Brooklyn Bridge. His house at East Seventy-third Street has been converted into several condominiums.

In 1912, his yacht was sold to James Ross, who renamed it *Glencairn*. Lord Tredegar bought it two years later and restored the name *Liberty*. Tredegar owned it for less than a year when the British Navy took it over during World War I, first as a patrol vessel, then as a hospital ship from September 1915 to January 1919. It was ideal for the purpose, with a medical staff of fourteen and a crew of sixty-two. The yacht was sold in 1920 to Sir Robert and Lady Houston, who kept it longer than any other owner. Lady Houston used it for her own war with the Britisn government—flying anti-government signs between the masts at various regattas—until the *Liberty* was broken up in 1937.

THE FAMILY

Pulitzer's fifty-eight-year-old widow, Kate, never remarried. She lived much of the rest of her life abroad, in Deauville, Cap Martin, and Nice, dying in 1927 at seventy-four, with her son Herbert at her bedside. She was buried next to her husband at Woodlawn. A *Post-Dispatch* editorial for July 30, 1927, credited her with helping Joseph overcome his doubts about buying the *World* in 1883 and so giving "New York the greatest free newspaper it has ever had." "Free," of course, meant "independent." She left each of her three sons $234,018 from her newspaper stock. Her other assets were equally divided among her five children.

Six weeks after Pulitzer's death in 1911, his daughter Edith married William S. Moore. She contested her father's will, which gave her $750,000, claiming that he suffered from "insanity as to the family"—a weak argument, Joe confided to his brother Ralph, against a man who had "sufficient sanity to run the *World* as he did." She dropped her claim when the brothers promised her a yearly income of $50,000. Edith died at eighty-eight in 1975.

Pulitzer's daughter Constance married William Gray Elmslie in 1913. He was her brother Herbert's former tutor and the son of a British judge. The couple settled in Winnipeg, Canada, where Elmslie worked as a businessman. Constance died at fifty in 1938.

Ralph Pulitzer and Frederica were divorced in 1924. She remarried soon after. Four years later he married novelist and historian Margaret Leech. In 1930 a nervous breakdown forced him to resign from the *World*, and his brother Herbert replaced him. Ralph died in 1939 at age fifty-six.

While Joe was fishing off the Florida Keys in March 1925, his wife Elinor died in a car crash. A year later he married Elizabeth Edgar. Although Joe had lost his sight in his left eye and had only partial "tubular vision" in his right, he was an avid duck shooter and salmon fisher and was said to be able to spot a pretty woman at two hundred paces. He closely supervised his editors or edited the *Post-Dispatch* himself until his death in 1955 at seventy. Because he loved both of his wives, he avoided the problem of which one he should be buried next to by requesting to be cremated and have his ashes scattered from a plane off Egg Rock in Frenchman's Bay. His widow Elizabeth died in 1974 at eighty-four, and her ashes were scattered in the same area. Daniel W. Pfaff wrote a revealing biography of Joe, *Joseph Pulitzer II and the Post-Dispatch: A Newspaperman's Life*, published by Pennsylvania State University Press in 1991.

Pulitzer's youngest son, Herbert, was a flying instructor in the U.S. Navy during World War I, and married Mrs. Gladys Amory in 1926. He briefly took over the *World* after Ralph's breakdown in 1930 but had neither the training, talent, nor inclination for the job. And he antagonized the staff by remaining aloof, smoking perfumed cigarettes, and speaking in an explosive British accent. Herbert suffered from eye trouble and in 1934 had one eye removed. Because of this he was at first turned down when he tried to reenlist during World War II, but he was later accepted by the RAF. After the war he spent much of his time traveling or at his shooting lodge in Scotland. He died at sixty in 1955. His son Herbert Jr. hit the headlines as a Palm Beach playboy involved in a sensational divorce in 1982.

THE NEWSPAPERS

For ten years after Pulitzer's death the *World* flourished with such notable recruits as Heywood Broun, Franklin P. Adams, Alexander Woollcott, and Herbert Bayard Swope, the latter considered by *World* city editor James Barrett as the best reporter in the world. In 1919 Swope won the first Pulitzer Prize for journalism for his series "Inside the German Empire," and became the paper's editor in 1920. John Leary Jr. also got the prize, in 1920, for articles on the national coal strike, and Louis Seibold the following year for an exclusive interview with President Wilson. In 1922 the *World*'s Rollin Kirby was the first cartoonist to get the award.

When Frank Cobb died of cancer in 1923, Walter Lippmann took over the editorial page. He aimed for a more intellectual reader—less fun and fireworks—and naturally circulation and income suffered. The *World* itself won the Pulitzer Prize in 1922 for airing the activities of the Ku Klux Klan despite threats of libel suits; in 1924 for exposing the peonage system in Florida farm camps, in one of which a young man was flogged to death; and in 1929 for a campaign to clean up the justice system.

Over the years, instead of preserving, perfecting, and perpetuating the *World*, as their father had ardently wished, his sons took $25 million of the dwindling profits to perpetuate their luxurious lifestyles and plowed back next to nothing to sustain and enrich the paper. By 1931 the *Times, Daily News*, and *Daily Mirror* all outsold the *World*, which was $3 million in the red.

Defying their father's wishes and betraying his trust, the Pulitzer brothers sold the paper to publisher Roy Howard of the Scripps-Howard chain for $5 million. They gave their 2,867 employees a fond farewell and two weeks' pay.

The new owner junked the daily and Sunday editions and merged the *Evening World* with the *Telegram* as the *World-Telegram*, which newspaper critic A. J. Liebling critic called "anti-foreign, anti-intellectual, anti-poor people, and anti-government (except for J. Edgar Hoover)." In 1950 it merged to become the *World-Telegram and Sun*, which folded in 1966.

However, under Joe Pulitzer's leadership the *St. Louis Post-Dispatch* survived and prospered. His brothers agreed that he should have full control of the paper, and to compensate him for being unfairly treated in their father's will, saw to it that he had a generous salary and bonuses. The *Post-Dispatch* won a Pulitzer Prize in 1937 for exposing wholesale voter registration fraud in St. Louis and for getting forty thousand "ghost" ballots invalidated; in 1941 for an effective campaign against the city's smoke pollution; and in 1948 for successfully demanding stricter safety regulations after a mine disaster in Centralia, Illinois. The next year it shared the prize with the *Chicago Daily News* for revealing that fifty-one Illinois editors and publishers had accepted payoffs totaling $480,000 to publish handouts from Republican party headquarters. The paper won again in 1952 for disclosing widespread corruption in the IRS and other government departments.

Post-Dispatch reporter John Rogers won the 1927 prize for his daring investigation that led to the impeachment of Illinois judge George English, and Paul Anderson got it in 1929 for an exposé of illegal naval oil leases, known as the Teapot Dome scandal. Charles Ross was a 1931 winner for an insightful look at the country's desperate economic plight. In 1940 Bart Howard joined the winners for a year of distinguished editorials on the menace of German militarism, cartoonist Daniel Fitzpatrick in 1955 for his entire career, and Robert Lasch in 1966 for editorials denouncing American policy in Vietnam.

Joe's son Joseph Pulitzer III succeeded him on the *St. Louis Post-Dispatch*. After thirty-one years as its editor and publisher he retired in 1986, at seventy-two. His thirty-five-year-old son Joseph Pulitzer IV remained as vice president and administrator of the company until he resigned in 1995. Today, in 2001, Pulitzer's seventy-one-year-old grandson Michael, chairman of the board of Pulitzer, Inc., is the only family member connected with the paper. The *Post-Dispatch* is still one of the country's great newspapers. The company also owned several TV and radio stations, which it sold to the Hearst Corporation (!) in 1999 for $1.8 billion, surely enough to resurrect the *World*. Instead the company bought thirty-nine weekly newspapers and five other papers.

When William Robinson Reynolds chose Joseph Pulitzer as his Ph.D. thesis at Columbia University, he wrote to Joe for help. He replied on January 24, 1941: "It occurs to me that before writing a life of my father you should see a man, now 78 years of age, who probably knew my father more intimately than I or any of his secretaries. That man is Jabez E. Dunningham, referred to as a 'confidential secretary.' The truth of the matter is that Dunningham was his valet, or, in a sense of the word, his 'trained nurse,' and, as such, came to know him more intimately, probably, than anyone on earth. . . . I'm sure he could tell you a great deal about my father's health, eccentricities, unhappy loss of temper, affection and intolerance for his family, and all the intimate details of his restless life. I urge you to see him before he dies." Reynolds took Joe's advice, and much of what he learned from Dunningham is in this biography.

Although Joseph Pulitzer has been dead for almost a century, he is still remembered anew each spring, when some two dozen outstanding editors, writers, cartoonists, photographers, and musicians gather at Columbia University to receive prizes in his name, what one winner, muckraker Jack Anderson, calls the Academy Awards of Journalism.

Notes

"CU" and "LC" in the Notes refer to Columbia University and the Library of Congress, respectively.

Introduction: Joseph Pulitzer and His "Indegoddampendent" World

1   *"any hitherto unprinted"*   John A. Cockerill, "Some Phases of Contemporary Journalism," *Cosmopolitan* 13, 1892.
2   *"I want to attack"*   J. P. to C. F., August 5, 1911 (LC).   *"a contest of madmen"*   Sydney Brooks, "The American Yellow Press," *Fortnightly* 96, 1911, p. 137.
3   *"Joseph Pulitzer had a shining"*   *New York Times*, October 30, 1911, p. 2.

Chapter 1: The Fighting Immigrant

6   *"Take that . . . little"*   Don Carlos Seitz, *Joseph Pulitzer: His Life and Letters* (New York: AMS Press, 1970), p. 44.
8   *"In my condition"*   Ibid., p. 51.   *"I still have a painful"*   Ibid.
9   *"Whether or not"*   Alleyne Ireland, *An Adventure with a Genius: Recollections of Joseph Pulitzer* (1914; reprint, New York: Johnson Reprint, 1969), p. 173.
10 *"The first thing he did"*   Ibid., pp. 221–223.
11 *"He stopped short"*   Ibid. pp. 173–174.
12 *"I could not believe it"*   Seitz, *Joseph Pulitzer*, p. 58.
13 *But . . ."it was not long"*   Ibid., p. 59.   *"One sultry day"*   Ibid., p. 60   *There he continued to work,*   Ibid., p. 61.
14 *"They think," said Brockmeyer*   W. A. Swanberg, *Pulitzer* (New York: Charles Scribner's Sons, 1967), p. 13.

Chapter 2: Upright, Spirited, and Dangerous

16 *"Mr. Pulitzer," it read*   Don Carlos Seitz, *Joseph Pulitzer: His Life and Letters* (New York: AMS Press, 1970), pp. 62–63.   *As Seitz explained*   Ibid., p. 63.
17 *Claiming his honor*   Ibid., pp. 65–67.   *There were conflicting*   Ibid., p. 70.
18 *Pulitzer's roommate*   Ibid.   *"Tonight [January 27]"*   Ibid., pp. 65–66.   *"Augustine called him"*   Ibid., pp. 66–67.
19 *"I know the correspondent"*   Ibid., pp. 67–68.   *"Pulitzer is blamed"*   Ibid., p. 69.
20 *It eventually came out*   Ibid., p. 72.

Chapter 3: Survives Fire and Marries

22 *As co-owner and*   Don Carlos Seitz, *Joseph Pulitzer: His Life and Letters* (New York: AMS Press, 1970), p. 75.
24 *"Not that I fail"*   Ibid., pp. 80–81.
25 *"I am not here, sir"*   Ibid., p. 84.   *"I heartily despise"*   Ibid., p. 86.
26 *Nevertheless, he addressed*   Ibid., p. 89.
27 *An impassioned Pulitzer*   W. A. Swanberg, *Pulitzer* (New York: Charles Scribner's Sons, 1967), p. 42.
28 *"almost every avenue"*   *New York Times*, April 12–14, 1877, p. 1.
29 *"first love letter"*   Seitz, *Joseph Pulitzer*, pp. 91–92.   *They married at*   Swanberg, *Pulitzer*, p. 49.

Chapter 4: Buys *St. Louis Post-Dispatch*

32   *"appraisingly about"*   Julian S. Rammelkamp, *Pulitzer's* Post-Dispatch (Princeton, N.J.: Princeton University Press, 1967), p. 19.   *"If it is a crime"*   Ibid., p. 46.   *"Democracy means"*   Ibid., p. 47.

33   *He opened with*   St. Louis Post and Dispatch, February 15, 1879, pp. 1–2.   *To cries of*   Rammelkamp, *Pulitzer's* Post-Dispatch, p. 53.

34   *He dramatized*   Ibid., p. 54.   *Nevertheless, he*   Ibid., p. 55.   *The result, wrote*   Brian Roberts, *The Zulu Kings: A Major Reassessment of Zulu History* (New York: Charles Scribner's Sons, 1974).   *"The most painful"*   Post and Dispatch, February 12, 1879, p. 2.

35   *As newsboys yelled*   Rammelkamp, *Pulitzer's* Post-Dispatch, p. 55.   *"It stamps the"*   Ibid., p. 54.   *But when Pulitzer*   Ibid.   *To this, Pulitzer replied*   Ibid., p. 56.

36   *"One day he rushed"*   W. A. Swanberg, *Pulitzer* (New York: Charles Scribner's Sons, 1967), p. 58.   *"I worked on that carcass"*   Rammelkamp, *Pulitzer's* Post-Dispatch, p. 65.

37   *Kate was a "remarkable beauty"*   Swanberg, *Pulitzer*, p. 62.   *"Where has the money gone?."*   St. Louis Post-Dispatch, October 16, 1879, p. 2.

38   *"Mr. Hermann is not"*   Rammelkamp, *Pulitzer's* Post-Dispatch, p. 72.   *In sensational terms*   Ibid., pp. 81–82.   *"We are ruled"*   Ibid., pp. 58–59.

Chapter 5: President Garfield Assassinated

40   *"A hard taskmaster"*   Ibid., p. 91.   *Typical was his*   Walt McDougall, *This Is the Life* (New York: Charles Scribner's Sons, 1926), p. 138.   *Depending on his mood*   Don Carlos Seitz, *Joseph Pulitzer: His Life and Letters* (New York: AMS Press, 1970), p. 106.   *But no one on the staff*   Julian S. Rammelkamp, *Pulitzer's* Post-Dispatch (Princeton, N.J.: Princeton University Press, 1967), p. 93.   *"Nothing escaped his"*   James Creelman, "Joseph Pulitzer—Master Journalist," *Pearson's Magazine* 21 (March 1909): 238–239.

41   *"Mr. Pulitzer was the"*   George Johns, "Joseph Pulitzer: His Early Life in St. Louis," *Missouri Historical Review* (1931–1932): 68.   *"I can never be president"*   W. A. Swanberg, *Pulitzer* (New York: Charles Scribner's Sons, 1967), p. 64.

42   *Pulitzer biographer*   Ibid.   *In a blatant about-face*   Rammelkamp, *Pulitzer's* Post-Dispatch, p. 133.   *"Although a soldier"*   Ibid.   *So the tall, handsome*   Ibid., p. 124.

43   *Restating his policy*   St. Louis Post-Dispatch, September 22, 1880, p. 4.   *"The Missouri Pacific"*   Rammelkamp, *Pulitzer's* Post-Dispatch, pp. 154–155.

45   *The following Sunday*   Post-Dispatch, January 10, 1881, p. 1.   *Pulitzer explained*   Ibid., January 11, 1881, p. 4.   *Once more Pulitzer*   Ibid., February 14, 1881, p. 4.

46   *In his editorial column*   Rammelkamp, *Pulitzer's* Post-Dispatch, pp. 252–253.   *A reporter nearby*   O. O. Sealey, *130 Pictures of Live Men* (New York, 1910), p. 349.

47   *He stated with astonishing*   Post-Dispatch, September 8, 1881, p. 1.

48   *Pulitzer exposed*   Ibid., September 12, 1881, p. 4.

Chapter 6: Jesse James "Shot Like a Dog"

51   *Conceding that prizefighting*   St. Louis Post-Dispatch, February 8, 1882, p. 4.

52   *He saw her as a lonely*   Ibid., March 4, 1882.

53   A DASTARD'S DEED   Ibid., April 4, 1882, p. 1.

54   *"However much we may feel"*   Ibid., p. 4.   *Pulitzer attacked*   Ibid., April 14, 1882.   *"It must not be thought"*   Ibid., April 10, 1882.

55   *"Frank James might find"*   Frank Triplett, *The Life, Times, and Treacherous Death of Jesse James* (New York: Promontory Press, 1970), p. 266.   *"A villainous and utterly indefensible lie"*   Ibid.   *"If this advice is followed"*   Post-Dispatch, April 14, 1882, p. 4.   *"another scandal"*   Ibid., April 3, 1882.

56   *"Let us throw"*   Wayne Andrews, *The Vanderbilt Legend* (New York: Harcourt, Brace, 1941), p. 182.   *"upon a filth begrimed"*   Post-Dispatch, April, 26, 1882.   *Rev. Lofton Goes Up"*   Ibid., May 16, 1882, p. 1.

57   *Pulitzer even persuaded clergymen*   Ibid., June 30, 1882, pp. 1, 5.   *This, explained British prime minister*   John Morley, *The Life of William Ewart Gladstone*, vol. 3 (New York: Macmillan, 1903), p. 81.

58   *"The Battle of Tel-e-Kebir"* Post-Dispatch, September 16, 1882, p. 4. *"about as honorable"* Ibid., September 11, 26, 27, 1882, p. 4.

59   *He counterattacked next day* New York Times, "Shot Down by an Editor," October 14, 1882, p. 1. *McGuffin later recalled* Ibid. *"fruits of aggressive"* Julian S. Rammelkamp, *Pulitzer's* Post-Dispatch (Princeton, N.J.: Princeton University Press, 1967), p. 289. *Harper's Weekly agreed* Ibid., p. 290.

60   *A slap on the wrist* Ibid. *William Rockhill Nelson* Ibid. *"The charge of blackmail"* Rammelkamp, *Pulitzer's* Post-Dispatch, p. 290.

61   *Even the cautious* New York Times New York Times, October 17, 1882, p. 1. *Hyde's hostile* Missouri Republican Ibid., October 11, 1882, and Cockerill's New York Times obituary, April 11, 1898. *"We are far behind England"* Post-Dispatch, October 30, 1882, p. 3. *"A reporter for the New York Mail"* Ibid., December 7, 1882.

Chapter 7: Pulitzer Takes Over the *World*

63   *"furtive as a deadly spider"* Maury Klein, *The Life and Legend of Jay Gould* (Baltimore: Johns Hopkins University Press, 1986), p. 2.

64   *"the skunk of Wall Street"* Ibid., p. 3. *"one of the most sinister figures"* Ibid. *"the largest white elephant"* Walt McDougall, "Old Days on the *World*," American Mercury (January 1925): 21.

65   *"keeping this little holding"* Don Carlos Seitz, *Joseph Pulitzer: His Life and Letters* (New York: AMS Press, 1970), p. 131. *"I hardly knew the place"* James Wyman Barrett, *Joseph Pulitzer and His* World (New York: Vanguard Press, 1941), p. 73. *"You have all been living"* W. A. Swanberg, *Pulitzer* (New York: Charles Scribner's Sons, 1967), p. 81.

66   *"There is scarcely a man"* Julian S. Rammelkamp, *Pulitzer's* Post-Dispatch (Princeton, N.J.: Princeton University Press), p. 299.

67   *"First-rate,"* Gould replied New York World, May 13, 1883, p. 1. *"French Scientist and Explorer"* Roger Butterfield, *The Fabulous Century* (New York: Time-Life Books, 1970), p. 172. *"the sordid aristocracy"* Seitz, Joseph Pulitzer, pp. 138–139. *"to their Korean names"* George Juergens, *Joseph Pulitzer and the* New York World (Princeton, N.J.: Princeton University Press, 1966), p. 209.

68   *"And it is to such men"* World, May 13, 1883. p. 4. *"Collis Huntington's extremely"* McDougall, "Old Days on the *World*," American Mercury, January 1925, pp. 22–23.

69   *"with your tender feelings"* Charles Gibson to J. P., May 14, 1883, Joseph Pulitzer Papers, Columbia University. *Editorial writer William Merrill* Barrett, *Joseph Pulitzer and His* World, p. 75.

70   *"that journals of this city"* Swanberg, *Pulitzer*, p. 92. *"We are delighted to receive"* World, May 1, 1883, p. 4.

71   *"LET ME DIE!"* Ibid., May 30, 1883, p. 4. *A few days later* Ibid., June 3, 1883, p. 1. *"As the voices of JP"* Barrett, *Joseph Pulitzer and His* World, p. 74.

72   *One day, a Tammany Hall politician* Ibid. *"Damn fool was making so much noise"* Ibid. *"They cannot help it."* World, September 9, 1883, p. 4. *"the un-republican spectacle"* Ibid., September 15, 1883, p. 4.

73   *"every blow is given"* Ibid., September 2, 1883, p. 4. VAST ASSEMBLAGE ALMOST FRENZIED Ibid., August 7, October 25, 1883, p. 1. *"it was a great exhibition"* Ibid., August 7, p. 4. *If Pulitzer didn't write this editorial*, he certainly approved it. *"I will bet $100"* Ibid., August 10, 1883, p. 6.

74   *A—Door stained with blood* Ibid., September 19, 1883, p. 1. *He used the same X-marks-the-spot* Ibid., November 19, 26, 1883. *"Inasmuch as the divine sunflower"* Ibid., December 17, 1883, p. 4.

75   *"It was about time for Rockefeller"* Ibid., June 2, 1883, p. 4. *"What respect is due"* Ibid., October 14, 1883, p. 4. *he calculated that Vanderbilt's* Ibid., November 12, 1883, p. 4. *"rabid victims of the Anglomania disease"* George Juergens, *Joseph Pulitzer and the* New York World (Princeton, N.J.: Princeton University Press, 1966), pp. 178–179.

76   *"New York under Cornwallis"* World, November 28, 1883, p. 4. *"Why should virtue"* Ibid., September 15, 1883, p. 4. MARY ANDERSON'S TRIUMPH Ibid., October 28, 1883, p. 1. *"the most brilliant private ball"* Ibid., December 11, 1883, p. 5.

77 "We have been accused" Ibid., October 14, 1883, p. 4. "criticism of the wealthy families" Juergens, Joseph Pulitzer and the New York World, pp. 196, 200. He also knew that
women World, October 1, 1883, p. 3. "The World attacked the titans" Juergens, Joseph
Pulitzer and the New York World, p. 209. "By exercising to keep fit" William Inglis, "An
Intimate View of Joseph Pulitzer," Harper's Weekly 55 (November 11, 1911): 7. "a newspaper should be" Alleyne Ireland, An Adventure with a Genius: Recollections of Joseph
Pulitzer (1914; reprint, New York: Johnson Reprint, 1969), pp. 113–114.

Chapter 8: Puts a Democrat in the White House

79 The World interviewed a clergyman New York World, January 26, 1884, p. 1. "The
attempt of a few narrow" Ibid., March 26, 1884, p. 4. "The complaint of the" Ibid.,
April 13, 1884, p. 4.

80 "Sinners do not shrink" Ibid., May 27, 1884, p. 4. "that a sensational newspaper"
George Juergens, Joseph Pulitzer and the New York World (Princeton, N.J.: Princeton Uni-
versity Press, 1966), p. 71n. "the destruction of property" World, April 1, 1884, p. 4.
"We cannot ride roughshod" Ibid., April 1, 1884, p. 4.

81 "the deaths of 45%" Juergens, Joseph Pulitzer and the New York World, p. 277. "Never
drop a thing" John Tebbel, The Compact History of the American Newspaper (New York:
Hawthorn, 1963), p. 198. Pulitzer concluded that "but for the" World, August 31, 1883,
p. 1. "milk from along the Harlem line" Ibid., February 24, 1884, p. 12. MARM MAN-
DELBAUM ARRESTED Ibid., December 9, 1883, p. 1.

82 "While some of our esteemed" Ibid., December 11, 1883, p. 5. Pulitzer's bête noire Journalist, December 13, 1883, p. 4. He also complimented himself World, April 27, 1884, p. 4.

83 "The insolence and impertinence" Ibid., January 25, 1884, p. 4. "The World ahead of the
pack" Christopher Silvester, ed. The Norton Book of Interviews (New York: W. W. Norton,
1996), p. 9. "Duelling is looking up" World, March 24, 1884, p. 4. "If any Mexican
greaser" Ibid., May 7, 1884, p. 4.

84 "the modern Greek" Ibid., February 15, 1884, p. 4. "These foreigners, who, it is said"
Ibid., February 21, 1884, p. 4. He dismissed the Chinese Ibid., February 18, 19, 1884, p.
4. As for the French Ibid., April 27, 1884, p. 11. The World again ripped into royalty
Ibid., October 12, 1884, p. 10. "I hope you will be back in the Crimea" Victoria to Cambridge, 30, 1854. In Queen Victoria in Her Letters and Journals, selected by Christopher
Hibbert (New York: Viking, 1985), p. 126n. "a fairly habitable apartment" World, February 24, 1884, p. 4.

85 "There was nothing that could be done" Journalist, July 19, 1884, p. 5. he deplored "the
use of dynamite" World, April 15, 1884, p. 4. "The Jew is accused of" Ibid., February
14, 1884, p. 4. "so long as they remain at home" Ibid., September 3, 1884, p. 4.

87 "Republicans went insane" Gil Troy, See How They Ran: The Changing Role of the Presidential Candidate (New York: Free Press, 1991), p. 91. "Wall Street was in the saddle"
James Wyman Barrett, Joseph Pulitzer and His World (New York: Vanguard Press, 1941),
p. 86. "more of a Reformer than a Democrat" Ibid., pp. 84–85. "repulsive to the
rascals" Ibid., p. 86. "a reform fraud and Jack-in-the-box" World, August 26, 1884,
p. 4.

88 "The opponents of Cleveland" Ibid., July 27, 1884, p. 4. "I should like to point out"
Juergens, Joseph Pulitzer and the New York World, pp. 79–80.

89 "baseless rumor" World, July 25, 1884, p. 4. "A villainous libel" Ibid., August 6, 1884,
p. 4. "the coarse debauchee" W. A. Swanberg, Pulitzer (New York: Charles Scribner's
Sons, 1967), p. 102. "indignant, deluded and outraged" Barrett, Joseph Pulitzer and His
World, p. 88. "cheerfully admits the indiscretion" Ibid. "a culpable irregularity of life"
World, August 8, 1884, p. 4. Twining was willing to forgive Cleveland Barrett, Joseph
Pulitzer and His World, pp. 88–89. "after the child was born" World, August 8, 1884, p. 1.

90 "Cleveland acted a heroic part" Ibid., p. 4. "a sporadic association" Ibid. "The casket
containing" Ibid., August 20, 1884, p. 4.

91 "incompetent Chief of the Signal Service" New York Times, November 15, 1884, p. 4.
"If he had left the scandal" World, September 23, 1884, p. 4. "always up to some meanness" Ibid., August 7, 1884, p. 3. Pulitzer himself was up to Ibid., September 24, 1884,

p. 5. *An admiring St. Louis friend* Charles Gibson to J. P., October 10, 1884 (CU). *"You have a right to ask"* John Dillon to J. P., September 5, 1884 (CU).

92 *Under the scare headline* World, March 24, 1884, p. 1. *"Everywhere we hear of"* Ibid., September 3, 1884, p. 1. *"demonstrated that the Eastern"* Ibid., p. 4. *"Notwithstanding all the calumnies"* David Saville Muzzey, *James G. Blaine: A Political Idol of Other Days* (New York: Dodd, Mead, 1934), p. 317.

95 *A REVOLUTION* World, November 2, 1884, p. 1. *DOING MURDER IN ARMOR* Ibid., November 3, 1884, p. 1.

96 *"I can never lose the vividness"* Don Carlos Seitz, *Joseph Pulitzer: His Life and Letters* (New York: AMS Press, 1970), p. 149. *"that dragged the sewers"* World, November 7, 1884, p. 4. *"the vileness of the* World's" Journalist, November 8, 1884, pp. 4–5. *"Despite great provocation"* World, November 6, 1884, p. 4. *WAS BLAINE HIMSELF* Ibid., October 17, 1884, p. 5.

Chapter 9: Saves Statue of Liberty

97 *"Our splendid society"* New York World, January 28, 1885, p. 4.

98 *"Dividends paid on"* Ibid., March 14, 1885, p. 4. *"in a population of a million and a half"* Jacob Riis, *How the Other Half Lives* (New York: Charles Scribner's Sons, 1903), p. 243.

99 *"gladly and zealously support"* W. A. Swanberg, *Pulitzer* (New York: Charles Scribner's Sons, 1967), p. 127. *"the able and aged"* World, January 19, 1885, p. 4. *"To what race of human beings"* Ibid., February 15, 1885, p. 4 *"with grammatical precision"* Ibid.

100 *"This letter [from Dana to the president]"* Ibid., February 18, 1885, p. 4. *"a sewer for the stream of vice"* Journalist, May 24, 1885, p. 5. *A REFINED YOUNG LADY* Ibid., July 5, 1885, pp. 1–2. *"for various kinds of loathsome diseases"* Ibid., January 17, 1885, p. 4. *"vouch for the honesty"* World, March 13, 1885, p. 4.

101 *"Zola is very fond"* Ibid., October 18, 1884, p. 4. *"to find his subjects"* Ibid., February 22, 1885, p. 20. *WIT AND LITERARY ABILITY* Ibid., March 2, 1885, p. 7. *"a divided city"* George Juergens, *Joseph Pulitzer and the* New York World (Princeton, N.J.: Princeton University Press, 1966), p. 272.

102 *"one of the families subsisted"* World, January 11, 1885, p. 20. *"pestilential human rookeries"* Ibid., April 23, 1885, p. 3.

103 *Reform would have to wait* Ibid., April 14, 1885, p. 4. *"own yachts or put on aristocratic airs"* Ibid., January 13, 1885, p. 4. *"are now more intelligent"* Ibid., February 16, 1885, p. 1. *"shows how eager the Republicans are"* Ibid., February 22, 1885, p. 4. *He despised both the self-indulgent rich* Ibid., March 8, 1885, p. 4.

104 *Despite his respect* Ibid., April 25, 1885, p. 1. *"it would be an irrevocable"* Ibid., March 16, 1885, p. 4. *Tens of thousands of positive replies* Don Carlos Seitz, *Joseph Pulitzer: His Life and Letters* (New York: AMS Press, 1970), pp. 157–158. *"the British Navy cannot"* World, April 10, 1885, p. 4.

105 *"that it is only a matter of time"* Ibid., May 8, 1885, p. 4. *"Cyrus H. McCormick invented a great reaper"* Ibid., May 16, 1884, March 11, 1885, p. 4. *BOREAS ON A BENDER* Ibid., February 12, 1885, p. 3. *"science" of "noseology"* Ibid., April 20, 1884, p. 1. *"people of refinement dropped"* Journalist, June 28, 1884, p. 6.

106 *THE PAROXYSMAL EPOCH* World, March 8, 1885, p. 20. *"the conversation will drift pleasantly"* Ibid., March 10, 1885, p. 4. *Just as New York City women* Ibid., October 26, 1884, p. 10.

107 *It doubted "whether a writer"* Ibid., May 23, 1885, p. 4. *"At the time of his marriage"* Ibid., May 23, 1885, p. 5.

108 *"You are suffering from something"* J. D. to J. P., July 8, 1885 (CU). *"the circulation rose"* Journalist, August 22, 1885, p. 5. *"looked on with an apathy"* World, August 11, 1885, p. 4.

109 *"He said that all the little"* Kate Pulitzer's diary, October 16, 1885 (CU). *"forever unsatisfied"* Allen Churchill, *Park Row* (New York: Rinehart, 1958), p. 38. *"It is doubtful if a woman"* World, April 18, 1884, p. 4. *"that he nightly read"* Walt McDougall, "Old Days on the *World*," *American Mercury*, January 1925, p. 23.

Chapter 10: Haymarket Square Massacre

110 *"of the high esteem"* Newsboys to J. P., New Year 1886 (CU).
111 *McDougall saw Pulitzer in a new light* W. A. Swanberg, *Pulitzer* (New York: Charles Scribner's Sons, 1967), p. 133. *"you have a much better position"* T. C. to J. P., April 13, 1886 (CU). *But the proposal was spiked* Allen Churchill, *Park Row* (New York: Rinehart, 1958), p. 39. *"the Broadway Railroad"* James Wyman Barrett, *Joseph Pulitzer and His World* (New York: Vanguard Press, 1941), p. 101.
112 *Sharp was arrested* Ibid., p. 102. *"hundreds of poverty stricken"* Page Smith, *The Rise of Industrial America* (New York: Viking Penguin, 1990), p. 242. *"Mother" Jones, as the labor leader* Ibid.
113 *"murdering our brothers"* Ibid., p. 244. *Facing a crowd* Ibid. *"You have nothing more to do"* Roger Butterfield, *The American Past: A History of the United States from Concord to the Nuclear Age* (New York: Simon & Schuster, 1957), p. 248. *Then he morphed into a peacenik* Ibid. *Pulitzer's response was fast* *New York World*, May 6, 7, 1886, p. 4. *Afraid that Americans* Ibid., May 7, 1886, p. 4.
114 *Calling anarchists "dynamite demons"* Ibid. *When the* Chicago News Ibid. *"Nearly every English journal"* Ibid. *The* London Morning Post Ibid. *To exonerate the Irish* Ibid.
115 *The* World *continued to cover* Ibid., June 22, 1886, p. 4. *Although the bomb thrower* William J. Adelman, *Haymarket Revisted* (Chicago: Labor History Society, 1986). *"state had never discovered"* *Encyclopaedia Britannica*, 11th ed., vol. 1, *Anarchism* (New York: Encyclopaedia Britannica, 1910), p. 917. *Pulitzer predicted that* Allan Nevins, *John D. Rockefeller*, vol. 2 (New York: Charles Scribner's Sons, 1941), p. 115.
116 *"If you can prove to me"* Swanberg, *Pulitzer*, p. 138.
117 *"who is something of a reformer"* Ibid., p. 142. *"You are doing excellently"* Ibid., p. 143. *the "bronze female"* Joyce Milton, *The Yellow Kids: Foreign Correspondents in the Heyday of Yellow Journalism* (New York: Harper & Row, 1989), p. 7. *"human joy has rarely been"* Ibid., p. 5. *"We will not forget"* Don Carlos Seitz, *Joseph Pulitzer: His Life and Letters* (New York: AMS Press, 1970), p. 159.
118 *"What is fame and fortune"* G. C. to K. P., November 27, 1886 (CU).
119 *Even Kate failed to* Churchill, *Park Row*, p. 38. *The rules, he wrote, "are just"* J. P. to K. P., 1886, office of Joseph Pulitzer III.

Chapter 11: Nellie Bly Goes Crazy

120 *"to fill a vast area"* W. A. Swanberg, *Pulitzer* (New York: Charles Scribner's Sons, 1967), p. 155.
122 *"Jerome-Churchill story"* J. P. to T. C., March 28, 1887 (CU). *"It is not the first time"* L. J. to J. P., April 1, 1887 (CU). *"The future king"* William Manchester, *The Last Lion* (New York: Dell, 1984), p. 136.
123 *"10,689 people of the first"* *New York World*, July 10, 1887, p. 1.
124 *"he cared little for"* Allen Churchill, *Park Row* (New York: Rinehart, 1958), p. 39.
125 *"I'm afraid to stay"* Brooke Kroeger, *Nellie Bly, Daredevil, Reporter, Feminist* (New York: Times Books, 1994), p. 90. *"somebody's darling"* Ibid., p. 91. *in their hands: "coarse, massive"* Ibid.
126 *"a raging crowd of"* Walt McDougall, *This Is the Life* (New York: Charles Scribner's Sons, 1926), p. 188. PLAYING MAD WOMAN *New York Sun*, October 14, 1887, pp. 1–2.
127 ALL THE DOCTORS FOOLED *World*, October 15, 1887, p. 5. *"men and women were sent"* Kroeger, *Nellie Bly*, p. 95. *"that cool courage, consummate"* *Pittsburgh Dispatch*, October 18, 1887, p. 2. *"On the strength of my story"* Nellie Bly, *Ten Days in a Mad House* (New York: Munro, 1887), p. 98. *"The* World *Their Savior"* *World*, October 28, 1887, p. 12. *"a very bright and very plucky"* *Pittsburgh Dispatch*, October 16, 1887, p. 10. *"Her appearance was at"* McDougall, *This Is the Life*, p. 186.
128 *"We have withdrawn from"* *Sun*, October 18, 1887, p. 4. *"Malicious lies"* *World*, October 19, 1887, p. 4.
129 *"How odd it was"* Swanberg, *Pulitzer*, p. 160. *"The boss behind Nicoll"* James Wyman Barrett, *Joseph Pulitzer and His World* (New York: Vanguard Press, 1941), p. 105. *"They*

know Dana's record" Ibid., p. 106. *Early that summer* Swanberg, *Pulitzer*, p. 159. *"The Jews have a special interest"* Ibid., p. 164.

130 *"The Jews of New York"* Ibid. DEMOCRACY TRIUMPHS *Sun*, November 8, 1887, p. 4.

131 *"no more rope than"* Ibid., November 9, 1887, p. 1. *"And now, Pulitzer"* Ibid., November 8, 1887, p. 4. *"the largest ever printed"* *World*, November 9, 1887, p. 4. *"For nearly three weeks"* Ibid., November 10, 1887, p. 4.

132 *"we have been getting out"* Don Carlos Seitz, *Joseph Pulitzer: His Life and Letters* (New York: AMS Press, 1970), p. 166. *"The* World *had been conducting"* Alleyne Ireland, *An Adventure with a Genius: Recollections of Joseph Pulitzer* (1914; reprint, New York: Johnson Reprint, 1969), pp. 218–220. *"On my way downtown"* Ibid., p. 220. *"Is it true that"* W. C. W. to K. P., December 22, 1887 (CU). *"I am not quite dead yet"* J. P. to W. C. W., December 26, 1887 (CU).

Chapter 12: Tries to Save His Sight

133 *"reminds me of your generous"* J. Mc. to J. P., February 13, 1888 (CU). *And the* World's *business* G. T. to J. P., February 25, 1888 (CU). *Pulitzer was always "kind"* T. G. to J. P., March 31, 1888 (CU). *he faced the group* Allan Nevins, *John D. Rockefeller*, vol. 2, p. 792A (New York: Charles Scribner's Sons, 1941), p. 119.

134 *"the father of trusts"* Ibid. *"It was a glorious picture"* Ibid., p. 118. *"proved conclusively that"* Ibid., p. 119. *"the most active and possibly"* Ron Chernow, *Titan: The Life of John D. Rockefeller Sr.* (New York: Random House, 1998), p. 297.

135 *"Would gladly face"* R. C. to J. P., March 16, 1888 (CU). *Conkling had once confided* W. A. Swanberg, *Pulitzer* (New York: Charles Scribner's Sons, 1967), p. 163. *Bly's account captured* New York *World*, April 1, 1888, p. 1. *"the giggling, rather pretty"* Brooke Kroeger, *Nellie Bly, Daredevil, Reporter, Feminist* (New York: Times Books, 1994), p. 113. *"the most beautiful reporter"* Ibid., p. 115.

136 *"dreads being overshadowed"* *World*, April 11, 1888, p. 4.

137 *"heard him frequently"* Swanberg, *Pulitzer*, p. 117. *"He came against his doctor's"* Allen Churchill, *Park Row* (New York: Rinehart, 1958), p. 42. *"For Cleveland"* James Wyman Barrett, *Joseph Pulitzer and His* World (New York: Vanguard Press, 1941), p. 133.

138 *"long hours of reading"* Don Carlos Seitz, *Joseph Pulitzer: His Life and Letters* (New York: AMS Press, 1970), p. 166.

Chapter 13: "An Instrument of Justice, a Terror to Crime"

140 *"Never fear of troubling"* W. A. Swanberg, *Pulitzer* (New York: Charles Scribner's Sons, 1967), p. 178. *"I decidedly object"* Daniel W. Pfaff, *Joseph Pulitzer II and the Post-Dispatch: A Newspaperman's Life* (University Park: Pennsylvania State University Press, 1991), p. 19. *"the strangest mixture"* Alleyne Ireland, "A Modern Superman," *American Magazine*, April 1912, p. 670. *"My Dearest"* J. P. to K. P., June 11, 1889 (CU). *Ponsonby wrote to Kate* C. P. to K. P., June 21, 1889 (CU).

141 *"a dreadful fizzle"* Walt McDougall, *This Is the Life* (New York: Charles Scribner's Sons, 1926), p. 188. *Promoted as "one of the most"* New York *World*, February 17, 1889, p. 9. *waiter rushed upstairs* Brooke Kroeger, *Nellie Bly, Daredevil, Reporter, Feminist* (New York: Times Books, 1994), p. 136.

142 *But one who signed himself* *World*, November 10, 1889, p. 27. *"God grant that this structure"* Don Carlos Seitz, *Joseph Pulitzer: His Life and Letters* (New York: AMS Press, 1970), pp. 171–172.

143 *"If it is an extraordinary thing"* Ibid., pp. 173, 174; J. P. to W. D., November 23, 1889.

Chapter 14: Nellie Bly Races around the World

144 *After her visit* New York *World*, December 26, 1899, p. 2.

145 *"much talked about prejudices"* Brooke Kroeger, *Nellie Bly, Daredevil, Reporter, Feminist* (New York: Times Books, 1994), p. 152.

146 *because, he shouted, "Death"* Ibid., p. 158. *"My God!" he said with a gasp* Ibid.

147 "You can't leave until" Ibid., p. 166. "I never doubted the success" World, January 26, 1890, p. 1.
148 concluded that "a young woman" Journalist, February 1, 1890, p. 5.
149 "He is certainly better" C. P. to K. P., December 23, 1889, office of J. P. III. "I am certainly no worse" Ibid., J. P. to K. P., December 23, 1889, office of J. P. III. "I really feel that my health" Ibid., January 1, 1890.
150 "How suddenly it has gotten dark" Don Carlos Seitz, Joseph Pulitzer: His Life and Letters (New York: AMS Press, 1970), p. 177. "All his life thereafter" Allen Churchill, Park Row (New York: Rinehart, 1958), p. 59. THE FIRST ELECTROCIDE World, August 7, 1890, p. 1.
151 "in a state so feeble" James Wyman Barrett, Joseph Pulitzer and His World (New York: Vanguard Press, 1941), pp. 137–138. "Yielding to the advice" World, October 16, 1890, p. 4. "A great vacuum" New York Herald, October 17, 1890, p. 4.
152 The Texas Newspaper Union Joseph Pulitzer II Papers, Pattee Library, Pennsylvania State University.
153 "THE GREATEST NEWSPAPER" World, December 10, 1890, p. 1. "Is God in?" Churchill, Park Row, p. 43.
154 "Mr. Pulitzer had issued" New York Times, December 11, 1890, p. 3. "THE PULITZER CELEBRATION" Ibid.
155 frustrating "scheme after scheme" World, December 10, 1890, pp. 3, 4.
157 plagued with insomnia Daniel W. Pfaff, Joseph Pulitzer II and the Post-Dispatch: A Newspaperman's Life (University Park: Pennsylvania State University Press, 1991), p. 15. "sounds that others would" Ibid.

Chapter 15: Running the World by Remote Control

158 "Mrs. Pulitzer," Hosmer noted James Wyman Barrett, Joseph Pulitzer and His World (New York: Vanguard Press, 1941), p. 142.
159 "HENNESSY AVENGED" New York World, March 16, 1891, p. 1. "long-continued separation" Barrett, Joseph Pulitzer and His World, p. 143. "a tendency to asthma" W. A. Swanberg, Pulitzer (New York: Charles Scribner's Sons, 1967), p. 193. "no one ever came into" Don Carlos Seitz, Joseph Pulitzer: His Life and Letters (New York: AMS Press, 1970), p. 186.
161 "wobbles about" Town Topics, November 26, 1891, p. 6. "suspicion, jealousy and" Walt McDougall, This Is the Life (New York: Charles Scribner's Sons, 1926), p. 107.
162 noting that "the news editor" Swanberg, Pulitzer, p. 196. "divided their domain" Ibid., p. 197. "I'll make it a hundred" Ibid. "I want to say" S. W. M. to J. P., December 15, 1891, office of Joseph Pulitzer III.
163 "most wealthy socialites" Daniel W. Pfaff, Joseph Pulitzer II and the Post-Dispatch: A Newspaperman's Life (University Park: Pennsylvania State University Press, 1991), p. 20.
164 "Suppose Ballard Smith" Swanberg, Pulitzer, p. 201. "Please assume this hypothetical" Barrett, Joseph Pulitzer and His World, p. 147.
165 "Kill the hired thugs!" World, July 7, 1892, p. 4. As expected, the Ibid., July 3, 1892, p. 4. "The First Fruit" Ibid., July 7, 1892, p. 4. "There is but one thing" Ibid., July 12, 1892, p. 4.
166 He wrote to Kate, instead H. P. to K. P., 1892 (CU). "Dear Mr. Pulitzer" J. P. to K. P., 1892 (CU). Perhaps to escape from Barrett, Joseph Pulitzer and His World, p. 145. "about 200 cigars" Swanberg, Pulitzer, pp. 203–204.
167 "My regard for you" Ibid., p. 204. "Perhaps fifty different" Ibid., pp. 204–205. "Grateful memories" Seitz, Joseph Pulitzer, p. 190.
168 "Remember that fault-finding" J. P. to G. H., after August 1892; Swanberg, Pulitzer, p. 206. "jelly-fish, with the" Journalist, October 22, 1892, p. 9.

Chapter 16: Pulitzer's "Satanic Journalism"

169 Past midnight, Harvey stood Don Carlos Seitz, Joseph Pulitzer: His Life and Letters (New York: AMS Press, 1970), p. 192.
170 Resenting his promotion Ibid., p. 194.
171 "It's because I'm not yet" W. A. Swanberg, Pulitzer (New York: Charles Scribner's Sons, 1967), p. 214. "Such, Mr. Olney" Ibid. Day after day the World exhorted and at times

commanded Olney to investigate the sugar, rubber, lead, copper, cordage, whiskey, tobacco, cotton-oil, and cash register trusts, and General Electric's attempted monopoly. Each published report concluded with the text of the Sherman Act and Cleveland's inaugural address against trusts. *"Havemeyer knows that"* John L. Heaton, *The Story of a Page: Thirty Years of Public Service and Public Discussion in the Editorial Columns of the New York World* (New York: Harper & Brothers, 1913), pp. 95–96.

172   *a "fire-eating anarchist"* Brooke Kroeger, *Nellie Bly, Daredevil, Reporter, Feminist* (New York: Times Books, 1994), p. 209.

173   *The* Journalist *welcomed* Ibid., p. 207. *"There is only more"* *Town Topics*, October 5, 1893, p. 12. *"I would rather live in hell"* James Wyman Barrett, *Joseph Pulitzer and His World* (New York: Vanguard Press, 1941), pp. 154–155. *"Can it be possible"* Ibid., p. 155. *"crime, underwear and pseudo-science"* Joyce Milton, *The Yellow Kids: Foreign Correspondents in the Heyday of Yellow Journalism* (New York: Harper & Row, 1989), p. 28.

174   *"two weeks salary"* Barrett, *Joseph Pulitzer and His* World, p. 155. *"the longest and most delightful"* Swanberg, *Pulitzer*, p. 215. *"the apparently pangless"* Ibid., pp. 215–216. *"I am not afraid"* Ibid., p. 215. *"If you send Pulitzer"* Ibid.

175   *"when a little pet-secretary"* G. H. to K. P., January 7, 1894 (CU). *"Writing to me is 'headachey'"* J.P. to K.P., April 27, 1894 (CU). *"I have frightful rheumatism"* Daniel W. Pfaff, *Joseph Pulitzer II and the* Post-Dispatch: *A Newspaperman's Life* (University Park: Pennsylvania State University Press, 1991), p. 22. *"a coarse, bloated millionaire"* Ibid., p. 25.

176   *"It is incredible"* Ibid., p. 24. *"It takes me every moment"* Ibid. *"after hours of torture"* Ibid., p. 26.

177   *"because he never stops"* Ibid. *"way of keeping all your nerves"* Ibid., p. 36. *"was entirely incompatible"* Ibid. *"Lord Randolph Churchill's"* *New York World*, July 11, 1894, p. 7.

178   *"We are born in a Pullman"* *The Parable of Pullman* (Illinois Labor History Society), p. 1. *Colonel Jones responded* Seitz, *Joseph Pulitzer*, p. 196. *"paradise" was more like purgatory* World, July 13, 1894, p. 3.

179   *"the most bitter striker in town"* Ibid., July 15, 1894. *"It's already been printed"* Ibid., July 17, 1894, p. 5.

180   *He had "called on Col. Ingersoll"* New York Times, September 1, 1894, p. 6. *Pulitzer's "satanic journalism"* Swanberg, *Pulitzer*, p. 217. *atrocities committed by the Japanese* World, December 12, 1894, p. 1.

181   *"The Chinese fired on"* James Creelman, *On the Great Highway: The Wanderings and Adventures of a Special Correspondent* (Boston: Lothrop, 1904), p. 33. *"cursed him up hill,"* Swanberg, *Pulitzer*, p. 219.

182   *"snarling savage"* W. A. Swanberg, *Theodore Dreiser* (New York: Bantam Books, 1967), pp. 78–79. *"They might as well have asked"* Ibid., p. 79.

183   *"I have accepted your advice"* Seitz, *Joseph Pulitzer*, p. 198. *"You like to emphasize"* Pfaff, *Joseph Pulitzer II and the* Post-Dispatch, p. 21. *"It is, I hope"* Swanberg, *Pulitzer*, p. 216.

Chapter 17: Prevents War between the United States and Britain

185   *"I don't object to Gladstone"* Hesketh Pearson, *Disraeli: His Life and Personality* (New York: Grosset & Dunlap, 1951), p. 193. *He also accused* Ralph G. Martin, *Jennie*, vol. 2, 1895–1921, p. 176. *When someone repeated the libel* Randolph S. Churchill, *Winston S. Churchill, Youth, 1874–1900* (Boston: Houghton Mifflin, 1966), p. 240. *"I am the loneliest man"* W. A. Swanberg, *Pulitzer* (New York: Charles Scribner's Sons, 1967), p. 223.

186   *"When I did not hear"* Ibid., p. 226. *MR. AND MRS. NELLIE BLY* New York World, April 21, 1895, p. 17.

187   *"Such is the degradation"* *Town Topics*, April 25, 1895, p. 12.

188   *ROOSEVELT AS JUDGE* World, May 17, 1895, pp. 1–2. *This delighted the likes of* Roger Butterfield, *The America Past: A History of the United States from Concord to Hiroshima, 1775–1945* (New York: Simon & Schuster, 1947), p. 268.

189   *To scare Salisbury* Swanberg, *Pulitzer*, p. 229. *As historian Barbara Tuchman remarked* Barbara Tuchman, *The Proud Tower: A Portrait of the World before the War, 1890–1914* (New York: Macmillan, 1966), p. 30. *When he did not reply* Samuel Eliot Morrison, *The*

Oxford History of the American People, vol. 3 (New York: New American Library, 1966), p. 114.

190 *Salisbury ridiculed the Venezuelans' claims* John A. Garraty, *The American Nation: A History of the United States* (New York: Harper & Row, 1966), p. 628. *Salisbury's supercilious response* Henry W. Bragdon and Samuel P. McCutchen, *History of a Free People* (New York: Macmillan, 1967), p. 463. *In that mood he addressed* Swanberg, *Pulitzer,* p. 229. *The House gave him unanimous* Ibid., p. 230. *"to interfere in South America"* World, December 21, 1895, p. 4.

191 *"This Venezuelan boundary"* Ibid. *"Under the teaching"* New York Times, December 20, 1895, p. 4. *Pulitzer now launched* Swanberg, *Pulitzer,* p. 230. *He sent scores of cables* World, December 24, 1895, p. 1.

192 *"Dare not interfere"* Ibid. *"I absolutely disbelieve"* Ibid. *"Would prefer Venezuela"* Ibid. *"unnatural strife"* Ibid., December 25, 1895, p. 1. *"We are too closely bound"* Ibid., December 24, 1895, p. 1. *With Queen Victoria's approval* Ibid., December 25, 1895, p. 1. *Because the British had* Ibid., December 24, 1895, p. 1.

193 *"The statute cited"* John L. Heaton, *The Story of a Page: Thirty Years of Public Service and Public Discussion in the Editorial Columns of the New York World* (New York: Harper & Brothers, 1913), p. 122. *"It would give me great"* Swanberg, *Pulitzer,* p. 232. *"[T]he war clamor ceased"* Don Carlos Seitz, *Joseph Pulitzer: His Life and Letters* (New York: AMS Press, 1970), p. 206. *"The World led"* Ibid., p. 207. *"The country is open"* World, December 6, 1895, p. 11.

194 *"Two young English"* Ibid., December 15, 1895, p. 59. *"Mr. Churchill had"* David Stafford, *Churchill and Secret Service* (Woodstock, N.Y.: Overlook Press, 1998), p. 12. *"While the Spanish"* Rene Kraus, *Winston Churchill* (New York: J. B. Lippincott, 1941), p. 49. *"I have been civil"* Winston Churchill to his mother, November 10, 1895. Randolph S. Churchill, *Winston S. Churchill, Companion,* vol. 1, part 1, 1874–1895 (Boston: Houghton Mifflin, 1967), p. 597. *"The essence of American journalism"* W. S. C. to J. S. C., Ibid., November 15, 1895, p. 600.

195 *At year's end* Winston S. Churchill, *A History of the English-Speaking Peoples: The Great Democracies* (New York: Dodd, Mead, 1958), p. 330 fn. *"From Japan westward"* World, December 15, 1895, p. 4.

Chapter 18: Fighting Crime and William Randolph Hearst

196 *"in that it appeals"* John K. Winkler, *William Randolph Hearst: A New Appraisal* (New York: Avon Books, 1955), p. 15. *"broke into New York"* James Wyman Barrett, *Joseph Pulitzer and His World* (New York: Vanguard Press, 1941), p. 171.

197 *He adapted the idea in a series* Allen Churchill, *Park Row* (New York: Rinehart, 1958), p. 72.

198 *"I knew when I appointed you"* John K. Winkler, *William Randolph Hearst,* p. 83. *"only remained in their nest"* Don Carlos Seitz, *Joseph Pulitzer: His Life and Letters* (New York: AMS Press, 1970), p. 212. *What most infuriated Pulitzer* Barrett, *Joseph Pulitzer and His World,* p. 173.

200 *"Please don't write in Delphic phrases"* Brooke Kroeger, *Nellie Bly, Daredevil, Reporter, Feminist* (New York: Times Books, 1994), p. 278. *To dramatize the need for them* Ibid., p. 286. *"The outcry against me is tremendous"* H. W. Brands, *T. R.: The Last Romantic* (New York: Basic Books, 1997), p. 291. *"Of the forty-five highway robberies"* New York Times, March 19, 1896, p. 8.

201 *"We present a simple statement"* New York World, March 19, 1896, p. 4. *"She performed feats"* Ibid., February 23, 1896, p. 1. NELLIE BLY PROPOSES TO FIGHT Ibid., March 8, 1896, p. 25.

202 *"Do you think," she asked* Ibid., p. 17.

203 *When Creelman arrived* James Creelman, *On the Great Highway: The Wanderings and Adventures of a Special Correspondent* (Boston: Lothrop, 1904), p. 162.

204 *Instead he reported a wild rumor* Ibid., p. 167. *Creelman was so disturbed* Ibid., p. 168. *"the real cause of the war"* World, May 1, 1896, p. 1.

205 *"Blood on the roadsides"*   Roger Butterfield, *The Fabulous Century* (New York: Time-Life Books, 1970), p. 276.   *"How do they want me to"*   John Tebbel, *America's Great Patriotic War with Spain* (Manchester Center, Vt.: Marshall Jones, 1996), p. 22.

206 *"Tall, cadaverous, reddish beard"*   Ralph Blumenfeld, *In the Days of Bicycles and Bustles* (New York: Brewer & Warren, 1930), pp. 66–67.   the *"Custer of Journalism"*   *World*, April 11, 1896, p. 5.   *"Pulitzer let me see that"*   Wickham Steed, *Through Thirty Years*, vol. 1 (London: Heinemann, 1924), p. 76.

207 *"I am deeply touched"*   John L. Heaton, *The Story of a Page: Thirty Years of Public Service and Public Discussion in the Editorial Columns of the* New York World (New York: Harper & Brothers, 1913), pp. 126, 130.

208 *"One of the most important duties"*   Roger Butterfield, *The American Past: A History of the United States from Concord to Hiroshima, 1775–1945* (New York: Simon & Schuster, 1947), p. 272.   *"You shall not press down"*   *New York Times*, July 10, 1896, p. 3.   *"Is Bryan crazy?,"*   Ibid., September 27, p. 12.

209 *"in unceasing labor"*   Seitz, *Joseph Pulitzer*, p. 227.   The new owner-editor of the New York Times   Daniel W. Pfaff, *Joseph Pulitzer II and the* Post-Dispatch: A Newspaperman's Life (University Park: Pennsylvania State University Press, 1991), pp. 38–39.   *Geranium [Hearst's Journal] is never to be*   Ibid., p. 39.   *"report on the hours"*   J. P. memos, fall 1896 (LC).   *"paranoia querulenta"*   John A. Garraty, *The American Nation: A History of the United States* (New York: Harper & Row, 1966), p. 616.   *"This is the first time I have"*   Butterfield, *The American Past*, p. 272.

210 *"There is no doubt as to"*   Seitz, *Joseph Pulitzer*, pp. 226–227.   *"As we sat there on his"*   George Cary Eggleston, *Recollections of a Varied Life* (New York: Henry Holt, 1910), p. 320.

211 *Searching for a metaphor*   Ervin Wardman, *Concise Dictionary of American Biography* (New York: Charles Scribner's Sons, 1964), p. 1141.

212 *"Damn your impertinence!"*   W. A. Swanberg, *Pulitzer* (New York: Charles Scribner's Sons, 1967), p. 248.

Chapter 19: War Fever

213 *"I have thought of you every day"*   J. P. to K. P., January 14, 1897 (CU).

214 *"a woman of the people"*   Nathaniel Lande, *Dispatches from the Front: News Accounts of American Wars, 1776–1991* (New York: Henry Holt, 1995), pp. 132–133.   THE UNCLOTHED WOMEN   W. A. Swanberg, *Pulitzer* (New York: Charles Scribner's Sons, 1967), p. 268.   *"devotion to duty"*   Ibid., pp. 268–269.   *"I never heard"*   Ben Procter, *William Randolph Hearst: The Early Years, 1863–1910* (New York: Oxford University Press, 1998), p. 105.   AMERICAN SLAIN   John Tebbel, *America's Great Patriotic War with Spain* (Manchester Center, Vt.: Marshall Jones, 1996), p. 42.

215 *"The murder of Dr. Ruiz"*   *New York World*, February 20, 21, 1897, p. 1.

216 *"If the facts are true"*   John L. Heaton, *The Story of a Page: Thirty Years of Public Service and Public Discussion in the Editorial Columns of the* New York World (New York: Harper & Brothers, 1913), p. 160.   *Although the soldiers who*   Joyce Milton, *The Yellow Kids: Foreign Correspondents in the Heyday of Yellow Journalism* (New York: Harper & Row, 1989), p. 146.   *Scovel wrote a*   Scovel, *Letter from Calaboose #1*, February 28, 1897, S. S. Papers, Missouri Historical Society, St. Louis, Missouri.   *Apparently this did not include*   Milton, *The Yellow Kids*, p. 149.

217 *"Give Scovel my kind regards"*   Memo from J. P. to B. M., April 1897, S. S. Papers.   *This was an unhappy choice for*   Don Carlos Seitz, *Joseph Pulitzer: His Life and Letters* (New York: AMS Press, 1970), p. 232.   *"to exhibit his hoofs and horns"*   Ibid., pp. 232–233.

218 *"Mr. Pulitzer's attention"*   K. P. to A. B., June 8, 1897 (CU).

219 *"I wonder how Mr. Pulitzer"*   S. S. to F. S., May 19, 1897, S. S. Papers.   *"They would quietly rejoice"*   Ibid., S. S. to J. P., June 11, 1897.

220 *"under the direction of"*   John K. Winkler, *William Randolph Hearst: A New Appraisal* (New York: Avon Books, 1955), p. 111.   *"breathe the breath of truth"*   J. C. to S. S., July 8, 1897, S. S. Papers.   *"no ordinary woman"*   Ibid., S. S. to J. P., October 2, 1897.

221 *"This tenderly nurtured girl"*   Swanberg, *Pulitzer*, p. 273.   *"We've got Spain now!"*   Proctor, *William Randolph Hearst*, p. 106.   *"I answer the World"*   World, August 21, 1897, p. 1.   *"and finally imposed a condition"*   Ibid.   *"the Spanish in Cuba"*   Swanberg, *Pulitzer*, pp. 273–274.   *"I wish to correct a stupid"*   World, September 9, 1897, p. 1.

222 MISS EVANGELINA CISNEROS   *New York Journal*, October 10, 1897, p. 1.   *"a wonderfully able"*   J. P. to D. C. S., December 23, 1897 (LC).   *"find somebody in the Journal's"*   Ibid., December 3, 1897 (LC).   *"the precise degree of accuracy"*   J. P. memo to Seitz, Ibid., 1897 (LC).

223 *"You may do features"*   Ibid., p. 101.

224 *"Stop [your] column at once"*   Ibid., p. 102.   *"committing journalistic suicide"*   Ibid., p. 108.   *"Poor Lucille is still very ill"*   J. P. to T. D., December 8, 1897 (CU).   *"she was most like him"*   Seitz, *Joseph Pulitzer*, p. 236.

225 *"I hardly dare think how"*   W. B. F. to T. D., January 1, 1898, Davidson Papers, Yale University.

Chapter 20: Americans at War in Cuba

227 *"I am greatly indebted"*   New York World, January 16, 1898, p. 1.   *"beautiful, pale, and agitated"*   Ibid.   *"Outside of France"*   Ibid.   FRANCE REFUSES TO ALLOW   Ibid.

228 *"bands of students paraded"*   Ibid.   *"aimed against American citizens"*   Ivan Musicant, *Empire by Default: The Spanish-American War and the Dawn of the American Century* (New York: Henry Holt, 1998), p. 119.   *"in many towns the supply of coffins"*   Ibid., p. 118.

229 *"fat pigs for Spanish bayonets"*   World, January 14, 1898, p. 1.   *"The United States battleship"*   Ibid., February 16, 1898, p. 1.   MAINE EXPLOSION CAUSED   Ibid., February 17, 1898, p. 1.

230 *"Public opinion should be"*   W. A. Swanberg, *Pulitzer* (New York: Charles Scribner's Sons, 1967), p. 284.

231 *"Nobody is so foolish"*   New York Times, February 17, 1898, p. 1.   *"It is cheering to find"*   John K. Winkler, *William Randolph Hearst: A New Appraisal* (New York: Avon Books, 1955), p. 128.   *"written by fools"*   Ibid., p. 129.   *"gross misrepresentation"*   New York Evening Post, March 17, 1898.

232 *"War! War! We must get"*   James Wyman Barrett, *Joseph Pulitzer and His World* (New York: Vanguard Press, 1941), pp. 176–177.   *Charles Chapin and others*   Chapin, *Charles E. Chapin's Story* (New York: G. P. Putnam's Sons, 1920), p. 173.   *"though superlatively profane"*   Ibid., p. 177.   *Pulitzer was "wildly absorbed"*   G. L. to K. P., April 8, 1898 (CU).   *"Spain is a decaying, ignorant"*   World, April 10, 1898, p. 4.

233 *"the backbone of a chocolate éclair"*   Thomas A. Bailey, *The American Pageant: A History of the Republic* (Lexington, Mass.: D. C. Heath, 1966), p. 618.   *"criticizing, complaining, stopping"*   J. P. to B. M., April 1898 (LC).   *Hearst was in such a state*   Swanberg, *Pulitzer*, p. 288.

234 *"Colonel Reflipe W. Thenuz"*   Ibid., p. 289.   *"Confederate notes, Chinese cash"*   Ben Proctor, *William Randolph Hearst: The Early Years, 1863–1910* (New York: Oxford University Press, 1998), p. 124.   *"editors demanded hair-raising"*   R. W. Stallman, *Stephen Crane: A Biography* (New York: George Braziller, 1968), p. 359.

235 *"the highest and truest courage"*   Ibid., p. 371.

236 *"Well, you might file"*   Ibid., p. 383.   *"Spanish sharpshooters picked"*   Ibid., pp. 400, 401.   SLURS ON THE BRAVERY   New York Journal, July 17, 1898, p. 1.

237 EDITOR OF THE JOURNAL'S   Ibid., July 20, 1898.   *"were especially touchy"*   Margaret Leech, *In the Days of McKinley* (New York: Harper & Brothers, 1959), pp. 304–305.   *"jeered at this repentance"*   Swanberg, *Citizen Hearst*, p. 190.   *But Theodore Roosevelt proved*   Stallman, *Stephen Crane*, p. 392.

238 *There, under the headline*   Ibid., p. 407.   *"At this spectacular moment"*   Charles H. Brown, *The Correspondents' War: Journalists in the Spanish-American War* (New York: Charles Scribner's Sons, 1967), p. 403.   *"You son-of-a-bitch!"*   John Tebbel, *America's Great Patriotic War with Spain* (Manchester Center, Vt.: Marshall Jones, 1996), pp. 262, 264, 265.

239 *"had the Spaniards held out"*   Bailey, *The American Pageant*, p. 623.   *"Make your demand to send"*   J. P. to B. M., August 1898 (LC).   *"There is a proposition before me"*   Ibid.

240 *What must have disappointed* World, August 2, 1898, p. 3. *"the picture that does not make"* George Juergens, *Joseph Pulitzer and the* New York World (Princeton, N.J.: Princeton University Press, 1966), p. 106.

241 *"I do not discount the talent"* November 28, 1898 (LC).

242 *"this gross Falstaff"* Joyce Milton, *The Yellow Kids: Foreign Correspondents in the Heyday of Yellow Journalism* (New York: Harper & Row, 1989), p. 361. *"The moment it was informed"* Ibid., p. 363. *"for your kindness in looking"* S. S. to W. Mc., December 22, 1898, McKinley Papers (LC). *"Such papers as* The World" Elmer Davies, *History of the* New York Times, *1851–1921* (New York: New York Times, 1921), p. 232.

243 *"How little they know"* Creelman, *On the Great Highway: The Wanderings and Adventures of a Special Correspondent* (Boston: Lothrop, 1904), p. 177. *"can work himself into quite as"* Swanberg, Citizen Hearst, p. 192. *"stooped, snooped and scooped"* Bailey, *The American Pageant*, p. 555.

Chapter 21: For the Boers, against the British

244 *identified the "bishop"* Joyce Milton, *The Yellow Kids: Foreign Correspondents in the Heyday of Yellow Journalism* (New York: Harper & Row, 1989), p. 364. *"Cubans have been able"* Ibid., p. 365.

245 MRS. PLACE PUT TO DEATH New York World, March 21, 1899, pp. 1, 2. *"Amazing stupidity"* J. P. memo, March 26, 1899, in George Juergens, *Joseph Pulitzer and the* New York World (Princeton, N.J.: Princeton University Press, 1966), p. 31.

246 *He hailed it as* Ibid., April 29, 1899, p. 166. *"the pursuit of the White Mice"* W. A. Swanberg, *Pulitzer* (New York: Charles Scribner's Sons, 1967), p. 312. *"Gentleman, with somewhat indifferent"* Times of London, 1899 (CU). *"a tall gentlemanly young fellow"* Swanberg, *Pulitzer*, p. 313.

247 *"You have become so used to"* W. L. to J. P., October 9, 1899 (CU). *"received a line of affection"* J. P. to K. P., March 20, 1899 (CU). *"every stroke of which"* Ibid., June 20, 1899. *"so cowardly about criticizing"* J. P. to D. G. P., August 17, 1899 (CU).

248 *to stop the arms race* Barbara Tuchman, *The Proud Tower: A Portrait of the World before the War, 1890–1914* (New York: Macmillan, 1966), p. 230. *"the ruler of the most"* John L. Heaton, *The Story of a Page: Thirty Years of Public Service and Public Discussion in the Editorial Columns of the* New York World (New York: Harper & Brothers, 1973), p. 168. *"The Bear That Walks"* Tuchman, *The Proud Tower*, p. 230. *"triumph of the foreign element"* New York Times, May 18, 1899, p. 6.

249 *"electrified the chancelleries"* Don Carlos Seitz, *Joseph Pulitzer: His Life and Letters* (New York: AMS Press, 1970), pp. 249–250. *"Though we have no such powerful"* Heaton, *The Story of a Page*, p. 169. *The* World *summarized* Ibid., p. 170. *"deepen that obligation"* Ibid. *"establish a military"* Ibid., p. 171. *In one excited outburst* Seitz, *Joseph Pulitzer*, p. 250.

250 *"With all its faults"* J. P. to K. P., October 22, 1899 (CU). *a "$500 reward with"* J. P. to World, November 1, 1899 (LC). *"Utterly alone here"* J. P. to K. P., November 2, 1899 (CU). *"distinctly tends to lower"* Seitz, *Joseph Pulitzer*, p. 433. *"Who wrote that asinine story"* Ibid., pp. 433–434.

251 *"it can be done to death"* Ibid., pp. 429–430. *Write to them, Pulitzer advised* Ibid., p. 430. *"George Eliot living with"* Ibid., p. 432.

Chapter 22: "Accuracy! Accuracy!! Accuracy!!!"

252 *"Accuracy! Accuracy!! Accuracy!!!"* Don Carlos Seitz, *Joseph Pulitzer: His Life and Letters* (New York: AMS Press, 1970), p. 434.

253 PULITZER HOME DESTROYED New York Times, January 10, 1900, p. 3. MR. PULITZER'S HOME New York World, January 10, 1900, p. 3.

255 *"Please take five o'clock"* W. A. Swanberg, *Pulitzer* (New York: Charles Scribner's Sons, 1967), p. 308. *"ballroom, music room"* J. P. to McKim, Mead, and White, April 16, 1900 (CU). *"have been quoting"* Daniel W. Pfaff, *Joseph Pulitzer II and the* Post-Dispatch:

A *Newspaperman's Life* (University Park: Pennsylvania State University Press, 1991), p. 33. *"The World is to me"* Swanberg, *Pulitzer*, p. 310.

256 *"Were there any good ones"* Charles Chapin, *Charles E. Chapin's Story* (New York: G. P. Putnam's Sons, 1920), pp. 219–220.

257 *"because I am convinced"* World, April 4, 1900, p. 1.

258 *"tea with lords and their"* Chapin, *Charles E. Chapin's Story*, pp. 222–224. *"Darling, your telegram"* K. P. to J. P., 1900 (CU). *He was to treat him* J. P. to Seitz, summer 1900 (CU). *Dumant Clarke, a friend* D. C. to J. P., November 3, 1900 (CU).

259 *"What you tell me about Ralph"* A. P. to J. P., October 19, 1900 (CU). *"fine chaps, the best types"* Chapin, *Charles E. Chapin's Story*, p. 224. *"I then went up to the house"* Swanberg, *Pulitzer*, p. 311. *Unarmed English at the Mercy* Paul Ferris, *The House of Northcliffe* (New York: World, 1972), p. 76. MAFEKING RESCUED World, May 19, 1900, pp. 1–2.

260 BRITAIN DELIRIOUS OVER Ibid., May 20, 1900, p. 3. THE RELIEF OF MAFEKING Ibid., p. 6. *"And how shockingly"* Chapin, *Charles E. Chapin's Story*, pp. 218–219.

261 *"What about the rotten beef"* Roger Butterfield, *The American Past: A History of the United States from Concord to Hiroshima, 1775–1945* (New York: Simon & Schuster, 1947), p. 288. *"appears quite unable"* R. N. to C. J., October 23, 1900 (CU).

262 *"You are not to leave"* K. P. to J. P., in 1900 files; otherwise undated (CU). *"I beg to tell you"* K. L. to J. P., December 2, 1900 (CU). *"I would as soon give"* Pfaff, *Joseph Pulitzer II and the* Post-Dispatch, pp. 20–21. *"to be a good rather"* Ibid., p. 21.

263 *"People say that"* Ferris, *The House of Northcliffe*, p. 108. *"I look forward into this"* World supplement, December 30, 1900, p. 1.

Chapter 23: President McKinley Assassinated

266 *"closely resembles"* New York World, January 1, 1901, p. 14. *"The best thing about"* James Wyman Barrett, *Joseph Pulitzer and His* World (New York: Vanguard Press, 1941), p. 181.

267 *"Your idea of the 20th Century"* World, January 2, 1901, p. 2. *"In the great matter of"* Ibid., January 1, 1901, p. 14. *"had made twice as many"* Paul R. Baker, *Stanny: The Gilded Life of Stanford White* (New York: Free Press, 1989), p. 309. *"the smile of a happy child"* Ishbel Ross, *Ladies of the Press* (New York: Harper & Brothers, 1936), p. 89.

268 *"Tell Mrs. Astor," she said* Ibid., pp. 86–87. *"be ready day and night"* Mark Sullivan, *Our Times: The Turn of the Century: The United States 1900–1925* (New York: Charles Scribner's Sons, 1928), pp. 557–558.

269 *"to help save the boy"* Daniel W. Pfaff, *Joseph Pulitzer II and the* Post-Dispatch: A Newspaperman's Life (University Park: Pennsylvania State University Press, 1991), pp. 33–34. *"we spent a good deal"* Ibid., p. 34.

270 *"Why should I?" the president replied* Margaret Leech, *In the Days of McKinley* (New York: Harper & Brothers, 1959), p. 584. *"knocked down, pinioned under"* Ibid., pp. 595–596. M'KINLEY [sic] SHOT . . . ASSAILANT CONFESSES World, September 14, 1901, p. 1.

271 *His first message was* G. H. to J. P., September 13, 1901 (CU). *He believed that McKinley's assassination* World, September 14, 1901, p. 6. *"If bad institutions"* W. A. Swanberg, *Pulitzer* (New York: Charles Scribner's Sons, 1967), p. 322. *The bullet that pierced* Ibid. *"ignoring Geranium [the* Journal]" World, J. P. to D. C. S., September 30, 1901 (LC).

272 *"If you have no compassion"* Don Carlos Seitz, *Joseph Pulitzer: His Life and Letters* (New York: AMS Press, 1970), p. 253. *"the most damnable outrage"* H. W. Brands, *T. R.: The Last Romantic* (New York: Basic Books, 1997), pp. 422–423. *"One of the most learned"* World, October 20, 1901, p. 4.

273 *"We are going to print'"* John Graham [David Graham Phillips], *The Great God Success* (Ridgewood, N.J.: Gregg Press, 1967), pp. 116–117, 185. *"My experience has been that"* D. C. to J. P., August 14, 1901 (CU). *"I was never once asked"* Charles Chapin, *Charles E. Chapin's Story* (New York: G. P. Putnam's Sons, 1920), p. 233.

274 *was "keenly hurt"* Seitz, *Joseph Pulitzer*, p. 254.

Chapter 24: "Find a Man Who Gets Drunk and Hire Him"

275   *"and epidemic of scandal"* New York World, January 5, 1902, p. 8. *"When I was there someone"* Don Carlos Seitz, *Joseph Pulitzer: His Life and Letters* (New York: AMS Press, 1970), pp. 22–24.

276   *"sap the foundations"* World, February 9, 1902, p. 4. *"Prices That Stagger"* Ibid., April 29, 1902, p. 6.

277   *"all the more"* Seitz, *Joseph Pulitzer*, p. 432. *Pulitzer took the visitor's* Norman Thwaites, *Velvet and Vinegar* (London: Grayson & Grayson, 1932), pp. 51–53.

279   ÉMILE ZOLA FAMOUS WRITER World, September 30, 1902, p. 7. *he cabled Seitz an outline* J. P. to D. C. S., October 2, 1902 (LC). *Pulitzer's orders were obeyed* World, October 12, 1902, p. 6.

280   *"No other city on earth"* Richard O'Connor, *Courtroom Warrior: The Combative Career of William Travers Jerome* (Boston: Little, Brown, 1963), p. 38. *"Perhaps some day intelligent men"* World, November 5, 1902, p. 6. *"The rights and interests"* Roger Butterfield, *The American Past: A History of the United States from Concord to Hiroshima, 1775–1945* (New York: Simon & Schuster, 1947), p. 320. *Exasperated by the "extraordinary"* Thomas A. Bailey, *The American Pageant: A History of the Republic* (Lexington, Mass.: D. C. Heath, 1966), p. 650.

281   *Roosevelt of "negotiating"* Butterfield, *The American Past*, p. 320. *Roosevelt warned Baer's banker* Theodore Roosevelt, *An Autobiography* (New York: Macmillan, 1916), p. 488.

Chapter 25: Euphemisms for Abortion

282   *"I return this to you"* J. P. to D. C. S., January 7, 1903 (LC). *"cultivate the habit"* Daniel W. Pfaff, *Joseph Pulitzer II and the Post-Dispatch: A Newspaperman's Life* (University Park: Pennsylvania State University Press, 1991), pp. 37, 38.

283   *Joe thanked his father* Joe to J. P., May 30, 1903 (CU). *He should study* J. P. to J. C., March 18, 1903 (CU). *"name some great editor"* Don Carlos Seitz, *Joseph Pulitzer: His Life and Letters* (New York: AMS Press, 1970), p. 437. *a man "worth twenty editors"* Ibid., p. 455. *Burton apologized to Pulitzer* P. B. to J. P., April 11, 1903 (CU).

284   *"The highest satisfaction"* New York World, May 10, 1903, editorial section, p. 1. *ex-President Cleveland, who conceded* Ibid. *Foggo "was very pleasant"* J. T. to J. P., June 21, 1903 (CU).

285   *"Understand jealousy"* Seitz, *Joseph Pulitzer*, p. 457. SCHOOL OF JOURNALISM World, August 16, 1903, p. 1. *"The lawyer, who may imperil"* Ibid. *He asked for the building* Seitz, *Joseph Pulitzer*, p. 447.

286   *"particularly what other men"* Pfaff, *Joseph Pulitzer II and the Post-Dispatch*, p. 47. *"I have already doubts"* J. P. to S. L., September 18, 1903 (CU). *Two of his secretaries* Norman Thwaites, *Velvet and Vinegar* (London: Grayson & Grayson, 1932), p. 57.

Chapter 26: Breaking In Frank Cobb

288   *"sleepless nights, savage pain"* Allen Churchill, *Park Row* (New York: Rinehart, 1958), p. 271. *"Story wretchedly written"* J. P. to D. C. S., September 2, 1904 (LC).

289   *"human interest" news clips* Alleyne Ireland, *An Adventure with a Genius: Recollections of Joseph Pulitzer* (1914; reprint, New York: Johnson Reprint, 1969), p. 118.

290   *"A social instrument"* Norman Thwaites, *Velvet and Vinegar* (London: Grayson & Grayson, 1932), p. 60. *"You are typical of a species"* Ibid. *"in a clear, incisive voice"* Ireland, *Adventure with a Genius*, p. 131. *"please read that"* James Wyman Barrett, *Joseph Pulitzer and His World* (New York: Vanguard Press, 1941), p. 182. *"If a candidate"* Ibid.

291   *"Think I have found editor"* Ibid., p. 184. *"Rhodes, McMaster, Trevelyan"* Ibid., pp. 184–185. *"Cobb was joyously candid"* Ibid., p. 185. *"not incisive, terse"* Ibid., pp. 185–186. *"I hope you will maintain"* Don Carlos Seitz, *Joseph Pulitzer: His Life and Letters* (New York: AMS Press, 1970), pp. 257–258.

292   *"I am going away"* W. A. Swanberg, *Pulitzer* (New York: Charles Scribner's Sons, 1967), p. 355. *"say some manly ringing"* J. P. to B. M., May 4, 1904 (LC). *"wished there was more"* K. P. to J. P., May 13, 1904 (LC). *"a man of great strength"* Susan E. Tifft and

Alex D. Jones, "The Family: How Being Jewish Shaped the Dynasty That Runs the Times," *New Yorker*, April 19, 1999, p. 46.

293   *"Do give me the pleasure"*   Meyer Berger, *The Story of the New York Times, 1851–1951* (New York: Simon & Schuster, 1951), p. 153.   *In it Hearst repeated*   Ibid., p. 153.   *"Shut yourself up"*   Seitz, *Joseph Pulitzer*, pp. 260–261.

294   *"I hope Cobb will improve"*   Ibid., pp. 258–259.

295   *"in a very good humor"*   K. P. to J. P., June 18, 1904 (CU).   *He spat out a memo*   J. P. to D. C. S., August 30, 1904 (LC).   *"My only extravagance"*   K. P. to J. P., October 2, 1904 (CU).

296   *"we had youth, health"*   Charles Chapin, *Charles E. Chapin's Story* (New York: G. P. Putnam's Sons, 1920), pp. 140–144.   *"Good lead on the Kaiser"*   Churchill, *Park Row*, p. 272.   *"remember that nature"*   K. P. to J. P., September 15, 1904 (CU).

297   *"You know that these corporations"*   *New York World*, October 1, 1904, pp. 6, 7.   *"were clamoring for your"*   Ibid., p. 7.

298   *"the great scandal"*   J. P. to W. M., 1904 (LC).   *Roosevelt was enraged*   H. W. Brands, *T. R.: The Last Romantic* (New York: Basic Books, 1997), p. 676.   *"acted the perfect dolt"*   Seitz, *Joseph Pulitzer*, p. 306.   *One crisp winter morning*   Norman Thwaites, *Velvet and Vinegar* (London: Grayson & Grayson, 1932), pp. 54–55.

Chapter 27: Unmasking Corrupt Insurance Companies

300   *"For Heaven's sake"*   Joe to J. P., January 25, 1905 (CU).   *"You are wrong"*   Ibid., February 1, 1905 (CU).   *Joe warned his father*   Ibid., February 27, 1905.   *McKenna was also to try*   J. P. to D. C. S., January 31, 1905 (LC).

301   *"I thought the old man"*   James Wyman Barrett, *Joseph Pulitzer and His* World (New York: Vanguard Press, 1941), pp. 295–306.

302   *"Rejection of the Frick report"*   Ibid., p. 199.   *"kept a huge fund"*   Seitz, *Joseph Pulitzer*, pp. 268–269.   *"Nothing short of revolution"*   Ibid., p. 270.   *Someone had jokingly*   W. A. Swanberg, *Pulitzer* (New York: Charles Scribner's Sons, 1967), p. 363.

303   *Each morning, Pulitzer rode*   Norman Thwaites, *Velvet and Vinegar* (London: Grayson & Grayson, 1932), p. 56.   *Pulitzer biographer Swanberg*   Swanberg, *Pulitzer*, p. 363.   *To Seitz, "the pain"*   Seitz, *Joseph Pulitzer*, p. 11.

304   *Pulitzer biographer Barrett*   Barrett, *Joseph Pulitzer and His* World, p. 289.   *"the fierce determination"*   Louis Starr, "Joseph Pulitzer and His Most 'Indegoddampendent' Editor," *American Heritage*, June 1968, p. 19.   *"How dreadfully slow"*   Seitz, *Joseph Pulitzer*, p. 274.   *"review him but not"*   Ibid., pp. 274–275.   *"Every newspaperman in Albany"*   Barrett, *Joseph Pulitzer and His* World, p. 200.

305   *"If there is anything"*   J. P. to D. C. S., July 13, 1905 (LC).   *"My God, Seibold"*   Barrett, *Joseph Pulitzer and His* World, pp. 201–202.   *Less than a week after*   J. P. to D. C. S., July 17, 1905 (LC).   *"The news columns"*   Ibid., August 26, 1905 (LC).

306   *When one witness refused*   Swanberg, *Pulitzer*, p. 366.   *And when Governor Higgins*   *New York World*, October 15, 1905 (CU).   *"Republican influence"*   Seitz, *Joseph Pulitzer*, p. 279.   *without a particle of prejudice"*   J. P. to J. H. and F. C., October 11, 1905 (LC).

307   *"Men battered and bruised"*   Ferdinand Lundberg, *Imperial Hearst: A Social Biography* (New York: Arno Press, 1970), p. 104.   *"It was a great mistake"*   J. P. to R. P., June 11, 1905 (CU).   *"for your kindness"*   F. W. V. to J. P., August 26, 1905 (CU).

308   *"I wish for nothing more"*   J. P. to R. P., October 16, 1905 (CU).

309   *"I could give you"*   R. P. to J. P., October 16, 1905 (CU).   *"Please tell the editors"*   J. P. to W. S., October 25, 1905, Papers of Joseph Pulitzer II, Missouri.   *Pulitzer must have wondered*   Joe to J. P., December 8, 1904 (CU).

Chapter 28: "I Liked the Way He Swore"

310   *His letter crossed*   Louis Starr, "Joseph Pulitzer and His Most 'Indegoddampendent' Editor," *American Heritage*, June 1968, p. 82.   *Pulitzer seemed to agree*   Don Carlos Seitz, *Joseph Pulitzer: His Life and Letters* (New York: AMS Press, 1970), p. 265.   *"Go back to the office"*   Starr, "Joseph Pulitzer," p. 82.   *"My dear boy, don't"*   Seitz, *Joseph Pulitzer*, p. 266.

311 "My tastes are rather simple" Starr, "Joseph Pulitzer," p. 82. "There is seldom more" Ibid. "There is no partiality" Charles Chapin, Charles E. Chapin's Story (New York: G. P. Putnam's Sons, 1920), p. 226.

312 Joe took the advice Joe to J. P., May 25, 1906 (CU). "The office gasped" Chapin, Charles E. Chapin's Story, pp. 228–229. "I am out here to learn" Daniel W. Pfaff, Joseph Pulitzer II and the Post-Dispatch: A Newspaperman's Life (University Park: Pennsylvania State University Press, 1991), p. 64. Jerome hit back Richard O'Connor, Courtroom Warrior: The Combative Career of William Travers Jerome (Boston: Little, Brown, 1963), p. 244.

313 "With your knowledge of the facts" J. P. to W. T. J., April 20, 1906 (CU). "My poor dear" W. A. Swanberg, Pulitzer (New York: Charles Scribner's Sons, 1967), p. 375. "Mr. Pulitzer of the New York World" Ibid.

314 "Harry Kendal Thaw" New York World, June 25, 1906, pp. 1–2. "The story had everything" O'Connor, Courtroom Warrior, p. 198. "Alfred Dreyfus was completely" World, July 13, 1906, p. 1.

315 "worked a tremendous change" Ibid., p. 6.

316 The World revealed Ibid., July 15, 1906, p. 1.

317 "The World and I" S. W. to J. P., May 24, 1906 (CU). "a political cockroach" W. A. Swanberg, Citizen Hearst (New York: Bantam Books, 1967), p. 287. "to treat Hearst without" Seitz, Joseph Pulitzer, p. 287. "We are trying to treat" Starr, "Joseph Pulitzer," pp. 83–84.

318 "Please don't call Hughes" J. P. to F. C., August 18, 1906 (CU). "He is the brightest of your children" J. P. to K. P., September 27, 1906 (CU). "When I see you" Joe to J. P., August 20, 1906, in Pfaff, Joseph Pulitzer II and the Post-Dispatch, p. 66. "You don't need the money" Ibid., August 30, 1906, p. 67. "You were sent out to learn" A. B. to Joe, September 6, 1906 (Post-Dispatch archives).

319 "would feel justified" Joe to A. B., September 8, 1906, in Pfaff, Joseph Pulitzer II and the Post-Dispatch, pp. 67–68. "When I shut my eyes" Joe to J. P., Ibid., September 8, 1906, p. 68. Despite a fall from a horse Ibid., late September. "decidedly clever and attractive" Ibid., November 19, 1906, pp. 86–87.

320 "Your letter certainly did not bore me" Ibid., J. P. to Joe, December 5, 1906, p. 87. Infuriated by the World's support Swanberg, Pulitzer, p. 383. Joe immediately promised Pfaff, Joseph Pulitzer II and the Post-Dispatch, p. 71. "I usually mean what I say" Swanberg, Pulitzer, p. 384. Swanberg went with this Ibid. "It was a meeting" K. P. to J. P., November 24, 1906 (CU). "Amazed. You must certainly" J. P. to Joe, December 20, 1906 (Post-Dispatch archives).

321 "Railroad rate question" J. P. Notes, Galley II (LC).

Chapter 29: Protesting Jingo Agitation

322 "Joseph is becoming" F. O. to J. P., Daniel W. Pfaff, Joseph Pulitzer II and the Post-Dispatch: A Newspaperman's Life (University Park: Pennsylvania State University Press, 1991), p. 75. "a flat (2 rooms and a bath)" Joe to J. P., January 23, 1907, ibid., p. 78 "cause you to think" February 15, 1907, ibid., p. 79.

323 "to sacrifice everything" Joe to R. P., April 14, 1907, ibid., p. 89. "It's ridiculous to maintain" R. P. to Joe, April, 26, 1907, ibid. "Please urge Andes" Joe to J. P., late April 1907, ibid., p. 79. "be too much influenced" J. P. to R. P., February 10, 1907 (LC).

324 "You refused to let me" K. P. to J. P., February 13, 1907 (CU). "impossible people" Ibid., March 4, 1907. "I have just done" Frederic V. Grunfeld, Rodin: A Biography (New York: Henry Holt, 1987), p. 527. "a remarkable portrait" James Wyman Barrett, Joseph Pulitzer and His World (New York: Vanguard Press, 1941), p. 288. "Your father," she wrote K. P. to Joe, May 2, 1907, in Pfaff, Joseph Pulitzer II and the Post-Dispatch, p. 80.

325 "There is not one scintilla" J. P. to Joe, May 27, 1907, ibid., p. 82. "I quoted from memory" Ibid., May 29, 1907, p. 83. "stopped dead in his tracks" Norman Thwaites, Velvet and Vinegar (London: Grayson & Grayson, 1932), p. 67.

326 "whatever may have been true" Ibid. Especially after Count Barbara Tuchman, The Proud Tower: A Portrait of the World before the War, 1890–1914 (New York: Macmillan, 1966), p. 331. "I should like you to" J. P. to R. P., May 28, 1907 (LC). In a memo of

their conversation Joe's memo, June 5, 1907 (*Post-Dispatch* archives). *"when I feel sure"* Pfaff, *Joseph Pulitzer and the* Post-Dispatch, p. 84.

327 *a daring, fearless expression* J. P. to F. C., July 8, 1907, in Don Carlos Seitz, *Joseph Pulitzer: His Life and Letters* (New York: AMS Press, 1970), pp. 311–312. *"Attack on Roosevelt"* Ibid., p. 319.

328 *"It was my unfortunate lot"* Thwaites, *Velvet and Vinegar*, pp. 61–62. *"how much I would give"* W. A. Swanberg, *Pulitzer* (New York: Charles Scribner's Sons, 1967), p. 393.

329 *"door-to-door trying to pry"* Ron Chernow, *Titan: The Life of John D. Rockefeller Sr.* (New York: Random House, 1998), p. 461. *"The greatest breeder"* Seitz, *Joseph Pulitzer*, pp. 320–321. *And when the company was* Ibid., p. 322. *"Dear Ralph, One cold day"* Joe to R. P., September 30, 1907 (LC). *"Boy," he said, "I am"* Seitz, *Joseph Pulitzer*, p. 36.

Chapter 30: Secret Double Life of Rockefeller's Father

332 *"I love it"* Don Carlos Seitz, *Joseph Pulitzer: His Life and Letters* (New York: AMS Press, 1970), p. 290.

333 *"the most exquisitely"* Richard O'Connor, *Courtroom Warrior: The Combative Career of William Travers Jerome* (Boston: Little, Brown, 1963), p. 187. *"I think merely that"* Ishbel Ross, *Ladies of the Press* (New York: Harper & Brothers, 1936), p. 90. *The sight of these young* Ibid.

334 *Unlike its competitor* O'Connor, *Courtroom Warrior*, p. 222. *Cobb was disgusted* Ibid., p. 213. *"former Poo Bahs"* Ibid., p. 214.

335 *The* World *characterized* Peter Collier and David Horowitz, *The Rockefellers: An American Dynasty* (New York: Signet, 1976), p. 8.

336 *"My dear Joseph"* K. P. to J. P., May 4, 1903 (CU). *"my nerves [were] nearly 'busted'"* J. P. to R. P., May 28, 1903 (LC).

337 *"I have in my mind's eye"* John L. Heaton, *The Story of a Page: Thirty Years of Public Service and Public Discussion in the Editorial Columns of the* New York World (New York: Harper & Brothers, 1913), p. 54. *In late July* James Wyman Barrett, *Joseph Pulitzer and His* World (New York: Vanguard Press, 1941), pp. 209–214.

338 STRICTLY AND MOST J. P. to O. B., in Daniel W. Pfaff, *Joseph Pulitzer II and the* Post-Dispatch: A Newspaperman's Life (University Park: Pennsylvania State University Press, 1991), p. 94. *"I have been in heaven"* Joe to J. P., Ibid., p. 95. *In August Pulitzer gave* Seitz, *Joseph Pulitzer*, pp. 341–342.

339 *While the doctor* James Barnes, *From Then to Now* (New York: Appleton-Century, 1934), pp. 365–366.

340 *In his continuing battle* Seitz, *Joseph Pulitzer*, p. 343. *At Southampton* Ibid., p. 345. *"One thing I insist"* Ibid., pp. 345–346.

341 *"I honestly declare"* Ibid., p. 348. *When he learned that Taft* Ibid., p. 350. *Told of Pulitzer's orders* R. P. to J. P., December 6, 1908 (CU). *"so happy and exhilarated* Ibid., December 1907 (CU). *After blaming the snow* Ibid., December 6, 1908.

Chapter 31: Roosevelt Tries to Send Pulitzer to Prison

343 *"the most dangerous man"* James Wyman Barrett, *Joseph Pulitzer and His* World (New York: Vanguard Press, 1991), p. 225. *"clear as a baby's"* Ibid.

344 *"I knew damned well"* Don Carlos Seitz, *Joseph Pulitzer: His Life and Letters* (New York: AMS Press, 1970), p. 356.

345 *There was no corruption* Ibid., p. 357.

346 *"What proof have you"* W. A. Swanberg, *Pulitzer* (New York: Charles Scribner's Sons, 1967), p. 421. *"Turn over the files"* John L. Heaton, *Cobb of the* World (Freeport, N.Y.: Books for Libraries Press, 1971), p. 2. ROOSEVELT TO PROSECUTE *New York Times*, December 11, 1908, p. 1. *"Who got the money?"* J. P. to F. C., December 13, 1908 (LC). *After the memo was* Ibid.

347 *"inadmissible license"* New York World, December 14, 1908, p. 6. *"The New York* World *evidently"* Ibid., December 21, 1908, p. 10. *On December 15 Roosevelt* Seitz, *Joseph Pulitzer*, pp. 364–365. *Pulitzer was ill* Norman Thwaites, *Velvet and Vinegar* (London:

Grayson & Grayson, 1932), pp. 57–58. *When that same day* J. P. to Porter, in ibid., p. 58. *Headed LESE-MAJESTY* *World*, December 16, 1908, p. 8.

348   *ROOSEVELT'S BITTER ATTACK* Ibid., p. 1. *Questioned by the* New York Times *New York Times*, December 17, 1908, p. 4. *He also omitted* J. P. to F. C. and R. P., October 1, 1908 (LC).

349   *"Mr. Joseph Pulitzer must be"* *World*, December 16, 1908, p. 3. *"If you swear to be witty"* J. P. to F. C., December 23, 1908 (LC). *When, as Pulitzer expected* Ibid., December 24, 1908. *As Seitz recalled* Seitz, *Joseph Pulitzer*, p. 373. *"but he disliked discomfort"* James Barnes, *From Then Till Now* (New York: Appleton-Century, 1934), p. 367.

Chapter 32: "The Big Man of All American Newspapers"

350   *"This Panama deal"* C. C. to R. P., January 2, 1909 (LC). *"please be very, very"* J. P. to F. C., January 2, 1909 (LC).

351   *his "indegoddampendent" editor* Louis Starr, "Joseph Pulitzer and His Most 'Indegoddampendent' Editor," *American Heritage*, June 1968, p. 84. *"I don't care how much"* James Wyman Barrett, *Joseph Pulitzer and His* World (New York: Vanguard Press, 1941), pp. 187–188. *"I would not barter"* Starr, "Joseph Pulitzer," p. 84. *In a statement to* Don Carlos Seitz, *Joseph Pulitzer: His Life and Letters* (New York: AMS Press, 1970), p. 365. *"The French have perfected"* Ibid., p. 366. *"a giant intelligence"* W. A. Swanberg, *Pulitzer* (New York: Charles Scribner's Sons, 1967), p. 424. *"I don't like a hair"* Ibid., p. 425.

352   *"These libel proceedings"* John L. Heaton, *Cobb of the* World (Freeport, N.Y.: Books for Libraries Press, 1971), pp. 15–16. *"Mr. Pulitzer conducts"* Barrett, *Joseph Pulitzer and His* World, p. 240.

353   *"I won't allow you"* Daniel W. Pfaff, *Joseph Pulitzer II and the* Post-Dispatch: A Newspaperman's Life (University Park: Pennsylvania State University Press, 1991), p. 100. *"For years I have resented"* Ibid. *His inheritance was* Ibid., p. 101. *Eventually, after reconciling* Joe to J. P., March 29, 1909 (LC).

354   *"Tell me what you see."* James Barnes, *From Then Till Now* (New York: Appleton-Century, 1934), p. 371. *"Are you tired?"* J. P. to F. C., March 29, 1909 (LC). *He commandeered a cork mat* Barnes, *From Then Till Now*, p. 372.

355   *To ensure a peaceful stay* Ibid.

356   *On land or at sea* Ibid., pp. 374–376. *The* New York Times *reported* New York Times, October 5, 1909, p. 4. *ALBERT PULITZER A SUICIDE* New York World, October 5, 1909, p. 7.

357   *"The exquisite service"* Barrett, *Joseph Pulitzer and His* World, p. 284. *And when his son determined* Pfaff, *Joseph Pulitzer II and the* Post-Dispatch, p. 105. *But Joe was beginning to* Ibid., p. 106.

358   *"Real troubles never bother me"* Seitz, *Joseph Pulitzer*, pp. 392–393. *"It's no use, my dear boy"* Ibid., p. 392.

Chapter 33: Roosevelt Seeks Revenge

359   *Yet, not wanting to* Don Carlos Seitz, *Joseph Pulitzer: His Life and Letters* (New York: AMS Press, 1970), pp. 397–399. *"every editor to write"* Ibid., pp. 397–398. *"I have never known"* Ibid., pp. 401–402.

360   *"Who made up the paper"* J. P. to R. P., January 22, 1910 (LC). *Nicoll had argued* James Wyman Barrett, *Joseph Pulitzer and His* World (New York: Vanguard Press, 1941), p. 247. *"A victory for freedom of the press"* New York World, January 27, 1910, p. 3.

361   *"Knox's foreign policy"* J. P. to R. P., February 20, 1910 (LC). *Pulitzer's "peculiar history"* N. T. to J. T., March 9, 1910 (LC). *"My dearest [Frank] Cobb, I nearly fainted"* J. P. to F. C., March 14, 1910 (LC). *"for the sake of the party"* Ibid.

362   *"it made me realize"* Daniel W. Pfaff, *Joseph Pulitzer II and the* Post-Dispatch: A Newspaperman's Life (University Park: Pennsylvania State University Press, 1991), p. 108. *"this was one of the few times"* W. A. Swanberg, *Pulitzer* (New York: Charles Scribner's Sons, 1967), p. 440. *"It seems that the wonders"* Barrett, *Joseph Pulitzer and His* World, p. 297.

363   *"the* World's *Democratic sympathies"*   J. P. to F. C., August 6, 1910 (LC).
364   *"You must seize"* Cobb's notes, August 8, 1910 (LC). *"aboard the ship"* Charles Chapin, *Charles E. Chapin's Story* (New York: G. P. Putnam's Sons, 1920), p. 204. *"narrow escape"* Seitz, *Joseph Pulitzer,* p. 407. *"Would it not be better"* Ibid. *"My feeling about T. R."* J. P. to J. B., October 20, 1910, in James Barnes, *From Then Till Now* (New York: Appleton-Century, 1934), p. 384. *"Your diary states"* Pfaff, *Joseph Pulitzer II and the* Post-Dispatch, p. 113. *"What can I do about"* J. P. to R. P., October 16, 1910 (LC).
365   *"The man who wrote"* Seitz, *Joseph Pulitzer,* pp. 418–419.
366   *He thanked Lincoln* Ibid., p. 420. *"The place here is damnable"* J. P. to R. P., November 12, 1910 (LC). *"Delighted to hear of your house"* J. P. to Joe, in Pfaff, *Joseph Pulitzer II and the* Post-Dispatch, p. 113. *The* World's *angry response* J. P. to C. L., December 2, 1910 (LC).
367   *"No!" Pulitzer corrected him* J. P. to F. C., December 3, 1910 (LC). *"with the uttermost impersonality"* J. P. to G. J., December 5, 1910 (LC). *"put in the word"* Ibid., December 6, 1910. *"Not bad for a beginning"* Ibid. *The paper did not mention* Barrett, *Joseph Pulitzer and His World,* p. 300. *"perhaps the most extraordinary woman"* World, December 5, 1910, p. 10.
368   *"never preached that there"* Ibid., p. 2. *"Just read your letter"* J. P. to G. H., November 23, 1910, in Seitz, *Joseph Pulitzer,* p. vii. *"I never dreamt"* Ibid., December 22, 1910, p. viii. *"If you go over the last twenty years"* Ibid., January 7, 1911, pp. ix–x.
369   *"Sincere wishes for pleasant Xmas"* Swanberg, *Pulitzer,* p. 447.

Chapter 34: Victory!

370   *"Roosevelt's legal lackeys"* New York World, January 7, 1911, p. 10. *"miraculously prevented"* Walter LaFeber, *The Panama Canal: The Crisis in Historical Perspective* (New York: Oxford University Press, 1989), pp. 15–16. *Justifying his decisions* Ibid., p. 45.
371   *"not in sympathy"* Joe to J. P., January 4, 1911, in Daniel W. Pfaff, *Joseph Pulitzer II and the* Post-Dispatch: A *Newspaperman's Life* (University Park: Pennsylvania State University Press, 1991), p. 116. *Had the* World *libeled* Gable, interview, May 3, 2001. *"before we are exposed"* Ibid., p. 118. *"For the tenth time"* J. P. to Joe, February 28, 1911, in ibid., pp. 118–119. *He had been one of Pulitzer's* Norman Thwaites, *Velvet and Vinegar* (London: Grayson & Grayson, 1932), pp. 64–65.
372   *The* World *had given the tragedy* World, January 25, 1911, p. 1. *"Well, here you see"* Alleyne Ireland, *An Adventure with a Genius: Recollections of Joseph Pulitzer* (1914; reprint, New York: Johnson Reprint, 1969), p. 40.
373   *"Gentlemen, this is Mr. Alleyne Ireland"* Ibid., p. 46. *"I left my dinner untasted"* Ibid., pp. 48–50. *One moment lively* Ibid., p. 41. *"You'll find this business"* Ibid., pp. 62, 70.
375   *"My God! What's this?"* Ibid., p. 93. *Or, according to Ireland* Ibid., pp. 180–181.
376   *"My God, I can't stand"* Ibid., p. 184. *"Go on," Pulitzer said* Ibid., pp. 106, 107, 110–112, 114–115.
377   *"What do you feel when"* Ibid., pp. 159–160. *"The past year has been"* Joe to J. P., May 29, 1911 (CU). *"I don't believe"* K. P. to R. P., May 28, 1911 (LC).
378   *"I really think"* Ireland, *An Adventure with a Genius,* pp. 209–210. *"Now, step please"* Ibid., pp. 225–226.
379   *"strictness of the account"* Ibid., pp. 215–216. *Encouraged, but knowing* J. P. to J. H., July 2, 1911 (LC). *"that I am abroad"* Ibid.
380   *"Condense to the uttermost"* Ibid., July 4, 1911. *"Passed almost unanimously"* R. P. to J. P., July 21, 1911 (LC). *On the way Frank Cobb* J. P. to F. C., August 28, 1911 (LC).
381   *"without flapdoodle"* Ibid., August 30, 1911. *"I am hungry for him"* J. P. to K. P., September 7, 1911, in Daniel W. Pfaff, *Joseph Pulitzer II and the* Post-Dispatch: A *Newspaperman's Life* (University Park: Pennsylvania State University Press, 1991), p. 126. *"But don't smoke"* W. A. Swanberg, *Pulitzer* (New York: Charles Scribner's Sons, 1967), p. 468. *"The United States Steel"* J. P. to F. C. and C. L., September 25, 1911 (LC).
382   *"Please expunge my foolish"* Don Carlos Seitz, *Joseph Pulitzer: His Life and Letters* (New York: AMS Press, 1970), p. 411.

Chapter 35: The Last Days

383   "too *heavily upon sending*"   J. P. to F. C., October 2, 1991, in Don Carlos Seitz, *Joseph Pulitzer: His Life and Letters* (New York: AMS Press, 1970), pp. 412–413.   *To be fair to Roosevelt*   Gable, Interview, May 3, 2001.   *"There has been no bombardment"*   J. P. to F. C. and C. L., October 3, 1911 (LC).

384   *The* World *later praised*   W. A. Swanberg, *Pulitzer* (New York: Charles Scribner's Sons, 1967), p. 371.   *The editorial in the Tribune*   J. P. to F. C., October 19, 1911 (LC).   *It was not unusual*   Alleyne Ireland, *An Adventure with a Genius: Recollections of Joseph Pulitzer* (1914; reprint, New York: Johnson Reprint, 1969), p. 233.

385   *"Mr. Pulitzer wishes you"*   Ibid., pp. 234–236.

386   *As Mann reached the end*   Ibid., p. 236.   *Dr. Hosmer heard the news*   G. H. to F. W., October 29, 1911 (LC).   *"A man of wide culture"*   *New York World*, October 30, 1911, p. 10 (LC).   *He concluded that while*   Swanberg, *Pulitzer*, p. 473.

388   *"had not read that morning's"*   Ibid., p. 474.   *"one of the greatest men"*   *New York Times*, October 30, 1911, p. 2.   *"a towering figure"*   *World*, October 30, 1911, p. 2.

389   *"When I recall the capaciousness"*   Ireland, *An Adventure with a Genius*, p. 141.   *"my early fear of him"*   Norman Thwaites, *Velvet and Vinegar* (London: Grayson & Grayson, 1932), p. 60.   *"expose all fraud and sham"*   *World*, May 11, 1883, p. 4.   *"Is this a fair report"*   Seitz, *Joseph Pulitzer*, p. 433.

390   *Pulitzer himself, a few years*   John Hohenberg, *The Professional Journalist* (New York: Holt, Rinehart and Winston, Inc., 1973), p. 5.

Chapter 36: The Aftermath

391   *In his will Pulitzer urged*   W. A. Swanberg, *Pulitzer* (New York: Charles Scribner's Sons, 1967), p. 398.

392   *a weak argument*   Daniel W. Pfaff, *Joseph Pulitzer II and the* Post-Dispatch: *A Newspaperman's Life* (University Park: Pennsylvania State University Press, 1991), p. 346.

394   *"anti-foreign, anti-intellectual"*   A. J. Liebling, *The Press* (New York: Ballantine Books, 1975), p. 419.   *"It occurs to me"*   Joe to W. W. R., *Post-Dispatch* archives.

Bibliography

Adelman, William J. *Haymarket Revisited*. Chicago: Labor History Society, 1986.

Andres, Wayne. *The Vanderbilt Legend*. New York: Harcourt, Brace, 1941.

Bailey, Thomas A. *The American Pageant: A History of the Republic*. Lexington, Mass.: D. C. Heath, 1966.

Baker, Paul R. *Stanny: The Gilded Life of Stanford White*. New York: Free Press, 1989.

Barnes, James. *From Then Till Now*. New York: Appleton-Century, 1934.

Barrett, James Wyman. *Joseph Pulitzer and His* World. New York: Vanguard Press, 1941.

Beebe, Lucius. *Big Spenders*. Garden City, N.Y.: Doubleday, 1966.

Berger, Meyer. *The Story of the* New York Times *1851–1951*. New York: Simon & Schuster, 1951.

Bernard, Marc. *Zola*. Trans. Jean M. Lebon. New York: Grove Press, 1960.

Berryman, John. *Stephen Crane*. New York: William Sloane, 1959.

Blumenfeld, Ralph. *In the Days of Bicycles and Bustles*. New York: Brewer & Warren, 1930.

Bly, Nellie. *Ten Days in a Mad House*. New York: Munroe, 1887.

Bragdon, Henry W., and Samuel P. McCutchen. *History of a Free People*. New York: Macmillan, 1967.

Brands, H. W. *The Reckless Decade: America in the 1890s*. New York: St. Martin's Press, 1995.

———. *T. R.: The Last Romantic*. New York: Basic Books, 1997.

Brown, Charles H. *The Correspondents' War: Journalists in the Spanish-American War*. New York: Charles Scribner's Sons, 1967.

Bruns, Roger A. *The Bandit Kings*. New York: Crown, 1995.

Butterfield, Roger. *The American Past: A History of the United States from Concord to Hiroshima, 1775–1945*. New York: Simon & Schuster, 1947.

———. *The Fabulous Century*. New York: Time-Life Books, 1970.

Carlson, Oliver. *Arthur Brisbane: A Candid Biography*. Westport, Conn.: Greenwood Press, 1937.

Chambers, Julius. *Newshunting on Three Continents*. New York: Mitchell Kennerly, 1926.

Chaney, Lindsay, and Michael Creply. *The Hearsts: Family & Empire*. New York: Simon & Schuster, 1981.

Chapin, Charles. *Charles E. Chapin's Story*. New York: G. P. Putnam's Sons, 1920.

Chernow, Ron. *Titan: The Life of John D. Rockefeller Sr*. New York: Random House, 1998.

Churchill, Allen. *Park Row*. New York: Rinehart, 1958.

Churchill, Randolph S. *Winston Churchill, Companion*. Vol. 1, Part I, *1874–1895*. Boston: Houghton Mifflin, 1967.

———. *Winston S. Churchill, Youth, 1874–1900*. Boston: Houghtin Mifflin, 1966.

Churchill, Winston S. *A History of the English-Speaking Peoples: The Great Democracies*. New York: Dodd, Mead, 1958.

Coblentz, Edmond D., ed. *Newsmen Speak: Journalists on Their Craft*. Berkeley: University of California Press, 1954.

Collier, Peter, and David Horowitz. *The Rockefellers: An American Dynasty*. New York: Signet, 1976.

Cowles, Virginia. *The Kaiser*. New York: Harper & Row, 1963.

Creelman, James. *On the Great Highway: The Wanderings and Adventures of a Special Correspondent*. Boston: Lothrop, 1904.

Davies, Elmer. *History of the* New York Times, *1851–1921*. New York: *New York Times*, 1921.

Davies, Linda. *"Badge of Courage": The Life of Stephen Crane*. Boston: Houghton Mifflin, 1998.

Edel, Leon, ed. *The Diary of Alice James*. New York: Dodd, Mead, 1964.

Eggleston, George Cary. *Recollections of a Varied Life*. New York: Henry Holt, 1910.

Emery, Edwin, and Michael Emery. *The Press and America: An Interpretive History of the Mass Media*. Englewood Cliffs, N.J.: Prentice-Hall, 1984.

Encyclopaedia Britannica. 11th ed. New York, 1910.

Evans, Harold. *The American Century*. New York: Alfred A. Knopf, 1998.

Ferris, Paul. *The House of Northcliffe*. New York: World, 1972.

Gage, Nicholas. *Mafia U.S.A.* Chicago: Playboy Press, 1972.

Garraty, John A. *The American Nation: A History of the United States*. New York: Harper & Row, 1966.

Graham, John [David Graham Phillips]. *The Great God Success*. Ridgewood, N.J.: Gregg Press, 1967.

Grunfeld, Frederic V. *Rodin: A Biography*. New York: Henry Holt, 1987.

Hearst, William Randolph Jr., with Jack Casserly. *The Hearsts: Father and Son*. Niwot, Colo.: Robert Rinehart, 1991.

Heaton, John L. *Cobb of the* World. Freeport, N.Y.: Books for Libraries Press, 1971.

————. *The Story of a Page: Thirty Years of Public Service and Public Discussion in the Editorial Columns of the* New York World. New York: Harper & Brothers, 1913.

Henry, Lewis C., ed. *Five Thousand Quotations for All Occasions*. Garden City, N.Y.: Doubleday, 1945.

Hibbert, Christopher, ed. *Queen Victoria in Her Letters and Journals*. New York: Viking, 1985.

Hohenberg, John. *The Professional Journalist*. New York: Holt, Rinehart and Winston, Inc., 1973.

————. *The Pulitzer Prize Story*. New York: Columbia University Press, 1959.

Holroyd, Michael. *Bernard Shaw*. Vol. 1, *1856–1898*. New York: Random House, 1988.

Ireland, Alleyne. *An Adventure with a Genius: Recollections of Joseph Pulitzer*. 1914. Reprint, New York: Johnson Reprint, 1969.

————. "A Modern Superman." *American Magazine*, April 1912.

Jones, Robert W. *History of Journalism in the United States*. New York: E. P. Dutton, 1947.

Juergens, George. *Joseph Pulitzer and the* New York World. Princeton, N.J.: Princeton University Press, 1966.

Kaplan, Justin. *Mr. Clemens and Mark Twain*. New York: Pocket Books, 1968.

Klein, Maury. *The Life and Legend of Jay Gould*. Baltimore: Johns Hopkins University Press, 1986.

Knightley, Phillip. *The First Casualty, from Crimea to Vietnam: The War Correspondent as Hero, Propagandist, and Myth Maker*. New York: Harcourt Brace Jovanovich, 1975.

Kraus, Rene. *Winston Churchill*. New York: J. B. Lippincott, 1941.

Krock, Arthur. *Memoirs: Sixty Years on the Firing Line*. New York: Funk & Wagnalls, 1968.

Kroeger, Brooke. *Nellie Bly, Daredevil, Reporter, Feminist*. New York: Times Books, 1994.

LaFeber, Walter. *The Panama Canal: The Crisis in Historical Perspective*. New York: Oxford University Press, 1989.

Lande, Nathaniel. *Dispatches from the Front: News Accounts of American Wars, 1776–1991*. New York: Henry Holt, 1995.

Langford, Gerald. *The Richard Harding Davis Years*. New York: Holt, Rinehart, & Winston, 1961.

Leech, Margaret. *In the Days of McKinley*. New York: Harper & Brothers, 1959.

Letters of Charles J. Guiteau. File 14056, National Archives.

Liebling, A. J. *The Press*. New York: Ballantine Books, 1975.

Longford, Elizabeth. *Queen Victoria: Born to Succeed*. New York: Harper & Row, 1964.

Lundberg, Ferdinand. *Imperial Hearst: A Social Biography*. New York: Arno Press, 1970.

McCullough, David. *Mornings on Horseback*. New York: Touchstone, 1981.

McDougall, Walt. "Old Days on the *World*." *American Mercury*, January 1925.

————. *This Is the Life*. New York: Charles Scribner's Sons, 1926.

Manchester, William. *The Last Lion*. New York: Dell, 1984.

Martin, Ralph G. *Jennie*. Vol. 2, *1895–1921*. New York: Signet, 1971.

Mason, Gregory. *Remember the* Maine. New York: Henry Holt, 1939.

Maurois, André. *Disraeli*. Trans. Hamish Miles. New York: Appleton, 1928.

Miller, Nathan. *Theodore Roosevelt: A Life*. New York: William Morrow, 1992.

Milton, Joyce. *The Yellow Kids: Foreign Correspondents in the Heyday of Yellow Journalism*. New York: Harper & Row, 1989.

Morison, Samuel Eliot. *The Oxford History of the American People.* Vol. 3. New York: New American Library, 1966.

Morley, John. *The Life of William Ewart Gladstone.* New York: Macmillan, 1903.

Morris, Donald R. *The Washing of Spears: The Rise and Fall of the Zulu Nation.* New York: Simon & Schuster, 1965.

Musicant, Ivan. *Empire by Default: The Spanish-American War and the Dawn of the American Century.* New York: Henry Holt, 1998.

Muzzey, David Saville. *James G. Blaine: A Political Idol of Other Days.* New York: Dodd, Mead, 1934.

Nasaw, David. *The Chief: The Life of William Randolph Hearst.* Boston: Houghton Mifflin, 2000.

Nash, Jay Robert. *Bloodletters and Badmen.* New York: Warner, 1975.

Nevins, Allan. *John D. Rockefeller.* Vol. 2. New York: Charles Scribner's Sons, 1941.

O'Connor, Richard. *Courtroom Warrior: The Combative Career of William Travers Jerome.* Boston: Little, Brown, 1963.

Pakenham, Thomas. *The Boer War.* New York: Random House, 1970.

The Parable of Pullman. Chicago, Illinois: Labor History Society.

Pearson, Hesketh. *Disraeli: His Life and Personality.* New York: Grosset & Dunlap, 1951.

Peel, Robert. *Mary Baker Eddy: The Years of Authority.* New York: Holt, Rinehart, & Winston, 1977.

Peskin, Allan. *Garfield.* Kent, Ohio: Kent State University Press, 1978.

Pfaff, Daniel W. *Joseph Pulitzer II and the Post-Dispatch: A Newspaperman's Life.* University Park: Pennsylvania State University Press, 1991.

Pringle, Henry F. *Theodore Roosevelt: A Biography.* New York: Harcourt, Brace, 1931.

Proctor, Ben. *William Randolph Hearst: The Early Years, 1863–1910.* New York: Oxford University Press, 1998.

Pulitzer, Joseph P. Jr. and Michael E. Pulitzer. *Newspapers and Broadcasting in the Public Interest.* New York: The Necomen Society of the United States, 1988.

Rammelkamp, Julian S. *Pulitzer's Post-Dispatch.* Princeton, N.J.: Princeton University Press, 1967.

Richardson, James F. *The New York Police: Colonial Times to 1901.* New York: Oxford University Press, 1970.

Riis, Jacob. *How the Other Half Lives.* New York: Charles Scribner's Sons, 1903.

Roberts, Brian. *The Zulu Kings: A Major Reassessment of Zulu History.* New York: Charles Scribner's Sons, 1974.

Robertson, Priscilla. *Revolutions of 1848: A Social History.* Princeton, N.J.: Princeton University Press, 1971.

Robinson, Judith. *The Hearsts: An American Dynasty.* Newark: University of Delaware Press, 1991.

Roosevelt, Theodore. *An Autobiography.* New York: Macmillan, 1916.

Ross, Ishbel. *Ladies of the Press.* New York: Harper & Brothers, 1936.

Schurz, Carl. *The Autobiography of Carl Schurz.* Abr. Wayne Andrews. New York: Charles Scribner's Sons, 1961.

Schwarzlose, Richard A. *The Nation's Newsbrokers from 1865 to 1929.* Vol. 2. Evanston, Ill.: Northwestern University Press, 1990.

Sealey, O. O. *130 Pictures of Live Men.* New York, 1910.

Seitz, Don Carlos. *Joseph Pulitzer: His Life and Letters.* New York: AMS Press, 1970.

Silver, Christopher, ed. *The Norton Book of Interviews.* New York: W. W. Norton, 1996.

Smith, Page. *The Rise of Industrial America.* New York: Viking Penguin, 1990.

Stafford, David. *Churchill and Secret Service.* Woodstock, N.Y.: Overlook Press, 1998.

Stallman, R. W. *Stephen Crane: A Biography.* New York: George Braziller, 1968.

Starr, Louis. "Joseph Pulitzer and His Most 'Indegoddampendent' Editor." *American Heritage,* June 1968.

Steed, Wickham. *Through Thirty Years.* Vol. 1. London: Heinemann, 1924.

Steel, Ronald. *Walter Lippmann and the American Century.* Boston: Little, Brown, 1980.

Strouse, Jeane. *Morgan.* New York: Random House, 1999.

Sullivan, Mark. *Our Times: The Turn of the Century: The United States 1900–1925.* New York: Charles Scribner's Sons, 1928.

Swanberg, W. A. *Citizen Hearst.* New York: Bantam Books, 1967.

————. *Pulitzer.* New York: Charles Scribner's Sons, 1967.

————. *Theodore Dreiser.* New York: Bantam Books, 1967.

Tebbel, John. *America's Great Patriotic War with Spain.* Manchester Center, Vt.: Marshall Jones, 1996.

————. *The Compact History of the American Newspaper.* New York: Hawthorn, 1963.

————. *The Life and Good Times of William Randolph Hearst.* New York: Paperback Library, 1962.

Thwaites, Norman. *Velvet and Vinegar.* London: Grayson & Grayson, 1932.

Tifft, Susan E., and Alex D. Jones. "The Family: How Being Jewish Shaped the Dynasty That Runs the *Times.*" *New Yorker*, April 19, 1999.

Triplett, Frank. *The Life, Times, and Treacherous Death of Jesse James.* New York: Promontory Press, 1970.

Troy, Gil. *See How They Ran: The Changing Role of the Presidential Candidate.* New York: Free Press, 1991.

Tuchman, Barbara. *The Proud Tower: A Portrait of the World before the War, 1890–1914.* New York: Macmillan, 1966.

Tugwell, Rexford Guy. *Grover Cleveland.* New York: Macmillan, 1968.

Wardman, Ervin. *Concise Dictionary of American Biography.* New York: Charles Scribner's Sons, 1964.

Weintraub, Stanley. *Victoria: An Intimate Biography.* New York: E. P. Dutton, 1987.

Welch, Richard E. Jr. *The Presidencies of Grover Cleveland.* Lawrence: University Press of Kansas, 1988.

Wellman, Francis L. *The Art of Cross-Examination.* New York: Collier Books, 1962.

West, Ray B. Jr. *Kingdom of the Saints: The Story of Brigham Young and the Mormons.* New York: Viking, 1957.

Winkler, John K. *William Randolph Hearst: A New Appraisal.* New York: Avon Books, 1955.

Winks, Robin W., ed. *The Historian as Detective: Essays on Evidence.* New York: Harper and Row, 1970.

Index

ML   10/01